My True Course

Dutch Van Kirk
Northumberland to Hiroshima

Suzanne Simon Dietz

Red Gremlin Press LLC
Lawrenceville, Georgia

First Edition 2012.
ISBN 978-0-692-01676-3
Library of Congress Control Number: 2012900926

Layout and design by: BeauDesigns, Inc.
Youngstown, NY
www.beaudesigns.biz

Every reasonable effort has been made to trace present copyright holders of the materials used in this book. Any omission is unintentional, and the publisher will be pleased to correct errors in future editions.

Cover images of Sea Rescue Chart and Van Kirk are from the National Archives, College Park, MD.

Printed in the United States of America on acid free paper.

Dedicated to the memory of Mary Jane Young Van Kirk
who waited for her beau and four brothers
to return from the war.

(1923 – 1975)

National Archives Photo

Dutch Van Kirk
Navigator *Enola Gay*
Hiroshima   August 6, 1945

Contents

Voice from the Doolittle Raid

The month of March 1942 and the month of July 1945 may appear to have no particular historical significance together. However, on a closer look they were two of the most intensive training periods for the two bombing missions that began and ended the war against Japan. First was the attack on the Japanese homeland in April 1942 led by Lt. Col. (later General) James H. Doolittle with sixteen twin-engine medium B-25 bombers each carrying one ton of bombs and launched from a United States Navy aircraft carrier. The other was a mission to Japan by a single long-range four-engine B-29 bomber piloted by Col. (later Brigadier General) Paul W. Tibbets carrying one bomb in August 1945.

I had the opportunity to volunteer for the first mission and our leader assured us it would be the most dangerous we would ever experience. He cautioned that we were not to discuss the training we were undergoing even among ourselves and anyone could drop out at any time. Each plane was modified to carry 2,000 pounds of bombs and enough fuel to fly 2,000 miles.

Twenty-four volunteer crews took the training and each crew would consist of a pilot, co-pilot, navigator, bombardier, and engineer/gunner. The major part of preparation for the pilots was to take off in the shortest distance possible, but we were not told why we had to practice such dangerous takeoffs with heavy bomb loads. We all found that it could be done.

We flew to the west coast and boarded the carrier USS *Hornet* with sixteen planes on April 1, 1942, at Alameda, California. As we headed west, we were told that a sixteen-ship Navy task force would take us to a point off the Japanese homeland. We were to fly our planes off the extremely short deck of that carrier and bomb Tokyo and four other major Japanese cities.

We hoped to get within about 450 miles from Japan but were discovered by a radio-equipped enemy vessel and had to take off eight hours before we

The Crew of Plane No. 1
Left to right, Lt. Henry A. Potter, Lt. Col. James H. Doolittle,
Sgt. Fred A. Braemer, Lt. Richard E. Cole, and SSgt. Paul J. Leonard
(Air Force photo, National Archives, College Park, Maryland)

originally planned. All sixteen planes got off successfully on April 18, 1942, and proceeded to attack our assigned targets heading to China. We encountered bad weather at night and could not locate the intended airfield because a radio beacon had not been installed. Most crews bailed out and others ditched; one crew landed in Russia and was interned by the Russians.

The target damage was minimal and all planes were lost to the American cause, but we achieved our major purpose, which was to make a strong negative psychological effect on the Japanese militarists who had told their people they could never be attacked. But Americans had bombed five of their major cities in retaliation for the Pearl Harbor attack and thus proved that America could and would fight back.

My True Course: Northumberland to Hiroshima is the fascinating life story of Major Theodore "Dutch" Van Kirk leading up to his being the navigator on the famed B-29 Superfortress crew that dropped the first atomic bomb on Japan. His earlier war experience includes his missions with Colonel Tibbets over German-occupied Europe, but ultimately the intense training of the crew to prepare for dropping the most powerful weapon ever devised knowing that its anticipated capabilities might cause harm to their aircraft and themselves. All the other crew members have died which makes this memoir of Van Kirk, last surviving crew member, to be especially noteworthy.

Although Dutch and I did not know each other during our war years, the common experience we share is the outstanding leadership qualities shown by our leaders and the major factor in the success of our respective missions. Lt. Col. Jimmy Doolittle was an outstanding charismatic aviator of world note. His personal friendship with all of his Tokyo Raiders lasted throughout his life. I was extremely fortunate to be his co-pilot.

Colonel Tibbets also had an unusual professional and personal rapport with Van Kirk and his crew. Both leaders encouraged all who served under them to do the best jobs humanly possible. Perhaps we could say that it was their competent leadership that encouraged us to give them the best we were capable of as we completed the first air attack against the enemy homeland in the Pacific and the first atomic attack that brought the largest war in history to a close.

R E Cole

— Lt. Col. Richard E. Cole, USAF (Ret)
Doolittle's Tokyo Raiders

Foreword

"The Three Musketeers"
by D. M. Giangreco

Two names kept popping up when talking with Paul Tibbets. The retired Air Force brigadier general had piloted the *Enola Gay* in the first nuclear strike against Imperial Japan, ending World War II, and I knew who he was talking about. The men were long-time crew members from his time flying B-17s against the Nazis in Europe and North Africa, then the B-29 in the Pacific. He clearly had a deep respect for their abilities and the names came up again in a story involving a wild practical joke on a fellow airman after the war. I remarked that they must have been pretty good friends of his. "Friends!" said Tibbets, "we were the Three Musketeers. Tom Ferebee, 'Dutch' Van Kirk, and I were the Three Musketeers."

The men had first met in April 1942 when Second Lieutenants Van Kirk and Ferebee were assigned to Tibbetts' 340th Bombardment Squadron at Kelly Field, near Sarasota, Florida. Serving as navigator and bombardier respectively, Van Kirk and Ferebee shared the nose compartment of a B-17E as Tibbets, then a major, attempted to instill discipline in his squadron. Van Kirk had no complaints about the long hours of training and even referred to the 340th's hard-charging boss as a "swell guy" in a letter home. By August he would find himself and Ferebee flying deadly combat missions from England with Tibbets at the cockpit above them.

Navigating for the squadron leader on the missions where Tibbets was able to get away from his headquarters desk and other duties, Van Kirk guided the 340th to target. On one mission against the North African port of Bizerte they took their bombers in at just 6,000 feet, so low that tracers from the antiaircraft guns were coming "right up our butt." Weather, fuel consumption, timing, and routes calculated to hopefully minimize the German's fighter and ground defenses were planned to the finest detail. And Van Kirk never let the men down.

Being the squadron commander's navigator meant many special missions ferrying a variety of VIPs, including General Eisenhower about half a dozen times, to meetings, inspections, and conferences. It wasn't until Tibbets' fiery tongue got him in trouble with a senior commander and was sent home that Van Kirk's participation in combat missions increased under a new pilot. After his fifty-eighth strike against the Germans (eight more than the newly established limit for operational missions) in June 1943, Van Kirk was given the thanks of a grateful nation, ordered to pick up the decorations he had earned, and hitched a ride on a US-bound aircraft to take whatever desk job the Army Air Force could find for him.

The trio, which had become a duo, was finally broken up as he and Ferebee parted ways. Like countless other servicemen who had developed the special bond of those that had shared both good times and the risk of violent death, Van Kirk had no expectation of seeing Tibbets and Ferebee ever again. Some fifteen months later, however, while on leave in New Orleans, Van Kirk was surprised to find the phone ringing in his hotel room. Tibbets, now a full colonel and the commander of the mysterious 509th Composite Group, had tracked him down with an offer too good to refuse. "I am forming a new group. I want you as my group navigator. Tom Ferebee has agreed to be my group bombardier. I cannot tell you what we are going to do, but I can tell you that it's going to be important enough that we are going to end or significantly shorten the war."

Tibbets was a superb, experienced combat pilot, one of the very best. But there were many other such flyers in the Air Corps. What landed him the assignment was his organizational and leadership skills, combined with the fact that he had been the one to actually plan and execute the early B-17 strikes against the Germans and had been a key figure in the testing of the often-troublesome B-29, the only made-in-America bomber judged capable of carrying the still-undeveloped nuclear weapon.

Tibbets was given his choice of several remote bases to set up shop and the resources to create a completely self-contained — and secure — unit. The 509th Composite Group would field fifteen B-29s, six big C-54 cargo planes, maintenance, engineer, medical, technical support, and ordnance elements as well as a heavily augmented "MP company" that included an average of thirty Counter Intelligence Corps personnel whose other technical skills allowed them to work side-by-side with personnel that they were "monitoring." He also brought in about a half-dozen airmen he'd served with in the past.

Both in interviews and his book, *Flight of the Enola Gay*, Tibbets marveled at his navigator's ability to arrive at bomb aiming points precisely on schedule, and proudly declared that Van Kirk and Ferebee were "the best qualified airmen in the outfit." These were the men that he wanted at his side, and it was during the training, planning, and run-up to the atom bombing of Japan that the three became even closer; more so, in fact, than Van Kirk actually realized. More than once the self-effacing old navigator told Suzanne Dietz, the author of this volume, that "a lot of people had the idea that there was Tibbets, Ferebee, Van Kirk, and the rest of the 509th;" not the least of which was Tibbets himself! The impression was due to far more than just being the commander's navigator and bombardier and the officers responsible for ensuring that their colleagues throughout the 509th were completely in sync with how the boss expected them to carry out their jobs.

Tibbets, by his own admittance, had "put the screws on pretty tight" in terms of security. A sting operation created specifically to make examples of those with "loose lips" was set in motion shortly after the 509th was activated in December 1944 at Wendover Field, Utah, when a cross section of the Group's personnel were given Christmas leave. There were very few ways to get home from the desolate facility on the edge of the Bonneville Salt Flats and security agents in the guise of friendly civilians, reining in their prey at the bus and train stations in Salt lake City, had little trouble extracting just enough information from the airmen to get them in trouble. Immediately recalled to Wendover they were hauled before Tibbets who demanded, "Why didn't you keep your mouth shut?" The confused and thoroughly cowed serviceman were placed under arrest then given "one more chance" within a day or two.

The word that "talking wasn't healthy" got around very quickly, and the security efforts continued. "Some suspected that I had a personal gestapo watching their every move," said Tibbets. This was not far from the truth. Thus, the easy access, close working relationship, and obvious camaraderie with the boss — and little things like the MPs loaning them shotguns to go duck hunting — immediately set Van Kirk and Ferebee apart from "the rest of the 509th." This separateness would persist well into the 1960s. As for some of the hijinks that the trio engaged in, principally on Tinian Island and after the war, well, airmen will be airmen.

The trio's reputation as a sort of modern-day Three Musketeers spread far beyond the confines of Tibbets' organization. After an uncharacteristic mishap during the Bikini bomb tests in 1946, the men were at a party on Kwajalein Island when in walked General Curtis LeMay who, upon spotting them in the crowd, bellowed: "Over there are three guys who'll tell me where that bomb hit."

The US Navy was convinced that the Army Air Force could not accurately navigate its bombers over ocean waters. The Air Corps would soon prove their sea service critics wrong, but for some personnel it was a long learning curve. As for Van Kirk, his round-trip missions from England against German targets on the continent were mostly over land and a few hundred miles at most. When the squadron was transferred to the Mediterranean, his April 4, 1943, round-about approach and egress when guiding the 340th from its Algiers base against rail yards at Naples, Italy, was more than 700 miles over water but visual landmarks (if one could see them) were still plentiful. Radio direction finding (RDF) beacons were also set up on Allied-held territory to enable accurate bearings to be taken; yet tragedies still occurred.

On the same Naples mission mentioned above, a B-24 striking the harbor from another Allied base became lost when its RDF stopped working and the navigator and pilots became disoriented. The bomber flew past its airfield and deep into the Libyan desert where the crew perished of thirst. The possibility of similar occurrences was far greater in the vast reaches of the Pacific.

Variations in air pressure, and even dust in the sensors, would affect the critically important airspeed and altitude data from a navigator's instruments as well as the drift data supplied to him by the bombardier. His magnetic compass could be also be deflected by electrical fields created by an aircraft's own equipment and the gyrocompass by a virtually imperceptible unsteadiness in the gyros themselves. Even the slightest imperfection in a heading would throw an aircraft further and further off course — using up more and more precious fuel – during a long-distance flight.

By the time that the 509th arrived at Tinian in May 1945, long range navigation stations had been set up at Iwo Jima, half-way to Japan, and the still hotly contested Okinawa. Known by the acronym LORAN, the transmitters greatly minimized the risk to aircrews but the more than 3,000-mile round trips to Japan during practice and weather missions, as well as the atomic strikes themselves, necessitated that all the 509th's navigators — and the bombardiers who served as back-up navigators — be trained to the highest state of proficiency in celestial navigation. At this, Van Kirk excelled.

Author Dietz skillfully blends "Dutch" Van Kirk's story into the *Enola Gay* saga adding unique insights into group commander Tibbets, the atomic missions, and their aftermath. The young airman, who enlisted before Pearl Harbor and seriously considered taking advantage of an official US program to switch to the Britain's Royal Air Force, is followed through family correspondence, official records, and extensive interviews. Van Kirk's memory and perception are extremely valuable. Refreshingly, he always made clear whether he was speaking from direct personal knowledge or from something he had learned from other participants later or his own study. He was not afraid to say, "I don't know."

We are very fortunate that this Musketeer's story is finally told.

D. M. Giangreco
Fort Leavenworth, Kansas
November 13, 2011

Giangreco served for more than twenty years as an editor for *Military Review*, published by the United States Army Command and General Staff College at Fort Leavenworth, Kansas. He has written and lectured widely on national security matters and is an award-winning author of numerous articles and more than a dozen books, including *The Soldier from Independence* A Military Biography of Harry Truman and *Hell To Pay* Operation DOWNFALL and the Invasion of Japan, 1945-1947.

Introduction

Franklin D. Roosevelt ~ January 6, 1945, *In all of the far-flung operations of our own armed forces — on land, and sea and in the air — the final job, the toughest job, has been performed by the average, easy-going, hard-fighting young American, who carries the weight of battle on his own shoulders. It is to him that we and all future generations of Americans must pay grateful tribute.*

Theodore Jerome "Dutch" Van Kirk, "the average, easy-going, hard-fighting young American," grew up as the country wrestled with the economic hardship of the Great Depression and served in the Army Air Corps on four continents.

Born in the decade of the Roaring Twenties, Van Kirk's youth was characterized by a time of incredible change and societal transformation: the Red Scares, reappearance of the Ku Klux Klan, restrictive immigration, Prohibition, Babe Ruth, dance crazes, literary and musical greats, the Scopes "Monkey Trial," and the birth of the Model T. During his teenage years the radio found its way into virtually every home and became a national pastime as families listened to baseball and Franklin Roosevelt's fireside chats. In the backdrop of American society by the end of the thirties the tides of war surged closer to Northumberland.

Van Kirk began his military career before the United States declared war on Japan. This young man's censored letters home tell the story of an aspiring pilot who washed out and became the lead navigator for the early heavy bombing raids on German occupied Europe, the first on northwest Africa, and the first atomic bomb mission. His mother's intimate and almost daily letters provide a unique voice of life on the home front and worry for her son.

While her big brother went off to war, Jean Van Kirk wrestled with being a teenager and flirtations from a neighborhood boy who became a medic and sometime after the war her husband. Elwood "Mick" McAllister waited with his medic kit on August 6, 1945, ready to treat the wounded, if he survived the impending invasion of Kyushu. High school classmates like William Kelley stormed the beaches at Iwo Jima and battlefronts around the world.

No war story is complete without a love story and this one is no different. Mary Jane Young waited for her "dearest darling" beau and four brothers serving their country to return home. When her boyfriend returned to the states from the North African front, he married her, and within a year left for the battles in the Pacific. Mrs. Theodore J. Van Kirk now waited for her husband.

More than half a century later Robert W. Granston, a Prisoner of War held by Japan for most of the war, and James L. Starnes, Jr., Officer of the Deck on the USS *Missouri* during the surrender signing, became neighbors of Van Kirk in Stone Mountain, Georgia, and forever part of the brotherhood that fought to bring an end to this global conflict.

Dutch Van Kirk sat at his kitchen table and narrated the tales of B-17s and B-29s, the antics of young men amidst death and destruction, the early heavy bombing raids on German occupied Europe, the air attacks in northwest Africa, and the first atomic bomb strike. These are the stories from the past and recollections from the present that many offspring of Van Kirk's generation wanted to hear, but will never hear from their fathers who also took up arms to fight the Axis powers. A few of the events along the course of Van Kirk's life appear in this work as likely news of the day.

Other historians have written scores of books and articles about World War II and in particular the mission of the *Enola Gay*. More will be written. But this is the last word of Dutch Van Kirk, the sole living crewmember and navigator of the *Enola Gay* of his journey to take up arms.

My True Course is the authorized biography of a young man who dug potatoes on the family farm in a little town in the heart of Pennsylvania, worked as a clerk in a small local grocery store, and played with his fellow "river rats" by the Susquehanna River. Van Kirk's voice in the present and his written word during the war depict a man who served his country and followed his true course in life and throughout his military service.

Dutch Van Kirk's name is already in the history books, but he is much more than a figure of prominence in world history. He is a husband, a father, and a grandfather and for more than sixty years has spoken to countless community groups and high school students educating them about the war.

Van Kirk's story represents the sixteen million men and women who also followed a "True Course" and helped bring an end to the war when the world stood on the precipice of evil.

Notes about the voices from the past and present and editing.

Son, "Ted," "Teedy," "Dutch" .... Theodore Jerome Van Kirk

Mother .... Grace Snyder Van Kirk

Father "Fred" .... Fredrick Van Kirk

Sister .... Jean Van Kirk McAllister

Aunt Martha, sister of Grace .... Martha Snyder Van Kirk

Uncle Lee, brother of Fredrick .... Lee Van Kirk

Mary Jane, M.J., "Janie,"
    girlfriend of Theodore .... Mary Jane Young Van Kirk

Mickey, "Mick," husband of Jean Van Kirk .... Elwood M. McAllister

High school classmate .... William J. Kelley

Cousin Jim, "Jimmy" .... Leroy (Nancy) J. Van Kirk

Cousin Frances .... Frances Van Kirk

Robert, William, Albert, and Ray Young .... brothers of Mary Jane Young

Emma Seasholtz, "mother" to Mary Jane .... aunt of Mary Jane Young

George Seasholtz, "father" to Mary Jane .... uncle of Mary Jane Young

Arnold and Bill Seasholtz,
    "brothers" to Mary Jane .... cousins of Mary Jane Young

Present neighbor .... Capt. Robert W. Granston, USN (Ret)

Present neighbor .... James L. Starnes, Jr.

"Norry" .... nickname for Northunberland, Pennsylvania

The letters were transcribed as written. Grace Van Kirk wrote almost daily to her son and also her brothers serving in the military. Many of the letters had limited punctuation, use of possessive case, and typically no question marks for interrogatory sentences. The use of (sic) for the spelling of corse (course) or conclusion (conclusion) from the different writers in all cases would be distracting and added only where necessary for clarity. Corrections were made when the obvious intent was a different word, for example, think vs. thing. Several letter writers spelled Kelly Field "Kelley." Japanese were referred to as

Japs in the correspondence and not meant to be derogatory, but present the writing in its original form.

Grace frequently mentions M.J. (Mary Jane), her future daughter-in-law. Unfortunately, only a few letters of Mary Jane to Dutch survived.

The names in the manuscript were from available primary source materials. The author will be glad to receive information leading to corrections and additions for subsequent publications and apologizes for any errors or omissions.

All photographs that appear, unless otherwise noted, are part of the Van Kirk personal collection.

List of Tables

Chapter One

Japan's *American Prisoners of War*

August 5 - 6, 1945, lives lost in the Asian-Pacific war had reached unfathomable millions.[1] A brutal offensive launched by Japan in 1941 against the Chinese of "kill all, loot all, burn all" had caused countless civilian and military deaths. More than 100,000 Chinese, Korean, and Philippine women had been forced into sexual slavery for Japan's military.[2]

American casualties from battle deaths, other deaths, and wounds exceeded a million. The casualty figures of 1,076,325 did not include combat related psychological disability and non-battle deaths of Navy and Marines, which raised the number to greater than two million.[3]

The United States suffered from a manpower shortage and a decline in available inductees from the Selective Service since 1943.[4] The public grew weary of the war even though the criteria for reported casualties had been adapted to reduce the numbers. By August 1945 the war cost roughly 150,000 Allied and Axis lives (substantially civilians) a week.[5] As the battles moved closer to the main islands, the Japanese became better at fighting their enemy causing more losses.

On June 18, 1945, Gen. George Marshall at a Joint Chiefs meeting with President Truman compared the planned invasion scenario to the difficult and bloody Normandy invasion.

The Surgeon General ordered 471,000 body bags for the six months of the initial land attack on Kyushu, *Operation Olympic*.[6] The southern half of the island would be a staging area for the main invasion.

On the main islands of Japan kamikaze aircraft and fresh troops in

Manchuria waited in reserve.[7] The Empire's schools closed in March and children eight years and older were ordered to report for war service.[8] Civilian militia numbering close to twenty million prepared to fight to the death for the Emperor as the militants proclaimed "The Glorious Death of One Hundred Million" to defend Japan.

Incendiary bombings of Tokyo killed more than a hundred thousand and left more than a million homeless just in March 1945. Continued pounding by the Superforts did not bring Japan's surrender. The Japanese people faced starvation and homelessness. War Minister Korechika Anami and hard-core militants prepared to sacrifice the Japanese people to extinction rather than be dishonored by surrender.

American prisoners of war suffering deprivation, forced work, torture, and barbarous conditions for more than three years faced certain execution if foreigners stepped on the shores of Kyushu. One former prisoner saved by the end of the war lives next door to Van Kirk.

"At the Kitchen Table with Dutch"

Dutch ~ My neighbor moved in about two years ago. I started to hear reports that he had been captured at Corregidor. To me that set him up in my eyes as high as you can go. Mary Jane's brother had been killed on the Bataan Death March and another brother in an invasion of an island in the Pacific. And here is my neighbor next door who had been on Corregidor, a prisoner of war of the Japanese, practically the entire war. That in of itself says enough. I have great respect for that man and besides he is a damn nice guy.

"He Saved Me"

Twenty-six hundred miles from Northumberland in the Hamlet of Richmond Highlands, north of Seattle, Washington, Robert Wyatt Granston was born December 28, 1916, to John Harry Granston and Clara May Wyatt. His Granstrom grandparents emigrated from Sweden to the United States in 1880.[9]

"My parents, maternal grandparents, aunts, and uncles lived in a little enclave around the family farm where I grew up. During the depression we did not have a nickel, but an abundance of good food and nutrition that helped me survive later on during the war. After high school, I was fortunate to be in enrolled in the Navy ROTC program at the University of Washington. When

Ensign Robert W. Granston
(Courtesy of Sharon Granston)

I learned that six graduates of the NROTC program would be commissioned into the Supply Corps of the regular Navy; economics became my secondary major, and the Navy, my primary goal. I was elated to be one of the six chosen. After graduation I went to the Navy Supply and Finance School at the shipyard in south Philadelphia for six months.[10] I always wanted to be in the Navy. There must be a Viking in my genetic past," and Granston laughed.[11]

While attending the school, "I met Norma Beatrice Hiscoe from Upper Darby, Pennsylvania.[12] She soon became my all consuming interest and extra-curricular concern. We attended the Army – Navy game in 1940. Navy won.[13] At the Penn Athletic Club that night, I proposed. Norma said it was too soon to be committed, but she did wait for me. During my training I did poorly on one exam. Commander Walter Buck called me into his office and said my performance left much to be desired. I told him I had met this particular young lady and my attention had been divided. He was not amused. He read me off and hoped he would not see me again and refocused my attention. With renewed effort, I completed the curriculum."

Granston volunteered to go to the Philippines, which in hindsight "was at a very bad time" with his buddy Chuck Wilkins, a fellow classmate at the University of Washington and in the Navy Supply and Finance School. Granston and Wilkins drove back to Seattle in a new 1940 Nash, which cost $750.00. They crossed the Pacific on the Navy transport, the USS *Henderson*, and arrived in Manila on May 1941 after a "relaxing three week transit. Passing the SS *Washington*'s return with our nationals to the United States" did not evoke any sense of panic or impending disaster in the Pacific.

"My first duty assignment was at the Cavite Naval Yard as Assistant Supply Officer and subsequently as a Supply and Disbursing Officer of the Receiving Station. Chuck was the Commissary Officer. After duty hours I played golf and tennis. I traveled around the Philippines and enjoyed a trip to visit the summer capital of Baguio City. It was the good life. While in Manila I met Lucita Goyena, the reigning movie queen of the Philippines. She introduced me to the social life, but nothing in contradiction to my commitment in Philadelphia," referring to his fiancée Norma.

Following the bombing of Pearl Harbor, the "good life" came to a terrifying and screeching halt on December 10, 1941, when the Japanese attacked the Cavite Navy Yard. A United States Army Signal photograph of the yard in flames was one of the first to reach the states since the outbreak of the war.[14] Ensign Granston risked his life during the bombing and the explosion at the torpedo factory. He raced to the Receiving Station, removed the currency from the safe, and subsequently transported the monies to a bank in Manila. Granston also assisted in providing support to damaged ships and assisted in the burying of some 1,400 dead military and civilians. On December 24th the mandatory evacuation began to Bataan.[15]

Near the end of January, Granston was moved from the Section Base at Mariveles to the Island of Corregidor. "There I tried to reconstruct lost Navy pay records. My greatest satisfaction was sending the required financial returns to Cleveland, Ohio, and to register allotment of pay to their family members."

The epic Battle for Bataan during the first months of 1942 ended when Maj. Gen. Edward P. King, Jr., surrendered the Luzon Force to Japan on April 9, 1942, the largest mass surrender of United States forces, about twelve thousand American soldiers and also sixty-three thousand Filipinos. The prisoners were forced to march from Mariveles in the southern tip of Bataan to Camp O'Donnell more than sixty miles north in intense tropical heat and abused by their captors, known as the Bataan Death March. The March was characterized by horrific brutality, murder including beheadings and throat cuttings, and deliberate withholding of food and water.

Corregidor had been under fire from Japanese aerial, naval, and artillery bombardment since December 29, 1941. The Filipino and American Navy and Army troops inflicted heavy enemy losses, but on May 6, 1942, General Wainwright surrendered. "I was in Queen's Tunnel, the Navy tunnel, when we heard about the surrender. As the Japanese came in we lined up by a big table. A Japanese soldier walked up and down with his bayonet drawn. It was deathly silent. We were ordered to the Ninety-Second Garage area and held there for about a week. Then we were taken by ship to the end of Dewey Boulevard and then marched to Bilibid prison. After a week or so we were trucked to Cabanatuan and marched to Camp 3. Later we were moved to Camp 1. The bulk of my stay was in Camp 1."

Granston was moved several times while being held for the next three and a half years in various prison camps in the Philippines, Japan, and Korea subject to slave labor, regular beatings, and inhumane conditions. "I was fortunate that I was being bitten by the same mosquitoes as the other men, but didn't get malaria. I drank the same polluted water and ate the same food, but did not get

Chapter 1

dysentery. I came into captivity with good nutrition and as a stubborn Swede of faith. Malaria and dysentery wore many of the prisoners down. I lost about fifty pounds. I have always been an optimist and knew that the United States would evolve victorious. It was my personal battle to survive."

Roll call began the day at 5:30 a.m. "Ich, Ni, San, Si, Go, Roku, Sitchi, Hachi, Kyuu, Juu"[16] one, two, three, and so on. This is how Granston learned to count in Japanese. The count seemed to be endless and the Japanese guards were never sure of the number of prisoners. "After roll call we took our mess kits to the kitchen for lugao, a watered down rice mixture. You scrubbed your teeth with a piece of cloth and picked your teeth with bamboo. Work detail was from early in the morning until noon and then we marched back to the camp for a meager meal, something with a little greens from the fields we worked, and then returned to the farm in the afternoon. We pulled weeds by hand. The farm mainly grew potatoes and other vegetables. Sometimes I succeeded eating turnip tops. Always we were watched carefully. After work you might get a pass to the hospital ward, the Zero Ward, and talk to the sick prisoners about home and family. They knew they were dying. You knew they were dying, but we didn't talk about it."

The Japanese pilfered the first Red Cross shipment of food that reached the prisoners after about two and a half years of captivity. Many prisoners opened their personal packages from home only to find cookie crumbs and maggots. "I was very proud of my parents. They had gone to Doctor Bonham who recommended sending bottles of Vitamin B. I shared the vitamins with Lieutenant Commander Erickson and others. Also, I was fortunate to get letters from home and from Norma. When permitted we wrote abbreviated messages on three by five cards. Most of us pondered for days the carefully written permitted twenty-five words."

Evening conversation always centered on food and on a rare occasion women, if the meal portion was more than the typical meager ration. "We talked about what our first meal would be when we did get home. I talked about my mother's cake and rolls and the southern boys talked about Brunswick stew and rabbit. And we talked about our experiences during holidays like the Fourth of July. At home down on the beach my dad broiled salmon basted with butter and olive juice over a fire of alder-wood. My mother would arrive with a keg of beer."

Every morning a Catholic or Jesuit priest would say Mass. "I often attended. Occasionally on a Wednesday evening we had some local camp entertainment. Warrick Potter Scott III conducted talks on growing wine and his experiences at the Sorbonne. He was tall, gangly, and sensitive to the sun. While working he wore a pillowcase over his head with two holes for eyes and a hole for his nose and mouth. He looked a little like Ichabod Crane. The Japanese had no idea what to do with him. Later Warrick was killed on the Hell Ship, the *Oryoku Maru*."[17]

"Countless times during my captivity I said a prayer taught to me by my mother about Jesus Christ, above all my hero."

Jesus is my health. I cannot be sick. Jesus is my strength in failing quick. Jesus is my all. I know no fear and by His might and power I will overcome and by His Will I will persevere.

On December 13, 1944, about 1,600 Bilibid prisoners were loaded on the *Oryoku Maru*. The defenders of Corregidor and Mindanao and the survivors of the Bataan Death March were the last prisoners evacuated from the Philippines.[18] The Hell Ships also called Death Ships in news reports were unmarked and frequent targets of Allied submarines and fighter aircraft from the USS *Hornet* and *Hancock* unaware of the transported POWs crammed into the cargo holds. The *Oryoku Maru* was sunk in Subic Bay off Olongapo, Luzon.[19]

Many men already weakened after more than two years of captivity faced the darkness and indescribable nightmares of the hold including lack of air fouled by their own excrement and were driven quickly to dehydration, insanity, and death.[20] John Zale, a survivor of the Bataan Death March, the Hell Ships, and three and a half years of captivity in Manchuria, described the ships as much worse than the March. "We were down in the hold, no sanitary conditions, and guys full of lice. There was no food, no place to sleep. You stood or squatted; no room to lie down. When someone died they were thrown overboard."[21] The atrocities done to the prisoners and by the prisoners in moments of insanity and desperation were unimaginable.

After repeated attacks from American fighters targeting the *Oryoku Maru*, Granston and others jumped overboard. "George Petritz was one of two who escaped. Afterwards, he was used in the United States for war bond drives." On Christmas Day the survivors were transferred to the *Enoura Maru* that was bombed by fighters from the *Hornet* on January 9, 1945. The last transfer took place on January 11th to the *Brazil Maru*, which did not head to sea until the fourteenth of January and reached the harbor of Moji in northern Kyushu on January 29th. More men perished soon after the long ordeal that began seven weeks earlier.[22]

"When we finally arrived on the last ship to Kyushu with just remnants of our summer clothing, we were issued some warmer clothing when called topside by our rank. I was a Lieutenant Junior Grade. My buddy Bart Cross of the Cross Pens' family in New York was an ensign. He was very weak and emaciated. I was issued a coat, pants, and socks, which I gave to Bart. When his name was called, I went up for him. The American interpreter called out 'you had been up here before.' Hearing this the Japanese interpreter had me severely beaten."

News of the end of the war came one afternoon while Granston worked on a farm in Jinsen, Korea, traditionally known as Inchon. "Johnny Johnston was head of the work detail. He came up to me and said, 'It is over. The war is over.' I said come on you've been eating too many turnip tops. But it was true. The camp was awash of rumors. The Japanese commander approached Commander Beecher. 'The war will soon be over. Here are the keys. I suggest that all your people stay within the confines of the camp.' At the camp, there was jubilation. The storehouses were opened and we ate ourselves sick. With bolts of yellow cloth we spelled POW on the roof. I had the greatest respect for Colonel Beecher who was the American commandant. He was a remarkable person with the highest standards, which he never compromised with his dealings with the Japanese."

"An advance intelligence officer arrived and told us about Hiroshima and that a nuclear explosion had occurred. I felt elation. It shortened the war. He advised us that B-29s with supplies would come shortly. Industrial plants surrounded our camp. The camp covered about five acres. Three airplanes did come out of the east with 'POW supplies' written underneath their wings. The bays opened and containers of food, clothing, and other supplies were dropped. The supply containers hit some of the barracks and kitchens causing fires. The next day we got out of the camp and went to a nearby hilltop by a Belgian convent. On the third day we made arrows 'drop here' on the tidal flats. From the supplies I got the clothing that I wore back to Manila and eventually to the United States." The POWs were evacuated by ship to Manila.

"When we were liberated and boarded the Navy ships, the first thing I did was enjoy a hot shower and a ham and egg breakfast, and then wrote a letter to Norma in Philadelphia."

On board the USS Refuge can (destroyer)
September 9, 1945 6:00 p.m.
Norma Darling: It still is a dream, a glorious dream. My first letter to you in almost four years, the war over at last. American planes, ships, supplies, everything

happening so fast, on board this hospital ship, a shower, pajamas, ham and eggs, coffee, ice cream. Ice Cream – imagine.

Darling. I'm free. I can't believe it yet. Free to live, free to laugh, free to love again. And Norma how I love you. All I want to write is I love you, I love you. I have been planning this letter for years and now I am at a loss. It is impossible to crowd the past in one letter so I will wait until we are together. My head is awhirl with so many plans for us.

Norma, I feel great and my weight is back to normal. We were released yesterday at our camp in Jensin Korea and brought directly aboard this ship. We are being treated like kings, like white men again. What it all means you can well imagine, darling.

I am so anxious to receive the first word from you and the folks - how you are and where you are - can you meet me in San Francisco – can we be married right away - this and a thousand other questions. Best of all, darling. I'm coming home, home to you.

We sail for Manila in a few days. There we will be processed and segregated. I wish we might fly home from there. But by ship or by plane we are heading for the United States.

Norma, Chuck is not coming home with me. He died on January 10, 1945 in Formosa as a result of a bombing we sustained there. He wanted us to carry on for him and be terribly happy. I hope Earl and Gordon are safe and well. My sympathy to Chuck's mother and family. I'm very anxious to hear from Mom and Dad.

I will write every day and try to wire or phone from Manila, darling. Loving you and having your love is all that brought me through these past years. Norma until tomorrow – how wonderful to write again – to say I love you. I love you.

Yours As Ever
Bob
Darling, I love you

"My parents received my letter, which they forwarded to Norma with the first news of my liberation. Later my dad told me it cost more for my mother, Clara May, to court Norma never forgetting a holiday or birthday card for her, than it cost him to court my mother. Norma waited for me, but some guys did get 'Dear John' letters while being held prisoner."[23]

Captain Robert W. Granston received the Navy Cross, the Navy's second highest award for valor after the Medal of Honor. Granston is one of only two known Supply Corps recipients. He donated his Navy Cross to the Supply Corps Museum in 2009.[24]

In 2007 Granston moved to Stone Mountain, Georgia. "I joined the Men's Forum and was invited to speak for ten minutes to give a bit of my personal history. I learned from other neighbors about my distinguished neighbor next door, Theodore 'Dutch' Van Kirk. I went over and knocked on his door and introduced myself. I told him I was going to speak to the men's group and was going to give him full credit for saving my ass. I wanted to express publicly my life long appreciation to him and the crew of the *Enola Gay* for what they did to bring an end to the war. I have never ceased to be grateful to him."[25]

So, what kind of person is the "distinguished neighbor next door" who as a young man also wanted to serve his country? What is his story that began in another town on the other side of America?

Chapter One — Endnotes

1 From the invasion of Manchuria, Rape of Nanking, retribution for the Doolittle raid, biological warfare and human experimentation on Prisoners of War from Unit 731, forced labor, Bataan Death March, Hell Ships, brutality in labor and prisoner of war camps, and battles across the Pacific Ocean and Asia casualties reached in excess of twenty-three million according to data compiled by Werner Gruhl, former chief of NASA's Cost and Economic Analysis Branch.

2 George Hicks, *The Comfort Women* (New York: Norton, 1995). Chinese scholars estimate higher numbers. Research and debate on the figures is ongoing.

3 Total American battle deaths 291,557 and other deaths 113,842 totaled 405,479; wounds not mortal 670,846. Total casualties 1,076,245 United States Department of Defense. Non-battle deaths, psychological issues, and Merchant Marine and Coast Guard casualties are typically excluded from data. D. M. Giangreco, *Hell To Pay Operation DOWNFALL and the Invasion of Japan, 1945 – 1947*, (Annapolis, MD: Naval Institute Press, 2009), 4.

4 Men who entered military service peaked in 1943 at 3,323,970; 1,591,942 in 1944; and 945,862 in 1945. "Selective Service System: History and Records," http://www.sss.gov/induct.htm [accessed February 23, 2011].

5 The death rate was increasing as the war continued. Gruhl estimated that of the 150,000 lives 100,000 were Allied Asian civilians and 18,000 Japanese civilians. Werner Gruhl, *Imperial Japan's World War Two 1931 – 1945*, (New Brunswick, NJ: Transaction Publishers, 2010), 204.

6 The Surgeon General based the need for body bags on the deaths of American forces in the battles in the Pacific theatre plus 30% for margin of error. Thomas S. Walters, *Why, Must The World Be Like This*, (New York, NY: Vantage Press, Inc., 2006), 171.

7 Giangreco cites reports and other sources of significant numbers of Japanese forces at the time of the surrender of fifty-nine divisions, thirty-six independent brigades, and forty-five regiments, which did not include the Imperial Navy or Army Air Service in excess of the March 1945 estimates by MacArthur staff's. Giangreco, *Hell To Pay Operation DOWNFALL and the Invasion of Japan, 1945 – 1947*, 21 and 287.

8 The United Press also reported the announcement that Japan admitted the loss of Iwo Jima. "Japan Closes Schools, Children to Go to Work," UP, *Binghamton Press*, March 19, 1945.

9 The Granstrom surname changed to Granston by the next generation.

10 On August 1940 Granston accepted a regular commission in the Supply Corps of the United States Navy.

11 Robert Wyatt Granston, telephone interview April 20, 2010, and interview with author Stone Mountain, GA, July 11, 2010.

12 Norma Beatrice Hiscoe was born June 17, 1920, in Albany, NY, the daughter of Arthur Winthrop Hiscoe and Bertha Louella Bevens.

13 Described as the "swashbuckling sailors" by Harold Parrott in the *Brooklyn Eagle*, Navy beat Army 14 to 0 in front of 102,000 fans packed into Philadelphia's Pawling Municipal Stadium on November 30, 1940.

14 "Barges in Cavite Navy Yard Burn After Jap Raid," *Niagara Falls Gazette*, April 1, 1942.

15 George H. White, Captain, SC, USN (Ret), "The Incredible Story of Three World War II Supply Corps Heroes." Granston was awarded the Navy Cross for his duties during the defense of the Navy Yard.

16 Granston recited the numbers phonetically.

17 After the war Granston responded to a letter from Edgar Scott, brother of Warrick, and visited the Scott family. Ichabod Crane was a fictional character from Washington Irving's short story, *The Legend of Sleepy Hollow*.

18 John A. Glusman, *Conduct Under Fire*, London, England: Penguin Books, 454.

19 Glusman's book and the Weller newspaper accounts reported the numbers for deaths differently. Some survivors of the *Oryoku Maru* were killed after being transferred to the *Enoura Maru* when it was also bombed.

20 Glusman, *Conduct*, 455, and George Weller, "Cruise of Death series," *Chicago Daily News* Foreign Service. The series of ten articles ran in newspapers around the country in the fall of 1945 including the *Rochester Democrat Chronicle*, Rochester, NY.

21 John S. Zale's (né Zubrzycki) personal account of the Bataan Death March, Hell Ships, and three years captivity in Manchuria during his experience as a POW in World War II. Interview with Dietz July 23, 2007. Dietz, *Honor Thy Fathers & Mothers* Niagara Frontier's Legacy of Patriotism and Survival, Youngstown, NY, 125.

22 Weller articles, 1945.

23 Robert Granston and Norma Hiscoe married October 9, 1945, in Seattle, WA. Norma passed away in 1993. Captain Granston married Iris Marie Inman in 1997.

24 "WWII Supply Corps hero donates Navy Cross to Supply Corps Museum," *The Oakleaf,* November 2009, 6.

25 After 28 ½ years Captain Granston retired from the Navy. Following his military service Granston worked in private industry as a consultant and logistic staff assistant in a special weapons laboratory. On October 8, 2002, Judith Kent interviewed Robert Granston for the Library of Congress Veterans History project.

Chapter Two

Northumberland *Hometown America*

In 1772 Robert Martin, a prospector, settled the wilds of Northumberland, Pennsylvania. He established a tavern several hundred feet beyond the intersection of the west and north branch of the Susquehanna River in Pennsylvania, where centuries later a young man played in its waters and began to chart his course through life and history.

"My First Plane Ride"

Dutch ~ I was born at home on February 27, 1921, in a farmhouse between Northumberland and Danville on Route 11, on a large farm at that time.[26] My

parents were living with my Snyder grandparents. They were tenant farmers for a rich family named Greeno who also had a bakery. My mother's relatives looked at me and said, "Grace will never raise that one." It made me feel real good hearing that story.

My mother was Grace Snyder Van Kirk and my father Fredrick Van Kirk. Mother was Pennsylvania Dutch and my

Home where Van Kirk was born
(Courtesy of Leroy J. Van Kirk)

father Holland Dutch, but could not speak it. One of mother's Pennsylvania Dutch sayings when I did not clean my plate was "remember the starving Armenians." I did not know who were the Armenians.

Fredrick and Grace Snyder Van Kirk

We were a united family. I was very close to my maternal grandparents. My grandmother was a great cook. The grandchildren were always visiting. I do not know how my grandparents fed us all. It seemed as if my grandmother could take a pot of water and feed us.

Dad had bought me a .22 caliber rifle. My grandfather would egg me on in the back yard to shoot at the long radio antenna tubes. I also used that .22 to shoot rats that came up the riverbank. Everybody in town did that.

I was a depression kid. My father was a night watchman at a converting plant in Sunbury, Pennsylvania, before the plants all moved south. Then he worked on the farm with my uncle for a while under new owners. I hate to tell you how many potatoes I picked. Later, dad drove truck for Weis Pure Foods stores. They had about one hundred stores in the area. Eventually, I also worked for Weis at the store in Northumberland.

Nobody had any money at that time. I attended a small school and before graduation the WPA (Works Progress Administration) built a new school. WPA was big in our town. Northumberland is situated on the north and west branch of the Susquehanna River. We dug sand out of the west branch, and my dad and I dredged coal from the north branch. The coal had been dumped in the river at Scranton. We sold the coal for two dollars a ton.

The railroad followed the Susquehanna River and split just like the river. One branch went towards Buffalo and Williamsport and the other to the Wilkes Barre, Scranton, and Binghamton areas. The railroad and classifying yards, a forging company, and a stamping mill provided employment for many in Northumberland. Some worked in the surrounding areas of Sunbury and Danville, or drove to Harrisburg, the State Capitol, about fifty miles, a horrible commute in those days.

I was a river rat with several semi-rowdy friends, and always climbing trees

Dutch - My middle name was from this grandfather, Jerome Snyder. He lost an eye while working as a stonemason. The Snyders were my favorite grandparents. My grandmother was a good cook and made a great potpie.

and roaming the area on our bikes. We rode three or four miles to where we climbed the blue hill. One of our friends got stuck on the hill until the fire company rescued him.

In the summer I worked on my Uncle Lee Van Kirk's farm picking potatoes. It was a backbreaking job. I worked for a dollar a day and could pick up a hundred pounds of potatoes. I will tell you one thing. We did not loaf around.

The furthest I got away from home even in high school was Hershey, Pennsylvania, an amusement park, about sixty miles away. That was an event for us. Once we made a trip to Philadelphia about one hundred miles away. That was like going to the moon for heaven's sake.

During this time period I got my first plane ride with a pilot from town John Abusio. I still remember his name. I do not know how my dad financed it, but he did. John had an old bi-plane. Up along the river, the north branch, in a small town called Riverside, Pennsylvania, there was a park. We went to the Riverside Park for reunions. John landed on a nearby farmer's field and gave people a ride for four or five dollars. I went up with John and was hooked. I never wanted to walk again!

"The Younger Sister"

Jean - Jean Van Kirk McAllister, the younger sister of Dutch, lives in Locust Grove, Virginia, near the Wilderness battlefield of the War Between the States. "Daniel Van Kirk was wounded in Wilderness."[27] Daniel joined the 12th Ohio Infantry Regiment on June 20, 1861, and the list of ancestors who played varied roles throughout the history of the United States since the American Revolution.

"We grew up in the thirties, and it was very rough. We were kids of the depression. If we got two pennies for candy we thought gosh it was wonderful. We did not go joy riding. Portzline Dairy was the hangout where we met the fellows we would like to date." Everyone knew each other. There were no strangers. "Northumberland was a very small town, very provincial." Jean wondered how Joseph Priestley found their little town. He had discovered oxygen gas at Leeds, England, in 1774 and fled from the prejudice of England to settle in Northumberland. "Nothing can be more delightful, or more healthy than this place," Priestley said.[28]

"My aunt Emma Van Kirk, the oldest of the Van Kirk children, lived in the Priestley house. Emma married John Bingaman."

Honeysuckle vines covered the Van Kirk porch at their home at 672 Queen Street. "Mother liked a little privacy. The Biega family owned the home. They were Ukrainians I think. I adored him and called him Daddy Biega and I called her Mary. They had three sons and they all served too, I believe."[29]

Dutch ~ Mrs. Biega made the best beer in the world.

"River Rats and Squeaking Gliders"

Mick McAllister ~ "We were all river rats. Every man knew every man's privates because we all swam naked in the Susquehanna River. So those of us who were proud stood on land and those who were not stayed swimming. We went through the railroad tunnel on Seventh Street then out into the river."[30]

Mick collected arrowheads washed up on shore after the tides retreated and watched the daily ritual of Louie Santangelo, a local shoemaker and one of the Van Kirk's neighbors, fishing in the river.

"We had a card store downtown on Queen Street where we played poker." The young men including Van Kirk also played cards at the No. 1 Fire Company on the second floor.

"Mother didn't know about it. No, no," insisted Jean. "But in those days everything was nickel and dime."

A light over the pool table at Hennie's Pool Parlor had the glamour of Las Vegas for young men living on the edge. Mick called Hennie's "the dark room. Nothing illegitimate just a couple of pool tables and a place you could play cards. There wasn't much misbehaving in town." Everyone knew where you lived.

Jean often told her daughters, "If you misbehaved downtown by the time you got home your parents knew. That kept you on the straight and narrow."

Jean ~ "Ted was an extremely hard worker. Uncle Lee managed a farm for Weis Food on the Danville Road and they grew potatoes, fields and fields of potatoes. For a summer job Ted picked potatoes." Potatoes were dug by hand.

"It was hard work and hot work. He couldn't have been too old mid teen's maybe."

Dutch ~ I worked three summers on the farm from about fifteen to seventeen years old.

Jean ~ "Ted saved his money in the family's old fashioned attic under the loose floor boards." One day he went up in the attic "to get his last couple of dollars. Some mouse chewed up the money and carried it away. Mother and dad said, 'Well you know that is the last thing you should do. You do not put money in a mouse hole.' Oh boy, you can imagine after he worked that hard," Jean commented in sympathy.

"Ted was a tease. One of my aunts told me that 'He was a little devil.' I don't remember this because I was too young. My mother was one of the first ladies in town that got a license and drove a car. Mother was going some place and wanted Ted to go along. I do not know if he did not want to go or if he was just being ornery. Anyway, she said 'all right Theodore if you don't go with me I am leaving.' Mother started the car and he ran after her," chuckled Jean.

Dutch ~ We had a 1927 Chevrolet with running boards and disc wheels. Mick lived up on the corner. That corner was the highlight of our social existence; we used to play street games like "kick the wicket." We didn't have a baseball bat. We used a stick and a ball and kicked it and followed the rules of baseball.

Mick ~ "We sat on their front porch and the damn glider would squeak like hell. Ted's favorite expression was that 'every time I didn't hear that glider squeaking I went out to see what was going on. I told dad to get an oil can too.' We all grew up together."

 *February 27, 1921,* Warren Gamaliel Harding occupied the White House when Theodore Jerome Van Kirk was born. Harding defeated Ohio governor James M. Cox, a democrat, and vice-presidential candidate Franklin D. Roosevelt in the 1920 election. Harding ran on a pledge to return to normalcy following World War I.[31] Harding's administration began a resurgence of isolationism and an administration blighted by scandals.

Earlier in the month trade unions in Germany protested the harsh reparations imposed after the war. In a manifesto the unions stated, "We are not prepared to perish for the benefit of international capitalists."[32]

March 1, 1921, the first Japanese census registered seventy-seven million citizens.[33]

March 6, 1921, the Sunbury, Pennsylvania, police chief issued an order for women to wear their skirts at least four inches below the knee.

March 8, 1921, Germany rejected the European Allies demand to pay fifty-six billion dollars over forty-two years. The Allies turn down the German counter offer for less than a quarter of the amount. Troops from France and Belgium marched into Dusseldorf and several other cities and disarm their police forces.

April 2, 1921, Albert Einstein lectured in New York City on the theory of relativity.

July 29, 1921, Adolf Hitler became the President of the Nationalist Socialist German Workers Party.

November 7, 1921, Benito Mussolini proclaimed himself the Duce or leader of the Nationalist Fascist Party in Italy.

November 29, 1921, Prince Hirohito took the place of his ailing father as the Regent of Japan.

December 10, 1921, Niels Henrik David Bohr won the Nobel Prize in Physics for his work on the structure of atoms and the radiation emanating from them.[34]

June 1922, a student movement led to the formation of a Communist Party in China and called for the overthrow of the capitalists. Mao Tse-tung, a primary school teacher and library assistant, attended the first party congress.

September 4, 1922, Lt. James H. Doolittle in a modified DH-4B made the first transcontinental flight in a day.

November 9, 1922, the Royal Swedish Academy of Science announced the award of the Nobel Prize in Physics to Albert Einstein for his contributions to theoretical physics and his discovery of the law of the photoelectric effect.

January 25, 1923, the French Army occupied the industrial Ruhr Valley in response to Germany's failure to deliver reparations of coal and timber.

March 9, 1923, Vladimir Ilyich Lenin suffered a severe stroke and a triumvirate was created to lead the Communist Party. Lenin, the architect of Russia's revolution, had formed the first Soviet government on November 9, 1917, and served as its chairman until his death.

March 27, 1923, the Nazi Party rallied in the streets of Munich carrying swastika banners. Adolf Hitler called for the repeal of the Treaty of Versailles.

Margaret Young with her twins
Albert and Mary Jane.

September 1, 1923, the 7.9 earthquake in the Tokyo – Yokohama area, subsequent firestorms, and the tsunami generated in Sagami Bay damaged more than 694,000 homes and caused 142,800 deaths.[35]

November 8, 1923, Hitler attempted a coup against the German national government and was arrested.

November 15, 1923, twins Mary Jane and Albert Young were born in Point Township, Northumberland County, Pennsylvania, to George W. and Margaret Cooper Young. George worked in the Northumberland shops of the Pennsylvania Railroad as a mechanic. The Youngs had three other children, Ray, Robert, and William.[36]

April 1, 1924, Hitler sentenced to five years in prison for his part in the Beer Hall putsch served only eight months in the Landsberg Castle in Munich. During his internment Hitler wrote his autobiography with ghostwriter, Emile Maurice, and his chauffeur, Rudolph Hess, a student at Munich University. Hitler entitled his work *Four Years of Struggle against Lies, Stupidity, and Cowardice*. The publisher edited the title to *Mein Kampf, My Struggle*.

June 17, 1925, an International Law signed in Geneva banned the use of biological methods of warfare.

December 17, 1925, the court found Brig. Gen. William "Billy" Mitchell guilty for insubordination by accusing his superiors of treason for inadequate air defenses. Mitchell had commanded the air combat units in France during World War I.

December 25, 1926, after the death of his father Taisho Emperor Yoshihito Hirohito, the Showa Emperor (Enlightened Peace) Hirohito ascended the throne.

May 13, 1927, the economic system in Germany suffered a severe price drop and collapse known as Black Friday.

May 20, 1927, Charles Lindbergh left a muddy Roosevelt Field and crossed the Atlantic in his Ryan monoplane, *the Spirit of St. Louis*. He touched down at

Dutch and his sister Jean Van Kirk.

Le Bourget Field in Paris, France, on the twenty-first at 10:22 p.m. to be the first to solo across the Atlantic.

August 27, 1928, the Kellogg-Briand Pact, named for the United States Secretary of State Frank Kellogg and French foreign minister Aristide Briand, renounced aggressive war except in matters of self-defense in an effort to prevent another world war.

The Pact outlawed war as an instrument of national policy and called upon countries to settle their disputes by peaceful means. The Pact had little effect in stopping the rising militarism of the 1930s. The initial signatories to the Pact were the United States, France, United Kingdom, Japan, Germany, Italy, Canada, Ireland, Poland, Belgium, Czechoslovakia, India, South Africa, New Zealand, and Australia. An additional forty-seven nations followed suit and signed later.

September 24, 1929, Army Air Corps pilot and speed demon Lt. James H. Doolittle flew a Consolidated NY-2 biplane from Mitchell Field on instruments only making the first blind flight.

October 24, 1929, the Great Depression began with the devastating Black Thursday Stock Market crash on Wall Street and quickly spread to most countries of the world. The depression wreaked a chasm into the nation's economy, which did not completely recover until the war effort machine was well underway.

Ca. 1930, the Van Kirk household paid $20.00 a month rent for their home on Queen Street.

Dutch ~ My father worked as a night watchman at Sunbury Dye Marks.[37] We had a place out there in the country from the Rinehearts (family name), on the back road past the hospital, second house to the left near the black creek. Now it runs white, the Shamokin Creek. My dad loved the place and my mother hated it. It was kind of a feud between my mother and dad. We lived there for the summer then moved back to Queen Street in the winter.

November 14, 1930, a member of an ultranationalist right wing group attempted an assassination of Osachi Hamaguchi the "Lion" prime minister of Japan.

September 18, 1931, an explosion occurred on the Japanese controlled Manchurian railroad north of the Chinese City of Mukden (Shenyang). Japan blamed the incident on Chinese Nationalists and used it as an opportunity for the Kwangtung Army to move further into northern China, quickly take Mukden, and control Manchuria establishing the puppet state Manchukuo (Manzhouguo). Appeals to the League of Nations to enforce the Kellogg-Briand Pact were futile.

A civil war had existed in the Republic of China between the Kuomintang (KMT or Chinese Nationalist Party), the governing party of the Republic of China led by Chiang Kai-shek, and the Communist Party of China (CPC) since 1927. Other factions particularly warlords added to the divisions within the country. But after the Mukden incident the Kuomintang and Communists united against Japan until after World War II ended when they resumed the civil war.

Ca. 1932 James Chadwick, a British physicist, proved that the neutron exists.

January 28, 1932, for more than a month a short war, the *January 28 Incident*, ensued between the armies of the Republic of China and the Empire of Japan before the official hostilities of the second Sino-Japanese War start in 1937.

May 1932, military extremists in Japan killed Premier Tsuyoshi Inukai increasing the Army's power and ending parliamentary government.

January 30, 1933, Adolf Hitler became the Chancellor of Germany, which gave rise to official anti-Semitism and legislation against the Jews.

March 4, 1933, Franklin Delano Roosevelt won a landslide victory over Herbert Hoover to become the thirty-second President of the United States. John N. Garner served as his Vice-President from 1933 to 1941.

March 23, 1933, the passage of Hitler's Enabling Act legally ended democracy in Germany. The German authorities established concentration camps all over the country for political prisoners and what the Nazis considered social deviants.

May 1933, the Nazis burned books, broke up trade unions, and threatened to take children from parents who fail to follow Nazi programs.

September 1933, Albert Einstein and other scientists moved to the West. In 1905 Einstein determined the relationship between mass and energy and that the relationship could be explained in the formula $e=mc^2$.

"The Recovery Program"

 Roosevelt ~ *July 24, 1933*, " . . . For many years the two great barriers to a normal prosperity have been low farm prices and the creeping paralysis of unemployment. These factors have cut the purchasing power of the country in half. I promised action. Congress did its part when it passed the farm and the industrial recovery acts. Today we are putting these two acts to work and they will work if people understand their plain objectives . . .If I am asked whether the American people will pull themselves out of this depression, I answer, 'They will if they want to' . . . I do have faith, and retain faith, in the strength of common purpose, and in the strength of unified action taken by the American people."[38]

 *December 19, 1934,* Japan denounced the Washington Naval Treaty of 1922 limiting the naval armament of the United States, British Empire, French Third Republic, Empire of Japan, and Kingdom of Italy, and the London Naval Treaty of 1930 between the United States, United Kingdom, Empire of Japan, France, and Italy regulating submarine warfare and shipbuilding.

James Chadwick received the Nobel Prize in Physics in 1935 for his work on the neutron.[39] Physicists had learned that the neutron could act as a projectile for bombarding other nuclei.

October 1, 1935, four retired Japanese officers on an international peace and goodwill mission arrived at Fort Niagara in the Town of Porter, New York. The delegation of Capt. Hiroshi Nakamura, 2nd Lt. Paymaster Moichiro Fujita, Lt. Gen. Harushige Ninomiya, and Admiral Isamu Takeshita, the former commander-in-chief of the Japanese fleet, represented the Reservists Association of Japan at the thirty-sixth national encampment and convention of the Veterans of Foreign Wars of the United States held in New Orleans earlier during the week.[40]

During a radio broadcast from Buffalo, New York, Takeshita warned against agitators and jingoists who tried to impact the relationship of Japan and the United States. He declared that there should never be anything but the friendliest relations between the two nations.[41] In the afternoon following a welcome with a military salute at the entrance of Fort Niagara and witnessing the evening parade, Commandant Col. Charles H. Morrow, entertained the Japanese delegation at the Officer's Club. The Admiral toasted Morrow, decorated for his command in Siberia during World War I. Takeshita remarked that Japan and the United States would never go to war against each other.[42]

November 25, 1936, the Anti-Comintern Pact concluded between Nazi Germany and the Empire of Japan.

January 20, 1937, Chief Justice Charles E. Hughes, Sr., administered the presidential oath of office at the Capitol for the second time to Franklin Roosevelt. The 20th Amendment to the Constitution established the term of elected federal offices, which changed the inauguration date from March to January. "The terms of the President and Vice-President shall end at noon on the 20th day of January . . .and the terms of their successors shall begin."

July 7, 1937, a battle erupted between Chinese and Japanese forces near the Marco Polo Bridge outside Beijing (Peking) marking the opening of the Second Sino-Japanese War. Another incident of Japan's imperialistic policy toward China developed into a total war between the two countries and expanded after Pearl Harbor.

December 12 - 13, 1937, the Japanese Army marched into Nanking (Nanjing) and other cities. Gen. Prince Yasuhiko Asaka directed the bombing and heavy shelling assaults. Soldiers of the Kuomintang government of Generalissimo Chiang Kai-shek attempted unsuccessfully to defend the city. Six weeks of widespread executions, rape, and random murder took place.

Iris Chang in *The Rape of Nanking, the Forgotten Holocaust of World War II* claimed 260,000 – 350,000 Chinese deaths were caused by the aggression and atrocities perpetrated by Japan during the invasion. Chang describes diabolical acts of unimaginable scope against the people.[43] Reports by foreigners in the city corroborated the Chinese stories.

December 17, 1937, the Domei News Agency reported that Lt. Gen. Iwane Matsui on horseback led the triumphant entry into the conquered former capital city of Nanking through the Chung Shan gate. Adm. Kiyoshi Hasegawa, commander in chief of the Japanese naval forces in China, and other naval dignitaries followed a naval band through the Ksia Kwan gate.[44]

General Yang Yu commander of the Shanghai garrison had been executed per the orders of Chiang Kai-shek according to an official Chinese announcement. Officers and all Chinese soldiers even privates were to be executed if they made an unauthorized retreat.[45]

January 27, 1938, The Northumberland High School students moved into the new Dr. Charles W. Rice Senior High School.

"In Love with Miss Kelley"

Jean – The Northumberland High School was "the school up on the hill." The students helped with war recycling efforts. "We had paper drives. We saved everything even cooking oil and scrap metal."

Dutch – We had the finest bunch of teachers in high school. Boise L. Brewster was the principal. You did not mess around with him. Mr. Brewster also taught dramatics and got all the boys to come out for school plays. He always won the prize for the best play.

Neil Wormley, my chemistry teacher, always talked v-e-r-y s-l-o-w-l-y. Our high school was an old building. It looked like an old house. I am surprised we did not blow it up with the Bunsen burners in our chemistry class. Mr. Wormley walked around the room and instilled in me a love of chemistry. Bucky Bostian and I became chemical engineers. He was the brain of our class and went to Bucknell on a scholarship. He did not go to war and took a job with the Manhattan Project.[46]

Bill Kelley's sister was one of our teachers. She was the best looking girl I had ever seen. We told Miss Kelley: "You think we are taking your course because we were interested in dramatics? We love you." She made an impression.

William Kelley – "Some of her students were as old as she was."[47] Laura Kelley graduated from high school at age fifteen and started teaching high school at nineteen after graduating from college.

Dutch – I graduated in June 1938 from Northumberland High School. There were eighty in that class I think and only about nineteen of us left. We still have reunions. I attend when I can. No ballrooms we gather at one of the old Dutch restaurants look at each other and say, "You look good. You made it another year." The girls in Northumberland organize the reunions. Joseph Marotto was the first guy killed from my class. Frank Cooper was next.

Van Kirk graduated with classmates Charles W. Bollinger, Lewis Cellitti, Leroy V. Fenstermacher, Albert R. Pardoe, Nick Ponendo, William P. Shannon, and James C. Snyder who signed the *Pine-Knotter Yearbook*[48] and wrote "Army" next to their names. R. Dale Phillips and Frank Holtzapple signed "Navy." The "Inside Stuff" listed Van Kirk as fond of Scotch, usually found with (Arlo W.) Klinger, "wants to be a WPA Worker," and "probably will be a florist."

Vice-president of the Science Club, Van Kirk participated in research and experiments described in the Yearbook as "designed to demonstrate the value of science in everyday life." Van Kirk was one of the club editors for the 1938 yearbook. His classmates teased him with the senior question, "Do you remember what a time 'Teedy' Van Kirk had keeping his class ring for himself?"

Dutch - I should have bought two class rings or maybe three.

High School Graduation (With permission of Schindler Studio, Sunbury, Pennsylvania).

"Susquehanna University 1938 - 1939"

Dutch - Right after high school I attended college and majored in Chemistry at Susquehanna University. Charlie Steele, a guy from town who had money, gave me a scholarship for one hundred fifty dollars. The tuition was one hundred dollars. I hitchhiked back and forth from home to Selinsgrove.

Jean - "Ted had the year at Susquehanna, a wonderful liberal arts school. But for Ted it was not what he needed. So he stopped and went to work at Weis Market to save money so he could go to Bucknell and take engineering courses. He found out he did not make that much money and then that's when he went in the service. I always admired him. He always stuck to his guns. He wanted that engineering degree."

Dutch - The Masonic Lodge owns the Weis building now. The second floor is the Masonic blue room. It is beautiful up there.

Mick ~ Van Kirk was mentor and guide to Mick McAllister four years his junior. "Ted helped me through school. Just before he went into the service the teacher gave us a slide rule and said, 'it will save you all kinds of time in mathematics.' I went to Ted to help me. He showed me a few things and how you divide and how to multiply. I said, 'I don't understand.' He said, 'I can't help you. You are no damn Mathematician.' He did help me on the slide rule to get by, and eventually get through four years at Susquehanna University."

MOVIETONE NEWS *October 21, 1938*, Japanese troops take Hankou (Wuhan) and occupied Canton (Guangzhou) in effect surrounding Hong Kong.

January 1939, Enrico Fermi left Italy and immigrated to the United States. Fermi won the Nobel Prize in Physics in 1938 for his work on the artificial radioactivity produced by neutrons and for nuclear reactions brought about by slow neutrons.[49] He left Italy, immigrated to the United States and taught physics at Columbia University from 1939 to 1942.

Physicists Otto Hahn and Fritz Strassmann observed that the uranium nucleus split when neutrons bombarded the uranium. Lise Meitner interpreted the experiment as fission of the nucleus of uranium and release of incredible nuclear energy.

April 3, 1939, Congress passed Public Law 18 appropriating three hundred million dollars for the expansion of the Army Air Corps and permitting African Americans to receive flight training.[50]

"A Girl for Each Night"

July 18, 1939
Tuesday
Dear Teedy,
Since it is raining I'll start writing letters. It has been raining all day. I didn't get up till eleven. We played bridge last night till after one. So you see I'm still not getting to bed nights. Even if you aren't here. We were to the movies Sunday night. Tomorrow we are going shopping in Pittsburg.

How is Vic? What did you do Saturday night? The Girls Band played at Salem, did you go?

We have the cutest little dog it's a wire-hair terrier, and a holy terror. It's here at the desk wanting me to play ball with her. She's a pest.

We play lots of croquet. I haven't played any tennis yet. But, I haven't forgotten the bet. Have you? You probably have.

Have you been working hard; I always look at my watch about five thirty and think of you coming home from work. Isn't that nice?

I am going to Cumberland Maryland for the day, next Monday. I bet you are thinking, "I hope they keep her."

Were you to church or Sunday school on Sunday? If you weren't you should have been.

Well, how many girls has it been, one for each night since Saturday night or two for each night. I haven't met any people, because we either have been away or sleeping. If you see Jane or any of the other girls tell them to write to me first, then I'll answer them. Tell Jane that (mostly) maybe I'll write one after I finish this.

Have you been down to the carnival at Selinsgrove? You should go down. Have you been to any dances at the Green? Don't go out with too many girls? (none)

Well, I can't think of anything else you'd be interested in, or I want to know. But please answer, and don't wait a week or two. Sit right down and write. Break a date, (Kidding) I still think of you. Please answer!

Love,

Mary Jane[51]

"Mary Jane Young"

Dutch ~ Rolling Green Park about eight miles from Northumberland was a major summer amusement site. The park eventually became a golf course. I do not know why Mary Jane was worried about me dancing with other girls. I was always an innocent young man.

I met Mary Jane before the war while I was attending Susquehanna. She was a junior in high school at that time, several years younger. We met on a freezing cold night sleigh riding and sledding in the hills around Northumberland. Mary Jane taunted me pulling her sled back up the hill. You never quite know how these things happen. I asked her out.

Portzline's Dairy had the best milkshakes and was the local hang out where people met each other. We also went to the movies together. Movies were much cheaper in those days about a quarter. Things gradually developed and the next thing I knew we were considered going together and a couple.

Mary Jane's "father" George Seasholtz, a leader in the town, worked for the Pennsylvania Railroad and served on the school board. Mary Jane was the Seasholtz's niece and went to live with the family when she was very young. Her birth father died seeing how fast a Ford would go. Her older brothers Ray, Robert, and William Young, and twin brother, Al, were raised in an Odd Fellows orphanage near by.[52]

The I.O.O.F. Odd Fellows facility on the outskirts of Sunbury towards Elysburg in a valley by Black Creek named for the color of the water from large deposits of coal.

The Young brothers played on the football team. I hated to play with them. They were too damn good. Her brother Rip (Robert) was a fabulous athlete and could almost beat our team single-handed. He was the type of person you would predict to do great things. He was killed invading a beach. Bill joined the service first and was in the Philippines on the Bataan Death March. Mary Jane grew up separated from her brothers except for occasional visits. She loved them and spoke often of them.

Albert was drafted late and never went overseas. He was a few years younger than his brothers. Mary Jane went by the surname of Young. It took me a long time to understand the family relationship. When she spoke of her brothers I asked, "Are you talking about the Seasholtz or the Youngs?" She was born around the Sunbury area.

Mary Jane had two much older Seasholtz "brothers." Arnold and Bill (William Lee) Seasholtz treated Mary Jane like their little sister.[53]

July 18, 1939, Wellington bombers flew over London, England. The Air Ministry called the show of thirty bombers as routine, but considered it a public display of Great Britain's air strength.[54]

July 26, 1939, the United States notified the Japanese of its intentions to not renew the United States – Japan 1919 Treaty of Commerce and Navigation. America's protests of Japan's military actions against the Chinese had been ignored.

August 23, 1939, Germany and the Soviet Union signed the Treaty of Non-Aggression also known as the Molotov-Ribbentrop Pact in Moscow under a portrait of Lenin and stunned the world.[55] The two countries agreed to reinforce an earlier Neutrality Agreement from 1926 and to secret additional protocol of boundary issues and influence in Eastern Europe.

September 1, 1939, nine German armored divisions with more than a million troops tore into neighboring Poland without warning.

September 3, 1939, France and Great Britain declared war on Germany.

"A Devastating War"

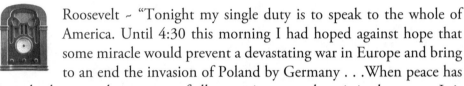 Roosevelt ~ "Tonight my single duty is to speak to the whole of America. Until 4:30 this morning I had hoped against hope that some miracle would prevent a devastating war in Europe and bring to an end the invasion of Poland by Germany . . .When peace has been broken anywhere, peace of all countries everywhere is in danger . . .It is easy for you and me to shrug our shoulders and say that conflicts taking place thousands of miles from the continental United States, and, indeed, the whole American hemisphere, do not seriously affect the Americas ~ and that all the United States has to do is to ignore them and go about our own business. Passionately though we may desire detachment, we are forced to realize that every word that comes through the air, every ship that sails the sea, every battle that is fought does affect the American future . . .I myself cannot and do not prophesy the course of events abroad . . .We have certain ideas and ideals of national safety, and we must act to preserve that safety today and to preserve the safety of our children in future years . . . I have said not once but many times that I have seen war and that I hate war. I say that again and again."[56]

October 11, 1939, Alexander Sachs, an economist and banker, delivered Albert Einstein's letter to President Roosevelt suggesting nuclear research. "The element uranium may be turned into a new and important source of energy in the immediate future." Through the work of Fermi and Leo Szilard "it may be possible to set up a nuclear chain reaction in a large mass of uranium" and that through this work an "extremely powerful bomb of a new type may thus be constructed."[57]

"The Aviation Cadet Entrance Exam"

Dutch ~ I took a summer job in 1940 cooking with the food store. Then I saw the signs about being an aviation cadet. Now most people around Northumberland did not know much about diddly squat. They did not read the newspapers. We had the *Sunbury Daily Item.* It would be a good

PTA bulletin right now. I knew the war had started in Europe. The National Guard was called up from around our area for the Twenty-Eighth Division of Pennsylvania and to me it was inevitable we were going to be in the war. I did not want to be in the infantry so I applied to the cadets. The response was "sorry you need two years of college or to pass a competitive exam." So I said, "good. I will take the exam." That in of itself is a story.

The exam was given in Middletown near Harrisburg, Pennsylvania, down the road from home about seventy miles. The exam including the physical took three days. I slept in the car at night and ate baloney sandwiches. I passed my physical but walked out thinking that I never came close to passing the exam. It was the same entrance exam for West Point with sections on architecture and things like that, which I did not know anything about. So I went back to college and got word that I passed the damn exam, surprise of surprises, and would be advised of a class opening as soon as possible.

In 1975 while living in Charlotte, North Carolina, I had tests and X-rays for back trouble. The doctor told me I had only one kidney and questioned how I got into the service. I said, "Where were you when I needed you?" I have lived my whole life with only one kidney.

Since the war was going on I thought the government would be anxious to get people and make them pilots to be prepared. I didn't return to college and went back to work.

MOVIETONE NEWS

June 14, 1940, German forces took Paris as the French and Allied forces retreated.

July 15 - 18, 1940, at the National Democratic Convention held in the Chicago stadium Roosevelt received the nomination for president by acclamation. Henry A. Wallace ran as Roosevelt's vice-presidential running mate.

September 7, 1940, sirens wailed as German bombers escorted by more than six hundred fighters filled the sky over London. Hundreds of civilians were killed in a matter of minutes during Black Saturday, the beginning of the Blitz.

September 14, 1940, Congress passed the first peacetime conscription in American history. Roosevelt signed the Selective Service Act two days later requiring males between the ages of twenty-one and thirty to register with their local draft boards.[58]

September 27, 1940, Japan, Germany, and Italy formed the Axis powers and signed the Tripartite Pact "to assist one another with all political, economic and military means."

October 8, 1940, the British Royal Air Force (RAF) formed the Eagle Squadron composed of volunteer American pilots, which subsequently became the United States 4th Fighter Group.

"Arsenal of Democracy"

Roosevelt ~ *December 29, 1940*, "Never before since Jamestown and Plymouth Rock has our American civilization been in such danger as now . . .

The Nazi masters of Germany have made it clear that they intend not only to dominate all life and thought in their own country, but also to enslave the whole of Europe, and then to use the resources of Europe to dominate the rest of the world . . .

Frankly and definitely there is danger ahead-danger against which we must prepare. But we well know that we cannot escape danger, or the fear of it, by crawling into bed and pulling the covers over our heads . . .

The history of recent years proves that shootings and chains and concentration camps are not simply the transient tools but the very altars of modern dictatorships.

. . .I want to make it clear that it is the purpose of the Nation to build now with all possible speed every machine and arsenal and factory that we need to manufacture our defense material . . .

I have the profound conviction that the American people are now determined to put forth a mightier effort than they have ever yet made to increase our production of all the implements of defense, to meet the threat to our democratic faith . . ."[59]

December 31, 1940, during the year 18,633 men entered military service under the Selective Service Act.[60]

January 20, 1941, Roosevelt began an unprecedented third term as President.

February 1, 1941, Pope Pius XI, head of the Roman Catholic Church, called for public prayers to avoid another war.

Late February 1941, at the University of California Berkeley, Glenn Seaborg and his colleagues discovered plutonium (Pu), in the form of an isotope.

March 11, 1941, Congress approved Lend Lease in the interest of national defense and authorized the Secretary of War, the Secretary of the Navy, or the head of any department or agency of the Government to "sell, transfer title to, exchange, lease, lend, or otherwise dispose of, to any such government any defense article" to assist its Allies.[61]

March 28, 1941, Dr. Glenn Seaborg and other scientists discovered Plutonium-239 (^{239}Pu) produced by the bombardment of uranium with neutrons and that the isotope was fissionable with slow neutrons.[62]

April 1941, the Japanese Army approved research into an atomic bomb.

"We choose human freedom"

Roosevelt ~ *May 27, 1941*, " . . . It is unmistakably apparent to all of us that, unless the advance of Hitlerism is forcibly checked now, the Western Hemisphere will be within range of the Nazi weapons of destruction . . .

Today the whole world is divided between human slavery and human freedom . . .

Our whole program of aid for the democracies has been based on hardheaded concern for our own security and for the kind of safe and civilized world in which we wish to live. Every dollar of material that we send helps to keep the dictators away from our own hemisphere, and every day that they are held off gives us time to build more guns and tanks and planes and ships . . .

I have tonight issued a proclamation that an unlimited national emergency exists and requires the strengthening of our defense to the extreme limit of our national power and authority . . ."[63]

June 1941, Mary Jane Young graduated from Northumberland High School and was active in sports and music. She received letters for basketball and cheerleading.[64]

June 20, 1941, the United States Army Air Corps (USAAC) became the United States Army Air Forces (USAAF).

June 22, 1941, in a pre-dawn offensive codename *Operation Barbarossa* Nazi Germany invaded the Soviet Union.

June 28, 1941, President Roosevelt signed Executive Order No. 8807 establishing the Office of Scientific, Research and Development (OSRD) for the purpose of providing adequate provisions for research related to national defense.[65] Dr. Vannevar Bush, an electrical engineer, chaired the National Defense Research Committee (NDRC) and led the OSRD.[66]

"Don't Go Out with any Girls"

July 3, 1941
Thursday
Dearest and Darling Precious,

I'm so homesick I could scream. I cry every night. I can't sleep or anything. Arnold and Louis went out tonite. I go to the movies in the afternoons and stay in nights.

I want to come home. What am I going to do I'll go nuts if I stay here much longer. Please don't say anything to anyone. When they go out I'm scared to death to stay alone, but of course I have Bitsey. I'm scared about Lindy she's not well. She has a lump back of each ear and she's getting so thin and she don't eat very much and she's cranky. Well enough of this kind of talk.

What have you been doing? Please I beg of you don't go out with any girl or girls. Please dear, I love you and only you remember. Please love me.

Johnny Abusio was here for supper last night. He's awfully nice. What did you do today.

Write to me every day please. You have more to write about than I.

(I love you very dearly and always.)

All of my love to you and Lots more of Love,

M Jane

please come out soon I love you. I'm sending you a piece they had in the paper out here.

 *September 11, 1941*, Roosevelt ordered the Navy and Army Air Force to shoot any German vessels on sight after several American ships were attacked and sunk with loss of life.

September 14, 1941, the first American action in the war occurred when the *Northland*, a Coast Guard cutter, destroyed a German controlled radio station in Greenland. A few days earlier a submarine torpedoed the destroyer *Greer*, which responded with a depth charge.

"Leaving for the Service"

Jean ~ "I was not included in the big party" for Dutch before he left for the service. "Oh no, he had his friends. He was six years older. I was the kid sister. But it sounded like a good party." The party and names of the guests made the local newspaper. "Everyone made the *Sunbury Daily Item*. If you went to

Harrisburg you were written up."

Jean and her friend Romaine Gresch walked to school each day. "We walked everywhere. Parents didn't drive you unless you were sick or there was a blizzard." The morning Van Kirk left for the service "I was crying so badly. Mister Gresch felt so sorry for me that he got the car out and drove us to school. I was heart broken when Ted left. I always admired him so much."

The farewell party was held at Mertz's cabin in Lithia Springs and attended by girlfriend Mary Jane Young, and Northumberland friends George Atherton, Jack Atherton, Malcolm Arter, Jean Babbitt, Robert Bastian, Shirley Beury, Dorothy Bingaman, Henry Brecht, Mary Brennan, William Brennan, Phyllis Brouse, Alice Fenstermacher, Joe Gallo, Pauline Gallo, Dick Gass, Davis Gross, Mary Haupt, Shirley Herman, Richard Hinkelman, William Hopewell, Olga Howzdy, Jack Kerwin, Mildred Kerwin, Agnes Lewis, Trevor Lewis, John Longacre, Jane Malone, Victor Meredith, Ned Mertz, Robert Miller, Milton Moeschlin, Laura Neidig, James Olley, Martha Jane Packer, Anna Petrullo, Lorraine Phillips, Sterling Post, Jean Pursell, Ben Reichenbach, Robert Saxton, Frank Shirk, John Snyder, Nelson Specht, Margaret Stephens, Marietta Taylor, Frances Van Kirk, Madelyn Zong, and Rhoda Zong. Donald Houtz and Mariethel Rothermal of Sunbury were also at the celebration. Van Kirk's friends gave him an Elgin wristwatch. In addition to mother Grace Van Kirk, Mrs. Emma Seasholtz, Mrs. Leroy Beury, and Mrs. W. P. Zong chaperoned the young people.[67]

Chapter Two — Endnotes

26 Van Kirk's birth certificate recorded his birth in Point Township, Northumberland Co., PA.

27 Jean Van Kirk McAllister interview with author, Locust Grove, VA, September 20, 2010.

28 "Northumberland The Story Of An Old Town 1829 – 1929," *The Susquehanna Press*, 3 - 10.

29 The 1930 Census lists children: Mike, William, and Steve Biega. William served in the Pacific with the 38th Infantry "Cyclone" Division from 1943 to 1945. Source: National Archives AAD file on-line, www.nara.gov and World War II Memorial database. Stephen Biega was named in the "General Marshall's Victory Report" in the tribute to Northumberland's men and women.

30 Elwood M. "Mick" McAllister interview with author, Locust Grove, VA, September 20, 2010. Mick, Dutch's brother-in-law, lived at the corner of Seventh and Queen Streets, a stone's throw from the Van Kirks. "Three generations lived in that house and never threw anything out," said Jean Van Kirk McAllister.

31 "Warren G. Harding," Encyclopedia Britannica, http://www.britannica.com/EBchecked/topic/255071/Warren-G-Harding [accessed May 18, 2010].

32 Clifton Daniel, ed., "War debts cause outcry in all Germany," *Chronicle of the 20th Century*, (Mount Kisco, NY: Chronicle Publications, 1987), 277.

33 World and United States time line events adapted from the *Chronology of the Modern World, Chronology of the 20th Century, The Encyclopedia of American Facts and Dates*, newspapers, and other historical publications referenced in the bibliography.

34 "The Nobel Prize in Physics," Nobel prize.org, http://nobelprize.org/nobel_prizes/physics/laureates/1922/ [accessed December 9, 2010].

35 Damage also occurred on the Boso and Izu Peninsulas and on O-shima during one of the most destructive earthquakes in the world. "Historic World Earthquakes," United States Geological Surveys Earthquake Hazards Program, http://earthquake.usgs.gov/earthquakes [accessed April 14, 2011].

36 The death notice for Robert Young listed the members of the family. "Ex-Orphanage Ward Killed In Saipan Battle," *Sunbury Daily Item*, July 1944.

37 The 1930 United States Census for Northumberland County in the Town of Northumberland lists a radio for the Van Kirk household: Fred (head), Grace (wife), Theodore (son), Jean (daughter), and Mildred (sister). Fred and Grace married at the age of nineteen.

38 President Franklin D. Roosevelt's Fireside Chat, July 24, 1933. Franklin D. Roosevelt Presidential Library and Museum. Roosevelt's speeches and writings are in the public domain.

39 "The Nobel Prize in Physics 1935," The Official Web Site of the Nobel Prize, http://nobelprize.org/nobel_prizes/physics/laureates/1935/ [accessed June 23, 2011].

40 "To Be Guests at Niagara Falls Tomorrow," *Niagara Falls Gazette*, September 30, 1935.

41 "Other Japanese Visitors," *Niagara Falls Gazette*, October 2, 1935.

42 "Complete Plans For Entertainment Here Of Japanese Party," *Niagara Falls Gazette*, October 1, 1935, and Dietz, *Porter Images of America Series*, Great Britain: Arcadia Publishing, 2005, 35.

43 Some historians and Japanese dispute the numbers of deaths and scope of the atrocities.

The "Crimes against humanity" were brought up during the International Military Tribunal for the Far East (IMTFE). The tribunal estimated more than 200,000 casualties. Gen. Kingoro Hashimoto, a vigorous advocate of expansion, participated in the seizure of Nanking. Hashimoto received a sentence of life imprisonment. "World War II War Crimes Records: Far East," Record Group 238, National Archives Building, College Park, MD.

44 "Formally Enter Nanking," Shanghai (UP), *Niagara Falls Gazette*, December 17, 1937.

45 Several officers serving in North China were executed for failure to carry out orders during the Japanese advance south to the Yellow River. "Report Commander Executed, Shanghai (UP), *Niagara Falls Gazette*, December 17, 1937.

46 According to *The Bucknell Alumnus* Robert B. Bostian died April 23, 1945, at Boston General Hospital while employed by the War Department in the chemical research RAD laboratory at Massachusetts Institute of Technology.

47 William Kelley email to author, January 25, 2011.

48 The 1938 *Pine-Knotter Yearbook*, published by the senior class of Northumberland High School and part of the historical collection of the Priestley-Forsythe Memorial Library, Northumberland, PA.

49 "Enrico Fermi – Biography," Nobel Prize, http://nobelprize.org/nobel_prizes/physics/laureates/1938/fermi.html [accessed December 9, 2010].

50 In 1941 the Army chose the Tuskegee Institute in Tuskegee, Alabama, for the training of the segregated 99th Pursuit Squadron. Franklin D. Roosevelt Presidential Library and Museum – The Tuskegee Airmen.

51 "Teedy" was the nickname for Theodore Van Kirk. Mary Jane Young's return address: c/o A. P. Seasholtz, 1108 Cochran Rd., Mt. Lebanon, PA.

52 According to the obituary for Lt. Robert Young in the *Sunbury Daily Item*, Mary Jane's father died in 1925. Her four brothers were admitted to the orphanage home on September 21, 1925. The three older brothers played on the Odd Fellows' orphanage baseball and football teams famed for "rugged strength and courage. Often with no substitutes to fill gaps in their ranks, they took on any team willing to play them, and built up a fine record of victories."

53 George Seasholtz, head of the household, worked as the "Chief Clerk Railroad" according to the 1920 Census, Northumberland, PA. The family lived at 456 First Street.

54 "British Bombers Fly Over London," *Brooklyn Eagle*, July 18, 1939.

55 Vyacheslav Molotov, the Soviet Foreign Minister, was one of the principal signatories to the Pact. After the war the German Foreign Minister Joachim von Ribbentrop was tried at Nuremberg and hung for war crimes.

56 Excerpt President Roosevelt's radio address "On The Outbreak of World War II," September 3, 1939.

57 Albert Einstein, Old Grove Rd., Nassau Point, Peconic, Long Island, letter to F. D. Roosevelt, August 2nd, 1939.

58 The age range changed to ages from eighteen to forty-five. "Selective Service System – US Military Draft," http://www.selectiveservice.us/military-draft/7-use.shtml [accessed March 25, 2011].

59 President Franklin D. Roosevelt's Arsenal of Democracy radio address, December 29, 1940.

60 The "Selective Service System" website is the source for the numbers of men entering the

military under the Selective Service Act for the years 1940 through 1946.

61 *Public Laws*. Part 1 of *United States Statutes at Large Containing the Laws and Concurrent Resolutions Enacted During the First Session of the Seventy-Seventh Congress of the United States of America, 1941-1942, and Treaties, International Agreements Other than Treaties, and Proclamations*. Vol. 55 (Washington: DC, Government Printing Office, 1942), 31-33.

62 "Plutonium is Discovered, Glenn T. Seaborg," *Explorers Journal*, Vols. 51-53, December 1973.

63 "Announcing the Proclamation of an Unlimited National Emergency," President Franklin D. Roosevelt's "Proclamation of a National Emergency" radio address May 27, 1941.

64 In addition to working at Weis Food Store, Mary Jane worked at the Westinghouse Electric and Manufacturing Company in Sunbury after graduation according to the wedding announcement in the *Sunbury Daily Item*.

65 The Office of Scientific Research succeeded the National Defense Research Committee. Irvin Stewart, *Organizing Scientific Research for War* The Administrative History of the Office of Scientific Research and Development, appendix I, (Boston, MA: Little Brown and Co., 1948).

66 Bush was considered Roosevelt's chief advisor on military research during the war. G. Pascal Zachary, "Vannevar Bush Backs the Bomb," *Bulletin of the Atomic Scientists*, December 1992.

67 "Hold Farewell Party For Theodore Van Kirk," *Sunbury Daily Item*, September 1941.

Chapter Three

Sikeston *Air Corps Training Detachment*

September 29, 1941, *Got in the army as an aviation cadet and sent to Sikeston, Missouri.*[68]

Dutch ~ Finally, I was called and told to report to Harrisburg as part of Class 41 dash something, which is the way they numbered the class. Good, I finally made it. Before I took the physical I had four teeth kicked out during a college touch football game.

Our group left Harrisburg on the train bound for Sikeston, Missouri. It was the first time I was ever in a Pullman car for heaven's sakes. We went as far as St. Louis. All I know is that I got to Sikeston and three days later was up in an airplane.

"Inspection"

October 1, 1941

Dear Mother and Dad and Diz,

I got here Tuesday afternoon about 2:00. We were assigned to barracks and given our stuff. Then given help by the upper-classmen who live in the other side of the barracks.

It's damn hard here. Harder than I ever worked in my life but everything (everyone) thinks it's worth it and nobody thinks of quitting.

Our beds must be made exactly. The fold must be 22 inches from the head and be 7 inches wide. We get our lockers and pillows fixed and don't use them for fear we will get them out of order for inspection. I had an interruption here for reveille.

If we're not drilling we're being inspected. We drilled today for 6 hrs. and exercised for 4 hrs. I got up at 4:45 all brass & everything must be highly polished.

We are drilling every minute.

I finished this letter on Oct. 2. The food is excellent. Ice cream twice a day and all you want. I can't write often. I got up at 4:15.

Write even if I can't.

They don't give us time to get homesick.

You could bounce a quarter off the bed.[69]

October 3, 1941 – 4 p.m.

Dear Ted,

Just received your letter that sure was a short one. After all the waiting we did for it. You did not say if you thought you were going to like it or not. I hope you do. Dad is not home from work yet and Jean and Francis went to Sunbury. Well Theodore I guess we will have to stay where we are I have been all over town trying to find a place but have not been successful so far. I was down to see Mary Jane last evening. She was as badly disappointed as I was. We thought we should have had a letter yesterday. She told me she has already counted the days until she thought you would be home. We got home Monday afternoon at 3 o'clock. Mary Jane drove all the way home. She said she liked to drive so I let her drive.

What time did you leave Harrisburg and when did you get to Missouri. Did you have to take any more exams? There has nothing new happened in town since you left and I should know for I have been down everyday. I don't know what to do with my self. Jean and dad are away all day so that leaves me with nothing. I haven't been in the store. Martha said "Buz" looks as if he is worked to death. The collector was just up this afternoon to collect the 50 cents for the radio. You said you were so busy. Well you won't be able to spend much money. Mary Jane was worrying last evening and wondering if you would save so you could come home when you get leave.

You say you drill so much. When do you go to school there? I suppose you are so tired you can go to bed early and sleep.

Jean & Dad will write later. I wanted to answer your letter right away and they are not here. Write as often as you can.

With lots of love from all

Mother

Dutch ~ Two brothers, Fred (my father) and Lee Van Kirk, married two sisters, Grace (my mother) and Martha Snyder. Each had two children. Frances and Jim are my cousins. Jim and I are still very close.

The heart of Northumberland. Dutch ~ I took the photo from the second floor of the Weis Foods Store. The five-and-dime store was across the street. Hershey's had a shop and sold ice cream for fifteen cents a pint. The movie theatre, behind the canopy, charged ten cents a movie. The "blue hill" is in the background.

Buz Gaugler worked at Weis Pure Foods Store where I worked in Northumberland. He managed the produce department, all sixteen feet of it, and then opened his own store in Middleton. Buz got married and never went into the service.

"The 'Subway Series' at Ebbets Field"

October 4, 1941

Dear Darling Mary Jane,

I wrote a letter the other day but didn't even have time to mail it. This afternoon it is the first second (and I do mean second) I've had to myself since I've been here. We've drilled and had exercises from 8 to 10 every day since I've been here. I've been so tired I didn't know what to do. This morning I learned to wear and use a parachute and start a plane. Monday I start to fly.

This first three weeks we get only a few hrs. off on Sat. and Sun. After that Sat. afternoon & Sunday are ours.

The food here is very good. Ice cream every day, twice every day and all you want of it.

I don't know what's going on in the world. They tell us here we'll be in the war in a month. I don't even know who's winning the World Series.[70] Tell Mrs. Phillip, the fellows at the store and the gang that I'm too busy to write. Even too busy to get homesick for anything but you and your love.

I give you all my love.

T.

Write often Janie please even if I can't.

Just to show you how tough it is here we get 4 yrs of West Point in 5 wks here and we get it or else.

"Brass Must Be Polished"

October 4, 1941

Dear Mother, Dad and Jean,

I wrote a lousy letter the other day and didn't even get time to mail it yet. I got here Tues. afternoon. I am stationed in C barracks. Half are upperclassmen & half are lower. Everything is very strict here. We are supposed to do our years of West Point in five weeks here.

Wed. Thurs. and Friday we had a drill and calisthenics from 8 to 6 and they are hard but you are really in condition when they finish with you. Today I sat in an airplane and started it and learned how to wear and use a parachute.

Here we must salute all upperclassmen and especially officers. All brass must be polished and uniforms must fit and be worn perfectly. The upper class rides us like the devil.

The barracks must be in perfect order for inspection every morning. The beds must be made perfectly.

We got our first shots this morning for typhoid, small-pox and tetanus. Monday morning I start to fly.

The food here is the best and all you want of it. Ice cream twice a day and everything. You earn it though. I may have more time to write hereafter – I hope.

Love,

Theodore

Write often even if I can't. They don't give you time to get homesick.[71]

"Confined to the Post"

October 5, 1941

Dear Jean,

You said you wanted a separate letter. Well here it is.

Today is the first time I had to myself. They made us work to beat the devil down here. We had to learn all our drill in the first three days. Starting tomorrow I go to school in the morning and fly in the afternoon.

We must be up by at least 5:15 but to get my work all done I get up at 4:00 and Friday I was up at 3:05.

We are confined to the post for our first three weeks but yesterday I went into town

C-1 Group

Written on the back: "The gang from C-1 and the watchman. The fellow with the dark glasses washed out today. This out of 21." Van Kirk standing fourth from the left.

for two hours to get my hair cut and today I went in for three hours to go to church.

Today was the first I saw a paper since I've been here.

Most of the fellows here are too old for you but write to me and I'll give them the letter and your address.

Love

Theodore

I got my hair cut short. I had too. It does improve my looks in my uniform though.

"Sick as the Devil"

October 6, 1941

Monday

Dear Mother, Dad and Jean,

I got Mother's letter this morning. It was the first letter I got and was I glad to get it.

I came in from the flying line early that's why I'm writing today. I was up for about 50 minutes today. I was flying the plane doing right and left turns, etc. and all of a sudden I got sick as the devil for a minute. I was disgusted as the devil with myself.

There's not much to do here except work. If it wouldn't be for being so busy I'd get pretty homesick.

I may be home sooner than you think if I wash out and about ½ do. If I do I'm going to try to be a navigator or bombardier and get a commission.

Starting today I spend 1 ½ hrs. in athletics about 4 in classes and fly for about 1 hr. each afternoon. Each night I attend study hall.

Write as often as you can.

Love

Theodore

"Mickey the Rat"

Postmarked October 6, 1941

Dear Brother,

This wonderful morning I got off some work. You know how good I am at that. I wish you lefted your pen home this thing don't work right maybe it is me.

Sr. High is terrible thank you. The kids treat us like . . .(illegible) *they treat us terrible. Of all the names they could call me they call me Arlene. I think Eddie Fisher has something to do with that. I had a fight with Mickey, the rat, we won't speak to each other. I am running out of news. Oh . . .* (name withheld) *ran away.*

I bet you wish I could make your bed for you. I am using your room for schoolwork. I like Latin, don't care much for plane Geometry.

Mom is yelling her head off. Don't mind the writing and mistakes. I write a better one soon.

Lots of love

Jean

PS Last night I got wet and now I have a cold.

Dutch ~ Mickey "Mick" McAllister lived right across the street and Jean later married him. I told my dad 'make sure you don't oil the hooks on the glider' while he was courting Jean. Mick made a wonderful husband and still plays tennis at eighty-five years.

Mick ~ "We lived down the street. From fifth grade on Jean blossomed and I knew that she was for me."

Jean ~ "I wasn't so sure. Remember Eddie was in there. My mother was not pleased that I was dating, but I did like Eddie Fisher, a classmate of Mick's. He was a very nice young man."

Mick ~ "We played basketball for the Junior Varsity team during high school, but we were too short for varsity, five feet seven and a half inches. Eddie was vice-president of our class, the class of 1942. He worked for American Airlines after the war. We communicate once a week. Eddie is a great guy. We remained friends all our life. He lives in Selinsgrove, Pennsylvania."

"Dad Dreamed about You"

October 6, 1941

Did you lose your camera or did you get it out all right.

Monday morning October 6.

Dear Ted,

Well how are you coming along by now all right I hope. It is only 9:30 and I have my wash all done.

How is the weather out there. It is terrible warm here. It has been trying to rain but so far it hasn't rained to amount to anything. What did you do yesterday. Did you have any work? Mary Jane was up Saturday morning. She said you said in her letter you would not have much to do on Saturday. Jean was to Sunday school and Church on Sunday and she and Mic had a good fight. She said that Virginia B. & Raymond said he went down to Beury and told Mrs. Beury, Jean talked about here.

How long do you think it will be before you can come home? I want you to save all your money so if you can come any time you will have the money. We all thought you might come home for Xmas. So save your money. You will not have to send any home. Dad and I will carry your bills along for October & November. But be sure you save it and in a safe place.

You will have to write to Jean sometimes she was very much disappointed on Fri. She said you did not say a word about her. And when you have time I wish you would write and tell us more about everything. Dad said he dreamed about you. I ask him what he said he dreamed. You took your course in 3 ½ months that would be going pretty fast wouldn't it. How are you getting along with your bed making. At least you will know how to make up your bed perfect when you get a wife.

I guess this will be all for this time. You know nothing happens around here. If there is anything you want tell us.

Lots of love

Mother

Dutch ~ My mother or my sister always made my bed at home. The Beury family lived on Queen Street. They were distant relatives of Mary Jane.[72]

"A Short Hair Cut"

October 6, 1941

Dear Mother and Dad,

I have time to myself on Sunday so I'll write this letter now. Tomorrow I start to ground school in the morning and flying in the afternoon. If you can't fly after 12 hours instruction you are washed out. Our upper class started with 110 men and now have about 60. This is the toughest primary training school in the country. I would get that one.

All the fellows here are very nice but everything is strict as the devil.

I filled out papers for $10,000 insurance to be paid by the government. The policy will be mailed to you.

I got summer uniforms and had to get a short hair cut. They go very well together. I gained 10 lbs. since I've been here.

Write and tell me the news from around home. I can't write so often. I'm too busy. If you see any of the fellows tell them what I said and that I'm too busy to write.

Love,
Theodore

"Speculation about Atomic Power"

October 8, 1941

Wednesday morning

Dear Mother, Dad and Sis,

The weather is bad so we're not flying this morn. My flying is O.K. and it would pass any place but I not sure it will pass the army. Yesterday I was learning to do stalls, spins and acrobatics. Every bit of flying here must be precision. In making turns around pylons one fellow picked as a pylon a crossroads with a mailbox on each corner. When they landed the instructor gave him the devil for not saying which mailbox his mark was. That's the way it is here.

I haven't gotten a demerit for over a wk. I feel good about that. My ground school average is also about 90. Next wk. I'll know whether I go or stay. I'll probably ride in the washing machine.

Did M. J show you the picture. I hope so.

I can't use a radio here except Sat. afternoon – Sun. and there are plenty of radios here for that time. See Mrs. Hine to stop the magazines.

There's nothing I want or need in fact I wish I could send some things home.

Let me know the news.

Love,

Ted
I just got my grades. My ground school average so far up till 12:00(today) is 94 ½

Dutch ~ I had outgrown *Boys Life* then and was reading a lot of magazines including *Popular Mechanics*. Several years before the war broke out I read an article in *Mechanics* speculating about atomic power by scientists. The Manhattan Project tried to confiscate magazines with similar articles during the war because of the possibility of using an atomic weapon.

"In Your Uniform"

October 8, 1941
2 p.m.
Dear Ted,

Had not heard from you since last Fri. Today and four letters in the noon mail so some one was holding out on us or you did not get them mailed. Madelyn Zong & Mary Jane were up last evening to see if we had a letter they couldn't understand why we hadn't heard from you. But with all you have to do I don't wonder. Where in the world do you get all the brass to polish you talk about and how do you get up at 4.15.

That Bingaman and Mary Jane were just here to see if I got any letters they are going over to the movies. They had a farewell party last night for Russel Clugston I suppose Mary Jane will tell you all about it. You told me to tell you the news well you know there is no news in this town. I seen Buz when I mailed your last letter he said that (he) had not heard from either of you boys yet down at the store. But they must have heard from Klinger for they were saying he had to push a peanut around with his nose.

Jean was so proud of the letter you sent her she took it along to school to show the kids. How did you get along with your flying the other day when you said you were going up. Do you think you will be able to fly with 12 hours instruction.

Do you need anything Theodore if you do write and tell us. You said you did not see a paper. Would you have time to read the (The Sunbury Daily) Item if I have it sent out to you. But if you don't have time to read it I don't see any use sending it out. Have you been getting your letters alright we have sent three. You said in your letter you did not use your pillows what do you sleep on then. I would like to see you in your uniform but I don't know how about that short hair cut remember the last one you had. You said you gained 10 lbs since you were there my goodness if you keep on gaining like that you won't be able to wear any of your clothes. Gilbert Strausser has been home since Sunday he has gained a lot of weight too. He has been made lieutenant already. I think that was fast work. How soon do you think you will be able to come home is your money lasting alright. Write

Lots of love
Mother

"Five Gallons of Gas a Week"

October 9, 1941

Thursday evening Do you want anything
Dear Ted,

Well how are you getting along now I suppose you are pretty settled by now. Are you still so thrilled about being a cadet. Have you been flying yet if you have how do you like it? I just seen in this evenings paper Charlie Stibish had a farewell party for Russel Clugston and gave him a gift they said they also sent Noll a gift. He must not have gotten in the cadets yet for the paper says he is planning to enter the Cadets. Jean was just telling me Bill Brennan ask if we heard from you yet. I seen Post the other day he ask about you and ask for your address did he write?

Edythe just came up to fix a dress and she and Jean are talking upstairs and I am trying to write this letter. Jean is telling her about one of the new teachers having a date with one of her pupils.

I started to work to day but I don't think I am going to last very long I am so tired and sore this evening I can hardly move.

Have you been gone out any where away from camp since you have been out there. I don't suppose you care about going every evening now. Really the car looks sick since you are not here we only buy 5 gallon of gas a week as you know how much we drive it.

Dad is going out to supper again tomorrow evening down in Hacky's trailer this is a ham and egg supper. I ask him if he wanted to write he said I was to tell you he was helping me write this letter but he is a big help he is reading the paper. Has Francis wrote you a letter she got your address so did Mildred. Mildred is going back to Butler on Saturday she wanted me to go along and stay a week. They got a six room apartment.

Have you been getting your letters? Do you get them alright with just the letters for address. How does Wendle Mertz like it? Lois Gresh ask me the other day if you said anything about him. Dad said I should tell you he just greased the car he just came too. Jean is reading what I am writing now but she said I should tell you she would write her school work almost has her down.

Is there anything you want? Do you have enough covers? I suppose you get tired of answering my questions like you did when you were home. It is getting cold as the dickens out how is it out there. I think I have said enough for one time it is only 7:30 but I think I am going to bed.

> *Lots of love*
> *Mother & Dad & Sis*

Ca. October 9, 1941, at a meeting at Arthur H. Compton's home several scientists discussed the British progress and prospects for separating U-235, and Washington's complacency in light of the compelling evidence of German's interest in atomic power.

After Roosevelt was presented with the MAUD (British) committee report that a bomb was possible during the estimated time frame of the war in Europe, he approved the atomic research program and created a Top Policy Group.[73]

"Try for the State Motor Pool"

October 10, 1941

Friday evening

Dear Ted,

Just got your letter today telling how sick you got when you went up on Monday. What was the matter was it the height or were you scared so darn bad it made you sick were you flying the plane if so that probably was the reason you were so sick thinking something would go wrong.

Write and tell me about it. Have you been up since. If you have been how were you? You said if you were washed out you were going to try for navigator or bombardier. What do they do they go up in a plane too don't they. How did Wendle make out did he get sick too. Jean and I are all alone this evening. Dad went over to Hackys trailer for ham and eggs for supper. So we didn't have any we are going down and get a milk shake after while.

Today was my second day of work I am not near as tired as I was yesterday I went to bed last evening at 7:30 but I don't like work anymore I don't think I will work long.

Well Theodore I can't tell you any news for there hasn't anything happened around here.

If you are washed out in the Cadets why don't you come home and try for the state motor patrol.

They say Chet Newcomer will be coming home soon. Dad said he heard some one say Monday but he did not know if it was true. Well I guess this will be all this evening. Hope you are making out alright. Write and let (us) know.

> *Lots of love*
> *Mother*

"Mr. Wormley"

October 11, 1941

Dear Brother,

I am sorry I didn't write last week, but I had so much schoolwork. School is coming along fine only I don't like Geometry or Mr. Wormley he isn't nice to the girls. Last week he made a fool of Betty Graham. You know how hard it is to do that.

You are going to miss a big fight, I think. Between Virginia Buery and me. We are at it again. This is going to be the last one because I'll smack her down and that will be that. (I hope)

There isn't much doing in town it just the same as it ever was. Mother and I were down at Sidlers last night. We were talking to Mary Jane. We went down about 7:00 and came home about 9:00.

Its getting terrible cold last night I nearly froze. I am going to wear a plaid skirt and sweater to the Sunbury Zion Chapel will that be alright? and we run down to Mr. Van Horn and get the answer.

I'll write when something important happens.

Love

Jean

I know you can't read my writing but I am in a hurry.

Jean - "Mother was getting pretty sick by the time I was in high school (in the fall of 1941). When she got sick I had to rush home from school. I didn't have many after school activities because of that, but I loved to play basketball."

"I had trouble understanding Mr. Wormley's soft deep voice."

Dutch - Mr. Wormley taught math and chemistry. He was a very good teacher and influenced my decision to major in chemistry. Sidler's was a small drug store and soda fountain shop with six stools. Mary Jane worked there during the war for a short time.[74]

"Write Whenever You Can"

October 11, 1941

Will do better next time

Lots of Luck

Saturday

Dear Ted,

Received a letter this morning you must be having more time to write we had a letter yesterday too. Jean has been writing you a letter for the last hour and I came up to write mine and she only had about 4 lines written. I ask her what she had been doing all the time and she said she wrote her letters right not like I did. She said she bet you thought it was a pleasure for you to read her letters after reading mine. How about it? Jean and I were down at Sidlers last evening for about 1½ hours talking to Mary Jane. Dad was out for supper so we did not know what to do with ourselves and Jean didn't want more than sandwiches for supper so she did not have to wash dishes you know how that is. So we went down and got a chocolate milkshake. Olley was in and wanted to know how you were getting along. Catherine is here we are going to take her over home as soon as dad comes home. He was supposed to come home for dinner and didn't so I don't know where he is. They took Kate Strausser to the hospital this morning in the ambulance. I guess she is pretty sick. They said the doctor was with her all night up until 5 oclock this morning.

Grandma Snyder & Martin's Catherine were over this morning to see if we heard from you and got your address so I suppose they will write. You said in your letter this morning you would be home 4 days in Dec. if you stayed but you still would not have much more than one day at home would you if you only had 4 days in all. How are you getting along with flying any better? Well I think I better close I will admit this letter is terrible like a puzzle. You won't be able to find the right pages but want to mail it when I go down town.

Love
Mother

"Pants Fly in a Perfect Line"

October 11, 1941

Dear Mother, Dad and Sis,

I have a little time to myself on Sat. and Sunday so I'll try to describe my life here. You probably know I'm pretty busy. 1, 2, 3 are barracks I'm in 1. 4 is recreation hall never used except for Sat. & Sun. 5 is the classroom building, 6 the medical, 7 the mess hall. 8 the administration build and 9, 10, 11, etc. are hangers. The field is extra large. But it seems that there's another plane too close on landing or taking off. I get up at 4:30 and make my bed & get dressed until 5:15 then we have reveille & breakfast. Then we have until 7:00 to clean barracks and things must be perfect. Shoes under our beds must be shined and in perfect line. Beds must be perfectly made and in line and bed rolls must be in perfect line. All personal brass and brass in barracks must be polished and everything must be dusted every day.

From 7 to 9 we have athletics and then we have 5 minutes to get into our uniforms and get to classes. At 11:30 classes are over and we get ready for flying line and eat until 12:15. We fly in special uniforms & jackets so we must change again. We come in from flying about 4:30 – 4:45 and must get into uniforms by 5:10 for retreat. We eat at 6:15 and got to study hall from 6:50 to 9:00. We must be in bed by 9:15. Now you know the funny part of it is we get so we can change clothes & be dressed well (we have to be) in about 2 minutes. You don't waste any time though.

Air Corps Training Detachment, Missouri Institute of Aeronautics, Sikeston, Mo.

Harvey Parks Air Port

PHOTO BY CELE POTTER

Van Kirk described in his letter the location of the buildings from left to right.

The barracks are inspected every day and everyone has certain duties besides making his bed etc. If anything is found wrong about any of your things you get a "gig." For every gig over 3 you get you must walk 1 hr. on the ramp on Sat. afternoon and Sun. morning. They gig you for a spec of dust on anything. Even the waste basket must be wiped out inside. We never use tables, chairs, waste baskets or ash tray because we don't want to get them out of order. We don't touch a door handle without using a handkerchief. There is a place and a way for everything in your locker and only so much can be in it. We fix our lockers and never use them. We use our suitcases in the attic. Every Sat. morning we have personal and barracks inspect by 3 lieutenants. They'll give you gigs for not having hair cut etc. Shoes and brass must glow. Shirt must be tucked in at sides and shirt, belt buckle and pants fly must be a perfect line. If you even roll an eyeball while they are looking at you

Chapter 3

get a gig. You must stand at attention for about 2 hrs. when it's all over your stiff.

The lieutenant gave us a talk yesterday. He said anytime it got too tough for us here we should just tell him and he'll see we get an honorable discharge and a ticket home. He said he knew this was the toughest school and he didn't want a bunch of babies. If you get through this school you're pretty sure of getting through. They flunked 60 out of 100 of our upper class.

I got a 95 in my first test here. If I can keep that up I can go to a different school if I can't fly. My flying instructor says I'm improving and about as good as anyone. Next week I start learning stalls, spins and dives, oh my stomach. Tell Mary Jane if she thought I yelled when she was learning to drive she should hear the instructors here. They're terrific.

I sent a card to Martha of the field so you can see what it looks like. I'm sending pic. 8 negatives to M.J. I told her to show them to you. Write
Love
Theodore
I'm putting something in for Jean.
P.S. I only got one gig all week hooray

"Our Barracks"

Dutch ~ We lived in three barracks. The upper class took great joy in hazing us. Sikeston was a civilian flying school. The only military people on the base were the commanding officer, a retread captain from World War I, and two lieutenants who had flight training before. The base had one redeeming feature; it sat next to a country club, but it really was a cow pasture with holes for the golf balls to go in.

The club was considered on the base. If your grades in ground school were high enough you did not have to go to ground school at night you could go to the club and meet the girls from town. It was a good deal. My grades were good enough so I could go and it was a ball.

We were told what our left foot was, what our right foot was, and when you march you start with your left foot and you put it in front of your right. Our flight training was in old Stearman PT-18s. After landing the ground crew could replace the bottom wings in three hours when necessary. My instructor, a fellow named Huntsinger, was an outstanding pilot. One day after about eight hours of dual training, we landed and taxied. Huntsinger crawls out of the airplane, looks at me, and said, "You are too dangerous to fly with; so take it yourself." So I soloed. It was a big achievement the day you soloed. After that the training was partially dual and partially solo.

I used to love to get up in the air and do chandelles and then at about eight thousand feet do spins to turn around and then put the airplane into a spin turning three times one way and three times the other way and lose altitude really fast.

We had lots of barrack's inspections. The guy would come in, open the window, and with white gloves run his hand on the outer sill to make sure it was clean. But it was fun and we were given a lot of freedom.

"Our Instructors Treat Us like Fathers"

October 12, 1941
Sunday afternoon
Dear Mother, Dad and Jean,

I don't know what to write about after so much last night. I just called M. Jane the phone down at the store. It cost $1.45. I wished you were there but I didn't know where to call you so that I could get you in a hurry.

Everything here is going fine. This is the last week of our confinement. Next weekend I can go out. They start the washing machine this week. If I get my check on one of my good days I'm O.K. That's the way flying goes. Your good one day and the next day your awful. A good flyer got washed out last week because he had a poor day when he had a check ride. My future will be better determined by next Sunday at this time.

The fellows here are really swell. We are told an aviation cadet is neat, well-mannered, but loud, nice appearing, honorable and above all cocky. The honor system works here to the nth degree. If you even loose a penny or a pencil it will be returned.

The two fellows I run around with most are swell. One was an engineer from Louisiana he was getting $350 a month from Du-pont. The other is a boy from Virginia. I'll send you some pictures of the three of us.

Our instructors treat us like fathers if we can fly. They won't look at one of their men soloing while he can see them but when he can't his eyes are glued to them. They invite you to their homes and everything. In the air they give you h. for every little thing and on the ground they are swell. And can they fly.

At first I didn't care whether I passed or not but now I really want to. I like it here even if they do only give you five minutes to change clothes and do a dozen other diff. things.

I was to church this morning and almost fell asleep in church.

That's all there is to write about just now. From 7 tonight until noon next Sat. I'll be busy as a man could be but I'll try to write.

Chapter 3

Love
Theodore

How are you feeling How do you like the Theodore picture If you ever call me call person to person $2.20 because it may take me 3 minutes to get to phone.

Tell Jean not to go get beat up and let Dad catch up on his sleep.

October 12, 1941
Sunday evening 5:30
Dear Ted,

What have you been doing with your self today. I suppose you got rested up for next week. How are you and flying coming now. Does it still raise the dickens with your stomach. Dad said I should tell you to keep your chin up. I wonder if he could.

I am up in your room writing this. Jean came up and tried on her band uniform and you should see her. I will have to move all the buttons over to the very edge. She weighed herself out at Martha and Lee's today and she weights 118 lbs. She is getting like a tub.

We were out at Martha and Lee's this afternoon and we had an argument about the time Lee says that your time out there is about 6 ½ hours slower than ours is. How about it? Theodore how about those magazines I want to stop them. Who should I see or write to about them.

Mildred went out to Butler Sat. morning but I don't know if she is going to stay or not. I guess they had a scrap again. They said Bob sent her a telegram and he talked for ½ hour the telephone bill was $2.85 and she had to pay it. That just makes me think would we be able to call you and talk to you on a telephone or don't you have them. Do you have radios. If so do you want yours? You know we just had our big one is broke again. Jean was just downstairs and came up and said I bet you can't guess what Dad's doing. I only made one guess sleep. Write

Lots of Love
Mother

October 13, 1941
Monday evening
Dear Ted,

I failed to get a letter today so I should not write any either this evening I guess. You must have been awfully busy over the weekend.

I told Jean and dad said if he did you could not read it any way so what was the use. And Jean with all her social duties is quite a busy girl. She went to choir practice and majorette practice she and Virginia Buery are having quite a time. Thelma Ruck quit and Betty Graham got her place now Betty wants to put Jean

Jean Van Kirk in her drum majorette outfit.

back in the majorette section all the time and Virginia thinks they should take turns so I don't know how they are going to make out. Every thing seems very quite (quiet) about the game this year you don't hear anyone saying much about it Jean says our players are all done up before the game I don't know what she means.

Dad said some fellow from Norry is working over at No 1 and he was asking about you today. Do you know who it might have been. Dad said he didn't know who it was.

How are you getting along do you still get sick when you go up in a plane?

Mildred is here and she is hunting a stamp for me in her pocket book. I think she has anything but a stamp. She was out to Butler over the weekend but she came back again this week to get her things ready to send out she says they got a very nice apartment.

Well I guess this will be all for this time I am tired as the devil and got some ironing to do.

Now if you don't get this letter it will be Mildred's fault she is going to mail it.

Write when you can

Lots of Love

Mother

"Do You Still Get Sick?"

October 14, 1941

Tuesday evening

Dear Ted,

Your letter telling us all about yourself came today that really was the first one we had that we found anything out. You sound as if you are getting more settled and more like your self.

Jean is pleased with her pin she had it to school showing it to everybody even Miss Savage. She sure is proud of it. I am awfully glad to hear that you made out so good in your test. Do your studies seem hard? And how about flying do you still get sick.

Jean said I should ask you what the gigs are you get is that one all you ever got? I hope you said if it ever gets to hard you could get a discharge have you ever thought of getting one? Dad just came home for supper he just said Sig Jr ask about you today. Today is my and (your) dads wedding anniversary I just ask him if he knew what it was and he said oh I almost forgot.

I ask you about 3 times about Wendle and you have never said anything yet so what happened to him.

They were just telling me to day that Frank Noll finally made it but they didn't know where he would go.

There is a case of infantile paralysis out on the heights a 10 yr. old Stuck boy.

He went to Priestly school they closed the school. I don't know what they will do about our schools there were 2 of his brothers come in here to high school. How are your eats? You probably would enjoy a pan of fried potatoes know I bet you don't get any of them. Have you gained any weight lately if you have I imagine you are pretty husky by now.

Jean is doing my ironing for me for 50¢ and she is worrying right now when she is going to get her 50¢.

She says thanks for her pin and she will write later well I guess this all I am running out of news writing everyday not that much happens around here.

Lots of Love
Mother
Write. Do (you) want anything

Dutch ~ Sig Weis, Junior, was one of the owners and founders of the Weis Food Store.

Clippings from the local newspaper accompanied the letter. Frank Noll, son of Mr. and Mrs. Roy D. Noll, 410 Queen Street, Northumberland, had been transferred from Maxwell Field to Dorr Field, Florida. Still in ground school training Noll had a very high average for the course. Noll and his roommate Bill McKee attended Bucknell. Bob Schuck of Hummel's Wharf, another close friend of Noll's but in a different squadron, and Louis Baylor of Northumberland attended Susquehanna.

William Diehl, son of Mr. and Mrs. Herbert Diehl, Front Street; John Kelley, son of Mr. and Mrs. Harry Kelley, King St., and John Kerwin, son of Mr. and Mrs. James Kerwin, Orange Street, enlisted in the Army at the Shamokin recruiting office and would be ordered to report for duty if they pass the examination for admittance.

October 15, 1941
Wednesday evening
Dear Ted,

Dad and I are all alone this evening Jean is out she is a very busy girl this week. Her schoolwork keeps her pretty busy and than they have had band practice almost every evening. They closed Priestly school and the Steele building. I don't know what they are going to do about the Jr & Sr high there is another case of Polio one of the L- kids down on Duke Street.

You say you don't like to fly well then I certainly would try for something else if there is any chance at all.

You say you would like to try for bombardier or navigator. Well I don't see what would be the difference you would be up in a plane anyway. You say when you take off you must be 300 feet from the ground do you cadets take the planes off of the ground and land them right away or does the instructor do that for a while. You say about being washed out well for my part if you don't like flying I don't care. You said you flew from 7-9 when you are up in the air what in the world do you do all that time. How long will you fly till you go up alone? Dad just ask me what I write about when I write a letter every evening he said he didn't see what I write about. I said well I ask a lot of questions like I always did and you answer what you feel like answering.

I haven't seen the picture yet you send Mary J. I haven't seen her this week I went down last evening but she must have Tues evening off she was not down at work. So when you get some pictures send us some.

I don't know why the other kids haven't written any letters. Sterling got your address the first week you were away I guess he is pretty busy with his school work to I see he was taken in one of the fraternities up there. Have you wrote to the fellows down at the store they were waiting for a letter from you the last time I seen any of them. Dad said you must have put on all your weight in your arms & legs if you still wear your belt one notch tighter I said no I guess you just have to keep your pants up. Write

> *Lots of love*
> *Mother*

Dutch ~ Priestley School was an elementary school with two classrooms, one with multi-grades in one room. The school was located in Caps Heights, part of the town of Northumberland. Grades second through fourth were held in the Steele's building.

"Progress Check Ride"

October 15, 1941
Wednesday morn
Dear Mother, Dad and Jean,

I got your box of cookies and candy yesterday. They were very good and did the fellows like them. I had a picture taken in my winter uniform. I send it to you.

I've got a light headache right now. I did too many stalls and spins this morning. I spun myself dizzy.

I got a letter from Klinger this morn. He likes it a lot. The dance Sat. night wasn't any good at all.

I go up for a progress check ride with the flight commander on Friday. They must think I'm doing all right. My instructor says I can fly if I keep my head up. He also says sometimes I fly like an army pilot and other times as though I never saw a plane. I hope I have a good day on Friday.

Well its time for dinner right now so I'll have to cut this short.

Love
Theodore

"A Cadet Is Cocky"

Wed. again 4:15
Dear Mother, Dad and Jean,

I got your letter this morning. I got my camera here all right but I haven't had time to use it yet. It's pretty warm here sometimes but when I get up in the morning its cool. On Sunday I haven't got anything to do but make my bed, study and get things ready for the rest of the week. I may come home sooner than you or I think but I hope not. If not I have 4 days in the middle of December but I must be back in Texas four days after I leave here. If I don't flunk out.

I just came in from flying. My instructor said I was improving but I think I'm lousy. Throwing a plane around in the air certainly raises ~~hell~~ with my insides though. It does everyones.

Well that's all for now I must shine my shoes, brass etc.

Tell Jean to write again and tell me how she is.

Love to all
Theodore
Write often

"Don't Tell Mary Jane"

October 16, 1941

Thursday afternoon

Dear Mother, Dad and Jean,

   This will be a short letter. I'm going to write it between classes.

   My flying this morning wasn't too bad. I don't get sick at all any more. I do spins, stalls, steep 360° turns and everything. I only hope I do them good enough. I'll find out in about a week.

   I'm writing this in math class. I know all this anyhow. There's not much to tell about the place. My ground school average so far is 94 ½.

   Oct. 25 all the cadets go to a girls' college in Cape Girardeau for the day to an athletic carnival & dance there. On Nov. 1 they come here for a dance. Don't tell M.J. this. They're the only things we've had so far and the only chance we get to do anything like that is on Sat. So it doesn't happen very often.

   In this class except for the time I spend helping others I have nothing to do. It seems I'm always helping someone else though. Tomorrow we have two tests. I'll have to study a little meteorology.

   Thurs. nite – Study hall.

   If you get a chance to look at Life Magazine look for the pic. of the one plane knocking the tail off of another. The fellow who did that was here last January.

   We have 2 tests tomorrow so I must study now.

   Tell me about the game.

   Love,

   T.

October 16, 1941

Thursday eve

Dear Ted,

   I did not get my letter today I feel awfully disappointed in the evening when I come home and don't have a letter. Are you still pretty busy? I wish you would not have told me you do not like flying. I worry about you now than ever now why don't you try to get something else. Tell me truthfully have you ever been homesick yet. I hope not. I have ask you three or four times about Wendle Mertz but you have never said anything about him yet.

   Dad wants to know if you ever get a chance to wear your own clothes and how your money is holding out It should last a long time since you are not buying all the gas you used too dad buys $1.00 worth every week and we don't use all that so you know how much we drive. The shock absorbers are getting bad again and

Millers are letting there car go back so we ask them what they wanted for the ones of there car Less Baker got 2 new tires off of it for $7.00 and the battery so we may as well get something off of it. Jean said I should tell you she learned to do a lot of new things with her baton such as putting it under her legs and throwing up in the air and catching it and she says tell him I am good at it. She is getting ready to go to a parade now she has on 2 sweaters and a coat and bandana you would think it was cold out.

There is another case of polio in town this little Jimmie Meyers right above us here they took him up to the hospital last evening they say the Lynn boy is very sick his dad told Joe he does not know anymore they don't expect him to live the night out. I have not seen Mary J all week so I did not see your picture yet. I might see her this evening if she is working.

Is there anything you want or anything you are hungry for that we could send you if there is tell us. Write

Love

Mother

Do you get a letter everyday you should. I write every evening.

October 17, 1941

Friday eve

Dear Ted,

I am writing this letter and trying to listen to the football game if you could call it that Sunbury is running away with Norry[75] the score right after the first quarter was 19 – 0 in favor of Sunbury of course but Bob Seebold just run 95 yds for a touchdown they just got about 15 min ago Sunbury just make another touchdown the score is now 26 – 6 Boy am I glad I did not spend any money to go to that game they have one of the biggest crowds they ever had up here on this field they say they will at least make some money.

I drew my first pay to day I really am making out good he pays me 40¢ an hour so that will give me $16.00 a week not bad is it I don't know how long I will be able to work so far I haven't minded it I really think I have been better I don't have time to set around and think.

It is just the end of the half with a score of 26 – 6 it will probably be 52 – 6 till its over. Mary Jane and Dot B were up last evening they gave me some pictures they are good but you still look like a crabby kid I think you have grown. Dad says you are just straightened up with your shoulders back. I think I mispel some words. But I am having and awful time trying to listen to this radio and write.

How are you and how are you getting along.

I am going to get a permanent tomorrow morning with my first pay. I drew

$6.34 for 2 day so I am going to spent it quick I am afraid you will not be able to read this letter I think I need a new pen too.

I will wait till I get the final score before I close and mail your letter they are just starting their last half.

The games over the score is 44 – 6 they say they have a crowd of about 5000

Love

Mother

"I Don't like to Fly"

October 19, 1941

Sunday afternoon

Dear Mother, Dad and Jean,

I'm at the country club right now. Its a place like the one a(t) rolling green. It's furnished swell. There are some people outside playing golf and a group of cadets inside doing the same as I am (writing). We have some very good piano players, singers, dancers etc. here and they entertain us. It's considered on the post and the only place we can go for 3 weeks and then only from Sat. noon until 5 Sunday. That's all the time anyone ever gets off.

Confidentially I don't like to fly a plane but I like to ride in it. I'm going to try to transfer to bombardier, navigator or something. My ground school average is high so I have a good chance. We can leave here anytime we care to but we can't transfer unless we can't fly.

Tell Jean I'm sorry I can't write to her more often. I hope she likes the emblem. I got out from 9:00 to 12:30 this morning and went to town for church and Sunday school.

There have been several new pursuit ships here the past several days. Yesterday there was a Douglas bomber here like the one that crashed down in Texas. When we take off we must be at 300 feet before turning or going over the school. He was about 150 feet. There is a landing T here that swings with the wind. The taking off and landing pattern is planned according to the way that swings and you must know the pattern for each degree of direction. We have a good night prayer as follows

"Now I lay me down to sleep I pray the Lord my pattern to keep if I should land across the T They'll wash me out – what's left of me."

We have several songs such as The Eyes of Texas, That Old Stearman Trainer and lots others. We have some (few) good times here. They take wonderful care of you though. I'm about 10 – 12 lbs. heavier and still wear my belt one notch tighter than I did when I came here.

Love to all,
Theodore
Write. Tell Jean to write.

"Only Bounced One Landing"

Bef. October 20, 1941
Dear Mother,

O.K. I'll start on this side (of the stationery) anyhow. I'm in a hurry. I haven't got much time. I got your letter you wrote on Tues. today. I also soloed. I flew about 50 min. by myself and made 5 take offs and landings. I only bounced one landing. All the others were good. Even my instructor said it was good (wow).

It only cost me $1.45 to call Mary Jane. Tell Cam S. I'll send him a card if I ever get around to it.

It's really swell to get up there by yourself. The plane handles a lot easier without the instructor. My instructor told me my hardest part was over but I still had a lot of work to do.

I must go now. Will write more later.

Love
Theodore

I'm still gaining and getting tan. It's hot down here yet and the wind in a plane really tans you.

October 19, 1941
Sunday eve
Dear Ted

I suppose you were over to the Club again this afternoon I think you are getting pretty ritzy going to Country Clubs.

I am sending you clippings of Sunbury Norry game I didn't know if Mary Jane would or not. You sure did not miss anything this year they say it was one of the lousiest teams Norry has ever had on the field. Martha & Lee were here this afternoon. We went down to Fetzers down in Snyder County for a ride they bought a farm down there and such a place we had Barry along did he enjoy that.

I hear you are going to solo this week so be careful.

Jimmie ask me if you said anything about his letter he wrote he is all thrilled he says that is what he is going to be. You will have to send grandma and Grandpa Van Kirk a card dad was out last evening and he said she felt slighted because you had not sent her a card.

My True Course

61

Russel Clugston left yesterday I was down at Sidlers yesterday talking to Mary Jane and Marjorie Russel came in she felt awfully bad about it she said Bain said he would be in Camp Meade they thought that would be grand they could go see him there Bain said ok that will only be about 3 weeks than he will be in Texas.

Mary Jane was telling me yesterday Chap Lewis and Jean Reed broke up they say Jean is making a play for Seebold now. Mary Jane said you fellows were having a dance out there on the 1st of Nov she wondered where you were getting the girls. I dont know but I think she felt slighted to that she didn't get any wings she admired Jeans an awful lot. Isn't Wendle mostly doing the same you are some one said he had a different address than yours is. I guess they are having quite a time with these boys down at the store Mary Jane was telling me Saxton almost got fired I guess Bill gave him another chance.

Martha said she was telling Bill about you getting sick the first time you were up in the air and Bill said "well that's what he gets for going and leaving us like this!" That Lynn boy I was telling you about having infantile paralysis died last evening but the other 2 are getting along good they say. Mildred and Larry left for Butler after the game Friday evening Walter Bingman and Grandpa Van Kirk took her things out last week one night.

Steve lost his job again so he is not working now he said he didn't know where he was going now to look for work he should have stayed down in Baltimore Martha said today Joe Stapwell is working down there now.

Jean started to write you a letter this afternoon I don't know when she will get it finished honestly she doesn't get a thing done since she goes to school.

How do you like flying now any better? You said you would find out this week if you would stay or not well I don't know how you feel but I for one don't care if you do flunk. You said about trying for bombardier well that would be still worse for you know than what you _would_ have to do. Mrs. Fetzer said this afternoon she didn't think our boys would ever see action well I hope she is right.

Well I think I have told you everything that has happened in this town in a week you know it isn't much. _Write_
Lots of Love
Mother
Dad cut the clippings for you

Seebold's ninety-yard run for Northumberland thrilled more than six thousand fans in the jam-packed Northumberland stadium.[76]

"Quit Mother"

October 20, 1941
Monday Morning
    I flew from 7 – 9 this morning. Got to barracks about 10:30 and had six letters, Jeans' three from mother & two from M.J.
    Why are you working. Quit right away before you get sick again.
    I don't get sick when I fly but I'm not crazy about it. We get all the covers we want and there is nothing I need. I wanted to send some pictures in this letter but they didn't come yet.
    Love
    Teedy
    Mary Jane and you are the only one's I've heard from. Quit work.

October 20, 1941
Monday eve
Dear Ted,
    I am writing this letter than going down to mail it and see Mary Jane. She was up last evening to tell me about the telephone call and I was in bed and Jean didn't wake me. I guess that was a rather expensive call wasn't it. If you keep that up you sure will not have enough money to come home. What was the matter were you homesick or don't you have time yet to get homesick. I am glad you are getting along so well if you really want to stay I imagine life around here would be rather dull for you know – Do you like so fly better now than you did when you first started? What do you think of the Norry football team I guess the same as every one else not much but every one around here seems to feel sorry for the boys they say it is all the coaches. You said I should not tell Mary Jane about the dance. Well I will not dare let her read that letter we always read one anothers letters. You said about that pic(ture) in Life being one of the fellows that was there, was he there as a cadet. Don't you ever try that. This will be all for now I have my ironing to do yet this eve write more news tomorrow Write
    Love,
    Mother

"Cleared the Tree"

October 20, 1941
Monday night
Dear Mother, Dad and Jean,
    I got your letter from Thurs. and Fri. today. I'm writing this in study hall. We aren't supposed to.

There were about 6 fellows soloed here so far. They had previous time. Some have also washed out. I flew in afternoon. One week I fly in the morning the next in the afternoon.

I made 12 take-offs and landings today. We were using a field where we had to come in over some trees and a drainage ditch. On my one landing my instructor yelled, "Are you going to land in that tree?" I gunned it and stretched my glide and cleared the tree by at least six foot. I hope I solo about the end of this week.

On Sat. night we all go up to a teachers college about 30 miles from here to a big party and dance. They provide trans. and everything. This weekend we can go out and have freedom from Sat. noon until Sun. at 7:00. You must sign in at a reasonable hr. on Sunday morning though.

That's about all there is to tell now.

I got a letter from Martha and Jimmie today.

Answer to question.

I don't get homesick they keep us too busy. Sometimes on weekends I wish I were home but it isn't bad. I'm getting so I like it here.

Love,
Theodore

"Washed Out Six Already"

October 21, 1941
Tuesday afternoon
Dear Mother, Dad and Jean

I just got your letter from Sunday. The game certainly must have been poor from the score.

Tell Jimmy I got his letter. I'll send cards as soon as I get any time.

I may send Mary Jane some wings if I'm sure I won't wash out. Wendle is in the same post but a different barracks.

I don't get sick when I fly and I love it now. I thought I was going to solo today. My inst. said to me when I got in the plane, "Do you think you can fly it." I shook my head yes. He said, "Well you can. Lets practice a few landings." While we were practicing the wind began to shift and they shifted the "tee" six times. Three times on one landing so he wouldn't leave (let me) try it. I made five good landing though. I need 8 hr. before I can solo and I've now got 7:55. One of my friends Mr. Briggs soloed today. They washed about 6 out already. There are 50 in the upper class out of 110 started. We started with about 120 so there are about 170 men here now.

One student dragged a wing today on a landing. He didn't hurt it a bit.

That's about all for now. We do the same here every day. Besides it's time for retreat. Write.

Love
Ted

Dutch ~ When the wind shifts, you must adjust your approach. The instructor changed the point we were supposed to land.

Postmarked October 22, 1941
Dear Ted,

I am writing your letter earlier than I do most evenings dad has not come home for supper yet I don't know what he is doing this evening he hasn't been working late the last few weeks. I still have some ironing to do since I have been working it is the same as ever I am never thru but I feel fine since I have been working. I have been working almost two weeks now and I don't think any one knows about it yet that is a miracle in this neighborhood. Jean is going to the movies to see "Aloma of the South Seas" She said I should tell you she is having a devil of a time with her teachers especially Wormley she does not like him at all. I was down at Sidlers last evening talking to Mary Jane she was still all excited about her telephone call she was telling me all about it. I guess she and Mrs. Sidler don't get along very well the way she says.

I suppose she told you about Frank Shannon getting married she said she was sending you clippings.

I seen Cam Snyder last evening he said I should tell you he ask about you he said he thought maybe he would have a card from you. I told him you were pretty busy.

Its to bad about Wendle I do feel sorry for him if he really want to stay. You don't know how much better I feel when I get a letter from you like the one I got today. Telling me that you like it and time seems so short. But whatever you do be as careful as you can when you solo. You must be pretty good though I guess or they wouldn't let you do it but be careful.

I will finish your letter now.

I just had to stop writing and go get dads supper he just came home it is seven o'clock. I wish I could see you when you bounce around like you say you do. Do you like flying any better I hope you do if you stay. I will make you some fudge and toll house cookies but won't promise how good it will be Jean says she is going to make the candy so I don't know if you will be able to eat.

I must tell you about Bob Weis you know he is down in Texas the other week he wrote to his dad and told him he bought a car he wanted the money to pay for it they said Harry Weis almost pulled his hair out he said to Bohner what would you do Bohner said why send him the money so they went to Texas last week. I suppose they took the money.

This will be all for this evening Jean is waiting for me to take her to the movies Take good care of yourself.

Lots of Love

Mother

Dutch ~ Frank Shannon lived right down the street from me and was one of my closest friends and a brother river rat. I knew the girl he married because I liked her myself, but I found something better.

October 22, 1941

Dear Brother,

I don't believe you can read this because of this darned pen. School is coming along find. I only got the dickens about ten times this year. In Biology Mr. Wormley socks the homework on you. We have six experiments to hand in on Monday.

What do you think of the Sunbury-Norry Game! I just had to write it up for English Class. (Did I like that)

The dance is going to be held Saturday night. I got a ticket from Eddie but I am going to sent it back. I am having a terrible time hes always after me. He don't give me five minutes peace. I am soon going to get mad and tell him to lay off.

The writing looks like the learning tower.

Thanks heaps for my pin. All the girls were green with envy. But I am afraid to wear it. I might lose it. It looks swell with my black sweater.

I use your room for studying and writing your letters. Do you mind? I like it better than mine. I wish you were home. For about a hundred reasons. 1. I don't have anyone to fight with. 2. You can't help me with my homework. 3. I don't have anyone to tell me if I look nice. 4. I don't have anyone to give me money. 5. Most important is because I love you.

Heap of love

Jean

Please excuse writing and what not. I can't write on paper without lines.

Jean ~ "I wrote to Ted probably when mother made me. Gosh I was a snotty teenager, but I loved him dearly."

Dutch ~ My sister Jean never missed a dance.

"Mr. Zong"

October 22, 1941
431 Water St.
Northumberland, PA

Hello old Man how is every little thing by this time the old town is about the same with the exception of the Store that damn place is dead. Even Bill seems to be in a trance but the other night at the run away or should I say Football Game I saw him. But we did not have any Battle. Your sweet is here and they are having some kind of a Sorority or bull fight I don't know just what it is. Well how do you like the army by this time and how are your eats in 16 – 17 – 18 (World War I) *the eats were louzy but it was mostly the poor cooks.*

How is your instructor I suppose hard boiled but remember they must be tough.

I hear you are going to So Low. Well just be careful. It is not to damn low for there is a Top and Bottom to Everything it is hot this evening or perhaps I should have a drink. Yesterday I went down to the Store and could not get every one to watch so I bought a Beer came home and went to bed. I guess I will call it cheerio for this time and you will hear from me later.

I remain as ever.
WP Zong

Dutch ~ Mr. (William P.) Zong served in World War I. He had three daughters and Mary Jane was one of their best friends. Mr. Zong and his wife were close to the teenagers in my group.

October 22, 1941
Wed. eve
Dear Ted,

You said you did not know what to write after that long letter the other night What do you think I write about every evening. But Jean says I always can find something to say because I am always talking.

Dad said I was to tell you about Buzz he was made manager of the Milton store I bet Bill is walking around in circles with those two dopes he has down there if you were still down you probably would have been made assistant manager but I guess the way your last two letters sound you would rather be where you are. You ask how I was feeling since I was working I have been feeling fine up until today but today it got me I don't know how much longer I will last. Have you soloed yet? Boy will I be glad when you have and that is over.

Dad is having trouble with the stove again he has it all apart you know the time he most always has with it.

Jean is having a terrible time with her boy friends and notes as usual.

I hope for your sake your check day is one of your good days for I really think you are getting to it. I think it would be pretty dull for you around here now.

Be careful

Love

Mother

Dutch ~ Buzz Gaugler and I worked at the Weis Food stores. He got married and did not go into the service. He managed the produce department and was made manager at a store up in Milton.[77]

October 23, 1941

Thur. afternoon

Dear Ted,

I am writing your letter this afternoon I did not go back to work I think I will have to quit I have a terrible headache again the first one I have had since you left but I think it all came from working I could feel myself slipping the last few days so I think I had better just stay at home before it costs more than I make again altho I would like to have the money but I guess we will get there somehow.

Don't say anything to Mary Jane about me working I don't think she knew it and I am not going to tell her.

Have you soloed yet?

I just had a letter saying you had not soloed unless you did since you wrote that. The letter I just had is the one you told about almost landing in a tree. Does it scare you when you do things like that or are you a past being scared. I guess Mary Jane is having quite a time with Mrs. Sidler and her mother she said last evening she was thinking about going to N.Y. to look for work she said her mother said if it wasn't for her she would not have to keep the home going here.

I feel sort of sorry for her. Dad said last evening maybe Bill would take her down at the store he said they had girls in Sunbury store now. So I am going to tell her when I go down. I guess Bill is left in a heck of a fix for heavens sake don't tell her I was discussing her. Will write more tomorrow

Write Be careful

Love

Mother

October 24, 1941
Fri. afternoon
Dear Ted,

You should be here right now Jean and I are having a good scrap. She just came home from school and wanted to know if Mary Jean could stay with her tomorrow night so they could go up to the high school and watch them dance and I told her she could not go up and watch them. You should hear her. What makes me so cross at her Eddie Fisher gave her a ticket to the dance and she send it back and said she couldn't go now she wants to go up and watch them and I said no.

I had a family for dinner today Jean come home and had Francis and then just as we were ready to sit down to eat Martin come in so he stayed. He was asking all about you and how you liked it.

Bill Brennan asked Jean for your address so I suppose he will write to you.

I am waiting for dad to come home than I am going down and mail a payment on the car and get my pay I hate to go down I just know what he is going to say. Have you soloed yet? I wait every day for my letter to see if you have. Lois Gresh was down last evening for money for the library and she said she had a letter from Kenneth Diehl he must have had a letter from Wendle because she said he told her to write because the way Wendle's letters sounded he needed some cheering up. You say in your letter you love to fly now do you really mean it at first I think you almost hated it.

Jean and I are going to bake some cookies and make some candy this evening than I will send you a box tomorrow. In case they are heavy don't eat to many or you sure will not be able to fly especially upside down.

Take care of your self. Write
Lots of Love
Mother

"Never Safe from a Washout"

October 25, 1941
Dear Mother, Dad and Jean,

Well another week is over. This weekend we can go out and do what we like.

We had inspection again and I came through that O.K. I finally got around to soloing on Thursday. I'm getting so I can land in my sleep.

I've made 44 landings in the past four days. About 25 of them were solo landings.

It really gives you a thrill when you try your first spins, stalls, dives, etc. all alone. I used to think a spin was awful before I came here now I put the plane in a spin for the fun of it. You can make a plane do most anything and you have the whole sky to do it in.

We have a devil of a lot of fun here. There's a West Virginia hillbilly here named Gus and a little red-headed freckled fellow from Mississippi named Pitts. They're a circus.

They washed about 25 men out of our class in the last two days.

You're never safe from a washout here. You just hope you're hot the day you ride with the captain.

Our upper class leaves for Randolph Field on Friday. They must report there Tuesday morning. That's how much time you get.

That will make us upper class on Friday and that will be swell. You treat an upper classman the same as an officer and you obey their orders. They're the ones who really ride you here but most of them are very nice fellows.

I have a ground School average of 96 ½ right now. That put me in class A which give me more privileges when I become upper class. It will really be nice then but I like it now.

Love,
Theodore

October 25, 1941
Dear Theodore,

I was glad to receive your letter and glad to hear the army makes you move. Via – Mary Jane I heard that you soloed, "Congratulations." I hear you are coming home in Dec., too bad that it won't be for a few weeks, you know what I mean, a few days of luxury, nice girls, nice hotel, etc. By the way, since I am being processed and seasoned to become a Sigma Chi I am also making out all right with the Phila. girls, that is one thing I don't object to. Up at Bucknell you can't walk through the quadrangle at the Sem. without being mobbed if you have a Sig pin or Sig pledge pin. (I'm afraid to walk through)

I haven't seen Reichenback too recently, when I did I told him to write to you. Probably he didn't . . .

I don't get much chance to write but I stop in at Sidlers regularly to get the latest data on you.

How are the girls out there? If I know you, which I do, I would say it's about time Van Kirk has some fun in Sikeston, Mo. The way I figure Mary Jane may not go out with any other fellows, but you won't restrain and not go out with some luscious piece of femininity if the opportunity is afforded. Not as any reflex on Mary Jane's faith in you, which I know reaches infinity, but I tell her frequently that you wouldn't go out with another girl.

Something in the way of local news: Jim Olley drives us up to school in their '30 Hudson. The first day he drove he dam near took out one of Judge Johnson's beautiful big trees. The first time he brought me home he hit this bump out here at the side of the house so hard it almost drove my head through the roof. The other day going up to Lewisburg he crowded one of the big "Horton" carriers off of the road. "Never a dull moment with Olley driving."

When I sit in some of the dull lectures I think of you flying around in a PT and I certainly wish I was with you. If you have some time when you answer this letter describe the thrill you get when you are in a spin, when you do an Immelman and tell me a little about landings. Every time I see an airplane I practically go nuts.

Dutch Snyder and I had one hell of a fight the other day, he said Sigma Chi was no good, I said he was full of shit and told him to go to hell.

You called up and wanted to know how Norry was making out. They are a bunch of bums, they are no darn good no matter how you look at it...

Have you had any gunnery yet or does that come later? Are you playing any tennis, if you get good when you come back I'll teach you how the game is played.

I can't give you much Norry news but I can say that town is primarily composed of a bunch of dull shits and sad apples, there are a few exceptions. However, if you want any dope on any specific thing tell me and I'll get it. Also, if in the event you want anything let me know.

Local News: (I just thought of this)

    "Thurman" Brennan and Jane Malone are going together again.

    Ben had a date with Lorraine Phillips recently.

    Jean Reed is nuts about "Jake" Seebold.

    "Torch" Post loves "Torch" Post (dearly)

    Mary Jane loves Theodore.

    I'm going out with "Zip" sometime in the near future, perhaps.

Sincerely,

Sterling

P.S. Does the Army Censor Mail? If they do somebody will be shocked.

"Upside Down in a Roll"

October 25, 1941

Sat. nite

Dear Mother, Dad and Sis,

Another week end to be confined to post. Next week we get out. I'm doing O.K. right now. I've only got 1 "gig" the past two weeks and that good. My ground school average at the end of this week was 93.

I asked my flying instructor if he thought I'd get through. He said, "You have the ability if you use your head. Unless you get worse you'll be O.K."

He's getting me ready to solo. He says he's getting afraid to ride with me. Yesterday he made me take off and land 8 times. My second landing I bounced sky high so he gunned it and kept on flying. He yelled into the phones, "Damnit you're flying this plane and your going to make this whole landing. I'm not going to touch the controls if you land in the cotton field and plow through the fence. The landing was good – I cleared the fence by every bit of 5 foot. I can go through spins, dives and everything and not even bat an eyeball let alone turn a stomach. I only got sick twice.

I was flying upside down in a roll on Fri. and my feet stayed on the rudder pedals perfectly until I wondered what was holding them there. Then my knees came up and hit me in the chin. That's a sensation – hanging there on a safety belt for the first time.

I like the place now. The time goes very fast. This past week seemed like a day.

We have telephones here. Just call M.I.A. – Sikeston, Mo., Don't call unless you have to though I'm never around where I can get to a phone in a hurry. I may call you some Sat. nite or Sun. It costs about $1.80. The time diff is 1 hr. It's 6:00 here and 7:00 there.

They start washing lower classmen out this coming week. Here's hoping.

Don't say anything to anyone but —— flunking ground school bad. His average is about 50. He's disgusted.

There's nothing more to write about now. Good night.

Love

Theodore.

P.S. Toll house cookies, fudge etc. is appreciated. Make enough because we always pass it around the barracks – 25 men.

October 25, 1941
Sat. eve
Dear Ted,

Did not get a letter today its the first day this week I did not get a letter. I might have got one but there was only one mail and that was early. I sent you a box this morning you will have that I suppose before you get the letter. Jean is getting dressed to go down town and dad is reading I don't think we are going anywhere but down town to mail the letter.

Jean got up this morning and said she dreamed about your last write I ask her what she dreamed she said she dreamed she came down stairs and you were sitting in the rocker she ask you why were home and you said I was washed out. How are you getting along? If you stay you said you had four days off in Dec that would not give you much time at home would it unless you could fly to Middletown.

Dad was home all afternoon he said they had the work all cleaned up over there he hasn't been making much over time lately I guess they have to many men now. This afternoon has seemed like a week. Do you think you would like to come back where you were again before you left or do you like the kind of life you have now better? I got my pay yesterday and have it all spent already I got Jeans coat today it is getting pretty cold here I think she will be able to wear it before long.

I haven't been feeling so good today dad wanted me to go down to the doctors this eve but I don't think I am I haven't been down since before you left.

I had to stop writing and sew Jeans buttons on her jacket she is the same as ever she wouldn't sew on a button if she had to pin it she is not improving any. She just told me I could get her a maid for Xmas.

We are going over to Grandma Snyders tomorrow for dinner they sure are getting ritzy over there they had these rooms all done over and got venetian blinds with drapes over them it looks swell I suppose you are already for the dance by now or maybe on your way it is 6:30 here.

Norry played Montgomery today they must have won that game we heard them going down Duke St blowing there horns Dad said if he was them after last Fri eve he would come home quiet.

Have you soloed yet? I wait for every letter to see if you have written. How are you have you gained any more weight.

Well I run out of news so this will be all until tomorrow I hope I can dig some up till then. Write

Love

Mother

"Tetanus Shots"

October 26, 1941
Sunday
Dear Mother, Dad and Jean,

Well another Sunday is here and not much to do. We have open post this wk. end so I think I go in town.

It seems that every other day is Sunday here. The weeks roll by so fast you don't know what happens to them.

Last night we were all up to a teachers college to a dance. There wasn't much doing there so we went swimming.

I told you you shouldn't have gone back to work. I don't want to here (sic) of you going back either. The first is payday and I'll send you money home.

Yesterday I got tetanus shots and they gave me the hives for about an hr.

I'm getting ready to go to church now so I'll finish the letter when I come back.

Well another Sunday is past and the long grind begins. Next wk. at this time I'll be upper class. Things happen fast around here.

Well I must go to study hall now so Good-bye.

(I feel homesick today) but business starts in about 15 min. so it won't be long.

Love,

Teedy

October 26, 1941

6:30 Sunday eve

Dear Ted,

I think your letter will be short this evening I am running out of news. Kate is here she was just asking me what I wrote about when I wrote everyday. But when I tell you all that happens around here in a day it almost makes a letter.

We were over to Grandma's all day to day we just came home all we heard today was Grandpa talking about the game he is going to get next Sat.

Aunt Alice and Uncle Ed were over last evening till 11.30. They were asking all about you. Aunt Alice got some of Jeans clothes to dress up in for Halloween.

Did you have a good time at the dance last evening what time did you get back to the post?

They had a victory dance up at the high school last evening Jean said there were about 25 there I dont know why they had a victory dance they haven't had a victory yet. Montgomery beat them yesterday 27 – 7.

Sunbury beat Wm. Penn 39 – 7

They say Sunbury has a swell team this year.

We have to go out to Grandpa and get some gas yet so I guess this will be all this evening. Write

Lots of Love

Mother

October 27, 1941

Mon. eve

Dear Ted,

You sure must be a busy man these days by the looks of some of your letters. The one I got today anyway it was backward and everything it keeps me hustling to read them lately. I am awful glad you have soloed for the first time and you like it so well but don't start handling those planes like you did your car. We can hardly wait until we see you with all that extra weight on and a good tan you always looked sick when you were home.

I guess we won't need to look for you home if your instructor says you are so good.

You know I was going to come out to see you next month (Nov) if I could have kept working but since I can't work I give up the idea.

Saxton isn't down at the store anymore Trevor Lewis took his place he went up to Rea & Derrick's warehouse.

I see in this evenings paper Frank S. really got married will send you some clippings when dad is thru with the paper.

Jean said everybody up at school is sick about the football team but Wormley said they should not feel that way they just got off to a bad start I think they have been for the last few years. Will write a long letter when I get down town to find out some news.

Write
Lots of Love
Mother

Hometown news stories enclosed with the letter announced a wedding and gave the local football scores. Miss Dorothy Bramley of Duke Street and Frank Shannon of Queen Street, a popular young couple, were married at St. John's Lutheran Church. The Sunbury High School's *Owls* crushed the William Penn *Tigers*, 39 to 6, at Fager Field, Harrisburg, before a mob of 3,000 howling fans, and a week of intense drilling was in prospect for the annual Selinsgrove - Northumberland High School football game.

October 27, 1941
Parks Air College
East Saint Louis, Illinois
Dear Ted,

Glad to hear from you. I guess I know what you're going through, we got a new class of cadets here shortly after I came & boy did they get an initiation! Some of them are still at it. Everybody stood around & gave them the horse laugh.

I hope you like it there. I sure like it plenty here. The work's plenty tough too. It's a known fact that only half of the class coming in finally graduates. We're really working.

Did you know that Parks is supplying some of the planes where you are? Also at Jefferson. I know that we have a new Rearwin instrument trainer down there, how many others I don't know.

We've had 2 weeks here. One of the Army fliers at Curtiss cracked up & got a broken arm. Saturday I had the luck to see a Republic pursuit crack up. I was standing in front of the hangar when 2 planes came over. The 1st landed at Curtiss, the 2nd was circling & right over Parks the fellow's engine choked off, vapor lock we later found out. He was going down wind & didn't want to bank so he just went straight. He hit in a plowed field & we saw him go over on his back. Everybody dropped what they were doing & ran like hell. No one was hurt, 2 prop blade bent, rudder smashed, & fuselage bent.

Did you hear that Buz is managing the Milton store now? Sunbury beat Norry 44 to 6. Seebold ran 90 yds. for Norry's only score.

How's Wendle?

Keep 'Em Flying,

Bob K.

P.S. Have you met any girls? I have, O, boy!

P.P.S. Don't they have rotten weather here?

"Washed Out About 10 Fellows"

October 28, 1941

Tuesday morning

Dear Mother, Dad and Jean,

I didn't have time to write yesterday so I'll get busy now. I'm using the blue paper because I'll need blue name tags when I get to be upper class on Friday.

Since I soloed last Thursday I've been flying about 1 hr. dual and one hr. solo each day. It's certainly nice to go up alone. I've found out your almost as safe in a spin as you are in your bed. One fellow fell out of bed and hurt himself but no one was hurt flying.

In ground school we study meteorology, math, theory of flight, engines and navigation.

We had a cold streak here today and our winter uniforms haven't been issued yet. I put my sweat suit under my summer flying coveralls and my flight jacket and gloves on. I was still damn cold. For winter we get leather boots, pants, jackets and helmets all lined with sheep-skin. Some stuff.

They washed out about 10 fellows so far this wk. and haven't even looked at me yet so I guess I'm doing all right. I hope so.

Love,

Theodore

October 28, 1941

328 King St.

Northumberland, PA

Dear Teedy,

How's the old hard working, lovesick, Weis employee coming with those flying machines.

First of all, I want to congratulate you! Mary Jane told me that you soloed last week. It just don't seem as if you have been gone so long that they would trust you with a plane by yourself already.

Boy, we sure do miss you here. It don't seem like the same old town without you.

Weis will soon have all new employees. First you and Klinger, then Bus, and Saturday was Saxton's last day. He got a job at Rea and Dericks warehouse starting Monday.

The football team isn't getting along so good. They lost to Sunbury and then to Montgomery in a lousy game.

What they really need is a couple of 60 and 70 yd runs – your specialty, you know.

Since you've gone we haven't played much tennis. The last time we played was about 3 weeks ago. Ben and I went out and play 2 sets but for playing at night it really was hot.

Well I bet you, you'll soon be a millionaire. With your salary and your smelly matching - whew!

This town is still the same way – bursting with energy and overflowing with doings. So, there's not so very much to write about.

I hope your having a great time and I'm sure you'll soon be showing those instructors a few tricks in flying.

Well that's about all from the prosperous town of Northumberland for now.

Wishing you the best of luck

Your pal,

Bill Brennen

P.S. "Keep em Flying"

October 28, 1941

Be careful when you try those spins that you say are fun

Tuesday eve

Dear Ted,

Just had your letter from Sat. telling about all those things you do for fun. You just better be careful you are not that good yet. I suppose if you ever got a fellow in a plane you would scare him to death. George Donachy was at the store this evening when Jean was up he was asking Jean about you and wanted to know how you were getting along Dad said I bet if Theodore took him up he would scare Geo half to death. I was down at Sidlers last evening talking to Mary Jane and Olley was down there he said he wanted to be one of the first to congratulate you when you come home for he said you sure do deserve it.

You do not want to tell Mary Jane anything about going to dances at those schools she will have a fit she said last evening that she bet you wouldn't write Sat. than I said well what could you expect it's there first Sat off they probably went out or something she said yes thats just what I was afraid of.

I do hope you will have some time off so you can come home before you go to Texas if you don't wash out do you still think you might I guess not with an average like you have. I suppose you won't like me saying this but I always sort of wished you would. I went to work again today he sent one of the girls up for me and said if I would come back he would see that I had all easy work well I'll try it and see how it works out.

Dad wants to know how your money is holding out. Sat is payday I suppose you will all go out and spend your money Sat nite. Write

Lots of Love
Mother

October 29, 1941
How were your cookies and candy pretty hard
Wed. eve
Dear Ted,

This is going to be a short letter for I want to go to the doctors I feel lousy again today I was in bed all afternoon but this is the first I have been in bed since before you went away so I done pretty good.

Kate is here she was down for supper this evening.

Dad was home by four o'clock he says work is getting awful slack over there but I guess they have too many men since Chet is back. You said it was pay day soon you would send some money I don't want you to send any money home for 2 or 3 pays so you have some money if you come home in Dec. Mary Jane said she hated to see you come home if you could only stay a day but I don't care if you can only stay a half day if you can come home.

Mary Jane said well if he only comes home a day we will have to go thru all that again but I still want you to come home if you can. Maybe you could fly to Middletown than we could get you there. I suppose you will make the other boys step now since you are upper classmen. I guess Frank Noll is giving up trying to get in the Cadets. Mary Jane said he is going to be married now. She said the girl he is marrying is on(ly) 18 yrs old. You should see how fat Mary Jane is getting you will make a nice looking pair.

Write Be Careful
Lots of Love Mother

Postmarked October 29, 1941

Dear Grandson

I am sending you this card to remind you I have not forgot you. Not much space to write will send a letter later we are O.K. Hope you are the same so long.

Grandma Snyder[78]

Left to right Dutch's great-grandmother Catherine Copenhagen Snyder, mother Grace Snyder Van Kirk, and grandmother Virgie Walter Snyder.
Jean ~ "My mother was real pretty. Grandma Snyder popped out babies like mad."
(Courtesy of Elwood M. and Jean Van Kirk McAllister)

October 30, 1941

Thur. eve

Dear Ted,

What's the idea of the blue paper you say you will have blue tags on Friday when you are upper classmen what do you mean. I would like to see you kids when you are upper classmen I bet you will think you are some one.

Jean is doing the supper dishes she is not in a very good mood I need her to do the ironing today too they do not have school to day & to-morrow they are having institute up here.

Norry plays Selinsgrove this week and Sunbury plays Milton. Honestly there hasn't been a thing happening around here lately really there isn't anything in

Norry news anymore. I was down to the doctor last evening my pressure is 196 and I have to go over and have my eyes tested on Sat morning he wanted me to up to the Gesinger to have it done but I am going over to Decker. I guess this will be all for this evening. I don't feel so good it is only 7 o'clock but I think I am going to bed. Be good and be careful.

Write
Lots of Love
Mother

"Upperclassmen Got the Devil"

October 30, 1941
Thursday
Dear Mother, Dad and Jean,

I got your letter today telling me to be careful. That's all you hear around here too. Never do anything foolish is the motto. The things I do are taught to us.

This morning the sky was overcast and measured ceiling was 900 ft. so we were given permission to fly dual. My inst. and I were the first ones to take off. At 700 ft I was in the overcast and couldn't see the nose of the ship so I came back down to 500 and my inst. told me to go back and land. I did but all the other ships took off and didn't come back so he say(s) "If they can fly in that we can too." So we took off again. This time I only got up to 580 before I was in it. We came back to land again but when I was about 10 ft. from the ground he told me to go to South field instead. So I zoomed over the field and started for S. field. On the way there we dodged about 6 planes and by the time we got there the ceiling was down to 300 ft. About 10 planes landed there. They sent a bus down to bring us back. You can't tell a thing in a cloud. You may be flying upside down, in a dive or a climb and you don't know it. We dare not fly in the clouds or above the clouds.

One of the upperclassmen got the devil the other day for flying along side a train and waving at the passengers. Another for dive bombing a steamboat on the Miss.

I become an upperclassman tomorrow. A new class comes in on Wednesday. More fun.

My instructor is a nice fellow. He's about 30 – 35 and only comes up to my shoulder but he can certainly fly. I'd trust him to do anything with me in the plane.

I'll be very busy tomorrow and Sat. moving my things to the upper class side of the barracks so I may not be able to write until Sat. afternoon.

We're having a dance here Sat. night. They are getting us dates and everything.

They are also having a good orchestra. That's one thing – everything we get is the best – If you don't think so our winter flying uniforms cost $80 each.

Love
Theodore

October 31, 1941
Fri. eve
Dear Ted,

Jean and I are trying to decide if we want to go to the movies or not dive bomber is playing its a miserable night here tonight it is pouring down rain and getting very cold.

I drew a pay today I only had 3 ½ days in and drew $14.45 dad said I was making almost as much as he is. I am in a bad way now I am working at Biebermans now and I am supposed to go to work over at Nite Craft on Monday morning I don't know what to do it really isn't bad down here and I don't intend to work long. Jean is reading the paper and if this letter gets mixed up that will be the reason. They had a write up in the paper about you soloing this evening I will send it to you when dad gets the paper read but you know how long it takes him to read the paper.

Dad said I should tell you he wished you would have taken that suit of underwear along you left home he is wearing them you should see him in them its some of those that were so long. You said you were going to have a progress check ride today how did you make out or don't you find anything out. You also said you spun yourself dizzy why did you do that or do you have to.

I am glad you boys liked the cakes and candy tell me if there is anything else you would like. I must close and take Jean down to the movies I don't think I am going.

Write
Lots Love
Mother

"Fairchild Trainers"

November 1, 1941
Air Corps Training Detachment
Harvey Parks Airport
Sikeston, Missouri
Saturday afternoon
Dear Mother, Dad and Jean,

I became an upperclassman on Thursday at 5:30. It feels good to wear a blue name tag instead of a white one.

I got paid today and cleared exactly $67.58. I'll enclose my envelope. When I get a chance I'll mail some money home. I never get to a post office or bank when its open so I guess I'll wire the money home. They fill out money orders at the Western Union office. I hope to get there tomorrow.

We're having a dance here at the post tonight. I hope it clicks. The new lower class comes in the beginning of next week.

Today we got leather face masks to cover our whole face. Not a thing on us is exposed in the cold weather.

I haven't flown since Wednesday. Thursday I flew for 30 minutes with the ceiling at 300 – 700 ft. and since that the weather has been so bad that a plane hasn't been in the air.

There is a new Fairchild trainer and a North American A-17-H observation ship in here today. We soon get new Fairchild trainers here so I'll be flying them. There was a big Douglas bomber here last wk. My instructor said I would probably be assigned to pursuit if I got through. That's where most small fellow go.

I'm in the barracks of shortest fellows here. They call us sand-blowers. It also the best barracks here in inspection drill and number of washouts. Well I'm running out of paper so I must quit.

Love,
Theodore

"Inspection by a General"

November 2, 1941
Sunday morning
Dear Mother, Dad, and Jean,

I'm sorry I haven't written sooner but everything seems to come at once around here.

Yesterday was supposed to be a Saturday but we had a regular day. Ground school and flying. To top that off the lower class had the worst inspection ever seen on the post so we were confined to the barracks area for the whole weekend.

I have two tours to serve but I can sit them out instead of walking them because I'm a cadet officer.

The upper class must do all the processing of the lower class. Besides my other things I've been drilling them and trying to teach them. They're a bunch from N.Y. and think they're pretty good. They won't for long though. I gave them each 12 laps around the ramp yesterday and I'm going to give them more.

I flunked a check ride with Lieutenant Shaw last Friday. It doesn't mean anything but if I happened to do that in a final check I may wash out. I couldn't fly a kite that day.

On top of being confined to barracks we had inspection last night and are going to have one tonight. That never happened before. The lower class is suffering though. They're the dumbest bunch I ever saw.

I'm on Class A again this week. I made 100, 92, 92 in three tests. My average is now 95. If it stays that high I can go to almost any other school if I do wash out. I may go to Canada too – don't blow a fuse I was only kidding. I feel safer flying a plane now than I would driving a car. I haven't driven for so long I think I'll have to learn all over.

Next Wed. a General from Wash. is going to be here to inspect us. That is going to be lovely too. Everything has to be in perfect order.

I'm running out of news so I'd better stop.

I feel and look better than I ever have in my life.

Next week we have open house here. Any one you invite can come and look over the post and then we have a dance Sat. nite.

That's all I have to write about and it looks like enough.

How is everyone.

Love

Theodore[79]

November 2, 1941

Sunday eve 6:30

Dear Ted,

I will have to write a long letter this evening I did not write any yesterday. I was over and had my eyes tested and they put drops in them and it made me so darn sick I had to come home and go to bed I was in bed all afternoon and part of the evening from the darn things.

I have to have glasses and must wear them all the time I went to Dr Decker and he says my eyes are very bad especially my left one he says that one is being strained when I just look at something 3 times as hard as his is when he reads with glasses on he told the nurse that they tested 50 – 75 whatever that is.

We were at Martha and Lee's today for dinner dad and I Jean wouldn't go along you should hear from all he talks about since you left Martha said is airplanes and he is always buying some or making some. Dad wants to know if you always use the same plane when you go up or if you use different ones.

I was over at the station yesterday to see what it would cost me to come out to see you he said as close as he could figure it would be about $30.70 round trip in just the day coach. But if you can come home in Dec I don't think I will come out but if you can't get home I am before you go to Texas. I was down at the store with Mary Jane on Fri evening for about 2 hrs I waited there while Jean was to the movies. We *were figuring how much we would have to save a week to come to Texas when you graduate in spring we thought if we started to come now if there would be about four of us we could drive down wouldn't that be nice than you could come along back with us. That is if you don't wash out I have my doubts if you will now. How did you make out with your progress check? I suppose you flew like you never saw a plane before that day.*

Well if you come home why you can get married like all the rest of them are than you will have a dependent. Jane is going to married at Xmas and she wanted Bill and Francis to be married than too but Martha wouldn't let them she said Francis was to young so I guess they are going to wait till June.

Norry played Selinsgrove yesterday the score was 20 – 0 in favor of Selinsgrove we have some team this year Sunbury played Milton the score was 12 – 0 in favor of Sunbury they say they have a swell team this year Well I guess this will be all or I won't have anything to write next time.

> *Write*
> *Lots of Love*
> *Mother*

November 3, 1941
Mon. eve
Dear Ted,

Well we had your letter today saying you were moving. Did you get your moving all done and get to the dance and what were your dates like? I am rather late writing this eve it is about 8 oclock but I had a busy evening. Dad did not come home for supper till about 6 oclock than he stopped on his way down from Williamsport for supper than I went over for him so I am just getting settled. Dad has a terrible cold I don't know where he gets them this is the second one he has had already but this one is worse than the first one he had.

Do you still get colds like you used to? I image those suits are awful warm. Jean said I should tell you that you went away one year too soon you should see the young teachers up here fresh out of college. She also wants to know if you smoke yet I don't know why she doesn't write and ask her questions. She is doing geometry right now she says she don't know what it has to do with her she will never use it.

You know I didn't think she would miss you the way you's used to scrap but she misses you an awful lot.

I haven't got my house cleaned yet we were trying to find an apartment but we can't get any in Norry there's a lot of them in Sunbury I would move over there if it wouldn't be for Jean. You said you were going to send some pictures I didn't get any yet.

Love
Mother
Write[80]

November 3, 1941
Monday
Dear Mother, Dad and Jean,

    I got two letters from you today. You have an awful time with your work. I'll send some money home. I'll get Mrs. Moore to send a money order for me as soon as I see her.

    I flew for 2 hrs. today. I shot my first stage landings and got an average grade.

    I was busy over the wk. end. We had a big dance here on Sat. yesterday I went to church and the movies and studied for a test. I got 92.

    I'm on Class A now and don't have to go to study hall but I must study tonight for a math test tomorrow.

    That's about all for now so I guess I'll study.
Love
Theodore

November 4, 1941
Tue eve
I'll have to get another pen or I won't be able to write
Dear Ted,

    We just got your letter telling about your pay how did you come to get $147. – but if you wouldn't have your expenses would of have been more than you get. You said about sending money home I told you to save it so you would have it to come home unless you want us to save it for you. We will be able to make it yet for another month or two.

    What do you mean by being assigned to pursuit when your thru and what do you mean by small fellows do they consider you small. I was telling Joe D. how much money you got to start with.

    And Jean was up to the store while ago and George D was up there and he ask Jean how you were getting along and Joe said "Well he drew a pay of $180 month how would you like to draw that he will leave George believing that after while Jean said George wanted to know how your marks were and Jean told him he said well you always were smart. I see in tonites paper F Noll made it in the Cadets he was assigned to Montgomery Alabama now I don't know what he is going to do last week he was going to get married. I must close we must go out and get some anti freeze in the car it is awful cold here.

Love
Mother

November 4, 1941
Dear Theodore,
    Was very glad to receive your letter yesterday and was sure glad you are doing so well keep up the good work we will all be very proud. I am sure. I let Mr. Weis read your letter and he said I should tell you he is glad to hear you are getting along so fine. Your mother and dad were out Sunday for dinner. We had pheasant and rabbit and we thought about your Jean. Would not come along I guess she is to busy to bother with us country folks. Frances said she would write when she once get all her lousy history outlined. She said I should tell you she had a notion to send it out for you to do. I'm glad you like your instructor that means a lot if you are with some one you like. Grandma showed me the card you send her and I was telling her how fine you are getting along. Jimmie wants to know if you could read his letter He just came home from grandmas with a ice cream cone and is half froze. He wants me to tell you he got a new BeBe gun and was out hunting with his daddy on Sat. in a pouring down rain. I am looking for him to get the measles the school is full of them Jerry got them right after Will went home. Frances wants to know if there are any nice girls out there. I guess the way I hear Mary Jane is pretty lonely without you. Frances is still all wrapped up in her Bill. Today is Election around here. Lee will know if he will be school Director for four years tomorrow. I almost forgot to tell you Buss left the store in Norry to manage the Milton store. I hope he will make a success of it. He is a nice fellow but I guess Bill misses you fellows. He always looks dead tired Sat. eve. when I go in there. It is starting to get pretty cold here and our water supply is running short. Lee has to pump again I dont know how long he will have to. I guess Jimmie gave up writing letters as a bad job. He went to bed. He hasn't gotten any whipping as yet this winter. He has another teacher and I guess she is to good to them. Well I guess I am running out of new so will say so long and good luck
    With lots of Love from all
    Martha

November 4, 1941
Wed. eve
Dear Ted,
    Well I did not have a letter today so should not write any what do you do now write Mary Jane one day and me the next so you don't have to write two letters in one day she was up last evening and said she did not have a letter yesterday but 2 the day before now I did not have any today I suppose she had. She showed me the

wings and locket you sent her is she proud of it she made a special trip up last eve to show it to me. It is 6.15 and dad is not home for supper yet so am writing your letter I just wrote one to James at Phila asking about that bungalow Roberts lived in that is going to be empty Paist resigned and is going to Bloomsburg. I ask his sister Mrs. Keithan but she said she did not know what he would do he wants to sell it he wants $2200 for it I think if I could borrow the money we would buy it.

I think it is real nice on the inside I was in it today so I wrote and ask him if he would rent it now I don't know how we will make out I hope we get it but I guess no such luck. I was over and had my glasses fitted today you should see me in them they are the real ritz kind $15.00 bucks should be. How are you getting along since you are upper classmen? Keep your mark high as you can. I have suppose you wonder why I say that but if your going to stay you may as well be good. Well my paper is all so must close. Write

Lots Love
Mother

November 5, 1941
Dear Mother, Dad, & Jean,

I've been busier than a one armed paper hanger here. The lower class came in and are they dumb. I'm on Class A and have to help them every night.

I've been made a cadet corporal here. It has a lot of privileges but it means a little more work right now.

I have a test tomorrow and must study. So good night.

Keep writing
Love
Theodore

"My Landing Check"

November 6, 1941
Dear Mother, Dad and Jean,

I've been pretty busy lately and haven't had much time to write. The new lower class is all in now. Most of them come from N.Y. and Wisconsin. One man is from Pa. – Wilkes Barre.

I was made a cadet corporal. I couldn't fly today because of the weather so I had to drill new cadets. I get out of ground school tomorrow to drill them. You should hear me yell. My lungs are twice as strong.

One of my buddies here got mixed up the other day and landed in a cotton field along side the South field. He just gunned it and pulled it right back up. Does he get razzed.

I got a 92 and 100 on two tests here last week so I believe I'll stay in class A. I got a good grade on flying on my landing check so I go for a ride with Lieutenant Shaw tomorrow. I'm not worried yet.

That's about all for now so I guess I'll have to close.

Love

Theodore

I got a nice new stripe on my arm now.

November 8, 1941

Sat. Afternoon

Dear Ted,

I suppose you think we neglected or forgot about writing but we didn't I felt discouraged we only had three letters this week and you didn't say why until the one we got today you said you were so busy we thought you had more time since you are upperclassmen but you must have less. I am awful glad to hear you are getting along so well do you still like it as well as you did.

I wasn't the only one discouraged Mary Jane sounded awfully disgusted last evening too. I have been busy too I work and try to clean my house in the evening I washed this morning before I went to Sunbury than I went over and got my glasses and Jean some things and it was noon until we got home I am getting along swell with my specs.

I was just up to the football field and took Jeans coat and a blanket up for there it is awful cold here right now. They play Montoursville today it was about 20 min till two when I was up and there wasn't anyone there yet so I imagine it will be a big game of course we will be beat. I seen Walt Riechenbach when I was up he ask about you he said Ben was busy hunting now.

Lois Gresh just told me Kenny told her Wendle is getting along good now. You still didn't answer my question I ask you if you would be home before you went to Texas. Dad is taking his afternoon nap again and I will leave to close and get my work done will write a long letter tomorrow.

Love

Mother

November 9, 1941

Sunday afternoon

Dear Ted,

This has been another long Sunday afternoon with nothing doing. We were over home awhile we went over to tell them about you being made a Cadet Corporal they really are about as proud of you as we are and I think Grandpa Van Kirk is too, but you know grandma she never says much I was down town yesterday afternoon and Mary Jane called me over and she was telling me she told Jane Witmer about you being made a corporal and she said Jane said Donald expected to make one soon. Mary Jane said she felt like saying well he should be something soon he has been there long enough Teedy has only been gone a month. She sure is proud of you. She has the picture of you in your uniform with the sheep skin lining she said don't he look darling she says she shows it to everyone that comes in the store so I left her have that one and I took the negative up to Rea's to get some. You do look swell and happy on that one I guess you are the talk of the town the way you are getting along. I seen Vic Meredith down town yesterday and he ask about you he said he heard you were getting along so good. He got your address he said he was going to write but I should say hello for him when I wrote to you for I would write before he would. What have you been doing this afternoon? We were over house about an hour but they were all very busy so we didn't stay long they were putting a furnace in they sure are fixing the place up swell over there.

Norry & Mountville were tie yesterday and Sunbury and Shamokin score was 19 – 9 in favor of Sunbury.

I am getting along swell with my specs the only trouble I have is behind my ears they make them sore as the dickens and my nose a little bit but I guess I will get used to them everyone else does Jean says I look terrible and everybody else says they are becoming so I don't know what you will think. Well I guess I will have to close and get these starved Indians something to eat really they are hungry everytime I look at them. How about you are you still the same way.

Write & be careful
All our Love
Mother

"Lower Classmen Dumb as Hell"

November 10, 1941
Dear Mother, Dad and Jean,

There isn't any more to write about since yesterday. I passed my civilian check ride today. If I'd have failed that I'd have been up for wash out ride. I'm safe for a while again.

We may get off Thurs., Fri, Sat, and Sunday for Thanksgiving. If we do I may come home and be home from Thurs. night till Sat. night. I believe it would cost too much though. Briggs, Parsons and I may go to St. Louis for the wk. end though.

The lower classmen are getting on my nerves. They're dumb as hell. I'm still on *class A. and still like the place. I've got to study now so I guess I'd better stop. I flew 2:36 today. My instructor says he's going to fly me until I tell him to quit. I'll never get tired of that though. It gets darn cold up there sometimes though.*

Now I've got to study.

Love,

Theodore

Dutch ~ Bill Briggs like me also did not make it as a pilot. I ran into him in North Africa.

November 12, 1941
Wed. eve 9 o'clock
Dear Ted,

I finally did get to write your letter I have been having an awful time this evening. I came home and finished house cleaning the rooms and had our supper and done the dishes and by that time Grandma & Edith were here so I had to stop and entertain them.

They want dad and I to take them out to Mildreds on Sat but dad won't go he had off yesterday and he said he wouldn't take off on Sat that was losing to much time so I guess Lee is going to take them out they want me to go along I don't know if I will or not.

We were up to Milton last nite to the parade we took a car load of majorettes up we darn near froze standing up there but the parade was not near as good as it was other years. Dad was home yesterday I worked so he done the most of the cleaning in the rooms and I finished this evening.

The gasoline stove was on fire this morning the darn thing scared me almost to death dad was still up stairs I screamed and he came tearing down stairs with one shoe on and the other off its funny since its over but I felt sick all morning from the scare. I won't light it now anymore I wait till dads here to light it. So I guess maybe I will leave to get another stove. You talked about going to Canada don't you ever let me hear you mention that again if you wash out you get right home here where you belong. Jean said you were not to go to Canada and fight those Englishmen's fight for them and Mary Jane and I just decided the other evening that we would sooner have you home working at Weis than in the Cadets.

Some one told me the other day that you didn't like it at all when you first went there do you really like it now? Ans. that question don't ignore it like you do most all of my questions.

I ask you in three or four letters if you thought you would get home next month and I still don't know for you have never answered that question.

Dutch ~ My Aunt Edith (on the left), dad's sister and one of the twins, with my mother by dad's Chevy in front of our house on Queen Street.

You said you were confined to the barrack over the weekend how come you were confined same as the rest if it was from poor inspection? Wasn't that the fault of the lower classmen or are the upper classmen confined the same as lower.

Well I guess I will have to close and get down and mail this letter and get to bed or I will never be able to get up in the morning.

You said you look and feel better than you ever have in your life didn't I used to tell you if you went to bed at night and got your rest you would feel better you should see how fat Mary Jane is getting too. Oh I just happened to think she just said the other evening the best birthday present you could have given would have been to call her on the telephone. I would have told you before but she did not tell me till Tue evening.

Well don't let me hear anymore about Canada or I will do more than blow a fuse

Write
Love
Mother

November 12, 1941
Wed eve
Dear Ted,

How are you feeling better I hope so. I did not get a letter today so must go down and see if Mary Jane did. It worries me when I do not hear from you especially since J- said you were sick the other day. Dad and Jean are washing the dishes. You

My True Course

should hear them they chew at one another from the time they start until they are finished.

Jean has the same tired feeling she always has had.

How are you getting along with your flying alright I hope since that is only thing you want to do. Have you had anymore check rides. How is the weather warm or cold it is very warm here now again almost like spring. Do you know if you will come home and when if you stay before you go to another training field.

Jean said Sterling and Bill Brennan ask if you were coming home for Thanksgiving she told them you couldn't and why she said they seemed awful dissappointed.

There is an airplane crossing over our house right now ever time the darn things fly over it makes me get the blues. Mrs. Conrad said yesterday every time one went over she thought of you she thought your pictures were swell. Well I guess this will be all for this eve I have a lot of work to do yet and till you get all my questions answered in this letter you will have a letter. But that is just the trouble you never answer them.

Dad said tell him. I just got done with the dishes Jean said tell him I helped.
Write
    All our Love
    Mother

"Final Test in Meteorology"

November 13, 1941
Dear Mother, Dad and Jean,

I'm just about out of ink but I may try to stretch it.

Well I finally had to go fill it – out of somebody else's bottle as you can see.

I sent some pictures to Mary Jane she'd bring them up to you then.

Our inspection here was one of the best the general saw he said. As usual "C" company was on the top of the group. I wish my flying were as good.

Some days I think I can fly and other days I don't. Today I flunked a 180° side approach. That's one of them spot landing tricks where you have to shave trees and polls to get into a field the size of a postage stamp.

There were 20 lower classmen in our barracks when we started so far 5 have washed and 5 more ride in the washing machine tomorrow. My instructor started with 5 students. Four lower classmen and an upperclassman. There are two of us lower classmen left and the other one rides in the washing machine tomorrow. Keep your fingers crossed.

We take a final test in meteorology tomorrow.

Sat. is our big open house here. Oh Boy.

I see F. Noll got in. He went to one of the poorest fields in the country.

Well I must go study.

Love

Theodore

November 13, 1941

Dear Brother,

I have to use a pencil Mom's using the pen. She is on the warpath. She has been terrible this week.

We get our report cards Friday they changed the marking systems. I'll send you my marks. I got 80 in my Geometry test 94 in Latin and 84 in History. I joined the typing club tonight and got the devil because I didn't come home and do my work.

I told Daddy I wanted a snow suit he said I should write to you (take the hint). I got my ice skates out and polished them up. I can use them soon if this weather keeps up.

Poor Ben I was supposed to give him your address last Thursday and I forgot it until today. Tell Mom to get a big Christmas Tree. They are going to put one on a table with no yard. Its terrible since you are not home to take my part they gang up on me. You should see Mom in her glasses she looks terrible (Don't tell her I said so) She has sore ear were the glasses fit behind them. I guess thats why she so mean. Daddy sticks by me.

Write to me I like my own letters

Love

Sis

P.S. Mom is putting something terrible in her letter about me don't believe it because I have been a good girl. Daddy says so. I haven't ask her for a thing she did not spend her last two pays on me I told her I would rather not have her work than get anything.

November 13, 1941

Thursday eve

Dear Ted,

Well I did not get my letter today but I will get big headed and write anyway. I am as grouchy as the dickens this evening so you might get a bawling out Jean just told me to get it out of my system so I would feel better. We were just trying to figure out about the letters we got from you yesterday you wrote on Sunday and they are post marked Nov. 6. I didn't notice it until Mary Jane said about it last evening she thought they were the letters you wrote Sunday a week ago but I knew it could *not be that by some of the things you said in your letters so we looked when the one before was postmarked than we knew that it was marked wrong.*

Grandma Snyder said she wrote you a letter did you get it she ask me Sunday if you said any thing about getting her letter.

I am going to send you a box as soon as I get my house cleaned and have time to fix it maybe you will be home till then.

Did you get Mary Jane's letter yet telling you about the dance. She ask me what I thought she should do. I told her I didn't want to tell her what to do she was to do as she pleased about it. She said well it does not mean a thing only I am so lonely and it is my birthday.

Jean wrote something in her letter about me and she won't let me see if she just left dad read it but he had to promise on his word of honor not to let me see it. I'll find out yet what she said she is a little brat lately so just ignore anything she says I have spent the bigger part of my last two pays on her and she still isn't satisfied. These are a tit for tat letters but we just dare not let you forget us. Don't believe what she says I just told her what I wrote now she is writing more out our way as usual. Write

Love

Mother

"If I Wash Out"

November 13, 1941, *Thursday afternoon*
Hotel De Soto, Eleventh at Locust St Louis, Mo.
Dear Mother, Dad and Jean,

We got here at 3 this afternoon and have been sleeping for the last 3 hrs. Parsons, Briggs and I are all in this room. We got special rates and its not costing much.

I called Klinger as soon as I got here. He was glad to here from me. I'm going over to see him tonight. He's afraid he may flunk over there too. Weis may get us both yet. I hope not. I couldn't stand that.

If I do wash out I can go into navigator, bombardiering etc. and get the same pay and commission. Or I could come home and look for work and if I didn't find it join the RAF and go to their basic school in California and when I get through there go to Canada as an instructor. I said instructor I don't know what to do.

We're going out to get our Thanksgiving dinner now. Write and tell me what you think.

Yours

Theodore

November 14, 1941
Friday eve
Dear Ted,

Had your letter today saying you might be home for Thanksgiving but you guess it would cost to much. You first better get yourself home if you can come home it won't cost you that much. It would only have cost me around $30 – 31 to come out there and you can travel for less than I could you can get special rates so you should be able to make the trip for around $20 and if you and those fellows go to St Louis you will spend darn near that much and as for saving for that other reason these will be a way to get around that too so you see Mary Jane has told me all about it. I am sending her a card for her birthday would like to get her something but I don't know what.

Jean said I should tell you she got a good report card B – C not an A on it do you think that is good. Well anyway she says its good so that is all that is necessary. Dad has to go out and tell grandma I am not going to Butler to-morrow I suppose she will throw a fit but I can't help it the trip would make me to tired and I am near dead now till Friday night. You say those lower classmen get on your nerves don't you think you kids got on the other ones nerves when you went there. I wish when they send you some place else they would send you to Langely field or somewhere nearer home so we could get to see you more often. Well I guess this will be all for this evening Jean says no wonder you don't answer my questions she don't think you can read half of my letters. Write

Lots of Love
Mother

"The USS *Boise*"

November 15, 1941, the USS *Boise*, a Brooklyn Class light cruiser, left Pearl Harbor and steamed towards Manila in the Philippines. On board Ensign James L. Starnes hoped to become "an officer and a gentleman" and see the world.[81]

James Starnes ~ The sailors "while at Pearl Harbor trained on how to conduct warfare and attack Japanese ships. We worked hard and played hard." During the week, "We practiced defensive exercises to defend against a Japanese attack."

The *Boise* escorted troop transports and supply ships of foodstuffs.[82] "We left Pearl Harbor with the convoy on November 18, 1941. We were the only combatant ship with the supply ships." While heading toward Manila one night, "We saw a ship in the far distance, on the horizon. They failed to identify 'friend or foe.' We were ready to be engaged. The next morning the ship was gone."[83] Starnes and his crewmates in the weeks ahead asked themselves the question, "What if we had attacked the ship on the horizon?" Would it have changed history?

November 15, 1941, *Saturday*
Dear Mother, Dad and Jean

I haven't got much to write about. We're having a pretty good time but I wish I could have come home. We went over to Packs this morning Klinger has been with us all day. We want to go out now so I'll let this go and write more soon.

November 16, 1941
Sunday eve
Dear Ted,

Gee if I don't get around and write you will soon think we died but I have had so darn much to do this week end that I have been busy every minute You might know we have been busy dad didn't even get his nap today. Yesterday I tried to clean house and had company most all day Mary and the kids were here and Catherine was down and she was down till ten oclock last eve Martha & Jim and Francis & Bill were in too Lee took grandma and grandpa to Butler we just came in from out at Lee's and he just came home it is 8.30 here we went out this afternoon for to get one of those big lights to put up in the kitchen we went out at about 3 oclock and were coming right back but to please Jim we had to stay for supper I guess he got lonely out there dad took him back to the woods for a walk and he thought that was swell.

They have to pump there water with an engine out there again so you know it must be pretty dry. I had 5 pictures made of you in your flying tags I gave over home and out home each one and gave Martha & Lee one and Jim thinks they are swell. He brought it out today and wanted to know if that was your plane and if you flew it alone and how many seats it had in it. Mary Jane told me you called her Friday eve Faye Seasholtz told me Sat. I was to come down M.J. wanted to see me I went down and she told me she said she just had to tell me it wouldn't keep I thought you called her at the store and I just missed it. I was down with her Fri eve from about 7 – 9. I guess she was still half asleep when you talked to her.

Write & be careful
Love
Mother

Ca. November 16, 1941[84]

Sunday

Dear Mother, Dad and Jean,

I'm sorry I didn't write yesterday but I took a tetanus shot (my last one) right after inspection and drill and it made me sick. I was in the hos(pital). For about 3 hrs. I had hives all over me. They gave me a shot of adrenlin and I was so shaky I couldn't do anything the rest of the day - and on open house too.

Last Monday I passed a check ride. On Thursday my instructor said I was going to wash out. On Friday my instructor was sick so I rode with the flight commander. He's a good instructor and really taught me some tricks. He said I was all right. Now I don't know whether I'm good or bad.

If I go through I will be going to Texas (I hope to Randolph) in about 3 ½ weeks.

The inspector general who inspected the school on Wed. said we had the best school in the eastern area. That may help us get to Randolph. Everyones hoping it does.

Well I guess I'd better go into church now.

Love

Theodore

"Complicated Acrobatics"

November 17, 1941

Monday

Dear Mother, Dad and Jean,

I got two letters from you and one from Jean today. It sounded just like home. I can't come home because we can only go 500 mile by railroad or 250 by car. So I guess I'll just go up to St. Louis and see Klinger.

They washed 5 more fellows today. That makes about 1/3 of our class. I think I'll last now. It isn't as long anymore.

I told you most of the news yesterday. The hives were awful.

There were some people down here from Butler, Pa. over the weekend to see their son.

I guess I'll have to go eat supper I'm half starved. I usually am. I flew 1 hr. 55 min. This afternoon. All solo. My head roar(ed) and my ears ache. Next wk. I start learning more complicated acrobatics.

There's the call for supper so I must leave.

Love

Theodore

November 17, 1941
Monday eve
Dear Ted,

Well another blue Monday just about gone I always hate to see Monday come because I have to start out to work again. I haven't felt so good over the week end I don't know whats the matter. Dad and Jean don't feel so good either this evening so its good around here Jean is doing the dishes and growling all the time. How did your open house turn out were there some nice girls there! You said we were to keep our fingers crossed for you I guess we most always do and hope you get thru all right. How soon will you be safe from a washout or won't you be safe as long as you are there? Martha was telling Mr. Weis you expected to go to Texas he said wouldn't it be nice if he gets where Bob is because they know one another. He said Bob has an office job.

I haven't seen your pictures yet you sent Mary Jane I am going down when I mail my letter and see if she got them.

Norry got beat again on Sat. Bloomsburg beat them 20 – 6 Sunbury beat Mt. Carmel 13 – 6. Everybody around here has given up hopes I don't think they will win a game this year for they sure will not beat Milton. Do you get the Collier's magazine Mrs. Hine was here a few weeks ago for the money so I stopped American Boy and had Collier's sent to you and I get Cosmopolitan for 38¢ a month well this is an evening I run out of news. Write
  Lots of Love
  Mother

Ca. November 18, 1941
No more talking about joining the R.A.F. I didn't sleep all nite the other nite when you said that in my letter.
Tue. eve
Dear Ted,

How are you now are you alright again. You never got sick before from those shots did you and what did they give you the shot of adrenalin for.

You said you did not know how your flying was good or bad you must think you are pretty bad. I thought you were getting along good. How is Wendle getting along with his flying or don't you see him very often.

We got your pictures they are the best pictures I believe you ever had taken. Mary Jane showed them to Olley last eve and he thought they were swell. He says ever body looks good on a picture but him. The painted one is darling but I let Mary Jane keep that one she thought so much of it.

Martha & Lee were in this eve and I showed them the pictures. I said I had a notion to have one made and painted. She said if I did I was to get her one they thought they were swell. We had Barry over for supper he is getting to be a little dickens. When we got over there we can't come home without him. We have to bring him along over he is crazy about dad. Martha and Lee butchered they brought us some scrapple and sausage in.[85]

Well I guess this will be all for now I still must dampen my clothes and I haven't been feeling so good it takes me a long time to get around and dad pussy foots around he makes you nervous. Write

Lots of Love
Mother

"Beat the Flight Commander"

November 19, 1941
Wed
Dear Mother, Dad and Jean,

This has to be short. Time is precious now.

Vacation stars at 6:00 p.m. tonite and ends Sunday at 7:00 p.m. I can't come home so five of us are going to St. L. I'm going to see Klinger and Parks Air College[86] *and the Airport there.*

My instructor said he was going to wash me out today. I told him I'd only beat the flight commander anyhow so I don't know what he'll do now. 43 out of 117 have washed out.

Well I must go now. I'll write more from St. Louis.

Love
Theodore

November 19, 1941
Norry, Pa.

Well young Chap how is it going by this time I hope well, I suppose you thought the Phillips have forgotten you, such is not the case. I have been after that Lorraine to write this long time and I would write a few lines and put in with hers; every time I say you write to Teedie she would say he wrote to you not to me, every couple days her daddy will say did you write to Teedie.

We miss you very much. I know I do a great deal especially when it comes to carrying my grociers home. When we go in Weis Sat. night Ann will say poor Teedie how he always took our things home.

Last Sat. Brecht delivered my things thats the first time since you left.

Nuck left Weis and is working at Rea & Derricks Warehouse. Trevor took

Nucks place Nuck took Lorraine to the movies to-night. She & Bobby Miller aren't on very good terms she told him what she thought of him here the other week and still he hangs around. You know what I think of them his folks moved to Phila this week, he is boarding up at Henry Glasses on King St, that is Wilmont Benner's Mothers, I wish he would move to then maybe Lorraine will forget him, and enjoy some one else, as he certainly won't show any girl a good time, he's to tight.

I guess you think I am terrible talking this way but you know me I say what I think. How do you like it by this time, I guess you don't get time to get lonesome you are so busy all the time, we often think of you, I hope you will make good, I know you will and we all wish you the best of luck, & God bless you, & be with you, know matter where you go & what you do, and I do remember you in my prayers often and don't forget your prayers & I am sure you will have luck always. Well Teedie I will close, Write when you can & as I always said (Bee good) I am as ever your friend.

Mrs. Phillips

November 21, 1941
Dear Brother,

Mother is tired tonight I don't think she will write. This town is as dead as can be. I only go out on Sunday and Saturday nights and maybe a movie once in a while.

I joined the typing club. Do you think its a good club? I thought it was a good one to join. I got my seat change in school aside of Doug Brennen we fight like the dickens. He is always picking on me. I have to tell you my marks. B is good C is fair English – B   Geometry – C   Biology – B   Music – B   Latin – B   History – C

I missed the honor roll by a point. I bet you think it isn't so hot, but I think its good.

Mother has been swell to me. I don't know what going to happen. Daddy is the same as ever.

I am surprise at you talking of washing out I never knew any Van Kirk losing out yet my brother yet to boot. I'll kick you all the way back to Sikeston if you wash out you can fly any of those old crates.

I got something funny to tell you Eddie is going to give Mickey a black eye if he don't stop hanging around me. Isn't that a hot one, boys fighting over me. (Ahem)

Daddy is in a session with the paper. Could you send me a gas mask he nearly has me smoked out. I have to get my beauty sleep.

Love
Sis

P.S. I have a birthday Dec 3 (take the hint) You can send me fur mittens or a pen.

"Don't Worry"

November 23, 1941

Sunday eve.

Dear Mother, Dad and Jean,

I found 3 letters from you, 2 from Mary Jane and from Mrs. Phillips when I got back today. If you don't feel good you'd better stop working.

I got through last week all right but I have a check ride tomorrow morning and the way I feel after a vacation oh no one is ever safe from elimination here. They're getting tougher every day. They're getting too many pilots for the planes they have.

While we were on vacation a colonel and his wife stopped and our captain took him through our barracks. They said our beds were better and neater than the ones at West Point. They have to be.

Don't have Collier's sent to me. I can get it in the recreation room and don't want to bother with it.

Don't worry about me being sick. That stuff only bothered me for about an hour. If you sprain your finger or sneeze more than twice around here they put you in the hospital with a doctor by your bed. They take no chances of anyone getting sick.

The weather was warm here until Thursday. Then it got cold and Saturday it snowed in St. L. but not here.

I don't think I'll be able to get home between transfers but we may get a long vacation and not report right away. I hope so.

There is a fellow here who washed out and left on Thurs. morning. I saw him Friday afternoon and he had a job in an arms plant in St. Louis making $60. a wk.

If I wash and go into armaments I'll go to Denver, Colo. and if I go in nav(igator). I go to Alabama. You get the same pay and the same commission all the way through as I get now or I would get. I'll know all about it tomorrow or by Wednesday at least.

We had a good time in St. Louis and with Klinger. Saturday is payday. I should get about $90. I'll send some home.

I'd better study a little now.

Love,

Theodore

November 23, 1941

Sunday eve

Dear Ted,

Well I suppose you are home from your vacation all played out it will take you all week to get rested up. I said to dad last eve now if you could have come home you would be home. But now you still have your trip home.

We just come home we were out to see Jimmie Van Kirk he has the measles you should see him he does look cute.

When we come home the gang of boys were in here with Jean raising the devil you should have heard dad the same as usual he hasn't been feeling good of late anyway I don't know whats the matter with him he looks awful bad.

Well I will finish your letter now.

Clifford was just here as I had to stop writing and help entertain him Jean says our place is Grand Central station every time we try to do something there is always some one comes in we were trying to clean house yesterday and there were only five or six in and Barry does not want to stay at home anymore he is always over here when I take him home he cries like the dickens and want to come back with me.

I showed Grandma Van Kirk your picture to day and she wanted to know if it was hers I told her no that was all I had I think I will try and have some made and give the grandmas each one Clifford just told me grandma Snyder is sick he was going to take her to the doctor. How are you since you had your shot and was sick. What is the matter with you and your instructor you are talking about being washed out than you say the next day you are alright than the next letter you talk of being washed out. Well I guess I better close and get these starved Indians some supper and there isn't much more to write there is nothing happen anymore

Write

Love

Mother

"Flying on Saturdays"

November 24, 1941

Monday

Dear Mother, Dad and Jean,

Well it looks as though I'll stay here for a little while longer. I passed my check ride today so I'll probably be safe until I take my final check.

Things are changing here. From now on we must fly and go to school on Saturdays the same as any other day. That means we'll only get a little time off each Sunday. We may get a longer Christmas vacation from it though.

A fellow got lost this afternoon and didn't get in until after dark. He landed in some farmer's field and asked him where Sikeston was. He was going in the opposite direction.

Well I'd better study now. We have a test tomorrow.

Love

Theodore

Dutch ~ As you get to the end of your course the Army started giving the check rides. You always had to be prepared for a forced landing. While taking off and getting to about two hundred feet altitude the instructor chopped the throttle and said, "forced landing. What are you going to do?" Sometimes I would say, " I am not going to hit that house over there. That is all I can tell you."

The military got involved and started giving check rides when we were close to graduating. Military flying was entirely different from what our civilian instructors taught. The civilian instructors told us to make our flying nice and smooth. When you flew with the military guys they would say "bring that goddamn airplane around."

November 24, 1941

Monday eve

Dear Ted,

Just got your letter today that you wrote there in St. Louis. You said you wished you could have been home you did not wish it anymore than we did we count the days till we think you will be home.

You ask what we think you should do if you wash out well dad and I were just talking and if you want to be a navigator or bombardier all right but as to going to California and go as an instructor for the R.A.F. no no for dad and I both feel this way if they flunk you they know that you will not make a flyer and if you would join the R.A.F. they would probably push you through no matter what kind of a flyer you are and before long you would be going to England. Dad said he didn't even care much about you being a bombardier or navigator I really think he misses you as any of us. There are so many things you could do at home here without going back to Weis you wouldn't have to come back to Norry to work you could get work somewhere else there are an awful lot from Norry working down at Middleton airport and the rail road is posting bulletins on there bulleting boards for men so you surely could find something you wouldn't even be in the next registration yet. But for your sake I hope & pray that you don't wash out but whatever you don't think of joining the R.A.F. in any way. Well I guess this will be all I have a lot of work to do yet this evening we have our Thanksgiving here this week

Well the best of luck and hope everything turns out all right

Lots of Love

Mother

Postmarked November 25, 1941

We were over home Saturday. I saw your large pictures. Mother and Dad were cleaning house got your card yesterday hope you wont wash out so wish you good luck so long

Grandpa. & Gma.

November 25, 1941

Tue. eve

Dear Ted,

I did not get a letter today but I will forgive you for I guess you have been pretty busy since you got back. How are (you) getting along since you got better I hope. Do they still talk about washing you out? I was down at Sidlers last evening Mary Jane was all alone and she seemed to be glad that you might wash out for my part I wouldn't care for then you would soon be home but I know that you would like to stay. But I guess we will just have to wait and find out and hope for the best.

I just finished my ironing it is 25 min. till nine Mrs. Miller and Freddie are over they have been over for about an hour now honestly they get to be a nuisance she is playing the piano now.

I have to tell you about Jean last evening. Eddie Fisher has been trying to get her to go out with him again I guess she had her mind about half made up to go out with him again than Bill Gross told her he walked a girl home from the Island on Fri. nite and Jean said Bill said he even kissed her good nite I had to laugh than she said to me well mother you need not laugh about it this is a very serious problem you should have seen Mary Jane laugh when I told her. She was telling me about getting new clothes I said gee you will be all dressed up she says well I want to look nice when Teedy comes home. Well tomorrow will be our last day till Friday morning thats a help. Do you know what we are going to Thanksgiving dad and I are going to clean house Jean is going to Milton to the game we got a 3 lb. chicken you don't think we will get sick do you. Well I guess this will be all for this eve. Do you know I always sort of look for you when I came home in the eve Write

Lots of Love and luck

Mother

November 26, 1941, the plan of Admiral Yamamoto, commander in chief of the Japanese fleet, to assault the United States was underway. Vice Admiral

Chuichi Nagumo commanded the strike force as the Empire's aircraft carriers left Hitokappu Bay bound for Oahu.

"Slow Rolls and Vertical Reverses"

November 26, 1941
Wednesday
Dear Mother, Dad and Jean,

I got Jeans letter yesterday and mothers today. You don't have to worry about me joining the R.A.F. I found out what they paid.

I've been forgetting to tell you this. About two weeks ago I was promoted to a cadet sergeant. I was only corporal about a week. That gives me another nice gold stripe to put on my sleeve.

I started learning advanced acrobatics today. My instructor made me do 13 loops in a row. (I got a new instructor) Then he tried to teach me snap rolls, slow rolls, vertical reverses, immelmans, split S's. Whenever you get upside down you just hang there on your safety belt. Some fun. Whenever you pull out it feels like a steam roller pushing you down in your seat. Some fellows black out but I never do. My nose only bleeds a little.

They start giving final military checks tomorrow. That tells you whether you do or you don't. Here's hoping.

I have to study now.
Love
Theodore

November 26, 1941
You do not have to send any money home this month yet you might come home, but save what you can
Wed eve
Dear Ted

Well I had a long letter from you today I can hardly wait till we get your next letter we will probably know by then if you stay or not I think we worry as much about you now yet as ever.

I don't understand what you mean you said you did not think you would get home between transfers but might get a long vacation and not report right away. I don't get that. You was worrying about what you were going to do if you washed out well if you can go and do like that fellow did get a job for $60 a week. Why you wouldn't have to worry. Well we don't need to worry about work tomorrow dad and I are both home tomorrow we are going to clean our kitchen and attic its about *time or it will be spring before I get there. Kate came in to stay tonite she is afraid to stay out there alone there is no one in the other side anymore Edna and her husband parted Kate wanted us to rent it but it is out a little bit to far for me we are out far enough. Altho I like the house. I was talking to Mrs. Donachy this evening up at the store she was asking about you I told her you liked it a lot she said well she guessed George would sooner be where you are than where he is to day she says he likes to fly but he does not have a license. Jean is having her usual evening session on the piano I think she pounds on that more than ever lately. Well I guess this will be all for this eve*

Write

All our Love

Mother

"My Flying Has Improved"

November 28, 1941

Friday

Dear Mother, Dad and Jean,

Today is Friday but tomorrow is the same as any other day from now on. I like the flying but I always fall asleep in classes.

I shot a B stage today and that is something. I was the first one - the only one so far – to get a B on a 360° overhead stage. You go over the field at 1000 ft turn off your motor and circle around like this (drawing of a circle with arrows clockwise) and try to land on a line. I hit the line 4 out of 5 times and was only 25 ft. away the fifth time. That made my new instructor smile. He said most of the instructors couldn't do that unless they were as luck as I was. My flying has improved 100%. It may get me to Texas in a week and a half. It better. I have to study for a test now. So I'd better learn something about carburetors.

Love

Theodore

November 28, 1941

Fri evening

Dear Ted,

I think your letter is going to be short this evening I am so darn tired I can hardly write dad and I cleaned the kitchen this evening and did we clean it is ten oclock and we are just finishing we were going to do it yesterday when dad had off but Lee came in for him and wanted him to help out on the farm yesterday he had to buy 150 bags of potatoes and his men would not work. Jean went to Milton to the football game so I was alone most all day I worked all day so I did not know if it was Thanksgiving or not we had a roast chicken but we did not have our dinner until 6.30. Milton beat Norry 47 – 0 I sure am glad the football season is over I guess everybody was ashamed of our team. Hazelton beat Sunbury 6 – 0 that is the only game Sunbury lost I will send you the clippings as soon as dad gets the paper read.

You said you were safe again for a while for how long. I thought you said you would know for sure this week. What are you going to do if you do. I wish you would come home and try to find something. Jean and I want to see that picture last evening A Yank in the R.A.F. that was terrible and it make me care still less to have you stay. You talk about your Xmas vacation do you really think you will get home for Xmas if you stay.

You said a fellow got lost and did not get in till after dark it wasn't you was it. I most always go down and spend Fri evening with Mary Jane but have only seen her once this week so you know how this will be all for now I must go to bed I can hardly stay awake any longer Write

All our Love
Mother

November 30, 1941
R. E. McCorkill
Susquehanna U.
Selinsgrove, Pa.
Dear Ted,

At the time you went into the Air Corps, I read an article in the paper about your going; and I wondered at the time if you would remember that you promised to write to me. Then you can understand how delighted I was to receive your letter. I wanted to write to you much sooner than this, but the month of November has been such a hectic month that not until now have I had chance to fulfill that desire.

You're really quite a distance from home, but as long as you like the place, you should be happy. It must be interesting to come in contact with new people and new places. You're to be envied.

It is terribly interesting to hear about your flying. In fact, I wouldn't mind being out there and soloeing also. If you remember I always was and still am a bit "baffy" about flying and all that goes with it.

Listen - you're good enough to fly, or else. So don't let me hear of your washing out. U.S. needs you as much as does Canada. You're probably a super-super by this time.

Susquehanna's football team could not boast of many victories this year, but we had a good bunch of fellows who desire a lot of credit for their pluck. Basketball season opens this Tuesday. We're looking forward to having quite a successful season.

I'll write and keep you posted.

As we had only one day Thanksgiving vacation this past Thursday we made up for it by having an Inter-fraternity dance Wednesday night. There is one more dance before Christmas vacation begins on December 18. That is the Inter-sorority rush dance on December 13. Fraternity rushing began a week ago yesterday. Last night Bond and Key had an Open House. Sorority rushing begins December 1 so we will be plenty busy for the next two weeks.

Tell Mr. H. E. Parsons that I'll write sometime this week. Is his first name Harry, Harold, or what? Glad to hear the fellows out there are swell. What makes you think I would like them? You should send me a picture of you and some of your friends. What about a picture of you in your winter flying uniform, so I can see what a polar bear looks like.

I saw Vic Meredith when I was at Dickinson for the game two weeks ago.

Friendly thoughts

"Scotch"

November 30, 1941
Sunday afternoon
Dear Ted,

Well this is just another of these dull Sunday afternoons it is 4.30 here and this afternoon has been like a day we want to go over to Grandma Snyders after while she has not been feeling so good but we want to wait until Jean gets ready for Church. We were away last Sunday afternoon and when we came home she had about ten kids in here and I guess they went thru the house from one end to another. She is down at Portzline's this afternoon I suppose she will have a gang gathered up until she comes home she is going out with Eddie F(isher) again. Congratulations on being made a Cadet Sargent but I guess it is a little late you sure are forgetful what is on your mind some pretty girl or flying. Won't you be home between transfers if you stay and if not do you have any idea when you will? You always say there is nothing to write do you know if you would answer some of my questions you would have something to write. What do you want Santa Claus to bring you this Xmas you are a problem child this year it is awful hard to think of something you can use Jean has told me so much she wants my trouble with her is which I really should get her out of all she wants beside that she has a string she wants for her birthday this week but that is all the good it does her. I am sending you clippings of the games on Thanksgiving day and you told me not to send you Colliers well I guess Mrs. Hine already has sent it so if you don't want it take it to recreation hall I don't know how long it will be till they are run out. We still have $2.45 to pay than we will have your radio paid off and the tires are just about finished to I guess we have about

10.00 yet. Well I guess will have to close and get some supper you know dad he is always ready to eat. I am glad that business about the R.A.F. is settled so I don't have to worry about that

> *Write*
> *All my Love*
> *Mother*[87]

"Kick My — Out of the Plane"

December 1, 1941
Monday
Dear Mother, Dad and Jean,

I haven't got much time I have to shine my shoes before I go to bed.

My instructor told me today I would go through to basic. I didn't have any check rides yet but he told me I should pass them and if I didn't he'd kick my — out of the plane at 5000 ft. He'd taught me plenty about flying in the past week.

> *I must go now*
> *Love*
> *Theodore*

AIR CORPS TRAINING DETACHMENT
HARVEY PARKS AIR PORT
SIKESTON, MISSOURI

December 1, 1941
Monday eve
Dear Ted,

I did not get a letter today but will write anyway but if I do not get one tomorrow I won't be so big hearted I have a lot of time I come home from work early and do not go back until they send for me I need the rest alright but I also need the money with Xmas so near it would happen just at this time I think I am going down and see Mrs Snyder about going over to Nite Kraft. *I do not have much to write about it is getting terrible around here there is only a half of page of Norry news in the paper anymore so you know how dead it is getting. How are you getting along this week? Do you think you will be home for Xmas answer these questions. Jean is going to choir practice Dad is having his usual evening session with the paper.*

They took Les Bakers wife to the hospital last nite and operated this morning Faye is working down at Andrews Hardware store now she got her divorce some one said she and Jimmie Bolig were going to be married he is to good for her I think. Mrs. Fleming went to Wisconsin her father died. There I guess that is all the news so I will close for this eve. Don't forget to write.

Lots of Love
Mother

December 2, 1941
Hope we will see you soon
Tue evening
Dear Ted

Well I will write you a letter this evening and try to remember what I do with it last evening I wrote you a letter I went down to Sidlers to get a stamp and Mary Jane said I had to stay and talk to her awhile so I was down there until about 8.30 than I came out and stopped down at Snyders and after I got home and get in bed I happened to remember I did not mail my letter I looked for it and could not find it so I don't know what became of it unless I left it lay down at Sidlers if I did Mary Jane probably mailed it so tell me when you write if you got a letter I wrote Monday evening if not I don't know what happened to it. OK I have a lot of news to tell you this eve I put a ding in the back fender on the right side of your car today the darn thing has me worried sick I took it down to Mertz I was going to have it fixed but they could not do it today they told me to bring it down Friday it would cost $2.00 to have it fixed and the whole fender repainted but dad says it is not that bad so I was to let it go until we have the motor fixed up and than we will have it fixed up. The fenders that the paint was bad on are getting pretty bad to be told yes he would repaint the four fenders so they looked exactly like the car for $8.00 so maybe I will have it done after we got the motor fixed up and I have work dad said I should not have told you about the fender he said its not that bad. You must be getting along fine right now with your flying we had your letter today telling about those fancy landings you were making I can believe its really you doing that with a plane dad says well sooner them than me doing those things with them planes. If you go to Texas in a week and half will you be home at Xmas time than do you think I hope so I just told dad this evening if I would have a pass I would leave been to Missouri *several times already. Mick M(cAllister) took Jean to the movies tonite I don't know if they will have a fight or not before they get home they remind me of Mary Jane and you the way they fight but Mary Jane still says ok we had fun. Well I guess this is enough of our happenings at home for one letter dad wants to know what all I was telling you tonite.*

Write & good luck
All our Love
Mother

December 3, 1941
Wed eve
Dear Ted

After that long letter last night I don't have much to tell you. I did not get my letter today you must have been pretty busy Jean is doing the dishes for once she is 15 yrs old today she sure is getting big

Dad is taking a bath he hurt his back today getting coal out of Harry Weis cellar so he is not in such a good mood. I do not have to go to work tomorrow so I can sleep tomorrow morning I bet. I will have to tell you about the scrap Jean got in to Eddie Fisher send Brub Diehl up to get him a date with Jean on Sat so Jean told Brub she would give Eddie a date Tuesday nite and in the time from Sat to Tue she seen Eddie smoking so she broke the date so Mick – come over last eve and ask Jean to go along to the movies and she did so today Eddie wrote Jean a note and told her what he thought of her

And Bill Gross came in her class room and I guess he gave her a good bawling out he went so far as to call her liar so these kids are having some time. Well I am going to come to the point and just ask you what you want for Xmas for it postively has me I do not know what to get you or what you can or can not use so give me a couple good hints.

Well I said I was not going to write a long letter but till I tell you all our days happenings I have a letter. Jean said Ben Reichebach ask about you today he said some one told him you were coming home in a couple week he wanted to know if it was true Jean said I hope so.

Well now this is all.
Don't forget to write
All our Love
Mother

December 4, 1941

Thur. nite

Sterling T. Post

ΣX

Dear Theodore,

I was glad I heard from you, also glad you are coming along ok. All I can say is I'm glad I am passing all of my subjects. Trig. & Chem. the two that I was worried about the most are the ones I have the highest grades in. As for the B.O. women they are really ok. I met one at our pledge dance the other week that I really go for in a big way, Mildred Dyer from Stubenville, Ohio. She is a brunette, about 5'3", lovely eyes, pretty teeth and a wonderful personality.

In case you are ever in here and in need of a date, I really believe I can fix you up with something that is ok. Last week and over vacation I was down at Susq. U. I must say I met some nice stuff. Not to brag or anything but since school stared my list of feminine acquaintances has increased 120%, which isn't bad. Also I don't ever think that it will be necessary to fix you up; but if you were a free man, that's a different story.

I can just imagion what a thrill acrobatics are. I can practically see you at Randolph now.

How did you make out in St. Louis? Also, are there any nice women located near you? Honest, I believe I'm falling in love with love. Anytime I don't have school work I'm either thinking about or out with dames. Had a good experience several Sat. nights ago. H. Brecht, C. Lewis, Boyer, R. Young, Saxton Pacher, Beury, & Bingamen & I went over to that hole in Kratzerville (dance hole, perhaps you remember something about it) well we almost got mobbed Saxton really beat some guy up then about 30 of them were going to mob us, you should have seen us leave that place. I'm sorry that I can't furnish you with all of the local news, however I don't associate with the yokels too much lately. I'm going to Phila. over Xmas, if I get a little work before Xmas. Fay & the girls inquired about you and sent their best regards.

I saw those pictures of you that Mary Jane had I must say they are really OK. Gee, it must be nice to be handsome and wear a flying corps uniform.

Noll is now in the Cadets at Maxwell field Ala.

When you can write & tell me what goes on.

Sincerely

Sterling

"BT-14s"

December 5, 1941
Friday evening
Dear Mother, Dad and Jean,

I haven't written for some time but I've been pretty busy. I got two letters from you today and will try to answer your questions.

I didn't get the letter you lost yet so it must really be lost. I'm not worrying about a ding in the fender. I have enough to do trying to put a ding in an airplane.

I don't care what I get for Christmas. I could use another suitcase but I think I'll buy that before I go to basic.

Here's the big news. We go to Enid, Oklahoma to an army school for our basic training. We get officers uniforms without the bars. The field has hard surface run ways and we fly the same planes that they fly at Randolph BT-14's – low wing monoplanes with 440 h.p. motors.

The town is about the size of Sikeston and we think we're the first class to go there. It's a new school.

I was scheduled for my final military check both yesterday and today but the captain didn't show up either day. So I have both military and civilian checks to take yet.

Wendle Mertz washed out. He'll be coming home in about a week or more. You can talk to him then.

We leave here Friday and must report there Tuesday morning. I don't know about Xmas yet.

I have over $100 in my pockets right now.

I'll write more later.

Love
Theodore

December 6, 1941
294 Orange Street
Northumberland, Pa.
Hi Cadet,

How is the flying coming along? I hope you like it as much as I've heard you do.

I read a letter you wrote to Post and it certainly didn't seem as if you had time to get homesick.

I started to write to you the day before Mother did but it took me till now to really get started.

Post probably told you that he, D. Gass, J. Olley, and John Snyder were playing *tennis one night a few weeks ago.*

It was so cold they must have had to shovel the snow off before they started.

You've probably heard what a successful season our football team had. Ann said they should have played "tag."

In October I received a letter from a fellow in Puerto Rico. He is a radio operator on a "Flying Fortress" I do not know him but he said he saw me at a football game last year and asked me to write to him to (boost the moral of the army 50%). I did but as yet I haven't gotten an answer.

Hiney was in Iceland, the last time we heard from him, head for "?"

Henry went hunting the other day and he came about 3 feet away from a rabbit, he aimed, fired, and hit; only to pick it up and find the head and 4 feet left. Some shot!

Well I'll probably be seeing you soon, so, until then,

Keep 'em flying,

Lorraine

While negotiations with Japanese envoys in Washington were taking place, the Japanese government under Gen. Hideki Tojo, the prime minister, completed preparations for war against the United States.

 The Japanese Navy's first-line aircraft carriers transported the First Air Fleet and launched a surprise attack against the United States Pacific Fleet at Pearl Harbor, Hawaii, on "a date, which will live in infamy."

Crawling out from the depression most Americans did not want to go to war prior to the attack on Pearl Harbor.

"Japanese Bombing Something"

December 7, 1941

Sunday

Dear Mother, Dad and Jean,

Well tomorrow will tell me the tale. I fly with the captain for my final check ride at 7:15 a.m. tomorrow.

We all supposed to go to Enid, Oklahoma. The R.A.F. was using the school but they moved out. We'll be the first U.S. Army class to move in. They have hard surfaced runway and everything.

The ships we fly are the same as at Randolph. They have 440 h.p. motors. The new airport has an altitude of about 1200 ft. above sea level. The higher the altitude the faster the plane lands. Oh boy.

Wendle Mertz will be coming home about the end of this week. I'll tell him to stop and see you.

I don't know how many days we get for Christmas but if we get less then 8 days I won't be able to make it. We're going 500 miles further west. They're getting me further and further from home.

Some one just said something about the Japanese bombing something or other. Our cadet Captain says Eleanor Roosevelt won't like that. She doesn't (like) w–a–r in a nice drawling tone.

Well I thing I'll go in town and go to the show.

Here's hoping I soon get home.

Love

Theodore

Dutch ~ Wendle Mertz washed out as a pilot, like me. We were cadets together. He re-enlisted in the infantry. I am glad the same fate did not befall me. Back home Wendle raised vegetables and had greenhouses.[88]

"Trouble with the Japs"

December 7, 1941

Sunday eve

Dear Ted

What are you doing you sure must be busy we did not have a letter since Thursday and than only about six lines are you getting ready to leave or what are you doing you are so busy. We all had a feeling you would be home over the weekend but we failed to see you. I wonder if the trouble with the Japs will keep you from coming home I just heard on the radio they canceled all leaves of the men that were home I hope it does not effect you boys. We were out at Martha's and Lee's today for dinner they are coming in this eve to go over to see Grandma Snyder she is sick in bed. We have Barry and his pup in here and they drive you darn near crazy.

I suppose you will be moving this week.

I hope you get a little closer to home when you move so we can see you a little oftener. Well I guess this will be all I just don't know what to write about this evening this war business has me all upset I hope to heavens they soon finish those Japs once and for all

Try and write if you can.

All our love

Mother

Dutch ~ On the day the Japs bombed Pearl Harbor I had gone into town on a date with a girl. We had left church when we heard the news. At first people couldn't believe it. How could this happen? How could these people be so audacious? Finally things sunk in and our training got tougher, but there was no sense of urgency. We went on just like we had been. It frustrated me no question about it because people went on like life was normal. You knew life was not normal at least I did. I was not at Sikeston much longer.

In those days we could wear civilian clothes off base. To me, this was hog heaven. I was flying and getting paid seventy dollars a month, eating good food, and was enjoying it. It was the best life I ever had. The previous weekend I had bought a bunch of new civilian clothes and was living it up. The next day after Pearl was bombed the order came out "you can no longer wear civilian clothes off base," so there went all my civilian clothes.

Jean ~ "We were visiting grandmother and grandfather Snyder. They lived in a little house in Sunbury. Mother was so upset that dad took her to visit her parents. Going home all of us were crying in the car because we knew that Ted was going to be right smack in the middle of it. We were all upset. It was a shock."

 *December 8, 1941,* the United States declared war on Japan.

James Starnes ~ "We got into Manila on the 5th of December. It was so obvious to Admiral Hart what was going to happen that he got us out and sent us south of the Philippines." On December 8th at 0500 a message was intercepted by the *Boise*. Ensign Starnes, the assistant navigator, headed to the bridge to take the four to eight watch.[89] "The captain showed me the communication from Knox[90] and said, 'Jim, old boy, we are at war with Japan.' Our orders were to carry out the battle plan. We did not know about Pearl Harbor."

"Military Check Ride"

Ca. December 8, 1941
Monday
Dear Mother, Dad and Jean,

They tell me that war has been declared. They seem to know it every place except here. We go on just as we have been and nothing is said about it.

I'm afraid that will spoil my Christmas vacation anyhow. They'll probably have us flying every day except Christmas and Sunday. Our instructors said they couldn't speed us up any more. We were thirty week wonders now – if we got through thirty week it was a wonder.

We were talking about it in navigation class. Someone wondered where the pilots were when the Japs were bombing Manila. Our instructor said they were probably making nice beds so they wouldn't get giged.

I flunked my military check ride today. Four out of six of us did. Nobody said anything about it so I guess it doesn't make much difference.

I tried to call you at Mrs. Conrad's tonight but the lines through St. Louis were all busy. I take it back.

We cannot have radios except on Sundays and we never get time to read the newspaper so we never know what's going on. We'll probably have to send all civilian clothes home and wear uniforms all the time.

Well I guess I'd better study. I hope I fly better tomorrow then I did today or I'll be heading for Pa. instead of Oklahoma on Friday.

Wendle Mertz leaves to come home on Friday.

I'm enclosing some pictures.

Love

Theodore

Don't worry about me I'm in the best place in the world for a fellow my age. The thing will be over before they'll let me fly a fighting plane. Some fellow (a cadet) is trying to tell us that cows do not have horns. Only bulls. You should hear Tex Brown. He owns a ranch in Texas.

December 9, 1941

Tuesday afternoon

Dear Ted,

Well I cannot say if I feel better or worse since I talked to you but it sure was good to hear you again. Jean wanted to know why we did not call her so she could say hello. I suppose you are getting ready to move I am very thankful that you still have six months and I do hope you get the whole six month I don't know if it will be better or worse I sure do wish you could have come home if you find you can not come home for Xmas I was thinking about coming to see you that is if we could see you if we did come to see you. Try and find out about that will you.

You said Wendle would be home don't you think he will have to go in the regular army or will he have some time off first. You were a big help in telling me *what you wanted for Xmas you tell me you need another suit case and than say you are going to buy it yourself. Mary Jane and I have been wearing our brains out trying to think of something you could use. Well I guess I will have to close and get supper try and find out about Xmas and let me know if you can. I will not write another letter now until you move and send me your new address it would not be much use.*

 Write
 All our love
 Mother

"In the Midst of a War"

 Roosevelt ~ *Evening of December 9, 1941*, "I can say with utmost confidence that no Americans today or a thousand years hence need feel anything but pride in our patience and our efforts through all the years toward achieving a peace in the Pacific which would be fair and honorable to every nation, large or small. And no honest person, today or a thousand years hence, will be able to suppress a sense of indignation and horror at the treachery committed by the military dictators of Japan, under the very shadow of the flag of peace borne by their special envoys in our midst . . .

 We are now in this war. We are all in it all the way. Every single man, woman, and child is a partner in the most tremendous undertaking of our American history. We must share together the bad news and the good news, the defeats and the victories-the changing fortunes of war . . .

 Your Government knows that for weeks Germany has been telling Japan that if Japan did not attack the United States, Japan would not share in dividing the spoils with Germany when peace came. She was promised by Germany that if she came in she would receive the complete and perpetual control of the whole of the Pacific area-and that means not only the Far East, not only all of the islands in the Pacific, but also a stranglehold on the west coast of North, Central, and South America . . .

 We are now in the midst of a war, not for conquest, not for vengeance, but for a world in which this Nation, and all that this Nation represents, will be safe for our children. We expect to eliminate the danger from Japan, but it would serve us ill if we accomplished that and found that the rest of the world was dominated by Hitler and Mussolini . . .

 We are going to win the war and we are going to win the peace that follows."[91]

MOVIETONE NEWS

Roosevelt called for all Americans to unite to work for the war effort. More than six million women joined the work force for the first time. By July 1944 women were thirty-five percent of the labor force.[92] Lockheed's "Rosie the Riveter" poster began appearing everywhere in response to the growing shortage of industrial manpower. Curtiss-Wright made a dramatic plea in the *Buffalo News* classified ads on January 2, 1943, for workers: "What American women do in industry during 1943 will determine the number of boys who will die in this war!"

December 11, 1941, the United States declared war on Germany and Italy.

"Pay for Navigator"

Ca. December 12, 1941

Friday

Dear Mother, Dad and Jean,

Well the time has finally come. I washed out yesterday. I've taken four check rides since Monday. I got by Major Rockwood. Mr. Glass and I rode twice with Lieutenant Stocking. He washed me out. (on my final check ride with about 60 hours flying time) He even had me thinking I can't fly. My instructor and Mr. Sanders say I can though.

My military and scholastic record is excellent. They want to send me to navigation school.

The R.A.F. man talked to me and sent me material. I can get in their basic school in California and be a 2nd. Lieut. in 2 mo. but won't be paid as well. I'd still be flying though and have more hours when this is over.

If I go to navigation I'll go to Maxwell Field, Ala. and may get home. If I go to the R.A.F. I'll have to get a discharge and then join the R.A.F.

I'll still be here for two weeks at least so continue to write. Wendle left this morning.

We were left out last night until 10:00. One of the fellows in our barracks didn't come in until 2:00 a.m. and they washed him out. He was one of the best pilots here.

Eight out of 21 men who started in C barracks got through. Fifty-six out of 121 of the class made it.

I think I go into navigation and then I may be called back as a pilot.

The course takes 7 ½ months so I won't be fighting for at least a year and it will probably be all over then.

Tell Mary Jane about this then I won't have to write all this stuff to her.
Tell me what you'd do if you had the choice.
Pay for navigator & pilot is always the same. (I still think I can fly)
Love
Theodore

From the diary ~ *While at Sikeston I met Bill Briggs of Baltimore and New Orleans, Hershell Parsons of West Virginia and many others. Liked the place and had a good time.*[93]

December 15, 1941
Monday
Dear Ted
I have just had the best news and feel better than I have any time since we are in war I suppose you know what that was. You know I have had a terrible fear inside of me ever since you have been flying so you can imagine how much better I feel. You ask me what I would do if I had the choice Navy or R.A.F. well what do you think navigation of course I think you would be foolish to even think of the R.A.F. if you were not good enough to fly for U.S. army why you are not good enough for R.A.F. so do not think about R.A.F. anymore but if you do not want to come home I would go to navigation you may still get a chance to fly if you want to fly so badly.
You have not got a letter from us for a long time because we thought you left Sikeston on Friday so we did not write.
I hope you will get home for Xmas. I was just over to Sunbury this morning to get the details about going to Okla(homa) if you could not come home it would have cost me $50.00 for car fare alone so this will save us some money
Don't worry about not being able to fly a plane you may still have a chance and I feel a lot better right now than I did yesterday so does Mary Jane
Love
Mother

"Got Papers from the R.A.F."

December 15, 1941
Monday
Dear Mother, Dad and Jean,
All I do since I've washed out is eat, sleep and go to one athletic formation. I don't care I'm getting paid $4.65 a day for it.

I got papers from the R.A.F. man today. All I have to do to get in there is fill out the papers after I get my discharge.

I'm waiting for my appointment to go to navigation school at Montgomery. Alabama. It may be next week or it may be next month. The pay goes right on through. I'm in charge of the lower class when they come in. If that happens a few more times I will be crazy.

I hope that after I get my commission (7 ½ months) I may be able to get back as air training for flying a multi-engined bomber.

I'm sending some presents home and also my civilian clothes. I don't know whether I'll get home for Christmas or not but I hope so.

Love
Theodore

"Decided to join the RAF"

December 16, 1941
Tuesday
Dear Mother, Dad and Jean,

Well I've finally decided to join the R.A.F. If I monkey around waiting a few months to go to navigation school I'll probably be caught in the draft and become a buck private. I just found that out today.

See Jerry Mertz and get another birth certificate for me.

I saw my instructor this morning. It's the first he knew I had been washed out. He thinks they're crazy and told me he gave me an excellent recommendation for basic. He says I would probably be assigned as an instructor when I get through there. He wants me to get in all the flying hours on multi motored ships that I can get too.

Well I've got to go out and see some more lower classmen.

Love
Theodore

Ca. December 18, 1941
Dear Brother,

Mother is sick tonight so I will have to write your letter. I missed school today to stay home with her. Don't worry it just one of the spells she gets sometimes. I have improved a hundred percent in my cooking. Remember the horrible meals I use to make you. I don't see how you got them down. You should see my new snow suit it's white and blue with a white hat and vest. It's suppose to be one of my Christmas presents but I saw it.

School is coming along fine. I love Latin. Most of the kids hate it I got 100's or above 90's in all my tests I have ever taken in it. Biology is swell too. I just finished a drawing of the heart and of the kidney. I think I know even vein, artery, and capellaries in our bodies.

We were play basketball in gym Wednesday and you know when you push or shove anybody it counts as a foul. A girl who never played it before pushed a forward when she was shooting a basket. Miss Swope said she shouldn't do that it counted as a foul. This girl turns around and said to the girl she pushed, "I beg your pardon." She thought it shouldn't be a foul after she said that. (Dumb girl)

I hope you get home for Christmas. It won't be Christmas if you don't.

Love

Sis

Mother and Daddy sents their love and hope you will come home for Christmas I gave boys up for good. I hope you can read this.

"Go to Hell"

Ca. December 18, 1941

Thursday

Dear Mother, Dad and Jean,

I went down and asked Lieut. Pierce for my discharge today so that I could join the R.A.F. He wouldn't give it to me. He says I'm going to navigation school.

He fed me a line then about how wonderful my record was and how good I'd be in navigation. I'd have told him to go to hell but he is a Lieutenant.

I don't know where or when they will send me. They keep everything a secret around here. We get 1½ days off for Christmas. If I were sure I would be here you could come down over Xmas but I may or may not be transferred before Xmas. I don't even think they know. Well it's just about time to go to bed so I'd better close. After I find out when and where I'm going I'll leave you know more.

Love,

Theodore[94]

Dutch ~ I washed out as a pilot because I took the landing gear off the BT-9 during my check ride. Under the rules they had to release you. You became a civilian and then went back home subject to the draft again. I wanted to show them and join the RAF. The RAF waited outside the gate very happy to have you. So I thought, that is what I am going to do. An old kindly captain, the commander at the base, called me in and said, "Mr. Van Kirk, you are about to be released. I understand you are going to join the RAF."

I said, yes sir those are my plans.

He looked at me and said, "You can do that if you want to, but you will be dead within a year."

He got my attention. I asked him: "Why do you say that?"

"You are only a marginal pilot," he responded.

I thought I was a hot pilot, but he called me a marginal pilot and added "The RAF will not give you much more training than what you have now. You will be sent to Canada for a little training, then to England, and then you will be flying against the best pilots in the world. You are not going to last."

I asked what were the alternatives.

He said, "We think you would be a good navigator." I asked what would I have to do to be a navigator and he explained it to me.

December 19, 1941
Friday eve
Dear Ted

I did not get a letter today and about six lines yesterday you must be a busy boy. I just came home from the movies the picture was Unfinished Business it was very good we went down to Sidlers than to see Mary Jane and take a book down I read she told me you might be home next week I hope so but than maybe you will not get home for Xmas and that will not be so nice. I have not been working for the last two days I have only worked two and a half days this week I feel all right and don't get me wrong we just do not have the work. And when I would like to leave it to just before Xmas.

Francis was in this evening for supper Bill wanted her to go along to church but she did not go now she wants me to go along with her tomorrow evening I don't know if I will or not. (Grandma and Edith were up last evening they invited us over for Xmas dinner they are all coming home they said there would be about forty some (illegible).

They are having three Turkeys and two chickens. I told them I did not know if we would come out or not if you were only home a day or two.

Well I guess I will have to close and go to bed I can hardly hold my eyes open anymore I cleaned house today and am I tired.

Write.
Lots of Love
Mother

"Home for Christmas"

December 21, 1941

Sunday eve

Dear Ted

I have not written to you for a long time so I will try to write you a letter this evening we just fixed you a box I hope you get it for Xmas Aunt Alice baked the cake she was over yesterday all day and helped me bake cookies and make candy the one box of candy she had made when she did came over I don't know what I would have done without her I have been in bed again for a few days again I am better now but still pretty jittery as you will see by my writing.

Mary Jane and I split the cost to call you the other evening it cost us $1.05 each you had me so worried with that RAF business I just had to call for that sure did not help me any you did not sound as if you were very glad to hear us. As for calling you at that time Wendle told us to call you at 10.15 our time that would be 9.15 your time but it took at awful long time for the call to go threw. I wish you could have come home for Xmas that is one reason we are late sending your things for we felt sure you would be home.

Well I guess this will be all for now but do write and tell me some news or something about yourself.

Love Mother

I wish you a very Merry Xmas and altho we cannot be with you we will be thinking of you[95]

"I Can Fly as Good"

December 21, 1941

Sunday

Dear Mother, Dad and Jean,

Well I've finally run out of writing paper both blue and white types so I'll have to start using my tablet.

I'm still in Sikeston and probably will be for a little while yet. When I finally get transfered I will go to Maxwell Field, Montgomery Alabama. The course lasts from 7 ½ to 9 months after my entrance. That will be about the middle of May. Being a Lieutenant will be pretty nice especially at $250 per month.

We get 1½ days off for Christmas. The people in Sikeston are inviting all of the cadets in to their homes for Christmas. I hope I find someone that can cook anyhow. We're thinking of having a big party at the country club the night before Christmas. None of us have anything to do.

I hope you got the presents and my civilian clothes. I'll send my other shirts and suit home one of these days.

My instructor is still trying to get them to send me to basic but I don't think he can talk them into it. He says I can fly as good as any of his other students. The Lieutenant who washed me out got transfered to a pursuit squadron. I hope he goes to Hawaii or the Phillipines where they show him he can't fly.

I sent almost everyone Christmas cards.

Well I guess I have to stop writing and do some work for a change.

I was in bed asleep when you called. I was half asleep while I was talking to you. I'd join the R.A.F. if I could get my discharge. I may be able to get it if I try hard enough but I don't think I'll bother.

Love
Theodore

"Christmas Plans"

December 23, 1941
Tuesday
Dear Mother, Dad and Jean,

I got Jeans letter today after figuring it out I was sorry to hear that mother is sick.

They haven't said anything yet about when I will be transfered so I just sit around, keep my mouth shut and wait. I'm still getting 4.65 a day for it.

I have two invitations to Christmas dinner in Sikeston. I don't feel like going to either place but I'll probably go to one of them. They'll probably ask me a lot of silly questions about flying and I'll have to answer them.

I hope you get your presents before Christmas. I still have one of Mary Janes presents here. I can't find a box for it and can't get into town to mail it anyhow.

Well thats about all for now. I have to go get this inch of hair on my head cut down to a half inch or I'll get giged at the next inspection.

Love
Theodore

December 23, 1941
Tue. eve
Dear Ted

I have not been writing my letter every evening for a while so I guess I had better get caught up on my letters since I am feeling better I don't suppose you will get this letter before Xmas so I can ask you how you spent your Xmas and where I hope you had a very nice Xmas. Our Xmas this year does not mean much to us I don't know but we just don't seem to be able to get into the Xmas spirit. We received your gifts yesterday they were all very lovely gifts in fact Jean and Mary Jane wonder where you get the good taste and wondered if you might have had some feminine help but thanks so much for everything and you should not have spent so much money our gifts to you seemed very small compared to what you sent us but it was very hard to buy anything you needed as there are such a few things you can use. Some of your clothes came with the gifts. Could you keep some or what that you did not send them all. It is 8.45 here now and dad has not come home from work yet.

Jean has been going down to church to practice she plays the part of Mary in a pagent on Sunday evening down at the church. I guess we are going out to Grandma Van Kirk for Xmas dinner they are all going out so I suppose we will have too I don't care about going out but I don't want to stay at home either this year.

I just got a Xmas card or I think it is from Milton for you I am to forward it I suppose it is from Buz I don't know it is sealed will send it to you. Did you get many cards? Do you know where you are going yet? I had intended to come and spend Xmas with you if you could not come home but since I was sick again and you don't know when or when you would be transferred I thought I had better give it up.

Write
Lots of Love
Mother

Jean – "Ted sent me a gorgeous purse. I used it as a pocket book. It was beautiful and leather, one of those things men wore with their kilts (Sporran). I kept it for a long, long while. He sent me that from England. He was always sending mother dress pins."

Japan's continued aggression against China and attacks on the Philippines and islands in the Pacific set the stage for the battles of the American military.

Chapter Three — Endnotes

68 Van Kirk, "My Life In The Service," is a personal diary of several pages. On the opening page he wrote: Theodore J. Van Kirk, Serial Number 13030940, Height 5' 9 ½", Weight 144 (Sept. 29, 1941), Religion Lutheran, Nearest Relative Or Friend Mr. Fred Van Kirk, 672 Queen St., Northumberland, PA, Sept. 29, 1941; Feb. 14, 1942, Weight 166.

69 "Diz" - Van Kirk's nickname for his young sister Jean. The return address for the unsigned letter: Aviation Cadet Theodore Van Kirk, A.C.T.D. C-1, Sikeston, MO.

70 The New York Yankees faced the Brooklyn Dodgers in the "Subway Series" at Ebbets Field before 33,100 fans for Game 3 on October 4, 1941. The first two games were played at Yankee Stadium. The Yankees won the first game three to two. The Dodgers won the second game three to two. Baseball Almanac, http://www.baseballalmanac.com/ws/yr1941ws.shtml [accessed August 9, 2010].

71 The envelope addressee: Mr. Fred Van Kirk, 672 Queen St., Northumberland, PA.

72 After graduation from the orphanage William Young, Mary Jane Young Van Kirk's brother, lived with his aunt (sister of George Young) and uncle, Mr. and Mrs. Leroy Beury in Northumberland, PA. Leroy Beury, a veteran of World War I, served as commander of Milton Jarrett Norman American Legion Post 201 in Sunbury, PA.

73 The Top Policy Group: Vice President Henry Wallace, Secretary of War Henry L. Stimson, Gen. George C. Marshall, James Conant, and Vannevar Bush. Jim Baggott, *The First War of Physics* The Secret History Of The Atom Bomb, (New York: Pegasus Books LLC, 2010), 110.

74 Sidler's Cut Rate at 80 Queen Street advertised patent medicines and cosmetics, Dolly Madison Ice Cream, and "Meet Your Friends at our Fountain." Advertisement, *Pine-Knotters Yearbook*, 1938.

75 The Northumberland football team's mascot is still the "Pineknotters."

76 "Figure 6650 At Grid Game," *Sunbury Daily Item*, October 18, 1941.

77 Van Kirk earned $18.00 per week at Weis Pure Foods Stores as a store clerk under his immediate supervisor William Hollenbach. Van Kirk's E. I. Du Pont De Nemours & Company Application for Employment.

78 Dutch's grandmother sent him a postcard of Fort Augusta, Sunbury, PA. Fort Augusta built in 1758 was an important early frontier fort and key to the vast area from Harrisburg to Fort Niagara.

79 The envelope addressed to Mr. Fred Van Kirk, 672 Queen Street, Northumberland, PA, had a string attached to the right side of the envelope with "Pull Rip-Cord Right and Down" printed on the front.

80 Pvt. Albert M. Lilley, of Northumberland, transferred over the weekend from Randolph Field, TX, to Jefferson Barracks, near St. Louis, MO, according to a news item enclosed with the letter.

81 James L. "Jim" Starnes, Jr. telephone interview with author, August 9 and October 8, 2010. Starnes born in 1921 in Little Rock, Arkansas, to James L. Starnes, Sr., and Maude White, grew up in Decatur, Georgia. After attending Emory University for two years he joined the Navy. Starnes made his decision to enlist quickly and wanted his father's permission. The senior Starnes accepted his son's decision. Starnes graduated from a V-7 training class. "We trained as if we were at Annapolis, but it was a compacted program." Starnes commissioned an Ensign in November 1940 chose active duty rather than

waiting to be drafted. The former navigators, Starnes and Van Kirk, are neighbors in a Stone Mountain, Georgia, retirement community.

82 Kermit Bonner, *Final Voyage*, (Paducah, KY: Turner Publishing Co., 1996), 30. Starnes added information about the supplies of foodstuffs.

83 Starnes said, "Later, we discovered the ship was part of the Japanese fleet headed toward Pearl. We were in Indonesia on Christmas Eve and met some PBY pilots. They told us the story of what happened at Pearl."

84 No date on the letter or postmark on the accompanying envelope. Date drawn from the content and other letters surrounding "Sunday."

85 Scrapple is traditionally scraps of pork mixed with cornmeal and flour.

86 Parks Air College, St. Louis, Missouri, one of the civilian facilities, which trained military pilots during World War II. St. Louis Downtown Airport History, http://www.stlouisdowntownairport.com/history.htm [accessed April 11, 2010]

87 *Sunbury Daily Item* article enclosed about Northumberland's home team final football game, "Norry Ends Jinxed Season In 47 – 0 Defeat By Milton."

88 Wendle Mertz reenlisted in the Army according to the National Archives enlisted records. www.nara.gov [accessed April 8, 2010]. Mertz served in France as a sharpshooter rifleman in the infantry per his obituary in the *Daily Item* on December 24, 2008.

89 West of the International Date Line is one day ahead of HAST – Hawaii-Aleutian Standard Time Zone.

90 Frank Knox, Secretary of the Navy, and at the age of fourteen served as a trooper with Teddy Roosevelt's Rough Riders in Cuba during the Spanish-American War. Jack Alexander, "Secretary of the Navy Frank Knox," *Life* Magazine, March 10, 1941, and the Naval History and Heritage Command website.

91 Excerpt of Roosevelt's radio address broadcast from the Oval Office on December 9, 1941.

92 Working married women became one of the most dramatic societal changes of the era. Ann McBride, "Women vital to war effort wives take their spouses' jobs," *Niagara Falls Gazette*, September 5, 1999.

93 Van Kirk, "My Life in the Service," 1941.

94 No envelope or date other than the day of the week. The references to joining the RAF occurred in other letters during December 1941.

95 The *Sunbury Daily Item* news clippings sent with the letter to Van Kirk reported on other Queen Street boys in the service. Pvt. Frank Noll, son of Mr. and Mrs. Roy Noll, 410 Queen Street, had been transferred from Fort Eustis to the Flying Cadets at Maxwell Field in Montgomery, Alabama, according to a telegram. His many friends were glad to hear of the appointment. Louie and Dick Hummel, sons of Mr. and Mrs. B.F. Hummel, also of Queen Street, left for Balboa, Panama Canal Zone.

Chapter Four

Kelly Field *School of Navigation*

Dutch ~ On Christmas Day of 1941 I found myself on the train from Sikeston to Kelly Field, Texas, for navigation school. It was a little tough not being home and riding on the train on Christmas. We were three G.I.s with about a dozen civilians. A man traveling with his family and two young teenage daughters had a bottle of liquor and invited us to have a drink. We made a family where there was no family.

We only had Mexican cooks and I had never eaten Mexican food in my life. A whole new class formed at Kelly. We were going to be navigators and started out with a lot of calisthenics. You had to be fit.

One of the foremost training centers of the Air Corps, Kelly Field was known as the "West Point of the Air."

"Christmas in Texas"

December 25, 1941

Dear Mother, Dad and Jean,

I left Sikeston at 4:00 p.m. yesterday and got in San Antonio at 7:00 p.m. today. Kelly Field is about 8 mile out of town.

I never thought Texas was so doggone big. I'm certainly seeing the country. I had a lower berth and slept all the way across Missouri, Arkansas and Oklahoma. We came through the center of oil field. Crossed the Colorado River and saw Austin and other towns in Texas.

It gets a little cool here at night but warms up during the day. A lot of places the grass and trees are green and some flowers are blooming especially that Christmas flower pon-setta something or other. I won't see any winter this year.

We're going to report to the field tomorrow and I may be pretty busy for awhile so write.

Love

Theodore

I sent all my things home so I wouldn't have much to bring and 1 hr. before I leave that big box of presents arrives. I brought everything but the eats with me and I brought along some of the candy and cookies.

"Only our Shirts On"

December 26, 1941

Dear Mother, Dad and Jean,

I got to Kelley[96] Field about 10:30 this morning and I'm ready to leave it right away. Things are really different here. It's a lot easier than Sikeston but I still don't care for it. We haven't done a doggone thing since we've been here and if we keep this up I will be bored to death.

We get to fly about 6 hr. a week and get uniforms that are the same as officers.

The country and the city of San Antonio are very nice but we never get much of a chance to see it.

It's warm down here. We're running around with only our shirts on.

I'll write my address on the back of this sheet.

Love

Theodore

Aviation Cadet Theodore Van Kirk

School of Navigation 42-5

Kelley Field

San Antonio, Texas[97]

"All I Need is the Bars"

December 28, 1941

Dear Mother, Dad and Jean,

I've been here three days now and still don't think much of the place. They haven't got much of a system and everything is much easier than it was at Sikeston. They aren't near as strict about anything.

We start classes tomorrow and we go on our first flight on Friday. We fly for about 500 miles.

The course has been cut down to twelve weeks and I will get my commission at the end of that time. That won't make me mad at all. I've been issued regular government stuff now. Towels, underwear and everything. My uniforms & clothes are just like officers. All I need is the bars. I hope I will be able to get home at the end of that time but I've found out you should never plan anything in the army.

Unsigned

December 29, 1941
Dear Theodore,

Just a few lines to tell you we are all well. Hope you are fine. Saw your Mother last night and she gave me your address so I want to thank you for the Xmas card and hope you got all your things we sent you. We were all hoping you could be home, but maybe when you get to come home you can stay longer.

We got very nice gifts for Xmas. Your mother and dad were up Sunday to see our tree. We were down to Grandmas for dinner Xmas so you can picture the gang, the usual big time. Lee is laying on the floor by the radiator asleep now and Jimmie is in bed. Frances and Bill went out some where so I am here writing to you. I hope you will like Texas. Bob Weis is down there some where he did not get home for Xmas either. Bill thinks he will get called about February. I suppose your Mother told you Jane was going to be married at Xmas and her boy friend could not come home so it's off for the time being. Saw your pictures in home and they are fine. Jimmie wrote you a letter but I cant read it he was in to big a hurry. So I guess I will not send it until he writes another one for you. He is a very busy boy he has been doing some trapping with out much success. He got one muskrat and was afraid of that. He is growing like a weed this winter. I guess because he is out so much. Bob and Will were here for Xmas. I guess Bob is going to loose his job on account of the ban on tires. After Jan. 5 so I dont know what he will do. They are putting the new road by our house this winter. You wont know the place when you get home. It is going to be a very nice highway. I just made a big blot (of ink) on this paper. It would be so near the end of the letter and I havent got enough ambition to write another tonight so youl have to excuse it this time I guess I better just do good night.

With lots of love from all
Martha

December 29, 1941
Monday afternoon
Dear Ted

Just got your first two letters that you wrote since you are in Texas so am answering those right away for I have not written for a long time it makes me feel ten times better when I hear from you but Xmas was terrible knowing that you were on the train all day. You say you do not like it now but I know you will like it a lot better when you are there awhile you know you did not like Sikeston at first when you went there. I hope you get to see some of the boys from home Sam Fletcher is there and they say quite a few more boys from Norry. You said you got your box just as your were ready to leave I was afraid of that did you eat any of the cake Aunt Alice baked you? Did you get Mary Jane's box she ask me if you did I told her you did not say.

She and Madlyn Zong were up on Friday evening to see our tree and the gifts you sent. You should have seen our tree it was terrible I took it down this morning.

Madlyn got a job down at Weis she has been working about a week so I told Mary Jane to go up and put in an application she did and she came up last evening to tell me she got a job there too she goes to work next Monday. She is tickled to death about it I hope she likes it she ask me to come down this evening and keep her company Mr. Sidler goes to Kiwanis meeting and Mrs. Sidler is sick. We got your application for drivers license today shall I send it to you. You said in your letter you fly six hours a week do you still fly a plane yourself? Do you think you will get home before so very long I certainly hope so it seems ages since we seen you. I thought sure we would get to see you at Xmas now that is over and we didn't so I do hope you can come home sometime. This Ditzel boy up here is in Texas he is coming home this week.

Write
Lots of Love
Mother

December 30, 1941
Tue afternoon
Dear Ted

How do you like Texas now better I hope. There really isn't anything to write about at home here for there is nothing ever happens. I was just over to Gladys Biega and one of the Beck boys is over there he is home on his second furlough since he has been there. He looks fine he says he weights 196 lbs and he looks it. I hear Lou Staddow left for Texas on Sat she went down to marry John Gulick. I guess she is going to stay down and work. You said you send the rest of your clothes home I have not got them yet. I was down to see Mary Jane last evening I was down about 2 hours and all she can talk about is you she really has it bad now she says she would never fight with you again when you come home. I think she was dissapointed she did not get her diamond for Xmas. She said ever her mother said she could not see why you did not give her a ring.

What do you wear to sleep in your bed your pajamas home? Don't tell me you boys sleep in the raw. Do you still fly a plane yourself answer these questions Mary Jane was so thrilled when she heard you were going to navigation school she thought you would not be flying at all when I said you would in a plane just the same she did not like that. Elwood has enlisted as a mechanic he expects to be called in about two weeks. You said you would not see any snow this winter we have not had any snow here yet either we have not had enough ice yet for the kids to go skating one thing it is easy on the coal pile it is a good thing for I am not working right now I don't know when I will be called back I haven't worked for about 4 weeks now. Well I don't seem to be able to write anymore so I guess I better close

> *Write*
> *Love*
> *Mother*

Jean ~ Grace Van Kirk wrote diligently to her brothers Elwood and Martin Luther Snyder and "especially her youngest brother Clifford. On the paternal side we had three uncles through marriage also in the service: Michael Twardy, Franklin Walker, and Robert Walker. Michael married Aunt Isabelle. Robert married Aunt Mildred and Franklin to Aunt Edith. They were married before the war and were drafted. We were concerned that daddy would be drafted. He was forty-two, the same age as my mother. Believe you me a lot of the windows had a lot of stars in it."[98]

"Regular Officer's Uniform"

December 30, 1941
Tuesday
Dear Mother, Dad and Jean,
We started to classes yesterday and they keep us pretty busy ever since. I like the work very much and I think it's pretty easy right now.

I have the regular officers uniform. They also issued me a mackinaw, a blouse, 3 pairs of winter & 3 summer pants, 3 summer & 2 winter shirts, 6 sets of shirts and shorts, 4 flight caps & 1 officers cap, 12 pr. socks, 6 hand(kerchief), *tooth brush, towel and everything else.*

We were issued rifles yesterday and it was a h. of a job getting them clean.

I must get to bed now so good-by.

> *Love*
> *Theodore*
> *And write too*

December 31, 1941

You must have written your letter in a hurry it did not have your name
Wed afternoon
Dear Ted

I was just getting my things to write your letter when I had a letter from you. You say everything is so much easier there it is a shame than that you could not go there for your primary training maybe you would have made out all right then. But if you fly now yet why you will have plenty of hours in the air any way to get a license. You say they have cut the course down to twelve weeks now does that mean that you will be commissioned at the end of that time. That would be in April. You say you hope you can come home then well I certainly do too for if you can't sure as the dickens I will have to come down to see you. I wonder why you boys don't get home as often as some of the others do. Is it because of the different course and being in the different services or what? This Ditzel boy that lives up on Wheatly Avenue is in Texas and he is home again. Tomorrow is New Year but it is just like another day. For us too only that dad is home. Martha & Lee want us to come up for dinner we probably will. Bill H. thinks he will have to go in about Feb. I wouldn't doubt he and Francis will be married if he does. Jane Witmer did not get married her boy friend was sent some where along the coast just before Xmas. You say you go on your first flight on Friday about 500 mile why so far? I know you will like it better after you are there awhile. The people in Norry are behind you boys in full they can hardly get the defense bonds and stamps in fast enough. I still did not get your clothes you send home when you left Sikeston. Write

Love
Mother
Can you read this letter it is written terrible

December 31, 1941, during the year 923,842 men entered military service under the Selective Service System.

Western Union telegram to Aviation Cadet Theodore Van Kirk
EVERY AFFECTIONATE THOUGHT FROM MOM AND DAD ON NEW YEARS AND THROUGH OUT THE YEAR
MOTHER

"I Like Navigation"

January 1, 1942
Dear Mother, Dad and Jean,
I got a letter from Mother yesterday. It was forwarded from Sikeston and the

first letter I had for ages. I haven't heard from Mary Jane for two weeks.

They left me have off from 7:00 p.m. yesterday until 7:00 p.m. today. It's the only time I get off for my first three weeks here.

It seems as though I've been away for an awful long time. I hope I'll get home after I'm through this place even if it is fifteen weeks from now.

I like navigation almost as much as I did flying but I don't like Kelly field near as much as I did Sikeston. Last night in town they had a Cadets party and I met a lot of the boys who were in my upper class at Sikeston. They're at Randolph field now.

Right around San Antonio they have Randolph, Kelly, Brooks and Duncan fields and Fort Sam Houston. There are more soldiers in that town then there are civilians.

I'll probably be graduated and get my commission about the end of March. I can do it if I like it but if I don't they can go to h. and I'll try to wash out.

I guess I'd better get to studying now and learn something.

Love

Theodore

P.S. The next time I get in town I'm going to buy Jean a pair of real Texas cowboy boots.

Dutch - In the classroom we learned to use a compass and plot three different headings on the Weems course plotter, how to take wind drift readings, and how to keep the airplane on course and talk to your pilot so he kept it on course.[99] In addition to ground school we flew a PT-18 twin-engine airplane, with three seats. During flight training the instructor flew as co-pilot. Each seat had a drift meter.[100] We flew from San Antonio, to Houston, to Austin, to San Antonio, a triangular course and had to hit each destination right on the nose every time.

Weems Course Plotter

A flying aircraft's course is subject to wind speed and direction. To determine how far the aircraft heading differed from the desired course, the drift meter and recorder on the B-29 calculated the amount of drift to make the necessary course corrections.[101]

January 1, 1942
When I get to the end of my letters I always think of a lot to say yet
Thur eve 8 oclock
Dear Ted

We just got home we were out to Martha & Lees all day Martha and I went up to Danville to the movies and Martha had seen the picture so we went to Bloomsburg and the same picture was playing there at the large theatre so we went to some little dumpy theater on a side and Jakie Coogan was playing in Glamour Boy I was bored to death till I came out.

It is raining like the dickens here this evening it snowed awhile this morning then it turned into rain and it sure is raining now. How did you spend your New Year write and tell us about what you do and yourself. Dad had off today he says and tomorrow seems like Monday to him now. He has been seriously thinking about going down to Baltimore to see about a job down at Glen Martin bomber he was talking to a fellow that works down there and he was telling him they are working 7 days a week now and expect to take 1400 more men this month. The pay would be swell but it would be very lonely for Jean and I here.

There was a young fellow killed in town this morning a fellow by the name of Hoover from Sunbury about 20 years old he was going to Penn State I guess the way they say he was out last nite and was coming home this morning from a dance somewhere up the road when it happened out on front street he ran into one of the trees in front of Bairds or Boligs I don't know which but I guess he never knew what happened he was killed instantly. I ask dad if he wanted me to tell you anything he said just tell him he is not missing anything in this burg he really is disgusted with the place especially when these other fellows tell him about big money they are making. He said young Sig Weis told him to send best regards when we wrote to you. I still have a Xmas card here for you from Milton I was to forward to you I will some day.

Love
Mother

January 2, 1942
Friday afternoon
Dear Ted

I did not get a letter today so you must be pretty busy now. How are you getting along do you like it better. You know I have been thinking about you all day today I guess because you had told me about that 500 mile flight how did you come through? Theodore you said about sending all your things home before you left Sikeston do you mean you send your other suit and topcoat if you did we did not get them Mary Jane has not got her present either if you sent it. Did you have them insured? I hope so just in case we do not get them it is over a week now if you sent them before you left Sikeston. I told you last evening it was very warm here and raining like the dickens. Well today the wind is blowing and it is cold. I just heard over the radio today that they are not going to make anymore new cars and I guess you can not buy tires anymore. Do you know if we could get enough money out of the car we may as well sell it. Jean is still at home this week the kids over at Sunbury had to go back to school this week and had yesterday off but had to go back today the kids over here have not been in school since day before Xmas.

The A&P store has moved out of town so Weis will have a still better business no wonder they took two new girls. Dad gets so disgusted he just said the other day they bought Bud Inns another new car he said the way things are now he could have used his old car but don't you worry about them over doing themselves to help. Does anyone get leaves now to come home? I hope they do for I sure hope you get to come home. Do you think you will?

Well it is four oclock I guess I better end my letter and get dad some supper he will be home in a few minutes. Is there anything you need or would like to have if there is write and tell us.

Write whenever you can
Lots of Love
Mother

I take back what I said about not getting your clothes we just got them and it cost us $1.63 to get them 58 cents express and $1.05 C.O.D. to be sent to Pitman Tailoring Company Sikeston Missouri. What I can't figure is what the $1.05 C.O.D. was for and what happened your good gray topcoat we did not get that all we got was your dark suit and sweater and ties and belt. Now write and tell us what this is all about and where your top coat is if its the tailors pulling that stuff or what is the matter.

Answer these questions in your letter. Did you by any chance sell your top coat it does not matter to us but dad thought some one might have kept your top coat. If you did not sell it dad said you had better write to Sikeston and find out about it.

"Answers to Your Questions"

January 2, 1942

Dear Mother, Dad and Jean,

I got three letters today so I guess I'll get busy and answer your questions.

1. *We ate the cake Aunt Alice baked in a hurry it was very good.*
2. *I did not get M.J.'s box. I got a lot of cards today and the box will prob. soon come. Six letters, & 9 cards today.*
3. *Save my application for drivers license until I get home some time.*
4. *I don't fly myself but I use the copilots or navigators seat and fly in lg. two engined ships.*
5. *We fly so far so they can tell how close we come to the place we are going. We are supposed to find the place without even looking out of the plane.*
6. *We sleep in our shorts. We don't have time to change in & out of p. (pajamas)*

That answers all the questions so you should like this letter.

When I get out of here for a while I'm going to try to find Sam Fletcher and some of the other fellows. See if you can get some of their addresses.

I got 3 letters from both you & M.J. so far and a lot of cards that were forwarded from Sikeston. We're running out of stamps down here and can't get out to buy any.

I have to go over and go to bed now. I'm writing this in our classroom where we each have a separate desk with drawers and a briefcase and maps and everything. I spend about 10 or 11 hrs. a day in the classroom except when I fly.

Love

Theodore

"I'd Quit the Whole Army"

January 3, 1941[2]

Dear Mother, Dad and Jean,

I start this letter tonight and finish it tomorrow. That way I'll save a stamp. I didn't get any letters from home today. I guess I got them all yesterday.

We went to classes today the same as we always do and have study hall tonight and tomorrow. They're certainly rushing us.

Today they were teaching us how to walk guard duty and I walked guard for about 20 min. with that rifle. My arm is still sore. If I had to walk for 4 hrs. I'd quit the whole army.

I got a letter from Martha today. She didn't have a whole lot of new things to say. I guess I'll have to stop waiting now and finish this tomorrow.

We get another class in on next Sat. They have six classes here at one time. Most of the classes had only 30 men in them but ours has 120 and from now on they will be big classes. They may leave us go out next week. I hope so.

They say this next class will come in partly from Maxwell Field. If they do I may know some of the fellows who were in my class at Sikeston.

I'm getting so I like it a little better here but I still get disgusted. One nice thought is that I'll only be here twelve weeks and one of them is over already.

I didn't get any letters from you since I answered all of your questions so I don't have any questions to answer.

I slept until late this morning and spent the rest of the time reading. I get tired of studying all of the time. The thing I dislike most of all is that drill.

Last night I walked over to the P.X. and got myself a milk shake. That was thrilling. I also bought myself a big foot locker so that I have some place to keep all of my new clothes. The ones the army gave me.

Don't say anything to Mary Jane but what was in that box she sent me? The only box I got was the one that you sent. Maybe she had a box in there that I didn't read the name tag on. I unpacked that in a hurry. I had to get on the train in exactly 1 ½ hrs.

I guess I better stop writing now or you'll fall over from the surprise of getting a long letter. I have a lot more time to write. Now if I only could get stamps I'd send a lot of letters.

Love
Theodore

Postmarked January 6, 1942
Dear Brother –

I can imagine how you hate to get my letters, but you have to get them and like them.

We had a deep snow. We have a lot of fun in it but Norry is terrible dull I do mean dull. We went back to school today after a week and two days vacation. I hated to go back. No ice-skating yet in fact no nothing in Norry. Church on Sunday night thats all. Did Mother tell you I had the part of Mary in the Christmas play. I was well I won't say.

I am writing big so I won't have to write much.

Because there is no news to tell you.

Thanks for my Christmas present it was swell. The girls say they want a brother – like you. I wouldn't give you up for all the money in the world.

Mother don't feel well she can't write a letter tonight.

Love
Sis
P.S. If you find any mistakes please excuse them.

January 6, 1942

Dear Grandson,

Just a card to tell you we have not forgot about you hope this card will reach you O.K.

Grandma[102]

"Government Insurance"

January 6, 1942

Dear Mother, Dad and Jean,

I thought I'd better write and tell you about my clothes. I didn't send my topcoat or raincoat home because I used them to wear on my way down here.

The money to Pitmas should have been taken out of my pay from Sikeston. I didn't get my pay from there yet and can't tell until I get it.

There isn't anything new around here except that we must stay in again this week end and study. So far the stuff hasn't been so hard and I hope it stays that way.

I must plan a flight for tomorrow. We fly over almost half the state of Texas tomorrow and I hope I know where we're at when I'm done.

I'll send some money home as soon as I get my back pay because I won't be needing any here for a few months.

Love

Theodore

Don't sell the car now. It may be worth more in a few years. You can cash that insurance policy of mine if you can. I have $10,000.00 worth of gov. insurance in case anything happens to me.

Wednesday.

I forgot to take these letters last night so I'll add this and make sure I send them tomorrow. Nothing happened today anyhow. The weather was bad and we didn't fly so we went to class some more.

January 8, 1942

Thur Afternoon

Dear Ted

Just got that long letter of yours. You said your arm was stiff from carrying that rifle are you sure it wasn't from writing that long letter. That almost floored me after some of those short ones you have been writing. You said you did not have any questions to answer you will have by the time you get this letter. I wrote one yesterday asking some. It has been very cold here the last few days it has been below zero for 3 days now and this morning it was colder than ever I don't now just how cold it was dad fixed the garage so he could put the car in but it was still so cold he could not start it this morning he was supposed to be to work at 6 oclock and he got the 20 after six bus so I think he was a little later. You ask about the box M.J. sent you well I doubt if you got it before you left Sikeston for I sent mine early Monday morning and she did not send her box until Monday noon we did not want to send them the Saturday before because they had cookies and candy in. Her box was sent seperate it was not with mine Mrs. Seasholtz had some cookies in it and M.J. had candy and a very good flash light and a small zipper kit with a razor & blades tooth brush & paste and shaving cream. So I think she should know if you did not get it for she had it insured did you get everything we sent you. You have never said Jean sent you a nice box of Woodbury shaving things (M.J. told us to buy it she liked the smell) dad and I sent you a large pack of razor blades, a shoe shining kit and a Bible I had a flashlight and when M.J. told me she got you one I exchanged it for the razor blades. You never did say anything about getting it you never said if you got the telegram we sent you for New Year than you wonder why we ask questions. I still think that was terrible being sent away like that just before Xmas when you had waited around like that for about 2 weeks you did not get your things right or anything I think Arnold & Louise had sent you a gift too now I won't say for sure but I am almost sure M.J. said they did. You said in one of your letters you still had a gift for M.J. you could not find a box for did you ever send that she never got it unless she did this week I do not see her as much since she works down at Weis but then I was in bed again for 3 days as a lot could have happened Dad was down to Dr Ennis last evening he said all that is the matter with me is war nerves and worry he ask dad about you and wanted to know where you were. When dad told him he thought that would be a swell place to be. You ask me to get some of the boys address I will try to when I get out again I would like to go down town this afternoon if I do I will send you a few stamps as you can write. How are you getting along with your work are you getting as good a marks as you did at Sikeston or don't you get marks there. Wendle Mertz is working for Mertz brothers now you know in the hot house I imagine it is quite a change for him too. Do you think I would be able to see you if I come out there some time or don't you ever have days off. Now I guess you have some questions to ans.

    Love
    Mother

Dutch ~ We had three doctors in town: Ennis, Rice, and Rudder. Rice and Rudder were the old timers.

Postmarked January [illegible]1942

Wed afternoon

Dear Ted

You will have to take this letter written in pencil if you like it or not I am still to jittery to write with ink I finally got out of bed this morning it took me three days to get over it this time. You said you have not been getting any letters I don't know where they are for I have been writing everyday so has Mary Jane since we have had your new address and that was last Monday and we both wrote and mailed a letter Monday evening yet, you said about sending Jean a pair of boots I think you had better save your money or someday you will have a leave and will not have any money to come home. I don't see what you do with all your money your $60 seemed to go twice as far down at the store as your money does now. I bet you wished you had waited awhile like we wanted you too and then went in the cadets you would probably have passed too later on. So you just had better do as good as you can now. Dad said I was to tell you he has to register Feb 16 he said it won't last long after he gets there. Well Ted I do hope you get home before long you are not the only one that thinks it seems a long time since you have been home. I guess I will have to close Dad is going to mail my letter when he goes back to work. I had to scold you a little bit it makes me feel better

> *write*
> *Lots of Love*
> *Mother*

January 9, 1942

Fri afternoon

Dear Ted

Boy can you be glad you are in Texas right now it is so darn cold here all you do is put coal on the fire and try to keep warm dad could not get the car started for 2 days now he could not stand that so he and some fellow came over with the truck today at noon and took it over to the garage he thinks the gas line is froze. I wanted him to try and sell it but he does not want to hear any thing about that. Chet Newcomer is going back to the army on Sat a week and he is going to sell his to the Weis Bros I guess they have a hard time trying to keep there district managers in cars since they can't get new ones any more Harry Gotshall just smashed his up again this week. If they keep that up they are going to have a time keep them going.

There has been an awful lot of scandal around our neighborhood lately the Straussers have been in the highlights lately first Jake lost his home and on New Years day I guess they were in a real brawl down at the Exchange Hotel it all started by Earl's & Rick's wife sitting on some mans laps. I guess till it was all over they had 3 good fights and a lot of publicity. Well Mrs. Miller just came over so I guess I may as well quit writing Bonnie is in my ink and got my envelope so I might as well close I wrote a long letter yesterday and sent you some stamps. Jean is having a swell time with this cold weather. She has been skating every day altho she does almost freeze to death.

    I will send you more stamps as soon as I get down town. Am sending this with the mail man. Don't forget to write and do you think you will get home.
    Love
    Mother

The *Sunbury Daily Item* newspaper clipping enclosed with Grace's letter revealed the secret marriage of Corporal Monroe S. Myers and Miss Elizabeth Ann Harbster's almost a year ago on February 4, 1941. Corporal Myers was stationed with the 109th Field Artillery, Medical Detachment at Indiantown Gap.[103]

Jean ~ "Minnie (Monroe) Myers turned out to be the dentist in town. I had a terrific crush on Minnie. There again I was not allowed in the kitchen when Dutch and Minnie were working. They would work away studying, and often I would hear Ted say 'no, no, no that is not how you do it.'"[104]

"Ten Weeks to Go"

January 9, 1942
Dear Mother, Dad and Jean,
    I haven't got much to write about and not much time to write. Tomorrow we fly in the morning and have tests and a formal, white glove inspection tomorrow afternoon.
    There is a class graduating here tomorrow. There are twelve men in it. I only have ten weeks to go if I can stand this place that long.
    I want to go over and listen to the fight now.
    I'll write more tomorrow night because I have to stay in again.
    I didn't get any letters so I don't have any questions to answer.
    Love
    Theodore[105]

January 11, 1942
Sunday morning
Dear Ted

Well I am beginning to believe you can not get stamps or can't write anymore. I have not had a letter since Wednesday and that is terrible did you get the stamps I sent the other day I am sending you six more today I will send you a book some day. It is still very cold here I don't know just how cold but it is still below zero. So you can be glad you are where it is warm or you sure would freeze here. Jean and Mary Jean were down town last evening I guess there ears were frost bitten when they got home. You should have heard them. Franklin Walker was skating the other afternoon and froze the end of his nose. Dad and Jean are going skating this afternoon I think that will be good when dad gets on the ice. Dad said I was to tell you he dreamed he was in the army last night he dreamed he was in the tank division and they were going thru town and somehow his tank was fastened behind one of those big trucks and the truck went on and he and his tank were sitting down on Duke Street. I think what made him dream like that was him and Lee were talking last nite about the box but I think I will when I see her let them pay her for it since you did not get it for she sent hers along and had it insured. I never got your top coat either yet. Well I guess I will have to close and go get my dinner Jean just came home for Sunday school. She said M.J. was there and ask her how I was. Dad is taking his usual Sunday morning nap. Now if you have time write a few more letters. How are you getting along?

Love
Mother

January 12, 1942
Monday eve
Dear Ted

Had your letter today telling me you had your other two coats that is a relief I thought sure they were lost. You said you had not had your pay yet from Sikeston. Do you need money? That has been long between paydays. So if you did not get it and need any we can send you a little. I seen Mary Jane yesterday she says she likes her job down at Weis a lot. She said she was called at Bell Telephone too but she liked it down there so she was going to stay her Mother thought she would have just as much for she does not have any bus fare or lunch to buy.

How are you anyway? You never tell us anything about yourself anymore. Did you take that flight yet? And did you know where you were? Dad said I should tell you if you ever had a long enough leave to come home and did not have money you should telegram us we would get some to send you to come home sometime. But I guess there is no such luck as you might get a leave.

I think I am going back to work again as soon as they open. There is no work right now. I really think I felt better when I worked I did not have as much time to think. The weather is getting a little warmer now again it is about time. We sure had plenty of cold weather for awhile. Dad and Jean were up at Walter's skating on the river yesterday they had a good time I guess Jean was going to show dad up but I guess dad showed Jean up Jean can hardly sit down to day. Dad said he seen Bill Rhinehart over at Sunbury the other day he told dad he did not know what to think about Charles. He said he did not know what he wanted he is down at Washington now Bill said taking up something else. Bill said he did not know what he had been in the Signal Corps. Elwood goes to Middletown Airport on Thursday.

Well I guess this will be enough for one letter now I wish you would write me a letter and really tell me something for once do you know I did not have a letter from you from last Wednesday until today (noon) so you must be busy or something again if you can not go out You should have a lot of time to write.

Lots of Love
Mother
Always answer all my questions

"Good Marks"

January 13, 1942
Dear Mother, Dad and Jean,

I got two letters today so I'll be a good boy and answer them.

O.K. I'll save my money then. If I get a leave I may be able to catch a plane from here to Middletown. They make trips pretty often to get parts and things.

Your Friday's letter said told about how cold it was. It was a little cold here last week but the past 4 or 5 days have been like spring. We run around without coats or jackets.

I don't think I'll need any more stamps. I may get out pretty soon. I should get pay this week I hope so.

I got good marks in all my tests we took over the weekend.

That's all I have to say now so I may as well stop.

Love
Theodore

January 13, 1942
Tue eve
Dear Ted,

Well I got your letter today and you said you did not have any questions to answer so I guess I will have to ask a few. How did your formal white glove inspection turn out. You said there were twelve men graduated they did not have a very large class did they? How many are there in your class? Did the boys that graduated get to go home? I hope they still do. I was up to the store before supper Mrs. Kelley was up there and she ask about you. She was telling me that Billy has been trying to get in the Marines but so far he has not been able to get in on account of having four false teeth in the front when I told her you did. She could hardly believe it she said they must have missed them. I told her they did not that they almost kept you out at the last minute. Do you like navigation as good as flying? and do you like Kelley Field better. You have enough hours in the air for a private license don't you? I must tell you what happened today that box I sent you for Xmas I sent by express today then express man came and wanted to know if I still had my receipt for it someone sent it as far as Pittsburg by train and from there by air mail express and the charges to be paid on it for air mail express were $7.81 so the Express Company is going to be out some money. It is a good thing it got in air mail express though or you would not have got it. I was down to Dr. Ennis today and he put me on a diet so when you see me again I will have my girlish figure I hope. I am going over to Grandma Snyders tomorrow to spend the day I am not supposed to work so I may as well go visiting

Dad was looking on the other side of the sheet of your letter when he did not find any more he said that was short and to the point. Dad said Bud ---- got his papers about going I guess he was in the Reserves they think. John Hilbish will have to go he is a West Point graduate. Well there is no news around here to write about so I will close now answer all my questions and you will have a letter write as often as you can.

Lots of Love
Mother

"Ordered My Uniform"

January 15, 1942

Dear Mother, Dad and Jean,

I got a letter yesterday and today. The one telling about all your dreams. You and Dad must both have war nerves.

You <u>have got</u> everything that I sent home. I did <u>not</u> send my top coat or raincoat. I still have them.

I ordered my uniform last night. I paid $144. for it and I am allowed $150. You don't get it unless you spend it so I thought I might as well spend it.

They are making a lot of new rules and regulations here and everyone is yelling about it. Most of us don't pay much attention to them.

We fly again tomorrow and we have tests tomorrow afternoon Sat. and Monday. So far I have a 98 average and I think I can make it unless I get mad and tell some *officer to go to h(ell). We all tell the upperclass to go there and the way we feel about the officers I think they will be next. They act like a bunch of R.O.T.C. men. I have to study a little now. I'll write again tomorrow.*

    Love

    Theodore

    Its warm here and only rained 1 day since I've been here. You should come south for the winter.

January 15, 1942

Thursday eve

Dear Ted

    Well I just got that nice long letter you wrote on Sunday saying you had to work Sunday morning you sure are getting it lately aren't you. Dad was down at the store today he said M.J. wanted to know if we had a letter from you today. I have not seen much of her lately I used to go down to Sidlers when she was down there but I have not been in Weis Store since you left. You are going to get a letter from Ben Riechenbach but it will be addressed in my hand writing he sent a letter down with Jean for me to address Jean is so absent minded she can not remember your address. I was over to Grandma Snyders all day yesterday Elwood left yesterday but he only goes to Middletown Airport. You tell me not to worry about you. You are better off than any other boy from Norry what makes you think that? I only wish I could make myself believe that. But I try not to worry too much about it but some times you just can't help it and than I have the radio on most all the time dad says he is going to give the radios away until after the war is over. I told him he had better not do that because they are not going to make anymore. You said about not coming down now I don't think I will maybe I can when you graduate but I hope you can come home than so it would not be much use me coming than either if you come home but if you don't come home I think I will. Write as often as you can

    Love

    Mother

January 17, 1942

    Did you get a card from Gandma Snyder? If you did you better send her one she has been looking for one everyday.

Sat morning

    Dear Ted

    I did not write yesterday so I will have to get busy this morning I suppose you are working to the same as ever. I have about 100 and 1 things to do this morning I have to bake Jean a chocolate cake she has been dying for. I have not baked for *so long I don't know if I know how anymore. Jean said I was to tell you she was to the basketball game last nite but we lost and she does not even know what the score was. She said Madelyn Zong was there she ask her where M.J. was. She said home reading a book. She said she wanted her to come but she wouldn't. She told dad the other day she did not feel so good. She was coming up Wed afternoon but said she did not feel good enough to walk up. The girls do not work down at the store Fri nite. Dad said John Hilbish got his notice to report for duty Feb 1 his transportation and all he is trying to get out of it I don't know how he will make out. Chet leaves this morning dad was late coming home last nite he took Chet around to finish up his business he let his car go back Dad said he had $360 paid and he only got $50 back. But he said now he had everything paid up and had nothing to worry about that way. He has always been so nice to dad whenever dad did not have the car he always brought him up home so dad said he felt he could do that for him. He does not care about going back either he wishes he could get to Kelley Field Dad told him to let us know if he did and we would tell you he said. He will be a lieutenant before I get there. write*

Love
Mother

"Mechanics have the Easiest Life"

January 18, 1942
Dear Mother, Dad and Jean,

I got the letter from both you and Jean yesterday. She didn't have the right address on her's and it got in the wrong place for a while.

I don't need any money. I still have $38. left after buying all those presents so you can see how much I spend. In fact when I get that money from Sikeston I am going to send some home. I can never get out when a post office is open to send it. Do you think it would be all right to just stick it in a letter. It would probably get there.

I'll tell you all about myself. I'm fine and healthy. I take exercises 1 hr. every day by request of the army. I'm about 20 lbs. heavier then when I joined the army. Two weeks ago I passed a physical exam. I have one cavity in a tooth that they will fill for me when I get ready. If there is anything else you want to know just write and tell me.

It doesn't look as though I'll ever get a leave. We have been even working 7 days a wk. for the past four weeks.

Tell Elwood they had better send him to Texas. The mechanics have the easiest life I ever saw. When there is an empty seat in the plane they go along with us just for the ride.

I've been on four flights so far and haven't got lost yet. Last Tuesday we were supposed to calibrate an air speed meter by flying over a speed course between two roads. We flew around a town for an hour hunting the roads and would probably still be hunting if another plane hadn't come by and showed them to us.

They are expanding this school from 200 students to 1800 students and taking the ten students with the highest grades from each class as instructors. They grade here on a basis of A.B.C.D.E.F. and everything but F is passing. There are only 3 men out of 125 in my class who got B's and I was one of them. The class average is D. I told my instructor I didn't want to be in the first ten but I wouldn't mind being the eleventh.

There is a fellow from Kentucky here who sleeps along side of me and who I run around with. His parents came down to visit him over the week end. He's having a big time.

There are about 1500 cadets in the replacement center down here and I can't find any of them that are from around home. I guess they are sending all of them to Georgia. The only fellow I saw here that's new are the ones in my upper class at Sikeston. They are over at Randolph now. I never have time to look for any of the others. There are so many soldiers around here though that it would probably be a days work to find anyone you were hunting.

I guess I wrote enough for one day. You'll probably be surprised to get this.
Love
Theodore

From the diary - *At first I didn't like it* (Kelly Field) *but finally found it very interesting. Always managed to find something to do around San Antonio.*[106]

January 18, 1942
Sunday eve
Dear Ted

Well we had another big day today we were out at Martha & Lee's all day and dad and Jean were skating again but it was not much good today it is getting very warm and it is starting to thaw so it spoiled there skating. Mr. Weis was up today and he was asking about you and wanted to know where you were. He said Bob Weis is at Randolph he has been there since July he has never been home either since he has been there.

Did you have a letter from Martha? She said she wrote you a letter but she never had an answer she was wondering if you got her letter.

Martha said she was talking to Bill last evening down at the store she ask him how he liked Mary Jane he said they liked M.J. a lot but he said that other thing can never get around she is always late meaning Madelyn Zong if Madelyn know that it sure would be bad. Madelyn must be taking your place for always being late how about it.

Did you work and fly again this morning? They ought to get enough pilots now they have lowered the age limit to 18 and not the 2 yr college course or equivalent. You said O.K. you would save your money then. So Put it in a good safe place and save hard for you will need it when you come home. I think, and I do hope you get home do you think you will? I see the fellows that graduate from the Norry are still coming home. Do you know that if you don't come home you will not know us anymore I am putting on some weight through it all and dad is losing Jean and M.J. are also putting on weight.

You said about how hard and long you boys were working I guess the boys all over are. John Clugston is at Camp Dix as a cook for the Air Corp and they went on a seven day week too. I guess John does not like that he had been coming home about every two weeks before that. Well this is a terrible letter but really there is never anything happens around this town to write about and I have not been going out much so I do not know what to write. Just now I am waiting for Jean to come home from church I don't know where she is. It is about 9.30. Mick is still trying to rush her but not progressing very well. write

All our Love
Mother

"Raised Hell"

January 19, 1942
Dear Mother, Dad and Jean,

I got your letter today and it didn't even have any questions in it. You're getting wonderful.

I fly again tomorrow. We dare not ever look out of the plane and must fly by instruments. They call it dead reckoning and you'd better reckon right or you'll fail the flight.

I got a little more rest yesterday then I usually get on a Sunday. All I did was sleep. Our class raised h. so much we got ourselves confined for 3 weeks. I slipped out Sat. night and went to the movies but had to be back before the 10 o'clock bed check.

There is another class graduating on next Sat. That will move me up the ladder another step. If I keep up my good grades I probably never will see action except as an instructor.

I had better plan my flight for tomorrow or I'll get lost. It will cover about 450 miles and be with in a ½ mile of Mexico when I get to my one destination. My instructor told me not to get lost and cross the river. It's against the law.

I'll write more later.

Love
Theodore

January 19, 1942
Monday eve
Dear Ted

Well I bet I can guess something I bet you got pay. Do you know what makes me think that well I will tell you that pretty new stationary you are using Jean liked it so well she wanted to cut out the emblem to take it to school. What do you mean by you are allowed $150 and you don't get it unless you spend it don't you even get your $75 a month to do with. I was wondering about that I found one of your pay envelopes it had on it total balance $50.80 is that what you got I never could understand it. And what do you mean by they act like a bunch of R.O.T.C. men I do not understand your slang you will have to explain it to me. Right now I am listen(ing) to a radio program and they just ask if a uniform always gets them. They should don't you think. I hope you get home so we can see you and yours. I am trying to write and listen to the radio at the same time as if I have part of a radio program in your letter you will know why. I am very glad that you have been having such a high average and hope you can continue with your high marks. Jean said I was to tell you she is not doing bad either she did only have one C on her report card. She has been making 100 in her Latin tests. How she does it I will never tell you. When she read your letter saying how much you had to pay for a uniform she said gee I could buy clothes for a whole year for that. How long will it be before you are a upper class. You said it has only rained one day since you have been in Texas. Well it is raining like the dickens here right now. As for coming south for the winter I certainly wish I could but that takes money.

If you have time you should write to Martha and Grandma Snyder they look for letters from you once in a while almost as anxiously as I do. I don't know what we will do when you are thru if we don't hear from every day or every other day. Well I guess this will be all for this evening. I have run out of news. write

All our Love
Mother

January 20, 1942

Hello old Man you know we missed you on Xmas, but Bill was on hand. I had to work on Xmas but was home in good shape I see your Sugar everyday and she is about as usual.

We are working every day even on Sundays. You say it is nice around Kelly Field well I don't know much about that place but as I told you Ft Bliss three mile N of Elpaso is not so nice. Not even a tree for 50 miles. Oh say have you met any of the Senoritas yet. I mean the dark kind well if not just fly to Elpaso and go down near the Bridge when I left there were plenty there of corse (sic) I did not know them all. Say the other night I heard some of the boys from your Post on the air and I was listening for you but of corse I suppose your horn was just to short.

Well I must Register you know of corse they will not put me in the Air Corps for I am a damn good mule skinner. Say if you have a brake down any time just go to Middletown Air Port and ask for Dodo Zettlernoyer he is in Civ Service. Well I guess I will give some one else a place to rite so good luck as ever.

W.P. Zong

Hello Tedy,

This is mom Zong now trying to put her little say in. Tedy we sure was glad to hear from you for we sure did miss you on Christmas. Well Tedy I don't know how army life is for you but it can't be as bad as the people in North'd is going through for every time we go to the store they get you one way or the other. When you first go in and stop at the green counter there stands the Clerk making goggle eye at the opposite sex. They you go looking for the Manager and you finally find him on the top shelf trying to play air warden then you come around to the dairy counter and the young lady there stands in aisles and you get your butter in 50 pieces or more. Then the time comes to be checked out there stands the lady with a sweet smile and slow hand but not to slow to make a mistake on the customer side. Now what I am trying to tell you things are not the same but I think we will live through it all and be here to welcome you home. Madelyn just rushed in to say she was going to eat up at Mary Janes but when she left she had half of my supper with her. Now Tedy if you can make this out write again and we'll answer

good night

Mrs. Zong

"Officers Think They are Hard"

January 21, 1942
Wednesday
Dear Mother, Dad and Jean,

I can't find the letter that I got from you yesterday so I can't answer the questions. I flew last Tuesday (yesterday) and did O.K. I fly again on Friday. We fly a couple of hundred miles each time and never get out of the state of Texas.

We are through with all of our tests for a while now. I didn't get any of my grades yet but I don't think I failed any of them.

We got a few new officers around here who think they are pretty hard. Our athletic director told us to stop picking on them so much.

The weather here is just like spring. It gets cold at night but in the afternoon it gets hot when you're out in the sun. I should have a nice tan. I'm out in the sun for two hours every day.

I am going to take some pictures on Sunday if it is nice and I will send you one of me in my uniform. I won't be too long any more until I am out of here. I think I'll go to bed and read now.

I'm sending you some money to go to the movies on.

Love

Theodore

"Japs Over Sunbury"

January 21, 1942

Dear Ted

Well no one wrote you a letter yesterday I guess if I died no would write to you any more I was sick all day yesterday so no one wrote I had one of my terrible headaches again. I thought I was going to get thru with out the doctor but I could not make it I have been having them more lately again than I did for a while. I have not had a letter from you since Monday in that one you said you would write the next day but you could not leave you have not answered my questions I ask about those other boys that graduated. I ask you if they had a chance to come home you never said they did or did not. Jean and Mary Jean want to go to the movies I do not know if they will get there or not Mick came over before they got started. Right now they are having an argument about going to the dance Sat eve.

Dad got his notice today about blackouts if they are out on the road. Jean has been having air raid drills up at school she says it will be just to bad for her if there is an air raid she is right under two big pillars. Dad told her she did not have to worry the Chamber of Commerce would not let the Japs or Hitler fly over Sunbury. How are you getting along (have) you been flying lately. When will you get that uniform you order you should look like a million in that. I have not seen Mary Jane for an age I thought sure she would be up today but she wasn't. Well I guess this will be all for this evening I don't know anymore to write about I never get out of the house anymore to get news. Don't forget to write when you have time.

Love

Mother

More news from home accompanied the letter about Pvt. Robert Fletcher of Water Street an acting corporal with Company E, 179th Infantry Regiment, and 2nd Lt. Gilbert Strauser of King Street who left from an undisclosed port for England to join other Army officers as observers.[107]

January 22, 1942
Thur eve
Dear Ted

Well I got that nice long letter today that is the kind I like to get. You told about them going to keep the highest ten for instructors and you wanted to be the eleventh. Don't you let me hear you say that again you keep yourself right where you are and if they really do that boy will it be a load off of my mind for a while anyway. You said about that fellow's parents being there from Kentucky well we would have been there long ago if we could afford it. You talked about sending money home well I don't think I would take a chance on just putting it in a letter. I would not do that unless you could have the letter insured for the amount you have in it but that is the only way. But if you save it there be sure to keep it at a good place so it is safe. Dad said that long letter was a surprise he just got thru reading it. He said I was to tell you about Bill Hollenbach you know we have only been buying a few things down there so E[illegible] Gearhart came to him and told him he wanted to tip him off that Bill was yelling about us not buying down there dad is so darn cross he said now he will go to Sunbury at one of the stores to do his buying he Bill has about the whole town since the A & P left but he still isn't satisfied. Dad and Jean are doing the dishes you should hear them Jean is quoting him some of Wormleys stuff about carbon dioxide and plants it really is good. Jean just got thru telling him she learned a lot from Wormley. Dad said (she) will get it that is where Ted got his. I do not know if you will be able to read this or not but Jean wants the ink to do some experiments and she stands here yelling.

I think I will go to the movies. Do you think you will get home?
Don't forget to write
All our Love
Mother
Jean told me to let this space for her she wanted to write something but she says she is insulted now and will not write. There is no change in her

"Marriage Under the Crossed Swords"

Postmark January 23, 1942

310 West College
Bucknell University
Lewisburg, PA

Dear Tedie: - I got your letter of a few weeks back and it's high time I answered it, I guess. It's great to hear you're making out so well and I hope you keep it up. I suppose you'll be leaving Kelly Field one of these days; in fact, you may have even left it now for all I know, so keep in touch with me and let me know whenever you change your address.

The second semester is now in full swing and it feels great to be on the home stretch at last, although there is still a lot of hard work to be done before graduation.

In case you are wondering about the stationery, I am privileged to use it now that I am a full fledged lab assistant. Vic was up to see me about a week ago and I gave him your address, so he'll probably be dropping you a line, if you're still there.

Mariethel was talking to your Mary Jane the other day and she was told that you write Mary Jane usually twice a day. I didn't know you had the bug that bad, chum! I thought I was the only one who did simple-minded things like that! Oh well, live and learn, and I'll be waiting for that marriage under the crossed swords!

I suppose you are working harder than ever, and no relief in sight! As just as the foreign situation gets more reversed, I suppose life gets harder for you.

I don't have the slightest idea what your plans are for the future, but whether you ever get in the danger zone or not, I wish you all the luck in the world and take good care of yourself. Military funerals are nice, but you have plenty of time for one of them when you're old and gray and can't take one even if you wanted to!

Well that's all! Write soon, and be good!

Your pal
Buck

"Big B-19"

January 23, 1942
San Antonio, Texas
Dear Mother, Dad and Jean,

I got that letter with all your questions and decided I had better answer them.

I mean that when we get a commission we get $150. allowance to buy an officers uniform with. We get that besides our regular pay. Here I draw $75. a month minus my laundry. At Sikeston I got $147.50 minus my room, board, laundry etc. It all comes out to be about $70. a month.

I become an upperclassman tomorrow. That will make things a lot easier.

I saw that big B-19 take off this morning at the same time we were taking off. That thing is really big. The pilot flys it with kid gloves too.

I can't think of anything else to write about. I think I'll write to Martha & Granma Snyder now.

Love
Theodore

January 24, 1942
Don't forget the pictures if you took some
Sat eve
Dear Ted

I am at home all alone this evening so I will write you a long letter dad went out house to play cards and Jean went down town. I think I will walk down town and mail the letter after while. I don't think you got any for a while did you? But I will tell you what happened I wrote you a letter Thursday evening and mailed it after I got home. I happened to think that I did not put a stamp on it so yesterday I went down to the post office to see about it and they said well they sent it out to Mary Jane they thought it was her letter so last evening I went out to M.J. to see what she did with it she said she put a stamp on it and mailed it but she did not know whose letter it was so I guess you will get it but a little late. I got my letter you sent today that had the money in it boy you must think I am going to the movies a lot with $10.00 dollars that would take me to the movies over a year all I have been going. Mary Jane said you were talking about coming home some time when I was sick but it would put you back three weeks well I would like very much to have you come home and the putting you back three weeks would be alright too because if you would have to go away it would keep you here that much longer, but if you would like to graduate with the class you are in now and that would keep you from doing so why I would not want you to do it don't worry about me I am O.K. I get one of those head aches every once and a while and I have had them quite often lately but the doctor said it is a flare up from that kidney condition but I hope you can come home when you graduate for a long stay and any other time you can that does not hurt your marks in any way for I sure do hope you can be one with the high marks so you can stay as an instructor you do not know how much better I feel since you wrote home and said that and I only hope it turns out alright. You know how much I worried about you when you went in the air service but now I do not worry about that near as much as I do about this war and where you might go. So whatever you do keep up the good work and keep those marks up as high as possible. Aunt Alice and Uncle Ed were over last evening and we were talking about pilots and flying Uncle Ed said well I advise the pilots but those navigators certainly must know there stuff. He did not know that you were studying navigation either we told him than after he was thru talking about them. Don't forget to write

Lots of Love

Mother

January 26, 1942

Monday eve

Dear Ted,

Well dad and Jean are doing the dishes so I will write your letter. I did not get a letter from you today. Well I have some news for you I started to work over at Nite Kraft and I feel fine this evening I think that was about one half of my trouble I was around the house alone most all the time and it gave me to much time to think. I do not know how long it will last they have not any work over there since before Xmas until last week and I heard someone say they do not have much work now so by the time I get started right I suppose it will be all (over).

We were over home yesterday afternoon and Elwood was telling us about his work down at Middletown he likes it very much. Martin is going down too I guess. I told Elwood what you said about him coming to Texas he said he wished he could but everybody down there is sent east. He said they had some repair work for Kelley Field down there now. I ask Jean and dad if there was anything they wanted me to tell you well Jean had a string a mile long she still does not have much ambition or she would write herself. These are the main things she said I was to tell you that she had. Jimmie Van Kirk has been very sick the Dr. thinks he has pneumonia. How are you? How are your grades coming along? Keep them high. Well I guess this will be all I bet you get tired of all this nonsense I write if you do just tell me. Well be a good boy and don't forget to write.

All our Love

Mother

"Tired When We Landed"

January 27, 1942

Dear Mother, Dad and Jean,

I'm sorry I haven't written for some time. I haven't got your letter here right now so I don't know what questions to answer.

I got open post on Sat. and went into town. It's real nice in there, rose garden, parks etc. is hot as the devil here right now. I don't know what I'll do when summer comes.

We flew this morning for 5 hours. I was really tired when we landed.
I have to hurry and get in bed before the lights go out so I'll write more tomorrow.
Love
Theodore

"Sub off Aransas Pass"

January 28, 1942
Dear Mother, Dad and Jean,

I got your letter today and also have two others here so I will answer all of there questions at one time.

I'll get that uniform in about eight weeks. I may as well answer the question of coming home right now. I don't think I'll get home. Neither of the last two classes that graduated got a chance to go home.

I got a picture but it wasn't very good. I'll send it to you anyhow.

We really had an awful time flying yesterday. It was very rough and the plane was bouncing all over the air. I was trying to read drift and the plane bounced. The driftmeter came up and hit me in the eye – Result one black eye. I'm not the only guy though. The winds were up as high as 50 knots.

A sub was reported off Aransas Pass today. We fly around there. I wish they'd send us out to look for him. We'd get all of our planes out he wouldn't have much of a chance.

I'll make someone a good wife when I get through here. Today we house cleaned the barracks and I make swell beds.

I have to work a few problems now so I'll have to stop writing.
Love
Theodore

January 28, 1942
Camp Beauregard, La.
Dear Mrs. Vankirk,

What is Theodor's address? I think of him quite often and would like to write to him.

You will find enclosed a self addressed envelope for you to send his address to me.

Thank you very much.
Yours truly,
Maxine S. Myers

January 28, 1942
Wed eve
Dear Ted

    Well I must be slipping I did not get around to writing your letter last evening but I was so tired and had a slight head ache I went to bed at about 6.30 and got up again at 8.30 and went back at about 10.30. But you are slipping a little bit yourself I do not get as many letters as I used to but the way Martha said you worked in her letter I guess you do not have the time. I called her to ask how Jimmie was and she read your letter over the telephone to me. She said she was writing you a letter when I called. She and Grandma Snyder are so proud of the letters they get from you. Well how is it to be an upper classmen? I suppose you like the place better now. I forgot to thank you for the money you sent I made very good use of it. I paid some bills that had piled up.

    Your said in your letter you seen the B-19 take off I suppose you wished you were in it dad said we would have to tell Grandpa Snyder about that you remember you said you wanted to fly it well you got pretty close to it. Clifford bought another car one of those small Fords a 1937 it really is a good looking car he said if he could save enough we would come to see you this spring.

    But I am still hoping you will come home. That would be the best thing ever. Franklin Walker trys to tell me you sure will have some time off when you graduate so I am still hoping. Did you take any pictures on Sunday? If you did don't forget to send some. Mary Jane said she was coming up this afternoon. I don't know if she was up or not because since I work over there it seems I am never home. Jean said I should tell you this was one of her bad days she could not find her seat or chair when she went to school and got the dickens then she came home at noon and had locked her self out. She had to pull the Xmas tree off of the cellar steps and climb over the coal pile. I wish I could have seen her. I just heard on the radio that the Coast of Texas is blacked out after spying two Axis submarines in the vicinity is that anywhere near where you are. You hear so much on the radio about war that you do no know what is what. But we never miss Gabriel Heatter and it is time for him now so good nite and be good. write

    All our Love
    Mother – Dad – Jean

January 30, 1942
Thur eve
Dear Ted

    Well another day gone and no letter if I do not get any tomorrow I think I will come to Texas and see what is the matter down there.

But if you keep those marks up in the high places I can forget about not getting a letter do you know I have only had one letter so far this week. Well I will have to finish with the pencil Jean left the pen fall and you should see the point now. So I will have to buy a new pen before I can write again so you see I will have a better excuse than you.

Well I just heard on the radio that our planes can land for twenty four hours so you can cross that river now you were talking about if you want to. Edythe was just telling me today Bob Walker was called for examination for the army I don't know how he will make out this time when he was called before he was deferred for six month but I guess he can not do that this time. Well I do not have any thing to write about I have not been down town all week. So I guess I may as well quit. Dad is taking his usual evening nap and Jean is in bed already it is only nine thirty she sure does get her rest. I bet we could not keep you in bed now anymore in the morning that use to be a terrible job for you to get up

Good night write
All our love
Mother

"Off Course"

January 31, 1942
Dear Mother, Dad, and Jean,

I got a letter from you today but I haven't got it here so I can't answer all of your questions. I think I just leave this letter open until tomorrow and just answer all of your questions.

I believe you had better stop working. It doesn't do you any good. Today was payday so I will send you some more money. I haven't spent my last months pay yet.

They worked us a little harder this week then they have before. They can't make us work much faster.

On my flight last Friday the wind blew me about 25 miles off course. It was blowing about 65 mph though so I didn't do so bad after all.

The other day there were two planes that couldn't get their wheels down so they landed on their bellies. The pilots said it was a lot of fun. I'll finish this letter tomorrow when I have more time.

January 31, 1942
328 King Street
Northumberland, Pa.
Dear Teedy

You probably think I've forgotten all about you – but I haven't.

This has been a terrible day. Its been raining and every once in a while snowing.

Everytime I go into Weis' I always ask Mary Jane how the Husband is. She always knows too.

This town is deader than a dead door nail. It you don't have the spondulex to go someplace else you stay dead with it.

Ben has picked up some chicken in Sunbury named June Reed. She seems to have fallen for him awful hard because she always seems to go where Ben is – quite coincidental. Last Sunday night I had a date with Lorraine and we took Ben & his chicken to Sunbury. After it was over Ruckenbach rolled in bed at 2:30 a.m. the next morning.

You better apply for a little vacation so you can get here before summer is over, then we can get a little tennis in. After all we'll take on all comers and beat em I hope.

I want to try and go to Bucknell next year if I can get a fairly good job this summer. If things work out I'm liable to land up being a college boy. I guess Post is going right on through.

By the way I don't need to join the army to quit fighting any more because Malone & me is no more. It seems some divine power has come to Brennen's rescue and saved him from further battering at the hands of that blitzkrieg. Anyway I'm glad it is finally all over, after a long war.

It won't be long for me anymore before my days in school are over. They ought to sign Doc Phillips up with the entertainment division. That numbscull don't need to act to put on a show he does it natural.

Well someday drop in around Northumberland – I mean the right way now.

Well take it easy Cadet and don't sleep too long.

Bill B.

February 1, 1942
Sunday

I just took a nice long nap. I'm getting worse than Dad. I can sleep anyplace, anytime.

Nothing new happened around this place except that we learned a lot more about navigation. I never learned stuff so fast in all of my life. So far they haven't washed any of my class out but they will start soon. A lot of them flunked their exams. We have our second 3 wks. exams this week so we haven't got much longer to go.

All I hope is that they don't make us go longer.

Love Theodore

February 1, 1942
Sat eve
Dear Ted

What is the matter I have not had a letter from you since Tuesday and that was written last Friday so I am beginning to get worried about you I went out to M.J. last evening to see if she had heard from you but she said she had not had a letter since Tue. either but she thought you were cross at her for some reason and I have been thinking everything from you being sick to a plane crash. I have been seriously thinking about calling you today but did not have any idea where or how to get you. Well then dad and M.J. had some more of these bright ideas that you were coming home. We were over to Sunbury at about five oclock and some one got off of the train and went out Arch St that I would have sworn was you from the back.

Dad finally got the car all fixed up I mean with stickers we had to have it inspected the end of this month and get a sticker for $2.09 at the post office beside and have our new drivers license. I think I am going to send you your application for drivers licenses and you can sign it and sent it back than you will have your license when you come home well I guess this will be all for now dad wants to go out to Grandpa.

> *Try and write*
> *All our love*
> *Mother*

February 2, 1942
Sunbury, Pa.
Dear Grandson

I am writing you this short letter and tell you we received your Post Card also your letter last Tuesday eve we took Aunt Kate home and stoped and had a little chat with Dad - Mother and sister Jean all are O.K. so are all of the rest of us Jimmie had been sick but is O.K. again Uncle Pud was home over the week end all fixed up in his uniform he looks fine. Black Mill running again Grandpa had been working every day until last week had a let up for a few days

You are lucky to have warm weather pretty cold here this morning of corse to day is Ground Hog day Well, Theo. so long giving our Best wishes and all good to you

> *Grandpa & Ma and Cliff,*
> *Will be looking for card or letter soon*

February 2, 1942

Dear Ted

Well I finally had a letter today after waiting a week within one day for one you must be a busy boy since you have before an upper classmen. Your picture looks like your in a bad mood. But you should have had your month open for they are the only ones that really look like you.

I just wrote a note to Monroe Myers I had a letter from him today asking for your address, so you will have a letter from him in a short time I suppose.

Well your telling me you did not think you would be able to get home at graduation certainly has taken the joy out of the coming of the last of March for me. Well if you can not come home I would like to come to Texas if I can afford it I was thinking about getting M.J. and Mildred said she would come with me that way it would not cost so much that is if we get the car going dad has been having a devil of time with it It is 9.15 now and he just came home I thought he was working but he was over there trying to get the car going it stopped for him right after he left the warehouse so he had some one tow him to the garage I don't know what is the matter with it. It has done that a couple of times already dad thinks it is the carburetor.

You had something in one of your letters about sending your drivers license dad and I were talking about it the other day he thought I should send it to you so you could sign it and send it so you would have it when you come home. Well I guess I will have to close and do my dishes you should be here now if you are getting to be such a good housewife

Well try and write if you can.

All our Love

Mother

February 4, 1942

Dear "Teddy,"

I wrote to your mother for your address & also to my father to find out your address for me. I received a letter from my father today & he sent it to me.

How is the Air Corps? I have been thinking about transferring to the Air Corps but Bethe & my parents talked me out of it.

What courses do you have to take to be a flying cadet? What pay do you get at the beginning? How long is the course? In fact what about the Cadets & the Air Corps? A lot of boys are transferring to the Air Corps.

I got a letter from Bill Rothenberg the other day. He is O.K. & still kicking.

I am going to M.O., La. over the week-end.

At present we are located beside Esler Field, La. It is about 12 miles from

Alexandria, La. But my address is Camp Beauregard. The big planes are taking off
& landing at all hours.

If we could only be back at S.U. with Rothenberg, Nevins, Lewis, etc.

Write & let me know how everything is.

Your Pal,

Monk.

Corporal M. S. Myers

M.D. 109th F.A.

Camp Beauregard, La.

February 4, 1942

Wed eve

Dear Ted

Well I got another one of those nice letters today with a bill in it, but do you know someday you might be able to come home and will not have enough money. If you cannot come we are going to try and come to see you at graduation time dad said he could hardly afford to take off. He would have to take about two weeks so I was thinking about driving down myself if some one will come with me. Dad just told me this evening he believed Lee would like to come down with me if I come down he told dad today he could drive down in three days. I don't know I suppose if we do come down we will be freezing here and roast down there. Dad said I was to tell you you will have to go some to beat his record in napping. He smashed the end of his one finger yesterday over at work he let a barrel of turpentine fall on it I don't think it is very bad he does not say anything about it hurting and you know how he moans about everything he went to Dr. Ennis and had it bandaged before he came home he must go down again tomorrow evening but I think Dr. Ennis knows the Compensation Company pays it.

Jean said I was to tell you she was one of the sophomores to be taken in the Kiwanis lassies there were only five sophs so she feels big. She is cramming now for a Geometry test she has a terrible time with that she just said she did not see why she did have it when you were still at home. I see in the paper to nite that Monroe Meyers and Betty Harpster are celebrating their first wedding anniversary all ready they sure kept it a secret for a long time. Sam Lewis is going to be married too he is marrying a Swineford (Pennsylvania) girl her dad runs a hotel so Tommy should be right at home. Well I guess this will be all for now or I will not have anything to write about the next time. How is your black eye. write

Lots of Love

Mother

Sergeant and Mrs. Monroe Myers celebrated their first wedding anniversary while Myers served with the Twenty-Eighth Division. Capt. Clayton H. Shunk had been transferred to the Forty-First Air Base at Tallahassee, Florida. Mrs. (Sgt. Bill) Levan gave birth to a son. Cpl. Robert Powell, Pvt. Louis A. Vecere, and Eugene Coster graduated from the surgical technicians course at Fort Sam Houston, Texas. Parents were given advice not to worry if their son or daughter did not notify them when transferred to another location, but to "keep quiet" because instances of unguarded remarks had led to serious leaks about troop and ship movements.[108]

"Not to Worry"

February 5, 1942

Dear Mother, Dad and Jean,

I'm sorry I haven't written for quite a while but we have tests and everything else this week. We got busier and busier.

I flew today for about 400 mile and I'm tired as the devil. We have another test tomorrow morning. I wear two watches around now. They issued us one here that costs about sixty dollars and I don't want to let either of my watches laying around so I wear one on each arm.

I told you a dozen times not to worry about me if you don't get a letter. If anything happens to me you'll know about it long before a letter would reach you.

I have to study for my tests now but I guess I'll have to write twice a day any how.

Love

Theodore

"Not Much Time"

February 6, 1942

Dear Mother, Dad and Jean,

I got another letter from you today but don't have much time to answer.

We started celestial navigation this week so that now we have classes day and night. It's seven o'clock now and we're just starting our night class. We go to class until 11:00 then go to bed in the dark and get up at 5:30 and start all over again.

I take my physical exam tomorrow morning. It's the one I take to get my commission so it doesn't make me mad.

I think I'll get a chance to go to town tomorrow night. I hope. Our instructor just came so I must stop.

Love

Theodore

"Celestial Navigation"

Dutch ~ The first lesson at navigation school was on using a compass then how to do dead reckoning and celestial navigation.[109] The teacher stood with a flashlight pointing to the stars saying "that is Polaris." Hell, I couldn't see anything.

I always liked Sirius, the brightest star in the heavens, and after a while I could identify other stars. Can still name them: Polaris, Sirius, Vega, Arcturus, Antares, and Spica. The appearance of the constellation changes in the far north. Sirius is the brightest star in the heavens and I can still identify it. Most people think Polaris, the North Star, is the brightest star, but it isn't and it is hard to find. Orion is the constellation I know best and prominent in flying school studies.

The North Star is the most valuable because you shoot it for sixty degrees of your latitude. At Kelly Field we studied the stars during only one season. On my own I learned to recognize the positions for other times of the year. If you only learned the constellations at one time a year you were licked. Now if you take me out during October, November, December and I look up I don't know what the hell the stars are.

I went out in the yard at night and practiced celestial navigation. In England you could see the ground. If you couldn't see the ground you were dead. By the way, I was good at celestial navigation. In celestial navigation you shoot the altitude of a star and that gives you a line all the way around the earth that has that same elevation. When you get three lines like that, that cross at a point that is where you are. I could get the celestial fix and do all calculations in ten minutes and there were a lot of calculations, all the things that the navigator Fred Noonan did not learn that lost Amelia Earhart; that's all I can say.

Aeronautical charts aided the navigators for long flights within the United States. The Great Circle Chart was used to plan overseas flights and round the world. The Magnetic Chart determined the magnetic variation at a particular spot.[110] Van Kirk studied the principal methods of navigation: pilotage, dead reckoning, aeronautical radio, and celestial. In addition to the compass the navigator used air speed and drift indicators, altimeter, and a watch.[111] Duties also included calibrating the altimeter, compasses, airspeed indicators, astrograph, and drift meter.[112]

Pilotage is the art of navigation by landmarks and requires the use of maps and charts. Dead reckoning utilizes instruments and keeping track of distance travelled and direction, and an accurate log. Radio navigation rides the beam from one known station to another. Many locations where American aircraft were flying at the time had no radio beams to guide the navigators. Knowledge of the stars and other celestial bodies in all quarters of the sky and at all times of night and day is key to celestial navigation.[113]

February 7, 1942
Sat. morning
Dear Ted

I am getting as bad as you are I have not wrote a letter since Thursday but that is not quite as bad as you are. I was down to the store last evening and M.J. was telling me about the grouchy letter she got from you this week so I suppose we will get one too if we do not get at and write you a letter but really since I have been working it seems I just can not get around. I guess I am getting old but you should not talk to M.J. like that she is being a very good girl. Last evening she worked in Lewis place and when Madelyn went home she ask M.J. if she was going down town after work and M.J. said no I am going right home Madelyn got cross and said well than stay at home you old stay at home. She still thinks you are coming home at graduation time. She told me last evening that Betty Harpster wants to go to see Monroe so bad and she wants M.J. to go with her to see you she told her she would only have about 100 mile to go alone but I think she would have more than 100 mile it is more than that across Texas to where you are isn't it? The weather here has been terrible on Thursday it snowed all day. Yesterday it started to rain and this morning it is coming down in buckets full the way it sounds and you should see the slop. You know I do not know how we are going to do about the application for license for the car you should sign it I guess. Dad said he did not know if he should try signing it or not. We did not get there yet but dad is already wondering about them. Jean is going to a dance up at the Jr. high school tonite the Jr. class is having she did not want to go but Mick gave her a ticket and they are 35 cents this year so she thought she had better go. I went to the movies last night the first in an age I seen, Babes in Broadway with Mickey Rooney did you see it? It was like all their musicals. Write

Lots of Love
Mother

"Parachute in the Proper Stall"

February 8, 1942
Dear Mother, Dad and Jean,

I have a bunch of your letters here so I have some questions to answer. I had letters from Martha and from M. Myers yesterday. I also got a letter from Bill Brennen the other day. And one from Grandma Snyder.

Jimmie sent me a picture of himself on the car and also wrote a note.

All our tests are over for the third three weeks. I didn't learn my marks yet but I think they are pretty good. We have to learn the names of and be able to locate seven stars by looking in the sky now.

A new class came in yesterday. One of the fellows in it was in my upper class at Sikeston. He washed out at Randolph. He made me write "I will put my parachute in the proper stall" for him 500 times one day. – Oh boy.

They are getting a devil of a lot of Cadets down around here. I don't know what they'll do with them all. I have to go out and look at the stars now.

Love

Theodore

February 9, 1942

Monday afternoon

Dear Ted

Well I had letter today that you said you guessed you had to write twice a day no matter how much you had to do. You do not have to write twice a day. If you do not want to write you won't have to write all. The only reason I ever said anything was because you used to write so often now I am lucky if I get one letter a week but if you do not have time that is alright.

You said you had two watches you should be alright. You can have one on war time and one on regular time. It is seven oclock here now and it seems so funny it is still daylight.

I do not know if I will get down to see you or not the Dr thinks it would be too much for me. I had one of my swell heads last evening again and he was up. I have to go down this evening again I don't know what for. I could not go to work today I don't know how I will make out tomorrow. Lois Gresh was just in I showed her the picture I got last week she said gee he looks crabby in that

Well I guess this will be all for this evening or I will never get down to Dr's.

All our love

Mother

The United States Western District Court ordered the immediate possession of 7,500 acres in the Towns of Porter and Lewiston, Niagara County, New York, in the interest of national defense to construct the Lake Ontario Ordnance Plant (LOOW) for a federal munitions project.[114]

February 9, 1942
Tue eve
Dear Ted

Well I wrote you a grouchy letter so I will have to write you another one today, but I really did feel grouchy yesterday I feel better today. Well than on all that you wrote a grouchy letter and that was the finish. I feel better again today. I went to work this morning. Our evenings are so long since we are on war time. I have not had our supper yet but I have to wait until dad comes home to go and get us some water some where we do not have a drop of water the main water pipe into town broke this morning and they do not have it fixed yet they said it would be 12 oclock tonite before they got it fixed. I was just talking to Mr. Kelley he told me Billy enlisted in the Marines he was sent to Paris Island he said it is a small island some where near South Carolina.

I will finish your letter now we went out to Grandma Van Kirks to get some water to get supper and when we got out there they had supper ready so we ate anyway I got out of getting supper. Well we just about have our plans made to come to Texas when you graduate if you can't come home. Mildred said she will come along and we figure if we have about five at $25 apiece we can make the trip but if you can come home we want you to come home. I was talking to Mr Baker yesterday he said Charles is in Louisiana and he thinks he will be getting a furlough to come home soon. Bob leaves on the 18th of this month Mr Baker says he does not want to go. Do you ever hear from Wendle Mertz? He goes on the 21st of this month he will have to start out as a buck private after all he said when he was here he did not want to do that. Than I see in tonites paper he is in jail for 3 days for driving his car without a stamp on it. It never rains but what it pours for him. How are you? still grouchy. How are your marks coming along? Well be good and get over that grouch.

All our love
Mother

"Half the Class Got Sick"

February 12, 1942
Dear Mother, Dad and Jean,

I haven't got much to write about and haven't got much time. We have classes every night now from 7 until 9:30. They don't give us any time at all.

I don't know what made M.J. mad. I didn't put anything in any of my letters to make her mad. In her letter she really sounded hot. I guess I'll have to buy her a ring and send it home on pay day. Do you think I should?

I have to fly tomorrow. It was so rough yesterday that over ½ of the class got sick. I didn't.

They washed 30 men out of our class yesterday.

I may be able to get home at graduation time but I don't know. We got on a new schedule and according to that we should graduate on April 11th.

I have to stop now.

Love

Theodore

"Wish I Was Graduating"

February 13, 1942

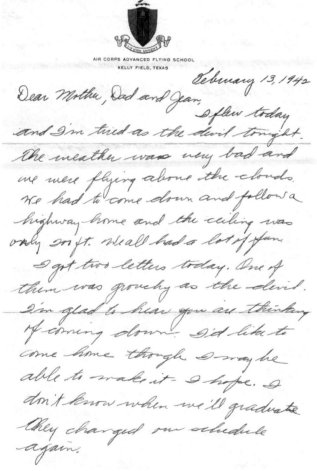

Dear Mother, Dad and Jean,

I flew today and I'm tired as the devil tonight. The weather was very bad and we were flying above the clouds. We had to come down and follow a highway home and the ceiling was only 200 ft. We all had a lot of fun.

I got two letters today. One of them was grouchy as the devil. I'm glad to hear you are thinking of coming down. I'd like to come home though I may be able to make it. I hope. I don't know when we'll graduate. They changed our schedule again. There is another class graduating tomorrow. I wish I was one of them.

I'm going to go down and got to bed now because I have a headache and everything else. I'll write soon.

Love

Theodore

February 14, 1942
Sat eve
Dear Ted,

I really am getting terrible I have not written a letter for two days as I had better get busy or you will think we all died in here. We are all still going dad is having a terrible time with the car. I guess its almost wore out I don't know we were planing to come to see you the last of next month now I do not know if we will make it or not. M.J. will be very dissapointed if I can't come down they say that is all she talks about. In the first place I hear they are going to start to ration gas five gal a week to a person if they do that I surely will not be able to drive down. But dad says they do not believe they will do it until the new licenses are out. I do not know what it will take to fix the car this time dad had it to the garage the other week when it would not start and they done something to the carbureator and charged him six dollars. Now there is something the matter with the gears we can not go in reverse at all. You can put it in reverse gear but the car will not move at all dad worked on it all afternoon and took it a part now he is going to try and get Elwood to come over and look at it tomorrow. As for me making the trip I ask the Dr about it last evening and he said it would not do me one bit of harm in fact he thought it would be good for me to go by car and take our time. I ask him what about my headaches and he said he would give me some medicine and a note so I could stop at any Dr if I did get a bad one so I don't think I would need to worry at all about that part. But maybe you will be able to come home after all yet I seen a fellow over at the station yesterday I sure thought for a minute it was you. They are having a birthday party for grandpa and grandma Van Kirk this evening but I guess we will not get there I ask dad if he was going out he said well he certainly was not going to walk out I am really glad that we can not go but I suppose we will still have to pay 1.12 they raised it again. Jean just got a big Valentine box of Schrafts chocolates from Mick and dad is teasing her about opening it she has not opened it yet. How are you? How have your marks been? and what has happened to the poor fellow from Randolph by now?

All our love
Mother

"Rationing"

Jean ~ War impacted the home front. "Everything was rationed. We had a little book with blue stamps and red stamps, for meat, canned goods, and sugar, and stamps for shoes. We had auctions in the high school for war bonds.

While Daddy was working at Weis he would get me a little can of Hershey's syrup. I would take it as one of the things to get auctioned off. My gosh, people did anything for that little can of Hershey's syrup."

"My teenage years were marred because of the war. It affected all of us. We had bond drives and civilians had to give up a lot of things. We all had brothers, uncles, cousins, or fathers in the service. Someone came to school crying and you knew they got bad news and that was tough.[115] It was your teenage years. All able bodied men in town went (into the service)."[116]

"Emergency Furlough"

February 15, 1942

Dear Mother, Dad and Jean,

It's been raining here for two days and this place is a sea of mud.

I was in town all weekend and I fell tired and lousy right now.

I got your valentines. Thanks a lot.

I don't know whether I'll get home or not. I suppose if you should get an imaginary sickness I could get an emergency furlough.

I got a letter from Myers today. He certainly doesn't care for the army.

I can't think of anymore to write and I have a lot of studying to do. I'll write soon.

Love

Theodore

"Exams Next Week"

February 18, 1942

Dear Mother, Dad and Jean,

I got a letter from you today. The first one in a long time.

I'm sorry to hear your having trouble with the car. If you want to you can have the car transferred to your name. If I must sign any papers send them to me and I will sign them. I doubt if I'll have to though.

We have had classes three nights so far this week. We kicked about it now so we don't have to get up the next morning until 8:00 after we have a night class. That suits us fine.

I've got very good grades in my last three flights. I think I am beginning to learn something about navigation. We have our nine weeks exams next week. They will all be on celestial nav. and that's tough.

It finally stopped raining here. Last night we went to bed and it was nice and warm. About the middle of the night we woke up and almost froze to death. It got cold as the devil and changed in about two hours.

I hope you finally get your plans made to come down. If you make up your mind leave me know before you get here so I can reserve a hotel room. They're hard to get around here.

I can't think of anything else and besides it's time for class to start again.

Love

Theodore

February 18, 1942
Cpl. M. S. Myers
M.D. 109th F.A.
Camp Beauregard, La.
Dear "Teddy,"

One year ago yesterday I was inducted in to Federal service. It doesn't seem that long.

I know the Air Corps isn't a picnic. But the Army isn't either. The maneuvers in Carolina wasn't a picnic & I survived it. I think I could stand the Air Corps.

This outfit I am in is crazy. We moved the infirmary last night after supper & the first thing this morning we had to move it back where it was. This week-end we are to move to a new area in Camp. If I move that infirmary again I go crazy. Everyone is trying to get out of the outfit.

What day would be a good day to come out to see you? Would it be able to go for a plane ride? Do they have a guest house?

Every mo. the best man in his grade gets a day off & I won it this mo. I am going to try & hold it over to next mo. so I can have a week-end & Fri. or Mon. off.

Do you have inspection Sat?

We are just changed from a square division to a triangular div. A triangular div. is like a German Panzer Div.

All I have to do is persuade my parents & wife that the Air Corps is O.K. & I'll be with you.

The year I spent at S.U. & the year in the Army are lost. I haven't learned a thing in this army.

If we could only be back at S.U. & know what we know now.

I wonder how Houtz is getting along.

I'll try & get out to see you next mo.

We moved to Camp Livingston last weekend but my address is still Beauregard.

Good luck old Top

Monk

President Roosevelt signed Executive Order No. 9066 authorizing the internment of Japanese Americans in the interest of national defense. An estimated 110,000 were held in camps generally in the west. Other groups of Italian and German descent and naturalized citizens were also detained under the Order.

February 19, 1942
Thur eve
Dear Ted

You are being a real good boy by this week we have had three letters and that is real good to what we have been getting. I have a lot of big news to tell you this evening things have really been happening around here this week. The Westinghouse Electric Company leased the dye work building and will open in a few weeks they will employ about 1200 men and about 200 women – that is the biggest thing that has happened around here for a long time. And there is some kind of a big plant going up between here and Milton.

You said Meyers does not like the army so well. You know why that is don't you I don't think you would care much for the army either if you had just got yourself a wife.

It would not be a hard thing for me to do what you suggest in your letter but when and in what way, by letter, or how. Don't you think you will have some time off when you graduate. I don't know but I don't think it would be wise for us to try to come right now either since they are starting to ration gas in some states we would be in a terrible way if we got in some states where we could only get five gallons in a week.

Rev Crouse's wife and son Junior were up the other day they wanted your address so you will probably hear from him sometime. We are going to have a blackout on Sat evening from 10 to 10.15 in Sunbury, Norry, and Milton. I think we will all stay in. You say it is a sea of mud down there it had been here to until this morning. Yesterday it was like spring today it is down to about zero again.

I said I had a lot of news when I started but I am run out already. So I guess I will close and go to bed. You said you were in to town over the weekend could you stay away from the field over nite. Now I will close before I think of any more news.

All our love
Mother
Dad is sitting on a chair asleep he did not get as far as his studio coach this eve.

 *February 20, 1942*, Brigadier Gen. Ira C. Eaker took the Eighth Air Force Bomber Command Headquarters to High Wycombe, England.

February 20, 1942

Dear Teedy:

I have finaly came to the conclusion there is not any danger in doing this, as you have taken a rigid physical examination and in condition to take it, but really I am not much of a letter writer.

Well here is hoping you are a (shave tale) by the time you receive this letter, I suppose you know what is meant above it being very common in the last skirmish meaning a second Lt. if not here is one whom is writing for you.

So you are working very hard in camp and ice many crack ups are very common, will some of us back home one working a little harder these day, every Wednesday night from 8 to 12 I spend on watch at the Legion observation post spotting planes going in all directions, if you can picture in mind the hill directly back of the senior high school better known as Davis hill, it was moved to this location the first of this year, at first was out at Post's home, and we rented a trailer for same, now we have a building about 12 feet wide by 24 ft long with six windows, a stove, table, 6 chairs, a desk and telephone some one is on duty 24 hours a day. This Saturday night at 10 pm we are having our first black out starting fifteen minutes every thing is war every place you go.

I guess you have heard about the girls working in Weis's store, as the young men are getting very few they are leaving town pretty fast if they do not enlist its either the draft or leave for work in a defense plant the paper has good news in tonight Westinghouse electric is leasing the Dye work also news about a large plant to be erected near Montandon.

The family is feeling fine hope you are the same.

I guess this is all for this time hoping you can read my writing, it is a job.

Hoping to hear from you soon wishing you all the good luck

Joe

Ann sends a X

294 Orange St.,

Norry Pa.

Lorraine has signed up for me now each night for defense her work is to put diapers on lighting lugs during a black- out.

P.S. Mom would like to have a couple snap shot small pictures of you in uniform.

My True Course

"Shoot the Stars"

February 20, 1942

Friday

Dear Mother, Dad and Jean,

I haven't had a letter from you since Monday but I have a little time so I will write.

I have to fly tomorrow afternoon so I won't get out on Sat. night. On Sunday a pilot I know has to make a flight so I'm going along with him just for the fun of it and for the ride. It will be nice to go for a ride without always worrying about where you are going and how you are going to get there.

It got nice and warm today. It gives me spring fever.

I got some pictures developed today that I took up at Sikeston. I'll have some of Kelly Field in a few days. I may get some from the air on Sunday.

I have to go out and shoot the stars now and figure where I'm at from them. Just like they do with ships.

Love

Theodore

February 21, 1942

Mrs. R. S. Bickel

15 W. Washington St.

Bradford, Pa.

Dear Theodore:

Well now that I have gotten your Address why I will be able to write to you.

How do you like flying by now. You haven't been home since you went away have you. I wanted to send you a Xmas card but no body knew where you were at.

So on Wednesday I got a letter from your mother and she told me.

It sure is cold here today and snowing like everything. Charmaine went to the show and Jr is helping his dad today, he never know's what to do on Saturdays, so that is a good place for him.

Theodore there were a couple of Nurses from here sent down there I think, the one girl I knew, her name is Josephine Monto Calvo. she took care of Charmaine when she up in the hospital.

Will you be staying there at Kelly Field or will they be sending you some place else.

Well Theodore I don't know any thing else to tell you, I don't know what is going on in Norry because I only get home once a year.

Every body is ok here and hope you are in the best of health.

Drop me a few lines I would like to hear from you.
Love Mart.
If you can't write why fly up some week end.

February 21, 1942
Dear Theadore.

How do you like the army air corpse? It is snowing here. I suppose that you like the army air corpse. Theadore have you seen any snakes in Texas? Well Theadore I have to close my letter.

love Charmaine Bickel

February 22, 1942
Sunday eve
Dear Ted

Well you know how much has been happening around here I have not written since Thursday evening and I still do not have anything to write about. We had our first test blackout last nite it lasted for fifteen minutes the town was dark as the dickens without lights the cars all had to stop and turn out there lights the buses were stopped and all trains that went through the towns the blackouts were in were turned low the towns were Sunbury & Noth'd & Milton.

We were out at Martha's & Lee's today for dinner it was her birthday. Lee had a big birthday cake baked and got her an automatic toaster it is swell. She was telling me about your admirer you have up there. There are people by the name of Goves bought the mansion and gas station and they have a daughter by the name of Vera and I guess the way they say she likes all men. Well anyway she seen your pictures at Martha's so she wanted your address she was going to write you and she told Martha she just had to bring you over when you come home. Martha told her she better be careful before some one found it out. Do you still think you will get home? I do not know what to do if you don't everybody thinks we would be doing the wrong thing to start out by car now. Mr. Weis said we should never think of it on account of the tire part alone and the other evening I was down to Dr Ennis and he said did you say you were going to Texas I said why yes he said well I guess you changed your mind I ask why he said why on account of the gas question some places he said you would only be able to get five gal a week. So I do not know what to do. I hope you can come home that would clear up everything. And end my worries.

Wendle Mertz left yesterday. The local draft got him after all. I really feel sorry for him he would have liked anything better than that. Bobby Snyder and his wife have a little baby boy. Well I guess that will be all

All our Love
Mother

"Radio Fixes Were Falling"

February 22, 1942

Dear Mother, Dad and Jean,

Something happened to the weather last night and today the weather is lousy. The ceiling is 0 and it's raining again. As a result I don't go on any flight today. This must be the raining season for Texas.

I got a letter from you this morning. One of the fellows brought it over to me. I didn't get up until 12 o'clock. It feels good to lay in bed. I don't get a chance to do it very often.

One letter you are talking about coming down and the next one you aren't. I only said that if you do come down to leave me know. I'm probably be able to get home sometime soon after I get my commission.

I get about two letters from M. Myers every week now. He's like(ly) to join the Air Corps but he says his wife and parents won't let him.

Did you ever get the papers from my government insurance policy. The policy should have been sent to you. It is for $10,000. so I would like to know.

I got a new instructor here. He's just a young fellow and a devil of a nice guy. On my flight yesterday my radio fixes were falling 30 and 40 miles away from where I was. I turned around to him and said, "Hell, this radio is broke." I never did find out whether it was me or the radio, but he couldn't make it work either.

I have a lot of notes that I must copy and a lot of studying that I must do so I will have to stop now. I wrote to Martha and Lee last night and sent Jimmie a lot of pictures of airplanes.

Love

Theodore

"Defense Bond"

February 23, 1942

Monday eve

Dear Ted.

This letter is going to be short it is getting late. I just fixed a box for your birthday I hope you get it till then you should see dad and I it takes us a whole evening to get a box fixed about the time I think that sure is alright he says now do you think that is alright and starts me wondering all over again. I had a letter today and in it you said you had a letter the first for a long time I do not know why. I always write if not every evening every other evening.

You said we were to let you know about our plans about coming down I am afraid we will have to give them up. Everybody tells me I should never undertake

that trip the way everything is right now meaning the gas – tires and when you
need repairs or parts for a car. You can hardly get them now. Mr Weis said I should
never try that trip by car now. He said he knew what a trip it was when you could
get anything without trouble he advised us to go by train but I could never think
about that right now it would cost about $80 just for train fare. So you try real
hard to come home. It would not cost you near as much. And we could all see you.

I am enclosing a note Jean wrote you it must be important she has it all sealed
up. So it must be important. I bought our first defense bond last week I hope I can
buy some more. Well I must close we want to hear the Pres. speech and than to bed.

Be good and don't eat too much on your birthday and we would all like to be
with you to help celebrate it
All our love
Mother

"The President's Speech"

 On the 210th anniversary of George Washington's birthday President Roosevelt warned the public of giving up and pursuing a course of isolationism. He asked his listeners to look at a world map, follow an illustration of the consequences of pulling out warships and airplanes to the home front, and justified the continuation of military efforts in Europe and the Pacific.

Roosevelt contrasted the advantage of Japan's control in the Pacific and ability to strike the North American continent in contrast with the range of our bombers and pursuit aircraft and other factors. " . . . your map will show that it would have been a hopeless operation for us to send the Fleet to the Philippines through thousands of miles of ocean, while all those island bases were under the sole control of the Japanese."

The president criticized American countrymen who spread "widely exaggerated" accounts of the casualties, ship and aircraft losses at Pearl Harbor, and the Axis propaganda. He called on the American people to keep up "uninterrupted production" of airplanes, tanks, guns, and ships.

Roosevelt cited the suffering of the Chinese people who had suffered grievous losses and their capital city of Chungking "almost wiped out of existence."[117]

February 23, 1942

Dear Brother

I know that the perfect letter writer would say I am off my beam. But I hope you don't care. Would you please do me a favor sent me a big pair of wings. I want to wear them on my sweaters. That is if you can.

Did Mother tell you I got in the Kiwanis Lassies. I wanted that more than anything else in High School. Schools going swell. I love Latin.

I hope you can come home. I want to show you off. You probably will not know me. Mick says I have grown up. He would like to know what you will think of me.

I can't think of anything to tell you.

Happy Birthday

Love

Jean

February 23, 1942

310 West College

Bucknell University

Lewisburg, Pa.

Dear Tedie: - I am pleased to say that I finally got some signs from you that you are still alive! A post card and a letter in one week too much; I imagine that maybe Mary Jane must have suggested something to you in one of her letters for I remember saying something about it to her in Sunday school a few weeks ago.

I am glad every thing is going good for you. I wish you would explain to me though just what your standing is now as well as your duties and what you expect to become as the years roll by. Outside of knowing you have something to do with the Air Corps, I don't know very much about you except the little that I've read in the papers (you're becoming quite a hero in Norry!)

Mother said that M.J. is now working in Weis's so I guess she's trying to fill your shoes. One of these days you'll be coming home and have a big military wedding with crossed swords and all.

My life is very much the same as ever. I'm still spending a good bit of time in Sunbury. How much longer I'll be doing that, I can't say! However, I have accepted a job for after graduation. It is with the Niagara Alkali Co. in Niagara Falls, N.Y. and my duties will be those of a research engineer, if I can avoid Uncle Sam long enough. It seems funny – you were trying hard to get in the service and I'm trying just as hard to stay out of it, because I see no future in it for me. I had several other offers – one from Standard Oil Co., Bethlehem Steel Corp., Civil Service, M.I.T., and I almost accepted one from Illinois Ins. of Technology to do graduate work; however, the salary offered by this firm in Niagara Falls was to good to miss.

It seems funny how quickly our lives have changed in such a short time. If you do not get a furlough before June, we probably won't be seeing each other again, or at least not often! I hope anyway that we've been good enough friends to at least exchange a few letters once in a while!

Well time and paper is getting short and I have some exams coming up so I'll sign off! Answer this when you get time and tell me more about yourself! Incidentally, Olley and all your friends are well as far as I know and we're all rooting for you! Best of luck and "Keep 'em flying" (or isn't that your motto?)

Your pal

Buck

X – This isn't for you but for some of those good looking "senoritas" down there! Who are Bucknell Men?

February 25, 1942

Hello ole Boy,

Well, I know it would happen sooner or later.

I arrived here yesterday with a bunch of other guys. Most of the sandblowers were sent here too.

Call me up for I would like to talk to you. I am in bldg #422, the new barracks. Start flying tomorrow.

Bill Briggs

"Class Until 10:30"

February 26, 1942

Dear Mother, Dad and Jean,

I haven't written because I am busy as h. We have tests all day Friday and Saturday and they are keeping us busy as the devil. We're studying all of the time.

I haven't got my drivers license here so I won't be able to sign it and send it home. It's down on my bed.

I got a letter from Martha Bickel yesterday. She said you sent her my address. I haven't got time to write the letters I have to and I get still more to answer.

There is a new class here. They came in last night. We were to class until 10:30 last night and had to come and start in again at 7:30.

I won't be able to write until after the tests so don't look for a letter.

Love

Theodore

February 27, 1942
328 King Street
Northumberland, Pa.
Dear Cadet

Happy Birthday! even though it is a little late. I should have written before, but, you now how I am.

I just was thinking about you and so here's my thoughts. I was just looking over a few catalogs I got from some air schools and I thought of A/C Van Kirk. I guess I'm getting pretty air minded or I'm walking on air or something.

I've sent away to some air schools for some information, and the way I feel now I would like to go to one of them. I've received catalogs from Parks Air School – (I guess thats where Klinger is), Spartan School of Aeronautics, in Tulsa Oklahoma, Lincoln Aeronautical Institute in Lincoln, Nebraska, Curtiss-Wright Technical Institute in Glendale, California. I received a letter from Dallas Air School, but I didn't get the catalog yet.

Bucknell doesn't seem to interest me anymore. I was thinking about taking up Commerce & Finance, but I could never picture myself enjoying life couped up in offices.

Right now I think I would rather go to Curtiss-Wright than any of the other air schools. For one reason its not as expensive as the others and I always did want to go to California. That must be hereditary – that's where my Dad & Mother were hitched.

Curtiss-Wright Technical Institute is at Grand Central Air Terminal at Glendale. That's where Howard Hughes finished his world flight. It was originally organized by Curtiss-Wright Corporation, but in 1934 they turned it over to Mayor C. Moseley. He was a member of Eddie Rickenbackers Squadron in the last war.

Hows everything going with the A/C these fine days.

How did you and that Mexican de-icer get along. Mrs. Phillip told me you were stepping out with a young chicken with a rich old man. Don't worry I didn't tell M.J. I usually secure full data on A/C T.V. every time I go into Weis!

Its a good thing they put Zong in the dairy dept. because those checking booths were about to collapse under the terrible strain.

When your seven months are up you better get the hell back home and surprise everybody. I'm starting to itch for a little tennis so start to practice up a little if you have time.

Well paper is getting a little scarce right here so I'll just say so long and don't forget to write.

B.B. (Bill Brennen)
P.S. I shave twice a week – I'm a MAN. Wahoo!

Eddie Rickenbacker, a World War I flying ace, survived dogfights with the Red Baron. He raced cars in 1914 at 134 mph earning $40,000 a year. When he entered the service, Eddie was the staff driver for Gen. John Pershing. Rickenbacker received his commission as a lieutenant after only twelve flights in a Spad.[118] During the North African campaign Rickenbacker spoke to the troops at Chateaudun du Rhumel.[119]

"Getting Religious"

February 28, 1942

Dear Mother, Dad and Jean,

Well the nine weeks tests are over and I haven't flunked any yet. I don't know what all of my grades are but I know three of them were 92, 94 and 88. I don't think many of the boys have much better grades then that.

We just got through eating and I got ready to go to town. Today is payday and we're waiting to get paid before we go in.

I got a letter from Charmaine Bickel today and a box of writing paper and a card from her parents. Lee and Martha sent me a dollar and a card. I got cards from almost everyone.

Today I got a letter from the Golden Rule Sunday school class with a book of Lenten devotions. The fellows said I was getting religious. This is some of the paper that Martha Bickel sent to me.

I don't think it's such a good idea for you to start down here either. If I stay here as an instructor I won't be able to get home but then you can come to see me any time. If I stay here I'll send you the money to come down. If they send me out on tactical duty I will get a 30 day leave. I'd like to be sent to Atlantic patrol work from Mitchell Field in N.Y.

Jean wants a pair of wings to wear so tell her I'll send them to her as soon as I get to the store to buy them.

We have to fall out for pay formation now and I don't want to miss that.

Love

Theodore

Most the boys who were in my class at Sikeston were sent here to Kelly for advanced training. I was with them last night and we had a good time.

March 1942, the first B-17E was delivered to the RAF in England and designated Fortress IIA.

"Party at the Hotel"

March 1, 1942

Dear Mother, Dad and Jean,

I wrote you a letter yesterday and never did get around to mailing it so I will put it in with this one. I have so many letters to write today that I don't know where to start.

I signed my driver's license finally so you soon will be getting that.

Last night I was in town and I saw all of the boys from Sikeston. My class and my upper class are both here now. Some of them are at Kelly and some are at Brooksfield. We got together and had a party at the Hotel last night.

I'd like to write to everyone who sent me a card and thank them but I haven't got time so you can tell them thanks for me. I am going to write to M. Bickel, Martha and Lee and Grandma Snyder and a lot of others.

I didn't get the box you sent yet but I probably will tomorrow the mail isn't brought in today.

I don't think you should start down here in the car either. These days a car is something to look at not to drive.

I had a letter from Bostian again today. He'll soon be through and I guess he's got a good job. He can have his chemistry. Since I've been flying, a lab or a store would seem like an awful boring place.

I haven't got anything else to write about so I'll have to stop. I hope I have enough stamp(s) to mail all of the letters I want to write.

Love

Theodore

Tell Jean I have a pair of wings but they're not the large ones like she wants so she'll have to wait until I get time to get them.

March 1, 1942

Sunday eve

Dear Ted,

Really if things keep up like the(y) have been I will have to take time off from work to write to you. We have had company every evening lately till late. Yesterday Martha and Jimmie were in all day until late well you know when they come in we always have such a big day I am so tired I can hardly get to bed at nite. Well on top of that Martin and Catherine and their two kids were over today now they have me just about worn out they just went home dad missed some of his radio programs and that did not please him any too well. I just said to dad when I sit at home here and would have liked to had company before I went to work no one ever came.

Oh yes there were some more here Grandma Snyder, Clifford and Kathryn and Betty. Now Clifford just came in again he is trying to find Jean and Mick to help solve a problem for Elwood that he has to have down at Middletown. They were all wishing you were here to work it for them. Right now they have Mick and Jean and Cliff working on it. I have some other big new to tell you Dr. Ennis is leaving town. I'll tell you that was a let down to me I don't know what I am going to do or who to get now he leaves near (the) 15(th) he is going to the Willis eye hospital at Phila. they say it is a very large hospital. Do you think you will get home?

Bob Fletcher is home again and he was just home about six week ago. Bob Weis is in Texas to he left in July and has never been home now he is coming home on a ten day leave but they said he would only be home four days it would take 3 days to come and 3 days to get back. I said gee I only wished you would get home four days.

Dad is in a terrible bad way you know Westinghouse is going in the Converting works and everybody says it is going to be so good and pay such big money and he would like to make some of it and he does not know what to do. I do wish he would get some thing else to do and make more money so I could quit work because I don't think I can keep working for long I am so tired all the time I an hardly move when I get home.

How were your things when you got them I hope you could eat them. Well I finally got rid of all the kids now I think I had better go to bed or I will not be able to get up in the morning.

When I am not writing I can think of dozens of things I want to tell you I guess I will have to write them down when I think of them.

Be good
All our love
~~Theodo~~ Mother
You can tell who I am thinking about

March 2, 1942
Cpl. M. S. Myers
109th F.A. Bn.
Camp Beauregard, La.
A.P.O. #28
Dear "Teddy,"

This is a moving outfit. We are gong to move again Thurs. to a new area. Then our next move is to ?.

I'll let you know about a week before I come down to see you. At present I am hoping they will give us a furlough. So I am holding on to my money.

It is impossible to convince my wife & parents that it is O.K. to join the Air

Corps.

This outfit has me about nuts. All I do is sit around. Loaf day in & day out. This medical outfit doesn't do a thing.

Congratulations on your birthday "Teddy." I got this clipping out of the S'by paper. A fellow in service battery got the paper. His name is Charles Rodenbush from S'by.

I'll be seeing you soon.

Your Pal,

"Monk"

March 4, 1942

Wed eve

Dear Ted

We got your license today with the money in it. You must think they have raised but gee it was a big help thanks a lot. Are you sure you are not cutting yourself short. You might still get a chance to come home and you are supposed to buy a ring you know. I have not seen M.J. for an age I don't know what become of her I have not been down and she has not been up.

Did you get your things alright and how were they? How many cards did you get? Jean was going around telling all the kids it was your birthday.

How did you come through your tests?

You said in one of your letters about Martha Bickel writing to you and you did not have time to answer what you had. Well Martha has been asking me for your address before Xmas already so I could not stall any longer.

Jean just come home from the movies she went to see they "died with there boots on" she said mother you missed something. She said it was a good picture she had a good cry over it.

I don't know if you can read this letter or not but I have quite a bit of work to do yet it is nine thirty now. I have some scandal to tell you about (name withheld) when I write you the next time and have more time. I cleaned your room good this evening dad wanted to know why. I told him I thought you were coming home.

I dreamed the other nite you came home during the nite and went to bed so when I got up in the morning I went over and looked. But you were not there. I hope it does come true sometime.

Do you think it will?

Well I guess if you read this you will have an evenings work will do better next time

Love

Mother

"First Night Flight"

March 6, 1942

Dear Mother, Dad and Jean,

You certainly must have had an awful time with all of your company. One thing I miss is the relations not sticking their nose in my business while I'm down here.

I went on my first night flight last night and it was a doozey. Everything went wrong. It's really nice flying at night though especially the big cities like Houston and San Antonio.

Next week we go on two flights to New Orleans. I hope we get fogged in and spend a few days there. It is about 482 mile.

The things I got were in very good condition. None of the cookies were broken and everything was fresh.

I flew this afternoon and had to fly last night so I'm pretty tired today.

We'll have all of our work done in about two weeks and then it will just be review until we graduate. I think I flunked that flight last night and if I flunk many more I may get a chance to fly again in the R.A.F. It's the first one I flunked so I'm not worried very much.

I'm going to go to bed now.

Write

Love

Theodore

March 8, 1942

Sunday eve

Dear Ted,

We are still alive up here but I suppose you thought we were dead. But you said you had so many letters to I thought I would give you a chance to get caught up on some of your other letters. We were out to Martha & Lee's tonite for supper. You should hear Jim I bet he ask me twenty five times this afternoon when you would be home. I wish you could see him with those wings he is as proud as he can be of them. You said in your last letter if you were made an instructor you would not be home but if you went on tactical duty you would get a furlough. Well we would all like to see you I cannot tell you how much but I still would like to see you as an instructor I suppose you think that sounds funny but you do not know how much I have worried already about you being sent out of the states. When you are through and if you stay as an instructor I will feel better about that. I hear they had a party for you for your birthday. I am glad you had such a good time on your birthday I suppose you think you are your own boss now and really feel grown up. How are you getting along with your horse back riding? Did you get your box yet I sent you for your birthday?

Elwood is finally going to be married on Easter. He can't back out now anymore Bert has already bought her clothes I guess she thought she had better get them before he changed his mind again. Grandma Snyder and grandpa and Cliff were up at Martha's too. Grandma said she had not heard from you for quite awhile.

Mary Jane was telling me the other evening that Olley has to go to the army I guess as soon as he is thru school this spring. She told me that Monroe Meyers is getting a furlough for Easter. It would be nice if you came home. If you could come home for the prom Mick is here as usual I just ask him where it is he said they have not set a date yet. He is getting to be a regular visitor.

Donald Steele and Bob Baker go to the army on Sat they are getting our town pretty well thinned out and I forgot Bill Riechenbach and Bob Bell. Jean and I were to the movies this other evening we seen Ben Riechenbach Jean said "hello Benjamin" he said my name is just plain Ben. Jean says he hates to be called Benjamin. Well I guess I will have to close I still have to get my and dads clothes ready to go to work that is a job every Sunday evening. Cliff just come in again he is our visitor to every Sunday evening.

Well be good till I see you hope that will be before long.

All our Love

Mother

March 11, 1942

Wed eve

Dear Ted.

I will answer your letter we had yesterday. I told Jean to answer it last evening but she always has so much to do she never gets around to it especially when she has to do some work around the house yet. I have had one of my headaches again I have been in bed for the last three days. I am feeling better now. I think I will go back to work again tomorrow. The letter we had from you yesterday said you thought you flunked your flight don't tell me that you are going to fail in navigation at the last minute. You always get to the last couple of weeks than something happens. So you get to work and so something about it. As for going to R.A.F. I don't think the chances of getting in there are so good anymore two fellows from Shamokin were in Canada trying to get in it last week I seen in the paper and couldn't get in it. They said they had plenty of flyers right now. Well I started this letter at 7 oclock now it is ten and I will finish it Martha and Lee came in Lee goes to air raid warden school. He said they learned how to bandage tonite. Did you take your flights yet that you were going to take this week? You had better not flunk them. You know I will be worrying about you now until you are thru and I know what you are going to do.

Dad said John Hilbish went to Baltimore today to see about getting a Commission in the army he said he was getting tired of taking there you might know what over around there I guess there are about 4 or five fellows from over there that must go.

Jean said she bet you look like a baby blimp if you weigh 172 lbs how about it maybe that is your trouble you are to heavy for the planes.

Do you still like it in Texas? and how warm is it? it has been terrible warm up here I just ask dad if he thought it was that much warmer where you are my goodness I will never be able to stand the heat if I came down this summer.

You can be glad you are in the army you do not need to think any thing about these things you can't get and I'll tell you can tell it around here when you go the stores. Well I had better close I am writing this in bed and dad just got in and is shaking the bed. I don't know if you can read it

All our Love
Mother

March 12, 1942
Dear Ted,

When you read this letter you will know by the paper that I did not have much. But I thought I had better hunt up some paper and write to you for by the way the letter sounds I got today I think you are being a very bad boy no wonder you flunked your flight the other night. You have been telling about the big parties at hotel and beautiful women. I wonder if you are going to have money to come home if you do get a furlough. I wish you would make up your mind so I know what you are going to do. One letter you say you won't get home another you will.

Don't you think you will have a chance to be an instructor you said if you did you would not be home. You say you are not going to spend a fortune for that ring either you must be stringing her along. She thinks you have it. As for paying a fortune you can get nice ones at home here for $35.00 but I don't suppose you save that much or probably if you see so many beautiful girls down there you do not want to get it for her. You say you would get a pay before you get home if that is all you have you won't even have enough to come home.

You said about having some fellows car all day Sunday. What did you do for a driver's license? This letter sounds like old times doesn't it I still have to scold you to make you behave. What do you think you will do or go when you are thru there?

Jean was just telling me Mary Jane got a $1.00 week raise down at the store. I guess she is tickled to death with it. I have an awful lot of things to tell you when *you come home.*

Jean has Barry over here. He is standing by the door trying to get her to take him out you should hear them.

I suppose by the time you get this letter you will have made your flight to La. I hope you make out better on that one than you did on your other. I worked today again I just came home now I must get dad's supper so I will write later when I get paper and have more time. Now you behave and be good.

All our Love
Mother

March 13, 1942
Dear Mother, Dad and Jean,

I haven't anything to do until 11:00 o'clock tonight and I have a class at that time so I may as well write letters for a while.

I had a letter from you yesterday but I can't remember any questions to answer.

Today we all got ready to go to New Orleans and the flight was called off. Then we got all ready to go to Wichita, Kansas and that was canceled. I wish they'd make up their minds.

Next Saturday our class will be the top class around here. Then we'll be able to go out every night until 12:00 and have things pretty easy. It looks as though I'll finally get through being a cadet.

Today they put me in a Link trainer to see how much I remembered about flying. I'm still supposed to be able to fly. I was alright until they told me to try a steep turn and then I went into a spin. I never did get out of it. It's a good thing I wasn't flying a real plane.

They had us filling out Reserve Officer's forms today and wanted to know how long it would take us to get ready to leave home. As though I were home.

It's hot as h. here. It's as hot here now as it ever gets at home. They haven't even got a river big enough to swim in.

I have to go out and learn some new stars now. So good bye.
Love
Theodore

March 15, 1942
Sunday afternoon
Dear Ted

I will have to write your letter now because I am so filled up I can not move around much we were over to Johnnie and Bettys for dinner today and we ate so much we can hardly move. We just come home it is five oclock. I bet you can guess what we are doing listening to the shadow we still always listen to that on Sunday evening. What have you been doing today? Have you made your nite flight to New Orleans yet? I have only had one letter all week so you must be pretty busy again.

I have been feeling pretty good the last couple of days I went back to work again. Mary Jane and Madelyn were up to see me the other evening and I was not home Jean said M.J. said she heard I was sick she came up to see me. Jeans said I never stay home long enough when I am sick for some one to come and see me. You should see dad right now he has a black eye and is it black he looks like one of those dogs have one black eye and one white eye. There was a chain on the garage door flew around and hit him in the eye. He sure has some shiner. Dad said I was to ask you what you thought about selling the car. Some fellow over at the garage told him he knew where he could sell for $550 dad said he would not take any less we have been having some trouble with it lately. The gears in the transmission went bad dad took it to the garage and they had to put all new gears in it but that was all we could do we could not drive it at all we could put it in reverse but it would not move. We had to have all four new gears put in. I said to dad I hate to let it go now we have put so darn many new things on it.

But if we did I could quit working so I do not know what to do. What do you think? Do you have any idea what you will do? Do you think you will get home? Do you think you have a chance of becoming an instructor? I hope so. Where are those pictures you were going to send me?

The weather is beautiful here right now I don't know how long it will last but I hope it last I am tired of winter this year it has been a very cold winter up here. Of course you don't know anything about that. Dad said I should tell you Cam Baker was asking about you. You know who I mean don't you the National Biscuit salesman. He told dad he always knew you were smart. He said he has a son wants to get in he said he wasn't very bright so he did not know how he was going to make out. I must tell you about my dream last nite I dreamed we had an air raid here we were raided twice I had a terrible time all nite. Well this is enough for one day I won't have anything to write next time.

Love
Mother

"Parties at the Gunter Hotel"

March 15, 1942
Dear Mother, Dad and Jean,

It's a good thing Sunday rolls around once a week or I wouldn't have any time at all to write letters.

Our flight to New Orleans was cancelled on account of bad weather so we have to fly it tomorrow. I don't know whether I'll fly or not. Yesterday we had a track meet here and I was running a race with only shorts on. I tripped and fell and tore all the skin off of my hands, elbows, knees, legs and stomach. They took me to the hospital and now I'm all bandaged up.

I've only been horseback riding a few times and it's O.K. except when the horse starts or stops suddenly.

I saw some fellows last night that knew Sam Fletcher and Bob Weis. They're out at Randolph Field. I never get time to go out to see them.

You don't have to worry much about flunking that flight. My instructor said it wasn't me it was night effects on radar waves so he passed me. On my first two celestial missions we went to Jackson, Miss. and I got a 90 & 92. I haven't flunked a flight yet. I know I can get in the R.A.F. though. After all I had 64 hours and navigation training.

It's hot as the devil down here. I hope they send me some place that's cooler if they send me out of here.

Every weekend from now until we graduate our class is having big parties down at the Gunter Hotel. They're really some parties too.

I have to stop now and go to bed.

Love

Theodore

"Paid for the Ring"

March 16, 1942

Dear Mother, Dad and Jean,

Our flight to N.O. (New Orleans) was called off again today. They said the weather in N.O. was bad again.

It's getting dry, hot and dusty down here. We just got two big electric fans from the store room and turned them on.

I had to go over to the hospital today and get my wounds dressed again. They always wash them out with alcohol and it burns like h.

I bought Jean a pair of big navigators wings today so I'll send them home with this letter. You don't have to worry about me spending too much. All of them parties are costing me only 8 dollars. I paid for the ring already but the jeweler still has it in his safe. $48.

I haven't got anymore to write about now so I may as well stop. We have our twelve weeks tests this Friday but I don't worry much about them any more.

Love

Theodore

March 18, 1942
Dad's draft no. is 390
Wed eve
Dear Ted.

I am all alone this evening so I will write you a long letter that is if you can read it I am writing it in bed. Jean and Mick went to the movies to see how green is my valley and dad has not come home from work yet. It is eight oclock but I guess he is up at Lewisburg they are opening a big store up there tomorrow. Did you go on your flight this week? You must have done something we have not heard from you. I see in this evenings paper one of the Fentschermacher boys from town is at Kelley Field. Jean is being initiated in Kiwanis lassies you should see them they have to wear their clothes all wrong side out braid their hair and wear ribbons on them paint a K.L. on their forehead with lip stick and put a big sign on their backs with "I am a lemon squeeze me" on it. You can tell spring is coming you should hear the kids out side. I think there must be about 150 out there the way it sounds Faye Seasholtz was taken to the hospital yesterday I guess they are going to operate for appendicitis. Runyans wife left him she is over at Bakers with her two kids they are just one big happy family.

I see Earl Strausser is moving to Phila. I wonder who will get Seasholtz's apartment now. You said in one of your letters that you did not get a letter with questions so you did not have any to answer. Well to tell you the truth I have run out of questions I don't have any to ask. Now I guess you really know I don't feel good when I don't have questions. I have been feeling like the dickens every since last week. I was so darn sick last nite from 12 to 4 I thought I'd die and Dr Ennis isn't here any more. I went down to Freline the other evening he tried to tell me my pressure was 270 I don't know if he knows what he is talking about or not but that is how high it was when I went to the hospital. He gave me some medicine but it makes me sick enough to die every time I take it. I don't know what I am going to do if I don't get someone to do for me like Ennis did.

I don't know if I told you about George Mertz or not. He was a brakeman on the railroad and he got caught between the cars somehow over in the yards and his arm was all mangled they had to take it off at the shoulder. Dad just stopped in on his way down he has to take the truck over yet and put it away he said he would be home at 9.30 or 10 so that makes a pretty long day. He just brought your drivers license home so I will put it in this letter some fellow over there brings them along up from Harrisburg for us. We haven't got the license for the car yet I don't know what we are going to do about it yet. We haven't even seen about leaving it changed or you will probably have to sign the application. You know I could still give you and dad a swift kick for buying that car if it wasn't for that we wouldn't have to

worry so much. Good way to end isn't it.
   Love anyway
   Mother

March 19, 1942
   I won't be here long but I'm going to look the place over. We flew over the Gulf all afternoon. You can't tell where you are without seeing land.
   Teedy[120]

March 19, 1942
Thur eve
Dear Ted,
   We got two letters from you today you must write them and save them and mail them all at one time. You should not have anything to say about me not writing this week. I have written You a letter every evening this week if you get them all you should have one every day. How are you? Were you skinned real bad or were they just brush burns when you fell? Are they getting alright? Goodness you must be getting heavy to bruise yourself up like that when you fall. Dad was scared you should have seen his face when I told him about you falling he thought you fell out of a plane. They are having there flood supper tomorrow nite he said he guessed he would have to go. You said in your letter you knew you get in R.A.F. if you tried what would you want in R.A.F. for I think we need plenty of fellows for ourselves so you just tell me why you would want in R.A.F. than you said you went into a spin the other day and never did get out of it so you would probably have to learn all over again. I only wish you were 15 and Jean 21 I would not have half the worries I am having right now. You said they wanted to know how long it would take you to get ready to leave home maybe they will let you come home for awhile. But I know it will be just twice as bad for us than when you go back again. You say it is so warm are you getting use to the heat you should be now. We could use some of that heat here it is very cold again and the river is almost flood stage again so if you had some of it you would have a place to go swimming.
   I suppose after this Saturday you fellows will think you are the head men around Kelley Field I suppose now your parties will last all nite. Dad said I should tell you to have a good time he only wished he was with you boys I ask him what about Jean and I he said well he would have to make enough to keep us too.
   You know if this keep up very long I am afraid he might have to go. I said that at supper this evening he said now don't start and worry about that yet. His no. is 390 and it has already been drawn. I don't know what in the world they are going to do with all these men there are about two coaches of draftee leave the Pennsy

station every day. Well I did not moan or complain about one thing in this letter dad said he bet you hated to get a letter I was always grumbling about something I told him I only wanted to make you feel at home. Do you know when you really will graduate? And do you think you will get home? Take good care of yourself.

All our Love
Mother

March 21, 1942, Robert D. Young, an older brother of Mary Jane Young and resident of Northumberland, Pennsylvania, and a graduate of four years of high school enlisted at Fort George G. Meade.[121]

March 22, 1942
Sunday eve
Dear Ted.

Well Sunday is just about gone again that and Saturday are two days that always go fast for me we had a big day today we were over at Grandma Snyder's all day. This afternoon Cliff wanted to go for a ride he wanted to go to Indiantown Gap but he wanted to go by Shamokin and come home by Harrisburg well we went out by Shamokin and in place of going the way I always went he crossed about four mountains and finally ended up by being within about four mile of Pottsville in place of Indiantown Gap when I found we were on the wrong road I told him we needed a navigator. We finally did get back to where we turned wrong and got to Indiantown Gap. You should see that place now to what it was when we were down there. Cliff drove all around it I told him we could not get in but when we got there we seen other cars in there so he said well if they go in we can so we drove in and all around it. I think it is about as big at Norry. They say there are about 2000 there. Elwood just told us he believes he will have to go in about June. I don't know if I told you or not but he is being married on Easter he said well he would not have been married yet but that was one way of getting some time off for Easter.

Grandpa Van Kirk smashed up his car the other evening he smashed it up right it can not be repaired so I guess he is going to buy another one but Grandma does not know that. He told dad he was.

How soon do you think you will be home after you graduate? and for how long. I sure hope you get home for I don't know how I could stand it to come down and see you if it is as hot as you say it is down there. I guess I did not tell you about the gang over at the warehouse ask for a raise and Bohner told them if it didn't suit them they knew what they could do he could get a lot of men that were willing to work for that. Well I guess this will be all for this evening I am darn tired.

How are your skinned arm and legs getting?
   All our Love
   Mother

March 23, 1942
Dear Theodore,
   I guess you thought I forgot to answer your letter but I didn't.
   I had been pretty busy I was going to the cooking school they had here at the theater for a week and I am just getting caught up on my work.
   Well I suppose you know by now where you will be going but I hope you stay at Kelly Field as an instructor.
   I know that your mother would feel a lot better.
   You said you haven't had very many cold days, boy it has been snowing all day yesterday and today. I wish we had some warm weather.
   I had a letter from Mill last week they are in Baltimore now boy they sure do get around.
   We heard Claudette Colbert on the Air tonight with Lowell Thomas and she said she thought that Uncle Sam should give boys in the Air Corp 2 weeks or a month at Sun Valley before they are sent away.
   It would be pretty nice wouldn't it.
   Well now I guess I can finish writing your letter Sissy up sleigh riding down front and fell and cut her lip so we had to take her down to the doctors and he put 3 stitches in it she sure has tough luck.
   Well I guess that is all for this time write and leave us know where you are as we will be anxious to know.
   Mart
   Please excuse the paper & pencil and we will keep our fingers crossed for you.

"Navigators Needed"

March 23, 1942
Dear Mother, Dad and Jean,
   I'll have to make this letter short because I haven't got much time but I do have some news. They took the best 30 men out of our class and we are going to graduate us on April 1.
   I don't know what for but my class commander told us that they needed 30 navigators someplace in a hurry and we were elected. I don't know whether it's to stay here as instructors or not but they do need some instructors. He also told us that we would have to work like dogs until April 1 so I don't know whether I'll have

much time to write or not. I'll try to answer all your questions though because I know you'll have a lot of them.

Love

Theodore

Dutch ~ We were in formation when thirty names were called out. What is going on here? We were pulled off. We asked some questions and told that it was enough for us to know that navigators were needed for a group going overseas and we were going to be it. Okay with us. But what they forgot to tell us was that we are going to do it in half the time. Doubled up on the calisthenics and class work they damn near killed us. We were going to school day and night. It took us about a week to convince the instructors that we couldn't do all the calisthenics for Christ's sake. Some of the exercises were cut out and we did graduate and finish in half the time. I still have the orders with the thirty names (See Appendix A). Teddy Hokenstad, one of my best friends, was flying overseas when a shell burst in the bomb bay. Abraham Dreiseszun became a major general in the Supply Corps after the war.[122]

"Don't Worry"

March 24, 1942

Dear Mother, Dad and Jean,

I finally got the low down on being hurried up. They picked the thirty men in the class who would get through early and have to graduate them on April 1. We will go out on tactical duty but we don't know where to probably West Palm Beach, Washington or Atlantic or Pacific patrol.

Boy we really have to work to get through. We fly tomorrow and have final Metro tests the next day. Saturday we fly to Oklahoma City and from St. Louis. Sat. night we fly from St. Louis to New Orleans. We spend the night in New Orleans and the next afternoon fly back to Oklahoma City and Sunday night return to Kelly. We have tests Monday and notebook critique on Tuesday and graduate Wednesday morning. We'll probably leave for our new posts the next day.

I leave you know where I'm going as soon as I find out. Until I tell you where I'm going I'll be at Kelly Field. If it's someplace around the east I may stop in at home.

Don't worry about me going any place for a long time because they won't send me out of the country for at least six months.

You can see Mary Jane. & tell her about this I haven't got time to write until at least Thursday.

Love

Theodore

My True Course 197

March 28, 1942

Hi Honey

I'm on my graduation flight – I hope. I'll be in New Orleans about three hrs. from now. I'll let you know where I'm going as soon as I know.

Teedy[123]

Dear Mother & Dad,

I'm on my graduation flight – I hope. I'll hit New Orleans about three hours from now. I'll send you another card from there.

Ted

March 29, 1942

Sunday eve

Dear Ted

Well I will write one more letter and send it to Kelley Field I guess you will still be there to get it.

I just said to dad I wondered what you were doing right now. It is 8.45 our time Sunday eve.

We just come in from Martha and Lee's we were out there for supper. On our way in I wanted some pussy willows out where Mrs. Feasters house use to be so dad had to climb the tree it was so big you should have heard him. It is terrible stormy out all day it has been snowing and melting all day so you can imagine what slop we have here and dad on a pussy willow tree in it.

Jim wrote you a letter while I was out there in case you do not know what he means by that robbets he is getting he means rabbits for Easter. As soon as you find where you are going and have time to write let us know. I don't suppose there would be such luck as you getting a chance to become an instructor.

Well I guess you don't have much time to read and I want to hear Gabbriel Heatter so I guess this will be all.

I told M.J. what you said about where you thought you would go.

I suppose this is the last time I will address a letter Cadet Van Kirk.

Lots of luck.

All our love

Mother

Navigation School — Gulf Coast Air Corps Training Center Field, San Antonio, Texas

Theodore J. Van Kirk satisfactorily completed prescribed courses of instruction at the school and completed:

Navigation Ground School	427.00 hours
Navigation Flights	108.45 hours
Meteorology	40.00 hours
Military Training	<u>59.00 hours</u>
Total Composite	634.45 hours

which qualified him for Aeronautical rating of Aircraft Observer (Aerial Navigator).[124]

March 30, 1942, ground broke for a new Bell Aircraft plant near Atlanta, Georgia. General Arnold advised Larry Bell on December 22, 1941, that Bell Aircraft had been selected to build B-29s at the plant.[125] The unique Bell facility built complete combat ready airplanes for the Army Air Forces. The other heavy bomber plants delivered their finished product to modification centers.

The Bell Aircraft plant in Marietta, Georgia, built nearly seven hundred B-29s. (Bell Aircraft photos courtesy of Niagara Aerospace Museum)

March 31, 1942
Dearest Teedy, Will be thinking of you even though I am not there. Sending all my love and luck to you. Let us know your destination.
Love = Mary Jane.[126]

The interior of the Bell Aircraft facility at Marietta.

April 1, 1942
Headquarters — Gulf Coast Air Corps Training Center

Office of the Commanding General Major General Harmon
Randolph Field, Texas

To:Aviation Cadet Theodore Jerome Van Kirk, A 0-659,024
Kelly Field, Texas (Appointed 2nd Lt., Air-Res.)

Subject: Appointment under Section 37, National Defense Act, as
amended.
1. The Secretary of War has directed me to inform you that the
   president has appointed and commissioned you in the Army of
   the United States, effective this date, in the grade and section
   shown in address above. Your serial number is shown after A.
2. You will not perform the duties of an officer under this
   appointment until specifically called to active duty by competent
   orders.

3. There is enclosed herewith a form for oath of office, which you are requested to execute and return promptly to the agency from which it was received by you. The execution and return of the required oath of office constitute an acceptance of your appointment. No other evidence of acceptance is required. This letter should be retained by you as evidence of your appointment.

By command of Major General Harmon

April 1, 1942 . . .each of the following named Aviation Cadet, now at Kelly Field, Texas, upon acceptance of his appointment as Second Lieutenant, Air Corps Reserve, is, with his consent, ordered to extended active duty, at this station, and transferred as indicated, effective April 1, 1942.

Each officer will rank from April 1, 1942
TO THIRD AIR FORCE, SARASOTA, FLORIDA

No.	Name	Serial Number	Home Address
28.	Van Kirk, Theodore Jerome	O-659024	672 Queen Street Northumberland, PA.

The travel directed is necessary in the Military Service...No leaves of absence will be granted . . . The original report of entry upon active duty will be accomplished at this station.

By Order of Colonel Prosser[127]

April 1, 1942, Personnel Orders No. 78 ordered Van Kirk and the group of navigators "to participate in regular and frequent aerial flights, at such times as they are called to active duty with the Air Corps...and are authorized to participate in regular and frequent aerial flights while on an inactive status" by command of Lieutenant General Arnold. (See Appendix A for list of navigators.)

April 2, 1942, the USS *Hornet* left the San Francisco Bay from the port of Alameda and headed west across the Pacific.

"Leaving for Florida"

April 2, 1942

Dear Mother, Dad and Jean,

Well I finally got my wings and them two gold bars to pin on my shoulders and it certainly feels swell.

The only trouble about the thing is that you have a lot more to take care of. Now you have to keep yourself, and before the army kept you. I've signed enough papers the past two days to keep me going the rest of my life.

We're leaving for Florida tomorrow. I have five days and could have come home by taking an airliner but it would have cost me almost $175 and that's too much. I'll be a lot closer to home in Florida and if I get five days there I can come home.

I don't know what my exact address will be there but on my orders it has Lt. T. J. Van Kirk, Third Air Force, Sarasota Florida. I know that there we get training in four motored ships and probably as patrol work.

I haven't got any more to say until I get there and then I'll tell you all about the place.

Love

Theodore

I didn't get the egg before I left. It seems that every time you send something for a holiday I move.

From the Diary - *Along with 29 others I was picked to graduate early. Graduated on April 1, 1942 and made a 2nd Lt. and assigned to Sarasota, Fla. 97th Bomb. Grp. and B-17E's. I left Kelly Field on April 3, 1942.*[128]

By Direct Wire From WESTERN UNION

SAB 13 25 3 EXTRA NT XC=SUNBURY PENN 31
AVIATION CADET THEODORE VAN KIRK=
NAVIGATION SCHOOL KELLYFIELD TEX=

    CONGRATULATIONS HIT A COUPLE HUNS FOR US. SAVE THAT
ARM FOR SOME TENNIS CAUSE WE'RE STILL CHAMPS HOWS THE
MEXICAN? HAPPY EASTER=
    BILL AND BEN AND DORLET TOO

Chapter Four — Endnotes

96 Kelly Field was spelled Kelley Field in many of the letters to and from Van Kirk.

97 The return address used by Van Kirk while at Kelly Field.

98 Jean Van Kirk McAllister thought that Franklin served in the Navy, Robert in the Air Force, and Martin and the Snyders all Army. "The Snyders lived in the Sunbury area and the Van Kirks in Northumberland."

99 A Weems plotter is a combination protractor and straight edge designed to aid in drawing and measuring lines in desired directions. Department of the Air Force, *Air Navigation Manual No. 51-40A*, (Washington, DC: United States Government Printing Office, 1962), 4-3.

100 The navigator looked in the drift meter through the floor of the airplane to locate an object on the ground catching it in the parallel lines of the eyeglass. The side of the instrument gave the measurement of the side drift. John Steinbeck described the training, instruments, and the role of the navigator in *Bombs Away*.

101 The navigator made readings of wind direction and velocity from the drift recorder to calculate the true ground speed. *The B-29* Pilot Flight Operating Instructions for the Army Model B-29 airplanes, (Eagan, MN: Flying Books Publishers, 1986), 40. The manual was a reprint of the restricted flight manual AN 01-20EJ-1 revised 25 January 1944.

102 Postcard "Scene Near Sunbury, PA" addressed to Aviation Cadet Theodore Van Kirk, School of Navigation, 42-5 Kelly Field, San Antonio, TX.

103 Monroe Myers and Elizabeth Ann Harpster graduated from high school with Van Kirk in 1938. Myers served in the Air Force from January 13, 1941, to September 23, 1944. Monroe S. Myers obituary, *Sunbury Daily Item*, May 10, 2010.

104 Monroe "Minnie" Myers joined the Air Force and served in the 109th Field Artillery Medical Detachment from January 13, 1941 to September 23, 1944. A graduate of Susquehanna University and the University of Buffalo Dental School Doctor Myers practiced dentistry in Northumberland for forty-two years. Myers obituary.

105 In several letters the year was not written correctly according to the postmark, which is common in letters and documents dated in January.

106 Van Kirk, "My Life In The Service."

107 "Robert Fletcher Sent To Camp Barkley, Texas" and "Visits England As Observer" *Sunbury Daily Item* news clipping, no date. Another article of the Van Kirk family interest was "H. W. Hackenberg Buys Orange Street Property."

108 Grace Van Kirk enclosed news clippings about local men in service with her letter.

109 The navigation students studied the globe, meridians, latitude, longitude, great circle and Mercator course, statute mile and nautical mile, and different projections of maps. John Steinbeck, *Bombs Away* The Story Of A Bomber Team, (New York: NY, The Viking Press, 1942), 100.

110 *Complete Examination Questions and Answers Aerial Navigation for Student, Private, and Commercial Pilots*, (Ithaca, NY: Carlton L. Wheeler, Certified Instructor, 1941), 4.

111 The altimeter reading gives the indicated altitude, which governs oxygen needs. True

altitude is calculated from the indicated by mathematical correction for instrument error and outside temperature. Aero Medical Laboratory, *Your Body In Flight*, (Dayton, OH: Air Service Command Patterson Field, 1943), 12.

112 The navigator also inspected his sextant and watch. Headquarters, AAF, Office of Flying Safety, "B-17 Pilot Training Manual for the Flying Fortress," 17.

113 Advanced navigation curriculum described in "The Advanced School" Selman Field's history in *The Zero Zero Reunion Program*.

114 The atomic uranium-235 residue from the Manhattan Project was transported to the LOOW site and initially contained in a 166-foot concrete silo. Dietz, *Honor Thy Fathers & Mothers*, 20.

115 See Appendix D for "Northumberland's World War II dead."

116 *General Marshall's Victory Report* On the Winning of World War II in Europe and the Pacific featured an added section of "Contributions made by Our Own Community Toward the Winning of the War." More than eight hundred Northumberland men and women's names were listed.

117 Fireside chat February 23, 1942. In addition to the Roosevelt Presidential Library and Museum website the "American Presidency Project" http://www.presidency.ucsb.edu/ also has many documents of FDR on-line.

118 "American Ace May Race," *Buffalo Express*, March 26, 1919, and "Eddie Rickenbacker Died In Switzerland," *Amsterdam Evening Recorder & Daily Democrat*, July 23, 1971.

119 A photograph of Rickenbacker speaking to the troops appeared in *The Hour Has Come* p. 88. Van Kirk served in North Africa during this time.

120 New Orleans Airport Buildings, New Orleans, LA, postcard to Mary Jane Young, 456 Front St., Northumberland, PA.

121 Young's weight 138# height 68, "U.S. World War II Army Enlistment Records," National Archives and Records Administration 1938-1946.

122 Major Gen. Abraham J. Dreiseszun participated in the first American daylight-bombing raid with the 97th Bombardment Group. From July 1944 until November 1944, Dreiseszun was assigned as Assistant Director of Academic Training for the Army Air Forces Navigation School at Selman Field, LA. Recalled to active duty several times after the war he was appointed deputy chief of staff, procurement and production, at Wright-Patterson Air Force Base, Ohio. Dreiseszun assumed command of the Defense Personnel Support Center in Philadelphia in July 1972 and two years later became commander of the Air Force Contract Management Division at Kirtland Air Force Base, NM. "Air Force Biographies," http://www.af.mil/ [accessed February 22, 2011].

123 Van Kirk's note to Mary Jane and his parents were sent on postcards of the sunken garden and entrance to Morningside Park on the Parkway, Memphis, TN.

124 James S. Cheney for David Rankin, 1st Lt., Air Corps, Secretary, signed the Proficiency Certificate. Copy Van Kirk personal papers.

125 The first "All Georgia" production B-29 was completed on December 20, 1943. Bell had a highly successful training program converting housewives and farmers into aircraft employees. Major Gene Gurney, USAF, *B-29 Story* The Plane That Won The War, (Greenwich, CN: Fawcett Publications, Inc., 1963), 10-11.

126 Direct Wire Western Union to Aviation Cadet Theodore Van Kirk, School of Navigation 42-5, 31 March 1942.

127 Special Orders No. 89, Extract, Headquarters Kelly Field, TX, March 31, 1942.

128 Van Kirk, "My Life In The Service." The HQ, 340th, 341st, 342nd, and 414th Bomb Squadrons composed the 97th Bombardment Group, and between 1942-1945 flew 483 missions under the Eighth Air Force in England, the Twelfth Air Force in Africa, and the Fifteenth Air Force in Italy.

Chapter Five

Sarasota *97th Bombardment Group*

Dutch ~ Practically all thirty from our group were assigned to the 97th Bombardment Group, which was located in Sarasota, Florida. Our B-17Es were old planes, and we were going to take them into combat.[129] I thought, Lord help us. Anyway, we went over to Sarasota because they needed navigators quickly. While I was there I started to keep a diary about that time, but only kept it for a few days.

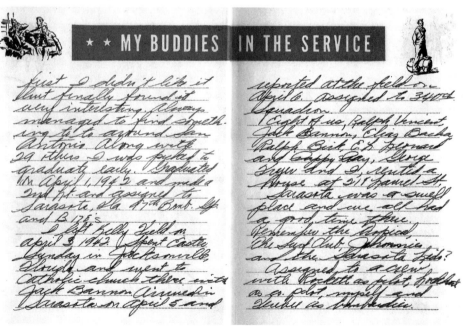

A page from Van Kirk's diary "My Life In The Service"

"Tom Ferebee"

Dutch ~ Sarasota was a nice town and had a brand new airfield. We were the first people on it, but there were no quarters by the airfield. I met my commanding officer, Paul Tibbets, and was assigned to the 340th Squadron 97th Bomb Group. Tibbets had three or four years in the military on the rest of us and was about six years older than me. I got assigned to a crew and did not know any of the guys.

(James) Rockett was the pilot and (Eugene) Lockhart, the co-pilot. Tom Ferebee and I met when we crawled up in the nose of the B-17 for the first time. I had never seen Tom before. We were almost inseparable and he became my best friend for life. On our first training flight Rockett couldn't get the plane started. Poncho Kendall, the crew chief, came up through the airplane hollering, "For Christ sakes lieutenant if you can't start it you can't fly it." Rockett eventually did get it started.

Tom and I had trouble understanding each other in the beginning. He said, "I was speaking Dutch." That is how my nickname became Dutch.

I told Tom that he talked as if he had a mouthful of grits. From then on Ferebee and I socialized a lot. He liked to tell me often about how great things were in Davies County in North Carolina.

We were equals and could say anything to each other. We didn't watch our language either. We were always that way with each other. I never found out until we went out to Yosemite in the late 1970s that Tom was afraid of heights. He sat next to me in the passenger seat. The road dropped straight down on the other side. Tom was leaning this way and that way. I asked him if he was afraid of falling out of the car. Maryann (Ferebee) piped up that Tom was afraid of heights! It never bothered him in an airplane.

Everyone had nicknames. John Holbrook "Chomp Chomp" Chalmers was great at story telling and a voice that went with it. He loved to tell stories about the Indians from his home state of Oklahoma. Theodore "Teddy" Hokenstad was flying in formation with us when his airplane took a .88 shell burst in their loaded bomb bay. About two years ago I read a magazine article that relatives were trying to find out what happened to him. I was able to call and tell them. Ralph Vincent, one of my best friends, always sat behind me in class. In the Army everything was alphabetical and organized. Levon Ray was from Texas and never said more than two words at a time. Ray was the navigator on the first mission. George Freyer, "Happy Freyer," lived in the house with us. Ben Rushing, Jack Bannon, Abraham Dreiseszun, and "Len" Leonard too, these are the guys I remember most from my navigation class.

TABLE 5.1 — SPECIFICATIONS OF B-17E

Armament:	One .30-cal. and eight .50-cal. machine guns and 4,200 lbs. of bombs
Engines:	Four Wright R-1820-65 turbo-supercharged radials, 1200 hp each
Maximum speed:	317 mph at 25,000 ft.
Cruising speed:	226 mph
Service ceiling:	36,000 ft.
Range:	3,200 miles (maximum ferry range)
Span:	103 ft. 9 in.
Length:	73 ft. 10 in.
Height:	19 ft. 2 in.
Weight:	51,000 lbs. gross weight (actual - normal load)
Serial numbers:	41-2393 to 41-2669 and 41-9011 to 41-9245
Crew:	9

Source: National Museum of the USAF, Fact Sheet for Boeing B-17E. Boeing Airplane Co. built 512 "E" models.

"The Ringling College of Art"

In front of the house at 218 Laurel Street, Sarasota, Florida.

Dutch ~ We lived in town. It was rough living with the all female student population of the Ringling College of Art nearby. The men were off fighting the war by this time. We had a big old time there, but also worked hard. Since we had no quarters, seven of the navigators got together, rented a big house, and bought an old 1936 or '37 Ford. If you wanted to use it and it was there, you took the car. If the car was not available, you were out of luck and got back to the base the best way you could. We had a few parties in that house and that is all I have to say about that.

There was never a shortage of dates. If one girl wasn't available, another was to go

Left: Ralph Vincent, one of Van Kirk's closest friends on the left, with girls from the Ringling School and another un-identified navigator.

Below: Jack Bannon sitting on the navigators' Ford.

out to dinner or the movies, and we had plenty of money. We thought we were rich getting second lieutenants pay. If you wanted a date to go out to dinner with, to go out to the movies with, there was a girl always available. No one paired off we were just a bunch of people male and female having a good time together.

Any time you put a bunch of guys together in a house you are going to have parties. Parties and dates at the house or on the beach were impromptu. We tried to get the girls to wash the dishes telling them they had to work for their food or drink.

We cooked as little as possible. Generally, somebody tried to make breakfast but we were flying at all odd hours or in ground school and not on the same schedule. We ate most of our meals in a mess tent.

"Paul W. Tibbets"

Dutch - Paul Tibbets tried to instill discipline in us. He had attended a military school before and was a second lieutenant stationed at Fort Benning when he met General Patton. Tibbets and Patton would shoot skeet together. Tibbets was a very good shot. He used to fly from Sarasota up to Columbus, Georgia, to see his wife Lucy and also to shoot skeet with Patton. A skeet round is twenty-five shots. Tibbets and Patton would break twenty-five out of twenty-five every time. They would be in the third or fourth round before one of them would miss. Tibbets thought Tom Ferebee and I were that good too and were going to shoot down planes. Hell, we couldn't shoot down anything.

One of the fellows, Mickey Miller, was always getting in everybody's hair. Tibbets used him for a gopher. One day Mickey somehow had the tractor pull out from under the trailer of gasoline. Mickey walked in while we were in the operations tent. Tibbets looked at him and said, "Mickey get that damn tractor up and under the trailer of gasoline."

There sat this trailer down on the ground and the tractor was out from under it. An hour and a half later Mickey comes back and says, "Sir is there anything else you want me to do?"

Mickey put guys on KP if they did not salute him. He had a bunch of about one hundred guys prop several big straight trees under the trailer to lift it and backed the tractor up.

At Sarasota we lost only one airplane. Eric Leland clipped a pine tree on take off and was lucky he did not kill himself. Surprisingly, no one on the crew was hurt either. We were getting ready to go overseas and flew to modification centers with our old B-17s, the "E" model. They did not have enough guns on them and needed modification and repair.

"Boston Red Sox"

April 5, 1942
Lt. T. J. Van Kirk
Third Air Force
Sarasota, Florida
Dear Mother, Dad and Jean,

I just got into this town and haven't had a chance to look it over yet.

The trip from San Antonio on the train was very slow. I found out that I can get from here to Philadelphia in less than twenty hours.

It seems that every holiday I land in a new town. Christmas day I came into San Antonio and Easter I got into Jacksonville. There was a man on the train who used to live around Sarasota. The air base is the only army outfit there so the town won't be over run with soldiers. The Boston Red Sox are in spring training there so dad should like it. Ringling Bros. circus has their summer headquarters there. It's

just a small town and we have the nicest beach in the world there. It sounds like a nice place.

I won't be getting there until about Wednesday so I'll write and tell you what I really think about it after I get there.

Love

Theodore

April 5, 1942

From the diary - *Spent Easter Sunday in Jacksonville, Florida and went to Catholic church there with Jack Bannon. Arrived in Sarasota on April 5 and reported at the field on April 6. Assigned to 340th Squadron.*

Eight of us, Ralph Vincent, Jack Bannon, Elias Bacha, Ralph Birk, E. L. Leonard and "Pappy" Ray, George Fryer and I rented a house at 218 Laurel St. Sarasota was a swell place and we all had a good time there. Remember the Tropical, The Surf Club, Johnnies and the Sarasota Lido?

Assigned to a crew with Rockett as pilot, Lockhart as co-pilot, myself, and Ferebee as bombardier. While there I made trips to Chicago, New York, Atlanta and many local flights. Had engine trouble in N.Y. and got wire that Mother was sick so I got home for a week.[130]

Dutch - Jack Bannon was a great guy. He said we ought to go to church since it was Easter.

"I have to go to the Catholic church," said Bannon. So we all went because we did not know where the other churches were.

During our training we were going to bivouac over in a field. We were told to take our pup tents and cooking gear to the other side of the airfield to learn how to pitch our tents and cook out. Rockett thought this was kind of foolish and put all the stuff in the car and drove over. Tibbets didn't think too much

Chapter 5

of that and the next day said to Rockett, "Your crew can now dig a ditch." So we all got shovels and started digging. After we were finished Tibbets said, "Now take the dirt and put it back." He was the commanding officer of our squadron. I didn't know Tibbets well until we got over to England and he became our pilot.

We went out and dropped barrels off the coast of Mexico and flew around shooting at them. That was our gunnery training.

"Looking for a Girl"

April 7, 1942
Hotel George Washington
Jacksonville, Florida
Dear Mother, Dad and Jean,

I'm finally here. I haven't settled down yet and haven't been out at the field yet but we got here yesterday afternoon.

We really hit something nice this time. This town is really swell. It is a resort town where all the people come for vacations and its really some place.

They have two golf courses here and the nicest bathing beach in the country. They have a lot of places to go and a lot of things to do.

The field just opened up here and the people treat us swell.

I report out at the field tomorrow and find out then what I do – as though I don't know. All they have here is them big flying fortresses and my job it to navigate one of them things around.

There isn't any place built out there for us to live at so I guess we'll have to live in town. Four of us are going together and renting an apartment with a living room, screened porch, kitchen & two bedrooms for $50 a month and everything furnished. I'll have to learn to cook.

I was out at the beach swimming today and got a little tan. It was certainly swell.

It is very hot down here but every building is air conditioned and if you stay out of the sun it isn't so bad.

What I'd like to do is get married and stay here for the rest of the war but I guess that's impossible. They say we'll be sent out of here in about 5 wks.

Don't go start worrying now.

Right now I'm looking for a girl with a car. The only way to get around this place is on little buses and they only run every hour so you spend most of your time doing nothing. I wish you & M.J. would come down here because you'd really like this place – and I'd like to see you.

I have to stop now & get some sleep.

Love
Theodore
I don't know what my address will be until we get that apt.

"340th Bombardment Squadron"

April 9, 1942

Dear Mother, Dad and Jean,

I reported out to the field today and didn't find out as much as I did by not going out.

I was assigned to the 340th Bombardment squadron. We fly on flying fortresses. One good thing is that we have the best ships made.

The set-up here is this. I may as well tell you so you can stop worrying. Each squadron is a separate unit and can go any place it is sent on short notice. We haven't got all of our equipment yet but we have several 1000 mile trips planned. We are supposed to be here five weeks or more but even that is uncertain. After that we don't know where we'll go. The place is just a new camp started last week and every thing is disorganized as h. but my commanding officer is a swell fellow.

Eight of us fellows went together and rented a furnished house. Its costing $12.50 a month and its a mansion. Six of us went together and bought a '37 Ford. That cost me $27.50 but now we're pretty well settled.

The house is a typical Florida white stone with a lg. lawn & trees and flower lined walks with a driveway of sea shells. Inside it has a breakfast nook, pantry & kitchen with electric refrigerator, stove & water heater and all pots, pans, dishes etc. that we need. Then it has a lg. dining room with a small walnut suite in it. It has a living room with a suite, writing desk, fireplace and all and a sun porch with a radio, studio couch and several large chairs. Upstairs it has four bedrooms with twin beds and three baths. It's swell.

I made an arrangement with a bank down here to send them $100 of my pay every month and I want that put in a joint checking account between you and dad and I. I gave them mothers name so that she will have to sign the card I am enclosing at the two places I have checked.

Right now I have $59. in there and every month from now on $100. will go in there. I can live off of the rest I will get but I may have to write some checks but they will keep us informed of the balance. After I go across you can have it all. That $10,000 insurance is being paid too from my check and if you ever want to find out anything about that write to National Service Life Insurance, Veterans Ad., Wash. D.C.

I doubt very much whether I'll get home or not but I'd certainly like too.

All the display is gone from the army down here. We work from 7 a.m. to 6 p.m. We put on old Khaki and comfortable shoes and go to work but after 6 p.m. we have a nice place & a nice town to come to.

My address here is

   Lt. Theodore J. Van Kirk

   218 Laurel Street

   Sarasota, Florida

Love

Theodore

April 9, 1942

Dear Ted

Well I will take a chance on writing you a letter I do not know if you will get it or not. I have so much to tell you and so much to ask you I know I will not get it all done in this letter. I started to write this letter at about 7.30 and I had company so it is 10 oclock now so I know I will not get half of all my questions asked. If I get anything in this letter about gym why I have a good reason for it Jean just come home she had part in a gym exhibition and just come in and is telling me about it. There were four very sick people over the weekend we were so sure you were coming home Jean and I cleaned all day Friday so we would have all our work done we were sure you would be home on Friday nite or Sat. Dad looked for you till Sat noon than he gave up hopes. M.J. was up on Thur eve she was here for about 3 hours she thought sure you would be coming home. Now I guess I will start and ask my questions. Do you think you will get home any time? How do you like your new place? Is it warm there now? and what kind of clothes do the ladies wear I want to know for I think we will be down next month or the beginning of June if you don't get home and if we can get to see you if we do come down.

I have a lot more to tell you but I am so tired I will have to wait until my next letter. Bob Walker left today for Wellston Georgia he is a 1st Lt in the Air Corps there how he ever done it I can't tell you. He wanted me to come along with him he said than it would not be far for me to go to see you.

Tell me in your next letter how to address your letters. write

All our Love

Mother

Did you get your Easter egg yet. The weather is terrible it is raining and snowing

"Bataan Has Fallen"

April 10, 1942
Fort Jackson, S.C.
Hello sister dear,

How's the girl? Boy what a pleasant surprise it was to get a letter from you. I almost couldn't believe it but now I think I've gotten it figured out. My Aunt made you write I guess not exactly made you but kept telling you about it so much you figured well what do I have to lose. O well knowing how you like to write I guess even at that I'd better consider myself lucky.

There's only one part of the army you want to keep the morale strong so don't kid me about wanting to keep the morale up.

Well I'm tired of walking already so when you get to it you can send your bike. Did you ever stop to think how heavy the pack is an infantryman carries on his back? It weighs between 50 & 70 lbs. We will soon have to march just 10 then 15 up to 25 miles a day with the full pack on our back. Ho hum!

I tried to get in the air corps but they wouldn't transfer anyone from this division. I got high enough mark in my I.Q. for machinists in the air corps but since they only needed men in the infantry they put me here classified as a gunsmith. I was trying to transfer up to a wk. ago but I've given it up as a bad job. Aw nuts I was put in the army for only one thing – that is to train to fight so I can do it just as good maybe even better in the infantry. Somebody has to do the dirty work & if it isn't done pretty soon you & I and everybody else will wish we were dead or something.

The practise I had walking up to Jeanne's comes in handy but it isn't like marching in step for the distance we have to travel. We already had a 6 mile march & gradually we will work up to a 20 than 25 mile march – in one day. During maneuvers we will march 25 miles a day for possible 7 to 10 days. Of course when we get over "there" it's hard to say how far we will have to go each day. They expect to have this division ready to go abroad for battle in 5 mo. and that isn't baloney. Of course if things get too bad I may be there before 5 mo.

I wonder what happened to our brother now that Bataan has fallen. If those dirty yellow rats got him & they don't get me on the way over I'll get enough for both of us. I haven't heard exactly whether some escaped from Bataan or whether all were killed or captured.

Glad to learn your boyfriend (Van Kirk) was made an officer. If I should see him I would have to salute him now.

What do you want to know if there are only nice fellows down here? You wouldn't even look at them anyways. Gosh you don't even go out with a fellow other than Teedy once or even look at another. Well maybe that's the way it should be for all I know.

Last night I was on guard duty here at the post. It was raining & I do mean raining. I had to walk for 2 hrs. in the rain with a gun then I was off 4 hrs. at which time I had to stay at the guardhouse with the wet soaked clothes on then after 4 hrs. I had to go out & walk my post for 2 more hrs. in the rain. I was out in the rain walking from 6 to 8 & again from 12 to 2 a.m. So far I haven't gotten a cold or anything so it isn't bad. Of course I had yesterday afternoon & all today off of any duty at all.

Tad I guess is going to school to study radio. I hope he likes it and gets along good. The army isn't bad if you get in a branch or line of service you like. Of course it is my own fault that I got in the infantry – which I don't like at all – and so I have no one to blame but myself & I am the one who is & will continue to suffer for it. But I guess I can take it I hope.

Well be good & take good care of yourself.

Good luck & Best wishes,

Love,

Bob[131]

"Navigating Without a Map"

April 10, 1942

218 Laurel St.

Sarasota, Fla.

Dear Mother, Dad and Jean,

I don't get very much time to write because they keep us busy as h. We have to go there every other day from 3 A.M. to 6 P.M. and the other days from 7 A.M. to 8:30 P.M. That includes Sat. Sun. and holidays. I may be able to get three days off before we leave which will be 4 wks. from Sunday. I don't know where we're going but I think it's England. Don't say anything to anyone but Mary Jane about what I tell you & keep it under your hats because after I fly clear across the ocean I don't want a reception on the other side.

This is a new type of outfit and everyone seems to be in a rush to get things done. I can't say that I blame them because we'll be fighting in four weeks.

This is still a pretty nice town and we are able to go out a little while a(t) night but we're usually so tired that we don't feel like going any place.

Maybe the reason I'm so mad is because we haven't got any navigation equipment and don't know when we'll get it. They send us up on a flight and we haven't even got a map. They say we'll get them before we leave but every time they tell me to fly now without any equipment I almost blow a fuse.

The waitress just brought my food so I can eat now.
Love
Theodore

April 13 1942
Dear Ted.

Got that letter today telling us the news so right now I do not know if I am coming or going. Mary Jane was just up to see what we were going to do that is about coming down. Her and I were going to come down to spend about two weeks with you now I don't know what to do. You said you would have about 3 days off do you want to try to come home some how? or want us to come down.

Do you think you could make it by plane so that you would have about a day at home we would meet you anywhere or if some one came down for you do you think you could make it that is if you want to come home of course than we could only spend the day together but you could see them all but if M.J. and I come down we were going to spend 2 weeks with you. We intended to leave here either on Thursday April 23 or early Friday morning April 24 and stay about 2 weeks but if you think you can make it home somehow and want to come home why let us know. Whatever you say is all right with us but answer this letter as soon as possible so we get it and know what to do. You will get this letter about Thurs or Fri and than till we get yours it will only about give us time to pack if you want us to come down.

I only hope that what you think is wrong and will not happen.

I have an awful lot to tell you but will wait till I see you.

I went over to see about coming down if we come down I think we will come by bus. The fare round trip is $30.00 I don't think that is bad. I don't know we probably could get a room in some private home to stay while down there. Now you write and tell us what you want us to do. If you want to come home and have enough time to do it in and don't have enough money I can give you what I had saved for my trip down for I won't need it if you come home. This will be all for now write as soon as you get this so we know

All our love
Mother
Did you get your Easter egg let me know I had it insured

Postmarked April 14, 1942
Dearest Teedy,

I received your letter about leaving if you can't come home or we couldn't come down maybe we could meet halfway. I feel as though your mother should see you before you go, and I want to see you terribly.

We'll see what we can do about it.
X luck
All my love
M Jane
I love you darling

Dearest Teedy,

I just wrote to Mother and Bob (Young) and so will write to you. Did you get the telegram I sent, you didn't say anything so I thought maybe you didn't get it. Bob is down at Fort Jackson S.C. They'll have their hands full I've been hearing from him about as often as I hear from you. He put his application in the Flying Cadets I hope he makes it. He's just like you he sent mother a card & said "Tell M Jane I said "hello" and that she should comb her hair. I thought sure you'd be home I was up to see your mother Thursday night and your Dad was holding Barry and giving him his bottle. He bought produce this morning to the store he told me to help unload the produce but you know how weak I am. Don't say it I know what your thinking. I think I'm lucky I have three brothers and a sweetheart in the army.

Thanks a lot for the wings and bars it was very sweet of you. I hope you do get home soon.

Bill Brennan & Ben told me to tell you to write, Ben thinks you're mad at him for inviting me to the prom I told him that you weren't.

I thought maybe you'd like to see Bill & Hazel's (Seasholtz) little baby if you want too just throw it away after you see it. They are going to write to you as soon as I send your address.

It's been terribly warm here the last couple of days it was hot here Easter.

I hear your uncle is going to go to Georgia to take up the same as Uzal Ent. That will be awfully nice.

Well write when you get time.

I wish you a lot of luck and success at Florida and always remember I'm thinking of you.

All my love
M. Jane

"First American Air Attack on Japan"

April 18, 1942, the planned date and launching point about four hundred miles from the main islands of Japan was moved up when an enemy picket boat the *Nitto Maru* got off radio warnings to the 5th Fleet flagship *Kiso* while

Lieutenant Colonel Doolittle wiring Japanese medals on a bomb before the raid.
(Air Force photograph National Archives)

the aircraft carrier *Hornet* was six hundred miles from the coast.[132] Sixteen B-25 Mitchell medium bombers led by Lt. Col. James Doolittle launched from the carrier on the first daring American air raid to strike the Japanese home islands.

The Doolittle Raiders trained at Elgin Field, Florida. Co-pilot of Plane No. 1, 2nd Lt. Richard Cole described Doolittle as friendly and not pompous, treating everyone with respect, persuasive, and led by example.[133] "Colonel Doolittle made the take off. After that we traded off while the other watched the tachometer. We had twenty to thirty feet left off the deck. We did not fly in formation. There was no problem on the flight to Japan. On the bomb run the ack-ack was pretty active, but not accurate. We got out unscathed. Hank (Potter), our navigator, couldn't use the drift meter and relied on his magnetic heading over China. We had high overcast. Midway he said we are going to be 180 miles short of the coast. No one was interested in ditching. We could see the sharks."

"We flew low level all the way and did not have oxygen. Doolittle gave the order to bail out at about nine thousand feet over Quzhou (Chuchow, China)." He landed in a rice paddy spread with manure and water up to his

B-25s tied to the deck of the Hornet waiting for takeoff. No. 02298 was the sixth bomber to takeoff for the raid. (Air Force photograph National Archives)

waist. Doolittle told Cole, "I remembered and was very happy with myself that when I got to the ground to flex my knees. I was very happy that I did what I was supposed to do. But what did I do? I sat down."[134]

The surprise raid caused minimal physical damage, but bolstered the morale and spirit of America and her allies. The raid and support of the Chinese of the downed crews incited the Japanese Army. Generalissimo Chiang Kai-shek advised Roosevelt that the Japanese in retaliation "may have" massacred 250,000 Chinese civilians.[135] Biological warfare against the Chinese ensued as additional punishment. Diseased microbes of cholera, dysentery, anthrax, and typhoid were tossed into rivers and reservoirs. Japanese aviators sprayed fleas carrying bubonic plague germs over Shanghai and Ningbo.[136]

April 19, 1942
Dear Ted,

Had a letter from you the other day you said you thought we all died you hadn't had a letter from us since you were there. You should have had I have written but the first one had the first address on you gave us. I began to think the same about you I thought sure we would have a letter from you yesterday telling us what too do. I wrote and mailed you one last Tuesday telling you we were planning to come down to see you. We have been waiting for an answer so we know what to do. We are just about all ready to leave now if we hear from you. If we do and come down we will be there about 4.08 Friday evening we are leaving by train Thursday at 12.28 noon and should be at Sarasota Florida by 4.08 Friday afternoon. You should see M.J. she is so excited she don't know if she is going or coming. Your picture was in the paper last evening and a very nice write up sent to the Item office right from Kelley Field. Dan Swenk is the reporter now for the Item and we could not imagine where they got a picture like that so M.J. ask him he said it was sent from Kelly Field.

How did you make out on your flights? I only wish you could have become an instructor. Jean had her picture taken they are real good she wants to send you one but I think I will wait now and if I come down I will bring it along. Grandma and Clifford were first here to see if we were really going down to see you and to tell us they seen that picture in the paper. Well I guess this will be all for now I hope to see you soon than I have a million things to tell you now if you can come home we still would like you to come home.

All our love
Mother

"First Furlough"

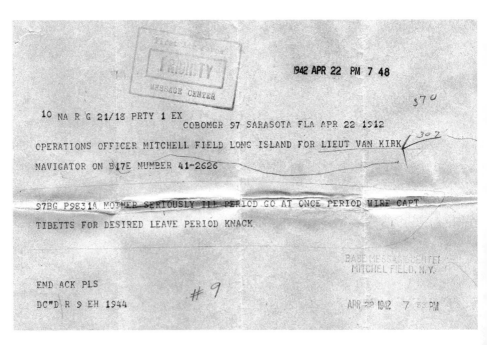

April 22, 1942

6:57

Sarasota, Fla.

Lieutenant T. Van Kirk grounded Mitchell Field New York, Military authorities contacting him.

Mae G. Meier

Sarasota Co., Red Cross

COBOMGR 97 SARASOTA FLA APR 22 1912 OPERATIONS OFFICER MITCHELL FIELD LONG ISLAND FOR LIEUT VAN KIRK NAVIGATOR ON B17E NUMBER 41-2626[138]

97BG P9831A MOTHER SERIOUSLY ILL PERIOD GO AT ONCE PERIOD WIRE CAPT TIBBETS FOR DESIRED LEAVE PERIOD KNACK[139]

Dutch ~ My mother was in and out of the hospital a lot, so I returned home at every opportunity.

Western Union Telegram

LT T J VANKIRK, CARE PRR TRAIN 554 =

ARRIVING 440P FM HARRISBURG WASHDC=

REQUEST FOR ADDITIONAL LEAVE GRANTED LEAVE TERMINATES MIDNITE APRIL THIRTY =

MOTHER.

April 24, 1942, Major Gen. Carl "Tooey" Spaatz arrived in England to establish the headquarters of the Eighth Air Force at Bushy Park.

"National Economic Policy"

Roosevelt ~ *April 28, 1942*, "My fellow Americans: It is nearly five months since we were attacked at Pearl Harbor . . . American war planes, manned by Americans, are flying in actual combat over all the continents and all the oceans . . .

Our planes are helping in the defense of French colonies today, and soon American Flying Fortresses will be fighting for the liberation of the darkened continent of Europe itself . . . It is even reported from Japan that somebody has dropped bombs on Tokyo, and on other principal centers of Japanese war industries. If this be true, it is the first time in history that Japan has suffered such indignities . . .

Yesterday I submitted to the Congress of the United States a seven-point program, a program of general principles which taken together could be called

Dutch ~ This was my first furlough home because my mother was sick.
Left to right back Frances Van Kirk and Martha Snyder Van Kirk, front Lee Van Kirk,
Dutch, and Jean Van Kirk, Jim Van Kirk (in front of Dutch)

the national economic policy for attaining the great objective of keeping the cost of living down . . .

Never in the memory of man has there been a war in which the courage, the endurance and the loyalties of civilians played so vital a part . . .

Many thousands of civilians all over the world have been and are being killed or maimed by enemy action.

Our own American civilian population is now relatively safe from such disasters. And, to an ever-increasing extent, our soldiers, sailors and marines are fighting with great bravery and great skill on far distant fronts to make sure that we shall remain safe."[134]

"97th Bombardment Group"

Postmarked May 1, 1942

Dear Mother, Dad and Jean,

I didn't go out some place and get lost but they've been trying to lose me in work.

I had to fly Friday night but it was called off because all the enlisted men in the crew showed up drunk. It was funny as the devil but the next day they had to move sand piles all day.

Today I am officer of the day and I've got to be here all of the time for 24 hrs. I also have to go around and inspect all of the guard posts tonight at 2 a.m. I'm going to sleep for a little while.

Next Wednesday our squadron moves up to Henderson field for a camping trip. It's only about 60 mile and when we go we find out what we have and what we don't have.

We got a lot of new officers in while I was home and we don't have much work to do any more while we're on the ground. The only trouble is that we aren't on the ground long enough.

I told the boys about me hunting submarines and stuff. You should have heard them laugh. They all think I got married while I was home.

I'm going to bed now until 2 o'clock. We keep the darndest hours down here. We never get a good nights sleep

Address my letters to

340th Bomb Sqd.

97th Bomb Group

Sarasota, Fla.

That way I'll get them out here at the field. I'm not in town very much anyhow. Take care of yourself & write.

Love

Theodore

"Our Flight Pay"

May 7, 1942

Dear Mother, Dad and Jean,

I just got back from a practice moving yesterday and it took me almost all of today to get clean from it. I was dirtier then I ever was.

I have three days off now but I have so much to do that I won't get any rest anyhow. I had an idea to fly home for the three days but it would have cost too much and I could only have been home one day anyhow.

While I have this time off I am going to clean up my things and pack up the things I don't need and send them home. I have a hundred and one things to do.

I got pretty lucky the other day and won fifty dollars but then everyone who got 3 days off and wanted to go home borrowed ten from me so it didn't do any good. I'll get it next month though. Whenever you loan money you can be sure of getting it back. I also have $70 more pay coming. There was a mix up and we didn't get our flight pay. We should get it in a week or so.

I tried to get you a Mother's Day card but you can't get anything in this town. This will have to do instead. If you want me to I could make up a little poem but that would probably put you in bed again.

I have more work to do now so I'll have to stop.

Love

Theodore

"William C. Young"

May 10, 1942, Staff Sergeant William C. Young of the 31st Infantry Regiment died while serving his country.[140]

"Like Hank Buck"

May 10, 1942

Dear Mother, Dad and Jean,

I haven't written for quite a while but I haven't received a letter for the last two days either.

Everything down here is all mixed up. We are getting ready to move out. We are going to a supply depot to get more equipment and our planes fixed up. We are going to Duncan Field, San Antonio Texas. Two of our squadrons are going to Middletown. I don't know how long we will be at Duncan. We may go to a field in Michigan after we get our equipment and stuff.

I have more stuff now then I know what to do with. I'm sending some stuff home that dad may be able to wear. I'll probably be able to get him some more stuff at Duncan. Maybe a jacket and a pistol, etc.

I feel pretty big when I get a tropical hat on and a .45 automatic pistol strapped on my waist. I look like Hank Buck.

Keep addressing my letters just as you have. I'll get them sometime.

Love

Theodore

May 11, 1942

Pursuant to authority contained in teletype 3BC M0498E dated 8 May 42 and 3BC M0621E dated 11 May 42 Headquarters 3d Bomber Command, the following named personnel will proceed by air on or about May 12, 1942 from Sarasota-Bradenton Airport, Sarasota, Florida to San Antonio Air Depot, Duncan Field, Texas, via the best available air route for the purpose of installing certain items in airplanes of this unit. Upon completion of this duty they will proceed to destination "T" by air via the best available air route.

TABLE 5.2 — TIBBETS' AND ROCKETT'S CREWS TO ENGLAND[141]

B-17E Airplane No. 41-9174
(P) 2nd Lt. James D. Rockett, O-436538, AC
(CP) 2nd Lt. Eugene M. Lockhart, Jr. O-437973, AC
(N) 2nd Lt. Theodore J. Van Kirk, O-659024, AC
(B) 2nd Lt. Thomas W. Ferebee, O-443490, AC
(AE) Sgt. Warren K. Hughes, 14037338, 340th Bomb Sq
(AAE) Pvt. James P. Fitzgerald, Jr., 20310037, 340th Bomb Sq
(R) Sgt. Orville S. Splitt, 16026620, 340th Bomb Sq
(AR) Pfc. Frederick J. Rich, 13038740, 340th Bomb Sq
(G) Sgt. John T. Tittsworth, 14043315, 340th Bomb Sq
(Maint.) Cpl. James Kowalski, 16035436, 340th Bomb Sq

B-17E Airplane No. 41-9020
(P) Capt. Paul W. Tibbets, O-361713, AC
(P) 2nd Lt. Christopher J. Karas, O-364573, AC
(CP) 2nd Lt. Charles R. (Dick) Wiley, O-443034, AC
(N) 2nd Lt. Edward L. Leonard, O-659016, AC
(B) T/Sgt. Rudy P. Lenser, 6994860, 340th Bomb Sq
(AE) Pvt. Charles H. McDowell, 20756301, 340th Bomb Sq
(AAE) 2nd Lt. Otis W. May, O-289323, AC
(R) Sgt. Jason C. Lancaster, 14038102, 340th Bomb Sq
(AR) Pvt. Hinton C. Witt, 14064684, 340th Bomb Sq
(G) Pvt. Edward T. Shifflet, 13043351, 340th Bomb Sq
(Maint.) S/Sgt. Roland V. Anderson, 6146248, 340th Bomb Sq
(X) 1st Lt. Eugene L. Griffin, O-342914, AC

The travel directed is necessary in the military service.

Source: Operations Orders No. 3 Headquarters 97th Bombardment Group (H) Army Air Force Offices of the Operations Officer, By order of Colonel (Cornelius) Cousland, Sarasota, FL, May 11, 1942.[142]

From the diary - *We left Sarasota on May 12 at 1300 hours with ten men on our ship with all their baggage. Started for Duncan Field in San Antonio but landed at Mobile, Ala. on account of weather. Left Mobile the following day and went to Montgomery, Ala. where we stayed for four days. Montgomery is a pretty good place. Mobile isn't.*

Finally arrived at Duncan. We got a room in the Gunter where we stayed while our plane was getting fixed up. Had a party one night and had a little trouble.

Stayed at Duncan for about two weeks. Renewed my opinion that San Antonio isn't such a good town but I'd like to visit it again.[143]

Dutch ~ From Sarasota we flew to the modification center in San Antonio and had two guns installed, one on the right and one on the left. All we had shooting straight ahead was a .30 caliber and it wasn't worth much. From San Antonio we went to Wright Pat for more modifications of weaponry and communications equipment before we went over to Presque Island, Maine.

We couldn't get our planes very high because they were pretty well beat up in training. If we got up to nineteen thousand feet, that was pretty good.

May 14, 1942

Pvt. Robt. D. Young
77th Division U.S. Army
307th Inf. Co. M.
Fort Jackson, S.C.

Hiya Sis,

How's the girl? I thought I'd write you a letter though I realize you owe me one. Well I'll forgive you this time cause I know it'll happen again.

Well yesterday I was informed that I was promoted to Sergeant. It doesn't become effective till a few days have elapsed so possibly tomorrow, Sat. or by Mon. I'll be a Sgt.

Congratulations kiddo! So you even beat your big brother. I always thought you'd be married before me but now I know it. Well good luck & be good.

I'm sending you a few pictures of your brother. They may help to scare the rats away.

I must close as I'm afraid you'll be getting tired of reading so be good & congratulations again.

Love,
Bob

"Duncan Field"

May 20, 1942

Dear Mother, Dad and Jean,

I wrote some letters the day before yesterday and thought that I had mailed them but I left them lay in a fellows hotel room so I don't imagine you got a letter for some time.

They have our planes out at Duncan field fixing them all up and I do mean fixing. They are putting four more guns on and a lot of other improvements.

Out of our four squadrons two of them went to Middletown and two came to Duncan. It was just my luck to come to Duncan. A fellow who lived here in San Antonio went to Middletown.

I'm getting six dollars a day plus my regular pay for every day since I left Sarasota until I get to wherever I am going I don't know what I'll do with all of my money. I forgot to get a checkbook for you before I left Sarasota but I'll write to the bank there and tell them to send you one.

I'm keeping a list of all the places I've been and the trips I've taken since I've been in the army. I was just looking it over and I've really been places. More places then I ever expected to see.

How much gas are you getting each week now. It's a good thing I'm not home because I could never get along with a gas ration card.

I have to go get a haircut now. I haven't had one for a long time so I really need it – or a violin.

All of us fellows are living here together and we're really having a good time. We have a party every night and sleep almost all day.

If you want to write address it to the
340th Bomb. Sqd.
Operations Office, Duncan Field
San Antonio, Texas but be sure to put a return address on it because I don't know how long I'll be here. I'm staying in Room 501 at the Gunter Hotel.

Love
Theodore

"To be Young"

Dutch ~ Many of our group had their flight training at Randolph Field and stayed at the Gunter Hotel. We had four rooms in a row for the officers. Rockett, Lockhart, Ferebee, and Van Kirk each had a room. Our stay was just one big party. A crap game or poker game was always going on in one of the hotel rooms.

We went out to the bars every night. One night, I was tired and said, "I am going to bed early." Strangely everybody agreed with me, which I thought was a little funny. When I returned to my room I found a four hundred pound woman in my bed. Tom Ferebee had paid her to be there. Until the day Tom died he was afraid that I was going to get even with him for that.

Years later Tibbets, Dick Nelson, George Hicks and myself were at the Marine base in Mesa, Arizona. Tom was going to fly in late. Several of the wives who were sponsoring the program took a limousine to the airport to meet Tom. He opened up the door to the limo and all he could see were legs, women's legs. He said, "Finally that damn Van Kirk got back at me."

Rockett was hot headed and we got into a major scrape in San Antonio while we were getting the first modifications to our airplanes. Tom and I had returned to the hotel after seeing a movie. A big party including the enlisted men was going on in Rockett's room, which was against the rules. Everyone was drinking and half crocked. Tom and I were relatively sober. The phone rang and I answered it thinking someone was pulling a joke on us and gave a wisecrack answer. It was the front desk. A few minutes later the house detective was knocking at the door. Rockett opened a drawer, grabbed his .45, and went to the door. He was going to shoot the guy because he was complaining about the noise. Tom and I looked at each other and realized this is serious. Tom takes Rockett and walks him out the hall one way. I took the house detective and walk the other way. We thought we had reached an agreement and things were settled, and Tom and I try to break up the party. About ten minutes later all hell breaks loose and twenty MPs barge into the room and take us to headquarters to "arrest us."

A couple of days later we left for Presque Isle and stopped at Wright-Pat for another modification. Tom and I figured we are on our way and out of trouble. What we did not know was that the major MP commanding officer wrote a long report that had followed us to England. The only thing that saved Tom and me was that the MP in his detailed report included that "Lieutenants Ferebee and Van Kirk appeared to be sober and did their best to contain a bad situation and tried to break up the fight."

What a wild trip out of San Antonio until we got over to England. It was great to be young!

"Orders for the Bolero Movement"

May 22, 1942
Orders from the Headquarters Eighth Bomber Command

1. The information and instructions contained in these orders are issued for the purposes of assisting pilots, to acquaint crews with a multitude of details, provide accurate information relative to the recognition of aircraft in the United Kingdom and to safely guide them to their ultimate home stations. Since flying conditions, weather, aids to navigation and communication are totally different in the British Isles a system of safety devices has been organized for the purpose of giving every possible assistance to all United States aircraft. Certain consideration must be given to the fact that this is a zone of combat and that active defensive organizations must be co-operated with at all times. It is imperative and fundamental to the safety of all concerned that each individual be thoroughly informed of all conditions that may arise and to this end crews should be thoroughly instructed in the following details:-

a. Enemy. It is known that enemy air and sea forces will be operating in the North Atlantic in the form of submarines, armed raiders and shore based aircraft operating from Norway. Both enemy fighter and bomber raids can be expected at any time over or near England. *Enemy long reconnaissance airways have recently been active over – Iceland.*[144] Intelligence Reports show that enemy reconnaissance has been active over ports used by our troops, and it can be assumed that he will have information on areas and stations which our airforces will occupy. It is possible that our forces will meet opposition enroute to and upon arrival in the United Kingdom.

b. Friendly. Considerable friendly activity is likely to be encountered when approaching United Kingdom. Friendly Fighter and Patrol units will operate normally along the route Iceland to United Kingdom, and our forces must be prepared at all times to show the recognition signals if and when challenged. Ground Anti-aircraft forces are so organized as to give complete protection of the coastal and industrial areas and planes must conform to flying regulations and recognition procedure to prevent being fired upon.

2. Mission.

a. Purpose. To fly combat, transport and reconnaissance type aircraft from United States, Canada, and Iceland to the United Kingdom with the highest regard for the safety of personnel and equipment.

3. Routes.

a. Into United Kingdom.

1.	Goose Bay	Prestwick, Scotland	2160	miles.
2.	Gander Lake	" "	2100	"
3.	"	B.W. 8 Greenland	970	"
	B.W.2	Reykjavik, Iceland	500	"
	Iceland	Stornoway, Scotland	657	"
	"	Prestwick	844	"
4.	Gander Lake	B.W.1	777	"
	B.W.1	Reykjavik	770	"
	Reykjavik	Stornoway	657	"
	"	Prestwick	844	"
5.	Gander Lake	Reykjavik	1635	"
6.	Reykjavik	Prestwick	844	"

b. Arrival Point in United Kingdom to home station.
1. Fighters.

Stornoway	Ayr, Scotland	203	miles
Ayr - home station (Chelveston,			
Kimbolton, Thurleigh (Podington area)		273	miles

These are the direct route distances only and not the ones that will be designated by Fighter Command and Flying Control. Routes to be taken will depend on enemy activity, weather, location of ground defense, danger areas, balloon barrages, etc.

2. Bombers and Transports.

Prestwick	Polebrook area	265	miles
Prestwick	Warton	135	"

Same remarks apply as in 3b (1) above.

4. Organizations.

a. Bombardment (H)35 B-17E's
1. 97th Bomb Grp. (H) to Polebrook and Grafton Underwood
b. Bombardment (L) (44 A-20's)
1. 15th Bomb Grp. (L) to Molesworth
c. Fighter.
1. 31st Pursuit Grp. (100 P-39's) to Chelveston and its satellite, Kimbolton.
2. 1st Pursuit Group. (100 P-38s) to Thurleigh and one squadron to Kimbolton.
d. Transport.
1. Two Transport Groups to Warton.

5. Operational Instructions.

a. Flight Plans. Prior to departure of any aircraft bound for United Kingdom Transatlantic Control (T.A.C.) at Prestwick will be contacted through Control Officer at point of departure for the purpose of determining the maximum number of aircraft that can be accommodated. (Prestwick will also be the control for Stornoway for this purpose). After this number has been determined the Flight Commander will provide Ferry Command and T.A.C. Prestwick with a warning order giving the following information.

1. Number of aircraft and destination (U.K.)
2. Types of aircraft and serial number of each.
3. Names of Officers, civilians and enlisted men in each crew by rank and initials.
4. Number of boxes, bags, etc. and weight of mail, freight or cargo to be removed at Prestwick for shipment to other points in the United Kingdom.
5. Personnel requiring rail transportation from Prestwick to other points in United Kingdom.

b. T.A.C. will then prepare and submit a weather forecast based on the Estimated Time of Departure (E.T.D.). If it becomes necessary to change the E.T.D. another E.T.D. must be submitted in which case T.A.C. will again prepare another weather forecast.

c. When it is apparent that the flight can be made, a Flight plan will be
1. Time of departure.
2. Number of aircraft and crews if different from that in the warning order.
3. Flight plan giving times at major latitudes or longitudes.
4. Estimate time of arrival.
5. Altitudes.
6. Course to be flown, i.e., great circle or rhumb line.[145]
7. Other pertinent information.

d. Control in flight. RAF will assume control of all aircraft after take-off from Iceland and continue in control until planes have reached 61°N at which place TAC Prestwick will take over.[146]

e. If weather permits, all approaches from the sea into UK will be made below 5,000 feet. In clear weather (unless otherwise ordered) planes will circle the field to the left at 2,000 feet. All landings will be made through instructions from the control room by radio. Most stations are equipped with landing T's, which normally are placed in front of the control tower. Other signals such as a black ball (land by T only) or yellow pyramid (aircraft making instrument landings) are used. Considerable construction is in progress at most fields and these must be well observed due to the fact that obstructions are not marked except by night. Traffic at all stations will be congested and pilots <u>must</u> be on the alert to avoid collisions since no information is given over the radio except when blind approaches are necessary. A white dumbell (sic) shaped panel within the signal panel in front of the control officer indicates "runways only."[147]

"Patterson Field"

May 28, 1942
Lt. T. J. Van Kirk
Patterson Field
Dayton, Ohio
340th Bomb. Sqd.
Thursday
Dear Mother, Dad and Jean,

I called home last night and told Mary Jane to tell you where I was and so you wouldn't think I was lost.

I'm sitting here on the balcony of the officers club writing this. It's on the third story and over looks the whole field. It's very nice and it's also cool which is one thing I appreciate today.

I don't know what's going on or anything else. We just seem to be jumping from one field to another and not getting much done at any one place. I hope we soon make one of our stops Middletown.

I've been into town twice now. It isn't such a bad town. It is a lot different to be north again though.

I don't think we'll be here very long but I'll write or call and let you know.
Love
Theodore

From the diary - *Left Duncan and went to Patterson Field, Dayton Ohio where we stayed for four days. Had a good time in Dayton at the Merry Go Round. Left there and went to Bangor, Maine after landing at Mitchell Field, N.Y. to check the weather.*[148]

Dutch - When we were in Bangor, Maine, going overseas Mickey Miller came around and said, "Guys, they do not have good shoes over in England. You better stock up on shoes." So we all bought two or three pairs of shoes in Holton, Maine. I think Mickey was making five dollars a pair. When he left for

England he did not take an ordinary footlocker with him. He took nothing but silk stockings and things like that. He knew what he was getting into.

"American Expeditionary Air Force"

May 31, 1942

Dear Mother, Dad and Jean,

Well here I am in another State. It seems that every time I write a letter I put a different return address on it.

We are here with a squadron of P-38s and the other two squadrons are at another place with a squadron of P-39s. The three groups make up what is known as the American Expeditionary Air Force. I don't know how soon we'll go across but we can't go much farther and still be in the U.S.

They say we will stay here for about a month and while we are here the navigators will make about three trips across with the ferry command just to get some practice.

I've only had laundry done once since we left Sarasota. I was always afraid to send it out because if we did we'd leave the place before we got it back.

On the way up here we went to N.Y. first and went right between Harrisburg and Norry. We were going to stop and buzz the town but we got in a thunderstorm and had a hard enough time getting through that without stopping and buzzing towns.

There is (not) a darn thing to do around here. But it is very nice country all full of mountains and lakes. It is a lot cooler here too. In fact we almost freeze to death here at night.

I'll write you a long letter and tell you all about it soon.

Love

Theodore

Address on Back

Lt. T. J. Van Kirk

340th Bomb. Sqd.

Dow Field

Bangor, Maine

"Getting Ready to go Across"

June 2, 1942

Fresno, Calif.

Dear Mother, Dad and Jean,

This time I'll write you a letter before I leave and try to let you know what's happening.

Last evening the navigators in our group packed up and got on a transport ship and went to Presque Isle, Maine, twelve miles from Canada. We were going to take some cargo ships across while the rest of our squadrons are waiting here for us.

This morning they got us up at five o'clock and told us to get ready to go back. We got back here at 9 o'clock this morning and our ships are all loaded ready to take off. We're just standing around waiting for the weather to clear up. Now we're going to the west coast, Tacoma, Washington to be exact.

Last night it was cold as the devil up at Presque Isle. I slept with two blankets and a comfort on.

All of the things that are on the boat to England have gone already. I didn't have anything on it except what they issued to me and I can get all of that stuff again.

I'll have to finish this in a hurry because we are getting ready to leave. I let you know more when I get there.

> *Love*
> *Theodore*

From the diary ~ The afternoon of May 31 they sent all the navigators to Presque Isle for duty on transports while the others were getting ready to go across. The next morning they sent us back.

June 2 we left Bangor for Fresno Calif. Got as far as Westover Field, Springfield, Mass. where we were weathered in for four days. Finally took off for Fresno. Refueled in St. Louis and spent the night in Albuquerque, N.M. The next day we flew on to Fresno. The trip was made via N.Y., Pitt., Dayton, St. Louis, Kansas City, Amarilla, Al., Bakersfield and Fresno.

We stayed at Fresno for about 10 day. I saw some of the fellows I had gone to school with and who were now flying in B-25s.

The scenery on this trip was beautiful. I got a good view of the country from one end to the other. Don't know whether I like Florida or Calif. the better.[149]

The Japanese had launched an air assault in early June on Dutch Harbor, but were repelled by American forces. Several days later they invaded the islands of Kiska and Attu. The Attu villagers were interned in Japan for the remainder of the war.

Dutch ~ We had been sitting in Maine waiting to go overseas and all of a sudden we were flying across the country to Fresno. When we landed in St. Louis to refuel Newt Longfellow railed at us. By the way Colonel Longfellow never wore insignia.

Japan had attacked Alaska and the Battle of Midway had started. The only thing between the Japanese and the west coast were our thirty-six B-17s. We were told to fly patrols. A funny thing happened. The flight crews took out the bomb bay tanks and put in the bombs. Finally, after we were loaded, some guy comes out and said to take out the bombs and put in the bomb bay tanks. Ferebee said, "Oh shit." He gets up in the bomb bay, takes the fuses out of the bombs and goes up in the bombardier compartment and pulls the toggle switch, which drops all the bombs right on the ground. We stood there and looked. None of them exploded! So Tom decided we might as well just roll them away.

We were ordered to go back to Maine then to England. Our laundry wasn't ready and we hadn't had clean clothes for ages. Mickey Miller went out with his .45 and came back with the laundry.

"Battle of Midway"

A decade earlier Japan had conquered Manchuria and established a Japanese controlled state. Six months after Pearl Harbor Japan had overrun Hong Kong, seized the naval base at Singapore, invaded Thailand, and taken the Philippines, Wake Island, Guam, and the British Gilberts. Conquering the Dutch East Indies (Indonesia) provided vital raw materials and oil resources for Japan during the war.

Admiral Chuichi Nagumo launched aircraft off half the carriers of the Imperial Japanese Navy to attack Midway Island. The nearby American carriers, the USS *Enterprise, Hornet,* and *Yorktown,* surprised the Japanese and destroyed four of their carriers, which six months earlier had attacked Pearl. The *Yorktown* was lost on June 5th.

June 4 – 7, 1942, the Battle of Midway is considered one of the most significant naval battles in history and a turning point as the United States and her Allies took the offensive in the Pacific Theatre. But Japan still controlled significant geographic areas with essential natural resources.[150]

"Every B-17 in the Country"

June 6, 1942
Lt. T. J. Van Kirk
Building 262
Hammer Field

Fresno, California

Dear Mother, Dad and Jean,

Well I finally got to California. I thought for a while that I wasn't going to get to see the West Coast but I suddenly changed my mind.

I have a letter here for you that I wrote in Bangor, Maine and never did have a chance to send. I've been trying to send you telegrams so you know where I'm at.

Since we left Sarasota I've had one letter from both you and Mary Jane. We went to Duncan Field and stayed there for about two weeks. From Duncan we went to Patterson Field in Dayton Ohio for a few days. Last Saturday we flew from Patterson field for Bangor, Maine. We were supposed to stay there for about a month and then go to England. Monday afternoon they took all the navigators off our ships and sent 14 of us to Presque Isle, Maine – 12 miles from Canada. The following morning we were to take about 35 transport ships to Greenland and Iceland and come back to our old squadron. In the middle of the night the orders were changed and they put us on a plane and took us back to Bangor. The next day Tuesday we started for here but ran into bad weather and had to land at Springfield, Mass. We spent two days there and left for here Friday morning. We stopped at St. Louis for gas and spent the night in Albuquerque, New Mexico and got here this morning.

That's the story of my life for the past month or so. Ever since we left Duncan we've been afraid to send out laundry because as soon as we do leave a place. We've moved so often that I haven't been paid yet this month. I have $315 coming to me.

The trip out here was really nice. From Maine to Canada I've seen almost all of the country now. I flew right over Lykens and Millersburg (PA). We wanted to buzz the town but the Major said we didn't have time.

About the prettiest country I saw was in Pa. It got awful monotonous at times flying across the plains. You couldn't see a hill for miles. Across the Rockies it was beautiful. The air was so clear that you could see the snow-capped peak of Mt. Whitney from a distance of 100 mile or more. This California air is really invigorating. It's not bad out here but we're on 24 hour alert and don't get out all of the time. They say this is a war zone. It looks as though we're going to stay here for a while. I think they're waiting for an attack on the west coast. They have every B-17 in the country out here and almost all of the B-25s.

I can't think of anymore to tell you but will write more often.

Love

Theodore

June 10, 1942, *Wed eve*
Dear Ted.

Had two letters from you today the first for a long time you say the same about mine but I don't know where they are for I have been writing and always have a return address on but have never got any back we just come in from grandma Van Kirks we took Mildred out she has been in with us all week she done my washing and ironing. I wish we would have had your laundry here. You must like Calif the way you say in your letter. I sure do envy you. You have seen more of the world already than I ever expect to see. I was down to M.J. a long time on Monday eve Jean went down with me M.J. lend Jean one of her evening gowns to go to the Alumni Dance. She looks very nice in it. Well I will finish your letter now I just finished putting Jean's hair up for the dance she said she just wondered what she was going to look like till I got thru with her. She is also invited to the senior class dance at Rolling Green on Tuesday eve so you know your sis is really growing up. You said in your letter you thought you would be out there for awhile I only hope you do. For I would ten times rather have you here than across. But I suppose you feel the other way. I wish you could come home again I really could appreciate it a lot now I was so darn sick all the while you were home the other time. Doug Portzline went to the army he only had a month to finish at law school and they wouldn't let him finish I don't know how some of these fellows in town here stay out and can finish school and all. Well I guess this will be all for now it is getting late will write often since I know where you are.

All our love Mother[151]

"On the Way to Bangor"

June 14, 1942
Hotel Statler St. Louis
Dear Mother, Dad and Jean,

I am on my way back across the country again. I left Fresno last Thursday and got weathered in here ever since.

We're going back to Bangor, Maine as soon as the weather clears up. I sent you a telegram today giving you my address at Bangor. It is Bldg. 122 Dow Field, Bangor, Maine.

It got very cold here last night.

I was down at Sikeston yesterday and saw my old instructors and a lot of other fellows. They're building the school a lot bigger.

I haven't anything more to tell you so I'll tell you about everything from Bangor, Maine.

Love
Theodore

"Orphans of the Air Corps"

Postmarked June 15, 1942[152]
Lt. T. J. Van Kirk
Bldg T-122, Dow Field
Bangor, Maine
Dear Mother, Dad and Jean,
*   I sent you a telegram last night letting you know that I was on my way back across the country again.*
*   We left Fresno last Thursday and landed at St. Louis. The weather was so bad that we had to stay there until today. We got as far as Springfield, Mass. today before we ran into bad weather so we landed here for the night.*
*   I just happened to think of Metzgers today and forgot whether I mailed them the check or not. I'll send you $20 and if I didn't you just give it to them & find out how much I owe. I haven't got last months pay yet. I still have money left from April. I'll send you some money as soon as I get paid.*
*   I don't know how long I'll be in Bangor this time. Things are so mixed up they don't know where they want us. Our commanding officer Major Tibbets calls us the orphans of the Air Corps.*
*   I'll write as soon as I can tell you more. My address will be*
Bldg. T-122
Dow Field
Bangor, Maine.

A loaded oil tanker off the coast of Florida was sunk by Axis submarines, which had begun to stalk the Gulf and Florida coasts.[153]

"Call Signs for Bolero"

June 16, 1942, the Office of the Operations Officer assigned tactical radio call signs and airplane call letters for use during the Bolero movement, the buildup of American military in Great Britain. The personal call signs were to be used for "communication with commanding officers without regard for airplane number" and not to be used for training purposes.[154]

TABLE 5.3 — CALL SIGNS AND AIRPLANE CALL LETTERS FOR 340TH BOMBARDMENT SQUADRON

Personal Call Sign	Pilot	
CO BomWg One	OU7Q	(Colonel Longfellow)
CO Bomgr Ninety Seven	B6RW	(Colonel Cousland)
CO Bomron Three Forty	F7XA	(Major Tibbets)
CO Bomron Three Forty One	1CAG	(Captain Knox)
CO Bomron Three Forty Two	WR9H	(Captain Musselwhite)
CO Bomron Four Fourteen	3YDA	(Captain Flack)
CO Bomron Three Fifty Nine	F7XQ	(Major Thomas) same as B-17E No. 41-9098
CO Bomron Four Nineteen	WR9V	(1st Lieutenant Traylor) same as B-17E No. 41-9119

Airplane Call Letters for 340th Bomb Sq.

41-2588	F7XB	(Lieutenant Lee)
41-2626	F7XE	(Lieutenant Wikle)
41-2578	F7XF	(Lieutenant Beasley)
41-9051	F7XG	(Lieutenant Summers)
41-9107	F7XJ	(Lieutenant Hoffman)
41-9174	F7XK	(Lieutenant Rockett)
41-9020	F7XM	(Lieutenant Karas)
41-2629	F7XO	(Lieutenant Aenchbacher)
41-9175	B6RZ	(Lieutenant Lipsky)

Source: "Signal Operations Instructions," WWII Combat Operations Report 1941-46 Eighth Air Force, Record Group 18, Entry 7, Box 5668, National Archives Building, College Park, MD.

June 17, 1942, the United States Army Corps of Engineers established the Manhattan Engineer District to develop the atomic bomb.

"A Crap Game"

June 19, 1942

Dear Mother, Dad and Jean,

I'm still sitting around Westover field trying to find out what we are going to do. We are going to take off and go to Bangor, Maine in about an hour. We're going to Bangor now instead of Houlton.[155] *They'll probably change it all in about five minutes.*

We've been here since Monday and at first they had us going to Bangor, then to Houlton and then to the far north fly the weather service and then staying here and now they're going to send us to Bangor. They change their minds once ever half hour.

Did you get your checkbook from the bank yet. At the present time I have a balance of 154.50 and I want to try to keep $125 there all of the time. We're going to take off now. I'll finish my letter in Bangor.

I got in Bangor about an hour ago. It took us 1 hr & 15 min. to go 270 mile. I don't know how long we're going to be here but I'm pretty sure our next move will be across. Two B-17s are going across with 8 – P-38s.

I got in a crap game right after I got here and won so I'll send you some money and also a check. After this check I'll have $125 left in the bank and then you can check out $88 for the next four months and $118 every month after that. Let me know how much a month you plan to check out just in case I have to write a check for something. I shouldn't need any now that I got a raise & I'll soon get 10% for foreign duty.

I'm going to town now to eat so I'll close at once.

I got 3 letters from you and four from M.J. waiting here for me.

Love

Theodore

Write out a check for Metzgers every month until that is paid and if you wrote out a check for the car this month tear this check up.

From the diary – *Left Fresno on June 15, 1942 and flew directly to St. Louis where we were weathered in for four days. I visited Sikeston again and had a good time in St. Louis.*

We flew on to Westover field where we were again weathered in for three days. We finally reached Bangor on June 23.[156]

"Bombardment Boys Took Over Town"

June 23, 1942

Dear Mother, Dad and Jean,

I got a letter from you today. That was really quick.

Don't take that money and finish paying Metzgers. Wait until next month and write a check for Metzgers and the car. The first five month – April, May, June, July & August, there will be $88 going into the bank every month and after that

$18 so you can check out more than $25.00 I'll very seldom use any of it I just got a raise and I soon be getting 10% extra for foreign service. Besides I always was lucky. And don't you go back to work either.

I didn't get your telegram until Monday but I don't think it was best for you to come anyhow. They made everyone send their wives home and the weather up here gets rough sometimes.

I don't know what all those kids back home are joining the army for. They don't know what its all about. Of course I didn't either but I learned fast. They'll be disgusted the first few weeks but they'll learn a lot.

I haven't been away very long but I'll bet I've learned more then I ever would have in Norry. I'm seeing all of the country too and I'll probably see a lot of other countries.

I'll let you know anything I find out as soon as I can. Don't worry about me. I wouldn't miss this for anything.

We have a lot of fun. One of the captains who is stationed up here said to me last night in town "You bombardment boys certainly took over this town."

Love
Theodore

June 26, 1942
Headquarters VIII Fighter Group
Dow Field, Bangor, Maine

Subject: Emergency Rations
To: Captain of each C-47 and B-17

1. You are responsible for each member of your crew and each passenger having the following:
   a. 5 "Bail-out" Rations (2 packets per ration)
   b. 1 "K" Ration (15 packets)
2. The "Bail Out" rations are to be stored on the person of each crewman and passenger.

The "K" rations are to be stored in the airplane, so as to be easily available.[157]

"Gun Under my Pillow"

June 26, 1942
Dear Mother, Dad and Jean,

I got your last telegram yesterday. I was sorry to hear that you weren't coming up but glad that you finally made up your mind.

We will probably leave on Sat. morning. Six ships. I will be on the first ship to leave so I'd better find my way. The first six ships to go will stay in Iceland with 24 P-38s as protection until all the rest go through and then we'll leave so we'll be the last ones to get to England. Just keep sending mail here and they will probably forward it and the last ship can bring some along.

I'm very busy now getting everything ready to go and still doing some flying. I walk around with my maps and route manual under one arm and my .45 in the other hand. If a route manual gets lost or stolen we'll probably have to go down to Australia instead of England. I'm sleeping with it and my gun under my pillow tonight.

We're going to a place about 500 miles north of the tip of Greenland from there to Iceland and Iceland to England. We could go straight across but the pursuit ships can't. It's daylight all the time up there and we have to fly across the ice cap. I'll have a lot to talk about when I come home. I've seen plenty and about to see a lot more.

I've got to sleep now. I hope you can read this.

I'm sending a jacket, sweater and .45 home tell dad to take my name & the bars & maybe the shoulder straps off the jacket before he wears it & take good care of the gun. There is a full clip there for it. Be careful with the gun its vicious & shoots so fast you can hardly count them.

Love
Theodore

From the diary ~ *We left Bangor on June 27, 1942 and landed at Presque Isle, Me. for final briefing.*[158]

"Indian Gloves for Jean"

June 29, 1942
Dear Mother, Dad and Jean,

You'll have to excuse the pencil but I'm out of ink and the bottle is in the airplane.

I'm in Goose Bay, Labrador. Don't look for it on the map because it isn't there. All it is is three lousy runways and a few buildings. The only contact with the outside world is by plane, radio or boat. There isn't a town within several hundred mile of here. There is an Indian and Eskimo village about 5 mile away and a Hudson Bay trading post 20 mile away.

Money doesn't mean a thing here. All you can use it for is gambling. You wash outside in cold water and never shave. It gets pretty cool here at night too. The sun sets about 10:00 o'clock and rises about 3 the next morning. The days are so

June 29, 1942

Dear Mother, Dad and Jean,

you'll have to excuse the pencil but I'm out of ink and the bottle is in the airplane

I'm in Goose Bay, Labrador. Don't look for it on the map because it isn't there. All it is is three lousy runways and a few buildings. The only contact with the outside world is by plane, radio or boat. There isn't a town within several hundred miles of here. There is an Indian and Eskimo village about 5 miles away and a Hudson Bay trading post 20 miles away

Money doesn't mean a thing here. All you can use it for is gambling! You wash outside in cold water and never shave. It gets pretty cool here at night too. The sun sets about 10:000 o'clock and rises about 3 the next morning. The days are

long we have a lot of time to do nothing.

We got here Sat. from Bangor and will continue our trip as soon as the weather gets good.

I got a pair of Indian gloves for Jean. I can't send them to her so I'll keep them until I get home.

All my mail from now on will be censored so I'll just write to let you know I'm O.K. Don't worry if you don't here from me because it will be darn hard to get mail through.

My address is
A.P.O.- 1066
Postmaster
New York City
The A.P.O. stands for Army Post Office but don't put that on. I'll write as soon as I can and try to call you from Iceland.

Brig. Gen. H. L. George requested improvements to widen the one hundred by six thousand foot gravel airstrip at Goose Bay, Labrador, and add additional housing. Spruce trees marked the Goose Bay military airport's runway sides and ends with portable lights. A smudge pot was placed on the edge of the runway, which was into the wind.[159]

July 2, 1942, Boeing Fortress No. 41-24444 was delivered and assigned to the 92nd Bombardment Group. Lt. Charles Austin flew the Fortress to England.[160]

"When I get to England"

July 9, 1942
Lt. T. J. Van Kirk
A.P.O. – 1066

ARMY AIR BASE
DOW FIELD
BANGOR — MAINE

Postmaster
New York City
Censored by T. J. Van Kirk
Dear Mother, Dad and Jean,

I don't see much use writing a letter because when they get through telling us what we can't write there's nothing to write about.

There's nothing to do here except sleep and eat. If I keep this up I'll be fat before I come home. I can't think of an easier way to clear $15. a day though.

By the time I get to where we'll settle down and get paid I'll have two months pay and over a months per diem coming. Besides the fellows owe me over $100. The only trouble is that we don't get paid in American money and it mixes me all up.

Yesterday I was showing the plane to a Lt. in the engineers and found he was from Pa. He asked me what part of Pa. and I told him Norry. He was from Sunbury. Some relative of Col. John Bains. I know of two fellows from home up here but can't locate them.

I don't know how long we'll stay here but not too long I hope. I hope we soon settle down in a permanent place. I had enough of this traveling to last me for a while. Besides all my clothes will soon be dirty.

There isn't much more I can write but I hope I have a lot of letters waiting for me when I get to England.

Love
Theodore

I can't write very often because I haven't got anything to say. I'll write as often as I can. I don't know how long it take you to get them so let me know that too.[161]

July 14, 1942
Dear Mother, Dad and Jean,
I finally ran across some writing paper that I don't have to dig in the bottom of my bag for so I'll write another letter.

I hope we soon get out of this place. There is no place to go in this town and there isn't anything to do there. The only trouble is that it's the only town too.

The food we have been getting since we left isn't anything to brag about but it keeps you alive and it isn't so bad when your hungry. I'd be glad to sink my teeth into a nice steak too. Tell Martha and Lee that when I come home I want a big chicken dinner.

I hope I soon get over there and get a newspaper. The only thing I've seen since the end of June has been an army paper printed on July 8. I'd like to see the ball scores.

When you send me letters put the address as

340th Bomb Sqd., 97th Bomb Gp.

A.P.O. 1066 c/o Postmaster

N.Y.C.

I hope I soon get the address right. I should have a lot of letters waiting for me. I hope.

Love

Theodore

"Icebergs and Mountains"

Postmarked July 14, 1942

Dear Mother, Dad and Jean,

It is now 1:30 a.m. here but I can't sleep so I'll write a letter. I haven't any light but I don't need it. It never gets dark here.

I'm trying to write a letter at every stop. I sent one about five days ago but I don't know how long it will take you to get these letters.

It's very pretty here with a lot of icebergs and mountains. There is a big glacier about 5 miles from the camp. They built a landing field on the only spot of level land I've seen yet. There isn't anything around here but the airport. I hope I soon get to a place in here I can go to a town.

We're going to leave here tomorrow if the weather is clear and I hope it is.

I'm going to try to find some of the fellows from home. I know some of them are there but I don't know whether I'll be able to find them or not.

I'm feeling as good as I ever did even though I did eat a lot of beans at our last stop. The food here is a lot better.

I gave you my address. I don't know how soon I'll get the letters sent there but I'll pick them up sometime.

The mosquitoes are getting bad now so I'll have to get under the net.

I'll write as often as I can.

Love

Theodore

From the diary ~ *The first leg of the flight across took us to Goose Bay, Lab*(rador) *where we spent a few days waiting for good weather.*

Our next stopping place was Bluie West One in Greenland. The flight was over water and in good weather. In Greenland we saw icebergs in the fjord and glaciers. We climbed a mountain until we were played out and still didn't reach the top. We spent about five days in Greenland and were pleased to leave. It never got dark here.[162]

Dutch ~ The Air Force put together the Bolero movement to get airplanes over to England. We had thirty-six B-17Es and some C-47s and P-38s. Each B-17 had four P-38s assigned to it. We had two bases in Greenland Bluie West One and Bluie West Eight. We were the navigation ship for the P-38s. One of the biggest problems was the weather and there were some mishaps.

If there were clouds you had to fly low and make a U-turn. If the weather was bad you might not be able to pull up without running into the sides of a fjord. You also had no depth perception between the ice and the sky. Rolf had guys throw baggage over the ice caps and then come around to land. He was the first guy to land on the ice. The crew cut the hub of the propeller off in order to get power to the radio and get word back of their location. A squadron of two B-17s and six P-38s were forced to land on the ice. *Glacier Girl* was one of the fighters lost over Greenland. Her crew was rescued on the ice after several days. Fifty years later the plane was recovered.

We couldn't land the first time because of the weather and had to return to Labrador. Eventually we landed at Bluie West 8 because it was the most open. Rockett told us we were going to be the weather scouts and fly due north to find Iceland again. It was an elementary course in navigation.

Lt. Gen. Dwight Eisenhower and Admiral Stark shook hands with Gen. Charles de Gaulle in London while the troops of the elite German Guard, paraded down the Champs-Elysees in Paris on Bastille Day, La Fete Nationale, July 14, 1942.[163]

"Hearst Newspapers"

July 15, 1942
Dear Mother, Dad and Jean,

I haven't mailed my letter from yesterday yet so I'll write some more and send with it.

I slept until noon again today. All we have to do is eat and sleep and it doesn't matter when we sleep.

I was introduced to Bill Wade along with the rest of our crew. He's a foreign correspondent for Hearst newspapers and International news. He wrote a story about our crew and sent it in so it looks as though I'll be getting my name in all the Hearst papers and most of the International news papers. The only trouble was that he put Sunbury as my home.

Today was the warmest day since I've been here and it's still cold. When I get to Eng(land) and get all the money people owe me and my pay I'll send some money home if I find a place to cable it from. Use what you need and put the rest in bank.

I'll write again soon.

Love

Theodore

Jean ~ "A lot of the time we did not know what was going on until we saw it in the paper or heard it on the radio. Mother adored Theodore; yes she did. Dad even more so I think. They were so proud of him. Grandpa Van Kirk ran a gas station on the Danville Highway. Uncle Lee's farm was about twenty miles up the road. The first time there was a release in the newspaper Grandpa Van Kirk got in the car and rushed up to the farm to show Uncle Lee because he did not get the paper until a couple of days later in the mail. Grandpa was so proud of Ted."[164]

"Stuck for the Duration"

July 17, 1942

Dear Mother, Dad and Jean,

There is nothing new going on around here. I was in town today and bought a few odd things and some candy bars. They put everything from peanuts to raisins in their chocolate bars.

We haven't moved on yet. I'm beginning to think that I'm stuck here for the duration but I hope not.

I wrote a letter to Zong's yesterday. That's one thing I can do to pass the time. The only trouble is that I haven't got anything to say.

There isn't anything to say now so I'll have to stop. I'll write more often and let you know what going on.

Love
Theodore

"Co-pilot Started Cursing"

July 22, 1942

Dear Mother, Dad and Jean,

I thought that I would be writing the next letter from England but we're still stuck in this place.

I saw Russel Hine about two days ago. He is driving a navy truck up here. I didn't know him. He stopped in front of our plane and left a fellow out and then drove on and backed up and asked me if my name wasn't Teedy Van Kirk. I recognized him then even if he did have a mustache. I saw him about three times after that and will probably see him again. He had the latest news from home. That is later than any I had. He told me Jean and his sister were going to visit his aunts.

He told me where John Naecker and Steamy Dodge and Bud Morris were. Steamy and Bud are together. I haven't seen any of them yet but I probably will if I stay here much longer.

Chapter 5

You can't get any laundry done up here in less than a week so I started doing my own. We wash a little each day and hang in on the barbed wire in back of our hut. We'll soon have everything clean and then we won't do any more until we get everything dirty again.

I met several fellows in the R.A.F. who are stationed here. They gave me their addresses and told me if I ever had a few days leave to go visit their parents. Some of them aren't so bad but most of them are the typical Englishman. Dumb as h.

The other day we took the chaplain of the post along for a ride. I gave him a pair of ear phones to wear and the co-pilot didn't know it. Something happened and the co-pilot started cursing and the chaplain could hear every word he was saying. Was his face red.

The next time I write I hope I'll be in England but I probably won't be.

Love

Theodore

"Real Poker Games"

July 25, 1942

Dearest Mary Jane,

You will have to excuse the paper because it's all I have. The other is all in the bottom of a pile of baggage.

I put this in my pocket to take notes on when some limey was briefing us. I didn't think he said anything worth writing down.

I think we will be leaving here soon. We were supposed to go today but Rockett was in the hospital and the doctors wouldn't leave him out. I think he'll get out tomorrow.

I haven't seen Russel Hine lately but I think I'll go down to see him before I go. He said he was going to write a letter to you I told him to tell you what a good boy I've been.

I soon be getting over there where I'll catch up with my mail again. I hope I have a few letters waiting for me. We'll be the last ones in our gang to get there. I hope they wait for us. The weathers been nice here the past few days and it's just about like a nice day in spring back home, except that the sun is up much longer. Its full moon up here tonight and the moon looks bigger then I've ever seen it. The only trouble is that the right girl isn't here to go with it – meaning you dear.

Today was Sunday – I think. It doesn't make any difference. Ever since I went to Sarasota Sunday has been the same as any other day. Now I don't do anything on any day so what's the use of wanting Sunday off.

Tell Bill and Benner they should be up here if they want to get into some real poker games. Money really changes hands fast but there isn't any use having it because there's nothing to spend it for. It's nice to win just the same.

This is the only sheet of paper I have so I'll have to stop. All my love and wishing I was with you.

Teedy

July 29, 1942, the USS *Boise* left Pearl Harbor assigned a mission to divert attention from the impending attack at Guadalcanal. She stopped at Midway Island before heading west to within five hundred miles of Tokyo.

James Starnes - "Our mission was to imitate the Doolittle raid and let it be known that we were there. We launched two scout airplanes with a catapult. Our presence was known. We broke radio silence trying to find the two planes, but lost them. We turned and headed back."

Chapter Five — Endnotes

129 The B-17E "Flying Fortress," an all-metal monoplane, was easily recognized by its broad expanse of wing surface, dihedral angle of the wings, and four engines. National Aeronautics Council, Inc., *Aeronautics Aircraft Spotters' Guide*, No. 1, January 15, 1942.

130 Van Kirk, "My Life In The Service."

131 Robert "Bob" Young, 77th Division, 307th Inf. Co. M., Fort Jackson, SC, letter to his sister, Mary Jane. Their brother William Young served in the Philippines.

132 The *Nitto Maru* radio warning went out at 0630 giving the position of the *Hornet* as 650 nautical miles east of Inubo Saki. Clayton K. S. Chun and Howard Gerrard, *The Doolittle Raid 1942: America's First Strike Back at Japan* (Oxford, UK: Osprey, 2006), 43.

133 Co-pilot of Plane #1 Richard Cole and Sgt. David Thatcher's, engineer gunner on Plane #7, speech at the "Gathering of War Birds" Air Show at Reading, PA, June 8, 2010.

134 Cole gave his account of Doolittle bailing out to Van Kirk and Dietz at Reading, PA.

135 Several crews ditched in the East China Sea and ten crashed in the interior of China. Chun and Gerrard, *The Doolittle Raid 1942*, 83. Chun used the phraseology "may have." *The Doolittle Raid* by Glines quoted Chiang Kai-shek's cable to Roosevelt that Japanese troops had slaughtered every man, woman and child in the area. Chang also used the figure of 250,000 Chinese massacred and added that the Japanese plowed up every Chinese airfield within an area of 20,000 square miles believed to have served as landing areas. Iris Chang, *The Rape of Nanking the Forgotten Holocaust of World War II*, (New York, NY: Basic Books, 1997), 216.

136 Ibid, 216. In addition to the Doolittle raid, Chang concludes that the basis for the massive campaign to "kill all, loot all, burn all" resulted from the Japanese military's contempt for the Chinese people and imbuing violence with religious overtones.

137 B-17E 41-2626 arrived at MacDill on March 1, 1942, and assigned to the 341st Bomb Squad 97th BG, and eventually transferred to the 92nd BG per "Individual Histories" of B-17s in Freeman's *The B-17 Flying Fortress Story*, 76.

138 Red Cross note, First Air Force priority message from Base Message Center at Mitchell Field, NY, and Western Union Telegram, Van Kirk personal papers.

139 "Total War and Total Effort," radio address of President Roosevelt, April 28, 1942.

140 Staff Sgt. William C. Young, Service No. 7025287, Manila American Cemetery, Fort Bonifacio, Manila, Philippines, Plot G Row 12 Grave 3. American Battle Monuments Commission, http://www.abmc.gov/home.php [accessed July 27, 2010].

141 The crew photograph of the *Red Gremlin* at Polebrook in *The Tibbets Story* included a "Sergeant Walker," but not Splitt or Kowalski.

142 Also by Operations Orders No. 3: B-17E Airplane No. 41-9051 (P) 2nd Lt. John C. Summers, B-17E Airplane No. 41-2588 (P) 1st Lt. Charles D. Lee, B-17E Airplane No. 41-9175 (P) 2nd Lt. Clarence W. Lipsky, B-17E Airplane No. 41-2578 (P) 2nd Lt. Harold H. Beasley, B-17E No. 41-2626 (P) 2nd Lt. Jesse O. Wikle, B-17E Airplane No. 41-2629 (P) 2nd Lt. Arthur E. Aenchbacher, B-17E Airplane No. 41-9107 (P) 1st Lt. David C. Hoffman O-417632. See Appendix B for crew lists.

143 Van Kirk, "My Life In The Service."

144 Corrections were handwritten insertions on the "Operations Instructions" and italicized.

145 A rhumb line intersects all meridians of longitude at the same angle. Holding a constant true heading would be flying a rhumb line. Department of the Air Force, *Air*

Navigation Manual, 2-8 and Glossary xv.

146 Extensive directions for "control in flight" were outlined in the Operations Instruction.

147 The secret instructions also included information about ground procedures, flight to home stations, and administrative matters. "Secret Operations Instructions," Headquarters Eighth Bomber Command USAFBI, May 22, 1942, WWII Combat Operations Report 1941 - 1946 Eighth Air Force, Record Group 18, National Archives Building, College Park, MD.

148 Van Kirk, "My Life In The Service."

149 Van Kirk, "My Life in the Service." The 97th Bombardment Group and the P-38s of the 1st Fighter Group quickly deployed to the west coast in response to the critical situation in the Pacific and impending Battle of Midway. The Groups returned to the east after about a week to prepare for the overseas flight. William Hess, *B-17 Flying Fortress*, (New York, NY: Random House, 1974), 53.

150 *General Marshall's Victory Report*, Biennial Report of the Chief of Staff of the United States Army, 1943 to 1945, to the Secretary of War, Washington, DC, September 1, 1945.

151 The Post Office stamped "moved, left no address" on the envelope addressed to Lt. T. J. Van Kirk, Building 262 Hammer Field, Fresno, CA.

152 Letter dated May 15, 1942, envelope postmarked a month later from Springfield, MA.

153 *Life* Magazine, May 1942, 48 – 49.

154 The confidential Signal Operations Instructions from the headquarters of the Ninety-Seventh Bombardment Group complied with SOI No. 6-3 Hq. Eighth Air Force, Grenier Field, NH. Airplane call letters were also assigned for the 341st, 342nd, 414th, 419th, and 359th Bomb Squadrons. NOTE: "O" in call signs and call letters (not the airplane Serial number) represents the letter of the alphabet and not the number zero. See Appendix C for airplane call letters for 414th, 341st, and 359th Bomb Squadron.

155 A large part of Houlton Army Air Base, established in 1941, converted to a Prisoner of War camp in 1944 and closed in 1946. Maine Historical Society, http://www.mainehistory.org [accessed April 26, 2010].

156 Van Kirk, "My Life In The Service."

157 Memorandum signed by Capt. Cass S. Hough, AAF, for the Commanding General, June 26, 1942. WWII Combat Operations Report 1941-46 Eighth Air Force, Record Group 18, Entry 7, Box 5668, National Archives Building, College Park, MD.

158 Van Kirk, "My Life In The Service."

159 "Airport Description Northwest River Labrador," Goose Bay folder, Record Group 18, Records of the Army Air Force, WWII Combat Operations Report, March 5, 1942.

160 No. 41-24444 was transferred to the 340th Squadron 97th Bombardment Group and named the *Red Gremlin*. Steve Birdsall, *Pride of Seattle* The Story of the First 300 B-17Fs, (Carrollton, TX: Squadron/signal Publications, Inc., 1998), 31.

161 "T. J. Van Kirk" frequently written as the censor on approved stamp for his letters home.

162 Van Kirk, "My Life In The Service." The United States constructed the air base at Narsarsuaq known as BW-1 Bluie West One near the southern tip of Greenland. The airfield provided a link in the North Atlantic Ferry Route during World War II.

163 Eisenhower got average marks and had a stellar record of demerits while at West Point (Class of 1915). "Bastille Day," *Life* Magazine, August 10, 1942.

164 Jean Van Kirk McAllister added that their grandfather Charles Theodore Van Kirk, Dutch's namesake, "did not live to see the Hiroshima mission either."

Chapter Six

European Theatre *Operation Bolero*

Dutch ~ Polebrook near Peterborough was our home base.

By July 27th the Bolero movement of the 97th Bombardment and 1st Fighter Groups was complete with the loss of five B-17s and six P-38s. The headquarters and squadrons of the 97th settled in at Polebrook and nearby Grafton Underwood.[165] The runways at Polebrook had been extended to accommodate the heavily loaded B-17Es.[166]

Back home during August, the *Holiday Inn* premiered at the New York Paramount Theatre while Bing Crosby and Fred Astaire delighted audiences around the country with Irving Berlin's music especially *White Christmas*.

"Dress up Every Night"

August 1, 1942

Dear Mother, Dad and Jean,

I got a letter from you today that you had written on July 20th so you can see that the mail service is O.K. when you get the right address. It is the first letter I got since I left. When I got here I found some letters waiting for me but they were all old. Some of them had been sent to Sarasota.

I got here a few days ago. It's very much like home. We have a very nice place. We have good rooms, pave roads too so we don't have to walk in mud. The food isn't too bad but it's not near as good as it was in the states. You can't go out here and buy a good thick steak for a buck and a half either.

We are doing a little work now. Getting a lot of instruction and practice. I hope we learn everything good.

Dutch ~ Mail call was frequently irregular sometimes twice a day, other times once in three or four days. Our base was outside Polebrook. Some rich babe (the Rothschild estate) had a house near by.

I broke all the braces off of my teeth but one. I can still use them but I think I'll have to get another set.

There aren't many cars in use over here but most of us have bicycles. They are high bikes and hard to ride. There will be more fellows killed on bicycles then in airplanes if we keep it up.

I'm going to collect two months back pay one of these days. If I get the chance I'll cable some of it home. I don't need much. I get all mixed up with this money over here. I still can't count it but I do know a pound is a lot more then a shilling. The stuff weighs a lot too.

Send my cadet blouse over to me. Over here we have to dress up every night for dinner and you need a lot of clothes. Also some candy etc. but no cakes and things.

My address is changed to
    340th Bomb Sqd.
    A.P.O. 875 c/o Postmaster
    New York City.
Keep writing and don't worry about me - unless I fall off my bicycle.
Love
Theodore

Chapter 6

Dutch ~ We each had bicycles in England but very quickly took whatever bike was available. The British were very proprietary about their bicycles.

I met with other navigators to discuss calculations about handling formations and to swing their compass for deviations on twenty-four headings over scotch and sodas in the Officer's Club. We got along at Polebrook.

The Polish pilots always wanted to buzz the towers.

"Letters Getting Censored?"

August 3, 1942

Dear Mother, Dad and Jean,

This has been one of the typical English days. We had a lot of mist and rain with very little sunshine.

Nothing has happened since I wrote my last letter so there isn't much to tell you. We hear and learn a lot of new things every day but of course we can't say anything about that.

We can't use electric razors or radios over here because we have a 250 volt electrical system. I don't know whether all the systems are like that but it certainly fooled the fellows who brought radios etc. along.

I think I'll finish this letter tomorrow and write to Martha & Lee and a few other letters I should write.

August 4

I got another letter from you today. The one telling about Frances getting married. I was surprised to find that Bucky was getting married so soon. How about getting his address for me so I can write to him.

Right now I'm heating some boiling water to wash some clothes in. I haven't had any laundry done since June 24 and it takes two weeks to get it done over here.

I've received two of your air mail letters so far but none of the Vmail. I haven't had a letter from M.J. since I've been here except old ones. You'll have to get after her.

I'll have to stop now or the censor will cut the words on this side when we want to cut them out on the other. Tell me if my letters are censored much. Keep writing and give me the news from home.

Love

Theodore

"Landing at Guadalcanal"

August 7, 1942, the Marines attacked the Solomon's and stormed the shores of the Tulagi, Guadalcanal, and the Malaita Islands.

James Starnes ~ "We heard rumors and stories over what we felt was great concern among the administration over where to put the most effort in Europe or the Pacific." Fleet Admiral Ernest King wanted to keep the sea-lanes open to Australia and stop the Japanese Navy's destroyers supplying replacement troops and supplies for their garrison on Guadalcanal by making round trips via the New Georgia Sound through the Solomon Islands. "We were assigned to the Task Force to stop the Tokyo Express. We received word from recon that the Jap fleet was on the way to Guadalcanal."[167]

"Flying with the Commander"

August 7, 1942

Dear Mother, Dad and Jean,

A few more days have passed and there is still nothing new. Nothing ever happens that we can tell about.

I haven't had any letters from you for the past three days. They usually come in groups of twos and threes.

I haven't had any time off since I've been here but one of these days I'm going to get a short leave and look the place over. Especially London.

I'll finish my letter now. I thought that I'd get a letter from you this afternoon but I doubt it very much.

The pilot I always flew with got sick and has taken a few weeks off I am now flying with the commanding officer of our squadron. He's a major and has been flying for a long time and is really good.

There isn't anything going on around here except what you can read in the newspapers so it's no use trying to tell you about it in a letter.

I'm O.K. and having a lot of fun. I'm getting more money then I know what to do with and don't know how to send it home. I'll write and let you know if anything happens.

Love

Theodore

"Training in England"

Dutch ~ While we were in England someone got the wise idea that we should do low level bombing. It wasn't very wise. The commanding officer at the time was ill so most of our training fell on Paul Tibbets' shoulders. Tibbets was the only one taking the war seriously. He had us out there one day flying low altitude missions over England. That came to an end when we wrapped most of England's power lines around our props.

Tibbets taught the gunners how to wash their guns down in gasoline so they would not gunk up or freeze at high altitude. We used gasoline for everything in those days. Tibbets was more experienced and had flown B-18s for submarine patrol up and down the coast. He became an old professor during the explanation to the gunners and was patient, but would only tell you once. If you didn't do it right the second time he lost his patience a little bit.

Kermit Beahan studied the bomb shackles because the British had the largest bombs at that time. He told us, "It is not like before when we were home. Now we are trying to avoid V1s, V2s, and VD."

At El Alamein the British Eighth Army slowly drove the Germans and Italians back towards Libya.

"First Heavy Bombardment Mission"

Pilot Maj. Paul Tibbets and 97th Group commander co-pilot Col. Frank Armstrong led the first American heavy bombing raid on Europe crossing the English Channel carrying British-made high explosives.[168] Four squadrons of RAF Spitfires escorted the dozen B-17s to attack the Sotteville railroad yards at Rouen, France.[169]

Gen. Ira Eaker observed aboard *Yankee Doodle*. Eaker described coming back towards the Channel coast when a Focke Wulf 190 attacked the No. 2 airplane astern of *Yankee Doodle* and two other German Fw190s fired from below him then pulled away. The RAF wing had climbed above and behind the B-17s and engaged in a "spectacular dogfight" with about thirty-five German fighters.[170]

Dutch ~ Tibbets was the only one from the 340th on that mission.[171] Tom Ferebee and I did not fly with him that day. Our group had been split between two different airfields: Polebrook and Grafton Underwood. Tibbets airplane was supposed to be sent to the other airfield to get loaded for bombs. The wrong airplane was sent so Paul switched planes and went with another crew. That is why Tom and I were not on the first one. Armstrong led us on a number of missions. He and Paul Tibbets turned the 97th around.

"Partying with the RAF"

Dutch ~ The RAF guys were outstanding pilots. We had a party at Polebrook and invited our friends from the RAF who escorted us.[172] They flew Spitfires and Hurricanes. One group that escorted us a lot was a Polish group flying for the RAF. They were one of the groups that we invited to the party. If you want to see a bunch of nuts they were it. When they came in the first thing they would do was buzz the field. They would be so low that their props would almost be hitting the ground. They put on the best flying show you saw here.

In the beginning we only had limited fighter support. The RAF took us in as far as they could with their Spitfires.[173] Then they let us go in by ourselves, drop our bombs, and on the way out would meet us again. The RAF pilots used to say that the most hazardous duty in the world was meeting us coming back out because we would shoot at anything. They said, "We were lucky though you could never hit anything!"

We could see the fighters turn around. It was like seeing your mother leave. You knew you were on your own. The formation of pilots automatically tightened up. That was our protection. Pilots would pride themselves by sticking their wing in the tail of the waist gun of the lead airplane. Your eyes got a little sharper. You would see spots out there that you would think were fighters or not. You called them out "fighters at 3:00 o'clock" or something similar. Sometimes the "fighters" were birds and there were a lot of false reports.

Tibbets said that in the fall of 1942 you were obliged to carry other officers, generally higher ranking officers. How do you tell a Brigadier General or a Colonel "no" who asked can I fly with you today? They stood right behind the pilot or the co-pilot just in front of the top turret gunner. There was not a lot of room in a B-17. Col. Frank Armstrong flew co-pilot.[174]

August 19, 1942, operational mission for Van Kirk [97th Bombardment Group (BG) – mission #2] Abbeville Drucat aerodrome, France[175]

The fortresses bombed the German controlled Abbeville aerodrome in a combined operations attack escorted by the RAF and Royal Canadian Air Force fighters.[176]

"My First Mission"

Dutch ~ My first mission was with Paul Tibbets. I was scared to death and did not know how I was going to react. I had never flown at twenty thousand feet before and fortunately that day I didn't get shot at.

We went in and bombed the Abbeville-Drucat aerodrome in northern France. This was the base for the Abbeville Boys, a fighter group of the Germans.[177] This raid occurred concurrently with the British commando raid on Dieppe.

Use of aerodrome or air depot depended on what group you were with. When with the British typically we said "aerodrome" and with Americans "airfield." Bombing missions became almost daily events. I could have gone crazy if I had been up on every mission.

"Scared as Hell"

Dutch ~ Our earlier training was useless once we started flying combat missions. I had never been above ten thousand feet before and now we were at twenty thousand feet. I looked down and said, "Christ that looks different," and had to teach myself. Tom Ferebee had never dropped a bomb from above ten thousand feet either and had to learn that too. Tibbets, Ferebee, and I used to joke that we got on the job training when we were in England. We were lucky we lived through it. That is all I can say. Later on the training got much better and more extensive than what they gave us.[178]

The *Pilot Training Manual* for the B-17 emphasized the essential pilot-navigator preflight planning and their relationship in flight. They studied the flight plan, weather conditions, and synchronized their watches.

Dutch ~ We did not hear about radar until we got over to England. The

British used it for a very good purpose, to defend their country. Their radar stations picked up the German raids. We seldom got flak until we got near the target. At the briefings we were told the location of the flak fields. Sometimes we came back cursing the intelligence officers because they told us wrong, but to the best of their ability. We tried to avoid the fields as we were going in and usually saw flak for no more than a half an hour while going in and coming out.

I can remember being scared as hell the first time we were hit with flak. During the fighter attack I looked out at the right hand window. You were as much a gunner as a navigator and better be able to shoot straight. Generally the gun I used was on the right side of the plane. There was another one on the left side. I turned around and looked at the left side for just a minute for other airplanes. When I turned back to the right side there were four bullet holes where my head had been. I thought they are not paying me enough for this job. That is what I mean about why it is better to be lucky rather than being good.

Tom Ferebee and I were always shooting behind. If we were not going to hit anything, we decided we might as well scare them to death.

The *Luftwaffe Gunnery Techniques* manual for German fighter pilots and gunners emphasized the importance of staying alert and that seeing the enemy first was "half the victory." Maneuvers and techniques for the approach, range, and cautions in facing stern attack from directly behind, pursuit curve attack, a dog fight, or frontal attack provided tactics against two and four engine bombers and their formations.[179]

Dutch ~ I was really close to Tom Ferebee up in the nose, but over the intercom you could hear the word "flak" or "here's one coming in at nine o'clock" and usually there was a bit of profanity like "get that bastard." Every once and a while Tibbets came over the intercom and said "cut it out on the intercom" or "too much chatter on the intercom."

Guys were always calling out where the fighters were coming from and Tibbets wanted them to be paying attention.

We always got a shot of bourbon when we landed. I did not drink much in those days. There was always someone who would drink it for you.

"Three Musketeers of the Army Air Forces"

Life magazine nicknamed the pilot, navigator, and bombardier as the "Three Musketeers of the Army Air Forces."

Dutch ~ Tom and I were late getting back from London. When we got to the base, we climbed over the fence. Our group was going on a mission. Tibbets saw us and said, "Where the hell have you guys been?" He had another navigator and bombardier on board. "Well, since you are here," Tibbets made us go on the mission in our dress uniforms. It cemented our relationship between the three of us because he protected us by not reporting that we weren't there.

 August 20, 1942, operational mission for Van Kirk [97th BG - #3 mission] Amiens/Longeau marshalling yards.

The 97th Bombardment Group bombed the Longeau marshalling yards in Amiens after photo reconnaissance informed Bomber Command of a large number of engines and railroad cars at the site.[180]

"Willie's Lucky Charm"

Dutch ~ John "Willie" Tittsworth said he had forgotten his rabbit's foot.[181] Tibbets pulled out of line and let Willie run back to get his good luck charm. That was Tibbets for you. If we ran true to form we razed Willie. I never carried any good luck charms or practiced any rituals, just get my maps together and go.

"Margaret Bourke-White"

August 21, 1942

Dear Mother, Dad and Jean,

I haven't written for so long that I don't know when the last letter was I know it was a long time ago.

I have been pretty busy the past few days. The newspapers and radio probably told why I'll send you a clipping too.

Yesterday a photographer for Life magazine Margaret Bourke White took a picture of our crew for the magazine. I'll soon have my picture there so look for it.

There isn't anything else to write about. The weather here has been pretty lousy as usual.

I haven't had a letter from home for the past two weeks. I don't know what the hold up is. I haven't had a letter from Mary Jane since I've been here. Maybe you aren't putting the whole address on them.

Lt. T – J. Van Kirk

340th Bomb Sqd.

97th Bomb Gp.

A.P.O. 875 c/o Postmaster

New York City

There's not a thing to write about. That was no. 3 for me and there isn't much too it. Had a lot of fun and did pretty good too. I'll try to write more often and hope I soon here from you.

Love

Theodore

Dutch - We were practicing getting our formations together and Margaret Bourke-White was taking pictures of our group flying and getting into formation. She was assigned to one of the pilots and was berating him on what she thought was the intercom. "Young man, young man, you are not doing what I am telling you to do."

The pilot turned around and said to her, "Ma'am, if you talked into the intercom instead of the pee tube I could hear you."

Margaret Bourke-White was the first female photo journalist hired by Henry Luce for *Life* Magazine, the first female correspondent to work in combat zones in World War II, and one of the first to document the concentration camps.[182] In the October 19, 1942, issue of *Life* more than a dozen photographs in England of the 97th BG by White appeared in the piece "U.S. High-Altitude Bombers Hit Nazis." White shot pictures of briefings, navigators looking over maps, the interior of a Fortress, B-17s in formation, and the bombing near the Abbeville airfield.

A telegram home that Van Kirk was safe also made the local news. Tibbets had made a hurried descent causing minor injury to Van Kirk's eardrums.[183]

Dutch - About the time my mother had one of her heart attacks, I was written up in a newspaper in France. My dad received an anonymous letter threatening him to stop giving out information about me or "your wife is going to have another heart attack." It infuriated my dad. He didn't give out the information. The newspapers did. If dad could have found out who wrote the letter he would have killed him.

My dad belonged to a Moose Lodge. After I got back from the atom bomb mission, someone stood up at a meeting and proposed giving me a life membership. Some of the members objected. My dad stood up and said, "My son would not take a membership in this lodge if you gave it to him," being the feisty old guy he was. It was a small town and there were animosities, but most people were glad to see me when I came home.

August 21, 1942, the 97th BG - #4 mission shipyards at Rotterdam, Holland. Several B-17s aborted for mechanical failures. The nine remaining unescorted Fortresses near the Dutch coast received a radio order to abandon the mission. As they turned twenty-five German fighters appeared, Fw190s and Me109s, and were beaten off by the American bombers. Co-pilot Lt. Donald A. Walter was killed, the first crewman of the Eighth Air Force to die in action, and Lt. Richard Starks' hands were badly burned. Sconiers, the bombardier, took over the controls and crash landed on two engines.[184] Due to a problem of coordination between the Eighth and the RAF, the Spitfire escorts did not appear, emphasizing the problem of coordination between the two Air Forces.[185]

August 23, 1942
Headquarters
97th Bombardment Group (H), Army Air Forces
Office of the Group Commander

To the Officers and Enlisted Men of the 97th Bombardment Group.

It is my privilege to express my gratitude to you for the services you have rendered. I cannot meet you all personally, as much as I would like to, so I am taking this manner of expressing my personal gratitude to you individually and collectively.

Our combat crews go into action, bomb the enemy, shoot down their planes then successfully return to our stations. For that they are acclaimed Heroes and decorated by our government. All this is very well deserved. However to me the entire Group, you men on the line are the unsung heroes of all our successful engagements. I, as Group Commander, and the combat crews of this organization fully realize and appreciate all that you have done. Without you(r) co-operation, the 97th would not have accomplished what it has. Continue you(r) good work and no more could be asked of any man.

It is my desire that every soldier under my command feel that he has a personal interest in having the 97th Bombardment Group among the foremost fighting organizations the United States Army Air Force has ever produced. You no doubt fully realize that during our few days of day operations in this theater we have revolutionized day bombardment. The whole world has been astounded and amazed by our accomplishments. After our first daylight raid, the traffic in New York City was blocked when the news was flashed by electrical signs on Broadway. The British Bomber Command and RAF Fighting Command has acclaimed the bombing of Abbeville as one of the outstanding accomplishments of the successful withdrawal of British troops from Dieppe.

The 97th has made history. We shall continue to accomplish the seemingly impossible. On the last raid the 97th was attacked by 25 enemy fighters when it had no friendly pursuit protection. The Hun paid for that with three enemy aircraft confirmed and a total of 12 probable aircraft shot down. That makes a total of one entire enemy fighter squadron - - and they never had the satisfaction of seeing even one of our aircraft shot down.

So I give you a toast. "Here's to the Hun – a splendid fighter. And here's to the 97th - - His master!" All because of you men and your untiring efforts. God bless you.

> Frank A. Armstrong, Jr.,
> Colonel, Army Air Forces,
> Commanding Officer.[186]

August 23, 1942, Columbia Pictures released the George Stevens Production *The Talk Of The Town* starring Cary Grant, Jean Arthur, and Ronald Colman. Doors opened at Radio City Music Hall in New York City for a gala stage revue and symphony orchestra.[187]

Dutch ~ As our group navigator I planned the missions. You wanted to be at the target at a certain time and planned the mission backwards. During our training in the states, you did not do that. The instructor would say "we are going to go over Houston and back to San Antonio," but we did not plan.

August 24, 1942, the operational mission for Van Kirk [97th BG - #5 mission] hit the shipping yards of Ateliers et Chantiers Maritime de la Seine at Le Trait.

Poor bombing characterized the Le Trait mission. Only a quarter of the 48 bombs dropped within 500 yards of the aiming point.[188] A 20 mm shell hit the cockpit of Van Kirk's airplane badly injuring the co-pilot Lt. Eugene Lockhart's hand. Tibbets had minor wounds. Flak damaged several Fortresses.[189]

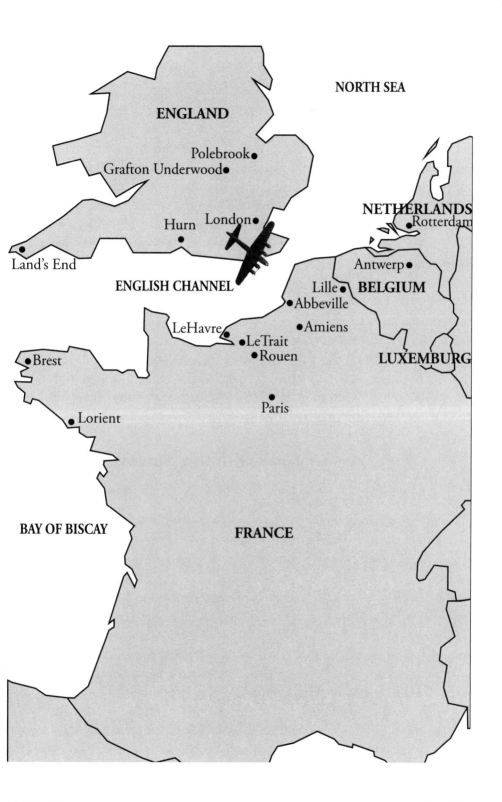

NORTH SEA

ENGLAND

Polebrook

Grafton Underwood

NETHERLANDS

Rotterdam

Hurn

London

Land's End

ENGLISH CHANNEL

Antwerp

Lille

BELGIUM

Abbeville

LeHavre

Amiens

LeTrait

Rouen

LUXEMBURG

Brest

Lorient

Paris

BAY OF BISCAY

FRANCE

Dutch ~ Paul Tibbets got wounded from shattered glass. We had a colonel with us that day as an observer, Newton Longfellow. Tibbets was a major at that time and the highest-ranking officer in our squadron. Longfellow stood back between the pilot and co-pilot. He was one of these old-time fliers and when we got hit as Tibbets put it, "Newt started grabbing handfuls of throttles." Tibbets took his elbow and clunk; he knocked Longfellow flat on his ass. When we got back to the airfield he told Tibbets, "You did exactly the right thing." Ferebee and I were below. Hydraulic fluid was running down from the instruments and a reddish color liquid. I asked Tom if it was blood and he said, "Nah, it doesn't look thick enough for blood."

No one made any comments at the debriefing about Longfellow. It was pretty much a private matter between him and Tibbets. Lockhart and Tibbets had been wounded. We just reported on the attacks and the injuries.

August 27, 1942, the 97th BG - #6 mission hit the Wilton shipyards at Rotterdam, Holland.

August 28, 1942, the 97th BG - #7 mission bombed the Avions Potez airplane factory at Méaulte, France, a repair depot for the German fighters.

August 29, 1942, the 97th BG - #8 mission targeted the Focke-Wulf 190 aerodrome at Kortrijk (Courtrai) Belgium.

"Good Time with the Nurses"

August 29, 1942

Dear Mother, Dad and Jean,

I have finally started receiving my mail so I have some to answer. I got your letter yesterday which was written on August 12 and one today from the 15th.

I'm glad to hear that you are sending the candy. I miss that and good milk shakes more then anything.

I had a pass the last two days and really had a good time. This place has its good points as well as the bad.

I got a letter from Rev. Crouse today. He told me all about everything. If you see him tell him I thank him for the letter but I'm too busy to write so much.

I've had a few more experiences that are worth telling about. Two of the fellows on our crew were wounded in one of them. They're both in the hospital now and probably having a good time with the nurses. I think I lead a charmed life.

The newspapers probably tell you all of the things that I can't tell you.

Don't you go back to work. If you need any money take it out of the checking acc. and if you need any more write and tell me. My cable address is:

Lt. T. J. Van Kirk
AM. EU40 Platform.

I'm not sure this is right but I think so. I'll make sure and tell you again.

Love
Theodore

Tell Jean thanks for the 4 leaf clover. I was always pretty lucky without it.

"Broadcast from London"

August 31, 1942

Dear Mother, Dad and Jean,

Since I haven't yet mailed my last letter I'll write a little more and put into it.

I haven't had any letters since the ones I told you about. I haven't written to Mary Jane for so long that I must get busy. Every time I think of starting to write something else happens and I forget it.

Some of our fellows made a Broadcast from London yesterday. You may have heard it. I didn't.

I'm sending you a clipping that will show you what I mean when I say we have the best planes and know how to use them. I'd like to describe a nice fight to you but I can't.

I think I'll get my first promotion next week. I'll be promoted to first Lt. I'll get a little more pay but not much.

I hope you can read this I wrote it in a hurry. I'll write more soon.

Love
Theodore

September 1, 1942
Headquarters
European Theater Of Operations
United States Army

Subject:Promotion
ThruCG, 8th AF, ETOUSA
To: Theodore J. Van Kirk, 2nd Lt. A.A.F.

By command of Lieutenant General Eisenhower, 2nd Lt. A.A.F. Theodore J. Van Kirk received a temporary promotion to 1st Lt. A.A.F. effective 1 September 1942. "This promotion, unless sooner terminated, will terminate automatically at the expiration of the present emergency and six months thereafter at which time you will revert to your permanent grade."[190]

"Fifth Mission"

September 2, 1942

Dearest Mary Jane,

They say everything happens at once and it certainly did to me today. I got promoted to a first Lt., got paid and best of all, got three letters from you.

I'm sorry now that we weren't married before I left. If we would have been you wouldn't have to be working and going to school now.

I was glad to hear all of the latest town gossip. It seems to me that some of the older boys like Boyer & Klinger either should join the army or go with older girls. They shouldn't be having too much trouble since everyone's away.

I was glad you had news of your brother even if he isn't in such a good place. I hope I never have to go to one of the camps but it could easily happen.

Tell Bill and Benner to take care of everything back home. I wouldn't mind seeing one of Benners steaks right now.

I got Ben's address so I want to write to him and to Bucky Bostian. Are he & M.E. together or apart.

The weathers kept me pretty active lately but I have already sent you the clipping of the fifth one for me. I hope to send you lots more.

I'll always love you.

Love,

Teedy

Mary Jane's brother Sgt. William C. Young had survived the Bataan Death March and was held at prison Camp #4 – O'Donnell, Tarlac, Luzon, Philippines 15 – 120. The family did not learn of his death on May 10, 1942, until later. [191]

Dutch ~ Cliff Heflin's B-24 outfit flew to France with armament and supplies for the partisans. He asked me one day if I wanted to go along. "We will go and visit Paris," he said. The partisans put out burning pots to guide him to land.

I couldn't believe we could walk around and see Paris. (The Reich still occupied Paris.) Heflin said, "Yeah, we can go in and walk around." I did not go.

"Promotion"

September 2, 1942

Dear Mother, Dad and Jean,

Today has been a big day for me. I only wish I had more of them. I got a promotion. It is now 1st Lt. Theodore J. Van Kirk. I got paid and also got seven

GPH PLK NR PLK 13/5   US CONFIDENTIAL IMPORTANT PRIORITY NOT WT

PASS TO

051700A

TO: 1ST WING SIGNALS

FROM: 97TH BOMB GROUP COMMUNICATIONS

PLK S0031J

A- 9

B- 5/9/42 0830-1145

C- 340 (ACDFGJM) 341 (BHLPT) 342 (DHGJKMN) 414 (ACLORQS)

D- 342-D MODULATION POOR ON INTERPHONE: INTERFERENCE ON LIASON

RECEIVER, 414-R NAVIGATORS JACK BOX US, 342-N INTERPHONE TOP
TURRET BUTTON STUCK, 414-C VHF CHANNEL C POOR OPERATION,
BC/375/ D US

E- NIL

BX

F- NIL

G- 340-C OBTAINED QDM

H- NIL

J- 340-J HAD DIFFICULTY UNDERSTANDING SPEECH ON INTERPHONE:

    341-L OTHER GROUP USED VHF FOR INTERPHONE OVER ENGLAND

    ON WAY OVER : 341-P REPORTS TOO MUCH TALK ON VHF AROUND

    TARGET, SOMEONE SEXXX SWEARING AT ~~RXXXXXXXXXX~~ PLANE,
TRACED TO OTHER GROUP. BOMBARDIER THOUGHT HE HEARD SOMEONE SAY
FLYING FORTRESS ON INTERCOM: 340-C RETURNED EARLY, LACK OF POWER:
340-A RETURNED EARLY BALL TURRET US, NO.2 ~~XXXXXX~~ ENGINE US:
340-F RETURNED EARLY NO.3 ENGINE US: 414-A DID NOT TAKE OFF

    BECAUSE OF BAD ENGINE: 414-L RETURNED BECAUSE RADIO OPERATOR
    FAINTED AT 22,000.

    END.

    HOLD

    TOD 1743 WS E VA+

    PLK   R 1743/5 BPF VA

(Photograph of record from National Archives)

letters from home. If it weren't raining now it would be a good day.

I got Bostains address so I'll write him a letter while I have time.

The weathers been so bad that I haven't been very busy for the last few days. It certainly is tiresome sitting around waiting for the weather to clear up. There's nothing drearier then a rainy day at an airport.

Mary Jane tells me that Bill is quitting down at the store Weis will soon have to close up if they keep on losing men.

I haven't got any packages yet but I'm expecting them soon. I('ll) certainly be glad to get that candy.

I haven't got any more newspaper clippings since the last letter. I'll try to send you one every time. I missed a few so far because there should be five for me.

I have a lot more letters to write so I'll have to close. I hope I keep getting your letters. Address them the same as always.

Love

Theodore

September 5, 1942, Van Kirk navigated for the largest heavy bomber raid of the Eighth Air Force [97th BG - #9 mission] to the marshalling yards at Rouen.[192]

The 1st Wings Signal received a confidential report from the 97th Bomb Communications about squadrons 340th (ACDFGJM), 341st (BHLPT), 342nd (DHGJKMN), and 414th (ACLORQS) during the mission from 0830-1145: "340-J had difficulty understanding speech on interphone: 341-L other group used VHF for interphone over England on way over: 341-P reports too much talk on VHF around target, someone sexxx swearing at plane, traced to other group. Bombardier thought he heard someone say flying fortress on intercom: 340-C returned early, lack of power: 340-A returned early ball turret us (useless or unsatisfactory), No. 2 engine us: 340-F returned early No. 3 engine us: 414-A did not take off because of bad engine: 414-L returned because radio operator fainted at 22,000."

Back in Northumberland the Van Kirk family read the news of the ninth daylight raid and the first loss of the "American Flying Fortress." The article added an editorial comment with hope that the Air Force would meet the challenge against the Nazis by sending fighter support.[193]

"Being Shot At"

Dutch ~ You were not taught how to be a good combat person. What do you do when you are shot at? People all react differently. Some people were shot at, came back, went through debriefing, and the next day they were ready to go again. Others came to the debriefing and said, "I am not going back up there again." No one pressured them to go. Sometimes after another three or four missions the guy would say, "I have to get my twenty-five missions so I guess I will do it again." Your psychological makeup influences your reaction to different things. One day someone who you thought was the most stable guy in the world and came back and goes completely off his rocker.

People reacted differently to being shot at. What helped me I attribute to Tom Ferebee. After five or six missions we sat around talking and decided we were not going to live through this. How could you? At the rate we were losing people and aircraft no way were we going to live through it. Once we accepted that, we went on and did not worry any more. Paul Tibbets saved my butt a number of times. A couple of times I had my feet at the door, but never had to bail out.

Tom and I, being on the same crew, knew that what was going to happen to one was going to happen to the other. We took the brunt of the action because Tibbets led the formations and the Germans attacked us head on. If you didn't think so for any other reason that was enough to start thinking. At that point there were two options: quitting, which meant facing a court martial and being shot, or keep on going and hope to be lucky and we were.

September 6, 1942, the operational mission for Van Kirk [97th BG – mission #10] again targeted the factory at Méaulte, France.

The 97th and the 301st were joined by the 92nd, on its first mission, to hit the Avions Potez factory in Méaulte.[194] The first 97th BG B-17, piloted by Clarence Lipsky, was lost near Flesselles and the 92nd also lost a bomber to the Hermann Goering squadron attacks.

The communication problems experienced during the mission by the 97th BG 340th Squadron's six B-17s (GJCFRS) and reported to the 1st Wings Signal Officer were: 340G-IFF shorted out: 340S-VHF XMTR failed: 340S-interphone bad on two positions: 341H-interphone shorted out: 341P-VHF poor: 341B-liaison receiver failed: 414S-VHF out, IFF out, interphone intermittent: 414Q-interphone temporary failure for five minutes: 414B-interphone distorted at high altitude: 342N-VHF poor operation: 342D-interphone in turrets interfered with liaison receiver: 342-IFF out, upper turret interphone out: 342M-interphone intermittent: 340G-TT interphone shorted out, and 340J-T gun jack shorted out for two minutes, CO-P and TT mike switch sticking. Colonel Armstrong reported "much use of VHF by bombers on way to target from English coast" and the 3410 reported one aircraft using VHF interphone, which could have been picked up by the enemy.[195]

"Horizontal Hague"

Dutch ~ Herman "Horizontal" Hague had been flying with Lipsky. Horizontal earned his nickname because he was sleeping all the time.

While Hague recovered in the hospital, his pilot Lipsky had the honor of being the first from the 97th who got shot down and surprisingly enough landed on the sand bar on the Seine River.[196] We never figured out why the airplane went down. There were some rumors at the debriefing because the airplane was under control and made a wheels up landing.[197]

Hague came out of the hospital and now did not have a crew and we needed a replacement for Blackie Hughes, our top turret gunner. Blackie had female problems. Hague said, "I will only fly with Paul Tibbets."

We asked Hague, "What is the matter with you that you will only fly with Tibbets?"

Hague said, "I will never fly back of Willie Tittsworth again. He is the bastard that put me in the hospital." On an earlier mission Lipsky's crew had been in a firefight. Lipsky had flown behind us in the formation. Hague claimed that it was not a German who shot him, but Willie.

 September 7, 1942, the operational mission for Van Kirk [97th BG – mission #11] dispatched the heavy bombers to the Wilton shipyards at Rotterdam, Holland.[198]

"North'd Aviator Shines In Raid On Rotterdam"[199]

The crew shot down two Focke Wulfs and one probable during the pelting on the Holland capital without fighter protection and under heavy fire. The press correspondent wrote that Van Kirk was "extremely busy manning two guns when the bombardier was sighting the target. At the same time Van Kirk managed to navigate directly to the objective." The news quoted top turret gunner Hughes description of the attack from a Fw190 20 mm cannon shell that made a direct hit on the vertical stabilizer and ripped a large hole in the tail, which nearly put their rudder out of commission. While returning to the base

Tibbets' plane fell back in the formation due to the difficulty of steering with their rudder according to Lieutenant Ferebee. Lieutenant Summers gave permission for anyone to bail out, but no one did. Another time their instruments were shot out and two crewmen were wounded.

News captions proclaimed "U.S. bombers down eighteen of Nazis best airplanes."

"FDR Chat"

Roosevelt ~ *September 7, 1942, evening* "Today I sent a message to the Congress, pointing out the overwhelming urgency of the serious domestic economic crisis with which we are threatened. Some call 'inflation,' which is a vague sort of term, and others call it a 'rise in the cost of living,' which is much more easily understood by most families . . . The nation must have more money to run the War. People must stop spending for luxuries. Our country needs a far greater share of our incomes . . . .

For this is a global war, and it will cost this nation nearly one hundred billion dollars in 1943 . . .

We have stopped one major Japanese offensive; and we have inflicted heavy losses on their fleet. But they still possess great strength; they seek to keep the initiative; and they will undoubtedly strike hard again. We must not over-rate the importance of our successes in the Solomon Islands, though we may be proud of the skill with which these local operations were conducted. At the same time, we need not under-rate the significance of our victory at Midway. There we stopped the major Japanese offensive . . .

Several thousand Americans have met death in battle. Other thousands will lose their lives. But many millions stand ready to step into their places -- to engage in a struggle to the very death. For they know that the enemy is determined to destroy us, our homes and our institutions -- that in this war it is kill or be killed . . .

All of us here at home are being tested -- for our fortitude, for our selfless devotion to our country and to our cause.

This is the toughest war of all time."[200]

"The Red Gremlin"

Dutch ~ We probably spent more time getting in formation than getting to the target because Rotterdam was not far. The total mission was about four

The Red Gremlin
(Air Force photograph National Archives)

hours. The Germans shot the hell out of us.

Paul Tibbets said we needed a new plane. We had been flying the "E" model. There is a difference between the models.[201] The B-17E didn't have as many guns as the "F" model. The B-17E had a .30 caliber gun, a squirt gun. There were sockets in the nose and you pulled the gun out of one socket and put it in another when you saw a fighter coming at you. By the time you did that the airplane was gone. A lot of times I told Tom Ferebee, "Don't pull it out, and keep your finger on the trigger by God!"

We looked over a B-17F, number 41-24444 [B-17F-10-BO 41-24444].[202] Tom and I both said "that is a winning poker hand no matter how you look at." That plane was a lucky plane. The *Red Gremlin* came back.[203] Our guys made up a poem for her. If things were true to form Orville Splitt, our radio operator, probably wrote it.

TABLE 6.1 — SPECIFICATIONS OF B-17F

Armament:	11 .50-cal. machine guns and carry 8,000 lbs. of bombs
Engines:	Four Wright R-1820-97 turbo-supercharged radials
Maximum speed:	325 mph at 25,000 ft.
Cruising speed:	160 mph at 5,000 ft.
Service ceiling:	37,500 ft.
Range:	2,800 miles (maximum ferry range)
Span:	103 ft. 9 in.
Length:	74 ft. 9 in.
Height:	19 ft. 1 in.
Weight:	56,500 lbs. gross weight (actual - normal load)
Serial numbers:	Boeing production: 41-24340 to 24639; 42-5050 to 42-5484; 42-29467 to 42-31031; Douglas production: 42-2964 to 42-3562; 42-37714 to 42-37720; Lockheed-Vega production: 42-5705 to 42-6204
Crew:	10

Source: National Museum of the USAF, Fact Sheet For Boeing B-17F.

The R-1820-97 engines with the "F" model gave improved high-altitude performance and the increase in fuel capacity extended the range. The *Aeronautics Aircraft Spotters Guide* described the B-17 Flying Fortresses as the "scourge of the Axis homelands" because of their range and load carrying ability. The refinements in performance and armament data were highly restricted. The "F" model was visually similar to the B-17Es. Modifications included a frameless plexi-glass nose, improved propellers, and renovated electrical and oxygen systems.[204]

"Cursing the Germans"

Dutch - The temperature in a B-17 could go way below zero. It wasn't real common but could happen depending on the humidity in the upper atmosphere and Tom and I didn't have to worry about that. We were up in the nose of the B-17, the most comfortable place to be, not like back in the waist or in the tail. We still wore our real heavy flight jackets.

You could get frequent freezing of your oxygen mask and had to check them. Sometimes in the heat of the battle people forgot to keep the oxygen mask clear.

Tom Ferebee would kick me if I nodded off. Every once and a while Tom looked at me and asked, "Do you know where you are at Dutch?"

Yeah, don't worry I would tell him.

The navigator sat right up front. We did not wear flak suits; they came later. Tom Ferebee and I substituted by putting armor plate on the floor to protect us, but I did get some flak once. Got shot in the butt. But that is another story. After the war at a reunion in Albuquerque, one guy said, "You guys flew the *Red Gremlin*. I took it after you. How did you get that plane up? It had so much armor plate in the nose." We had traced the *Red Gremlin* over to Maxwell Field and surmised it ended up in South America as a chicken hauler.

The worst anti-aircraft probably was on the mission to Rotterdam. The first time we went in we had the B-24s with us. The Germans defended Rotterdam very well. We usually saw the Messerschmitt Me109s and the Focke Wulf Fw190s. I don't remember if we ever saw any two-engine fighters. Later on the Germans sent everything up at the Americans.

Ferebee cursed the Germans a lot. Those bastards were shooting at us you know. We shot a lot of ammunition.

"Getting in Formation"

Dutch – We burned a lot of gas putting a formation together. Oh my God that was hairy especially in bad weather. The first airplane to take off flies straight and levels out quite a ways. The second one flies not as far and starts turning.[205] There was a knack of getting it together. If you started to chase the leader you were never going to catch up. In good weather it was no problem. Every once and a while a plane popped out from the cloud underneath you. There were lots of accidents. At other times a collision occurred when the plane would be flying straight and level and one of the guys chasing him trying to catch up popped out of the clouds and hit him.

When it was overcast the navigator had to use dead reckoning to inform the pilot of the position and used other methods to determine the position in relation to the target. Overcast conditions made the navigation more difficult. When it was nice and clear that was called pilotage. You could look out and see where you were. It was easy to find a railroad down here and steer the airplane.

In cloudy conditions you had to keep better track.

When Tibbets flew he was the leader so everybody was following us. I kept Tibbets apprised every time we passed something significant and how far we were from the target. But if Van Kirk, the navigator, was lost and not taking the group where we were supposed to be going that was tough luck. The others had to follow. If someone didn't follow and dropped out of formation chances are he would be shot down. The Germans always picked on a single airplane.

The biggest formation I saw get together was a hundred airplanes. Later in the war there were four or five hundred planes. I don't know how they did it. Other navigators tell me they had one group in one part of England and another group in another part of England. Each had their sector to fly in, got wings together, and trailed each other.

"It's Exciting"

September 9, 1942
Wednesday
Dear Mother, Dad and Jean,

I got three letters from you, six from Mary Jane and others from Zongs and Martha and Lee. It will take me a month to answer all of them.

Your letters are coming through very good now. My stuff hasn't arrived yet but it will one of these days. Don't bother sending me anything for Christmas. It takes too long and is too risky. Besides there are rumors about that we may be moving again.

I was up to the hospital today to see some of the members of our crew who were wounded in action. They're getting along fine. We had a hot time in our last few trips but they can't get me. Our crew is learning and getting better every trip and they were pretty good to start with. I'll have plenty to talk about when I get home.

I'll send you a few more clippings. I'd like to send you the one that tells about us getting 12 in one day. Our ship got two of them. It's so exciting that I'm afraid life may be very dull after the war.

My address is A.P.O. 875.

Don't worry about me. I'm O.K.

Love

Theodore

Our crew was interviewed yesterday by A.P. and United Press war correspondents. Keep these clippings in a scrapbook. The underlined fellows were with us when they got hurt.

September 12, 1942, General Spaatz decorated men from the B-17 crews who had been wounded including Tibbets and Lockhart from the first mission and other awards for valor.[206]

"Big Headlines"

September 14, 1942

I need more stamps please

Dear Mother, Dad and Jean,

I haven't received a letter from you since the last time I've written so I don't know any more news of home.

I had a few days off and spent the last two days in London. I had a nice time but I don't think much of the town. It has a few nice places but there isn't a baseball or football game going on the way there usually is back home.

I'm sending you a picture taken the other day when the general decorated some of the fellows. We were all dressed up and had a big parade. Four members of our crew got decorated because they were injured. I'm too lucky. I couldn't even cut my finger.

I saw a newspaper from back home today. It had big headlines about bombing something or other. The first few times I guess we made the headlines but that will soon be commonplace.

Don't send me anything for Xmas unless it's a fruitcake or something that gets better with age. Take care of yourself & buy yourselves & Mary Jane presents with some of my money in the bank.

Love

Theodore

"German Hun Head"

Dutch – In England the officers clubs were always decorated with a German Hun head and a corny sign something like "here is the Hun. He is a great fighter. Here is to the 97th Group his master." Baloney, the Germans were winning all the fights I was in. If you were going on a mission the next day the Hun's head was turned one way or if you were going to stand down that day the head was turned another way. I suppose to the young flyers the club was like a fraternity in college. You always had a crap table too, a place to play cards, and a quiet place for reading. Some people played bridge.

September 17, 1942, Leslie R. Groves was appointed director of the Manhattan Engineer District and receives a promotion to Brigadier General several days later.

September 21, 1942, large orders were placed for the unproven Superfortress designed to succeed the B-17. The first prototype of Boeing's heavy bomber, the XB-29, took off. [207]

"Too High Altitude"

September 26, 1942
England
Dear Mother, Dad and Jean,

I've been trying to write this letter for the past four days. I started it twice but never did get it finished.

There's nothing new to tell you about. It's starting to get pretty cold over here at times. They give us coke to burn and little stoves in each room. I haven't found how to regulate them yet so my room is either too hot or too cold.

Yesterday we were too high altitude and had to come down pretty fast. The sudden change in pressure hurt my left ear and I'm having a little trouble. The doctor's taking care of it and says it will be O.K. He hasn't taken me off flying or sent me to the hospital so it isn't bad. They usually send you to the hospital if you have a little headache.

I have a picture here of the crew that I fly with. You'll probably recognize me O.K.

I got some pictures and a letter from Grandma Snyder yesterday. I probably won't get around to writing to her so in case I don't, tell her I mentioned it.

I haven't had any letters from home for the past four days I'll probably get a lot of them all at once.

I'll finish this letter tomorrow I may have more news then I may have to get up about five o'clock tomorrow. That's bad when you usually sleep until noon.

England
Sept. 28.

Two more days and still no letter from home. I had a letter from Bud and Bertha today. I couldn't figure out who it was from at first.

My ears are O.K. again and I'm over a slight cold so everything's fine again.

I have a new address. It's the same as the old except that the A.P.O. is #634. Don't forget the 340th Sqd & 97th Gp. part. I'll send you my new Cable address soon.

Back row, left to right: Paul Tibbets, William "Junior" Ryan, Tom Ferebee, Van Kirk, Sgt. Warren Hughes, and Orville Splitt. Front row: Charles H. Peach, Morris Quate, James Fitzgerald, Zackie Gowan, and John "Willie" Tittsworth.

Write to the bank down at Sarasota & find out how much money I have there. It should be about $155. but I lost track. It will build up a lot faster because I'm not going to write any more checks.

I want to write to M.J. tonight so I'll stop this and write to her.

I'm sending you a pic(ture) you can save for me. I also have one to send to M.J. Love

Theodore

September 26, 1942, operational mission for Van Kirk [97th BG – mission #12] targeted Morlaix Ploujean aerodrome, France.[208]

September 27, 1942, Col. Joseph H. Atkinson became commander of the 97th Bombardment Group.

September 29, 1942, the American fliers with the RAF's Eagle Squadrons (the 71st, 121st, and 133rd) were transferred into the USAAF. The American pilots had been in the fight for almost a year before the attack on Pearl Harbor.

"The World Series"

September 30, 1942

England

Dear Mother, Dad and Jean,

I've decided to stay home tonight and catch-up with my letter writing. I'm writing yours first because I usually get tired after the first letter and don't write anymore.

I haven't had any packages from home yet. Sometimes it takes them two weeks and sometimes two months. For that reason don't send me anything for Xmas.

While I'm on the subject of presents I believe I forgot Mary Jane's birthday. I'll write and explain that to her. Take some of the money from the bank and buy her an Xmas present. Also one for Jean and Dad and don't forget yourself either.

Tell Gugin he's crazy as h. Airmail is faster than V-mail. Besides I like a letter better. You need a microscope to read that V-mail.[209]

That picture I sent you has on it from left to right standing Major Tibbets, 2nd Lt. Ryan, 1st Lt. Ferebee and me. The rest of the men are Sgts. Hughes, Sgt Splitt, Sgt Peach, Sgt Quate, Sgt Fitzgerald, Sgt Gowan and Sgt Tittsworth. It's a pretty good gang.

There isn't anymore to write about. I've been trying to get a review of the first game of the World Series but can't get it.

As usual I'm tired of writing after my first letter so I'll probably read awhile and go to bed. I have a nice fire burning tonight and it certainly feels good.

Write often and take care of yourself.

Love

Theodore

I just got the score of that game. They announced it over the public address system here at the field.

The New York Yankees played the first game of the World Series against the St. Louis Cardinals on September 30, 1942, in Sportsman's Park, St. Louis, Missouri. The sports writers focused on the comparison of Joe DiMaggio and Terry Anderson, the two centerfielders, to predict the winners of the series. The Yankees won the first game 7 to 4.

Results										R.	H.	E.
New York	0	0	0	1	1	0	0	3	2	7	11	0
St. Louis	0	0	0	0	0	0	0	0	4	4	7	4

Batteries - Ruffing, Chandler and Dickey; M. Cooper, Gumbert, Lanlee and W. Cooper.[210]

The Cardinals won the series in five games.

The Navy, Coast Guard, and Marines received summaries of the sports news from their hometown newspapers. The Navy Department in Washington condensed the events into short articles, which were radioed to ships and stations throughout the world.[211]

While the Yankee - St. Louis game was underway Hitler pledged that Stalingrad would be taken.[212]

October 1942, General Groves appoints Dr. J. Robert Oppenheimer scientific director of the Manhattan Project.

 October 2, 1942, the operational mission for Van Kirk [97th BG – mission #13] hit Méaulte, France, and the 97th BG – mission #14 St. Omer. Eighteen B-17s took off to bomb the Avions Potez factory while six others attacked the airfield at St. Omer.[213]

"Briefing"

Dutch ~ A large map hung on the wall of the briefing room. Black thread or tape connected the pins stuck in the map outlining the route we were supposed to follow. Flak fields' locations and bombing altitude also were identified. We were told the target for the day such as the shipyards at Rotterdam, the altitude to fly, who would lead the mission, list of all the airplanes and their order in which they were going to fly, the order in the formation, and weather information en-route and over the target.

Now we were told to stand up and empty our pockets. We were never to carry anything on our person that would identify us as a member of the 97th or our squadron. The air sea rescue kit was passed out. We would stick it in the knee pocket of our coveralls. The kit always contained two gold pieces or currency to bribe the French, chocolate bars, mini rations depending on where we were, and fish lines if we were near a body of water. I tried to collect the gold, but never had much luck. The real necessity was a silk map.

Churches or historic structures like that would be pointed out in the briefings. For example, "This is the target. This is the rail yard. Now over here in this southwest section is a large cathedral. It is a major historical artifact. We do not want to bomb it so try to not have your bombs hit over here." This was well discussed, but hard to do. Towards the later part of the war in Europe the Germans started to put snipers in churches. Everyone took advantage of the situation and put flak towers in the tall buildings, as we did too.

"Wrong Target"

Dutch ~ When you came back from the mission, you always met with the intelligence officer to be debriefed. Where did you get the most enemy action? Where did you get the most flak? Did we send you on the right route? Did we send you over any flak fields? Where were the fighter bases? Where did you see the fighters come from? What kind of attacks did they do? Did they all do head on attacks? Did anyone try and attack you from the tail? Did anyone make any ninety degree attacks or of anything of that type? Did you hit your target? Was the target camouflaged in any way? Did the enemy put up any smoke screens to try and hide the target? Could you pick out the target clearly? Did you have good identification marks to point you toward the target and where you were supposed to aim at?

Some navigators wrote down the location of the flak fields. I did not. I had a good memory and figured if someone were going to be shooting at me I'd know it.

You looked for signs of a camouflaged area to determine the real bomb target. Your senses had to be sharp. Were their homes missing? The clever Germans would pick out an area with the same general characteristics and camouflaged it to look like the natural target.[214]

Tom Ferebee and I came back from the mission at Méaulte I think. We had done a great job bombing and were in the officer's club celebrating when we heard, "Will Lieutenants Van Kirk and Ferebee report to headquarters." We get there and the intelligence officer said, "You guys bombed the wrong damn target today."

Well that was news to me.

Intelligence thought that the Germans had camouflaged the target, an aircraft factory, and that I had picked out the wrong one. Tom to his credit did a good job of bombing it. We were called a number of things when we were reamed out that day. I will never forget it. We were sent back and told to "get the right one."

We got the hell shot out of us from flak and fighters and that airplane never flew again. That was our second B-17E.

"My Purple Heart"

Dutch - You had to get medical attention for any injury while on the mission. Once I got a few small pieces of flak. Hell, it was not bad. I covered it with a band-aid. We came back for the debriefing and Tom Ferebee piped up "Hey, Ted - Dutch got a few pieces of flak in his butt." So I had to go to a doctor. I did not deserve a Purple Heart until after the doctors probed for the flak. A lot of jokes and bantering went on and it was an easy mission.

If you lost men you were down in the dumps. You just cannot imagine what the debriefing was like or the next morning. The closest thing that came to it after the war was when Tibbets, Ferebee, and I were at a model show in Ida Grove, Iowa. The Confederate Air Force had a show they put on; it was called the *Tora, Tora, Tora Show.* During the reenactment of the bombing of Pearl Harbor with airplanes painted like the Jap Zeroes a pilot got his turn a little bit too tight, spun in, and got killed. The next morning at breakfast where all the pilots had gathered we were talking and I asked, "Does this remind you of anything? Does this remind you of coming back from a tough mission and we had just lost a lot of people?" Right away it hit them. Everybody was silent.

It was devastating. We flew a few missions and were a cocky bunch. We did not need anybody to boost our morale. We had lots of it. The Germans shoot at you. They take a few hits. You come to think of yourself as invincible. They cannot hurt me, to hell with them. Then all of a sudden you start losing one or two planes and it suddenly comes to you that you are not invincible and they can get to you. We could be shot down. We could be captured. But I do not think it affected us with the attitude that we had. I always thought Paul Tibbets was invincible. He was invincible period.

If an airplane was shot down we were asked where was it shot down and how many parachutes came out of it. That was very important at a debriefing.

"Red Gremlin Poem"

October 7, 1942
England
Dear Mother, Dad and Jean,

I haven't written a letter for a long time. I started writing one to Mary Jane on Oct. 1 and I just finished it.

I got your letter with the clipping two days ago. What a line that was.

I sent M.J. a copy of a poem that one of our crew wrote about the name of our new plane. I haven't got any more copies or I'd send you one.

That last letter sounds as though your trying to get me married. The next time I come home I won't have a chance against both of you. It's going to take a lot of talking.

There still isn't anything to write about. I haven't got my packages yet. I believe the boat sunk.

I've got a pass tomorrow so I think I'll leave this afternoon and go to London. Nice town London. That's about the only place that anything stays open after 11 o'clock.

I have a lot of things to do and I have to dress and catch a train by 2 o'clock so I'd better get started. I'll write and tell you all about it as soon as I get back.

Love
Theodore

The Little Red Gremlins — In Tribute To The "Red Gremlin"
When you're five miles up in the heavens (That's a hell of a lonely spot)
And it's fifty degrees below zero (Which isn't exactly hot)
And You're frozen blue like your fortress • And scared a mosquito pink
You're a thousand miles from no-where
And there's nothin' below but the drink.

It is then you will see the Gremlins • Green and purple and gold
Male and female and neuter • Gremlins both young and old

It's no use trying to dodge them • For the lessons you've learned on the link
Won't help in evading a Gremlin
Though you climb and you dive and you jink
White ones will wiggle your wing tips • Orange ones will muddle your maps
Grey ones will guzzle your glycol • Green ones will flutter your flaps
Pink ones will perch on your perspex • and dance pirouettes on your prop
And there's a lively old Gremlin • Who'll spin on your stick like a top.
Black ones will jam your machine guns
Gold ones will mess up your "chute"
While a couple of little young Gremlins • Disconnect your electrical suit
They'll freeze up your camera shutters • And bite through your aileron wires
They'll smash and they'll jam, and they'll batter
And stick toasting forks in your tires

BUT

Don't be too quick to condemn them • Don't cus every Gremlin you see
For the little RED GREMLINS will help you • If ever in trouble you be

They'll keep your interphone humming
Though your batt'ries are nearly run down
And they'll keep at least one engine running
"Till you're back again on the ground
They'll stick by your side during battles • And if, by chance, you are shot
They'll give you first aid if you need it • And fire your gun till it's hot
They'll "beat up" all the bad Gremlins • And keep them out of your plane
And they'll keep your bombardier sober
So he won't drop his bombs in the Seine
And up in the nose you will find them • Cleaning the windows of frost
And there's a special crew been appointed
To keep Van Kirk from getting lost.

And so, as sort of a tribute • To the Little Known Guys On Our Crew
We've named our fortress "RED GREMLIN"
We thought that's the least we could do.

To The Crew Of Airplane No. 124444

(With Apologies to the Original Writer – if any O.S.S.)

"High Stakes Gambling"

Dutch ~ Tom Ferebee and I were not choirboys by any stretch of the imagination. Tom was an outstanding poker player and crapshooter. I inherited it somewhat. Tom was at one end of the crap table and I was at the other end. We would be partners and gambled for sums of monies anyone in their right mind would not even think of. My dad in his depression days would turn over in his grave and my grandfather would be spinning about the amounts of money we gambled. There was always a good crap game going on even when we went down to North Africa. One night a crap game ended with only Tom and a general with about twenty thousand dollars on the table.

"One of us is going to leave here broke and it won't be me," Tom told the general.

Tom won, but the general did not pay all the I.O.U.s.

Margaret Bourke-White's photograph (*Time* & *Life* Pictures/Getty Images) which appeared in the October 19, 1942, issue of *Life* magazine in the article "U.S. High-Altitude Bombers Hit Nazis." Van Kirk sitting near the front in the briefing hut turned around at the moment the photo was shot.

"Oxtail Soup and Beer"

Dutch ~ We made occasional trips to London. About the only fine experience in London was finding your way around in a black out. Everything was blacked out. You did not know where you are at and no street signs. You couldn't use a flashlight.

Sometimes we went to dances in Cambridge, which was closer than London. I scratched my head at the odd way the British danced around in a circle. It was like they were going around a racetrack. During the day we took chances to do sight seeing. I dated a British girl or two. The typical thing would be to go to a movie. Before and after the movie they played *God Save The Queen*.

Tom went up to Peterborough because he had a girl friend up there. Tom came back during the night while the Germans bombed Peterborough. The fog made it very difficult at night and was so thick sometimes a guy sat on each fender of the car to direct your way.

I do not know what there was about England, but they must have had great crops of Brussels sprouts. We always had lots of Brussels sprouts. American rations were bad enough, but British rations were beef and kidney stew or canned oxtail soup. Did you ever drink British tea made by a G.I. cook boiled in a cleaned out garbage can? It was foul stuff, but something you got used to. And there was always a shortage of vegetables. In a war you had to expect those things.

American C-rations looked like hamburger soup with potatoes with flavoring. Depending on your cook and unit the food was better or worse. Some cooks could take the lousiest food and make something decent out of it. Other cooks could take the best food in the world and make something lousy.

We always had lots of doughnuts. When we came back from a mission the Red Cross girls were there with doughnuts or our cooks made doughnuts. One of the good things in England was that when you had time to visit on a British base a nice young lady, a British WAAC (Women's Army Auxiliary Corps), came in and woke you up every morning. Good morning sir it is such and such a time. Breakfast will be in fifteen minutes and that sort of stuff. That is almost pleasant to wake up to.

We took a B-17 to fly over to the Isle of Man one time. When we got over to a British training base we did not have enough space to turn the B-17 around. A bunch of the girls helped to push and turn our B-17. I have to admit we got real good treatment that day.

The British pubs always had so much beer and stayed open as long as the beer held out. There were stronger drinks occasionally, but not very often. Civilians ran the pubs. Sometimes the British and American soldiers would get in a fight. Alcohol did not get rationed like at Wendover, but if you found a couple of bottles you saved them for a special occasion for example, like not getting shot down. If you went to London you always took a good bottle of Scotch with you. You never knew when you might need it for heaven's sake. It was in short supply.

I was never invited to the Rothschild's. As a second lieutenant the only invitation was to the local pub. The Brits had a saying about Americans: we were "over paid, over sexed and over here."

We always wanted something better. When we were flying B-17Fs and saw the B-17Gs we wanted that chin turret, but we couldn't have it. We knew that they made enough of the "G" models, but we did not think we would last long enough to get one. Every once in a while we questioned the information the intelligence officers gave us. What stupid bastard sent us over that flak field? Or maybe the church or cemetery was right next to the target we were supposed to bomb and we would say what ##!! picked that out? People were always griping about things like that. Sometimes you took it seriously sometimes not. I thought in general looking back on it yep, the military did a pretty good job of supplying us what we needed considering what was available and what the demand was over in the Pacific as well as in Europe. There was never enough to go around. You always wanted more, but couldn't have it.

One of my best friends Hazen Payette ended up with us on Tinian with the 509th and also was our intelligence officer in England and North Africa. He had been a lawyer in Detroit before the war. You knew he was a competent man, but still questioned some of the things.

You could voice an opinion at briefings for what it was worth, but the target was cast in stone. The only things that interfered with the mission were number one, bad weather, or two, the engines did not start and an airplane was missing. Some pilots had a reputation that they were going to abort and turn back when the least little thing went wrong. Others turned back if the tail gunner got a cut on their little pinkie. You always knew who those people were too.

"Keep on Course"

Dutch ~ Some pilots had a hard head and did not keep on course. Paul Tibbets always flew a heading for me as close as he could. He was good at that. One time we jumped in the airplane and Tibbets said, "What is the heading navigator?"

I said, "380 pilot." Now you know there is only 360 degrees.

Tibbets got it off the ground and was almost all the way around. He said, "What the hell did you say?"

I said, "20 degrees!"

 October 9, 1942, operational mission for Van Kirk [97th BG – mission #15] steel and locomotive plant in the Lille industrial area.

"Eighth's First 100-bomber Raid"

Headed to Lille, France, to strike heavy industries 24 B-24s joined 108 Fortresses for the first 100-bomber raid. Five hundred Allied fighters escorted the bombers during the greatest single daylight aerial attack under strong

German opposition.[215] Mechanical failures impacted the large group reducing the aircraft over the target by about twenty percent. The 97th had twenty-two B-17s take off and only one did not reach the target. Gunners claimed fifty-six German fighters destroyed.[216]

Dutch ~ Our third B-17 took us into Lille and weren't going very far in. We took two new groups with us: one B-17 group and one B-24 group. The Germans jumped on the B-24s right away and never picked on us. A B-24 did not have near the firepower of the B-17. The rule when you go in to bomb is that everyone follows the leader. We were the leader. They were new groups and did not follow the leader. They broke off and decided to bomb on their own. So here we were coming at the target one way and another group coming another way and the third another way all headed for the same point. Ferebee said, "to hell with them. We have the right of way. We know what we are doing. They don't."

I told Tom, "that is not going to do us any good if we run into them for Christ sakes." It was a damn mess, but the Germans had heavy losses that day.

"Biggest Hazard in England"

Dutch ~ Large formations attracted German attention. It was nice that the Eighth Air Force was growing, but we were losing more men and airplanes. The fact that we reached one hundred airplanes was in of itself a landmark and at that particular time I might have said that would have been all we could handle, but we got up to five and six hundred airplanes. Putting those formations together was not easy. Airplanes were taking off from different bases. They all looked the same until you saw the large identifying marks on the tail.

The first pilot to take off goes straight and level climbing a little bit then he starts his turn gradually. The next one takes off and starts his turn sooner and cuts inside. They keep cutting inside until the formation gets together. During bad weather you do not know where all the airplanes are. The biggest hazard in England was running into other airplanes. That was almost as big a hazard as the Germans shooting at you over the target. I saw one B-17 hit another and pancake him. Another time I saw a pilot fly right into the formation above him. There were all kinds of accidents.

We carried high explosive bombs. You thought about civilians because you were bombing rail yards next to towns and looked back on it after the war. I think the average bomb missed its target by over a thousand feet. You tried not to do it and tried to hit the target as close as possible. If you stop to think about it you realized that your bombs were not going to always go where you wanted them to go. Some people were better than others. Tom Ferebee was the best bombardier I ever knew.

Some people just dropped the bombs and got out of there. They did not want to be in the flak area any longer then necessary. You did not know where the bombs were going. You obviously were killing civilian people. Hopefully the civilians would have the sense to move far away from what were obviously military targets. Sometimes they did and sometimes they did not. You come back and you rationalize this is war. We used to say, there is no morality in warfare.

According to the United Press report from London, the Lille raid set records for the largest American Air Force operation of the war in any theatre, the first American manned fighters, and that the Germans lost more planes in one day on continental targets.[217]

"Battle of Cape Esperance"

October 11, 1942, between Savo Island and Cape Esperance, off the northern point of Guadalcanal, the *Boise,* other cruisers, and destroyers closed in on the Solomon Islands.

James Starnes ~ "We were not the flag ship. Admiral (Norman) Scott was in command. His ship did not have radar.[218] At 2300 we picked up a ship on our radar eight or nine miles away. Captain Moran was denied permission to open fire. When the ships closed in at about 4,000 yards the captain said, 'open fire.' The Navy policy was that if in danger we could start the battle. We immediately became the target of torpedoes and naval gunfire, our first experience in belly-to-belly warfare. After about fifteen minutes of active naval engagement, we did a lot of damage. But, we were damaged by one of their torpedoes and had to withdraw. Total darkness turned into total light." An enemy shell had detonated in her forward magazines from the Japanese *Aoba* and *Kingusa.* The *Boise* limped back through the Panama Canal to the Philadelphia Navy yard for repairs. The explosions and burning gases killed 104 men and 3 officers and wounded about 200 sailors.[219] The *Boise's* prominent role in the Battle of Cape Esperance helped turn back a Japanese cruiser-destroyer force en route to bombard the Marines on Guadalcanal.[220]

October 13, 1942
Candidate Robt. D. Young
24th Co. 4th Bn. 2nd S.T.R.
Fort Benning, Ga.
Hiya Sis (Mary Jane Young),

How's the new job doing these days? Thanks for writing every day last week – gosh you must use a lot of your time just to write to me - I sure feel good about it too.

You sure have to study here. They just rush you & you get it or you don't & if you don't by the way – you go out.

Well be good & keep writing.

Good luck –

Your Bro.

Bob

MOVIETONE NEWS *October 19, 1942,* found guilty on trumped up charges Doolittle raiders 2nd Lt. William Grover Farrow of Darlington, South Carolina, 2nd Lt. Dean Edward Hallmark of Dallas, Texas, and Sgt. Harold A. Spatz of Lebo, Kansas, were forced to kneel before shallow graves with their hands strapped to small crosses and then executed by a Japanese firing squad.[221] Their cremated ashes were located after the war and reinterred in Section 12 of Arlington Cemetery.[222]

"Not Getting my Letters"

October 19, 1942
Dear Mother, Dad and Jean,

I haven't had a letter from home for a long time. Our mail isn't getting to us and most of ours is not getting to you. I haven't written for quite a while but I've sent several cables.

I had a letter from Bucky Bostian last week. He told me about his job and where all of the fellows are. I also had another letter from Grandma Snyder.

I'm a little busier now then I had been for a few weeks. I'm still not being overworked though. I haven't got any more time to write so I'll have to stop. I'll keep writing but I doubt if the mail service will be much good.

I haven't written for so long I can't think of anything to put in a letter. Notice the beginning. It's a little different from the last letter.

Tell Mary Jane I haven't forgotten her. She's just not getting my letters.
Don't worry.
Love
Theodore

 October 19, 1942, special mission for Van Kirk, England to Gibraltar.

"Gen. Mark Wayne Clark"

Dutch ~ The first time we went to North Africa we took General Mark Clark. Junior Ryan had replaced our co-pilot Lockhart. In the meantime before we took Eisenhower Junior got dysentery so bad he ended up in the hospital. He told us that his weight went down to eighty-five pounds. We took Junior's uniforms and all his stuff because we thought he was going to die. Dick Wiley took over as co-pilot.

One day we got word that two passengers were going to arrive and to be ready to take off at a certain time. We were briefed in a closed room but did not know what was the mission. We were told to stay low all the way four hundred feet. That was new for me. You just had to do it.

I suddenly remembered that at some time around Portsmouth, England, about a conversation with an old British sea captain. We talked about the weather and he said, "You can always read the waves, the wind off the waves."

I asked the captain to explain.

"Always remember the wind is perpendicular to the white caps."

That makes sense after a bit. If there are just regular white caps you know your wind is about twelve miles per hour, but if they are breaking and the wind is strong enough to break the caps at the top and foaming then you know the wind is about eighteen miles per hour. Putting that together with what you are seeing on the water you can take a guess at the wind speed. It was a guessing game; believe me. You learned little pieces of information to store away in case you needed them. And that was the one thing that saved me on that particular mission.

Mark Clark was a patrician reserved type. On the Clark mission when we got down to Gibraltar on the runway I went with two enlisted men to get the "cargo" off the plane. We unloaded these little boxes about six inches square.

I remember passing it off the plane and said, "Gee what is in this, they are so heavy."

One of Clark's officers said, "Oh, that is ammunition." But it was the gold that we had taken down there to pay the French off. Clark gave each of us two gold pieces. I must have lost them in a poker game.

The ammunition story made a lot of sense. Every officer on the crew, in fact every man on the crew, had a Thompson submachine gun, a carbine and an army .45 automatic because we thought we might have to land in North Africa and pick Clark up. We wanted to have plenty of firepower. I could not hit anything with the gun, but could have hit something with the carbine. We had the record for the most ammo, but not hitting anything![223]

The funny part about the mission was that as soon as Clark got to Gibraltar all he wanted to do was get back to England. It was a rush, rush trip. I looked at the weather that night and said, "I do not want to take off."

Tibbets said, "We have got to get back."

So we took off, but I will tell you that night coming back with Mark Clark, I deserved every navigation kudos that I ever got in my life. I swear we flew through about six fronts between Gibraltar and England. If Tibbets was anywhere within about ten degrees of either side of the compass course I let him go because he couldn't hold the airplane any better than that. It was the worst weather I had ever flown in my life. We were flying up northeast and I knew Germany was close so I kept putting myself over to the left. If there was any place I did not want to fly over it was Germany.

Some radio stations helped me a bit until we flew over the north coast in Portugal and Spain. That was one of my most difficult navigations. It was too cloudy and you couldn't use the stars at all. So you looked at your compass and by guess and by God, and hope that God was taking care of you. I used primarily the compass, a few wind drift fixes from the radio station, and the approximate wind from that particular source then followed the Charles Lindbergh principal. Lindbergh did not really fly across the ocean. He was blown across the ocean.

We flew all night. About daylight I could see islands down there. Tibbets called me. "Navigator, do you know where you are at?"

Hell no. I answered that I had a pretty good idea, but not to hold me to it precisely.

Tibbets, "Well they are not the Channel Islands down there. Are they?"

"No way they are the Channel Islands," I insisted. Mark Clark was standing right beside us.

Tibbets turned to Clark. "Well they are probably not the Channel Islands.

Let's drop down and circle them. If they are the Germans they will start shooting at us and then we will know where we are at."

We went a little longer and fortunately I could pick out some islands. I figured that we were about twenty miles from where I thought, which was pretty damn good with the way things were that night. So coming up we had to make a right turn to about a heading of sixty to sixty-five degrees from Land's End into our base, so I did. Suddenly the radio operator (Orville Splitt) comes on and says, "Radio operator to navigator, I have got a QDM."[224] He says we are going the wrong way. Orville was a pretty sharp guy.

Orville, what the hell do you mean we are going the wrong way?

He said, "Well the QDM says we are supposed to be going 60 plus 180 that would be 240. We are supposed to be going 240."

We are?

"Well that is what the QDM says."

The British trained their navigators well. They had a system so you could contact a common radio frequency; they would get a fix on you and tell you which direction to fly to get back to your base. And that is what they were doing. I was supposed to be flying 240 and I was flying 180 degrees opposite. I had to think about it for a little while and thought gee, could he be right? That cannot be right. If I was supposed to be flying 240 I would be flying into Germany for Christ's sakes and the Germans would be shooting at us. Since they are not shooting at us I am not flying into Germany. On the other hand if I turn and fly 240 we are going to end up in the Atlantic Ocean without any gas. So I decided the hell with it, which we did.

We went on to our base and landed. The two RAF group captains were apologizing for giving me the wrong QDM. Never rely completely on mechanical gadgets when you are navigating, especially flying over the Pacific. So I stayed with the methods taught in navigation school for the rest of the war. A lot of our guys learned the British navigation system. I didn't because of my experience on the Clark mission. I don't think the British navigation training was near as good as ours. I would have hated to turn them loose over in the Pacific.

October 21, 1942, the 97th BG – mission #16 strikes a submarine base for the first time and hit U-boat pens at Lorient, France.[225]

 October 25, 1942, special mission for Van Kirk, Gibraltar to England.

"Tootsie Rolls and Candy"

October 26, 1942

Dear Mother, Dad and Jean,

I have been very busy and haven't written many letters. I haven't had many letters from home either. The mail service is very bad. That is the reason I send a cable every once in a while.

My last letter from you was a week ago. I've had one from Mary Jane, Ben Reichenback and Martha since then. We've got a new A.P.O. number. I think I told you in one of my cables. It is #520. It takes a cable about a week to get to me now. It took Mary Jane's last airmail letter about three weeks to get here. It took Martha's 10 days.

There still isn't much to write about. I have a lot of things I'd like to tell you about but I'll have to wait until I get home to do it.

I had a long letter from Mary Jane yesterday. It was the first letter I had from her for some time.

I got a box of stuff today. It had some Tootsie rolls, peanuts and fudge candy in it and it sure was welcome. I guess my blouse and the other box you sent were lost.

I had a letter from Bucky Bostian last week. He told me all about himself and Olley and Meredith. I think they're all missing a lot by not being in the army. They say experience is the best teacher so I've learned a lot since I've been away. Bucky also told me all about married life.

I got Jean another present. She'll have things from all over when I get home. They won't be of much use but they'll be nice to have.

That's about all for now. I want to write to M.J. tonight so I'd better save some energy.

Love
Theodore

Chapter Six — Endnotes

165 The first B-17E to land at Prestwick was Serial No. 41-9085. William Hess, *B-17 Flying Fortress*, (New York, NY: Random House, 1974), 54.

166 Earlier the RAF Squadron No. 90 carried out operational trials with Fortresses supplied to the British. Roger A. Freeman, *Airfield of the Eighth Then and Now*, (London, England: Battle of Britain Prints International Ltd., 1977), 185.

167 The Allied forces named the Japanese route to supply their troops the "Tokyo Express."

168 The other men who flew with Tibbets on *Butcher Shop* A/C No. 2578, navigator Lt. Levon Ray, bombardier Lt. Frank Beadle, engineer Sgt. Francisco Rebello, radio operator Sgt. Zane Gemill, waist gunner Sgt. Joseph Cummings, ball turret gunner Sgt. Richard Williams, gunner Sgt. Chester Love, and observer Lt. Glen Leland, Jr. "Crew Loading First Mission, 17 Aug. 1942," Gulley et. al., *The Hour Has Come*, 249. The other Fortresses were from the 342nd and 414th Bomb Squadrons, Roger A. Freeman, et. al., *Mighty Eighth War Diary*, (New York: NY, Jane's Publishing Incorporated), 10. The daylight attacks by the Americans became the key to success in the strategic air offensive against Germany.

169 A diversionary force of six B-17s made a sweep along the French coast. Hess, *B-17 Flying Fortress*, 55.

170 Eaker surmised that the Luftwaffe had been reluctant to engage the Fortresses with their "big guns bristling from every angle." "General Eaker Leads First U.S. Bomber Raid," and tells the story of how the Flying Fortresses smashed the Rouen railroad yards in the *Life* magazine September 14, 1942, issue. This issue also contains several photographs of the Abbeville raiders on Van Kirk's first mission.

171 Churchill did not welcome the first American daylight raid. He wanted the bombers to join the RAF at night. Churchill had been pressuring Roosevelt to disband the newly formed Eighth. Donald L. Miller, *Masters of the Air* America's Bomber Boys Who Fought The Air War Against Nazi Germany, (New York: NY, Simon & Schuster Paperbacks, 2006), 27.

172 The British escorts for the first American heavy bombing raid were identified as Spitfire Vs in Martin Bowman's *Flying to Glory*.

173 Gen. Ira C. Eaker agreed with the RAF echelon to utilize Spitfire IX escorts for the high altitude bombing missions of the B-17s until the Eighth Fighter Command was fully operational. Fredriksen, *Air Force Chronology*, 80. On September 7, 1942, Spitfire MK IX Wing escorted B-17s. Bowman, *B-17 Flying Fortress Units of the Eighth Air Force*, 14. From February through October 1942, Spitfire VB and VC were operational according to J. Rickard article (7 December 2010), No. 122 Squadron (RAF): Second World War, http://www.historyofwar.org/air/units/RAF/122_wwII.html [accessed May 6, 2011].

174 Armstrong was Tibbets immediate superior at the time. In several publications about the mission including Tibbets' autobiography, Armstrong flew as co-pilot and Tibbets did not fly with his regular crew.

175 The Abbeville raid received extensive coverage in the Sept. 14, 1942, *Life* magazine. Sources for missions: Van Kirk personal list of missions and World "War II Combat Operations Reports 1941-1946 97th Bomb Group," Records of the Army Air Forces, Record Group 18 Box 688 ARC ID 596339 NM-6 Entry 7, National Archives

Building, College Park, MD, and Thomas F. Culley et. al., *The Hour Has Come* (Venit Hora) The 97th Bomb Group in World War II, (Dallas, TX: Taylor Publishing Co., 1993).

176 RAF used the term "aerodrome." *The Hour Has Come* terminology was "airdrome" or A/D. Freeman's *Mighty Eighth War Diary* notes for A/D was "Air Depot." For consistency "aerodrome" is used in this publication.

177 The British and Americans used the nickname "Abbeville Kids" or "Abbeville Boys" to describe the exceptional pilots of the German Luftwaffe Jagdgeschwader Schlageter (JG 26).

178 Pilots had little if no formation time. Likewise, gunners had little experience with their turrets. Hess, *B-17 Flying Fortress*, 54.

179 George G. Hopp, Series Editor, Translated by H. G. Geiss, *Luftwaffe Gunnery Techniques* The Official Gunnery Techniques Instruction for German Fighter Pilots and Air Gunners, 1943-1945, (Ottawa: Valkyrie Publications, 1979), 23 - 40.

180 According to the 97th BG "Mission Summary" for August, 12 aircraft T.O. (took off), 11 Over T. (over target), 11 Sorties, 18.45 tons bombs, 2:45 time 'n flight, "Weekly Operations Summary," Record Group 18, National Archives.

181 In particular gunners and radio operators commonly lacked formal instruction for their position. Tittsworth and many other gunners had never fired a machine gun prior to their assignment and some radio operators left for Europe without studying the Morse code. Tittsworth's informal training came from other gunners who had received some formal instruction. Culley, *The Hour Has Come*, 15-16.

182 Women in History, Margaret Bourke-White biography, Lakewood Public Library, http://www.lkwdpl.org/wihohio/bour-mar.htm, [accessed April 27, 2010].

183 "Flier Wires Parents Here After Raids," scrapbook newspaper clippings of Van Kirk's personal papers.

184 The Spitfire escort left the bombers half way across the Channel. Col. Stanley M. Ulanoff, ed., *Bombs Away!* True Stories of Strategic Airpower from World War I to the Present, (New York: NY: Doubleday & Company, Inc., 1971), 162.

185 John C. Fredriksen, *The United States Air Force A Chronology*, (Santa Barbara, ABC-CLIO, LLC, 2011), 83.

186 Copy of Frank A. Armstrong, Jr. letter, August 23, 1942, Van Kirk personal papers.

187 "Talk Of The Town, Brightens Music Hall," *Brooklyn Eagle*, August 24, 1942

188 One wayward bomb luckily hit a submarine tied to the docks. Gulley et. al. *The Hour Has Come*, 36. "Mission Summary" for August, 12 aircraft T.O., 12 Over T, 18.00 tons bombs, 3:30 time 'n flight.

189 The top turret gunner received serious wounds according to Bowman's account of the mission in *Castles in the Air*, but all the injured men recovered.

190 Promotion letter from Headquarters European Theater of Operations, United States Army, to Theodore J. Van Kirk, September 1, 1942.

191 Sgt. William C. Young, "World War II Prisoners of War Data File, National Archive Archival Databases (AAD), http://www.nara.gov, and American Battle Monuments Commission, Manila American Cemetery, Manila, Philippines.

192 "Mission Summary" for September, 24 aircraft T.O., 23 Over T., 28.10 tons bombs, 3:00 time 'n flight, National Archives. The 301st BG on its first mission joined the 97th BG to Rouen.

193 The reporter added that the bombers had shot down at least five Nazi fighters, probably destroyed another thirteen and damaged at least twenty-five more Focke Wulfs. "Ganging Up on Flying Fortresses," news clipping, September 1942.

194 "Mission Summary" for September, 27 aircraft T.O., 27 Over T., 1 Lost, 12 Enemy Aircraft Destroyed, 63.50 tons bombs, 3:25 time 'n flight. The summary for the 97th BG did not include the lost bomber from the 92nd noted in the 97th group history and the National Museum of the United States Air Force fact sheet "AAF enters combat from England."

195 Seven Fortresses from each of the 341st (BLTQKPH), 342nd (EHDNGWM), and 414th (BCLRQSO) participated in this mission.

196 The radio operator/tail gunner, Charles A. Travinek, of Lipsky's crew wrote "The Gliding Fortress" for the 97th BG history about the "miracle" that six of the crew survived the crash. Lt. Lipsky, Ship No. 41-2445, Squadron 340, Cause Fighter. List of ships lost signed by Captain Orville Chatt, Group Intelligence Officer, Headquarters Ninety-Seven Bombardment Group (H) Army Air Forces, March 24, 1943, World War II Combat Operations Reports, Record Group 18, National Archives.

197 The Fortresses were intercepted by two dozen Fw190s. The Spitfire escort missed its initial rendezvous with the Fortresses. Lipsky flew B-17 Serial No. 41-24445, which went down under control followed by five fighters. Lipsky and several crew members became Prisoners of War (POWs). Martin W. Bowman, *B-17 Flying Fortress Units of the Eighth Air Force*, 13. Travinek's account states that two hundred plus Luftwaffe fighters were waiting for them.

198 "Mission Summary" for September, 17 aircraft T.O., 17 Over T., Enemy aircraft destroyed 12, 22.50 tons bombs, 3:10 flight time.

199 Headline from the *Sunbury Daily Item* clipping in the Van Kirk scrapbook.

200 "On Inflation and Progress of the War," last radio address designated as a "fireside chat" in Master Speech file of Franklin D. Roosevelt.

201 Fortresses B-17E and B-17F were four-engine aircraft powered by Cyclone R. 1820-65 or R. 1820-97 engines with Hamilton Hydromatic propellers, and turbo-superchargers. These models differed in their hydraulic systems. *Pilot's Notes For Fortress*, Air Ministry A.P. 2099 B, C, D, E & F. – P.N., supersedes A.P. 2099 B (Dec. 1942). In Birdsall's *Pride of Seattle* the prominent visual difference between the "E" and the "F" was the one-piece frameless molded plastic nose cone in addition to other improvements.

202 The B-17F-10 BO 41-24440 to 41-24489 had a modified tail wheel structure.

203 The aerial pixies also called gremlins by the aviators caused mechanical difficulties according to the crews. The *Red Gremlin's* artwork was described as the "demon from hell." John M. and Donna Campbell, *Talisman* A Collection of Nose Art, (West Chester, PA: Schiffer Military History, 1992), 183.

204 Several hundred modifications to the B-17E were incorporated in the "F" model. A new Boeing factory at Wichita, Kansas, a Douglas Aircraft plant in Long Beach, California, and Lockheed-Vega Corporation at Burbank, California, built 3,405 "F" models. Hess, *B-17 Flying Fortress*, 65.

205 The "B-17 Training Manual" explained "Formation Takeoffs:" the lead airplane flies straight for 90 seconds for each airplane, then makes an 180° half-needle width turn. The second airplane starts its turn ten seconds after the leader turns and pulls into position below and behind the leader's outside wing. The next airplane, another ten

seconds after the second airplane, pulls into position on the leader's inside wing. All airplanes take off at thirty-second intervals.

206 "Gen. Spaatz Decorates 22 Fortress Fliers and 11 Other U.S. Airmen," (AP) news clipping, September 12, 1942.

207 David Mondey, *Pictorial History of Aircraft*, (London, Octopus Books Limited, 1977), 48, 172.

208 "Mission Summary" for September, 18 aircraft T.O., 18 Over T., time 'n flight 4:30.

209 A microfilm machine could photograph more than 2,000 letters in an hour. The letters were written on a special paper provided at the Post Office. One roll of film held about 1,500 letters. The microfilmed mail service was known as V-mail. "V-mail," *Life*, December 14, 1942.

210 "Results First Game at St. Louis," *Brooklyn Eagle* Sports, October 5, 1942.

211 "Sailors Get Series News In Quick Time," *Brooklyn Eagle* Sports, October 5, 1942.

212 "Russian War," *Niagara Falls Gazette*, January 8, 1943.

213 "Mission Summary" for October, 18 aircraft T.O., 14 Over T., 1 enemy aircraft destroyed, 35.00 tons bombs, 3:30 time 'n flight.

214 Film from photo reconnaissance of an oil refinery near Bremen, Germany, showed before and after images of netting applied on a supporting framework over the entire storage tank area. Elaborate disguises were applied to even airfields such as the Nantes-Château Bougon airfield in 1942. Source of the images of the German efforts to confuse the bombers: Dr. Alfred Price, *Targeting The Reich* Allied Photographic Reconnaissance Over Europe, 1939-1945, (London, UK: Lionel Leventhal Limited, 2003), 58, 59 and 82, 83 respectively.

215 Wes Gallagher, "U.S. Fliers Blast Lille In Biggest Day Raid; 4 of 600 Planes Lost," (AP), *The Philadelphia Inquirer*, October 1942.

216 The 8th Bomber Command decided to review the gunners' high claims. After several months of examination the amount reduced the number of destroyed aircraft to twenty-one. The same aircraft racing through a formation could lead to duplicate claims. The German quartermaster records document the improvement of the American gunners' marksmanship. Hess, *B-17 Flying Fortress*, 58 – 59.

217 "Germans Seek Revenge After Smashing Raid," (UP) London news clipping, October 1943.

218 Admiral Norman Scott, buried at sea, was killed in action aboard his flagship, the cruiser *Atlanta* November 13, 1942. Winston Groom, *1942: The Year That Tried Men's Soul*, (New York: Grove Press. 2005), 302.

219 Starnes' recollections, Bonner in the *Final Voyage* described the damage to the *Boise* and the casualties during the Battle of Cape Victory at Esperance, 33, and the Naval Historical Center, http://www.history.navy.mil/photos/per-us/uspers-m/ej-moran.htm [accessed September 5, 2010].

220 Lieutenant Commander Edward J. "Mike" Moran assumed command of the *Boise* in late January 1942 bringing her back to the states after the ship accidentally grounded during the East Indies campaign. Moran led the ship to the South Pacific war zone for the campaign to hold Guadalcanal and awarded the Navy Cross for his "extraordinary heroism and courage" during that action. "Rear Admiral Edward J. "Mike" Moran, USN (Retired), 183 – 1957," Dept. of the Navy – Naval Historical Center, http://www.history.navy.mil/photos/pers-us/uspers-m/ej-moran.htm [accessed September 8,

2010].

221 Carroll V. Glines details the torture, mock trial, and executions in the dramatic account of *The Doolittle Raid* America's daring first strike against Japan.

222 "William G. Farrow First Lieutenant Army Air Corps," Arlington National Cemetery, http://www.arlingtoncemetery.net/wgfarrow.htm [accessed June 26, 2011].

223 Captain Theodore J. Van Kirk completed courses "for Pistol Automatic M-1911 A-1 .45 Cal" on February 29, 1944. Van Kirk part of HQ & HQ Squadron 41st Navigator Training Group received a score of 35 "Pistol Unqualified (Dismounted)." Another lieutenant scored 16. Special Orders No. 68, Headquarters Selman Field, Monroe, LA. Van Kirk personal papers.

224 QDMs were given as a magnetic course heading corrected for magnetic variation, but not for deviation or wind. "Operations Instructions" Item 7. c. (2) Weather, Headquarters Eighth Bomber Command, May 22, 1942, WWII Combat Operations Report 1941-46 Eighth Air Force.

225 "Mission Summary" for October, 21 aircraft T.O., 15 Over T., 11 Sorties, 3 aircraft lost, enemy aircraft destroyed 9, 30.00 tons bombs, 5:15 time 'n flight. Ships lost per "Group Intelligence Office" Lt. Schwarzenbek Ship No. 441 Squadron 342, Lt. Stenstrom Ship No. 443 Squadron 414, and Capt. Bennette Ship No. 344 Squadron 341; "Fighter" listed as cause for each ship lost.

Chapter Seven

North African Theatre *Operation Torch*

Dutch ~ We flew a few missions no more than two then suddenly they detached six airplanes from our group to Hurn, England. We were there maybe three or four days at most. The word was we were going to ferry some people. I had my picture taken as a "civilian" in case we had gone down probably somewhere into Spain. If we found the right band of partisans, they could have made us a passport. I took my military jacket off and put my necktie and civilian coat on. We were not allowed off the base. Everything was secret. The only one who left the base was one officer on payday who took our paychecks to get them cashed before we went to North Africa. Money was worthless there anyhow.

I think we found out at the briefing the night before where we were going. I remember thinking to myself this is another one of those damn low level missions. We still did not know who was going to be on what airplane, but we surmised it was going to be Eisenhower and his staff going down. It was a low level mission and we were given warnings and precautions about being detected by German patrol aircraft or their radar off the coast of the Brest peninsula.

Almost like the Clark mission they wanted to get it done come hell or high water and if something happened to poor Mark Clark that was tough fellas, you are with him. In the Eisenhower mission the preparations and dire warnings about German interceptors were more intense. For the Clark mission we only had two B-17s and for this we had six of our B-17s.

A lot of navigators used celestial going overseas, but some did not learn celestial navigation very well. As a result when they were going to fly over to join our group in North Africa they ended up in the Sahara Desert. They did not know their celestial navigation.

I saw Eisenhower more than Clark. Eisenhower had more stature, talked more, and associated more with his men. Clark stayed in the radio room. He was more of a cold fish, but both men were impressive.[226]

Jean ~ "Ted said that (Gen. Mark) Clark gave him some coins. Ted was very impressed with Clark, maybe because he gave him the coins."

"Gen. Dwight David 'Ike' Eisenhower"

 November 5, 1942, special mission for Van Kirk, England to Gibraltar.

Dutch ~ Eisenhower sat in the best seat in the B-17, the radio operator's area back of the bomb bay, when he got up to do something else. Eisenhower was not a guy who would sit on his butt just to observe what was going on. He walked up and spoke to Tibbets and walked back to talk to the waist gunners. Part of the time Eisenhower sat on the board between the pilot and the co-pilot. Eisenhower did not always require or demand special treatment. He was just another G.I. you might say, a good guy, and a gentleman.

Eisenhower did speak to me, but I do not remember what he said. I felt that I better damn well not screw up. We all had that feeling especially after the way we took off. We got up the next morning to take off and were delayed. The weather was absolutely horrible. For the first time we lined up to take off on a Gyro compass. I think it was the first time we could not see the end of the runway to take off, but we took off anyhow.

Eisenhower's group came out in buses and each one got off at the airplane he was going to fly in. Do we take off or do we not take off? Is the weather going to clear? We were all standing around talking and Tibbets spoke to Eisenhower. "Sir, I do not know if we can take off here today with this weather" or something of this type.

Eisenhower asked Tibbets, "What would you do if this was you alone?"

"Oh I would have been gone already," he replied.

Then Eisenhower said, "Well then son we better go. I have a war to fight down there." I think those were his exact words. That made up our minds.

This was the only mission that when we took off I could not see the wing tips and took off on a compass heading.

We did not fly in formation and stayed down low and not within sight of each other just one following the other. We took off from Hurn on the south coast of England, made a roughly right turn, and went out to Lands End. Lands End sticks out there pretty far. Then we turned south. We wanted to get far out beyond German radar and hopefully beyond German patrol planes too.

One of the other airplanes was delayed taking off with a brake problem. Lt. John Summers was the pilot. They took off the next day following the same route we went down on. Summers' airplane was spotted and attacked by German patrol airplanes. The co-pilot Thomas Lohr was injured during the attack. One of the passengers took over as co-pilot. His name was James Doolittle. How nice to have "Jimmy" Doolittle on your airplane to take over when your co-pilot was shot.[227] They turned around, went back to the base, and did not complete their mission. The next day with another co-pilot they took off fortunately because Doolittle was to take command of the Twelfth Air Force when he got down there.

One of the six airplanes did not show up. It happened to be John Knox, another one of our squadron commanders. By this time Tibbets was an operations officer. As near as we could figure the airplane caught on fire and went down in the ocean. Everyone on board was lost. That plane happened to be carrying General Duncan who was going down to Africa with Eisenhower.[228]

The squadron commander and operations officer were two different jobs. The squadron commander was only responsible for his squadron. As operations officer Tibbets was responsible for the operations of the entire group and also for receiving the information about the missions and responsible for the briefing. The operations officer was the better job although the rank connected with either position was the same.

Tibbets as a squadron commander could say for example, I am going to take my 340th squadron and fly tomorrow for training. As operations officer he could say our entire group is going to do a training flight.

 *November 7 - 8, 1942,* Spitfires from the 31st Fighter Group launch from Navy carriers to support the landing.[229] *Operation Torch* began before daylight as the Allies under Eisenhower invade northwest Africa.

"The Invasion Fleet"

Dutch ~ We got down to Gibraltar and land. Since we had been there before with Clark some of the people knew Tom Ferebee and me. Anyhow Tom and I had been invited on board one of the British vessels anchored at Gibraltar. Tom was always last because when we got on board we were given British grog, a kind of rum. I did not realize it at the time but the British issued a certain amount to their sailors every day and diluted it about two to one or better with water. I drank the grog without diluting it.

Tom said, "For Christ's sakes Dutch, you came down the gangplank swinging your arms like a limey sailor."

Shortly after we got to Gibraltar we had a briefing. One of the senior officers, do not ask me who it was, came up to us and suggested if we wanted to see a nice sight to come out to a certain point at the rock at a certain time that evening.

The officers said, "You will see a sight worth seeing."

During a beautiful moonlit night right on time this armada comes streaming through the Straits of Gibraltar headed towards Oran and Tripoli. Patton's group was attacking Casablanca on the east coast of the Atlantic while the fleet comes through the strait. Ships standing out like you have never seen before and you wonder why the Germans are not sinking all those guys. But it was a sight to behold and peanuts compared to the number of ships we had on D-Day.

Seeing the ships coming into the Mediterranean that night is something I will never forget.[230]

 November 9, 1942, special mission for Van Kirk, Gibraltar to Maison Blanche aerodrome at Algiers.

"Curse of the RAF"

Dutch ~ Word was going around about the possibility of supporting Air Marshal Welsh by bombing Bizerte. Our five or six B-17s ought to be able to do something. The next thing you know we get a call that we will fly General Clark to Algiers to take command of the ground invasion.[231] But we were told that it was unclear if the airfield had been captured or not. We pick up General

Clark, take off from Gibraltar, and had maybe a dozen Spitfires to escort us in case we ran into the Germans.[232]

About fifty miles away while approaching Algiers, I heard chatter over the radio, "Where the hell is that god damn Yank taking us? We don't see anything, but water down there."

I was the curse of the RAF believe me. Finally I couldn't stand it any longer and called Tibbets. "Pilot, do you mind if I tell them where the hell to go?"

Tibbets replied "No. And get them off our backs a little bit."

I got on the radio and said, "To all you Limey pilots wondering where to go, fly fifteen miles straight ahead, drop down through the clouds, and you will see an airfield there. Land on it. I hope it is captured."

When we reached Algiers the British aircraft were at the limit of their fuel. So we followed them in and landed. The airfield had been captured and was being bombed at the time. So Clark got out amidst the bombs and all the other generals disappeared.

Here we were in Algiers with our crew. We had the presence of mind to take our flight surgeon Doc (Eugene) Griffin with us, but no food, no ammunition, no place to sleep, no place to eat or anything. What do we do? We were on our own.

November 14, 1942, special mission for Van Kirk, Algiers to Oran[233]
November 14, 1942, special mission for Van Kirk, Oran to Gibraltar.
November 15, 1942, special mission for Van Kirk, Gibraltar to Algiers.
November 16, 1942, the 97th BG launched mission #17, another operational mission for Van Kirk, on the Sidi Ahmed aerodrome at Bizerte while the British First Army continued into Tunisia.[234]

"The Luckiest Mission"

Dutch ~ Tibbets went to Welsh, the RAF fellow at the base, to see if we could do some good and if we could get bombs and fuel. Welsh gave us a bomb trailer and fuel from the dock. Fortunately we had shackles on the airplanes so we could convert to carry the British bombs. We filled five-gallon cans, loaded them on the same trailers, made a little ladder, and created a bucket brigade to dump the fuel into the airplane. It took a lot of five-gallon cans to refuel our six planes. Welsh had told us that the Germans were bringing in a lot of

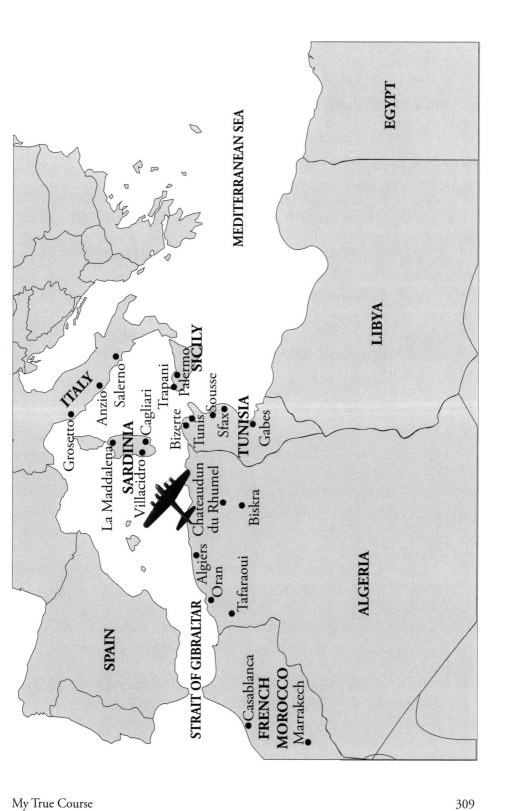

supplies and material to Bizerte so it would be a good target. I asked where the hell is Bizerte?

We did not have any maps of the area. I told the RAF Captain I needed some maps. His aide came back with a Standard Oil road map. That is what I used to navigate for our first mission in North Africa. I could not get lost because if we went too far south you hit the Sahara Desert. My navigation method was to fly near a port, and if they started shooting at you, you knew where you were.

Tibbets called us together early in the afternoon. We had six airplanes. Three went in and bombed the airfield and the others bombed the Bizerte Harbor.[235]

That was the luckiest mission I ever flew in my life. We found out why afterwards when Tibbets went to NATO. Some officers told him that fortunately or unfortunately depending on how you looked at it we hit the mess hall and wiped out almost all the German Me109 pilots of a fighter group.[236] We were at six thousand feet, which was scarier than twenty-two thousand. It was the first time I ever saw ground tracers coming up from the ground right up our butt. It was our first mission in North Africa.

"Fold Up Your Own Maps"

Dutch ~ Tom Ferebee and I always did our independent thing and never interfered with each other. Coming back from this mission toward dusk Tom looked at me and said, "What is your ETA?"

I meant six minutes past the hour, but said "six minutes past" nonchalantly. The next thing I know Tom is looking at maps, which was brand new for him. I never saw him look at maps before. "What the hell are you doing," I asked him.

He said, "I am trying to find where we are. You are six minutes past your ETA." We were not due for fifteen minutes. I meant six minutes past the hour.

Tom shot back. "The hell with you. Fold up your own maps." He never could fold up a map. That was the one and only time he ever tried to help me navigate.

Hell, I know where I am. I will just see where the Navy is shooting at us. We had Navy ships in the docks along the harbor and if you got too close to them they would shoot at you. The Navy never hit you, so it was not to worry about.

Tom tried to teach me how to operate the Norden bombsight. I said, "Tom that is too damn complicated. You do the bombing." My major role was telling Tom the wind direction and velocity so that he could have the drift killed before he sat down on his seat and looked through the bombsight. Tom was an exceptional bombardier!

"High Stakes Gambling"

Dutch ~ When we flew down to Gibraltar with just the crew and nobody else was around we became closer to Paul Tibbets. The four officers on the crew were inclined to do things together. There was no organized mess hall. We ate together and definitely talked about girls and occasionally something related to the war like the fall of a Russian or an Italian city. Tibbets liked to play blackjack, which evened things out a bit. He was smart enough to not get in a poker game with Tom Ferebee.

Tom was one of the best poker players in the service. I do not know where he got his ability to read odds and everything else for poker and crap games. He had natural instincts and was always winning money.

Several of the biggest pots were in the twelve to fifteen thousand dollar range. Our favorite game was seven card high low. You are betting three bets at a round, four cards every time you turn a card. So you are betting twelve different times. Tom usually had a table six and some pretty good size pots. Seven or eight hundred dollar pots were commonplace.

Tibbets told us "to gamble the way you guys do you need a salary of a million dollars a year back in the states." But in England we gambled with pound notes. At that time a pound was worth four dollars.

We frequently sent money back home. While we were in North Africa the value of the franc changed. Both Tom and I had saved a lot of money and made more converting currency back and forth. Tom sent money home more often than I did.

"Our Still"

Dutch ~ We had a sergeant who set up a still beside our airplane. We ran a fifty-five gallon drum of red wine through the still. The night we held our first dance we invited a group of British nurses. Nobody could figure out why all these nurses were passing out on the dance floor. They drank our two hundred proof distillate mixed with fruit juice and then all of a sudden clunk!

Every Monday morning I had to go and get one of the crew out of jail for having his way with the mayor's daughter. This happened a lot of weekends. The mayor threw the crewman in jail and I took a bottle of whiskey to the jail and bailed him out.

"Terrifying Moment"

Dutch ~ A few days after arriving in North Africa one of our B-17s was taxiing for takeoff, got a direct hit by a bomb, and caught fire. I will never forget it. The next morning we were faced with the horrible sight of the burned out B-17. Someone had to get the bodies out. Tibbets turned to me. We got all the good jobs as well as the bad. Tom and I always remembered that smell and the experience of carrying the bodies out of that airplane.

The following night we were bombed. It was the most terrifying thing that happened to me during my service. In the Tibbets' books he stood downstairs blowing a whistle, but he was nowhere around that night. I don't know where he was, but it was not with us. We were on the second floor of a French barracks during the attack. About five o'clock each night an airplane came by and dropped a bomb. We called it "five o'clock Charlie" and joked about it. We were frying eggs for dinner that night and had eaten eggs for breakfast and lunch too.

Along comes *five o'clock Charlie* and a couple more bombs were dropped and several drop in line with us. I dove under a bed figuring plaster was going to come down and it does. Ferebee runs down the stairs and hollers, "Dutch come on. Come on. We got to get out here!"

Another string of bombs came in and I said, "Tom, you are right buddy." We ran about fifty yards and I said, "God, Tom this is far enough. I can't go any further." We dove into a slip trench thinking we are safe and along came another bomber and he drops a string of bombs on one side of us, and then the other.

I responded, "Tom, you are right. We are not far enough way!" By now everyone is running up the macadam road including us. This time the Stukas are bombing too.[237] It was a clear moonlit night and you could look back and could see the Stukas dropping their bombs strafing the road and the line of sparks coming up the road. We knew we had to get off the road.

The area around Maison Blanche was small vineyard country. Tom always ran faster. He hit the wires first, running as fast as he could. I don't know how far he flew, but he was airborne for a good twenty feet. We ran through the vineyard and Tom got ahead of me. I don't know how far he ran that night, but he never got back to the base until the next morning.

Ferebee told me, "I ran into some anti-aircraft gunners and stayed with them."

I stopped in the vineyards. A few fires were still burning and the bombing stopped. I went back to our barracks and crawled into bed.

An officer walked in and said, "What the hell are you doing in here anyhow?"

I told him I was going to bed. The bombing was over.

"You can go to bed if you want, but there is a thousand pound bomb downstairs unexploded," the officer said.

"You are right. This is no place to sleep tonight," and I left pretty damn fast.

We were waiting for a mission when the photos were taken in the *Life* magazine. The guys emptied their pockets before we would take off. That was me with my head sticking up at the right time in the picture.[238] We were almost on the run in southern Tunisia in 1942.

"Pennsylvania's No. 1 War Mother"

Six sons of Mrs. George Kistner from Northumberland were serving in the military. Two more were eligible and a ninth if the age for the draft was lowered to eighteen. A "Bomb with Bonds Day" event featured Mrs. Kistner unveiling a Roll of Honor for Northumberland and Point townships.[239]

"North'd. Flier In Attack On Tunisia Base"

November 19, 1942, the operational mission for Van Kirk [97th BG – mission #18] raided the El Aouina aerodrome, Tunisia, escorted by P-38s.[240]

From the headquarters of the United States Twelfth Air Force somewhere in Algeria, Capt. Andrew Bing, a fighter escort pilot, called the daylight attack on the Axis-held Tunis aerodrome "the most beautiful bombing" he had ever seen. Major General Doolittle's boys destroyed five aircraft on the ground, four in combat, and damaged others in the third successive day attack. Sgt. Russell Ofala, a gunner on the *Red Gremlin* piloted by Lt. Col. Paul Tibbets, Jr., shot down one of the three Messerschmitt 109s after Sergeant Splitt "threw a load of lead" into it.[241]

November 21, 1942, the 1st Fighter Group of P-38s arrived to replace the 14th and escort the operational mission for Van Kirk [97th BG – mission #19], the aerodrome again in Tunis.[242]

"Doolittle Off Course"

Dutch ~ On occasion Doolittle flew with us. We were flying all over the country and I thought Tibbets was going sightseeing. I wanted to get back to the base. So I called up and said, "Navigator to pilot, you are about thirty miles off course. Are you going to get back on course?"

Doolittle came over the headphones and said, "Thank you navigator I will try." I did not know that Tibbets had let Doolittle take the pilot's seat as a courtesy![243]

"Move to Muddy Tafaraoui"

Dutch ~ We moved to a base called Oued Tafaraoui (ca. November 22, 1942).[244] God, the mud would be about a foot thick. We landed, but then couldn't move the airplane because of the mud. So we nicknamed the base "Gooey Tafaraoui." We pitched our pup tents right under the wing of the airplane. Tom Ferebee and I decided hell this was no way to live. We went out and got some cheap champagne. As long as it was raining we stayed drunk and drank more champagne. Paul Tibbets came out one day and said, "We are going to try to get off the ground."

"I am going to take Dutch," Tibbets said and I think also Junior Ryan, our co-pilot at the time. The three of us were going to try and get the airplane off the ground. Tibbets told Tom to stay put and that we would come back and pick him up. First one wheel would stick and Paul gunned the engine. Then another wheel would stick and Paul gunned that engine. Finally we got enough speed, took the weight off the wheels, and were airborne. We came and turned around over the place where Tom was standing.

As we flew over Tom he was growling and later told us, "You were going to come back for me. You did not come back you bastards!"

We went down to Maison Blanche and operated out of there trying to find an airfield that wasn't so muddy and had some decent weather. The airports had no runway lights and no facilities. We used our landing lights, but unfortunately visibility was limited.

The formations depended on the airfield and the location with one big difference. In England the air space was more crowded. In North Africa at Maison Blanche or Oued Tafaraoui, with a single runway you would take off one airplane after another. North Africa was easier than England because the weather was generally better and not as many airplanes in a confined space.

A Douglas transport stuck in the mud in Tafaraoui (National Archives).

November 23, 1942, the headquarters of the Twelfth Air Force moved from Gibraltar to Algiers while the 97th BG - mission #20 to Elmas aerodrome in Cagliari, Sardinia, aborted due to weather.

November 24, 1942, the 97th BG – mission #21 Bizerte docks, Tunisia.

November 27, 1942, the 97th BG – mission #22 Sidi Ahmed aerodrome, Bizerte.

November 29, 1942, the 97th BG – mission #23 Bizerte docks.

November 30, 1942, the 97th BG – mission #24 Bizerte docks.

"Critical of the Mission"

Dutch ~ Down in North Africa we wondered why we were going up to bomb Bizerte again; it had to be rubble by this time. At other times we bombed Naples or Sardinia, and we questioned. Why are we bombing this? Apparently the upper echelon thought there was something worth bombing. But as a crewmember especially when you were getting shot at, you questioned the mission. It was just griping.

December 1, 1942, the 97th BG – mission #25 El Aouina aerodrome.
December 2, 1942, the first sustained controlled nuclear chain reaction was achieved at the University of Chicago under the direction of Enrico Fermi.[245]

"Two Million Jews Perished"

The call for Christians and Jews to unite in a day of mourning and prayer for the "Jewish victims of Hitlerism" echoed across America's newspapers. The proclamation followed the previous week's revelation by the State Department of an alleged new order by Hitler for the extermination of the Jewish population of Europe. Jewish leaders in the United States announced that two million Jews had already perished and five million more faced extinction.[246]

December 3, 1942, the 97th BG – mission #26 Bizerte Harbor.
December 4, 1942, the 97th BG – mission #27 Bizerte Harbor.

"The Distinguished Flying Cross"

December 5, 1942
Saturday
Dear Mother, Dad and Jean,
I hope your getting these letters better than I'm getting yours. I'm not getting any of yours. They say our mail is getting home in about a week. I hope so.
I'm still in North Africa and doing the same old thing. About a week ago Gen. Doolittle went with us on one of our raids and I was the navigator on his ship. I don't know whether it made the papers or not but there were newspapermen there and I had my picture taken. It doesn't mean a darn thing though.
I was in the hospital a few days last week with a sore throat. I never was very sick but I got a good rest. I'm out now and back on flying.

This country isn't much like you'd expect it to be. There's plenty of water at some places. Its very mountainous and there aren't too many people around.

The Arabs are dirty people who run around bare footed with old sheets on. We trade them old clothes for eggs, oranges and tangerines. I've eaten so many tangerines I'm sick of them.

I thought of Jean's birthday the other day. I have some nice presents for her. I've picked them up clear from Fresno, Calif. to North Africa. Colonel Tibbets tells me I'm going to get the Distinguished Flying Cross the next time they give the decorations. I asked him what for and he said it would have that on the orders.

That's about all for now. I want to get this mailed.

Love
Theodore

Dutch ~ If Tom Ferebee and I spoke about Tibbets we said "Paul." If we were speaking to him, we always addressed Tibbets by his rank. We never called Paul by his first name until the war was over.

 December 5, 1942, the operational mission for Van Kirk [97th BG – mission #28] hit the Tunis docks and enemy shipping.[247]

"Japan Will Not Relent"

December 7, 1942, on the first anniversary of the attack on Pearl Harbor, Joseph C. Grew, the United States ambassador to Japan from 1932 until the war began, published *Report from Tokyo*. His speeches warned the government of the danger of a sudden attack by Japan.

Grew was emphatic in his evaluation of the character of the Japanese people and their fanatical obedience to authority. He warned of Japan's strength in an extensive article published in *Life*. Grew said that the Japanese will not relent even when eventual defeat "stares them in the face . . . Only by utter physical destruction or utter exhaustion of their men and materials can they be defeated."[248]

December 13, 1942, intense rains impeded most air operations for a week. The 97th heavy bombers resumed operations with mission #29 against the Tunis docks.

December 14, 1942, the 97th BG – mission #30 Tunis docks.

December 15, 1942
Savoy Apartments
Northumberland, Pa.
Hello Ted,

I am sorry that I did not write sooner but I have been to busy doing school work and working around town. This is the longest and hardest year I ever put in school.

Everyone is well in this lovely town of Northumberland. I don't know about Post because I only get to see him about once or twice a Month. I guess college life is to much for him.

Another thing that kept me from writing your lovely sister forgot to bring your new address.

I wrote one when you was in Mo. and I was going to mail it and your sister said that they moved you.

Jack, Bill, Diehl, and Bob Kelly joined the air force of the U.S. Army.

I just got paper to join the Marines.

Now all I have to do is to get Dad and Mother to sign off.

Keep away from the women and keep your nose clean.

How do you like the army? I got a letter from Jack and he says that he like it and said that he was on K.P. because his bed was not made right.

Well I am in study period and don't have much more time so I will shut my trap and say so long till later. Thanks for the Christmas card and I member Christmas eve

> *Love*
> *Ben*
> *Kee Kem Flying*

"Tail Gunner a Good Shot"

December 17, 1942
Dear Mother, Dad and Jean,

I don't know whether or not you got some of my other letters and cables so I'll repeat that I am in North Africa and have been from the very beginning. It was our ship and crew which carried Gen. Clark on his special mission which was mentioned in the newspapers. We also carried the commander-in-chief, Gen. Eisenhauer, around during the beginning of the campaign. It was quite a thrill for me to meet these men and navigate the ship on which they rode.

The other day a lot of back mail came in. I think I'll just go through it and answer your questions.

Letter of Oct. 26 – I got the clippings about D. Gross & M. (Minnie) Myers. I guess a lot of fellows are trying to get in now. I'm glad I got there first. My ear got O.K. and I am feeling fine. Getting a good tan too. I got one package since I left and Francis wedding cake. I did not get my coat. They say we have a lot of packages coming but I think my coats lost for good.

That bank balance certainly looks good. There's been $236 go in since that and I got $400 to send home if I get a chance to. There's no place to spend money here although I like to buy souvenirs. Use any of that money that you need.

Letter of Oct. 23. All them packages are going to be good. Them fruit cakes should be real good by the time they catch up with me. Thank Steve and Gladys for the one they sent. I sure stuck my head up at the right time in that Life picture. Tell Jean that every time she makes the honor roll to let me know and I'll buy her something extra. I'd rather buy a few good things to bring home then load myself down with a lot of junk.

Oct. 21 Not many questions except the one about the packages and I've answered that already.

Nov. 2. I got the clipping of John Bakers wedding. The ending of the clipping is what I like quote "they will reside at their respective homes for the time being." Dad must be getting better if he can get 2 squirrels & a pheasant in one days hunting. Our tail gunners a good shot too. He got <u>two</u> German planes in one raid.

I also got Xmas cards from you, Jean, Kate & Johnnie, Betty & John, Joe Phillip, Grandma & Grandpap Snyder and a letter from Post & Martha & Lee and seven from Mary Jane which I was very glad to get. I answered M.J. already and think I'll answer the rest since I have the time.

Now that I've cleared that up I think I'll tell you a little about me. I've been on as many raids as any American over here and more then most of them. Our groups had more experience then any others. Since I've been down here I've flown over most of North Africa as far as the allies have gone. I've slept out in the open and got soaked one night when my tent blew down. I've even stole so our crew could get some food already. The old army took pretty good care of us as soon as it could and I'm none the worse for wear. I've learned a lot got a lot tougher and sometimes feel glad it happened.

Right now I'm living in a nice hotel in a very nice town over here. It's warm but not too warm. The climate is much like Arizona's. Everything is irrigated and palm trees grow everywhere. There are a lot of dates, oranges etc. grown. I can step out on the veranda of my room and pick an orange off of the tree.

The town is populated with Arabs with quite a few French. Everyone speaks French and we have a fine time making ourselves understood. We usually manage to get what we mean across.

Seasons Greetings

FROM

THE OLDEST FORTRESS GROUP OVERSEAS

THE

97TH BOMBARDMENT GROUP

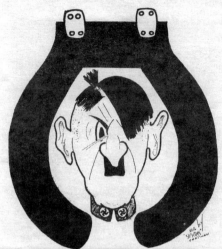

GENTLEMEN — THE TARGET FOR TO-NITE-

Best Wishes from the 97th

★

Take a dash of Florida sunshine, add a heaping six monthsful of England fog; plop in a portion of Tafaroui mud; sprinkle generously with the sands of the Sahara and the dust of Tunisia; stir with all the energy of the ground crews; boil under a burning African sun; add a beaker of the culture of historic Italy; top it off with a jigger of Russian vodka; squeeze into it the lives of those we have lost; chill with over 375 glorious sweat and thrill-filled missions; shake well in hellish reminiscence of stinking troopships, jostling jeep rides and the incomparable African railroads---then serve, and you have Schicklegruber's most abhoring and fearful high-ball... the 97th BOMBARDMENT GROUP!

✻   ✻   ✻

We are the oldest Fortress Group overseas... veterans of four campaigns; the first Fortresses to bomb Europe from England; the first Forts to strike at Germany from Africa; the first to land an American Fortress in Russia;--- and many more history making precedents

Our Group's pioneering and fighting spirit was aptly praised in a handful of words by General Armstrong in England when he said:

*"I give you a toast: Here's to
the Hun...a splendid fighter!
And here's to the 97th—his master!!*

"Somewhere over there"

GIFTS FOR SCHICKLEGRUBER

Another German aircraft factory falls behind schedule as Fortresses from our Group invade Germany and drop tons of "presents" on the Fishamend Markt Aircraft Factory.

Undated Seasons Greetings card from the 97th Bombardment Group

On the days when we fly we must go out to the field pretty early but other days we can sleep till about 8:00. That seems late to me now because for almost a month I got up every morning at the crack of dawn.

We usually fly about three days out of four and it's pretty hard on you. The work isn't hard but you always feel plenty tired when you come home.

You'll probably be surprised to get a letter this long but it makes up for a lot that I haven't written and maybe some I won't have time to write in the future. Besides it's the first time I've had a table to write on for almost two months.

I sent you a telegram with Christmas Greeting yesterday. I hope you get it because this letter will be too late. Don't worry if you don't hear from me sometimes because if I can't take care of myself now I never will be able to. I'd better stop before I fill this sheet.

All my love
Ted[249]

Soviet headquarters reported that Russian troops killed eight hundred Germans in one battle southwest of Velikiye stopping a series of Nazi counter attacks. The Germans were trapped in heavy fighting in the Stalingrad sector.[250] An Allied communication reported in the *Niagara Falls Gazette* that 107 Japanese warships and other vessels were destroyed or damaged since July 23, 1942.

December 17, 1942, Spitfires and P-38s escorted the operational mission for Van Kirk [97th BG – mission #31] on the Bizerte docks.[251]

December 18, 1942, the 97th BG – mission #32 Bizerte Harbor and offshore shipping.

December 22, 1942, solid overcast during the operational mission for Van Kirk [97th BG – mission #33] prevented bombing of the Bizerte docks.[252]

Christmas 1942
Telegram

MR FRED VAN KIRK
=672 QUEEN ST (NORTHUMBERLAND PA)=
CHRISTMAS GREETINGS AND HAPPY NEW YEAR TO YOU HAVE
ARRIVED SAFELY IN NORTH AFRICA AND AM WELL =
THEODORE VAN KIRK[253]

December 26, 1942, operational mission for Van Kirk [97th BG – mission #34] Bizerte docks.[254] Twin-engine Lockheed P-38s escorted the bombers over the Axis controlled naval port of Bizerte. On the ground Gen. Sir Bernard Montgomery pursued German Field Marshal Erwin Rommel west of Sirte about 220 miles east of Tripoli.[255]

December 28, 1942, the 97th BG – mission #35 Sousse Harbor, Tunisia.

December 30, 1942, the 97th BG – mission #36 Sfax docks, Tunisia.

December 31, 1942, during the year 3,033,361 men entered the service under the draft.

January 1, 1943, the 97th BG – mission #37 Tunis Harbor.[256] B-26s hit the marshalling yards at Tunis and the mission for the B-25s against the shipyards near La Goulette aborted due to weather.

January 4, 1943, operational mission for Van Kirk [97th BG - mission #38] Bizerte docks.[257]

January 5, 1943, P-38s covered the B-17s during the bombing of the Sfax power station, an operational mission for Van Kirk [97th BG – mission #39].[258] General Eisenhower appointed Maj. Gen. Carl A. Spaatz commander of the Allied Air Force in northwest Africa, which included the Twelfth Air Force, Eastern Air Command (RAF), and certain French air units.

January 8, 1943, the B-17s of an operational mission for Van Kirk [97th BG – mission #40] attacked the optional target of the Ferryville docks, Tunisia, after weather conditions prevented bombing Bizerte.[259]

"Four More Missions on This Round"

January 11, 1943

Dear Mother, Dad and Jean,

At long last but I have plenty of time to write. We're back here from our base getting our plane fixed up and getting a rest. We're living in a hotel by the ocean and getting swell food. Last night we had chicken and this morning we had real eggs. I also saw my first bread since leaving England.

I wrote a letter about three days ago. I can't find it now but I can't remember mailing it either so I don't know what happened to it.

This place we're at right now is about the nicest place I've seen since we left the states. What makes us so mad is that the fellows who are fighting the war don't see much of it. A bunch of guys who haven't done a damn thing since they got here live here and enjoy it all the time and make a bunch of rules about wearing full uniform at all times etc. They sure do get mad when we wear our old dusty clothes and tell them to go to hell if they don't like it.

I think I catch up on my back writing while I'm here. I haven't written to anyone but you and M.J. for about three months.

Nothing more to write about. Everything's O.K. and I only have four more missions to do on this round. Don't know what will happen then but I'm hoping.

Love

Theodore

January 11, 1943, the 97th BG – mission #41 bridge at Oued El Akarit, Tunisia.

January 11, 1943, the 97th BG - mission #42 the Fort held by the Italians at Ghadames near Tripoli, Tunisia.

January 12, 1943, the 97th BG – mission #43 Castel Benito aerodrome Tripoli.

January 14, 1943, the 97th BG – mission #44 Sousse docks.

"Casablanca Conference Opens"

President Roosevelt, passenger #1, became the first president to fly while in office. He left the United States aboard a commercial Boeing 314, the *Dixie Clipper*, and made the last leg on a C-54 to attend the conference and meet with Prime Minister Churchill, General Charles de Gaulle, and General Henri Giraud.[260] The leaders discussed the offensive in the Mediterranean and pledge to accept only unconditional surrender from the Axis.

Dutch ~ I did not see Roosevelt or Churchill, but their airplane crews stayed in the Hôtel Suisse with us. We got to know those guys very well.

"Spaatz and Tedder"

January 14, 1943

Dutch ~ Later on we flew Eisenhower around a lot. When he needed to go someplace Eisenhower called up and said, "Give me Paul Tibbets airplane and crew." He had to fly to the Casablanca Conference I think and then we flew him back to Algiers or Oran.

We also flew other brass around quite a bit.[261] One time we had General Spaatz and Air Vice Marshal Tedder, a British commander.[262] Spaatz and Tedder were up front with me. We were taking them to Tripoli, why I don't know. Both men were high up in their respective Air Forces. They got into an argument discussing something about air tactics and were going at each other. Spaatz looked over at me and said, "Isn't that right lieutenant?"

"Sir, I am sorry I was not listening," which I thought was very diplomatic of me at the time.

Another time, either in Oran or Tafaraoui, we were taking Eisenhower some place. Willie Tittsworth had a hangover and was sitting underneath the tail of the plane with his oxygen mask hanging out sort of breathing oxygen, eating an orange, and throwing the peels on the ground. An officious colonel came around and said, "Sergeant don't throw the peels around like that. Pick them up. Don't you know that General Eisenhower is going to be out here in a while."

Willie looked at him and said, "ah Colonel, don't worry. Me and the General is old friends."

We had flown Eisenhower around so often the crew got to think that way about him. But we weren't the only ones. Another crew he used quite often was Gene Aenchbacher's. Gene was one of the better pilots in our group.

January 15, 1943

From the headquarters of the Twelfth Air Force by command of Major General Doolittle the following named personnel were awarded three Oak-Leaf Clusters for participating in twenty sorties against the enemy in North Africa; in lieu of a second Air Medal.[263]

Maj. Robert E. Coulter
1st Lt. Thomas W. Ferebee
1st Lt. Edward Leroy Leonard
1st Lt. Theodore J. Van Kirk
1st Lt. Charles R. Wiley
Sgt. Zackie T. Gowan
Sgt. Willis D. Harris
Sgt. Jason C. Lancaster
Sgt. Thomas B. Roberts
Sgt. Richard A. Williams

"Arabs Plowing"

January 18, 1943

Dear Mother, Dad and Jean,

I've finally found enough ambition to write again. I don't know anything to do but just sit around and it's making me lazy.

We got some new magazines to read so they'll keep me busy for a while. We've played ping pong so darn much that we're sick of that.

We see a lot of fellows over here who have just come over from the states with mail etc. They say they're starting to ration a lot of stuff back there. If I get back there and find that place like England I'm going to quit fighting.

Our plane will be fixed up in a day or two and I'll have to go back to the base and start working again. I'll probably wish I had some time then.

How is the gas situation back home. Over here a lot of the people have coal burners in their cars and others have horses puling their cars around. The army has taken over most of the cars now.

We just had a good meal of chicken again so I feel more like writing.

Most of the people that stay around the hotel are French and it seems strange to see white people again even if you can't understand them. The girls are all anxious to teach you how to speak French. The funny part of it is that every time you say something in English you don't want them to understand they usually understand it.

The other day I walked home from the airport and saw the Arabs plowing. One of them had a mule & a camel together and one was plowing with oxen and another with camels.

I'll probably be going back soon and the mail service won't be so good so don't worry if you don't get any letters for a while.

Love
Theodore

January 18, 1943, the 97th BG – mission #45 Castel Benito aerodrome Tripoli.

January 19, 1943, the 97th BG – mission #46 marshalling yards at Jabal al Jallud and an industrial area south of Tunis.

"British Have Taken Tripoli"

January 22, 1943

Dear Mother, Dad and Jean,

Today is the last day of the vacation. I've put off going back as long as I could but I'm getting tired of sticking around here anyhow. I want to mail this letter before I leave so it will get home sooner. I'll probably have some of your letters waiting for me when I get back. I hope so.

The news that the British have taken Tripoli sounded good to us. That's one place we won't have to bomb again.

Last night a few of us were throwing a little party in a café near the hotel. Before the evening was over everyone in the place joined us and we had a devil of a good time. We had men from all branches of the army, navy, the RAF and nurses all raising the devil.

I picked up a few more souvenirs here. I have to start collecting small stuff or I'll have so much that I can't carry it with me.

I think I'll write a letter to M.J. and then go swimming once more before I go back to the desert. Don't worry about me.

Love
Theodore

"Move to Chateaudun du Rhumel"

Dutch ~ I made the best bedroll from collecting a lot of blankets and could stay warm no matter what. But I did not need it at Biskra. I was out flying someplace and when I got back to the base everybody was gone. Gee, where the hell did they go? I finally tracked them down. They had moved up to Chateaudun du Rhumel and not taken my bedroll with them. I had to go back and get a jeep. An army sergeant drove us in a jeep into the mountains towards Constantine. It was cold and snowing. I couldn't find anybody but I found our airplane and told the sergeant to let me out. I took my bedroll and slept in the radio area of the airplane with some K-rations so I would not starve and figured let them find me.

The next morning I heard something outside the airplane. I stuck my head out and said, "Who the hell is out there?" It was our crew chief getting the airplane ready to go. He tells me where the group moved so I could go and join them. So that is how it was in North Africa. They were moving around and you did not know where people went.

January 22, 1943, the 97th BG – mission #47 El Aouina aerodrome.[264]
January 23, 1943, the 97th BG – mission #48 Bizerte.

Postmarked January 24, 1943
Postcard of the Hotel Empire, San Francisco, to Miss Mary Jane Young
Lt. Rob't D. Young
Camp Roberts, Cal.
Hiya darlin, Hope you are OK. and things are going well. If you ever get time write me a card or letter.
Love
Bob

An unidentified serviceman bartering for eggs with an Arab (National Archives photo)

"Traded our B-17"

Dutch ~ We found a place to park the airplane and decided to scrounge around to find something to eat. Fortunately Arabs had lots of fresh eggs and also tangerines, oranges, and wine. So we started to barter with them. We were issued mattress covers, which you could fill them with straw for bedding. The first night we found the straw was filled with flees. We stopped using the straw and traded the mattress covers with the Arabs for eggs.[265]

Our subsistence became eggs, fruit, and wine. Within a day or so our flight surgeon, Doc Griffin found many civilians around the airbase who needed but were not getting medical attention. In gratitude Doc was paid in chickens, eggs, and fruit so we added chicken to our diet. We got so far that Tom Ferebee traded our B-17 to an Arab for 1,000 eggs. The old Arab stood out there every time we took off and waved to us as we left. One time we left and did not come back so the old Arab was out the B-17 and the eggs.

By this time also we were taking five-gallon gas cans and refueling our own airplanes. When you cut them in half they make a great cooking utensil. I remember Paul Tibbets sitting in the waist of a B-17 with a fire going cooking chicken. He was our cook.

January 24, 1943, the 97th BG – mission #49 Sousse Harbor.[266]
January 24, 1943, the 97th BG – mission #50 Sousse-Medenine.
January 28, 1943, the operational mission for Van Kirk [97th BG – mission #51] Sfax docks.[267]
January 29, 1943, the 97th BG – mission #52 Bizerte docks and shipping.
January 30, 1943, the 97th BG – mission #53 Ferryville docks, Tunisia.
January 31, 1943, the 97th BG – mission #54 Bizerte docks, Tunisia.
February 1, 1943, the 97th BG – mission #55 Tunis shipping, Tunisia.

German Me109s attacked the formation. Several of the Forts were damaged. The *All American* had no port horizontal stabilizer, a terrible gash through the fuselage, and damaged fin and rudder after being struck by a Me109. The pilot pitched up, recovered, and did land with her crew. A photograph of the miracle bomber became one of the famous aerial shots of the war. Another bomber was not so lucky.

Dutch ~ The Messerschmitt went over their heads. We thought they were all dead. Ralph Birk, the navigator, years later walked into one of our reunions. I said, "You are not here. You are dead." Birk, Knight, and Alfred Blair had been taken as prisoners of war, but the rest of the crew was killed.

"Grandparents"

Jean ~ "About once a week if we had the gasoline to drive we visited grandparents, the Snyders more so, the maternal side more than the paternal. Grandpa and Grandma Snyder had nine children, so did the Van Kirks. Farm families had a lot of children."

With many family members at arms in the war we "checked out where they were and how they were doing. We spent most of the time talking about the war. Grandpa Van Kirk was not a fan of Roosevelt so he usually had a tirade against him. The family was fiercely independent and did things for themselves. Ted was named for grandpa Snyder. Grandpa was gruff. We always called grandmother Snyder 'Virgie.' And grandpa Van Kirk was called 'Dory,' very stubborn too. It came down through the family. Grandpa Van Kirk passed away in February of 1943."

Dutch ~ Rattlesnakes and a creek ran in the woods back of grandpa Van Kirk's house. Someone had the idea to use the headwaters from the creek for a still. My uncle Lee's cows got drunk from drinking the water.

Charles Theodore "Dory" Van Kirk and his wife Bertha Boyer had recently celebrated their fiftieth wedding anniversary on January 17th. Dory was highly regarded in the community and one of the well-known farmers along the Danville Road.[268]

"French Cooks"

February 4, 1943

Dear Mother, Dad and Jean,

I've just washed the sand out of my eyes so I can see a little enough to write a letter anyhow.

There is nothing new to report from this section of the world. I have moved again but it was just from one hotel room to another. I now have a private bath. The thing only has cold water in it and I'm afraid the drains will be clogged with mud after I wash a few more times.

I have a little stove in the room that we use to make coffee on almost every night. They're running out of coffee so we've been getting tea to drink for the past month. I finally got used to the tea but now they're run out of sugar so we have to drink it unsweetened. The food is pretty good when the army cooks prepare it but these French cooks in the hotels spoil it when they start on it. It all comes from cans but it is substantial grub to say the least. I'm not losing any weight.

Right now there are a bunch of kids outside yelling, chewing gum, chocolate, cigarette etc. They start to cry every time they see an American. They never get anything but they sure do try.

I now have a bunch of pictures that we have taken at places ever since we left the states. I'd like to send them home but there are too many of them.

That's all for today. I'm really getting ambitious. I've written a letter a day for the past few days and that's pretty good for me.

Love

Theodore

February 4, 1943, the 97th BG – mission #56 Gabes airfield, Tunisia, and a landing ground west of the town.

 February 7, 1943, the operational mission for Van Kirk [97th BG – mission #57] Elmas aerodrome in Sardinia and the seaplane base at Cagliari escorted by P-38s. This was the 97th's first mission across the Mediterranean Sea.[269]

More than 25,000 Japanese perished during the brutal seven-month campaign for Guadalcanal. American Marines, soldiers, and Navy casualties numbered over 5,000.[270] The United States Navy lost twenty-four ships, which included fifteen destroyers, and the Japanese Imperial Navy lost nineteen ships.[271]

"Bet with Dick Wiley"

Tibbets had been transferred for duty as Doolittle's bombing expert reporting directly to Col. Lauris Norstad, the chief of operations. Norstad told Tibbets how to bomb Bizerte and the two tangled. Doolittle forced with the option of a court martial or transferring Tibbets sent him to the states for flight test work on the B-29.[272]

Dutch ~ Tibbets had left and Ferebee was with the Bomb Wing. Dick Wiley became our pilot and was going to be allowed to lead a mission for the first time. Junior Ryan was our co-pilot.[273]

We were going out on a sweep over the Mediterranean to find a luxury Italian liner, which had been converted to a troop transport. Our orders were to find and sink the ship. At the briefing we were told repeatedly to be back at the field by seven o'clock because it would be dark and there were no lights on the landing field. They kept emphasizing it. We take off and Dick reminds me we had to be back by seven.

I asked Dick, "Okay, what do I get if I bring you back at seven on the dot?"

"You bring me right back at seven o'clock and we will buzz the field," Dick said.

So I timed it. Sure enough we came right across the field exactly at seven o'clock at night. We flew a seven-plane formation at the time. Three planes up front, three planes behind and a little lower, and a seventh filling in the diamond underneath. Dick started to buzz the field. We were low and the second echelon even lower. Naturally we thought the guy filling in the diamond would slide out to the side. That didn't happen and he got trapped underneath and was so low he knocked the tents over. Needless to say we were not popular with the crowd down there.

February 8, 1943, the 97th BG – mission #58 Sousse shipping and railroad yards.

February 9, 1943, the 97th BG – mission #59 Kairouan, Tunisia, aerodrome fifteen miles west of Gabes.[274] Fighters strafed anti-aircraft, machine guns, and trucks in the Faid pass.[275]

Dutch ~ Chateaudun du Rhumel was in the Atlas Mountains and closer to the Mediterranean. It wasn't as muddy as Biskra and a much better place for an airbase, colder too and snowy. There was a bridge over a ravine near by in the town of Constantine, a major town in that area. Every one of our pilots had to fly underneath that bridge. I don't know why, part of their manly instinct I guess.

"Casablanca Conference"

Roosevelt ~ *February 12, 1943*, "We have lately concluded a long, hard battle in the Southwest Pacific and we have made notable gains. That battle started in the Solomons and New Guinea last summer. It has demonstrated our superior power in planes and, most importantly, in the fighting qualities of our individual soldiers and sailors.

American armed forces in the Southwest Pacific are receiving powerful aid from Australia and New Zealand and also directly from the British themselves.

We do not expect to spend the time it would take to bring Japan to final defeat merely by inching our way forward from island to island across the vast expanse of the Pacific.

Great and decisive actions against the Japanese will be taken to drive the invader from the soil of China. Important actions will be taken in the skies over China - and over Japan itself.

The discussions at Casablanca have been continued in Chungking with the Generalissimo by General Arnold and have resulted in definite plans for offensive operations.

There are many roads which lead right to Tokyo. We shall neglect none of them."[276]

February 14, 1943, first birthday of the 97th Bombardment Group.

February 15, 1943, operational mission for Van Kirk [97th BG – mission #60] B-17s hit the harbor and shipping at Palermo, Sicily. Major General Doolittle and Colonel Donovan led the raid on the docks.[277]

February 16, 1943, Adm. Sir Andrew Browne Cunningham announced at a press conference that the Allies had moved 780 ships totaling 6,500,000 tons of supplies safely to North African ports since the start of the operations. The United States Twelfth Air Force, the British Royal Navy, and the RAF had sunk almost one third of the Axis ships attempting to cross the Mediterranean to Tunisia.[278]

Dutch ~ Our B-17s were in formation over Pantelleria in the Strait of Sicily. The B-17s would try and stick their wing in the waist window of another B-17 for protection.

"Kasserine Pass"

On the 19th of February Field Marshal Rommel opened his command post near Feriana and prepared to commit the 10th German Panzer Division to strike against Tebessa and around the main Allied forces. The 21st Panzer

Division, the Afrika Korps, and the Centauro Division were also part of the Axis strength. The 1st Italian Army defended the Mareth positions. The United States Army II Corps commanded by Maj. Gen. Lloyd Fredendall suffered heavy casualties in the battles for Kasserine Pass, a two-mile gap in the Atlas Mountains of Tunisia. The II Corps fought as part of the British First Army.[279]

Dutch ~ The only time we saw the tanks from the air was when the Allies tried to break through at Kasserine Pass. We flew our B-17s so low the Germans were shooting down at us. This was first time I had ever seen B-17s in ground support.[280]

We had been down in North Africa for several months living in tents. Junior Ryan shows up, all 120 pounds of him, and he is going to beat the crap out of me and Tom Ferebee for taking his stuff down there. We told him we thought he was dead. Tibbets had already left for the states so Dick Wiley became the pilot and Ryan the co-pilot.

 February 17, 1943, operational mission for Van Kirk, [97th BG – mission #61] St. Elmas aerodrome in Cagliari, Sardinia.

February 18, 1943, fire broke out in the Frye Packing Co. plant in Seattle, Washington, after a flaming bomber crashed into the building killing more than two dozen people and dealing the highly classified B-29 project a serious blow. Testing of the XB-29 had been plagued with engine failures and fires. Boeing test pilot Edmund "Eddie" Allen and the entire crew died in the crash into the plant after an engine caught fire.[281]

February 22, 1943, the 97th BG – mission #62 Kasserine Pass, Tunisia.

"Living in Tents"

February 22, 1943

Dear Mother, Dad and Jean,

I think it's about time I start writing again. We moved to a new base a little while ago and in the moving I lost my brief case so I didn't have anything to write with or on.

We have moved from the desert to the mountains. It is cold as the devil where we are at now. Several mornings the water has been frozen in our canteens and it has snowed twice since we've been here. The mud is just as sticky as it ever was in Africa.

To top things off we are now living in tents. It isn't as bad as it sounds. I'm writing on a table that I made from some old boxes. It's the first thing I ever made that will stand up but it is pretty strong.

We also made a stove from a 50 gal. oil drum and old tin cans made into a pipe. We burn old engine oil and it gets hot as the devil. It gets so hot that I'm afraid the tent will burn down so I sleep with a fire extinguisher along side my bed.

I haven't any more letters lately. I guess they've been lost in the shuffle. I hope I get some soon.

Love

Theodore

February 23, 1943, the 97th BG – mission #63 Gabes Metlaoui, Tunisia.

February 23, 1943, the 97th BG – mission #64 entitled "Road (Maple at Walnut)" per the Mission Summary, hit the enemy troop concentration at Kasserine Pass.

February 25, 1943, the 97th BG – mission #65 Bizerte docks and ship.[282]

February 26, 1943, the 97th BG – mission #66 convoy en route to Palermo.

"Birthday in Oran"

February 28, 1943

Dear Mother, Dad and Jean,

I think that this is the first letter you will receive from me for a few weeks. I wrote some but I forgot to mail them before I left.

I am on another vacation as they call it. One thing we don't do is work too hard. The only difference between a vacation and working is that here we never have anything to do and while working we do something once in a while.

I have just finishing reading the Feb. 15 issue of Life. All the pictures they have in the magazine of U.S. airmen are pictures of fellows in my group.

We moved again and are now living in tents. I told you all about it in one of my other letter which I will mail as soon as I get back. I hope some of the other fellows mail them.

I celebrated my 22nd birthday (February 27) in Oran. I think most of the fellows were looking for something to celebrate because they sure did celebrate it.

I haven't had any laundry done for over 2 months. Every time my things get dirty I get some new ones. I don't know how many I have but it's a pretty good pile.

That's about all for now but I'll try to write more often.

Love

Theodore

The War Department announced that Van Kirk was awarded the coveted Air Medal for participating in five sorties against the enemy in North Africa. The men were living in tents and the temperatures had dropped so low in the mountains that water froze in the canteens.[283]

Lieutenant VanKirk Wins U. S. Air Medal In Africa

For participating in five sorties against the enemy in North Africa Lieutenant Theodore J. VanKirk, son of Mr. and Mrs. Fred Van-Kirk, 672 Queen street, has been awarded the coveted Air Medal of the United States Army, it was officially announced by the War Department today.

A member of the army air corps since prior to Pearl Harbor, Lieutenant VanKirk navigator of a Flying Fortress previously achieved distinction by participating in the first raid made by American fliers on German-held Holland. Considerable damage was inflicted in that raid and some outstanding results were achieved in combat with defending Nazi planes.

Lieutenant VanKirk was at that time based in England and subsequently participated in other raids over the mainland of Europe. He was in one of the first contingents of American fliers sent to North Africa at the time of the American invasion of that continent.

According to letters received by his parents, Lieut. VanKirk feels that he has had one grand vacation ever since he has been in the

LIEUT. THEODORE VAN KIRK

February 28, 1943, the 97th BG – mission #67 harbor shipping Cagliari docks.

March 1, 1943, the 97th BG – mission #68 Palermo docks.

March 2, 1943, the 97th BG – mission #69 Tunis Harbor shipping.

March 3, 1943, the 97th BG – mission #70 Tanks and transports in Gabes area.

Air Medal (*Sunbury Daily Item* article reprinted with the permission of *The Daily Item*, Sunbury, Pennsylvania)

"Sour Pickles"

March 6, 1943

Dear Mother, Dad and Jean,

About time I write again just to let you know I'm still kicking around.

I'm still on a so called vacation but I'm going back tomorrow. According to all reports the boys I left back there have the tent fixed up pretty nice. They improved the stove, put in electric lights and radio and got cots from some place. It will soon be like a nice hotel room.

Last night we played cards until late and four of us ate a gallon of sour pickles before going to bed. The surprising part of it is that none of us got sick.

It is now dinner time and we're having a little trouble getting two of the boys up. They want to wait until supper. I don't know how I got the ambition to get up for breakfast. I was pretty hungry.

A fellow moved in our room with us. He just left the states and he doesn't like Africa. He acts like a big baby and is homesick. I think we have him scared to death.

I saw a bunch of fellows who went to school with me in Sikeston. They're scattered all over the world. That was about the last class before the war started and it was also the last good class. Now the fellows are being cadets to avoid the draft and get more pay and they aren't eager.

I guess I'll go take a bath and get cleaned up. It's hard to tell when I'll get a chance to do it again. I hope I have some mail when I get back there.

Love
Theodore

March 7, 1943, the 97th BG – mission #71 shipping between Tunisia and Sicily.

March 8, 1943, the 97th BG – mission #72 shipping again off Bizerte.

March 10, 1943, operational mission for Van Kirk [97th BG – mission #73] El Aouina aerodrome and the Town of Gafsa.[284]

March 12, 1943, the 97th BG – mission #74 Sousse docks and marshalling yards.

March 15, 1943, operational mission for Van Kirk [97th BG – mission #75] hit a convoy in the Straits of Sicily.[285]

"Oran and Casablanca"

March 16, 1943

Dear Mother, Dad and Jean,

A shower has broken up our baseball game so I'll write a letter.

It looks as though spring has finally come. The days are nice and warm but at night it gets cold as the devil. It doesn't rain near as much as it used to.

When we don't fly we spent the day playing volleyball all morning and baseball all afternoon. We don't pay much attention to the rules and the games get pretty rough. Usually the side that can argue the best is the side that wins.

A little while ago I was running around with my shirt off and now, since it's raining it's so cold that I'm thinking of lighting the fire.

I had two weeks off as a birthday present. I spent them in Oran and Casablanca. It was the second time I had been to Casa. I was there on my other vacation too. I stayed in a grand hotel by the beach and had a good time. I'm not working too hard.

We finally got around to cleaning out our tent and it really needed it. It was the first good cleaning it's had since we moved in it. Last night we ate about five dozen eggs before going to bed and we had egg shells all over the floor. Eggs fried in butter is our midnight snack.

That's about all the news but I feel ambitious so I think I'll write to all the people I owe a letter.

Love
Theo.

March 17, 1943, Patton attacked in southern Tunisia.

March 21, 1943, operational mission for Van Kirk [97th BG – mission #76] Djebel Tebaga aerodrome, Algiers, in the morning.[286]

March 21, 1943, operational mission for Van Kirk [97th BG – mission #77] same target in the afternoon.[287]

March 23, 1943, operational mission for Van Kirk [97th BG – mission #78] shipping in the Bizerte Harbor.[288]

March 25, 1943, operational mission for Van Kirk [97th BG – mission #79] shipping at Sousse Harbor.[289]

March 29, 1943, the Eighth Army broke the Line after more than a week of battering from German air attacks. Rommel's forces were retreating. The major Nazi supply port of Gabes, south of Sfax, and the surrounding area were subjected to heavy naval bombardment.[290]

March 31, 1943, operational mission for Van Kirk [97th BG – mission #80] Monserrato aerodrome, Sardinia and Cagliari Harbor.[291]

March 31, 1943, the 97th BG – mission #81 Decimomannu aerodrome, Sardinia.

April 1, 1943, Capt. C. David Hoffmann, Air Corps, requested the promotion of 2nd Lt. Theodore J. Van Kirk to 1st Lieutenant describing the basis for performance of his duties as navigator as "excellent."[292]

April 4, 1943, the operational mission for Van Kirk [97th BG – mission #82] to the marshalling yards at Naples, Italy, was the first heavy bomber mission to the European mainland from North Africa.[293]

"Sleeping Bags"

April 5, 1943

Dear Mother, Dad and Jean,

Every time it stops raining around here the sun makes me so lazy I don't feel like writing. It's just like spring only it's a lot better. It must be spring fever.

I haven't written for so long that there should be a lot of news but there isn't. I just woke up from an afternoon nap and feel like the devil.

They got us up at 5:45 this morning. When they did that I was ready to hand in my resignation. It was cold as the devil and frost was all over everything. You freeze at night and roast during the day.

I forgot to tell you about my new bed. They gave us some air mattresses and sleeping bags. The sleeping bags are filled with duck feather stuff and a blanket lining that you can zip in or out. You'll never get cold in them and it's the softest thing to sleep on I've found. They didn't get many of them but the old officers of the squadron got the ones they had.

I had two letters from you yesterday. Both of them were V-mail and it took them a little over two weeks.

Almost time to eat again. I've missed a meal for the last two days because I was flying so I'm always there early for the next one.

Love

Theodore

April 5, 1943, the 97th BG – mission #83, Sidi Ahmed aerodrome.

April 5, 1943, operational mission for Van Kirk [97th BG – mission #84] El Aouina aerodrome, Tunisia.[294]

April 6, 1943, the 97th BG – mission #85 shipping sweep, north Tunisia.

April 6, 1943, operational mission for Van Kirk [97th BG – mission #86] shipping Trapani Harbor.[295]

"Cleaning up Tunisia"

No. _____

(CENSOR'S STAMP)

To Mr. Fred Van Kirk
672 Queen St
Northumberland, Pa
U.S.A.

From Lt. T. J. Van Kirk
(Sender's name)
340th Bomb Sqd 97th Gp.
(Sender's address)
A.P.O. #520. New York City
April 7, 1943
(Date)

Print the complete address in plain block letters in the panel below, and your return address in the space provided. Use typewriter, dark ink, or pencil. Write plainly. Very small writing is not suitable.

Dearest Mary Jane,

I'll have to use this paper if I want it to go by air but I still don't like it.

I had two letters from you today they were the first I had for a long time and it took them a month to get here.

Last night some fuel oil exploded in the tent next to ours and the tent burned down. One fellow was burned and they lost almost everything they had. We all played firemen for awhile but it didn't do much good.

The news reports say that the Eighth Army is moving again. I hope they keep right on going this time. The sooner they finish cleaning up Tunisia the easier it will be for me.

I'm sorry you think I didn't like your fur coat. You should know by this time that I like anything you wear or anything you do. In case you don't know it I'll tell you that I like everything about you. In fact I love you and always will.

I had a letter from Mr. Zong a few days ago. He also says _____
town. I guess _____
the unlucky _____
I'll make up _____

I haven't _____
wrote to May _____
can write to me _____
letters but I _____

Tent camp of the Twelfth Air Force in Algiers, Algeria. (National Archives)

April 7, 1943

Dearest Mary Jane,

I'll have to use this paper if I want it to go by air but I still don't like it.

I had two letters from you today. They were the first I had for a long time and it took them a month to get here.

Last night some fuel oil exploded in the tent next to ours and the tent burned down. One fellow was burned and they lost almost everything they had. We all played firemen for a while but it didn't do much good.

The news reports say that the Eighth Army is moving again. I hope they keep right on going this time. The sooner they finish cleaning up Tunisia the easier it will be for me.

I'm sorry you think I didn't like your fur coat. You should know by this time that I like anything you wear or anything you do. In case you don't know it I'll tell you that I like everything about you. In fact I love you and always will.

I had a letter from Mr. Zong a few days ago. He also says that everyone is gone from the old town. I guess I was pretty lucky getting in early. The unlucky part was being away from you but I'll make up for that.

I haven't found anyone with enough time to write to Mary Francis but I'm working on it. Tell her she can write to me if she wants to write. I like to read letters but I like yours best.

All my love
Teedy[296]
V-Mail

"Heating Our Tent"

Dutch ~ We took a fifty-five gallon drum cut a hole in the top for the tin cup chimney and another hole in the bottom with some dirt. Gasoline dripped on the dirt and burned keeping our tent warm. As long as you kept the fire going everything was fine. One day I walked into the tent and somebody apparently had just left and turned the fire off. The thing was still hot and I didn't know it. I turned on the gas, threw in a match, and woof flames shot up and singed my hair and eyebrows.

April 10, 1943, operational mission for Van Kirk [97th BG – mission #87] struck the heavy cruiser *Gorizia*, La Maddalena, Sardinia[297]

April 11, 1943, operational mission for Van Kirk [97th BG – mission #88] targeted shipping and the docks at Trapani, Sicily.[298]

"Biskra"

Dutch – Our 97th group was based at Biskra for a time. Biskra was one of the larger oases on the north edge of the Sahara. Bulldozers had leveled out a whole big area for our airfield. The problem was that when an airplane took off it would be so dusty you had to wait for another fifteen minutes for the sand to settle before you could see enough to take off. We took off in formation, three or six at a time. The others waited for the air to clear again. The dust caused numerous engine failures.

Biskra had three nice hotels, a great oasis, and date trees all over the place. The officers lived in the hotels and only one had mess facilities. We had reports that Biskra was a pre-war vacation place for gay people from France. I don't know if this was true or not. Guess what I got for Christmas that year, a box of dates. I hated dates.

We always carried our .45 automatic even when we went for meals because there were Germans around, saboteurs, and Arabs who would cut your throat for a dime. The .45 had a quirk. You cleared a .45 by slapping the chamber back and forth. It would not kick the last bullet shell out of the chamber. When we returned to the hotel we were required to clear the chamber.

One night in the lobby of our hotel I was clearing my gun. The bullet would not come out of the damn chamber. An MP watching me said, "What stupid lieutenant does not know how to get the bullet out of the chamber?" He grabbed my pistol. "Lieutenant, let me do that for you."

The MP did the same thing that I had been doing, pointed it at the ground, pulls the trigger, and shoots himself in the foot! He was the only man ever shot by that .45.

April 12, 1943, operational mission for Van Kirk [97th BG – mission #89] Bizerte dock area.[299]
April 13, 1943, the 97th BG – mission #90 Milo aerodrome Trapani, Sicily.
April 14, 1943, operational mission for Van Kirk [97th BG – mission #91] El Aouina aerodrome.[300]

"Yamamoto Killed"

The architect of the attack on Pearl Harbor, Adm. Isoroku Yamamoto, was killed when American fighter aircraft shot down his transport bomber. The

Admiral announced a year before Pearl that he looked forward to dictating peace to the United States at the White House.[301] Yamamoto had studied at Harvard University and was a Naval Attaché to Washington from 1925 to 1928.[302]

"Los Alamos Boys' Ranch School"

April 15, 1943, the contract between the Manhattan District of the Corps of Engineers and the University of California was signed for the secret *Project Y* operating under Oppenheimer. A wire mesh fence bordered the remote mesa compound about thirty miles northwest of Los Alamos, New Mexico, with posted signs of "Danger" in English and Spanish. The former ranch school became home to a community of physicists, mathematicians, and other fields.[303] Bright young scientists garnered from campuses across the country joined Fermi, Bohr, and Teller to create a think tank and develop a super weapon.

The bomb was developed in great secrecy and the tens of thousands who worked at the sites in Oak Ridge, Tennessee, and Hanford, Washington, did not know the exact purpose of their war related work. The Manhattan Project formally called the Manhattan Engineer District would cost more than 2 billion dollars and employ approximately 130,000 people by the war's end.

April 17, 1943, the 97th BG – mission #92 Palermo docks, Sicily.

 April 18, 1943, operational mission for Van Kirk [97th BG – mission #93] Boccadifalco aerodrome.[304]

"Volunteer or be Drafted"

April 18, 1943, Van Kirk's future brother-in-law, "Mick" McAllister enlisted in the Navy.

Jean – "We knew each other all our lives. We didn't get serious until Mick went into the service and I figured maybe I had better grab him."[305]

Mick – "I graduated at seventeen, too young in 1942 in the middle of the war so I went to college at Susquehanna for one year. Jimmy Kerwin, a World

War I veteran, headed the local draft board and knew everyone. I was eighteen in April. Kerwin called and said, 'If you don't want to be drafted to the Army I suggest you move quickly. You have one year of college. Either volunteer for where you want to go or I will have to draft you. I'll give you that choice,' which was damn decent of him. Everybody in town who was going to be drafted was called and told they were going to be drafted."

"I had been a Boy Scout and a Sea Scout. We had our rowboat in the Susquehanna River so I thought 'I am going in the Navy.' The irony of it was when I went down to register standing there naked the Naval recruiting officer said, 'What should we do with you?'"

"I don't know," Mick answered. "What do you want to know?"

The recruiter asked, "What have you done?"

"Not much, I am a musician."

The officer continued questioning him. "Were you a Boy Scout?"

"Yes. I have twenty badges and missed Eagle Scout by one, the Bird Study. I missed Bird Study because there were not thirty species of G-D birds in our hometown. I am interested in pharmacy work and medic and have a first aid merit badge."

"Great, you are a medic," said the officer.

"He stamped my wrist as I went through the line I heard, 'you are now a first class seaman.' The Navy sent me to the Great Lakes Naval Station to train as a lab technician. We marched every day. I volunteered to be the drummer during the march. After basic I was sent across the river to a training center for medics and had six months of that. I worked in the scarlet fever ward and picked up scarlatina from the guys who were in there."

April 18, 1943, a secret teletype sent to the Headquarters Fifth Wing General Atkinson was passed on to the men of the 97th Bombardment Group.

"The Commanding General Northwest African Strategic Air Force takes pleasure in transmitting the following paragraph of commendation recently received from the commanding general Army Air Forces quote while we are on the subject of congratulations CMA It appears to me that you and your Air Force are certainly on the receiving end. The Nine Seven Group especially should be commended for putting four seven of its four eight assigned airplanes into the air and getting em all back SMCN that is real maintenance. Then today CMA more good news in the form of your successful interception of a JIG uncle five two flight off the north conclusion of this war. I wish you would pass this on to your personnel CMA air and ground alike CMA that we at home are watching their progress with tremendous pride."[306]

April 19, 1943, operational mission for Van Kirk [97th BG – mission #94] shipping at Tunis Harbor.[307]

April 20, 1943, operational mission for Van Kirk [97th BG – mission #95] Sidi Ahmed aerodrome.[308]

April 20, 1943, the 97th BG – mission #96 La Goulette docks, Tunisia.

ADDRESS REPLY TO
HEADQUARTERS OF THE ARMY AIR FORCES
WAR DEPARTMENT
WASHINGTON, D. C.

WAR DEPARTMENT
HEADQUARTERS OF THE ARMY AIR FORCES
WASHINGTON

April 21, 1943.

TO ALL PERSONNEL OF THE ARMY AIR FORCES:

In violation of every rule of military procedure and of every concept of human decency, the Japanese have executed several of your brave comrades who took part in the <u>first</u> Tokyo raid. These men died as heroes. We must not rest – we must re-double our efforts – until the inhuman warlords who committed this crime have been utterly destroyed.

Remember those comrades when you get a Zero in your sights – have their sacrifice before you when you line up your bombsights on a Japanese base.

You have demonstrated that the Japanese cannot match you in aerial combat or in bombardment. Let your answer to their treatment of your comrades be the destruction of the Japanese Air Force, their lines of communication, and the production centers which offer them opportunity to continue such atrocities.

H. H. ARNOLD,
General, U. S. Army,
Commanding General, Army Air Forces.

3-8075, AF
1477AC

(National Archives)

April 23, 1943
Lt. Rob't D. Young 01306507
A.T. Co. 105th Inf.
A.P.O. 27
San Francisco, CA
10:00 p.m.
Dear Janie,

How is my little darling sister these days? Still love me ho! hum! I'll betcha I can see your lips answering that one now.

Well, darlin' I hope you had a happy Easter. Have lots of fun – some for me too

Say Janie how is your boy friend coming along these hot days. I guess he is in Africa or is he still in England?

Say hello to your Mother for me and also to anybody else around that I know. Be good & take care of yourself.

As ever

Love,

Bob[309]

April 23, 1943, the 97th BG – mission #97 shipping sweep Sicilian straits.

April 26, 1943, operational mission for Van Kirk [97th BG – mission #98] Grosseto aerodrome, Italy.[310]

April 27, 1943, the 97th BG – mission #99 Villacidro, Sardinia.

April 27, 1943, operational mission for Van Kirk [97th BG – mission #100] shipping sweep in the Sicilian Straits.[311]

April 29, 1943, operational mission for Van Kirk [97th BG – mission #101] shipping sweep of Bizerte.[312]

In the history of the 97th *The Hour Has Come* 90,000 leaflets were dropped during this mission and 2,000 during the following one.[313] The propaganda fliers were fired from Allied guns in shells that burst over the German lines in Tunisia.[314]

Dutch ~ I heard of the leaflets being dropped urging the German soldiers to surrender or face more bombing and die.

May 5, 1943, operational mission for Van Kirk [97th BG – mission #102] shipping off Tunis Harbor.[315]

"Promotion for Van Kirk"

From Headquarters, North African Theater of Operations, United States Army, by command of General Eisenhower, 2nd Lt. Theodore J. Van Kirk, 340th Bomb Sq (H) AAF was advised of his temporary promotion to First Lieutenant from May 8, 1943. "This promotion, unless sooner terminated, will terminate automatically at the expiration of the emergency and six months thereafter, at which time you will revert to your permanent grade."[316]

May 7, 1943, allied troops enter Bizerte and Tunis.

May 9, 1943, operational mission for Van Kirk [97th BG – mission #103] Palermo, Sicily.[317]

May 10, 1943, the operational mission for Van Kirk [97th BG – mission #104] Milo aerodrome, Sicily.[318]

May 11, 1943, the 97th BG – mission #105 Marsala, Sicily.

May 13, 1943, the 97th BG – mission #106 Cagliari docks, Sardinia.

"British Bar Fights"

Dutch – The best fight that I ever saw was after the war had been settled in North Africa. The British Eighth Army came back through to return to England. Tom Ferebee and I were in Algiers at that time. Some of the First Army units were also in Algiers.

We always went down to the bawdy houses because they were the best places in town to have a drink.

Tom said, "This is going to be fun in here tonight" seeing the British Army units and some Scots wearing their kilts.

The British First Army guys started fighting with the Eighth. The 97th Bomb Group history epitomized this time as the "comradeship of arms" as free men from across the globe served in North Africa.[319]

Both of us asked each other if we wanted to get mixed up in this fight.

Tom said, "hell no."

We got down behind the bar and grabbed a bottle in each hand. If any guy stuck his head over the bar we conked him. We weren't going to get involved in that fight. When it was almost over we sneaked out of there.

It was funny though, because in these big brawls no one got really hurt. It was like a fight back home in a baseball game.

May 13, 1943, the Allies defeated the Axis forces at Tunis taking about 250,000 German and Italian prisoners including many from Rommel's Afrika Korps. Prisoners began the process of being shipped to camps across the United States and by November 1944 POW camps operated in forty-six states. Hard core Nazis attempted to dominate the camps and the government and American people were slow to distinguish a typically nationalist German soldier from the fascists and those who supported the Nazi Party.[320]

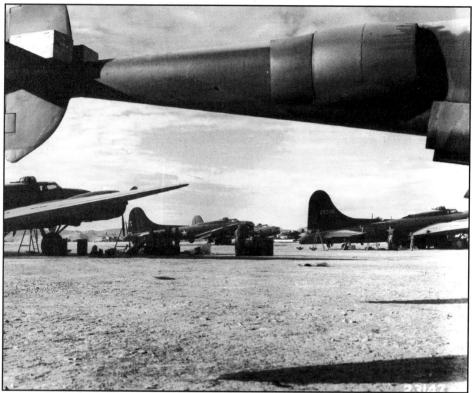

In the background B-17s were being serviced in Algiers (National Archives).

May 17, 1943, special mission for Van Kirk, Algiers to Malta.
May 18, 1943, the 97th BG – mission #107 Trapani docks, Sicily.
May 19, 1943, the 97th BG – mission #108 Milo aerodrome, Sicily.
May 20, 1943, special mission for Van Kirk, Malta to Algiers.[321]

Spring 1943, the Soviets purchased limited amounts of uranium approved by General Groves from the United States under Lend Lease, which resulted in a Congressional inquiry after the war.[322]

May 29, 1943, "1st Lieutenant Theodore J. Van Kirk, 0-659024, has been a flying officer of the 97th Bombardment Group, (H) AAF, since its inception in February of 1942. He has proven himself to be a creative officer whose resourcefulness and quiet manner inspire confidence.

This energetic young navigator has been extremely valuable to this command as a combat crew member and while he may be expected to perform in an outstanding manner any duty to which he may be assigned, it is suggested that in view of his very active career, he be assigned duties involving frequent aerial flights, such as are found in the Ferry Command, for example."[323]

May 29, 1943
340th Bombardment Squadron (H) AAF
Office of the Operations Officer
   Subject: Operational Missions and Operational Time
   To:Whom It May Concern
   This is to certify that 1st Lieut. Theodore J. Van Kirk, 0-659024, has completed fifty-four (54) operational missions for a total of two hundred fifty-six hours and twenty-five minutes (256.25).
   Signed: C. David Hoffmann, Major, Air Corps, Commanding[324]

"Fifty-eight Missions"

Dutch ~ Word came out that established a limit of fifty missions. I already had fifty-eight and was told I couldn't fly anymore. I said, "Good I can go home," but was told I couldn't do that either. And no one knew what we were supposed to do. My logs for the *Red Gremlin* were turned into the intelligence officer and were probably thrown out at some point.

Four of us who couldn't fly anymore got one of those big wheeled general staff cars threw our bedrolls, a bunch of canteens, and supplies in the back then toured North Africa and got into some of the damndest fusses. Dick Wiley led the foray into the native villages. The overpopulated mud huts in the villages usually surrounded an oasis.

When we got back I was given orders to go to Algiers and then orders to get our decorations and go home. When I asked about the transportation home the answer was, "that is up to you." I had to hitch hike home from North Africa to go home!

Tom Ferebee went to wing headquarters for several heavy bombardment groups. He had a girl friend over there.

When there was an especially difficult mission Tom volunteered for it. A letter granting him permission for exemption of the number limit was given and he had to sign agreeing to the extension. This went on until Tom reached sixty-four missions and he finally decided that he had been shot at enough and went home.

May 29, 1943, Colonel Donovan ordered the following officers and enlisted men to report without delay to headquarters for further instructions.[325]

(N) 1st Lt. James W. Hardwick	342nd Bomb Sq
(B) 1st Lt. Woodford R. Thompson, Jr.	342nd Bomb Sq
(TG) T/Sgt. James R. Boyd	342nd Bomb Sq
(RO) T/Sgt. Frederick R. Laite	342nd Bomb Sq
(E) T/Sgt. Wilmer J. A. Harverson	342nd Bomb Sq
(BTG)T/Sgt. Earl L. Love	342nd Bomb Sq
(CP) 1st Lt. Bernard A. Goncher	342nd Bomb Sq
(N) 1st Lt. Theodore J. Van Kirk	340th Bomb Sq
(CP)1st Lt. Joseph F. Di Salvo	340th Bomb Sq
(N) Capt. Dave W. Williams	341st Bomb Sq
(N) 1st Lt. Ralph L. Vincent	341st Bomb Sq
(RO) T/Sgt. Lloyd O. Burkholder	341st Bomb Sq
(BTG) T/Sgt. Chester H. Oliver	341st Bomb Sq
(E) T/Sgt. Felix A. Trice	341st Bomb Sq
(B) Capt. Irving P. Mac Taggart	Hq 97 BG
(E) T/Sgt. Paul W. Haygreen	414th Bomb Sq

May 30, 1943, Secret Orders from the Headquarters Northwest African Air Forces, by command of Lieutenant General Spaatz, ordered the "Return to U.S. of Combat Pilots and Combat Crews" and relieved 1st Lt. Theodore Van Kirk and others from their assignment and directed by military or commercial aircraft, surface vessel, belligerent or otherwise, and/or rail from their present stations in North Africa to the United States and to report upon arrival to the CO AAB nearest point of debarkation. A delay of more than seventy-two hours not to exceed fifteen days en route was authorized including a per diem of $6.00 for travel.

June 1, 1943, *10:00 p.m.*
Hiya darlin,
How is my little dimpled darling these dreary days?
Well, Janie I wrote to Teedy just a few minutes ago. I hope he gets it 'cause it is a lot of address to get on one letter and I'm not sure it is readable.

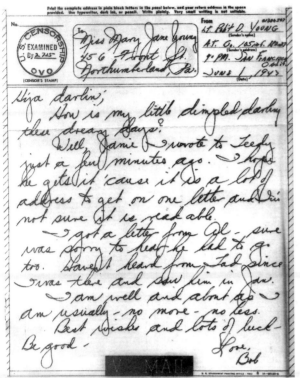

I got a letter from Al. Sure was sorry to hear he had to go too. Haven't heard from Tad since I was there and saw him in Jan.

I am well and about as I am usually – no more - no less.

Best wishes and lots of luck – Be good.
Love,
Bob[326]

Albert "Al" Young, Mary Jane's twin brother, was the fourth son in the family to serve during the war.

"Long Road Home"

Dutch - Joe DiSalvo and I were called in, told to get ourselves home, and that we were responsible for these twelve other guys too. All the Air Force guys knew each other from the Bolero movement. We had been together in England and in North Africa. So we went down to the airfield and it did not take us long to find a C-47 heading west to Oran.[327] We found an airplane and asked if we could go along. We hopped on board and as we were approaching Oran the pilot calls the tower and says, "I got fourteen guys who want to go to Casablanca. Anything going down to Casablanca?"

The tower guy checks and says, "Yeah I'll have one leaving in about fifteen minutes. Can you get here by then?"

The pilot said, "Sure, I will make it." He taxies one airplane and gets into another and we go to Casablanca. It is a pretty nice town by the way. We ask the transportation officer for help and he tells us that there is a ship down at the harbor we can take. We leave his office and I look at Joe DiSalvo.

"Joe, I am not sure about you, but I am not going to get on any damn ship and go across the Atlantic Ocean for Christ's sakes."

Joe says, "I am with you."

We put the other guys on the ship. We couldn't get out of there and had a great time in Casablanca for a month. Our orders read, "You are hereby authorized forty-five days delay en route."

While I was sitting around waiting to go home Tom Ferebee received a call to fly as a bombardier on an important mission with Bannon's regular crew. Jack Bannon lived with us in Sarasota, Florida. He got hit somewhere between his waist and knees. I am not going to say where. Tom bandaged him up. When they took Bannon out of the airplane he was all bloody. The medic looked at him and said, "Who in the hell did this bandaging job? I thought he was dead when I first looked at him."

Tom said, "Oh hell, Bannon is so full of morphine he doesn't feel anything anyhow."

After a month we decided it was time to get home and went out to the airbase. Fortunately another C-47 came in and landed. We knew the pilot and asked him what he was doing. He said, "I am flying the mail."

"Are you going down to Marrakesh?" we asked.

The operations officer had told us that if we could get to Marrakesh in time there was a C-54 down there leaving for England that night. The pilot did not have any mail for Marrakesh. He told us to wait a minute, walks behind the counter, gets an envelope, and a piece of paper. He scribbles something on the paper, turns around, writes 'free' on the envelope, and says, "Oh yeah, I must have missed a letter. Here is a letter to Marrakesh."

From Marrakesh we flew to Prestwick and soon we were in another C-54 back to LaGuardia field.

On June 5, 1943, at 5:55 a.m. Dutch and Joe DiSalvo on board an Air Transport Command TWA aircraft flight from Prestwick, Scotland, landed at LaGuardia Field, New York.[328]

In the states we were to report to the nearest air base. We called out to Patrick Air Force Base on Long Island and the adjutant sends a car for us. At the base he tells us, "I do not know what the hell to do with you. You are the first guys I have seen who came back." He reads our orders about the forty-five days delay en route and suggests we go home. We thought that sounded like a good deal and do not tell him we had already been in Casablanca for thirty days.

Joe went home to Batavia and we waited to hear from the guy at Patrick Air Force Base about where to report next.

The *Sunbury Daily Item* announced "Lieut. Van Kirk 'Veteran' of Air War, Home." The news described Van Kirk as one of Northumberland's colorful fighters. He told the reporter that he wouldn't have missed his military experience for a million dollars and that the RAF fighters were "a great outfit. I have been extremely lucky in not being grounded, but have added a few gray hairs." His many friends were glad to welcome him home.

Dutch ~ It is better to be lucky than good otherwise I would not be here. The forty-five days passed and we did not hear a thing. I thought that I couldn't spend the rest of the war at home and collect my pay so I called Joe. He got worried and called the airbase and was told that we would hear soon. Along came a telegram, "delay en route is hereby extended for thirty days."

June 5, 1943, General MacArthur's headquarters announce that Flying Fortresses and Liberators blasting Japanese aerodromes in New Guinea for the seventh successive day dropping eighteen tons of bombs today.[329]

"Coming Home"

Dutch ~ I was glad to be home. I was glad to be alive. My parents knew I was coming but not all the details. My mother had rented a place in a resort-like area outside of town. It had a spring fed swimming pool. The water had to be practically zero for heaven's sake, even though it was June.

The local Kiwanis and other groups asked me to come and speak. The high school wanted me to visit and come to an athletic event. School was still in session. Most of the people were glad to see me and that I made it back. Some did not, but that is another story.

Van Kirk spoke at the Kiwanis's weekly meeting at Bright's Café. He was swamped with questions and answered with the "frankness and truth that wartime censorship" permitted. He mentioned meeting some RAF pilots stationed at Malta and that one of his friends was the pilot who shot down the 1,000th German airplane from the Maltese skies.[330]

Dutch ~ Raw milk and ice cream were nonexistent in North Africa. I wanted milkshakes and some good German cooking. On Sunday nights one of my grandmothers cooked dinner for her eight kids and about thirty grandchildren. Several women in the kitchen would be peeling and frying more potatoes than you could feed an army. My uncle raised potatoes so we had lots of fried potatoes, country ham, and scrapple.

My mother repeatedly asked what I wanted for dinner every night. I weighed one hundred forty pounds and if I had followed my mother's advice I would have weighed four hundred. On the *Enola Gay* I weighed one hundred fifty pounds and was in good shape.

Chapter Seven — Endnotes

226 Van Kirk in an interview while at Selman Field for the article "He Flew Eisenhower and Clark" commented that Eisenhower had a sense of humor and told this story. While flying to Gibraltar the tail gunner, a sergeant, slapped the general on his back. "Got a match, bud?" Eisenhower turned around and with a smile gave him a light.

227 General Lemnitzer, Col. Thomas J. Davis, an Eisenhower staff member, and eight British generals were also on board with Doolittle. Tibbets, *The Tibbet's Story*, 111.

228 Brigadier Gen. Asa North Duncan, named the first commander of the Eighth Air Force activated January 28, 1942, followed shortly after by Spaatz, died in a B-17 crash in the Atlantic en route to Gibraltar. The *New York Times* "Air: To The Front" article on August 10, 1942, described the fifty year old Duncan as "tenacious and affable." General Duncan entered the service from Alabama and his name is listed as "Missing in Action or Buried at Sea" November 17, 1942, Tablets of the Missing at Cambridge American Cemetery, Cambridge, England. American Battle Monuments Commission, http://www.abmc.gov/home.php [accessed June 24, 2010].

229 Fredriksen, *The United States Air Force*, 93.

230 Convoys from England carried elements of the Twelfth Air Force and approached the Algerian and Moroccan coasts on November 7, 1942. Ibid, 93.

231 Tibbets flew Clark to Algiers the day after the initial landings according to his autobiography, *The Tibbets Story*, 114.

232 Biographies prepared for the *Enola Gay* mission crew note that Tibbets flew Clark and Canadian Gen. Andrew McNaughton to Algiers and "landed in an airfield, which they knew would be bombed. The Germans bombed the landing field before the plane stopped rolling on landing." Van Kirk personal papers.

233 Letter from John L. Pitts to Edward Neff's widow explaining that the Germans bombed the 97th out of Algiers and the group flew back to Oran. Gulley, *The Hour Has Come*, 53.

234 "Mission Summary" for November, 6 aircraft T.O., 6 Over T., 13.95 tons bombs, 3:55 time 'n flight. Tibbets group flew out of Maison Blanche.

235 The 97th BG's first mission in North Africa was to neutralize the enemy's air defenses at the Sidi Ahmed. Tibbets, *The Tibbets Story*, 116 - 117.

236 Germany controlled the strategic port of Bizerte from their airfield at Sidi Ahmed. Paul Tibbets had remarked that "we blew hell out of the place" and almost wiped out an entire squadron in addition to some of their airplanes. The wing spar of the *Gremlin* had been hit, missing the fuel lines and control cables, by 88 mm anti-aircraft guns. Van Kirk and Tibbets, *The Tibbets Story*, 117.

237 The Junkers JU-87 or Stuka (from Sturzkampfflugzeug meaning dive-bomber) was a German two-seat airplane.

238 Van Kirk's photo during a briefing is the top center photograph of page 32 – 33, "U.S. High-Altitude Bombers Hit Nazis," *Life* magazine, Vol. 13 No. 16, October 19, 1942.

239 "Northumberland Proud Of No. 1 War Mother And Six Soldier Sons, *Sunbury Daily Item* news clipping, no date.

240 "Mission Summary," 6 aircraft T.O., 6 Over Target 13.95 tons bombs, 5:45 time 'n flight.

241 The *Red Gremlin* crew was quoted saying the aerodrome was "badly smashed" according

to the *Sunbury Daily Item* article "North'd. Flier In Attack On Tunisia Base."

242 "Mission Summary," 11 aircraft T.O., 11 Over T., 26.40 tons bombs, 5:45 time 'n flight, National Archives.

243 Doolittle reported the destruction of nine enemy aircraft when he flew as an observer on this mission per the 97th BG history.

244 The field headquarters for the French at Tafaraoui was southeast of Oran.

245 Facilities at Oak Ridge, TN, and Hanford, WA, were constructed to produce the fissionable material needed for the bombs. Edward T. Sullivan, *The Ultimate Weapon* The Race to Develop the Atomic Bomb, (New York: Holiday House, 2007), 152.

246 Newspaper media coverage of the early reports from the State Department release of the Holocaust did not make the front page of even the *New York Times*. The *Post* report appeared on page fifteen adjacent to train schedules. "Jews to Observe Day of Mourning," *New York Evening Post*, November 30, 1942, and "Christians Should Join Jews In Special Day Of Prayer," *Brooklyn Eagle*, December 1, 1942.

247 "Mission Summary," North African Theatre Operations, 10 aircraft T.O., 10 Over T., 30:00 tons bombs, 7:45 time 'n flight.

248 Joseph C. Grew, "Report from Tokyo An Ambassador Warns of Japan's Strength," *Life*, December 7, 1942. Grew pointed out that the Germans and Japanese were very different and Americans generally were ill informed about the enemy in the Pacific.

249 T. J. Van Kirk censored the letter passed by US Army Examiner 11091.

250 "Russian War," *Niagara Falls Gazette*, January 8, 1943.

251 "Mission Summary," North African Theatre Operations, 18 aircraft T.O., 17 Over T., 2 enemy aircraft destroyed, 38.85 tons bombs, 4:15 time 'n flight.

252 "Mission Summary," 18 aircraft T.O., 10/10 overcast at target, 4:00 time 'n flight.

253 Postal Telegraph-Cable Company of Shenandoah, PA, received the telegram on January 18, 1943.

254 "Mission Summary," 18 aircraft T.O., 18 Over T., 1 aircraft lost, 5 enemy aircraft destroyed, 38.00 tons bombs, 4:10 time 'n flight. Freeman's *B-17* story puts the *Gremlin* at the Biskra base on Christmas Day 1942.

255 "Bizerte, Sfax, Tunis Battered; Axis Plane Losses Reach 277," (AP) Allied Headquarters North Africa, *The Philadelphia Inquirer*, December 28, 1942.

256 German fighter strength concentrated in Western Europe, about one-third in Russia, and twenty-five percent in the Mediterranean region. General Arnold believed that the direct strategic bombing of Germany by the United States and the RAF key to German's defeat. Henry H. "Hap" Arnold, General of the Army, USAAF, "Air Offensive-Europe," *Bombs Away!* True Stories of Strategic Airpower from World War I to the Present, (New York: NY, Doubleday & Company, Inc., 1971), 152. Arnold learned to fly at the Wright School, Dayton, OH. Norman Carlisle, ed., *The Air Forces Reader*, (New York: NY, The Bobbs-Merrill Company, 1944), 44.

257 "Mission Summary," 22 aircraft T.O., 17 Over T., 30.00 tons bombs, 4:00 time 'n flight.

258 "Mission Summary," 18 aircraft T.O., 14 Over T., 39.00 tons bombs, 3:10 time 'n flight.

259 "Mission Summary," 18 aircraft T.O., 15 Over T., 2 enemy aircraft destroyed, 27.50 tons bombs, 4:30 time 'n flight.

260 Douglas VC-54C *Sacred Cow*, National Museum of the US Air Force, —

http://www.nationalmuseum.af.mil/index.asp [accessed July 1, 2010].

261 The "Special Missions" were not listed in the "Report of Operations," "Mission Summary," or "Weekly Operations Summary." Some of the "missions" with Eisenhower and Clark were identified by location and date on a personnel type index card. "Van Kirk, Theodore J. 0-659024 1st Lt. Navigator" was typed across the top. The "Operational Missions" were identified numerically only i.e. 2, 3, 5, 9, etc. Van Kirk said he had a total of fifty-eight missions prior to returning to the United States.

262 Baron Arthur William Tedder, Marshal of the RAF and a senior commander, flew as a pilot and squadron commander in the Royal Flying Corps during World War I. Tedder was appointed RAF Middle East Commander in 1941 and served as Deputy Supreme Commander under Eisenhower for Operation Overlord. Arthur W. Tedder, *Air Power in War*, (Tuscaloosa, AL: The University of Alabama Press, 2010), 2, 3, and 7.

263 Restricted Awards of Oak-Leaf Cluster by command of Major General Doolittle, Brig. Gen. Hoyt S. Vandenberg, signed by Col. P.M. Whitney, (Section IV, No. 2), January 15, 1943, 23. Van Kirk personal papers.

264 The "Mission Summary," North African Theatre Operations Mission No. 47, in the National Archives had a notation of the mission coverage in *Life* magazine on March 1, 1943.

265 Several UP news clippings in the Van Kirk scrapbook were from Allied headquarters in North Africa about Americans being wined and died by Arab chieftains and dinners of fresh killed antelope, oranges, dates, cakes, and other local delicacies. "Arabs Dine Yank 3 Days," January 3, 1943.

266 Source for the targets: "Mission Summary" World War II Combat Operations Report 1941-46, 97th Bomb Group, Record Group 18, National Archives and *The Hour Has Come*. The *U.S. Army Air Forces in World War II Combat Chronology 1941 – 1945* by Kit C. Carter and Robert Mueller (Washington, DC: Center for Air Force History, 1991) also used to reconcile discrepancy in dates and targets of the missions from the other two sources. Van Kirk identified his operational missions by date and commented that the error could have occurred because their group had a male secretary.

267 "Mission Summary" for January, 14 aircraft T.O., 11 Over T., 1 enemy aircraft destroyed, 2 enemy aircraft damaged, 33.00 tons bombs, 3:00 time 'n flight.

268 "Dory Van Kirk Dies, Ending 50-Year Union," *Sunbury Daily Item*, 1943.

269 "Mission Summary" for Elmas target, 18 aircraft T.O., 14 Over T., 42.00 tons bombs, 4:40 time 'n flight.

270 Stanley Sandler ed., *Ground Warfare: An International Encyclopedia*, (Santa Barbara, CA: ABC-CLIO, Inc., 2002), Vol. 1, 344. References in other publications on the Guadalcanal battle vary on estimates for Japanese troops from 25,000 to as many as 37,000, which included non-combat deaths.

271 Included in the American naval losses were fifteen destroyers. The Imperial Navy lost two battleships and twelve destroyers (included in the nineteen losses). Theodore Roscoe, *United States Destroyer Operations in World War II*, (United States Naval Institute, 1953), 214.

272 Colonel Tibbets worked on the development of the B-29 and establishing a training program for pilots under Frank Armstrong. Tibbets was one of the first pilots to test the YB-29 Superfortress. The "X" models were built for experimental purposes and "Y" for service testing.

273 The photograph of the *Red Gremlin* on page 32 of *The Hour Has Come* was cropped. The photocopy shows Serial No. 41-34444 on the fuselage (not a number in the sequence of Boeing produced B-17s). Boeing historian confirmed No. 41-24444. In the front row holding an old rifle were John Tittsworth, Zackie Gowan, Arthur Napolitano, Joe Cifka, Howard Irvine. Standing in the rear left to right: John Hall, William Black, Theodore "Dutch" Van Kirk, Charles "Dick" Wiley, William Ryan, and Herman Haag.

274 The mission aborted due to overcast and the 97th BG's B-17s returned with their bombs. Gulley et. al., *The Hour Has Come*, 83.

275 The fighters also hit buildings near Mezzouna and trucks in another area. Carter et. al, *Combat Chronology*, February 9, 1943.

276 Radio address about the Casablanca Conference, Public Papers of F. D. Roosevelt, Vol. 21, 71.

277 Col. Stanley J. Donovan assumed command of the 97th Bombardment Group on January 5, 1943. "Mission Summary" for Palermo docks, 21 aircraft T.O., 17 Over T., 51.00 tons bombs, 5:40 time 'n flight.

278 The supplies arriving from the Middle East into Tripoli enabled Gen. Sir Bernard Montgomery to advance against the fleeing forces of Rommel in Tunisia. Phil Ault, Allied Headquarters North Africa, "Allies Move 780 Ships to North Africa," February 1943.

279 Martin Blumenson, *Kasserine Pass*, (Boston, MA: Houghton Mifflin Company, 1966), 243-245.

280 According to Blumenson on February 22, 1943, anti-aircraft gunners shot down five P-38s, but American ground troops were encouraged by the air support. Blumenson, *Kasserine Pass*, 282.

281 About two thousand changes to the B-29's Wright powered engines had been made prior to this tragedy. Gurney, *B-29 Story* The Plane That Won The War, 12.

282 The *Combat Chronology* lists the target for the date as the El Aouina airfield for the North African Air Force B-17s, but does not specify the 97th BG as part of the group.

283 "Lieutenant Van Kirk Wins U.S. Air Medal in Africa," *Sunbury Daily Item*, after February 1943.

284 "Mission Summary" for convoy, 41 T.O., 38 Target, 4 enemy aircraft destroyed, 3 enemy aircraft probable, 1 enemy aircraft damaged, 55.00 tons bombs, 3:29 time 'n flight.

285 "Mission Summary" for March, 20 T.O., 20 Target, 0 enemy aircraft destroyed or damaged, 54.00 tons bombs, 4:13 time 'n flight.

286 "Mission Summary" for March, 18 T.O., 15 Target, 21.06 tons bombs, 3:15 time 'n flight.

287 "Mission Summary" for March, 28 T.O., 26 Target, 23.08 tons bombs, 3:11 time 'n flight.

288 "Mission Summary" for March, 26 T.O., 22 Target, 1 enemy aircraft probable, 1 enemy aircraft damaged, 65.08 tons bombs, 4:30 time 'n flight.

289 "Mission Summary" for March, 26 T.O., 22 Target, 0 enemy aircraft destroyed, 66.00 tons bombs, 4:00 time 'n flight.

290 The Eighth Army took the Mareth positions of Matama, Toujane Mareth, and El Hamma and closed in further north to cut off the Axis retreat. "Mareth Line Falls, Trap

Closing on Axis," *Stars And Stripes*, Vol. 3 No. 126, March 30, 1943.

291 "Mission Summary," 20 T.O., 18 Target, 4 enemy aircraft destroyed, 120# bombs 25.09 tons, 4:06 time 'n flight.

292 Captain C. David Hoffmann's request to Commanding Officer 97th Bombardment Group for promotion of Van Kirk, 1 April 1943. Van Kirk personal papers.

293 "Mission Summary" for April, 45 T.O., 38 Target, 500# bombs 64 tons, time 'n flight 7:08.

294 "Mission Summary" for April, 23 T.O., 23 Target, 1 Fw190 enemy aircraft destroyed, 1 enemy aircraft probable, 120# bombs, 33.1 tons, 3:04 time n' flight. *The Hour Has Come* lists the two mission numbers of April 5, 1943, in reverse order from the military record. April 4, 1943, in the "Mission Summary" was listed after the two missions on the 5th of the month and numbered 84 instead of 82.

295 "Mission Summary," 22 T.O., 18 Target, 1/Rag destroyed, 500# bombs, 59.00 tons, 5:03 time 'n flight.

296 V-mail letter addressee: Miss Mary Jane Young, 456 Front St., Northumberland, PA.

297 "Mission Summary," 37 T.O., 37 Target 1000# bombs 108 tons, 6:00 time 'n flight.

298 Capt. Robert E. Kimmel Air Corps Group Operations Officer for the Group Commander, "Weekly Operations Summary" for week ending Saturday 17 April 1943, 21 T.O., 18 Over T., 18 Sorties, 0 Lost, 500# bombs, 59.0 tons, 5:15 mission time, 0 enemy aircraft destroyed or damaged.

299 "Weekly Operations Summary," 28 T.O., 27 Over T., 27 Sorties, 0 Lost, 500# bombs, 81.0 tons, 3:15 mission time, 0 enemy aircraft destroyed or damaged.

300 "Weekly Operations Summary," 25 T.O., 20 Over T., 20 Sorties, 0 Lost, Frag bombs, 27.4 tons, 3:25 mission time, 9 enemy aircraft destroyed, 4 enemy aircraft probable, 3 enemy aircraft damaged.

301 "Admiral Yamamoto Killed, Japs Report," *The Herald Statesman*, (Yonkers, NY), May 21, 1943. Hirohito ordered a lavish state funeral and Yamamoto's ashes were buried at a cemetery near Tokyo.

302 Edwin Palmer Hoyt, *Yamamoto The Man Who Planned Pearl Harbor* (NY: McGraw Hill, 1990), 55.

303 The former boys' school closed in February 1943. John D. Wirth, Linda Harvey Aldrich, and Linda Kathleen Aldrich, *Los Alamos: the Ranch School years, 1917 – 1943*, (New Mexico: University of New Mexico Press, 2003), 123.

304 Capt. Robert E. Kimmel Air Corps Group Operations Officer for the Group Commander, "Weekly Operations Summary" 97th Bomb Group for week ending Saturday 24 April 1943, 34 T.O., 29 Over T., 29 Sorties, 0 lost, 500# bombs, 59.0 tons, 5:50 mission time, 0 enemy aircraft destroyed or damaged.

305 Jean Van Kirk and Mick McAllister were married May 20, 1950, at St. John's Lutheran Church in Northumberland. "I was living with daddy and had not been anxious to get married." Our daughters asked, "How did it come about that you married dad?" Jean responded, "Northumberland was a very small town and the pickings were slim." Mick teasingly added, "Jean said there weren't many men left."

306 Brigadier General J. H. Atkinson circularized this commendation to the Commanding Officers of all squadrons 97th Bomb GP (H) and added: "personally I value this commendation above all others as it is from the Commander of all our Air Forces."

307 "Weekly Operations Summary" for 97th Bomb Group for week ending 24 April 1943,

21 T.O., 18 Over T., 18 Sorties, 0 lost, 500# bombs, 54.0 tons, 3:10 mission time, 0 enemy aircraft destroyed or damaged.

308 "Weekly Operations Summary," 25 T.O., 23 Over T., 23 Sorties, 0 Lost, Frag bombs 33.0 tons, 3:10 mission time, 0 enemy aircraft destroyed or damaged.

309 Envelope addressed to Miss Mary Jane Young, 456 Front St., Northumberland, PA.

310 Capt. Robert E. Kimmel, Air Corps Group Operations Officer, "Weekly Operations Summary" for 97th Bomb Group for week ending 1 May 1943, 27 T.O., 23 Over T., 23 Sorties, 1 Lost, 300# bombs 58.0 tons, 7:20 mission time, 0 enemy aircraft destroyed or damaged.

311 "Weekly Operations Summary" 12 T.O., 12 Over T., 12 Sorties, 0 Lost, 0 bombs, 5:15 mission time.

312 "Weekly Operations Summary" 28 T.O., 28 Over T., 28 Sorties, 0 Lost, 0 bombs, 3:50 mission time.

313 According to the "Weekly Operations Summary" no bombs were dropped on this mission, 28 T.O., 28 Over T., 28 Sorties, 3:50 mission time.

314 About 135,000 leaflets were fired over the enemy lines between April 22 and April 26. "Guns Fire Leaflets at Nazis in Tunisia," *Sunbury Daily Item*, April 29, 2011.

315 Maj. Robert E. Kimmel, Air Corps Operations Officer, "Weekly Operations Summary" for 97th Bomb Group for week ending 8 May 1943, 28 T.O., 26 Over T., 26 Sorties, 500# bombs 74.3 tons, 3:45 mission time, no enemy aircraft destroyed or damaged.

316 Promotion letter Commanding General NAAF to 2nd Lt. Theodore J. Van Kirk, May 8, 1943.

317 Maj. Robert E. Kimmel, Air Corps Operations Officer, "Weekly Operations Summary" 40 T.O., 36 Over T., 36 Sorties, 1 Lost, 500# bombs, 55.0 tons, 4:50 mission time, 19 enemy aircraft destroyed, 4 probable, 3 enemy aircraft damaged.

318 "Weekly Operations Summary" 30 T.O., 21 Over T., 21 sorties, 0 Lost, 1000# 9.0 tons and Frag 26.5 tons, 4:35 mission time, 0 enemy aircraft destroyed or damaged.

319 The American G.I., Jewish Brigade, Scot Highlander, London Division, Indian Division, Free French, Free Polish Brigade, and the "Desert Rats" of the Australian Army served in North Africa. Thomas F. Gulley, et. al., "Combined Operations – Africa Is Won," *The Hour Has Come* (Venit Hora) The 97th Bomb Group in World War II. (Dallas, TX: Taylor Publishing Co., 1993).

320 The first groups of POWs to arrive in America were held in the south particularly Texas, Louisiana, and Florida. The prisoners provided needed manpower for agri-business and other industries. Dietz, *POWs Interned At Fort Niagara* A Reference Work, (Youngstown, NY: Beau Designs, 2009), 13.

321 The 97th BG missions continued throughout the war in Europe to bomb Germany, Czechoslovakia, Yugoslavia, Hungary, and Austria.

322 The Soviets confiscated uranium from Germany, but by May 1945 the total was only seven tons of uranium oxide including the purchase from the Americans. Pavel V. Oleynikov, "German Scientists in the Soviet Atomic Project," *The Non Proliferation Review*, Summer 2000.

323 Letter of recommendation of Colonel Stanley J. Donovan by Major Howell Hollis, Air Corps, Headquarters Ninety-Seven Bombardment Group, (H) Army Air Force, Office of the Group Commander, to whom it may concern, May 29, 1943.

324 Major C. David Hoffmann, letter to Whom It May Concern, Van Kirk personal papers,

May 29, 1943. Special missions transporting Generals Eisenhower and Clark could account for discrepancy in the Hoffmann letter and total missions.

325 Headquarters Ninety-Seventh Bombardment Group (H), Special Orders No. 108 signed by Captain Alexander K. McGrew, Adjutant, 29 May 1943. Van Kirk personal papers.

326 V-mail from Lt. Robert D. Young, A.T. Co. 105 Inf. A.P.O. 27, 10 p.m., San Francisco, CA, to his sister Miss Mary Jane Young.

327 Oran (Ouahran) is located in western Algeria.

328 United States Department of Justice Immigration and Naturalization Service Air Transport Command Passenger List, Record of Customs Service, Record Group 36, National Archives, Washington, DC.

329 "War Grows More Grave Tojo Admits," *Niagara Falls Gazette*, June 5, 1943.

330 "Kiwanis Given Real Thrill By Lieut. Van Kirk," *Sunbury Daily Item*, 1943.

Chapter Eight

Selman Field *AAF Navigation School*

"Women Air Force Service Pilots"

Dutch ~ After another thirty days at home, Joe and I drove to the Training Command in Houston, Texas, in his old car and shared the gas expense. We reported for our assignments. I was assigned to a training base in Monroe, Louisiana. But before beginning my assignment I was told that I was out of date, rusty, and would need a navigation refresher school. I said, "Well, it sounds like fun. Where is it located?"

I got on the train for Mather Field in Sacramento, California, for thirty days of additional training. We were all veterans and went to school carrying our own beer. We had returned from combat and really did not care about more training. We paid no attention to the instructors because they had not been overseas. At the end of the course, I headed for the base in Monroe getting tired of going across the country except when I got to Los Angeles and had one of the biggest breaks in my life. Only two men were on the train, a Mormon missionary and me. At the train station in Los Angeles I was assigned to a berth in a Pullman car and in every other berth was a young lady going to Sweetwater, Texas, for pilot training. I insulted one right away.

My berth, the lower one, was loaded with what looked like very expensive luggage. I looked around and said, "What stupid bla bla bla would travel with this much luggage during a war?"

Some lady pipes up, "That is my granddaughter's luggage."

I replied, "Well ma'am, who would your granddaughter be?"

"She is a pilot and flew many hours up and down the Pacific Ocean on submarine patrol."

I asked what was she doing with the luggage. Well, she was going to Sweetwater, Texas, to join the Women Air Force Service Pilots (WASP). The rattlesnake roundup is held in Sweetwater every year. I hoped that I would have a place to sleep that night. Later on the pilot joined the conversation and said, "I understand you are complaining about my luggage."

"It is better than complaining about you," I responded.

I was not very diplomatic in those days either. It was a good trip as far as Sweetwater.

Numerous male crews were attracted to the female training site at Avenger Field in Sweetwater and requested emergency landings. Jackie Cochran ordered no more forced landings and the field was dubbed "Cochran's Convent." Cochran, an accomplished pilot, had proposed using women pilots in 1939.[331]

At Selman Field aviation cadets received pre-flight and advanced navigation training. Selman, a complete navigation training station, was activated in May 1942 under commander Col. Norris B. Harbold. During the then nine weeks of pre-flight training, the cadets received instruction in Morse Code, meteorology, mathematics and physics, naval forces, organization of the Army Air Forces, aircraft identification, and basic military science. Intensive calisthenics and drilling accompanied academics.[332]

"Outstanding B-17s"

June 30, 1943, a public relations release, approved by the RAF Field Press Censor, identified the *Red Gremlin* as one of the outstanding and significant B-17s particularly for the secret mission with Gen. Mark Clark and the first Fortress to land in Africa in November 1942. By the end of June 1943 the *Red Gremlin* had participated in seventy missions over enemy territory: fifteen in England, and fifty-five in Africa and credited with destroying eight enemy aircraft.[333] The release also recognized *Superman*, the oldest Fortress in North Africa, which had seventeen engine changes and collected over three hundred flak and bullet holes.[334]

July 2, 1943, by command of Major General Young, 1st Lieutenant Van Kirk was relieved from Hq AAFFTC, Fort Worth, TX, and assigned to AAFSETC with station at AAF Navigation School, Monroe, LA.[335]

At the end of June, Washington announced that 15,132 men were killed in action during the first 18 months of the war. The July 4th issue of *Life* magazine listed servicemen (including Frank Cooper from Northumberland, Pennsylvania) who gave their lives during the first eighteen months of the war, which did not include non-combatant accidents, diseases, or MIAs. (The Oran Cemetery Algiers photograph from the National Archives was taken at a later unidentified date.)

"USS *Boise* Enters the Mediterranean"

July 9, 1943, Operation Husky, the code name for the Allied invasion of Sicily began a large scale amphibious and airborne operation. More than 2,500 vessels transporting troops and escorts gathered near the Oran Harbor.[336]

James Starnes ~ The USS *Boise* painted with camouflaged colors had headed for the European Theatre in late spring. She sailed through Gibraltar to Oran and Algiers to "transport troops and join the fleet to invade Sicily for the first major invasion in Europe. We had unfortunate incidents shooting our own planes; there was a lot of friendly fire. The invasion of Sicily went quick. At Salerno the German buzz bombs created a great screeching sound and a lot of fear."[337]

The USS *Brooklyn, Philadelphia,* and *Savannah* also provided gunfire support to the landing troops.

July 20, 1943, at a press conference the Vice Adm. Frederick Horne stated the Navy planned to fight Japan until at least 1949. Secretary of the Navy Frank Knox disagreed with the current opinion over "winning the war in a hurry . . . We will have tremendous distances to cover in the Pacific, and we have to build bases from the ground up as we advance."[338]

"Progress of the War"

Roosevelt ~ *July 28, 1943*, " . . . our terms to Italy are still the same as our terms to Germany and Japan –'unconditional surrender.' . . .

In every country conquered by the Nazis and the Fascists, or the Japanese militarists, the people have been reduced to the status of slaves or chattels . . .

It is interesting for us to realize that every flying fortress that bombed harbor installations at, for example, Naples, bombed it from its base in North Africa, required 1,110 gallons of gasoline for each single mission, and that this is the equal of about 375 'A' ration tickets — enough gas to drive your car five times across this continent. You will better understand your part in the war — and what gasoline rationing means — if you multiply this by the gasoline needs of thousands of planes and hundreds of thousands of jeeps, and trucks and tanks that are now serving overseas . . .

We are pushing forward to occupation of positions which in time will enable us to attack the Japanese Islands themselves from the North, from the South, from the East, and from the West . . .

The plans we made for the knocking out of Mussolini and his gang have largely succeeded. But we still have to knock out Hitler and his gang, and Tojo and his gang. No one of us pretends that this will be an easy matter.

We still have to defeat Hitler and Tojo on their own home grounds. But this will require a far greater concentration of our national energy and our ingenuity and our skill . . .

We shall not settle for less than total victory."[339]

September 3, 1943, the Allies landed in Italy.

Newlyweds Captain and Mrs. Van Kirk (Courtesy Thomas L. Van Kirk)

"Van Kirk Wedding Bells"

Dutch ~ I arranged for Mary Jane to come down from Northumberland and to finally get married. One of her "brothers" Bill Seasholtz and his wife drove my car down, a second hand red convertible Chevy with black leather seats. It was a horrible car to have in Louisiana in the summer time and that is all I can say. If a girl sat down on the black leather seats she did not stay long.

Mary Jane was not twenty-one yet and I had a horrible time in Monroe, Louisiana, trying to get a wedding license. Bill offered to sign for her. These southern sticklers with their rules and regulations did not know if we could do that or not. Finally, about 5:30 one evening I got the marriage license and we drove over to Shreveport.[340] When we got there the preacher would not marry us until after he interviewed us. He wanted to know about where I was born and my background history. In retrospect it really was a good thing. He was being a fatherly figure and doing what a father would do to make sure this was not a quickie wartime marriage. It was a very nice wedding, just the four of us. We celebrated our honeymoon back at the airbase. Shreveport and Monroe are about roughly sixty to seventy miles apart on Interstate 20. We drove back

LT. VANKIRK, MISS YOUNG WED IN SOUTH

Word was received yesterday by Mrs. Emma Seasholtz, 456 Front street, from Miss Mary Jane Young, who made her home with Mrs. Seasholtz, that she and Lt. Theodore VanKirk, son of Mr. and Mrs. Fred VanKirk, 672 Queen street, were married Thursday evening, September 16, in the parsonage of the First Baptist Church at Shreveport, La., with the pastor, Rev. R. Dodd, performing the ceremony. They were attended by Mr. and Mrs. William Seasholtz, of New York City, who took Miss Young to Munro, La., where Lt. VanKirk is stationed, as an Army Air Force instructor. Members of the pastor's family also witnessed the ceremony.

The bride wore a powder blue silk jersey dress, trimmed with white lace, and navy blue accessories. The groom was attired in the customary military uniform of

Sunbury Daily Item
(article reprinted with the permission of *The Daily Item*, Sunbury, Pennsylvania)

to Monroe and found a place to live. I thought the war was over for me and stayed in Louisiana training navigators for about eight months.

September 16, 1943, Lieutenant Van Kirk and Miss Mary Jane Young were married Thursday evening in the parsonage of the First Baptist Church of Shreveport, Louisiana. Pastor Rev. R. Dodd performed the ceremony. Van Kirk was in uniform. His "bride wore a powder blue silk jersey dress, trimmed with white lace, and navy blue accessories."[341] A telegram to the Van Kirk's Queen Street home announced the marriage of Theodore Jerome Van Kirk to Mary Jane Young in Shreveport, Louisiana.[342]

Jean ~ "Hazel and Bill, her stepbrother, the Seasholtzs, took Mary Jane down to Shreveport. We were a little surprised. I don't think the family was expecting it really. They weren't unhappy. I think daddy was more perturbed than mommy because she was very fond of Mary Jane. The only thing was their youth. Mary Jane was nineteen and he was twenty-two. I think our parents wished they had waited a little bit. I don't think Mrs. Seasholtz was real happy either. Again, 'oh, why didn't they wait?' I think they all wanted them to come home and have a wedding. I am sure that is what they wanted."

September 1943, In *The Hour Has Come* the 97th Bomb Group claimed the *Berlin Sleeper II* to be the first heavy bomber to fly one hundred missions. The B-17F Fortress No. 41-24370 returned to the states to be part of the war bond tours.

November 1, 1943, the Fifteenth Air Force was activated and headquartered in Tunis, Tunisia. The 2nd, 97th, 99th, and 301st Bomb Groups were now assigned to the Fifteenth Air Force under the command of Maj. Gen. James Doolittle.[343]

November 15, 1943, the Reichsführer of the SS Heinrich Luitpold Himmler ordered all gypsies to concentration camps.

November 19, 1943, an announcement was made from the War Department of the temporary promotion to captain of Theodore Jerome Van Kirk by order of the Secretary of War: Official: Maj. Gen. J. A. Ulio, the Adjutant General, and Chief of Staff G. C. Marshall.[344]

November 20, 1943, the Marines engaged in one of the bloodiest landings on the beaches of Tarawa.

December 1, 1943, the Army Air Forces issued a directive to the Air Force Materiel Command for the modification of a B-29 under the *Silver Plated Project.*[345]

December 31, 1943, the highest conscription during the war of 3,323,970 men occurred during this year.

"From the Newlyweds"

January 27, 1944

Capt. T. J. Van Kirk 0-659024

Box 777, VN.T.G.

Selman Field, Monroe, LA.

Dear Mother, Dad and Jean,

I'm sorry I didn't write last week but I took a little trip and didn't get time to do it.

I had to go out to San Francisco on a business trip last Thurs. and was supposed to get back on Monday but I didn't get back until today.

I had a pretty good time. On the way out we stopped at El Paso, Tex. and spent the night at San Diego, Cal. The next day we went on to S. Fran(cisco) and stayed there two days. On the way home we had a little trouble with the weather so we stopped for a night at Fresno, Calif., another at Los Angeles, and then we had to spend two nights in Tucson, Arizona. It seemed like a tour.

Bob English was out there with me so Mary Jane and his wife, Bobby, stayed together while we were gone. They said they had a good time.

While I was in Los Angeles I was only 60 miles from Frances and I was going to go to see her but I didn't have her address along with me. I didn't feel very good that night either because I had caught a cold from the rain in "sunny" California.

Mary Jane fixed the house up some more while I was gone. She has so many pictures of swans and the other things in the bathroom that I feel like a bullfrog every time I take a bath. We have our book shelves and things up now and the place looks a lot better.

I was going to try to get home this month but after going to Calif. I didn't have time left to do anything. I'll try to make it next month.

Well it's getting pretty late and I'm tired so I think I'll go to bed. I flew almost as long today as I flew in the last couple months. I'm going to put a few pictures in here that you can give to Jimmy.

Love　　　　Love
Theodore and Mary Jane
Those numbers after my name is my serial number. It is supposed to be 0-659024 but I get it mixed up myself. I have to put them on when ever I send a free letter.

We haven't had our pictures taken yet but I'll do it as soon as I get time.

I hope you keep on gaining weight but stop when you hit the 200 mark. Mary Jane is just starting to pass that.

That is all.

Theo.[346]

January 31, 1944

Dear Janie,

I will have to break this long silence or go crazy. I haven't heard from either one of you for so long I don't know what to think. I have not been down town or seen anyone for so long. I do hope you still live in La. I seen Laura a few weeks back she said she had heard from you. She and Madelyn were going down to see you she said but could not until after school. I told her I hoped you would be here by then.

I read in the paper about those two planes at Selman Field I read it the next day but still I could not help but worry about it. I was sick over the thing for two days.

I told you in one letter about being so good. I'll take that all back I will never brag about it again that's what I get for it. I am having trouble with my one eye now so I hope you can read this, enough of that.

You used to think you had trouble with your hair Jean is having still more she had it set Friday she was going to have her pictures taken on Sat. when she got up Sat. morning it was all out so she still does not have a picture. Now she says she is going to take the five dollars you & Ted gave her for Xmas and get a permanent and then have them taken.

Does Ted have all his carpenter work all done yet? How did it turn out? Have you heard from Frances? Mother was telling me she quit work so she should have a lot of time to write now. Bill was moved again so I guess Frances will be moving again.

Oh I have something else to tell you Franklin Walker is going to the Navy.

I wanted to ask you where are your brothers stationed at now. I think I have only been down town once since Xmas so I don't know much. I have been wanting to go down to see your mother. I think until you answer all my questions you will have a letter so hoping to hear from you.

I close with lots of love.
Mother Van Kirk[347]

"Tired of Flying"

February 7, 1944
Dear Mother, Dad and Jean,

I'll finally write and let you know that I got back down here O.K. After we took off I watched you drive away and Lee's car was so shiny I could see it for a long time.

Mary Jane was out at the field waiting for me when I got back. She had it timed almost perfect.

I had a lot of work to do when I got back. It kept me pretty busy all last week and it looks like it will keep me busy for a few more of them. I took over the work of another dept. Things were all messed up and I'm having a devil of a time getting them straightened out.

There isn't much to tell you. I told you most of it while I was home.

Mary Jane says she will write tomorrow and answer all of your questions. Tell Lee thanks for taking me down. I could come home again this week but I'm tired of flying so I think I'll stay here for a while.

Love
Theodore[348]

"Mother Died"

Dutch ~ On my way to sign out, while going on a leave, the commander of the navigation school Colonel Egan asked me, "Captain, can you jump over that desk?"

"Well sir, I think I probably could make it." He wanted to see me do it so I bowled over the desk.

"When you come back from your leave, I want to make sure you can do that too," said the Colonel.

Kind of a Courtney guy, wasn't he?

A number of things happened during that year. My mother died during that year and I went home to Northumberland. I remember the day vividly. I was playing cards with Mary Jane and our neighbors and knew it was not good. We took a flight from Selman Field and flew home as soon as we could. It was hard for all of us. Dad wanted to move right away and found a desirable apartment on Water Street. Afterwards, Mary Jane wrote a lot to my dad and Jean.

I went home frequently and developed an auto trade with a cousin. I drove the cars from Northumberland and sold them in Monroe. One was a red Chevy convertible with hot sticky seats that I couldn't part with.

February 10, 1944, Grace Snyder Van Kirk passed away.

Jean ~ "High school was shaded because of mother's illness. I was missing so much school. Mother had been at grandmother Van Kirk's and had a stroke when she was out there. And then they took her to the Sunbury hospital. She died of kidney disease at only forty-two years old. She never heard of Ted's mission."

Jean Van Kirk was a senior in high school when her mother passed away. A few weeks later Fred and Jean Van Kirk moved to 250 Water Street in Northumberland.[349] While he was serving overseas Mick received a telegram from Jean about her mother's death and sent a telegram back to her.

Mick ~ "Grace was a marvelous lady. We loved her. But she had lived a long life, the perspective of youth."[350]

Jean ~ "Dad was concerned that I couldn't manage the furnace and all that sort of thing. He did work long hours. We moved into the Feaster's apartment. They were very, very kind to me. People were very kind and went out of their way to do things for us. I was just eighteen." The war stimulated the economy and helped the country come out of the depression, but the Van Kirk's had no medical insurance. "Mother's hospital bills were enormous. My father took two years after mother died to pay off her hospital bills. When he took up the last payment to the Geisinger Center (Sunbury, Pennsylvania), they said very few people did that. Our family did not take a hand out. If my dad did not have the cash we did not do it."

"Alvino Rey and the King Sisters"

Mick ~ "I was in Chicago for only ten days as a medic. We checked out the new recruits. The hospital had ten beds, one doctor, and six medics." After working in the scarlet fever ward the Navy picked up on Mick McAllister's musical background. He had learned to play the saxophone and clarinet and joined Ivan Faux, Mick's first Big Band at the age of fifteen.[351] Now the Navy sent him to Wright Junior College in Chicago. The college had been converted by the military to a radio technician training center. "We had a hundred radio techs. Alvino Rey, a radio tech striker, called out asking for any musicians." Rey joined the Navy and was trying to put together an armed forces orchestra.[352]

Alvino Rey and the King Sisters was one of the best of the Big Band era's names. The Armed Forces Radio often closed at night with *Nighty-Night* sung by Yvonne King accompanied by Rey's orchestra.[353] Mick met Rey at Wright Junior College and joined the Armed Forces Orchestra. "My medical training got bypassed a little with all the hottest places in Chicago the Aragon ballroom, the Sheridan, Edgewater Beach, and the Sherman."

"At the ballroom we were told, 'you will play an hour and take fifteen minutes off. We do not have booze at the Aragon; so in order to keep the people we are going to have a band rotating off stage so that the people keep dancing.' The alternate bands included Lawrence Welk, Eddy Howard, and Tony Pastor. Most of the Big Bands played there. I was with Alvino and the military band for a year and still carried my medical rank. The Navy never changed a damn thing and promoted me from 3rd Class Pharmacist Mate to 2nd Class Pharmacist Mate. I played music all the time but did some medical in the daytime when the band was not together."

February 13, 1944, Grace Snyder Van Kirk was buried in Northumberland's Riverview Cemetery.

February 19, 1944, "Capt Van Kirk, Theodore J 0659024 AC, Hq & Hq Sqdn – 41st Nav Tng Gp, is rld fr dy as Aerial Instr, Nav (Primary Dy); is then designated Tng O (2520-5) (Tactical Curriculum O (Primary Dy)" by order of Colonel Egan.[354]

"Captain Rommel"

James Starnes ~ *Sometime in April 1944* the *Boise* was in the waters around "Ulithi Atoll north of Australia when I received an order to return to San Francisco Naval Base for further orders. Detached from our ship a group of us became passengers aboard a Dutch freighter for a leisurely cruise to San Francisco. We played a lot of bridge. Every night we heard, 'This is Captain Rommel.' Usually several officers joined him for a cold beer. We asked him if he had any relationship to a very famous German general, Field Marshal Erwin Rommel. The captain said, 'He is my brother' and explained that a lot of Dutch were not Nazis and that he was fighting a war against Japan in the Pacific."[355]

April 4, 1944, The Twentieth Army Air Forces deployed to the Pacific Theater and operated initially from bases in India and staging bases in China, and later from the Marianas Islands.

Spring 1944, General Groves called on General Arnold to discuss the Manhattan Project and projections for the completion of the bomb even though the scientists were still unsure of the final size and weight of the implosion bomb. Groves discussed with Oppenheimer and his key men the use and need for modifications of the B-29 for the uranium and plutonium bombs.[356]

April 30, 1944, Capt. Theodore Van Kirk was relieved from assignment "Hq & Hq Sq-41st Nav Tng Gp (disbanded by CO #24 Hq AAFCFTC R/F Tex dtd 18 Apr 44) off 2359 hrs 30 April 1944; and then asgd to 2530th AAF Base Unit (Navigators School & Instructors School) as of 0001 hrs 1 May 1944 per GO #14 Hq AAFTC Ft Worth Tex dtd 14 Apr 44...No travel involved in this trf. No change in present primary duty..."[357]

"B-29 *Ladybird*"

Dutch ~ Many of the men assigned to the B-29 groups were a bit afraid of flying the airplane, because it caught fire a lot. Before we got to Wendover, Paul had the idea to train a couple of women and shame the college football guys who were afraid of flying it. He took two graduates from Sweetwater, Didi Johnson and Dora Dougherty.[358] Dora was a real sharp woman I will tell you and later got her PHD in aeronautical engineering. Both women were good fliers.

Dougherty and Johnson were at Elgin Army Air Base towing targets for gunnery practice. Neither woman at that time had experience piloting four-engine aircraft. Tibbets checked them out in the B-29 after a few days training and then flew to Clovis Army Air Field in New Mexico.[359] During the check ride with Tibbets and Dean Hudson, the Civil Aeronautics Inspector, the WASP took off with the number three engine feathered when the wheels were in the well. By the time the flaps were up number four feathered. Tibbets had Dougherty stall the airplane and other maneuvers. Hudson directed her to shoot some landings. At about ten thousand feet Dougherty was cleared to approach and join the pattern. She throttled back as the airplane filled with smoke because of an engine fire in number three engine and called the tower

Left to right: Paul W. Tibbets, Dorothea Johnson Moorman and Dora Dougherty Strother, and crew standing beside Boeing B-29 *Ladybird* at Elgin Field, Fort Walton, Florida. (Photo MSS 250.27.3 courtesy of Texas Woman's University)

to make a straight approach. Dougherty directed the engineer and her co-pilot Johnson to feather the engines and was the last one to leave the smoke filled bomber.[360]

Dutch ~ We let the word get out that a couple of women were going to come in at such and such a time and fly the B-29, and oh yeah they can't fly it. I think it was at Pyote, Texas.[361] A lot of people were standing on the flight line. I saw the airplane come in and bounce all over the place, make a horrible landing, and taxi in front of the ramp. The men were saying we told them that women couldn't fly that airplane. Then two male ferry pilots got out. Within fifteen minutes another B-29 comes in and this was Dora and Didi. They land touch and go and feather one end and take off again, go up, turn around, and come around again. That is when you feather an engine, never turn into that engine, and get that wing low. You must keep the wing high and turn it off. This time they turned into the engine and come around and put on a good display of flying, taxied up to the ramp right in front of operations, and these two little women get out. They did not have much trouble with the men after that.

The women did exceptional duty. While Dora towed targets it was strange how many guys mistook the airplane for the target. Later on Dora and (Mary) Helen Gosnell became the personal pilots for General Frank Armstrong.[362] Armstrong was from the 97th bomb group and now in the states.

I think Armstrong's wife really picked one of the women pilots because she was married.

TABLE 8.1 — SPECIFICATIONS OF B-29

Engines:	Four Wright R-3350s of 2,200 hp each
Maximum speed:	357 mph
Cruising speed:	220 mph
Range:	3,700 miles
Ceiling:	33,600 ft.
Span:	141 ft. 3 in.
Length:	99 ft.
Height:	27 ft. 9 in.
Weight:	133,500 lbs. maximum

Source: National Museum of the United States Air Force fact sheet.

The Boeing cutting edge technology and two turbo superchargers on each of the four radial engines enabled the B-29 to fly longer distances at greater speeds, which was critical in waging the aerial war in the Pacific. The pressurized cabin, pneumatic bomb-bay door device, remotely controlled gun turrets, and fire control system were only part of the innovations.[363]

"A Los Alamos Scientist"

May 19 -26, 1944, Oppenheimer sent Dr. Arthur L. Hughes a confidential memo about the news that a "first rate micro-chemist Leonard Pepkowitz is available."[364] Leonard P. Pepkowitz received his doctorate in chemistry from Rutgers University in 1943. He was teaching at the Rhode Island State College in Kingston and doing research for a federal project at the College's Agricultural Experimental Station. Pepkowitz received a telegram from Hughes enlisting his help with a project to bring the war to a close. The National Academy of Sciences in Washington conducted the search and made the recommendation of Pepkowitz to Hughes.[365]

Doctor Hughes wrote to Dean Mason Campbell about securing Pepkowitz's services. "We cannot go into detail regarding the nature of the work but can only say that it carries the highest priority." Doctor Pepkowitz accepted the call enlisting his help to bring the war to a close and the offer of $305.00 a month salary pending security clearance.[366] Rent for an available apartment would be approximately eleven percent of his salary plus eight to twelve dollars a month for utilities. Pepkowitz was advised of restrictions as a member of the project. "All contact with friends and relatives other than through correspondence must be severed. Your travel will be limited to a radius of approximately 75 miles."[367]

The Office Of Price Administration authorized Pepkowitz sufficient gasoline to drive from Kingston to "within fifty-five miles beyond Santa Fe, New Mexico, where the project is located." Leonard and Deborah did not think twice and jumped into their Model T Ford with doors held closed by a rope. They drove a circuitous route to Los Alamos and began for the next two years living under strict secrecy, censorship, and primitive living conditions. Some of the scientists were also talented artists and musicians and provided a cultural life on the mesa.[368]

Doctor Pepkowitz served as the group leader in analytical chemistry at Los Alamos.[369] His wife taught Fermi's children and other dependents of the scientists.

Animosity developed between Groves and Oppenheimer. Later, Pepkowitz told his children and residents in the Town of Porter that Groves wanted the scientists to be his "soldiers," but Oppenheimer was adamant that the scientists be left alone to do their creative work.

May 22, 1944, Captain Van Kirk was on leave for nineteen days effective this date.[370]

May 23, 1944, by Order of the Secretary of War, "Announcement is made of the temp promotion of the following named officers to the grades indicated in the AUS with rank from date of this order: 1st Lt. to Capt. Theodore Jerome Van Kirk."[371]

May 29, 1944, Adjutant Gen. Charles A. Fleming wrote to Captain Van Kirk at Selman Field that "by direction of the President, an Air Medal has been awarded to you by the Commanding General, Twelfth Air Force," by order of the Secretary of War.[372]

Jean ~ "Most of the young men in Northumberland were called up; it was a small town. I graduated from high school in 1944. By the time we graduated in June it looked like a girl's school. Our senior prom was pitiful." Young men received their diplomas and then often left during the first half of the school year before graduation.

Roosevelt ~ *June 5, 1944*, "My friends: yesterday, on June fourth, 1944, Rome fell to American and allied troops. The first of the Axis capitals is now in our hands. One up and two to go!"[373]

June 6, 1944, on D-Day the Allied forces land on the heavily fortified fifty-mile stretch of the Normandy beaches.

"My War Is Over"

Dutch ~ When D-day happened I was stationed in Louisiana, but was on leave in Pennsylvania. Left Northumberland early in the morning and drove back to my base in Monroe. I tuned into the radio and heard the news coming across about the invasion. It was so interesting I drove eleven hundred miles that day listening to the broadcast and almost made Monroe in one day's driving.

I still had the feeling, "I am glad I am not in that mess. My war is over. I will just sit here and keep my nose clean."

"Robert D. Young"

July 10, 1944, 2nd Lt. Robert D. Young, brother-in-law of Van Kirk, was killed in action against the Japanese on Saipan Island.[374] Young served with the 105th Infantry 27th Division.

July 18, 1944, Japan's Premier Hideki Tojo was ousted as Army Chief of Staff following the defeat at Midway and Saipan.

August 1, 1944, the United States Marines secured Tinian Island.

August 28, 1944, news of labor disputes and strikes at two war plants slowed production of key parts for the Liberator and Superfortress bombers. The Detroit Ford-operated Willow plant building B-24s closed furloughing 30,000 workers and production of B-29s halted at the Chicago Dodge plant.

Labor issues impacted the Pullman car manufacturing plant and Fairfield Steel in Birmingham (Alabama), Mosher Steel in Houston (Texas), a chemical facility at Mount Pleasant (Tennessee), a forging company in Washington State, and Walsh-Kaiser shipyards in Providence (Rhode Island). Closed coal mines in Pennsylvania and West Virginia over the rights of workers to unionize were seized by the government and production resumed.[375]

August 31, 1944, by order of Colonel Reid, Captain Van Kirk was relieved from duty as Training Officer (Tactical Curriculum O) (Primary Duty); and designated Training Officer (Primary MOS 1034) (Asst. OIC Special Projects).[376]

"General Ent, a Northumberland Son"

September 1, 1944, after testing a B-29 Paul Tibbets flew to Colorado Springs to report to Gen. Uzal G. Ent, the commander of the Second Air Force. Tibbets met with Ent, Security Officer of the Manhattan District Lt. Col. Jack Lansdale, Navy Capt. William "Deak" Parsons, and Dr. Norman Ramsey, a nuclear physics professor at Columbia University. The General told Tibbets that he had been chosen for a secret and important mission to organize and train a combat group to deliver a new powerful explosive that had not yet been developed.

Ramsey gave a brief account of atomic science during the past few years. Captain Parsons in charge of atomic bomb ballistics at Los Alamos attempted to answer Tibbets about what would be a safe distance for the bomber from the point of the blast and weight of the bomb. The scientists' best calculations to withstand the shock wave should be a distance of eight miles and the weight approximately nine thousand pounds, approximately the same bomb load usually carried by B-29s.[377]

General Ent had recommended Tibbets from three names suggested by Gen. Henry H. Arnold for the mission.[378] Ent grew up on King Street in Northumberland, Pennsylvania, and had attended Susquehanna University. He began his military career in World War I and was appointed from the regular Army to West Point. Ent led the B-24 Liberator raid on the Ploesti oil fields of Rumania that destroyed seven principal oil refineries and plants although the damage did not substantially reduce oil production.[379]

The front-line general returned to the United States in September 1943 and subsequently assumed command of the crews for the B-29 bombers, which were to be unleashed against the Japanese.[380]

Jean - "General Ent was a remarkable man, a hero. He visited Northumberland and we had a big parade for him."

Dutch - Uzal Ent was from my hometown. He was in a twin engine B-25 bomber. Hot shot pilots liked to quickly pull up the wheels, but he did it too soon. The plane dropped on its belly and the prop hit him in the back. (The propeller shattered and flew into the cockpit.) He was in the hospital for more than a month. Tibbets and I used to bring him cigars from Cuba while he was in the hospital.

Ent's co-pilot became ill before a flight and his replacement interpreted the General's nodding and singing while taking off to be a signal to raise the landing gear.[381]

His injury severed his spinal cord. Ent began a mission for better braces for Army patients. An improved stainless steel brace developed by the Veterans Administration aided about 3,000 veterans because of Ent's efforts.[382]

Maj. Gen. Uzal G. Ent died March 5, 1948, from injuries suffered in the 1944 accident. His ashes were strewn over the Pennsylvania hills near Northumberland.[383] Ent's tombstone stands near the Fred and Grace Van Kirk's monument at the Riverview Cemetery in Northumberland.

September 6, 1944, By order of Colonel Reid, Captain Van Kirk Section "B" Navigator Headquarters is designated Navigator (1034) (Examination & Testing Off) (Add Duty).[384]

"V-2 Rocket"

September 8, 1944, the Peenemünde rocket development program under Maj. Gen. Walter Dornberger had begun to transport rockets to the front. From Holland the Germans fired the first V-2 ballistic missile on London.[385] The rockets and components were produced at the central plant of Mittelwerk through forced labor. Slave labor from the Dora concentration camp carved out a key underground factory near Nordhausen.

Dornberger in *V-2 The Nazi Rocket Weapon* struggled with his decision to oversee the transition from the development stage to the actual operation after Heinrich Himmler appointed SS Gen. Hans Kammler, Commission General for the A-4 program. Hitler distrusted the "officer caste" according to Dornberger.

Chapter Eight — Endnotes

331 At the suggestion of Gen. Henry "Hap" Arnold", Cochran became a consultant to the Ferry Command in 1941 to study the issue of women in the Air Corps. Early in 1942 Cochran recruited twenty-five female pilots in the United States for the British Air Transport Auxiliary to assist Pauline Grower in England known as the "ATA" girls. An experimental squadron organized under the direction of Nancy Harkness Love and assigned to the ATC for ferrying duty at New Castle Army Air Base near Wilmington, DE. Twenty-eight women flyers comprised the initial squadron of the Women's Auxiliary Ferry Squadron (WAFS). Almost simultaneously, the Women's Flying Training Detachment created under Cochran trained at the municipal airport in Houston, Texas. The two organizations merged on August 5, 1943, into the Women Air Force Service Pilots. Dietz, "Women Air Force Service Pilots," *Honor Thy Fathers & Mothers*, 86 - 89.

332 The navigator known as "Little Tin Guy" must be "steady-nerved, cool-headed individual capable of making lightning decisions…plenty of grey matter between the ears." "Zero Zero" means perfection in navigation to hit a target "on the nose." "The Zero Zero Reunion Program," Army Air Forces Navigation School Selman Field, 23, 24, 32.

333 Capt. Charles R. Wiley from Lafayette, IN, piloted the American Flying Fortress, as of June 30, 1943. "Outstanding B-17's," War Theatre #15, Northwest Africa, with photograph and negative No. 203-JM-(NASHF-5W) 1-7-43. National Archives Building, Still Pictures Reference, College Park, MD. The *Red Gremlin* returned to the states on July 13, 1944, and was salvaged in June 1946 according to Roger Freeman's *B-17 Flying Fortress* publication.

334 First Lt. John A. Gallup from Upper Darby, PA, piloted the bomber on July 1, 1943.

335 Restricted Special Orders No. 98 from Headquarters Army Air Forces Flying Training Command, Fort Worth, TX, July 2, 1943. Van Kirk personal papers.

336 Bonner, *Final Voyage*, 48.

337 Starnes was made navigator of the *Boise*, which headed back to the Pacific.

338 "U.S. Prepared to Fight Japanese Until 1949," *Stars And Stripes*, July 21, 1943.

339 Address of the President broadcast nationally "On Progress of War and Plans for Peace."

340 Van Kirk received a receipt for $5.75 for a room and $0.22 for the telephone at the Washington-Youree Hotel, Shreveport, LA, for the night of September 16, 1943. Van Kirk personal papers.

341 "Lt. Van Kirk, Miss Young Wed In South," *Sunbury Daily Item*, September 1943.

342 The *Sunbury Daily Item's* coverage of "Miss Young To Marry Aviator" reported that Mary Jane and Lt. Van Kirk were planning to be married, but definite plans were not made until the party reached Louisiana.

343 The operational element of the Fifteenth Air Force formed from several groups from the Twelfth Air Force. Martin W. Bowman, *Flying to Glory* The B-17 Flying Fortress in war and peace, (Somerset: UK, Patrick Stephens Limited), 90. In the Mediterranean Theatre the 97th Bomb Group's markings on the fin and vertical stabilizers featured a black Y in a white triangle. A number inside a white circle indicated the squadron, "0" for the 340th squadron. Ernest R. McDowell, *Flying Fortress* The Boeing B-17, (Carrollton, TX: Squadron/Signal Publications, 1987), 61.

344 Special Orders No. 323, Extract, War Department, Washington, DC, November 19, 1943.

345 Richard H. Campbell, *The Silverplate Bombers*: A History and Registry of the Enola Gay and Other B-29s Configured to Carry Atomic Bombs, (Jefferson, NC: McFarland & Company, Inc., 2005), 110.

346 The envelope was postmarked Jan 28, 1944, Monroe, LA, addressed to Mr. Fred Van Kirk, 672 Queen St., Northumberland, PA. The year 1943 on the letter was in error.

347 Addressee on the envelope: Mrs. T. J. Van Kirk, 1300-A-South 4th St., Monroe, LA.

348 The return address: Capt. T. J. Van Kirk 0-659024, Box 777, V N.T.G., Selman Field, Monroe, LA.

349 Fred Van Kirk passed away May 4, 1969.

350 "Jean or Ted sent me a telegram," said Mick McAllister remembering his age of just eighteen years old and forty-two years old seemed like a long life.

351 Ron Counts, "Boogie Woogie Bugle Boy," *Culpeper Star-Exponent*, April 6, 2009.

352 Alvino Ray left the Horace Height's Band to start his own band in 1939 with the King Sisters. Ray's sax section became part of Woody Herman's Four Brothers. "Wanting a smooth sounding name he changed from Alvin McBride to Alvino Rey and married one of the sisters, Luise King. Alice was the lead singer," said McAllister.

353 Rey and his armed forces band recorded more than two-dozen of his arrangements of songs including *April In Paris, Lullaby Of Broadway, Three Little Words, Time On My Hands, Sentimental Journey,* and others. Charles Garrod and Bill Korst, *Alvino Rey and His Orchestra Plus The King Sisters 1938 – 1948,* (Portland, OR: Joyce Record Club, 1997), 14.

354 Special Orders No. 50 from Headquarters Selman Field, Monroe, Louisiana, relieved Van Kirk from duty as an Aerial Instructor and designated him as a Training Officer; copy of order by Colonel Eagan Van Kirk personal papers.

355 Starnes reported to the Naval Base and was given a thirty-day leave. "I called in everyday and eventually was told to report to Newport, Rhode Island. I was home on leave on D-Day June 6, 1944, and left a day or two later for my second tour of duty. My second duty assignment was to head the naval navigation school to teach the new crews being quickly put out to sea. Married now and with a child Starnes thought, "The war is over for me. I was running a naval training school in Newport, Rhode Island." Training comprised a thirty-day cruise to prepare the men aboard ship and compressed class instruction. "Trained crews were needed because ships were being built so fast."

356 Groves suggested a British *Lancaster,* and the certain cooperation of Churchill, if the B-29 could not be used. Groves, *Now It Can Be Told* The Story of the Manhattan Project, 253 - 254.

357 Special Orders No. 21, Headquarters Selman Field, Monroe, LA, by order of Colonel Galloway. Van Kirk personal papers.

358 Dora Dougherty Strother McKeon WASP Class 43-W-3 flew trainers, cargo aircraft, B-17, B-25, B-29, A-25, and Bell 47G-3 Helicopter and Dorothea "Didi" Johnson Moorman flew C-47 and B-24. Texas Woman's University Library, www.twu.edu [accessed January 31, 2011].

359 Wanda Langley, *Flying Higher*, The Women Airforce Service Pilots of World War II, (North Haven, CT: Linnet Books, 2002), 93.

360 Van Kirk and Tibbets' account of the B-29 check ride with the WASP. *General Paul*

Tibbets An Oral History interview by Dawn Letson on February 24, 1997.

361 Tibbets told Letson during the interview that Dougherty and Johnson demonstrated the B-29s at a number of airfields.

362 Dougherty and Johnson went to Grand Island, NE, Oklahoma City, OK, and Wendover, UT, with Paul Tibbets to support ferrying and transport. Johnson left and was replaced by Gosnell.

363 The USAF Museum fact sheets for the bomber specify the Performance Range as 5,600 miles maximum ferry range and 3,250 miles with 20,000 lbs. The Silverplates also had extensive electronic gear and a synchronizer to enable the pilot to twist a knob and maintain consistent RPMS in all the engines. Warren Thompson, "509th Bomb Group," *Wings of Fame* The Journal of Classic Combat Aircraft, Vol. 7, 1997.

364 Dr. Oppenheimer, Washington Liaison Office, Washington, DC, to A. L. Hughes, May 19, 1944, Los Alamos National Laboratory file, Los Alamos, NM.

365 M.H. Trytten, National Academy of Sciences, 2010 Constitution Avenue, Washington, DC, letter to A. L. Hughes, May 22, 1944, Los Alamos National Laboratory file.

366 Airmail letter and telegram reference, A. L. Hughes to Mr. Leonard Pepkowitz, May 26, 1944, Los Alamos National Laboratory file.

367 A. L. Hughes letter to Leonard Pepkowitz, May 26, 1944, Los Alamos National Laboratory personnel file.

368 Deborah Pepkowitz told her unreal spy story to the *Niagara Falls Gazette*. "Meet Mrs. Leonard Pepkowitz Los Alamos Experience Seems Unreal," April 16, 1967. The Pepkowitzes told their children, Samuel and Rebecca, that they did not think twice when posed with the opportunity to help bring an end to the war.

369 Jeremy Pearce, "Leonard P. Pepkowitz, 91, a Chemist In Atomic Energy, Dies," *New York Times*, November 4, 2006.

370 Headquarters Selman Field, Monroe, LA, Restricted, Special Orders No. 134 granting leave of absence, May 13, 1944. Van Kirk personal papers.

371 Special Orders No. 23, War Department, G. C. Marshall, Chief of Staff, Official: Robert H. Dunlop, Brigadier General, Washington, May 23, 1944. Van Kirk personal papers.

372 Adjutant General Charles A. Fleming letter to Captain Van Kirk, May 29, 1944. Van Kirk personal papers.

373 The opening of President Roosevelt's address "On the fall of Rome."

374 Margaret Young was "in nursing" in New York City when her son Robert died according to the obituary. "Mary Jane's mother was institutionalized in a New York City hospital and died shortly after the war," said Dutch. "Ex-Orphanage Ward Killed In Saipan Battle," *Sunbury Daily Item*, July 1944. Robert D. Young's grave Manila American Cemetery, Philippines, Plot G Row 12 Grave 12, Awards: Bronze Star, Purple Heart. American Battle Monuments Commission, http://www.abmc.gov/home.php [accessed July 27, 2010].

375 Associated Press, "Strikes Interfere with Production of Superfortresses, Liberators," *Niagara Falls Gazette*, September 9, 1944.

376 Headquarters Selman Field, Monroe, LA, Special Orders No. 244, 31 August 1944. Van Kirk personal papers.

377 Tibbets gave an account of the formation of his "secret Air Force" in *The Tibbets Story*, 152 – 155. Other publications use June 1944 as the time Tibbets learned of the

project. Nickname for the plutonium bomb detonated for the Trinity test was the "gadget."

378 Joe Diblin, "The story of the man who dropped the bomb," *The Standard Journal*, July 2007. The series of four articles reported on an interview by Studs Terkel and published in the *Guardian Unlimited*, "A Helluva Big Bang," August 6, 2002. Diblin flew B-17 and B-24s during World War II and trained other pilots to fly B-24s. Kevin Mertz, "Soaring through the Memories," *Standard Journal*, October 5, 2010.

379 "Ploesti Fields Still Blowing; Raid Success," *The Stars & Stripes*, Vol. 3 No. 234, August 4, 1943. Fifty-four bombers were lost and more than five hundred men, a high price for the raid. "Northumberland Proud Of Air Heroes" Exploits, *The Evening News* (Harrisburg, PA), February 16, 1950.

380 *Northumberland Point Township Pennsylvania Bicentennial 1772-1972*, 55.

381 Axis History Forum, interview with Ent's co-pilot, http://forum.axishistory.com/viewtopic.php?f=52&t=153316, [accessed May 24, 2010].

382 "Crippled Major (General) Plans Vets' Aid," *Stars and Stripes*, July 28, 1946, 2.

383 "Ploesti Oil Raid Commander Dies, Ill Since 1944," *Niagara Falls Gazette*, March 6, 1948.

384 Headquarters Selman Field, Special Orders No. 250, 6 September 1944. Van Kirk personal papers.

385 After the war Dornberger, Wehrner Von Braun, and more than 1,000 scientists were brought to the United States under *Operation Paperclip* and became key figures in the history of the American space program. Dornberger, an executive for Bell Aircraft, and his wife lived in the adjacent apartment to John, Salome, and Suzanne Simon at Campus Manor in Snyder, NY, in the early 1950s. The general gave an account of the German rocket program in *V-2 The Nazi Rocket Weapon*, (New York: NY, Ballantine Books, 1954.) Dornberger was a member of the Aero Club of Buffalo (NY).

Chapter Nine

Wendover *Silver Plated Project*

"A Mission to Shorten the War"

September 1944
Dutch - Suddenly the telephone rings in my hotel room while I am down in New Orleans on leave. Every once and awhile we had time off. The war was not very urgent here. The phone call was from Paul Tibbets.

"I am forming a new group. I want you as my group navigator. Tom Ferebee has agreed to come out and be my group bombardier. I cannot tell you what we are going to do, but I can tell you it is going to be important enough that we are going to end or significantly shorten the war. You do not have to go, but I want you and if you want to join us I will get the orders to transfer you."

I answered him right away. "I will be there whatever it is. If you, Tom, and I are going to get together again I want to be in on it." At that time I had lost track of Tom until Wendover.

Mary Jane was a wartime wife and realized what had to be done. I was going to be in danger again but had survived. Why not try another mission this was her attitude. We returned to the base in Monroe and waited. A few days later I secretly received orders to report to the Silverplate project at Wendover.

Until the day Tibbets died we argued about whether I volunteered for this job. When I received my orders they were dated two days before Paul called me, so much for volunteering.

TABLE 9.1 — VAN KIRK'S NAVIGATION RECORD FOR SEPTEMBER – OCTOBER 1944

Day	Aircraft	No. Landings	NAV. Time	Night Nav. Time
09/07/1944	AT-7	2	5:55	
09/10/1944	AT-7	2	3:00	
09/13/1944	AT-7	1	3:30	1:00
09/25/1944	AT-7	1	4:10	
09/27/1944	AT-7	1	4:15	
09/30/1944	AT-7	1	4:30	
10/23/1944	B-29	1	2:30	
10/25/1944	UC-78	2	1:45	

Source: Van Kirk's Individual Flight Records. September record certified correct by Capt. Dale J. Butterworth, Asst. Operations Officer. Van Kirk assigned to AAFCFTC 80th FTW Sec B HQ (Command), 2530th AAF Base Unit (Detachment). October record certified correct by Maj. R. H. May, Base Operations Officer. Van Kirk assigned to Second Air Force, 216th AAF, Base Unit Special, (Detachment).

October 3, 1944
R-E-S-T-R-I-C-T-E-D

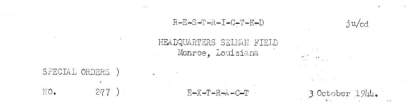

R-E-S-T-R-I-C-T-E-D   ju/cd

HEADQUARTERS SELMAN FIELD
Monroe, Louisiana

SPECIAL ORDERS)

NO.   277)   E-X-T-R-A-C-T   3 October 1944.

Headquarters Selman Field
Monroe, Louisiana
Special Orders)
No. 277) E-X-T-R-A-C-T

16. CAPT VAN KIRK, THEODORE J, O 659 024 AC (MOS 1034) 2530th AAF Base Unit (Navigators School & Instructor's School) Sec "B" is reld fr further asgmt & dy this sta; is asgd & WP 4 Oct 44 2d AF 216 AAFBU WENDOVER FLD UTAH for asgmt to Silver Plate Project. PCS TDN TPA 501-31 P 431-02 03 07 212/50425. Eff date of C on M/R: 8 Oct 44. Auth: TWX 11E-5287J Hq AAFCFTC R/F Tex dtd 30 Sept 44.

By order of Colonel Reid:

Official: Lawrence Conques, Capt AC, Asst Adj[386]

The isolated base at Wendover Field in the salt flats of western Utah became the training ground for the 509th Composite Group under top-secret conditions. The 393rd Bombardment Squadron (Heavy) detached from the 504th BG from Fairmont Army Air Field near Fairmont, Nebraska, and arrived to become part of the 509th and the welcome billboard: "What you hear here, What you see here, When you leave here, Let it stay here."

The initial training in the new B-29s was "slow and dull" and began with high explosive bombs similar to the implosion type of *Fat Man*.[387] General Arnold provided the new Superforts even though they were in short supply due to the tremendous demand for the heavy bombers in the Pacific.[388]

"Life at Wendover"

Dutch ~ Mary Jane and I drove to Wendover in three days. I was moseying along. We had stopped to eat along the way, came back to the car, and started driving again. I was not paying attention and drove about sixty miles back in the wrong direction. My wife said, "You are a great damn navigator."

We turned around and during the course of this I got a felon on the tip of my finger.[389] And it hurt. I stopped in Denver. A surgeon in the Army hospital said, "I can fix it up for you. It is going to hurt like hell, but it has got to be done."

The doc gave me a local anesthetic and told me to get a fifth of whiskey and drink it because I was going to need it when the anesthetic wore off. My finger bled almost all the way from Denver to Wendover. I looked at the airfield when we first reached Wendover. There was nothing but a couple

Van Kirk on the Wendover area hills, stone quarry in the background.

of Piper Cubs sitting on it. I thought what in the hell is this big thing that Paul has gotten us into now? We are going to do it with Piper Cubs! I went to the base operations to sign in about two o'clock in the afternoon. Paul and Tom were in his (Paul's) office already, heard me outside, and came out to greet me. When they shook my hand it started bleeding all over them. Paul said that the first thing was to get me to the hospital for a new dressing and then assignment of our quarters.

The barracks looked like tarpaper shacks heated by coal stoves and there were no separate accommodations for married people. If you were married with children you could get a small one-bedroom apartment, maybe two. Clothes were washed by hand and hung outdoors. Coal soot would cover the clothes. Since we had no children, we were assigned a dormitory like room. Couples cooked together or we could eat at the officer's club or mess hall. That was life at Wendover, very primitive.

Mary Jane and I did not think too much of the quarters, but as soon as she got to know some of the other women like Donald Berry's wife it was okay. Roberta talked constantly and still does to this day. Chuck Sweeney's first wife Dorothy, a nurse, was a good woman and a character. They met at Elgin Field and eventually had a large family. Sweeney was a good friend of Tibbets.

Wendover was very isolated, but we did have a nice swimming pool. I went to the pool just to see Jerry Slusky's wife. Jim Van Pelt flew out there and told his wife Sue to come and meet him. The train stopped just long enough to let her off with the two kids. They were standing by the railroad tracks while Jim was out flying someplace. The next thing you know Tom Ferebee and I get a call. "Mrs. Van Pelt is up here at the railroad station."

Tom said, "I guess we better go get her." Everyone was busy and off doing their thing. If it was official flying, we did it ignoring family and everything else.

509th Headquarters at Wendover (National Archives)

Tom and I took Sue to the hospital when she was in labor. Sue told the story that she got the best care when her third child was born "because Dutch and Tom took me to the hospital. Jim was out flying. With Jim, I probably would have had to walk to the hospital," and it was wintertime. Mary Jane helped Sue with the children.

Wendover had a pre-war population of a hundred and four residents. When Bob Hope performed here he called the town Leftover. People sat around and listened to the radio. We did not get much news. My recollection is that we followed the war on a map at the operations headquarters or the officer's club and plotted the progress of the war in Europe.

Compensations of Wendover living were the big State Line Casino and warm springs in the area. The casino sat on one side of the state line and the hotel on the other. The casino took extremely good care of us, but also took our money. A fella named Spikes on the Utah side of the line served the biggest, most delicious steaks of your life in his restaurant for two dollars. Spikes said, "You went out of your way to get here so we ought to go out of our way to take care of you."

Sometimes we checked out shotguns from the MPs to go duck hunting or hiking and did a lot of flying.

Very quickly Tom and I got a rather unique reputation of being buddies of Paul Tibbets. The guys had the impression out there that it was Tibbets, Van Kirk, and Ferebee and the rest of the 509th because of little things. Tom and I were there about a week or so and walked in to see Colonel Tibbets, Lieutenant Colonel at that time, and asked, "Colonel we would like to go into Salt Lake City this weekend. Do you have any objections if we go?"

Paul looked at us and said, "If you two guys want to go and do anything do it, but if I don't want you to do it I will tell you." That was the way things were from that time on and probably the reason why the rest of the people thought us as being close. In the 1960s I went to a reunion and when Tom and I walked in to register Fred Bock's wife said, "Why you two guys think you can do anything, don't you?" She was still giving us hell twenty years later.

"Flying with Paul Tibbets"

Dutch ~ On paper I was the group navigator in charge of training all the other navigators. I repeat "on paper" because we took an entire squadron out of the 504th Bombardment Group as our main flying personnel. The 504th had the best training record in the country. Tom Classen and his group had a really good navigator, William Wright. He trained the navigators in that group extremely well and was continuing to do that job. I decided to let Bill go ahead and do his job and stay out of his way, but checked the navigators' logs and training records. So basically I became Paul Tibbets' personal navigator.[390]

Paul had a habit of calling me up to meet him at the flight line at such and such a time. Generally, we would be gone for three days in a C-54 not a B-29. We flew into Washington and landed at the old Bolling Field.

Coming back one time we landed in Chicago. Paul was always very accommodating. "Do you have any cargo you want taken any place," he asked.

There were a bunch of airplane tires that needed to get to Albuquerque, New Mexico. Paul said to put them on the airplane. We landed in Albuquerque about three in the morning. Paul went in to operations, tells them about the tires, and that someone needs to unload them.

"We can't unload these," said the operations manager. "Nobody comes to work until about six o'clock."

"Well they are going to be unloaded, said Paul. "Come on Dutch; we will do it."

A C-54 stands about twenty feet high and when we rolled the first tire off the plane it hit the ground, bounced up again, and rolled across the field. The guy came out screaming at us, "Don't do that. Don't do that. We will get a guy to unload them."

Tibbets had the habit of telling me to be at the flight line at a certain time and that we were going to be away for a few days. If I did not have time to let Mary Jane know, I left word through Jim Van Pelt or Tom Ferebee. I told her not to lend Tom my car. He borrowed the car all the time. He was not a good driver and a worse navigator. I came back and found this big old crease down the trunk. "Tom what the hell did you hit this time?" He had backed into a pole.

We frequently flew to Los Alamos or Washington and got waylaid. At a stop in Chicago, we met up with a bunch of Navy WAVES. Paul from his days in Miami knew the commander of the detachment and asked her where the group was going? They were trying to get down to Miami so big hearted Paul offered to take them.

We had been headed back to Wendover and now all of a sudden we are flying to Miami. Interludes like that broke up the pressure and the work. Someone in our group wrote an Air Force song, which was going to be introduced on a radio program. That night we were coming back from some place with a stop in Los Angeles to go to that radio program. I remember the night very well because I was flying co-pilot for Paul. He never followed regulations and just got someone to sit in that co-pilot seat. We were approaching a peak and I could tell we were going to be damn close. You never could tell when Paul had dozed off, but he had dozed off.

I said, "Paul are we going to clear that peak up there?"

Paul looked at me and then looked up and said, "Hell no and wheels the plane around."

When we landed we saw Carmen Miranda on the show that night too. She was a show by herself. We get into Hollywood and were cavorting with all these women singing the Air Force song. I asked Tibbets, "Do we have to go back to that war for Christ's sakes?"

Infrequently on these trips, Paul gave me a separate mission at a base. On a rare occasion I would be with him during a meeting discussing targets, but most of our relationship was in the air. It didn't make any difference to me what target we were going to hit from the air, but I agreed later that it was a good decision to take Kyoto off the list. Most of my flight time was in a C-54 with Tibbets and often another man. I think his name was Sgt. Gagnon. (SSgt. Joseph A. Gagnon was Tibbets' crew chief at the time.) Usually Tom Ferebee was not with us. So it was just the three of us on this big damn airplane.

Tibbets and I played a lot of cribbage while we were flying. We had made a board to set between the two seats. Oh yes, the C-54 had an autopilot. In fact we were flying along and periodically he scanned the instruments. All of a sudden Tibbets said, "What the hell happened to number four? We do not have any oil pressure."

I turned around and looked out the window and said, "We don't have number four. It is feathered for Christ sakes!" I never figured out what happened except the feathering buttons were above and one of us must have thrown up our hands because we had lousy cards and hit the button without knowing it.

We broke even while playing cribbage, but if we were playing poker or shooting craps Tom Ferebee usually was the winner. If we played handball Paul Tibbets was usually the winner. I could hold my own though in cribbage.

We had flown from Wendover to Washington, DC, for a meeting at the Pentagon. Everybody there was a full colonel. Afterwards I asked Paul how he felt in that atmosphere with all those full colonels with chests full of ribbons who had not done a damn thing and here Tibbets was a lieutenant colonel with a record of flying combat, testing the B-29, and having a group to train for something special. "Doesn't that piss you off every once and awhile?"

Tibbets looked at me and said, "Dutch, I will tell you. I look at them and they look at me. I know how they got theirs and they know how I got mine, and I am happy."

"Training the Navigators"

Dutch ~ When the other navigators returned from a mission I checked their log. Some navigators got lazy. I believed that you never let the airplane get ahead of you. Keep the log and maintain the information so if suddenly you are lost you could find yourself and get back to the base. If the crews were flying at night, I checked to see that they did the correct celestial fixes.

In later years I went to some of the 509th reunions. Fred Bock's navigator, Len Godfrey, was a bit distant. Finally, I got to know him better and he said, "I hated your guts." I asked him why.

Len said, "You accused me of fudging my log," or something like that.

I did not recall anything of that type and to this day I do not know if I did. Len was a good navigator. But when you checked up on the navigators, they would be sensitive and get the feeling that you were accusing them of something.

October 11, 1944, "Lt. Col. Trowbridge ordered Capt. Theodore J. Van Kirk Sec A 216th AAFBU (Sp) assigned for duty with the Standardization Board."[391]

Sometime in October 1944, Women Air Force Service Pilots Dora Dougherty and Mary Helen Gosnell flew a shuttle mission to Albuquerque, New Mexico, to deliver top secret hardware. Before the cargo was loaded, the women were locked into the cockpit until the cargo was delivered and unloaded.[392]

"USS *Missouri* Leaves New York"

James Starnes - *Early November 1944,* "I received a telephone call. 'Jim, old boy, you got your orders.' What ship, I asked. The response was the *Missouri.* Orders were usually to 'proceed and report,' but this was 'report right now.' The *Missouri* was in New York. I got my parents to pick up my family. It was just before the presidential election in 1944."

"As the navigator I kept track of where the ship went and when it got there. I was just a lieutenant. A month later I received a spot promotion to Lieutenant Commander during my eighth trip through the Panama Canal. The beam on the battleship was one hundred eight feet. The canal pilots navigated us through the one hundred ten foot locks in the canal with only one foot on each side to squeeze through."

 *November 7, 1944,* Roosevelt won re-election for a fourth term as president.

Construction began in Alamogordo, New Mexico, for the Trinity test site.[393]

November 24, 1944, 110 Superfortresses of the 21st Bomber Command took off for Tokyo.

December 7, 1944, An 8.1 magnitude earthquake felt from northern Honshu to Kyushu damaged more than 73,000 houses and caused almost 1,000 deaths. A tsunami hit the east coast of Japan from Choshi, Honshu, to Tosashimizu, Shikoku. Wave heights of up to twenty-six feet were observed on the east coast of the Kii peninsula of Honshu. A small tsunami followed on Attu, Alaska, and San Diego and Terminal Island, California.[394]

TABLE 9.2 — VAN KIRK'S NAVIGATION RECORD FOR NOVEMBER – DECEMBER 1944

Day	Aircraft	No. Landings	NAV. Time	Night Nav. Time
11/16/1944	B-29	1	1:20	
11/26/1944	C-46A	3	7:20	3:40
11/27/1944	C-46A	1	2:00	0:30
11/28/1944	C-46A	4	7:35	6:20
11/29/1944	C-46A	1	3:00	2:30
12/06/1944	C-54B	2	4:50	1:30
12/07/1944	C-54B	2	8:20	2:30
12/08/1944	C-54B	1	4:35	4:35
12/10/1944	C-54B	2	8:50	1:50
12/11/1944	C-54B	3	4:30	4:30
12/13/1944	C-54B	1	3:25	
12/14/1944	C-54B	2	4:25	1:25
12/15/1944	C-54B	3	6:30	2:00
12/17/1944	C-54B	1	1:05	
12/18/1944	C-54B	2	7:35	6:20
12/19/1944	C-54B	1	3:35	
12/21/1944	C-54B	2	3:15	
12/27/1944	C-54B	1	5:40	1:00
12/28/1944	C-54B	1	2:20	
12/29/1944	C-54B	1	3:30	2:30
12/30/1944	C-54B	2	7:00	7:00

Source: Van Kirk's Individual Flight Record. November and December through the 19th records certified correct by Maj. R. H. May, Base Operations Officer. Maj. Hubert J. Konopacki, Group Operations Officer, certified the record for December 21 – 30, 1944. "Transferred from 216th AAF, Base Unit (Special) to 509th Composite Group, Wendover Fld, Utah."

December 17, 1944, the 41st anniversary of the flight of Orville Wright in the first powered airplane, the *Kitty Hawk*, coincided with the activation of the 509th Composite Group. The Group was assigned to the 315th Bombardment Wing of the Second Air Force headquartered at Colorado Springs.

December 19, 1944, Maj. Thomas W. Ferebee, Capt. Theodore J. Van Kirk, and other officers and enlisted men were relieved from assignment and duty with Sec A 216th AAFBU (Sp), and assigned to the Hq 509th Composite Group.[395]

December 20, 1944, the Women Air Force Service Pilots program was deactivated due to political pressure and increased availability of male pilots.

The WASP flew more than sixty million miles in twenty-eight different types of military aircraft from the smallest to the largest including the B-29. The women ferried new aircraft from the factories to waiting squadrons, towed targets for training raw recruits, instructed pilots, performed flight testing, and other missions except combat. Thirty-eight women pilots made the ultimate sacrifice.[396]

December 24, 1944, the USS *Missouri* arrived at Pearl Harbor on Christmas Eve and its "welcome to the Pacific Fleet," said James Starnes.

December 31, 1944, by the end of the year 1,591,942 men entered military service under the Selective Service.

January 1945, Gen. Curtis LeMay arrived at Guam and took over the Twenty-First Bomber Command of the Twentieth Air Force. General Arnold headquartered the Twentieth Air Force in Washington, DC.

"Batista Army Airfield"

Dutch ~ I was concerned with the navigators flying just around the western United States. If you flew out there long enough you could almost navigate by looking out the window, a mountain peak sticking up over here or a lake over there. This was not good navigation training. I went to Paul Tibbets with my concern. The navigators need some place where they would have to really navigate and couldn't tune into their radios. After some discussion, we picked Batista Field and I planned the navigation training.

Right away the rumors got out that we were going to Cuba. When we put the 509th together, we were supposed to be a very mobile outfit and could go anyplace, Europe or Japan, and operate almost independently with the exception of fuel, heavy maintenance, and things of that type. By moving the outfit to a distance like Cuba and giving additional training, we had the advantage of testing the mobility of the group too.

Everybody wanted to go to Cuba and looked at the signing boards each morning to see if they were picked to go or not. Going to Cuba was an opportunity to leave the lousy mud and snow in Wendover and go to some place that is nice and warm with bathing beauties around. I am not sure how we finally chose the crews, but eventually they all got their chance to go to Batista Field. We took them down. I was only there for two days. Then Bill Wright sent the navigators over the south Atlantic for very long missions.[397]

It must have been in Washington after we started the program when General Groves asked me, "Aren't you worried you are going to lose some crews out there?"

I told him, "General, would you rather lose them out there or when they are flying over the Pacific someplace?"

That was the end of that. Sloppy Joe's Bar seemed to be the favorite place in Cuba.[398] We found a cab driver down there who would take us to the good places. I smoked some good, cheap cigars. When I got back to this country I couldn't afford to smoke them.

Ferebee was with us on this trip the first time. We got to Miami and hadn't realized that going to Cuba was considered overseas duty. I didn't have all of my shots. The physician said, "You need eleven shots before you go" five in one arm and six in the other before I finally could get in the damn airplane and fly over across the street to Batista Field for two days.

We took a bunch of our MPs to secure our airplanes. Capt. Louis Schaffer was the commander of our MP unit. Lou had his MPs shoulder their arms and marched through the terminal in spick fashion to where they were going to stay temporarily while we were in Miami. An elderly gentlemen sitting on a patio watched the MPs march by. He looked at me and said, "the first group of soldiers we have seen go through here in two years."

We get to Batista about two or three o'clock in the morning. The men had not been fed for quite awhile. Tibbets turned to us and said, "You two make sure the men are fed before they get bedded down here."

Tom Ferebee and I went to the mess sergeant who did not want to get up and made an issue. Tom pulled his .45 on the sergeant and said, "These fellows haven't had breakfast yet and by God they are going to get breakfast." Incidentally, I don't think Tom knew how to shoot the .45. We helped make our men's beds too, all the officers did.

We didn't hear any complaints about what happened or anything from the people down there because we invoked the code name Silverplate, and also one of the reasons the guys could go to Sloppy Joe's with impunity. People left us pretty much alone. Our airplanes were guarded and separate from the others.

While we were down in Cuba, Tom and I almost beat a guy up in the shower one morning. We had been up until three or four o'clock the night before and now it is nine o'clock the next day. Another officer was taking a shower and all of a sudden the water goes cold. He starts bitching his head off and complaining, "This is the trouble with overseas duty no hot water."

Tom and I looked at each other and said, "What the hell is wrong with him" loud enough so the other officer could hear.

"Son, you have never been overseas. What are you talking about? This is not overseas," Tom said.

After several days Paul and I went back. I didn't even get to Sloppy Joes. But we had the ability to clear our plane secretly so the customs officers did not come on board. When people found out that we were running flights down to Cuba, the guys that ran the officer's club took up collections and gave us a lot of money to buy booze and everything of that type. We had by far the best-stocked officer's club in the country.

 *January 6, 1945,* Roosevelt's State of the Union address to Congress urged that the Selective Service Act be amended to draft nurses into the armed forces. The shortage strained the already overworked Army nurses. More than 18,000 additional nurses were needed for the Army and another 2,000 for the Navy.

Nurses served at station and general hospitals throughout the country and served in field hospitals, on beachheads, and hospital ships overseas.

"Security at Wendover"

Dutch ~ Security was always very intense. Maj. William "Bud" Uanna, a great guy, headed security. He had been a security officer for the Manhattan Project in Chicago. Bud stayed in Central Intelligence and disappeared after the war.

Every telephone line into Wendover was tapped. You could not have a private conversation if you wanted to. After the war we learned we had about twelve counter intelligence corps guys walking around and listening to what we were talking about. At the beginning Tibbets gave everyone a two-week pass to go home and put the security people on their tails to see what they talked about. If someone talked too much at a railroad station or airport, they were sent back to our base right away and Tibbets gave them a talking to and figured they learned their lesson.

Tom and I recognized another fellow as a cop. He had a typical cop look. His name was McClenahan, an Intelligence Officer. He was a quote unquote captain in our headquarters operations.

Tom and I played a lot of jokes on people including Henry McClenahan. After the war we found out he was a full colonel. We used to talk to him all the time. I don't believe he was really pumping us for information or anything. But if we slipped in our conversation, I am sure he would have reported it in a minute.

One of the pilots flew his B-29 home to show his parents. When he got back to the base Tibbets had his stuff waiting for him and sent him to the Aleutians, Paul's favorite place to send people. You could talk all you wanted in the Aleutians and nobody would listen to you.

TABLE 9.3 — VAN KIRK'S NAVIGATION RECORD FOR JANUARY 1945

Day	Aircraft	No. Landings	NAV. Time	Night Nav. Time
01/03/1945	C-54B	1	2:05	2:05
01/04/1945	C-54B	1	2:45	1:45
01/07/1945	C-54B	2	9:55	4:00
01/08/1945	C-54B	1	1:30	1:30
01/12/1945	C-54B	2	4:50	1:00
01/13/1945	C-54B	1	3:10	
01/14/1945	C-54B	1	5:00	3:45
01/15/1945	C-54B	1	1:45	
01/19/1945	B-29	1	2:05	
01/21/1945	B-29	1	2:00	
01/22/1945	B-29	2	4:25	
01/23/1945	B-29	2	5:00	4:15
01/25/1945	B-29	1	1:50	
01/26/1945	B-29	1	3:35	
01/28/1945	B-29	1	4:15	

Source: Van Kirk's Individual Flight Records. Record certified correct by Maj. James I. Hopkins, Group Operations Officer.

"Silverplate Bombers"

Dutch ~ If you wanted to see a bunch of ticked off guys, the 504th were it. The group believed they were ready to go overseas and bomb Japan. Instead, they faced more training. When Tibbets gave a speech to keep their mouth shut the guys were even more pissed off. You couldn't tell them what we were going to do. Only Paul Tibbets knew. I guessed and a number of others did too.

We did not have a bomb yet. The scientists were still working on it. It was the biggest poker game, and we were working on an inside straight.

I will never forget this. One of the scientists told us we think you will be okay if you are eleven miles away when the bomb explodes. I looked at him and said, "What do you mean, you think?"

He said, "We do not know." Some of the scientists were betting you have to be fifty miles away. Some are saying it may start a chain reaction in the atmosphere. The consensus was eleven miles, and if we were any closer we were not going to make it anyhow.

One of the first things we did was to strip down the airplane because the regular B-29 would not get high enough or fast enough to get ten miles away. We took about six thousand pounds out and all the guns except our tail guns.

The Silverplate B-29s had only one hook instead of multiple hooks for the bombs.[399] We practiced with dummy bombs, the same exact weight and same shape as *Fat Man*, the plutonium bomb. For all intensive purposes, we had an atomic bomb on board except it did not have the fissionable material.

The B-29s practiced bombing and the sharp turning maneuver to get away from the bomb over targets at Tonopah, Nevada, Salton Sea in southern California, and the abandoned Army Air Corps range near Wendover, Utah.[400]

According to Sweeney, he and Tibbets had been briefed on the aerodynamics of the Japanese Zero at thirty thousand feet, the altitude of the bomb drop for the atomic bombing missions. The Zero would literally run out of air and not have sufficient lift.

 *January 20, 1945*, Harry S. Truman was sworn in as Vice-President of the United States. He had resigned several days earlier as the Senator from Missouri. Truman served in the Senate since 1935 and as a member of key Armed Services Committees: Military Affairs Committee, Senate Special Committee to Investigate the National Defense Program (Seventy-seventh and Seventy-eighth

Congresses), and Military Subcommittee of the Appropriations Committee.[401]

While the nation was absorbed in the war effort, Roosevelt decided to forgo the traditional ceremonies for his fourth term and was sworn in by Chief Justice Harlan Stone on the South Portico of the White House.

"Hospital Ship USS *Tranquillity*"

Above: "The Tranquillaires" Band. Mick McAllister standing third from the right, Dr. Emory on the piano. (Courtesy of Elwood M. and Jean Van Kirk McAllister).

Left: Hospital ship *Tranquillity* (Courtesy of Elwood M. and Jean Van Kirk McAllister)

Mick – *February 1945* Mick McAllister was transferred to the hospital ship USS *Tranquillity*.[402] After the ship was commissioned in the Brooklyn Naval Yard "we went through the canal over to the Pacific.[403] On board the *Tranquillity* the captain told me to get an orchestra together."

"Captain Merritt D. Mullen said, 'I realize you are a medic but you are a musician, and I need a band.'"

McAllister told his captain, "I need five saxes, three trumpets, three trombones, and a rhythm section. He said, 'I will get you the people, the instruments, and the stage.' Within a few months we had a full seventeen-piece orchestra called the Tranquillaires."[404]

The *Tranquillity* docked at Saipan, Tinian, Peleliu, Wake, Guam, Ulithi, and other islands. "We went ashore for a couple of days and did a show" providing morale for the troops and also entertainment for the civilians. "We also picked up the deceased and those needing medical attention and brought them on board," said McAllister.

The *Sacred Cow*, a Douglas VC-54C, transported President Roosevelt to the Yalta Conference. Douglas Aircraft Company constructed the new transport specifically for presidential use. The aircraft featured numerous modifications to the C-54 including an elevator behind the passenger cabin to lift the president in his wheelchair.[405]

The conference laid the foundations for the post war world and democratization of Europe.

 *February 9, 1945*, while the Yalta Conference was underway the 9th Bombardment Group flew its first mission from Tinian to the Japanese held island of Truk.[406]

February 13 – 15, 1945, the nighttime firestorm raid by the RAF on the historic city of Dresden was followed by waves of American bombers.

"Iwo Jima"

James Starnes – *February 19, 1945*, aboard the *Missouri*, "At Iwo Jima it was a whole day of bombardment before the Landing Craft headed for the shores, but the Japs were so caved in. It was one of the most horrible battles."

The order for *Operation Detachment* was given to "Land the Landing Force" sending waves of Marines to the southern beaches of the island of Iwo Jima also known as Sulphur or Sulfur Island. The previous three days of naval and aerial barrage on Iwo filled the air with smoke as strong swells of the Pacific waters crashed on the shores.

William Kelley ~ "Our LCVP (Landing Craft, Vehicle, Personnel) hit the beach at 0930 as part of the third wave of assault craft," said former Marine Corporal William James Kelley, Radio Operator with the 5th Joint Assault Signal Company (JASCO) assigned to the 28th Marine Regiment.[407] "I was carrying a forty-pound radio in front of me along with a forty-pound pack in the rear. My buddy was carrying the matching generator, which also weighed about forty-pounds." Months of training and twenty mile hikes conditioned the Marines for this moment.

"For the first thirty minutes we lay partially submerged in the surf unable to move. We finally inched our way to the first level above the surf approximately two hundred feet from the base of Mount Suribachi. It was impossible to dig a foxhole because of the shifting black sands on the beach, so we used our spare radio equipment to build a protective wall."

"We set up our radio station with one man as the radio operator and one cranking the generator." Kelley reported to headquarters aboard ship the number of casualties, killed-in-action, wounded-in-action, and missing-in-action, suffered by the 28th Marine Regiment. "It was a big thing for headquarters to get an idea of the numbers. We continued to send messages into the night. Flares fired in the air during the night kept the area lit up as bright as day resulting in very little movement. The Japanese made two or three attempts to infiltrate our lines during the night but were thwarted each time."

"Last Rites on Iwo"

William Kelley ~ *February 20, 1945*, "At around 1300, while sending messages to request more supplies especially ammo for mortar shells, a Japanese mortar shell landed in our foxhole between my buddy and me. I was sending the voice message on the radio, and my buddy was operating the generator. I was facing the blast and ended up with shrapnel in my knee, arm, and foot. My buddy was facing away from the blast and his back was riddled with shrapnel. I was being hauled back down to the beach to be evacuated when machine gun fire from Suribachi cut down the two litter bearers and shot me through the neck.[408] I dropped to the sand paralyzed with blood streaming out of my neck. I lay there on the battlefield for more than six hours unable to shout out or talk because my vocal chords were numb. My dog tags had been shot off with the machine gun bullet, and I was taken for dead. The dog tags showed my religious belief. When a priest came by he gave me the Last Rites[409] assuming I was Catholic. A buddy finally came by and saw my eyes blink so he notified the medics.[410] At around 2300 I was finally taken off the island by amphibious tank with two other wounded.[411] We circled in the water to locate a ship that could take us aboard.

February 21, 1945, "At around 0130 or 0200, after three attempts to board various ships, we finally found a hospital ship that had enough room to take us aboard. I was raised up to the deck by a crane banging back and forth against the side of the ship all the way up."

President Roosevelt gasped when he was informed of 4,500 casualties and that the Marines were a long way off from securing Iwo Jima.[412]

Blasts from the battleships and bomber attacks launched off the carriers did not stop the deadly mortar and artillery fire as the Japanese fiercely defended their fortified positions from pillboxes, caves, and an extensive network of tunnels.

 *February 23, 1945,* finally, the Marines wrestled the 546-foot Mount Suribachi from the Japanese after more than fifty nightmare hours of fierce battle on Iwo.[413]

William Kelley ~ In the following days, "On board the hospital ship, the USS *Solace* (AH-5), I was operated on during a kamikaze attack. The lights went out. The ship lunged and I flew off the operating table. I only had a spinal injection to numb the affected area, so I was aware of my surroundings the whole time. While having breakfast one morning after the surgery, another Marine recovering from surgery was eating next to me and all of a sudden his head dropped. I tapped him to ask if he was okay, but he was dead." Eventually, Kelley was taken to Guam aboard the USS *Deuel* then transferred to the USS *Anne Arundel* and transported to the Army hospital at Schofield Barracks in Hawaii for recovery. "All the Navy hospitals were full."

The bloodiest fight yet in the Pacific cost 5,372 Marine casualties and the number was growing as members of the 28th Regiment raised the American flag on the volcano's crest. A larger flag replaced the first one and Joe Rosenthal's renowned photograph on Suribachi appeared in newspapers around the country.[414] Rosenthal, a photographer with the Associated Press, followed the Marines in the Pacific theatre.

TABLE 9.4 — VAN KIRK'S NAVIGATION RECORD FOR FEBRUARY – MARCH 1945

Day	Aircraft	No. Landings	NAV. Time	Night Nav. Time
02/07/1945	C-54B	2	4:50	1:05
02/10/1945	C-54B	1	2:35	
02/11/1945	C-54B	5	9:35	3:50
03/06/1945	C-54B	1	5:00	
03/08/1945	C-54B	1	7:50	
03/09/1945	C-47B	1	:40 (X)	
03/11/1945	C-47B	1	:40 (O)	
03/12/1945	C-54B	2	4:30	
03/13/1945	C-47B	2	6:20	4:45
03/16/1945	C-54B	2	4:15	2:15
03/17/1945	C-54B	2	3:10	
03/19/1945	C-54B	1	4:10	
03/20/1945	C-54B	1	3:10	
03/20/1945	C-54B	1	3:20	
03/21/1945	C-54B	1	4:50	4:45
03/22/1945	C-54B	1	3:20	2:20
03/23/1945	C-54B	1	4:25	
03/25/1945	C-54B	1	4:40	

Source: Van Kirk Individual Flight Records. (X) and (O) were listed under the heading "non-pilot." February and March records certified correct by Maj. James I. Hopkins, Jr., Group Operations Officer. Captain Van Kirk was assigned to Second Air Force, 315th Wing, 509th Composite Group.

 *March 4, 1945*, the *Stars and Stripes* covered the address of the Army ground forces commander Gen. Joseph Stilwell to the Cleveland Ordnance Association. Stilwell predicted that it would be necessary to defeat Japan in China. He said that Americans would face the best Japanese troops in Manchuria where two-thirds of the Imperial Japanese Army were stationed. Stilwell was quoted

as saying the Imperial Army was "as strong as it was when the war started."

March 5, 1945, Marines heated their ration cans from the steam of fissures on the slope of Suribachi.[415]

March 7, 1945, Sgt. Alexander Drabik with the 9th Armored Division was considered the first to cross the Rhine River at Remagen.

General MacArthur announced that six Japanese divisions, almost 100,000 men, were "destroyed" on Luzon and more enemy troops were holed up in the mountains. The Navy Secretary James Forrestal had returned from a tour of the Pacific and disclosed that the Japanese defense of Iwo Jima had been stronger and more skillful then expected.[416]

March 9, 1945, deafening sirens warned of the low-level incendiary attacks targeting Tokyo. Gen. Curtis LeMay sent the B-29s in at low altitudes that night upon the recommendation of Paul Tibbets following less successful bombings at thirty thousand feet.

Two thousand tons of incendiary bombs created a firestorm leaving more than a million homeless and yet Japan did not surrender. The Japanese metropolitan police reported 83,783 people killed and 40,918 wounded.[417] The raid devastated 15.8 sq. miles in the heart of Tokyo. Two nights later Nagoya was bombed and the following week Osaka and Kobe.

Nagoya had a population of about 1.5 million, the largest concentration of aircraft factories, an important port, and the country's greatest electrical and steel producing center.[418]

In addition to the surprising low altitude for the Tokyo mission the 9th BG were ordered that no ammunition was to be loaded in the guns to "avoid mistakenly shooting at other B-29s in the melee over the target."[419]

"Returning to Northumberland"

Dutch ~ We knew we were going overseas. I had an opportunity to go back to Northumberland and took Mary Jane and another couple that lived in the barracks. Mary Jane knew the wife and said, "We are going to take them back with us." If she said so, we were going to do it. We left Wendover in the middle of winter like the end of February beginning of March. We were going across the country, and Route 80 wasn't there yet. I think we drove on Route 6 until Laramie, Wyoming. The car engine was frozen solid. It took all day to get it thawed out. Then we had car trouble all the way across the country. A front came across and moving about the same speed, lots of snow. It was the most miserable trip across the country you ever saw in your life, but I never

got stuck. We dropped the other couple off in Michigan then went on to Pennsylvania to my wife's family house and got stuck in the snow for the first time.

I flew to Cincinnati, Ohio, to meet Paul Tibbets. He was visiting his friends from medical school. I went to the airport and our C-54 with two bunks on it was there, but Tibbets wasn't. I climbed in and fell asleep. The next morning I woke up and looked out. The field was flooded. Someone came to get me out of the plane. The Ohio River had overflowed.

The 509th ground echelon leaving Wendover for Fort Lewis, Washington.

March 14, 1945, British *Lancasters* dropped 22,000-pound bombs on rail targets in northwest Germany.[420]

March 22, 1945, R. B. Marshall, manufacturer of the M69 incendiary bomb used in B-29 fire raids, disclosed that the bomb burns at temperatures of 6,000 plus degrees centigrade for about eight minutes.[421]

March 24, 1945, President Roosevelt declared that the mobilization of "the largest armed force by far" in American history would be completed by the end of June. The Selective Service needed to draft replacements heavily from older and previously occupation deferred groups to cover losses and discharges.[422]

Tokyo Radio reported that almost three million citizens had been evacuated from the capital city. Minister Shigeo Odachi told the Japanese Diet that more people were scheduled to leave Tokyo.[423]

March 25, 1945, the Superfortresses had good results in the tenth bombing of the Nagoya area including the nearby Mitsubishi aircraft factory. The raid used 500-lb. demolition bombs instead of the incendiaries.[424]

Skipper Wayne Neal Gamet stood on the USS *Mount McKinley* and addressed his men of the danger ahead in their objective, Okinawa. Gamet warned them to not underestimate the Japanese, an enemy "who is well trained, well disciplined and utterly indifferent to death."[425]

March 26, 1945, intense fighting on the battlefield of Iwo Jima resulted in substantial casualties on both sides and a lesson for the Americans about the Japanese forces. Former Prime Minister Hideki Tojo was reported to have urged the Japanese Commander Gen. Tadamichi Kuribayashi to perform as the Battle of Attu in 1943 where the Japanese fought to the last man trying to obtain an honorable death by gyokusai or suicide attack.[426] General Kuribayashi had written several times to his wife and children that no Japanese would leave Iwo Jima alive.[427] Only a few hundred were taken prisoner as the fighting ended.

The United States gained control of the island and the airfields, a strategic site for the American B-29 bombers to land and refuel on their missions to the main home islands of Japan.

March 31, 1945, a Bell Aircraft P-63 *Kingcobra* shot down a Japanese Fugo balloon over Reno, Nevada.[428] Japan used the jet stream to send the balloons, about thirty-three feet in diameter and seventy feet top to bottom, filled with incendiaries to the states with the intention of causing panic and fires in the Pacific north-west.[429]

Continued bombing raids of the city of Hamburg targeted the Blohm & Voss shipyard construction of U-boats. Hamburg, the largest port city in Europe and concentration of crude oil refineries, had been the site of numerous attacks by the RAF particularly in July 1943 and later on the Allies. Estimates of 40,000 deaths and numbers exceeding the Nagasaki bombing have been used in accounts of the July firestorms.

Secretary of War Henry L. Stimson announced that as of the first of the month, the total casualties for Army and Navy reached 872,868 making it the costliest war in the nation's history.[430]

April 1, 1945, the USS *Missouri* and other battleships, aircraft carriers, destroyers, and cruisers fought one of the most significant amphibious battles. The island hopping strategy in the Pacific approached Okinawa with the objective of a base of air operations for *Operation Downfall*, the two-part invasion of the main islands of Japan.

Fourteen combat divisions would land on Kyushu after aerial and naval bombardment under the code name *Operation Olympic* scheduled for November 1, 1945. The second assault for *Operation Coronet* on March 1, 1946, would send at least twenty-two more combat divisions.[431] General Groves' autobiography notes that at this time the Japanese military action against the United States in no way lessened after Germany surrendered.

April 4, 1945, Japan claimed Americans were meeting furious resistance on Okinawa and forty-one ships of the American amphibious force had been sunk. The imperial communication contrasted Tokyo Radio's warning to the citizenry that it would be a "matter of short time before the rise or fall of our nation will be decided." A dispatch reported the death of Vice Adm. Noritada Ishi and 13 rear admirals bringing the death toll of Japanese admirals to 108 since May 1944. Retired Adm. Isamu Takeshita quoted by Tokyo Radio declared "the Americans are learning a great lesson now. They are beginning to realize Japan cannot be defeated."[432]

April 5, 1945, Moscow denounced Japan for waging war against its allies the United States and Great Britain and that it would not renew the Soviet-Japanese Neutrality Pact. Coinciding with Moscow's announcement Premier Gen. Kuniaki Koiso and his cabinet resigned according to Tokyo Radio. Koiso, an ardent member of Japan's militarist party, had recently broadcast that Japan was prepared to take an offensive toward the recapture of Iwo Jima, Saipan, and Guadalcanal according to an AP report. Baron Kantaro Suzuki, a retired admiral, was appointed in place of Koiso.[433]

James Starnes - *April 8, 1945*, "The Japs made the decision to go all out on the fleet with kamikazes and attacked the carriers. I was on the bridge when we were attacked. A kamikaze hit the deck level of the stern half in the water and half on the bridge. We tried to protect ourselves and lost no lives. We gave the pilot a regular Navy funeral with the part of his body that was on one half of the aircraft."

April 9, 1945, at an Army Day dinner at the Waldorf-Astoria Hotel Gen. Joseph Stilwell, Army ground forces commander, warned that despite the Japanese deaths in the Pacific the "enemy is stronger than when the war started." Ending the war would be difficult and the experience fighting the Japanese indicated that "a desperate struggle" awaited our forces in the Pacific.[434]

April 11, 1945, on the 9th day offensive the Eighth Air Force hit airfields, marshalling yards, ordnance depots, and oil storage facilities in southern Germany with more than 1,300 heavy bombers and 850 fighters of P-51s and P-47s.[435]

April 12, 1945, Franklin Delano Roosevelt, the thirty-second President of the United States, died at Warm Springs, Georgia. Shortly after 7:00 p.m. Vice-President Harry S. Truman took the oath of office to become the thirty-third president of the United States. After brief remarks to members of the Cabinet, the Secretary of War Stimson remained behind to give a short briefing of the new explosive.[436]

"Death of FDR"

Dutch ~ Roosevelt's death brought a great sense of loss on everybody's part. I was not a Democrat and my father and mother were Republicans. We had lost a great man, a great leader but did not know anything about Truman or what he was going to do.

I voted when I could, but not for Roosevelt. My father would have given me a good licking if I had voted for him. I had to vote Republican. The first time Roosevelt ran for president a staunch Democrat neighbor was talking about the election and how he had voted. My dad said, "I have got to go and cancel those damn votes." I don't know if he knew why he was a Republican, but he was. After I got out of the service, I did vote for Truman and am proud to say so.

Eisenhower, Patton, and Omar Bradley had just seen their first Nazi death camp at Ohrdruf when they heard the news of the president's death.[437] In McCullough's *Truman* the generals spent the evening ruminating about their opinions of Truman's qualifications or lack of them.

The cost of victory was rising steadily in the Pacific.

Several waves of B-29s escorted by hundreds of Mustangs attacked Japan at Koriyama, the Musashino aircraft plant in the outskirts of Tokyo, and the port of Shizuoka.[438]

Boeing disclosed that its Seattle and Wichita plants built their last B-17.[439]

"President Harry S. Truman"

April 16, 1945, President Truman addressed Congress for the first time and spoke of the heavy price for the defense of freedom. He called upon all Americans to help him and be united in the ideals of his predecessor and support of the military. "Our debt to the heroic men and women in the service of our country can never be repaid. They have earned our undying gratitude . . . Every day peace is delayed costs a terrible toll."[440] In an address broadcast to members of the armed forces Truman empathized with the troops. "I know the strain, the mud, the misery, the utter weariness of the soldier in the field, I know, too, his courage, his stamina and his faith in his comrades, his country and himself. We are depending upon each and every one of you."

The loss of American lives had reached more than 196,000. American casualties of all categories killed, wounded, MIA, and POW reached close to 900,000.[441]

MOVIETONE NEWS

April 17 - 18, 1945, the *Stars and Stripes* reported on the action of the Superforts strike against airfields and installations at Kyushu.

More than 1,000 B-17s and B-24s flew deep into southern Germany and Czechoslovakia escorted by Mustangs and Thunderbolts destroying 200 grounded enemy aircraft.[442]

April 26 – 27, 1945, the 97th BG was recalled at the beginning of their bomb run over the Fortezza railroad yards in Bolzano, Italy, because the air war had ended.[443]

A Senate ban on sending eighteen-year old draftees into combat without at least six months of training was approved by the House Military Affairs Committee.[444]

April 28, 1945, Mussolini was executed for high treason after his capture the day before by Italian Communist partisans near the Swiss border.

April 30, 1945, Hitler committed suicide in his Führerbunker at the Reich Chancellery in Berlin, Germany. Adm. Karl Dönitz made a nationwide radio address on Hitler's "hero's death" and announced that the war would continue to save Germany from the advancing Bolshevik enemy.

TABLE 9.5 — VAN KIRK'S NAVIGATION RECORD FOR APRIL 1945

Day	Aircraft	No. Landings	NAV. Time	Night Nav. Time
04/04/1945	C-54B	2	10:40	1:30
04/06/1945	C-54B	3	12:15	2:00
04/07/1945	C-54B	1	:35	
04/08/1945	C-54B	1	2:20	
04/10/1945	B-29	1	4:15	
04/16/1945	C-54B	1	4:00	
04/17/1945	C-54B	1	3:10	
04/18/1945	C-54B	2	2:25	
04/20/1945	C-54B	2	7:15	
04/21/1945	C-54B	1	5:05	
04/24/1945	C-47B	1	4:50	
04/25/1945	C-47B	1	3:45	
04/26/1945	C-47B	1	4:45	

Source: Van Kirk's Individual Flight Records certified correct by Maj. James I. Hopkins, Jr., Operations Officer.

Chapter Nine — Endnotes

386 Copy of Restricted Orders, which included relieving Van Kirk from duty at Selman Field for assignment at Wendover, Utah, to *Silver Plate*. Van Kirk personal papers.

387 Susan Grace interview with Van Kirk for "Dropping the Bomb," *The Free Lance-Star*, May 26, 1992. The practices were a change from the "follow the leader" missions in Europe.

388 Leslie R. Groves, *Now It Can Be Told* The Story of the Manhattan Project, (New York, NY: Harper and Brothers Publishers, 1962), 257.

389 A felon is a fingertip abscess deep in the palm side of the finger.

390 At Wendover Van Kirk and Ferebee also flew with Lewis in place of his regular bombardier and navigator. The Lewis crew returned the best flying records with the main competition from Sweeney and Eatherly. Gordon Thomas and Max Morgan Witts, *Enola Gay*, (New York, NY: Stein and Day, 1977), 67.

391 Headquarters Wendover Field Office of the Commanding Officer, signed by Captain Clayton A. Pearson, AC Adjutant, Special Order No. 285, October 11, 1944. Van Kirk personal papers.

392 Mary H. Gosnell, WASP, 44-6, Texas Woman's University, WASP Archives.

393 Sullivan, *The Ultimate Weapon*, 152.

394 "Historic Earthquakes," United States Geological Surveys Earthquake Hazards Program, http://earthquake.usgs.gov/ [accessed March 15, 2011].

395 Headquarters Wendover Field Office of the Commanding Officer, signed by Capt. Clayton Pearson, Special Order No. 354, December 19, 1944. Van Kirk personal papers.

396 The women pilots were not entitled to veterans' benefits at the time. Finally, in 1977 Congress passed legislation signed by President Jimmy Carter declaring the WASP active military service during the war.

397 The training also entailed high altitude visual bombing and operating singly rather than formation flying to be capable of independent navigation. Groves, *Now It Can Be Told*, 264.

398 The popular Sloppy Joe's Bar located in the central corner of Zulueta and Animas Streets in Havana opened in the 1930s and closed in 1959 after the revolution. The long mahogany liquor cabinet and celebrity patrons including Ernest Hemingway, John Wayne, Spencer Tracy, and Clark Gable added to its history. "Sloppy Joe's Bar History," http://www.sloppyjoes.org [accessed July 3, 2010].

399 A massive shackle held the bomb and a sway brace prevented horizontal or vertical movement. Warren Thompson, "509th Bomb Group," *Wings of Fame*. The total cost for a Silverplate B-29 was $814,700, which included $32,700 for the modifications of the bomber to the Silverplate configuration. Richard H. Campbell, *The Silverplate Bombers* A History and Registry of the Enola Gay and Other B-29s Configured to Carry Atomic Bombs, (Jefferson, NC: McFarland & Co. Inc., 2005), 107.

400 Sweeney described problems that occurred dropping the pumpkin bombs. The *Project Alberta* scientists studying the results made adjustments in the drop protocol and fin design. Maj. Gen. Charles W. Sweeney, U.S.A.F. (Ret.) with James A. Antonucci and Marion K. Antonucci, *War's End* An Eyewitness Account of America's Last Atomic Mission, (New York, NY: Avon Books, 1997), 93 – 96.

401 Truman served in World War I as a battery commander during the Meuse-Argonne Offensive. His regiment was called into service as the 129th Field Artillery Regiment on September 5, 1917. After the war Truman rose to the rank of colonel in the Reserves. Harry S. Truman Library, Military Personnel File, Record Group 407.

402 "The artist who painted the names on the ships at the Brooklyn Naval Yard painted the Tranquillity with one 'L.' We were being commissioned early January '45 so Captains Mullen and Hogan (medical) allowed the name to remain. 'No time to change. This is wartime; let's get going,' Mullen said. So the one 'L' stuck till the ship was decommissioned," said McAllister.

403 McAllister remained on the *Tranquillity* from February until November 1945.

404 The Tranquillaires flyer described Mick McAllister as "the man McAllister plays sax from the south and clarinet from the ankles up. The swaying maestro first led the 'Pinetones,' a high school orchestra. He graduated to Ivan Faux orchestra in his home state Pennsylvania. Then came the Navy stationed in Chicago. Alvino Rey brought him into the fold of his Navy orchestra."

405 Douglas VC-54C *Sacred Cow*, National Museum of the United States Air Force, http://www.nationalmuseum.af.mil/index.asp [accessed July 1, 2010].

406 The group described their first two missions to Truk and Iwo as "milk runs." Lawrence G. Smith, *History of the 9th Bombardment Group (VH)*, (Princeton, NJ: The 9th Bomb Group Assoc., 1995), 19.

407 William Kelley telephone interview with author, July 19 and October 21, 2010. Kelley, a high school classmate of Van Kirk lived on King Street in Northumberland, PA. Class president Kelley attended the 72nd reunion of the Northumberland class of 1938 in 2010. He said the convoy to Iwo took forty-five days from Pearl. "The convoy was slow, but Tokyo Rose always knew where we were."

408 Kelley estimated they were about forty or fifty feet from the beach.

409 In the Last Rites or Extreme Unction, one of the seven sacraments of the Catholic faith, a priest anointed a dying person with oil. The ritual is known today as Anointing of the Sick and performed to bring physical and spiritual strength during an illness.

410 "My buddy wanted my watch. It was the only one working. While he was taking the watch he saw my eyes blinking," said Kelley.

411 DUKW, an amphibious tank pronounced 'duck,' designed by General Motors transported troops and supplies over land and water.

412 Roosevelt had just returned from the Yalta Conference. Dr. Robert S. Burrell, *The Ghosts of Iwo Jima*, (Williams-Ford Texas A & M University Military History Series, 2006), 80.

413 "Mt. Suribachi, on Southern Tip of Iwo Isle Is Captured By Hard Fighting Marines," *Schenectady Gazette*, February 23, 1945.

414 Another AP Wire photo by Joe Rosenthal appeared in the *Niagara Falls Gazette* on March 1, 1945, under the headline: "Falls Marine Prays During Lull in Iwo Battle." Edmund Fadel of Niagara Falls knelt and prayed the rosary surrounded by the carnage at Iwo Jima with two buddies, Privates Walter Sokowski and Nicholas Zingaro, both from Syracuse, NY.

415 "It's an Ill Volcano That Belches No Good," *Stars and Stripes* London Edition, March 5, 1945.

416 "6 Jap Divisions Destroyed on Luzon, Remainder in Peril," *Stars and Stripes* London

Edition, March 7, 1945.

417 It took the Japanese twenty-five days to remove the corpses. Carl Berger, *B29 the Superfortress*, (New York, NY: Ballantine Books, 1970), 131.

418 "New Fire Bomb Used First Time," *Stars and Stripes* London Edition, March 12, 1945.

419 Smith, *History of the 9th Bombardment Group (VH)*, 21.

420 "RAF Uses 10-Tonner, War's Biggest Bomb," *Stars and Stripes* London Edition, March 15, 1945.

421 The manufacturer disclosed with the Army's approval. "New Fire Bomb Burns Hot Enough to Cut Steel," *Stars and Stripes* London Edition, March 22, 1945.

422 "Draft Drops to 93,000 A Month After June 30," *Stars and Stripes*, March 24, 1945.

423 Tokyo's pre-war population was around seven million. "Japs Admit Quitting Tokyo," *Stars and Stripes*, March 24, 1945.

424 "250 Deliver 'Worst Blow;' Shell Ryukyus," *Stars and Stripes,* March 26, 1945.

425 Radioman 1st Class Richard E. Berrien received his copy of the *First Cruise of the "Mighty Mac"* USS *Mount McKinley 1944 – 1945* on August 17, 1945, the day he left the ship. The *First Cruise* gave an account of the action at Kerama Retto, a group of islands near Okinawa, and the assault in April and May as Japan's suicide planes dived into the USS *Pinkney, Terror* and *St. George*. Copy of Gamet speech, Berrien personal papers.

426 Kumiko Kakehashi, *So Sad To Fall In Battle*: An Account of War Based On General Tadamichi Kuribayashi's Letters from Iwo Jima, (New York: Presidio Press, 2007), 18. Tojo had been forced to resign after the loss of Saipan.

427 Richard F. Newcomb, "20 Years Ago Marines Landed on Iwo Jima," *Niagara Falls Gazette*, February 14, 1965.

428 Fredriksen, *The U.S. Air Force A Chronology*, 149.

429 Japanese school children helped layer the paraffined rice paper for the balloon's hide. Several thousand balloons were launched, but most fell in the Pacific or were shot down by interceptors at Hawaii and the Aleutians. The original purpose of the Fugo balloon was in retaliation for the Doolittle raid. Bob Considine, "Jap Balloon Barrage Was Sidetracked," *Evening Recorder* (Amsterdam, NY), May 15, 1965.

430 "War Dead Already Exceed Civil War's," *Stars and Stripes*, March 31, 1945.

431 James Martin Davis, *Top Secret* The Story of the Invasion of Japan, (Omaha: NE, Ranger Publications, 1986), 1. *Operation Downfall* planned to be strictly American units with the exception of part of the British Pacific Fleet.

432 "Japan Reports Resistance On Okinawa," *Schenectady Gazette*, April 3, 1945. Takeshita, the last surviving Japanese who signed the treaty of Portsmouth that ended the Russo-Japanese war in 1905, taught judo to President Theodore Roosevelt. "Jap Admiral, 80, Dies," *Binghamton Press*, July 7, 1949.

433 Kuniakai Koiso replaced Premier Hideki Tojo in July 1944. "Crisis Makes Tokyo Form New Cabinet," *Stars and Stripes* London Edition, April 6, 1945.

434 "Stilwell Claims Japs Stronger," *Stars and Stripes* London Edition, April 9, 1945.

435 "1,300 8th Heavies Again Blast Reich as Nazis Hide," *Stars and Stripes* London Edition, April 12, 1945. The 56th Thunderbolt Group and 339th Mustang Group chalked up records of destruction.

436 Henry Stimson's letter to Truman on July 24, 1942, urged a meeting as soon as possible "on a highly secret matter" that he had mentioned briefly after Truman took office.

Confidential file Truman papers, Harry S. Truman Library.

437 Dietz's father John Victor Simon, a scout with the 353rd HQ Infantry Regiment 89th Division, participated in the discovery/liberation of Ohrdruf, a sub camp of Buchenwald.

438 "B-29s Hit Japan In Triple Wave," *Stars and Stripes*, April 13, 1945.

439 "B29s To Equal B17s If Pacific Needs Them," *Stars and Stripes*, April 12, 1945.

440 Truman's message was broadcast to members of the United States armed forces around the world. He knew their sacrifice. "I know the strain, the mud, the misery, the utter weariness of the soldier in the field." "Truman Assures Services Nation 'Will Not Falter,'" *Stars and Stripes*, April 19, 1945.

441 Newspapers disclosed more than six thousand casualties and the average in the Pacific of nine hundred per day the previous week. David McCullough, *Truman*, (New York, NY: Simon and Schuster, 1992), 354.

442 "8th Fighters Add 200 To Bag of Nazi Planes," *Stars and Stripes*, April 18, 1945.

443 The radio message advised the Group that the air war was over and to return with their bombs. Gulley et. al., *The Hour Has Come*, 234.

444 "House Unit Agrees to 18-Year-Old Ban" (ANS), *Stars and Stripes* London Edition, April 28, 1945.

Chapter Ten

Tinian Preparing for *Operation Centerboard*

"The Special 509th"

May 2, 1945, the battle for Berlin ended.

May 6, 1945, the USS *Cape Victory* sailed from Seattle for the three-week voyage to Tinian with 1,200 men from the 509th Composite Group. The 58th Bombardment Wing was already on Tinian's West Field area and the 313th on the North Field.

The runways on Tinian were considered the longest operational runways in the world at that time and necessary for the heavy bomb loads and fuel being carried on the B-29 missions to Japan.

Howard "Ted" Zobrist, a gunner on the *Umbriago* with the 304th Squadron 9th Bombardment Group of the 313th Wing, and his buddies learned that the 509th outfit was "up to something special, but no one knew what." The 9th BG was a neighbor to the 509th on Tinian.[445]

The 509th in addition to the 509th HQ and 393rd Bombardment Squadron now contained the 320th Troop Carrier Squadron, 390th Air Service Group, 603rd Air Engineering Squadron, 1027th Air Matériel Squadron, 1st Ordnance Squadron, 1395th Military Police, and *Project Alberta* under Captain Parsons. The 509th reported directly to the Twentieth Air Force. The Washington representatives were Brigadier Gen. Thomas Farrell, the deputy to General Groves, and Rear Adm. William Purnell.

 May 7, 1945, Germany surrendered.
May 8, 1945, VE Day (Victory in Europe) was simultaneously proclaimed by the leaders of the Big Three.

Dutch ~ Everybody was elated, but we didn't have any particular celebration because the war wasn't over for us.

May 9, 1945, the Interim Committee met informally for the first time in the Secretary of War's office. The members were Henry Stimson, chairman; George L. Harrison, alternate chairman; Hon. Ralph A. Bard, Dr. Vannevar Bush; Hon. James F. Byrnes; Hon. William L. Clayton; Dr. Carl T. Compton; and Dr. James B. Conant (not present). Harvey Bundy was present by invitation. Stimson explained the committee's initial responsibility to advise the President on atomic weapons, the background of the Manhattan Project, the Quebec Conference Agreement,[446] the Combined Policy Committee, and the Combined Development Trust.[447]

Ca. *May 10, 1945,* a smiling young flier appeared before Dorothy McKibbin. For the only time in her career at Los Alamos, New Mexico, McKibbin issued a pass without authorization. Col. Paul W. Tibbets had arrived late for a meeting of the Target Committee in J. Robert Oppenheimer's office.[448]

Dutch ~ In Europe and North Africa Tibbets flew straight ahead after dropping the bombs. How should he get away from an explosive weapon with the force of 20,000 tons of TNT? Flying straight ahead would put the aircraft over the top of the explosion and become part of the destruction. Oppenheimer's advice was to turn 159 degrees to gain the greatest distance in the shortest length of time from the point of the explosion.[449]

"On Tinian"

Dutch ~ Ferebee was already over on Tinian. I am not sure how he got there. He might have gone with Bob Lewis.[450] Everyone had left Wendover, but Tibbets and me. Tibbets was trying to drag his feet until my son was born, but finally we had to leave. He and I were late getting to Tinian.

We ran into Dick Wiley at Hickam Field in Hawaii. He was flying transports at the time and wanted to know what we were doing. Tom said, "We are coming over to win the war." We all laughed about that big joke.

After the war Dick wrote to us "That is the first damn time you guys told me the truth."

At Wendover we modified the B-29s ourselves and put in snap open bomb bay doors. Someone Tibbets knew offered him fuel-injected engines. I think they were made for B-32s. We took out guns and had put a patch where a turret was taken out. One of the pilots flying over San Francisco had a patch give way. The B-29 was the first pressurized airplane and when the patch did not hold the conditions were disastrous. One guy got a fractured skull. Another modification to the B-29s was the reversible pitch electric props, so you could actually back our planes up. Tibbets decided he wanted fifteen new airplanes built to our specifications. We were supposed to get anything we wanted by invoking the code name Silverplate.

We were given six new C-54 airplanes to transport the scientists. The Manhattan Project did not want the scientists flying in commercial airplanes. They might be recognized. Tibbets put in the request for the new planes and received a no. Tibbets sent the request again. This time he uses the Silverplate code, and again the answer is no. An officious brigadier general in the Pentagon was doing this by the way. Gen. Hap Arnold gets the word we wanted the new B-29s. The story goes that Arnold at a staff meeting said, "Good morning, major" to the general who had turned down our request. He got the message.

We had about 400 B-29s on Tinian and the biggest traffic jam in the air. There were B-29s on Saipan and Guam too, about 1,200 total with Tinian.

Tibbets shopped for his new B-29 at the Glenn L. Martin aircraft plant near Fort Crook in Omaha, Nebraska, to replace the well-used training Superfortresses from Wendover. The foreman pointed to No. 82. It was not built on Monday.[451]

 *May 12, 1945*, a joint press conference by Lt. Gen. James Doolittle and Maj. Gen. Orvil Anderson predicted more than 2,000 Superforts at a time would conduct bomb raids on Japan if she continued to fight. Deployment to the Pacific of Eighth Air Force personnel had already begun.[452]

May 22 – 23, 1945, during the night thirty Superforts hit the Shimonoseki Strait. One B-29 *Long Winded* No. 42-63509 was lost after severe flak damage. The crew bailed out over heavy seas. A submarine laying mines picked up three of the crewmembers.[453]

Dutch ~ The 509th Group did not lose any aircraft while on Tinian.

TABLE 10.1 — VAN KIRK'S NAVIGATION RECORD FOR MAY 1945

Day	Aircraft	No. Landings	NAV. Time	Night Nav. Time
05/01/1945	B-29	1	4:25	
05/02/1945	B-29	1	4:45	
05/04/1945	B-29	1	3:40	
05/07/1945	B-29	1	2:35	
05/08/1945	B-29	1	4:20	
05/11/1945	B-29	1	15:10	4:45
05/14/1945	B-29	1	5:25	
05/15/1945	C-54	3	5:50	
05/17/1945	C-54	2	8:05	
05/20/1945	B-29	1	1:30	
05/21/1945	C-54	2	5:25	
05/23/1945	B-29	1	4:00	
05/24/1945	B-29	1	2:45	
05/26/1945	B-29	1	13:50	
05/27/1945	B-29	1	2:20	

Source: Van Kirk's Individual Flight Records certified correct by 2nd Lt. Carl G. Ackerman, Asst. Operations Officer.

Few palm trees and coral remained on the tropical island of Tinian scorched by the bombardment from the Fifth Fleet in July 1944. Tinian was shaped like Manhattan, New York, with Broadway as the main thoroughfare and Riverside Drive paralleling the western shoreline. The airfield at Ninetieth Street east of Eighth Avenue had four paved runways, each about 8,500 feet long.[454] The Seabees of the Sixth Naval Construction Brigade and Army engineers built the runway extensions of the North Field that ran east to west across the northern tip of the island and supporting taxiways and hardstands.[455]

"Island Antics"

Dutch ~ We lived around 8th Avenue and West 125th Street, upper Manhattan (the "Columbia University" District). I barracked with General

Farrell, Tibbets, and Ferebee. Japanese troops hid in the caves and hills of Tinian and sniped at passing jeeps. In their spare time guys liked to go hunting for renegade troops and on occasion caught some of them to much fanfare.

Tibbets was the ringleader when we took the clothes off the beach from some lieutenants and nurses who had decided to swim in the nude. They walked back without their clothes and had to jump in the bushes every time a car came by. Occasionally on the ground Tibbets would cut loose on things like that, but when you got into an airplane with Paul Tibbets you were all business. You better be anyhow.

When flying with Tibbets I was always the lead navigator and never wanted to make a mistake. If you did when you got back, you would never hear the end of it. I never had it happen to me but have been on the giving end to other navigators who fouled up so I never fooled around either. Ferebee and I were professional when we were in an airplane.[456]

"Tooey Spaatz"

Dutch ~ Spaatz came over to the Pacific often, and debriefed us. He was a Pennsylvania Dutchmen born near Reading, Pennsylvania, and a gentleman, a nice guy, and smoked cigarettes like a fiend. I never met a general or officer who was an SOB. They were all kind to the lower ranks, and I was a lower rank.

May 18, 1945, the USAAF received Silverplate bomber B-29-45-MO-44-86292.

The *Missouri* broke the flag of Adm. William "Bull" Halsey, Jr., Commander of the Third Fleet, and again conducted shore bombardment against the Japanese positions on Okinawa. The USS *Missouri History* credits the battleship with shooting down five enemy airplanes, assisting with six others, and one probable, and shore bombardment destruction of several gun positions and other structures.

May 19, 1945, the Interim Committee at their second meeting agreed to establish a scientific panel to advise them. Doctors A. H. Compton, Ernest O. Lawrence, J. R. Oppenheimer, and Enrico Fermi were chosen. Consideration was given to organizing a military panel drawn from high levels of the Army and Navy and solicitation of the views of representatives from industries directly concerned with the project.[457] George Harrison reported that the British were considering establishing a similar committee.

The committee discussed publicity concerning the initial test of the "weapon." William Laurence under contract with the Manhattan District would be directed to prepare drafts of public statements to be made after the bomb was used.

May 24, 1945, General LeMay ordered another raid on Tokyo. Three-quarters of the bombs dropped from 562 B-29s were incendiaries.

May 28, 1945, "DOWNFALL," the strategic plan for operations in the Japanese archipelago to force the unconditional surrender of Japan, contained assumptions of the situation in the Pacific. The first point stated that "the Japanese will continue the war to the utmost extent of their capabilities and will prepare to defend the main islands of JAPAN with every means available to them. That operations in this area will be opposed not only by the available organized military forces of the Empire, but also by a fanatically hostile population."[458]

May 31, 1945, the scientists and several military officials including Generals Marshall and Groves met with the Interim Committee.[459]

June 1, 1945, industry representatives, George H. Bucher, President of Westinghouse; Walter S. Carpenter, President of DuPont; James Rafferty, Vice-President of Union Carbide; James White, President of Tennessee Eastman, appeared at the fifth Interim Committee meeting, and were solicited for their opinions on issues related to international cooperation and the length of time other countries would need to catch up to the United States in atomic energy development.

Carpenter made several recommendations including stockpiling bombs and securing supplies of uranium.

"Going to Church"

Dutch ~ Capt. Bill Downey, the chaplain, never pressured you. He was a good man and a perfect chaplain for 509th. Downey, Ferebee, and I were about the same age. Every once and a while he remarked to us, "I would like to see you guys in church one day."

So, we all decided one morning to attend church. Tibbets, Ferebee, Beahan, and myself sat in the chapel in the front row. Bill was a Lutheran pastor, a Protestant chaplain. He walked through the door and saw all of us sitting there and just stopped. Bill would take a drink once in a while. He was just one of the boys.

June 1, 1945, Undersecretary of War Robert Patterson issued a warning to the public not to approach strange objects after a long-range Japanese balloon containing explosives killed a mother and her five children on a picnic in the woods near Lakeview, Oregon. Hundreds of bomb carrying "Fugo" balloons had reached the United States. Any further damage or casualties would be censored in an effort to not aid the enemy in making improvements or encourage continued use of the balloons.[460]

"Blanchard and Baseball"

Dutch ~ Butch Blanchard was with us in the Pacific. He had been LeMay's Chief of Staff. We formed baseball teams and played with Blanchard. Tom Ferebee was an athlete and had letters in track, basketball, and football from college. Tom trained for a position with the Boston Red Sox as a catcher. He was that good. If you looked at his hands every finger had been broken.

Later on when we were in California, a guy wanted to make a cast of all our hands. He looked at Tom's hands and asked him, "What the hell did you do? Did you get them caught in a meat grinder?"

Tom was the catcher for our team. I played third base. Tom would throw the ball down to third. I was not going to get in front of it. He would yell "get in front of that ball Dutch god damn it!" Blanchard was on third base. It was a close play at the plate. Butch came barreling in and knocked Tom ass over teacups. Butch was a colonel at the time and Tom a major. Tom did not say anything.

Butch got up and said, "I guess you won't block the plate on me again."

Many ball games later the same thing happened. Butch was on third base again and Tom catching. This is going to be murder. Anyhow there is an infield play, the second baseman gets the ball, and pegs it home to Tom. He braces himself and tags Blanchard right smack on the nose. Butch came up all bloody.

Tom tells Blanchard, "I guess you won't try and bowl me over again." Tom took his baseball very seriously.

We swam a lot in the ocean. I found out later on that between Tinian and Saipan, that little pass in there, has the most sharks per cubic foot in the world. We went hiking and sightseeing. I must have slept a lot.

June 3, 1945, carrier pilots aboard Adm. John S. McCain's flagship off the Ryukyu Islands reported that expert Japanese pilots flying new airplanes outperformed their *Corsairs*.[461]

June 14, 1945, B-29 aircraft No. 44-86292, flown by Capt. Robert Lewis and crew B-9, stopped at Wendover before continuing its eventual journey to Tinian.[462]

Strategic bombing had not ended the war with Japan and a full-scale invasion was going to be necessary. In Washington the Joint Chiefs of Staff, Stimson, and Truman worked on *Operation Downfall*, the overall plan for the invasion of Japan. The plan for the two part operation was to begin with 800,000 troops for *Operation Olympic* at the end of October on the southern island of Kyushu to take the airbases and 1,000,000 plus men for *Operation Coronet* on the main island of Honshu in the spring of 1946.[463]

Prime Minister Suzuki explained at a press conference that the Supreme War Council composed of military men now functioned as the cabinet. During the preceding week the Diet approved a resolution making any cabinet decree law. Newspapers across the states reported Suzuki's remarks and Radio Tokyo's spin on the Japanese defeat at Okinawa as an embarrassment to the Americans because of the rejection of an offer to accept surrender from the commander Lt. Gen. Simon Bolivar Buckner.[464] Buckner was killed on the eighteenth by enemy artillery fire several days before Okinawa was finally taken.

June 18, 1945, 1530 hours, General Marshall presented the invasion plans at a Joint Chiefs meeting at the White House. Present at the meeting were the President, Fleet Adm. William Leahy, Gen. George Marshall, Fleet Adm. Ernest King, Lt. Gen. Ira Eaker (representing General Arnold), Secretary of War Stimson, Secretary of the Navy Forrestal, Assistant Secretary of War McCloy, and Brig. Gen. A. J. McFarland.

Marshall brought to the discussion the casualties from the Leyte, Luzon, Iwo Jima, and Okinawa campaign, the ratios of American to Japanese, and the casualties from the first thirty days of the Normandy invasion. The ratios demonstrated that as the war progressed the Japanese were more effective against the Americans. "It is a grim fact that there is not an easy, bloodless way to victory in war and it is the thankless task of the leaders to maintain their firm outward front which holds the resolution of their subordinates," Marshall told Truman. Admiral Leahy pointed out that the "troops on Okinawa had lost thirty-five percent in casualties…from the similarity of the fighting to be expected that this would give a good estimate of the casualties to be expected." Marshall added that the total assault troops for the Kyushu campaign were 766,700. Eaker had received a cable from General Arnold that a blockade of Honshu was dependent upon controlling airfields on Kyushu and also emphasized that delay only favored the enemy.[465]

The President concluded the meeting with his hope that "there was a possibility of preventing an Okinawa from one end of Japan to the other."

Dutch ~ Hospitals were being built on Tinian and Saipan. I wondered why. The hospitals were for the invasion casualties.

"No Acceptable Alternative"

June 21, 1945, a motion passed during the Interim Committee meeting unanimously favoring revocation of Clause Two of the Quebec Agreement providing that the signatories not use the weapon against a third country except by mutual consent.

Harrison presented a report from some scientists in Chicago through Dr. A. H. Compton that the weapon not be used in the war, only a test be conducted, and that other countries be advised of the test. The report was given to the scientific panel.

The scientific panel stated that they saw no acceptable alternative to direct military use. The Interim Committee reaffirmed their position taken at two other meetings that the weapon be used against Japan at the earliest opportunity, without warning, and on a dual target, a military installation or war plant surrounded by or adjacent to homes or other buildings most susceptible to damage.

Lengthy discussions ensued about the ramifications of what the President might say at the "Big Three" Conference about the atomic weapon and advising the Russians.

 *June 22 - 23, 1945,* the eighty-three day mammoth land-air-sea battle, codename *Iceberg,* was fought on the Ryukyu Islands of Okinawa, and resulted in the bloodiest battle of the Pacific War. Casualties (killed, wounded, missing, and non-battle casualties) of the Tenth Army for all units exceeded 65,000 from June 1 – June 30, 1945.[466] More than 107,000 Japanese and conscripts from the island, and about 100,000 natives of Okinawa perished.[467] The bloody battle for Okinawa ended as the Commanding Gen. Mitsuru Ushijima and Chief of Staff General Isamu Cho commit ritual suicide.

Representatives of the Republic of China, the United Kingdom, the USSR, and the United States, signed a letter on behalf of all the delegates to the United Nations Conference thanking the members of the International Secretariat for their work in creating the United Nations Charter.[468]

"Tom Ferebee's Namesake"

Dutch ~ *June 25, 1945*, I did not know my wife had gone to the hospital. At Tinian I started to get letters from Mary Jane. The baby did this, and the baby did that. But I did not know if I had a son or a daughter. It was just the baby, the baby. Mary Jane thought the Red Cross would be the fastest way to let me know. Well I still have not been notified from the Red Cross that I had a son. We had already picked out the name Tom for Tom Ferebee.

Mary Jane and Tom Van Kirk in front of what is now the Priestley-Forsyth Memorial Library in Northumberland. Dutch ~ My father lived in this building in a small apartment and took care of the furnace as part of the rent.

June 26, 1945, Truman flew to San Francisco for the official signing of the United Nations Charter.

June 27, 1945, Lewis and his crew left Wendover in B-29 No. 44-86292 with whiskey in the bomb bay that Jake Beser brought from Cuba arriving at Tinian on July 2nd.[469] The call sign for Victor 12 changed to Victor 82.[470]

Dutch ~ We decided the earlier B-29s we modified were not good enough and ordered new ones with the modifications from the Martin plant.

TABLE 10.2 — VAN KIRK'S NAVIGATION RECORD FOR
JUNE – JULY 1945

Day	Aircraft	No. Landings	NAV. Time	Night Nav. Time
06/10/1945	C-54	3	12:15	5:30
06/17/1945	C-54	1	3:30	
06/19/1945	C-54	2	8:30	
06/25/1945*	C-54		(no entry)	

*Entry written in pencil and dated after "Closed out – 24 June 1945 – Change of Station."

Record certified correct by 2nd Lt. Francis E. Griffin, Asst. Operations Officer. The remainder of the month Captain Van Kirk had no flying time at his assignment to the 20th Air Force, 21st Command, 313th Wing, 509th Group for the remainder of June certified by Capt. George W. Marquardt, Asst. Operations Officer.

Day	Aircraft	No. Landings	NAV. Time	Night Nav. Time
07/09/1945	B-29	1	8:40	
07/24/1945	B-29	1	3:00	
07/25/1945	B-29	2	6:45	
07/29/1945	B-29	1	13:20	3:00
07/31/1945	B-29	1	7:05	3:00

Source: Van Kirk's Individual Flight Records. Captain Marquardt certified the July flights.

July 1945, throughout the month the Twentieth Air Force's Superfortresses dropped incendiary bombs on Japan's principal industrial cities.

July 2, 1945, President Truman urged the Senate to ratify the United Nations Charter.

James Starnes ~ *July 8, 1945*, the Third Fleet set course to approach the Japanese main islands targeting Tokyo (Honshu) July 10th and several days later on Hokkaido.[471] Lt. Commander James L. Starnes, Jr., was responsible for navigating the Third Fleet. "Captain Murray asked, 'Are we there yet

Jimmy?' Finally we headed towards the shore through obstacles. The captain was anxious and asked the question again. I felt like I could beat the world. We turned parallel to the shore with no resistance."

July 9, 1945, Van Kirk navigated an 8:40 hour mission in a B-29.[472]

 *July 16, 1945*, Truman had left the states ten days earlier crossing the Atlantic on the *Augusta* passing tens of thousands of troops leaving the European Theatre bound for service against Japan.

President Truman, Soviet Premier Joseph Stalin, Prime Minister Winston Churchill, and Clement Attlee met at the Cecilienhof Palace in Potsdam, Germany, to discuss postwar matters and the continuing war with Japan. On July 26 the conference concluded with the proclamation of the Potsdam Declaration by the United States, Great Britain, and China that Japan must agree to unconditional surrender or face "prompt and utter destruction."

"The Atomic Age"

The location for the test site was in a desert region in the northwest corner of the Alamogordo bombing range in New Mexico two hundred ten miles south of Los Alamos.[473] The test had been delayed several days due to weather. A plutonium bomb was successfully detonated from the top of a 110-foot tower at Point Zero.[474] Doctor Pepkowitz, his wife, and other scientists watched from another mesa.[475] At 5:30 a.m. the first atomic bomb exploded.[476]

Dutch ~ Before the Alamogordo test, I had the feeling that we didn't have a bomb to drop and were spinning our wheels. There were very few of us that knew about the test and that it had been conducted. Two days later we found out about the Trinity test; now we had a purpose. Among Tibbets' group it was common knowledge about what happened.

To my knowledge there was not a great amount of secrecy after the test. Captain Parsons flew back to New Mexico to witness the detonation. Parson's report to Groves noted that he believed the bomb would not expose the crew to any danger.[477] I was happy to read that after our mission.

Some of the Manhattan Project people attached to our unit were to take care of and assemble the bomb. We knew they were not the plumbers. I recognized a Harvard professor from the cover of a national magazine.

Rank was around like General (Thomas) Farrell and Navy Captain Parsons and more open talk about the weapon, but still not using the words "atomic bomb." Parsons was a smart man and had more to do with our bomb than anyone else. We lived in the same Quonset hut.

We hadn't heard the name "Manhattan Project" at that time. People appeared visiting Wendover or we had transported them on our airplanes and might recognize them. Some wore Engineer Corps insignia. I recognized Norman Ramsey for heaven's sake because his mug had been in *Time* magazine as one of the outstanding young physicists. All of a sudden Ramsey was on our base; otherwise, I would have never guessed it was an atomic bomb.

A rivalry between the Navy and the Air Force for the bomb mission was going on at this time. A lot of people in LeMay's headquarters down on Tinian thought that we were not trained enough, not capable of dropping the bomb, that it shouldn't be done by us, and that some of their people should do it.

The Navy people thought the Air Force should not do it since the Navy was charged with carrying out the strategic mission. The Navy had two B-29s using them for test work before the 509th was formed.

When Tom Ferebee got wind of all this he sent Tibbets, who was in Washington for a meeting, a message to return at once because the Navy, LeMay, everyone was trying to get in the act.

Tibbets returned on July 16 in response to Ferebee's call. Colonel William "Butch" Blanchard argued with LeMay at a meeting the following day on Guam for the B-29 pilots who already flew missions to Japan. Tibbets suggested Blanchard or any of LeMay's staff fly a practice mission.[478]

Dutch ~ Tibbets, Ferebee, and myself had not flown together in the B-29s, and I was concerned. We had been flying in C-54s most of the time. In the B-17 we knew exactly what we were doing. Today, I still do not know what some of the gadgets were in the B-29. I wanted more time in the air together, and when the issue came up with Blanchard I welcomed the chance to do a dress rehearsal. Once prior to this, I flew with Lewis who carried out the turn. All the Silverplate pilots trained to do the maneuver.

Stateside the major part of the U-235 component left Santa Fe in a closed black truck with a seven-car convoy of security agents headed for Albuquerque, then a flight to Hamilton Field near San Francisco.[479]

"Think of the Kids Who Won't Be Killed!"

Berlin July 18 '45
Dear Bess: — I've only had one letter from you since I left home. I look carefully through every pouch that comes — but so far not much luck. I had to dictate you one yesterday in order to get it off in the pouch. I told you about Churchill's call and Stalin's calling and staying to lunch.

The first session was yesterday in one of the Kaiser's palaces. I have a private suite in it that is really palatial. The conference room is about 40 X 60 and we sit at a large round table — fifteen of us. I have four and they each have four, then behind me are seven or eight more helpers. Stalin moved to make me the presiding officer as soon as we sat down and Churchill agreed.

It makes presiding over the Senate seem tame. The boys say I gave them an earful. I hope so. Adm. Leahy said he'd never seen an abler job and Byrnes and my fellows seemed to be walking on air. I was so scared I didn't know whether things were going according to Hoyle or not. Any way a start has been made and I've gotten what I came for — Stalin goes to war ~~Apr.~~ August 15th with no strings on it. He wanted a Chinese settlement - and it is practically made in a better form than I expected. Soong did better than I asked him. I'll say that will end the war a year sooner now, and think of the kids who won't be killed! That is the important thing.

I told a 3 Star General as I got off the boat at Antwerp that I'd like to see my nephew Harry if it wouldn't upset things or detach him from his outfit. They found him on the Queen Elizabeth at Glasco(w), Scotland just ready to sail. They gave him the choice of sailing or comming (sic) to see his uncle. He is here — a sergeant and the nicest looking soldier you can imagine. He was as pleased as could be to see me — and am I proud of him! I gave him a pass to Berlin signed by Stalin and me.

He'll stay a few days and then I'll have him flown back to his outfit. He says it's the finest section (he's chief of it) in the Army - the right spirit sure enough.

Wish you and Margie were here. But it is a forlorn place and would only make you sad.

Please write and tell the young lady her dad can still read.
Lots of love
Harry[480]

"Special Bombing Missions Nos. 1, 2, 3, and 4"

July 20, 1945, "the 58th, 73rd, 313th, 314th, and 315th Bombardment Wings had inflicted widespread damage throughout Japan" per the Tactical

Mission Report limiting the potential targets that had not been bombed for the atomic missions.

The special missions familiarized the 509th crews with geographic areas for pilotage navigation and target recognition in the vicinity of the potential atomic strike and accustomed the Japanese to the sight of small groups of high-flying B-29s. The pumpkin shaped bombs, often orange colored, contained 5,500 pounds of high explosives and a proximity fuse that permitted an airburst similar to the atomic weapon.[481] A "fat man" in black was painted on the left side of the aircraft for each special pumpkin mission.[482]

Tibbets, Van Kirk, Ferebee, Beahan, and Van Pelt were combat experienced in Europe and North Africa. Capt. Fred Bock and Lt. Col. Tom Classen had tours of duty in the south Pacific. But for most of the 393rd the special bombing missions over Japan were their first combat assignments. Mission No. 1 targeted the Japan Refinery Company, marshalling yards, and an unidentified light industry plant, all in Koriyama. The Japan Refinery produced phosphorous and believed to be the largest such plant in Japan. The marshalling yards controlled traffic between the northern areas of Honshu and Tokyo in the south.

Mission Nos. 2, 3, and 4 were also carried out on the twentieth. For No. 2 the bombers hit an unidentified industry covering 1,500,000 square feet and 10 major buildings within the area. The Shinagawa manufacturing plant produced aircraft components, gauges, and altimeters. Mission No. 3 bombed an unidentified light industry facility in Nagaoka, in the center of Tsugami-Atagi manufacturing facility, also an objective of the mission. The Fujikoshi steel products and Higashi-Iwase plants in Toyama were selected because of their high industrial importance producing steel and ball and roller bearings. Also, part of this mission targeted the Nichimen Aluminum and Nippon Soda Companies, and the Toyama Steel Plant.[483]

The predicted weather in the Niigata area for these four missions was favorable for visual bombing.

"Special Missions Nos. 5, 6, 7, and 8"

July 24, 1945, Sumitomo Copper Refining and Sumitomo Aluminum Companies chemical facilities were attacked on the fifth mission. Pumpkins dropped over the Kawasaki Locomotive and Car Company in Kobe, Mitsubishi Heavy Industries, Kobe Steel Works, and I.G.R. Shops (an important rail yard) for No. 6. Shinko Woolen Mill and Furukawa Electrical Plant were targeted

Scenes from Tinian

for No. 7. The 509th struck heavy industry near the Yokkaichi Harbor, converted textile mill southwest of Yokkaichi, and the Utsube River Oil Refinery for No. 8.[484]

July 25, 1945, the Labour Party in the United Kingdom led by Clement R. Attlee won a surprising and overwhelming victory during the general election pledging rapid social reforms defeating Churchill's Conservatives. Attlee had accompanied Churchill at his invitation to the Potsdam Conference while the election results were tabulated.

July 25, 1945
TOP SECRET[485]
War Department
Office of the Chief of Staff
Washington 25 D.C.

O:General Carl Spatz (sic)
Commanding General
United States Army Strategic Air Forces

1. The 509 Composite Group, 20th Air Force will deliver its first special bomb as soon as weather will permit visual bombing after about 3 August 1945 on one of the targets: Hiroshima, Kokura, Niigata, and Nagaskai (sic). To carry military and civilian scientific personnel from the War Department to observe and record the effects of the explosion of the bomb, an additional aircraft will accompany the airplane carrying the bomb. The observing planes will stay several miles distant from the point of impact of the bomb.
2. Additional bombs will be delivered on the above targets as soon as made ready by the project staff. Further instructions will be issued concerning targets other than those listed above.
3. Dissemination of any and all information concerning the use of the weapon against Japan is reserved to the Secretary of War and the President of the United States. No inquires on the subject or release of information will be issued by Commanders in the field without specific prior authority. Any news stories will be sent to the War Department for special clearance.
4. The foregoing directive is issued to you by direction and with the approval of the Secretary of War and the Chief of Staff, USA. It is desired that you personally deliver one copy of this directive to General MacArthur and one copy to Admiral Nimitz for their information.

Signed: Thos. Handy
General, O.S.C.
Acting Chief of Staff

The First Nuclear Release Order[486]

July 26, 1945, the Armed Services Radio broadcasted the terms of the Potsdam Declaration calling for Japan's unconditional surrender.

"Little Boy Arrives at Tinian"

The USS *Indianapolis* docked at Tinian and delivered the uranium-235 core produced at Oak Ridge for the *Little Boy* bomb.[487] The cruiser left Tinian without a destroyer escort, made a brief stop in Guam, and sailed for Leyte to move into position for the invasion of Japan.[488] The ship did not have sonar or hydrophones nor told about an earlier attack by a Japanese sub. Officials denied Captain Charles Butler McVay's request for a destroyer escort from Guam.[489]

"Special Missions Nos. 8 and 9"

Weather conditions impacted the earlier July 20th attack and bombings were not successful. Reassigned for July 26th were the light industry at Nagaoka and Tsugami-Atagi Manufacturing (No. 8), Fujikoshi Steel Products, Higashi Iwase Plants, Nichimen Aluminum Company, Nippon Soda Company, and Toyama Steel Plant.[490]

"Receipt for Enriched Tuballoy"

Brigadier Gen. Thomas F. Farrell assumed "responsibility for the safe handling, storage and transmittal elsewhere of this material in accordance [illegible] existing regulations. The material, including enclosures and attachments, is identified as follows. (In identifying material, avoid any reference which might cause the receipt form to become classified.)

Projectile unit containing [blacked out] kilograms of tuballoy at an average concentration of [blacked out]" received from Dr. Norman F. Ramsey, Jr. General Farrell signed and dated the top-secret receipt.[491]

July 27, 1945, hundreds of thousands of leaflets known as the twelve-city leaflets rained down from the B-29s over Tokyo and other Japanese cities.[492]

TO THE PEOPLE OF JAPAN!
Do you want to save your own life and the lives of your loved ones? If you do, read this leaflet well.

Within a few days military installations in four or five of your cities will be destroyed by the American Air Force. It is necessary that the factories which produce military weapons and products and the military installations be destroyed, but bombs do not have eyes and so no one can tell where they will fall, and because humanitarian America does not want to kill innocent people needlessly, the people living in the cities written on the other side of this leaflet should leave at once!

AMERICA IS NOT WAGING WAR AGAINST THE PEOPLE OF JAPAN, but against the military clique who got you into this war. The peace which we all long for is prevented by the pressure of the military clique only. When you get rid of the military clique the new Japan can be built. This is what must be done to end the war and attain peace.

There is no telling which four cities written on the reverse side will be bombed, but they will be bombed, so be careful and evacuate at once.[493]

Dutch ~ We were flying training missions over Japan. The pumpkin bombs were the same size and weight of *Fat Man*, the Nagasaki plutonium bomb. We assigned crews a factory target to conduct the mission the same way as if the atomic bomb was on board like the steep turn, the whole bit. There was a lot of this going on. I helped plan many of these missions and did fly one with Bob Lewis.

I would not have gone on the Hiroshima atomic bomb mission if Lewis had been assigned as the pilot. I felt that strongly and neither would Tom Ferebee. When we were out socializing, we bought Bob two or three stiff drinks to get rid of him. We thought he acted like a brash kid.[494] We were all of twenty-four years old too you understand. We did not think he could make good command decisions.[495] If you have an atomic bomb on board, you better make good command decisions. He flew home across the country without telling his commanding officer or getting authorization to take the plane among other things. If I were Paul Tibbets, I would have kicked him out right then and there. Bob was a good airplane driver, but if you are leading an important mission being an airplane driver is not enough. You need to be prepared if something goes wrong.

A number of times I heard Paul being asked, "Why did you pick Tom and Dutch?"

Tibbets answered. "I wanted people on the airplane that I knew how they would react if something went wrong."

July 28, 1945, the Japanese Prime Minister Kantaro Suzuki issued a statement in response to the Potsdam Declaration. "…There is no other recourse but to ignore it entirely and resolutely fight for the successful conclusion of the war."[496]

"Special Missions Nos. 10, 11, and 12"

Dutch – Paul Tibbets and Tom Ferebee did not fly missions to Japan prior to the Hiroshima mission. I substituted for Bob Lewis' navigator at that time.

July 29, 1945, Van Kirk flew with Lewis on the 13:20 hour Koriyama mission (see Table 10.2). Lewis flew Sweeney's plane, the *Great Artiste*, while No. 44-86292 was being given a detailed inspection in preparation for Special Mission No. 13.

According to the Tactical Report the 509th flew strikes against the Ube Nitrogen Fertilizer, Ube Soda, and Nippon Motor Oil Companies for Special mission No. 10; heavy industry in Yokkaichi Harbor area, converted textile mill, and Utsube River Oil Refinery for No. 11; and the Japan Refinery Company, marshalling yards, and a light industry facility in Koriyama.[497]

"The USS *Indianapolis*"

July 30, 1945, 12:05 a.m., halfway to Leyte the Japanese sub I-58 under Lt. Commander Mochitsura Hashimoto fired the first of six torpedoes at the cruiser *Indianapolis*. The first torpedo hit the forward starboard side igniting a tank of several thousand gallons of aviation fuel and obliterating more than sixty feet of the bow. The next torpedo struck below the bridge and hit the boiler rooms damaging the electrical systems. A third torpedo hits the ship.[498] Within fourteen minutes the ship sunk and amidst the debris and black fuel oil slick, about 800 of the 1,196-crew members were in the water. The *Indianapolis* sent a distress call received, but disregarded on Leyte. "We have been hit by torpedoes. Need immediate assistance." Naval protocol at the time required confirmation of the message because the Japanese had been broadcasting bogus distress signals.[499]

July 31, 1945, Van Kirk navigated a 7:05 hour mission in a B-29.[500]

"Blanchard on His Butt"

Blanchard flew with Tibbets on a training flight to drop a pumpkin bomb on a Japanese installation on Rota. Van Kirk navigated to the aiming point at the exact time estimated and Ferebee released the bomb directly on the target. The 155-degree diving turn pinned Blanchard to his seat. This stopped further disagreement about Tibbets and his crew's qualifications for the Hiroshima mission.

Dutch ~ We practiced the turn and knew what we were doing and Tibbets also feathered an engine. The turn put Blanchard on his butt and he hollered, "What the hell is going on?" We laughed like hell because we had briefed him about what was going to happen.[501]

I am frequently asked if the diving turn maneuver has a name. Yeah, it is called "getting away from the bomb."

"More Leaflets Dropped"

For the second time within four days leaflets fell from B-29s over Japan with a warning by General LeMay to "evacuate these cities immediately." Six Superfortresses dropped 720,000 fliers. More than 1,300,000 people lived in the dozen cities. The first warning on the previous Saturday was released over the cities of Nagaoka, Nishinomiya, and Koriyama on Honshu; Hakodate on Hokkaido; and Kurume on Kyushu. Eight cities of industrial and military targets added to the earlier list were Mito, Hachioji, Maebashi, Toyama, Nagano, Fukuyama, Otsu, and Maizuru. The American news reported the eight cities as industrial and transportation centers on Honshu.[502]

Chapter Ten — Endnotes

445 Howard "Ted" Zobrist telephone interview with author, August 9, 2010. Zobrist received the Distinguished Flying Cross for his actions when a Japanese two-engine Betty, an American nickname for a Mitsubishi Jukogyo long-range medium bomber, attacked the *Umbriago*. Crew of the *Umbriago*: 1st Lt. Robert Kleeme, 2nd Lt John Gaudino, 2nd Lt. Vernon Worrell, 2nd Lt. Vaughn Riley, 2nd Lt. William Dutrow, TSgt. Robert Hill, Sgt. William Hauenstein, Sgt. Chester Tomaszewsi, Sgt. Benjamin Sikes, Sgt. Dennis Breen, SSgt John Kerr, Sgt. Howard T. Zobrist, and SSgt Harold Komarek. Smith, *History of the 9th Bombardment Group (VH)*, 25, 95.

446 The August 19, 1943, Quebec Agreement governed the collaboration between the United States and the United Kingdom in the matter of tube alloys (British code name for nuclear weapons) and agreed to bring the project to fruition, pool resources, and to "never use this agency against each other...not use it against third parties without each other's consent...not either of us communicate any information about tube alloys to third parties except by mutual consent." Foreign Relations of the United States The Conferences at Washington and Quebec, 1943, (Washington, DC: Government Printing Office, 1970).

447 "Log of the Interim Committee of the Manhattan Project, May 9, 1945," Subject File, Arneson Papers, Harry S. Truman Library & Museum, http://www.trumanlibrary.org/ [accessed March 3, 1945].

448 Dorothy Scarritt McKibbin, a 1919 graduate of Smith College, worked as a secretary for J. Robert Oppenheimer at Los Alamos. McKibbin's recollections documented in Conant's work provided insight into the top-secret project and her boss. Jennet Conant, *109 East Palace* Robert Oppenheimer And The Secret City of Los Alamos, (New York, NY: Simon & Schuster, 2005), 293. On May 11, 1945, Van Kirk navigated aboard a B-29 with one landing for 15:10 hours flight time according to his Individual Flight Record.

449 Joe Diblin, *The Standard Journal* articles, 2007. Tibbets returned to the airbase and practiced climbing to 25,000 feet and turning steeper and steeper until he brought the B-29 around in 40 seconds.

450 Robert Lewis, the first Second Lieutenant checked out in a B-29 with the 58th Wing, flew forty-four times in the first experimental B-29 before December 1943 according to his bio prepared for the *Enola Gay* mission. Van Kirk papers.

451 A total of sixty-five Silverplate B-29s were produced. A B-29 was modified at Wright Field to produce the prototype Silverplate. Campbell's "A Brief History of the *Enola Gay*" and *The Silverplate Bombers*.

452 Sid Schapiro, "2,000-Strong B29 Forces May Hit Japs," *Stars and Stripes* London Edition, May 12, 1945. Doolittle forecast unmanned aircraft in the next war responding to a question about robotics in aviation.

453 Back on Tinian the crew's regular navigator 1st Lt. Jack V. Wise of the 313th Wing 99th Squadron was in the hospital. He became a medical doctor after the war. Barbara Wise telephone interview with author, September 19, 2010. Wise's daughter, Susan Wise Strahan is a shirttail cousin of Dietz.

454 Doug Stanton, *In Harm's Way*, 61.

455 The Seabees also repaired the damage to the existing fields that occurred while taking the

island. Bureau of Yards and Docks, *Building the Navy's Bases in World War II: History of the Bureau of Yards and Docks and the Civil Engineers Corps 1940 – 1946*, Volume II, (Washington, DC: Government Printing Office, 1947), 361 – 362.

456 The news report speculated that Van Kirk operated as the lead navigator on the raids of German-held territory in Europe, but that his role could not be confirmed. Recently the Fortresses had been grounded due to bad weather. "Believe Flier No. 1 Navigator of U.S. Raiders," *Sunbury Daily Item*, 1941.

457 "Log of the Interim Committee of the Manhattan Project," May 14, 1945, Harry S. Truman Library & Museum.

458 United States Army Forces (Western Pacific), Twentieth Air Force and Staff GHQ. *General Headquarters United States Army Forces in the Pacific, "DOWNFALL," Strategic Plan for Operations in the Japanese Archipelago*, May 28, 1945.

459 All members were present at the fourth meeting of the Interim Committee.

460 "Six Are Killed by Jap Balloons," *Niagara Falls Gazette*, May 31, 1945. Maj. Gen. Hugh J. Casey reported after the war that only three to five percent of the nine thousand bomb balloons launched from the east coast of Honshu reached North America. "Three to Five Per Cent Of Jap Balloons Arrived," *Amsterdam Recorder*, July 25, 1946.

461 The news clipping of the United Press account did not identify the type of Japanese aircraft.

462 Norman Polmar, *The Enola Gay* The B-29 That Dropped The Atomic Bomb on Hiroshima, (Washington, DC: Brassey's Inc., 2004), 19.

463 Groves estimated the invasion force at 1,532,000 men, 36 divisions, and heavy casualties. Groves, *Now It Can Be Told* The Story of the Manhattan Project, 264.

464 "Suzuki Says He Won't Quit His Nation in Defeat," *Kingston Daily Freeman*, (AP) June 14, 1945.

465 "Minutes of Meeting held at the White House on Monday, 18 June 1945," Miscellaneous Historical Documents Collections, Harry S. Truman Library.

466 Roy E. Appleman, James M. Burns, Russell E. Gugeler, and John Stevens, *Okinawa: The Last Battle*, (Washington: Defense Dept., Army, Center of Military History, 1948), 490.

467 Several references for the Battle of Okinawa point out that numbers of casualties for Japanese and particularly Okinawa's residents were estimates due to those who fled or were entombed in caves, about one-third of the residents died. Some references state United States Army figures for civilian casualties were 142,058. The "Okinawa Operations Record of 32d Army," Japanese Monograph No. 135, (Washington, DC, 1949), gives 7,400 for the number of captured POWs being substantially natives who were less indoctrinated with the no-surrender order by General Ushijima and the code of Samurai to fight to the death. The casualty statistics referenced by Feifer emphasize that the Okinawan civilian deaths alone exceeded the deaths for Hiroshima or Nagasaki. George Feifer, *The Battle of Okinawa* The Blood and The Bomb, (Guilford, CT: The Lyons Press, 2001), 408.

468 "Certificate dated June 23, 1945," President's Secretary's Files, Harry S. Truman Library and Museum.

469 Gordon Thomas and Max Morgan Witts, *Enola Gay*, (New York: Stein and Day, 1977), 162. Crew B-9 commanded by Lewis, pilot Richard McNamara, navigator Harold J. Rider, bombardier Stewart W. Williams, engineer Wyatt E. Duzenbury, radio operator

Richard H. Nelson, radar operator Joseph S. Stiborik, gunner George R. Caron, and assistant engineer Robert H. Shumard. Van Kirk flew with six of the B-9 crew on the *Enola Gay* mission to Hiroshima.

470 Victor 82 also referred to as #292. Campbell, "A Brief History of the *Enola Gay*," 3.

471 "We led the Fleet to Hokkaido to bomb a munitions plant," said Commander Starnes.

472 Van Kirk's "Individual Flight Record" for the month July 1945 did not specify the aircraft number of the B-29. Van Kirk personal papers.

473 Terrence R. Fehner and F. G. Gosling, "Origins of the Nevada Test Site," (Washington: History Division Dept. of Energy, December 2000), 30 – 33.

474 Jim Baggott, *The First War Of Physics*, 316.

475 The Pepkowitzes felt strongly that the drop of the atomic bomb ended the war and that it was necessary. Dr. Pepkowitz became a member of the Atomic Energy Commission and advised the committee on the materials necessary for safely generating commercial power. In 1965 Pepkowitz, vice-president and general manager of Nuclear Materials Equipment Corp., managed the three-year boron production contract for the Atomic Energy Commission at the Pletcher Road facility in Lewiston, NY, situated on the former Lake Ontario Ordnance Works (LOOW) site. Virginia Miller, "Nuclear Unit Powder Produced in Lewiston, "*Niagara Falls Gazette*," May 2, 1965.

476 Some projects that Pepkowitz worked on during the war are still classified. Declassified: L. P. Pepkowitz, "Volumetric Determination of Microgram Quantities of Acid-soluble Sulfide Sulfur," "Microvolumetric Assay of Uranium," "The Microdetermination of Azide by a Kjeldahl Procedure" and Ernest C. Anderson, Leonard P. Pepkowitz et al, "Chemical and Spectrochemical Analysis of Uranium and Plutonium Materials." Los Alamos Scientific Lab, New Mexico.

477 Parsons arrived two days earlier after extensive travel during June and July to Wendover and related sites such as Cal Tech, Pasadena, regarding explosive lens matters and project connections at Inyokern. Initially, Parsons with physicist Luis W. Alvarez planned to fly over the tower and drop the instruments to measure the bomb blast. Due to a lighting storm at 1600 on Sunday, Oppenheimer after conferring with Groves ordered the B-29 to not fly directly over the tower. On Monday seconds before 0530, with Parsons standing behind the pilot to observe, the B-29 banked and flew in the direction of the tower about twenty-five miles away. Al Christman, *Target Hiroshima* Deak Parsons and the Creation of the Atom Bomb, (Annapolis, MD: Naval Institute Press, 1998), 169 – 171.

478 Tibbets details the controversy over which group should fly the Hiroshima mission and the flight with Blanchard in "Manhattan in the Pacific" from *The Tibbets Story*, 185 - 188.

479 The large crate and small metal cylinder were held in Groves' office and placed aboard the *Indianapolis* on July 16. Groves, *Now It Can Be Told*, 305.

480 Harry S. Truman's hand written letter to his wife Bess. Harry S. Truman Library, Independence, MO.

481 The orange color provided visibility during the drop. Polmar, *The Enola Gay*, 24.

482 A red caricature was painted on the airplane for the actual atomic bomb missions. Warren Thompson, "509th Bomb Group," *Wings of Fame*.

483 "Planning for Missions Number 1, 2, 3, and 4," Tactical Mission Report, Mission No. Special flown 20 July – 14 August 1945, Headquarters Twentieth Air Force, National

Archives Building, College Park, MD.

484 Yokkaichi was placed on the priority list for the B-29 assault. Incendiary bombs had leveled 1.23 square miles of the interior of the city of June 18, 1945. Planning for Missions Number 4, 5, 6, and 7, Tactical Mission Report.

485 Copy of the top secret (declassified November 25, 1956) nuclear release order, Van Kirk personal papers.

486 War Department directive to General Carl Spaatz, "The First Nuclear Release Order," 25 July 1945, copy Van Kirk personal papers.

487 Captain McVay had led the ship through the invasion of Iwo Jima and the bombardment of Okinawa. The *Indianapolis* antiaircraft guns shot down seven enemy planes before the ship was struck by a kamikaze inflicting heavy casualties and penetrating the ship's hull. The ship was in California for repairs when it received orders for Tinian.

488 Marc Tyler Nobleman, *The Sinking of The Indianapolis,* (Minneapolis, MN: Compass Point Books, 2007), 11, 12.

489 The I-58 Japanese B3 type submarine carried six kaitens (manned torpedoes) and other torpedoes. The sub fired on the cargo ship *Wild Hunter* and her destroyer escort *Lowry* prior to attacking the *Indianapolis*. Note referenced on "Imperial submarines" from Hashimoto Mochitsura. I-58 Kito-seri (Return of I-58), http://www.combinedfleet.com/I-58.htm [accessed October 18, 2010].

490 "No fighter escort was planned for these missions." Air-sea rescue for other units of the Twentieth Air Force could be used for these missions per the Tactical Report.

491 Captain W. L. Uanna authorized the one page document, dated 26 July 1945. Copy of document, Van Kirk personal papers.

492 The leaflets warned of the possibility of impending destruction and were dropped on more than thirty prospective bombing targets on July 27, July 30, and August 3, 1945. John W. Dower, *Cultures Of War:* Pearl Harbor | Hiroshima | 9-11 | Iraq, (New York, NY: W. W. Norton & Company, Inc., 2010), 190.

493 Eugene "Pete" Petersburg commanded the B-29 flight, which dropped the leaflets. Copy of translation Van Kirk personal papers.

494 Robert A. Lewis was actually three years older. He died in 1983 at the age of 65. Lindsey Gruson, "Robert A. Lewis. 65 Co-pilot on Mission over Hiroshima," *New York Times,* June 20, 1983.

495 Lewis wore a worn flight jacket, but he did not have combat experience. Lewis was described in the Thomas and Witts' *Enola Gay* as fiercely protective of his crew and flew by the book.

496 William S. Phillips, "World War II The Atomic Missions Of 1945," The Greenwich Workshop, Inc., 1994.

497 Stopping the production of special oils used for airplanes and diesel engines from the Nippon Motor Oil Company would hamper the aircraft industry.

498 After being rescued survivors of the *Indianapolis* told medic Mick McAllister that three torpedoes hit their ship.

499 Doug Stanton, *In Harm's Way*, The Sinking of the USS *Indianapolis* and the Extraordinary Story of Its Survivors, (New York: Henry Holt & Co., LLC, 2001), 123.

500 Van Kirk Individual Flight Record for July 1945 did not identify the target.

501 At the debriefing following the run to Rota, Jacob Beser asked scientist Ed Doll how many missions were planned. Doll answered "as many as it takes" to make the Japanese give up.

502 "12 Japanese Cities Are Earmarked for Ruin From B-29's," *The Kingston Daily Freeman* (Kingston, NY), July 31, 1945. "List 8 New Jap Cities for Quick Destruction," *Schenectady Gazette* (Schenectady, NY), August 1, 1945, reported that the eight cities and other targets for the leaflet drops now totaled nineteen. The numbers of the leaflets and the specific dates of the leaflet drops for the end of July differs in references. See note from Dower, *Culture of War*, regarding date and leaflet drops.

Chapter Eleven

Hiroshima *Special Mission No. 13*

"War is the most terrible tragedy of the human race and it should not be prolonged an hour longer than is absolutely necessary," Gen. George Marshall.

"Hiroshima, the No. 1 Target"

August 1945, Ferebee had accused Van Kirk of lying in bed just to get attention from the nurses.

Dutch ~ Tibbets told us we could not write home right about the time I got the hives and went into the hospital. Paul thought that I was nervous about the mission and sent Ferebee to check up on me. Hell, I had just eaten tomatoes or something of that type, that's all, and by the way we had the best mess on the island.[503] The hospital determined that I had eaten something that gave me hives, which I was very prone to do in those days.

We were supposed to have a series of shots when I first arrived at Sikeston. After the first one, I got a little itchy. After the second shot I walked out of the building and started swelling up. I went back into the building and the medical personnel threw me in a tub of cold water. It was not fun either. After that my tags were marked allergic to tetanus toxoid.

I can't recall a specific time. It was some days before when I knew about the target cities. We had to plan the mission and started getting our directions of what we had to do when the bomb dropped. I had it in the back of my mind that we were told if we couldn't drop it visually, then drop the bomb in the ocean and do not bring it back to the base. That made sense. If we were going to be landing with that much weight, there was a huge potential for crashing and one of our bases could be missing. I do not know if the bomb could have been disarmed if the green plugs were taken out and the red plugs put back. Morris Jeppson could have answered that question.

We formed a plan of who was going on the mission and how many planes we were going to take. We made the decision to have weather planes out over each of the three potential targets and to radio the information so we could alter our course.

In planning the navigation I took into account the winds, the air speed, and that we were going to stay at low altitude until Iwo because of the arming of the bomb. I picked points along the route and computed the time for each leg, governed primarily by the winds. The meteorological report gave the winds and their direction for specific latitudes, which determined changes in the airspeed.

Whenever possible, I used celestial navigation. It was the most accurate way of navigating.[504] A lot of people did not like it because of the hard work to calculate a fix. I loved it because number one, I was good at it. Number two, I knew it would be the most accurate method of navigation. Over in England or North Africa, generally you could look down at the ground and see where you were at so why mess around with celestial. But over in the Pacific I regularly used it.

Hiroshima was the number one target we wanted to hit, everything else being equal.[505] We were told to drop the instruments at the same time that the bomb dropped. The instruments measured the force of the blast. Sweeney had the instruments and a third plane, George Marquardt's, would take pictures.[506] That was the plan right along.

Hiroshima ranked as the largest city except Kyoto on the main islands undamaged by incendiary strikes. The city had a population of 344,000 in 1940, the headquarters for the Fifth Army Division, and a primary port of embarkation. An Army reception center, large military airport, Army ordnance depot, several shipyards and ship building facilities, the Japan Steel works, marshalling yards, and numerous aircraft component parts factories were also located in Hiroshima.[507]

"Getting Ready for the Invasion"

Mick ~ *August 1, 1945*, "My name showed up on the list for the invasion force with the 2nd Marine Division for the first wave on Kyushu the southern island. The Navy provided medical corps for the Marines. They had no medical corps of their own.[508] I asked the Chief Pharmacist should I take my medic kit or my sax?

He said, 'Take your instrument they won't kill a musician and wear your medic helmet.'

"I was not going to wear my medic helmet and be a target." Speaking of himself, "So Mick McAllister who had no combat experience was assigned to go ashore on Kyushu for the invasion of Japan date to be determined, but we had lined up at Leyte."

The officers in charge said, "We have eight hundred ships between the southern island and Tokyo."

"I looked out over the ocean and could see ships as far as you could see. You could walk out across the damn ocean. Until about May of '45 our ship had been lit. We had signs on the side of the ship. The kamikazes were getting so desperate trying to get our regular ships that they sunk two of our hospital ships because they were lit, which made them a good target. At that point around July we became part of the total body. In other words we blacked out, turned out the lights, and became part of the invasion force surrounded by destroyers and were still picking up the sick."

"We had Army. We had Navy. We had Marine Corps. We had the whole damn force left over from Europe that we were ready to go ashore and we knew that the kamikazes, the women, the kids were all armed waiting on us."

"Survivors of the *Indianapolis*"

August 2 – 3, 1945, Chuck Gwinn, pilot of a Lockheed PV-1 Ventura patrol bomber, sighted survivors of the *Indianapolis* and radioed Peleliu.[509] The second transmission asked for a rescue ship. Several B-17s from an Emergency Rescue Squadron dropped rafts and lifeboats into the water. Transports and destroyers rushed to the scene using LCVPs to rescue the men.[510] The last group of injured and delirious survivors had spent 112 hours in the water and drifted 124 miles. At 5:00 p.m. on August 4, the rescue operation ended.[511]

During the rescue Admiral Nimitz ordered the hospital ship *Tranquillity* to Peleliu to transport the 321 survivors to the Base 18 hospital on Guam.[512]

Mick ~ "I was a corpsmen and told to give Captain McVay his first shot, a new drug called penicillin."[513]

Field Orders Number 13

TOP SECRET
Auth: CG, Twentieth Air Force
Initials: /-+-2-4

FIELD ORDERS)
NUMBER   13)

TWENTIETH AIR FORCE
GUAM
2 August 1945 - 1500K

Map: JAPAN Aviation Chart 1:218,880

1. a. Omitted.

    b. (1) Omitted.

        (2) (a) No friendly aircraft, other than those listed herein,
                  will be within a 50 mile area of any of the targets
                  for this strike during a period of four hours prior
                  to and six hours subsequent to strike time.

             (b) Air-Sea Rescue facilities will be provided for this
                  mission through standard channels by Headquarters,
                  Twentieth Air Force.

2. Twentieth Air Force attacks targets in JAPAN on 6 August.

3. a. Omitted

    b. Omitted

    c. 313th Wing, 509th Group:

        (1) Primary target: 90.30 - HIROSHIMA URBAN INDUSTRIAL AREA.

             (a) Aiming point: 063096, Reference: XXI BomCom
                  Litho-Mosaic HIROSHIMA AREA, No. 90.30 - Urban.

             (b) IP: 3424N - 1330530E.

             (c) Breakaway (if target is bombed):

                  Right turn of at least 150 degrees
                  3400N - 13334E.

        (2) Secondary target: 90.34 - 168, KOKURA ARSENAL and CITY.

             (a) Aiming Point: 104082, Reference: XXI BomCom
                  Litho-Mosaic KOKURA ARSENAL, No. 90.34 - 168.

             (b) IP: 3343N - 1313830E.

             (c) Breakaway (if target is bombed):

                  Left turn of at least 150 degrees
                  3343N - 1313830E.

        (3) Tertiary target: 90.36 - NAGASAKI URBAN AREA.

             (a) Aiming Point: 114061, Reference: XXI BomBom
                  Litho-Mosaic NAGASAKI AREA, MITSUBISHI STEEL and
                  ARMS WORKS, No. 90.36 - 546.

             (b) IP: 3238N - 13039E

- 1 -

(National Archives)

F.O. #13

    (c) Breakaway (if target is bombed)

        Left turn of at least 150 degrees
        3137N - 13128E.

(4) Force required:

    (a) Strike force: 3 A/C

    (b) Spare: 1 A/C, which will proceed to IWO JIMA to stand
        by in case of abort. This A/C will be loaded with full
        gas load but no bombs.

    (c) Weather: 3 A/C, which will be dispatched one to each
        target at such a time as to be able to relay, from their
        assigned target, the target weather forecast for strike
        time, broadcasting this message between 060845K and
        060915K. This will enable strike force to select
        either the secondary or tertiary target in the event
        the primary is found to be cloud-covered. Each weather
        A/C will have aboard a weather observer furnished by
        the 313th Wing.

(5) C.O., 509th Group, will insure that necessary personnel and
    special equipment are dispatched to IWO JIMA to handle trans-
    fer of bomb load to spare A/C in case of abort.

(6) Route :

    Base
    IWO JIMA
    3337N - 13430E (Departure Point)
    341530N - 1333330E
    IP
    Target
    Breakaway
    IWO JIMA
    Base.

(7) Altitudes :

    (a) Enroute to target: Below 10,000 ft. until necessary
        to climb to bombing altitude. Below 5,000 ft. prior
        to passing Iwo Jima.

    (b) Of attack: 28,000 to 30,000 ft.
    (c) On route back: At or below 18,000 ft. when passing
        IWO JIMA.

(8) Time Control: Pass Departure Point at 060915K.

(9) Bombing Airspeed: 200 mph CAS.

(10) Bomb load and special equipment: As specified by C.O.,
     509th Group.

(11) Only visual bombing will be accomplished. Strike force
     will pass sufficiently close to primary target to assure,
     before going on to secondary target, that visual bombing
     is not possible on the primary.

- 2 -

T O P   S E C R E T

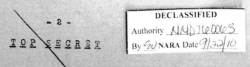

F.O. #13

        (12) Post-strike photography: C.O., 509th Group, will be respon-
        sible for briefing and dispatching two F-13 A/C, which will
        be detached to the 509th Group by the 3rd Photo Recon Sq.,
        for this strike. These A/C will not enter target area until
        4 hours after bombs away. To insure this schedule is main-
        tained regardless of whether the strike force has to make use
        of the spare A/C at IWO JIMA or not, the photo A/C will be
        required to check in with the ground stations at both TINIAN
        and IWO JIMA to obtain clearance to proceed past IWO JIMA.
        If these photo A/C do not receive notification of which tar-
        get has been bombed, they will photograph all three targets.

   d. Omitted.

   e. Omitted.

   f. 3rd Photo Recon Sq.:

      (1) Dispatch 2 F-13 A/C to NORTH FIELD, TINIAN, to land
      by 051600K, reporting to C.O., 509th Group, for post-
      strike photo briefing as specified above in par. 3. c. (12)

   g. CSC, IWO JIMA:

      (1) Participated in event of abort landing at IWO JIMA, making
      all necessary facilities available upon request of the 509th
      Group Project Officer.

      (2) Provide clearance to photo A/C, as provided for above in
      par. 3. c. (12), after assurance from 509th Group Project
      Officer that no abort has occurred.

4. No Tactical Mission Number is assigned to this mission. For record
   purposes, Special Bombing Mission Number 13 is assigned.

5. a. (1) Strike reports will be transmitted in accordance with Head-
      quarters, Twentieth Air Force Regulation 100-20, dated 15
      May 1945. 313th Wing Air-Ground Station will rebroadcast
      strike reports via the F method on all 313th Wing strike fre-
      quencies.

      (2) Contact reports will be transmitted in accordance with Head-
      quarters, Twentieth Air Force Regulation 100-19, dated 2
      July 1945.

      (3) IFF doctrine will be as follows: Turn IFF to position #1
      immediately before take-off. Turn IFF off when 50 miles from
      coast of Japanese mainland. Turn IFF on at land's end (enemy
      coast) when returning from target. Turn IFF off when landing.

      (4) Channel G (143.01 mcs) of the AN/ARC-3 will be used as inter-
      plane command channel.

      (5) Retune Channel 7 of AN/ART-13 transmitter of strike aircraft
      to 7455 kcs. Any strike plane aborting will immediately
      call the Twentieth Air Force Weather Station, IWO JIMA, call
      sign OOV181, on 7455kcs and transmit message saying "Aborting".
      The 313th Wing Ground Station will monitor 7455 kcs and pass
      any aborting message to C.O. of 509th Group.

      (6) Radio operators of strike aircraft will monitor 7310 kcs and
      intercept in-flight weather reports from weather planes over
      target. These weather reports will be addressed to 313th
      Wing Air-Ground Station, OOV670. The strike aircraft will
      intercept these in-flight weather reports.

- 3 -

(7) Photographic aircraft will return AN/ART-13 channels 1, 3 and 7 as follows: Channel 1 - 3410 kcs; Channel 3 - 10125 kcs; and Channel 7 - 7310 kcs. Photographic aircraft will be controlled by 313th Wing Air-Ground Station, 00V670. Photographic aircraft will monitor appropriate 313th Wing strike frequencies during their entire mission and intercept strike reports as rebroadcast by 313th Wing Air-Ground Station. Strike reports will determine which target will be photographed.

(8) Photographic aircraft of the 3rd Photo Recon Sq., attached to the 509th Group, will contact the 313th Wing Air-Ground Station, 00V670, on 7310 kcs, and the Twentieth Air Force Weather Station, IWO JIMA, on frequency 7455 kcs, call 00V181, and question both stations as to whether any striking aircraft of the 509th Group have aborted. This will determine whether the photographic aircraft will proceed to target or land at IWO JIMA.

(9) Annex A, attached hereto, will be the weather code used by the weather aircraft to transmit in-flight weather observations from over the target. The letter scramble indicated on the form will be used. Transmission of weather information will take the following form: letter indicated in column under letter scramble will indicate the weather element being reported. Each letter (weather element) will be followed by a number which indicate the actual condition. These numbers, one through zero, appear at the top of the weather code form. An example of an in-flight weather transmission might be as follows: ØØV67Ø V 21V675 - 16Ø7Ø3Z BT Y2Q1KØB1Z ØXQC2R1 BT IMI ØØV67Ø V 21V675 - 16Ø7Ø3Z BT Y2Q1KØB1ZØX C2R1. BT AR. The above message, when decoded, would indicate the following: low clouds, 1-3/10 small; middle cloud amount, none; height of tops, unknown; high cloud, none; height of base, unknown; height of tops, unknown, advise, bomb secondary; visibility in clear air, clear. This message will be handled by the broadcast method and repeated as shown in the example above.

(a) Each weather aircraft will be designated a specific target to observe. Each weather aircraft's radio call sign, together with the name of the target assigned to that aircraft, must be carried in both the Pilot's and Radio Operator's Folders. A simple way of designating this would be as follows:

Aircraft Call Sign	Target Observed
21V675	Primary - HIROSHIMA
7V675	Secondary - KOKURA
12V675	Tertiary - NAGASAKI

b. Command Post: Hq., Twentieth Air Force, GUAM.

BY COMMAND OF LIEUTENANT GENERAL TWINING:

R K TAYLOR
Colonel, Air Corps
Chief of Staff

OFFICIAL:

J B MONTGOMERY
Colonel, G.S.C.
D C/S, Operations

ANNEX "A" - Air to Air Weather Code omitted from this report.

- 4 -

The assembly crew for the atomic bomb mission painted on *Little Boy*, "This one is for the boys of the Indianapolis."[514]

"Briefing Hut August 5, 1945"

Dutch ‒ I found out the mission was scheduled maybe on the fourth. We were told to go ahead and drop the bombs at our convenience, which meant as soon as the weather forecast was clear over Japan. Somehow or other I knew that the president had to give the order for the release for the bomb. I may have heard this from casual conversation at the Officer's Club.

Captain Parsons explained at the briefing that the bomb was something new in the history of warfare and the most destructive weapon ever produced. Parsons headed *Project Alberta* for the Manhattan Project to develop the delivery of the bomb. He drew an image of the mushroom cloud on the blackboard. The scientists thought that the bomb would knock out almost everything within a three-mile area. Tibbets gave the impression that he believed that this mission would end the war.

Parsons attempted showing a movie of the Trinity test and the damn projector did not work. Here we had the ordnance engineer for the atomic bomb, but he couldn't make a projector work.

We were told how dangerous the mission was going to be and the fact that the bomb might cripple the airplane. I started thinking, am I going to live through it or not. We wanted to live. We had a purpose. We had families. The war was going to be over. We were not going to be shot at; so the attitude changed. We never, not any one of us, accepted the fact that this bomb was going to destroy the airplane. We always thought we were going to go up and be successful.

Our instructions were to drop the bomb visually. We could not drop it through the clouds by radar like in Europe near the end of the war. If we could not drop it visually, we were to take it out and drop it in the ocean. Do not bring it back to the base. It made a lot of sense.

I did not know until after the war around 1985 in Washington, DC, in the airmen's museum when for the first time I heard Paul talk about the cyanide tablets he had for each of us. I told him right there, "You might have had the tablets, but you would have had a hell of a time getting me to take it."

We manufactured sodium cyanide by the carload while I worked at DuPont, and I knew what it was.

Left to right, Captain Parsons and Colonel Tibbets conducting the briefing.
(National Archives)

August 4 - 5, 1945, during the night six B-29s from the 73rd Wing flew missions dropping leaflets over the Empire of Japan. One of the leaflets designed by the Psychological Warfare Section featured a photograph of five B-29s dropping bombs with the warning message around the border.

Translation:
Read this carefully as it may save your life or the life of a relative or friend. In the next few days, the military installations in four or more of the cities named on the reverse side of this leaflet will be destroyed by American bombs.

These cities contain military installations and workshops of factories which produce military goods. We are determined to destroy all the tools of the military clique which they are using to prolong this useless war. But, unfortunately, bombs have no eyes, so in accordance with American well-known humanitarian principles, the American Air Force which does not wish to injure innocent people, now gives you warning to evacuate the cities named and save your lives.

No. 82 the Enola Gay getting into position over the pit to load the bomb.
(Official photograph 509th Composite Group Photographic Laboratory United States
Army Air Forces, National Archives)

America is not fighting the Japanese people but is fighting the military group which has enslaved the Japanese people.

The peace which America will bring will free the people from the oppression of the military and mean the emergence of a new and better Japan.

You can restore peace by demanding new and good leaders who end the war.

We cannot promise that only these cities will be among those attacked but at least four will be, so heed this warning and evacuate these cities.

The cities named were: Miyakonojo, Saga, Yamata, Iwakuni, Akita, Otaru, Tokushima, Hachinoe, Imabari, Tottori, Takayama, and Urawa.[515]

August 5, 1945, per Field Order No. 14 the 58th, 73rd, 313th, and 314th Bombardment Wings made "normal-effort attacks" against the urban industrial areas of Saga, Maebashi, Nishinomiya, and Imabari.[516]

Dutch - Tibbets had the name *Enola Gay,* for his mother, painted on the airplane.

Dorr's Osprey *B-29 Superfortress* publication pointed out that an examination of publicity shots after the mission revealed that the name, *Enola Gay,* and the airplane number were quickly repainted in a more refined font. The forward facing arrow in a circle on the vertical stabilizer/rudder surface was changed to the letter R of the 6th Bomb Group.

"Operational Orders for Hiroshima Strike Mission"[517]

Date of Mission:	6 August 1945
Out of Sacks:	Weather at 2230
	Strike at 2330
Mess:	2315 to 0115
Lunches:	39 at 2330
	52 at 0030
Trucks:	3 at 0015
	4 at 0015
Combat Strike:	
29282	Tibbets As Briefed
35389	(Maj. Charles) Sweeney
29191	(Maj. George) Marquardt
35490	(Capt. Charles) McKnight
30488	Alternate for Marquardt
Gas:	#82 – 7000 gals.
	All others – 7400 gals.
Ammunition:	1000 rds/gun in all A/C
Bombs:	Special
Cameras:	K18 in #82 and #90.
	Other installations per verbal orders.
Religious Services:	Catholic at 2200
	Protestant at 2230
Briefings:	
Weather Ships:	General Briefing in Combat Crew
	Lounge at 2300
Special Briefings at 2330 as follows:	
	AC and Pilots in Combat Crew Lounge
	Nav – Radar Operators in Library
	Radio Operators in Communications
	Flight Engineers in Operations
	Mess at 2330
	Trucks at 0015
Strike Mission:	General Briefing in Combat Crew Lounge
	at 2400
	Special Briefings at 0030 as follows:

```
Nav and Radar Operators in Library
Radio Operators at Communications
Flight Engineers at Operations
Mess at 0030
Trucks at 0115
```

Note: Lt. McKnight's crew need not attend briefings.
Signed: James I. Hopkins, Jr.

"Mission Briefing"

Dutch ~ Finally, the sun came up and the weather report for Japan was good, and we had the final briefing for the mission itself. We were given the latest meteorological information about what we could expect for the winds and anything that had come up in the meantime from the intelligence people. Many navigators entered the meteorological data about the winds in their log to use during the flight if they did not or could not get their winds otherwise. The only time I wish that I had that information was on the trip back from Gibraltar, but I paid very little attention to it on the Hiroshima mission.

My recollection of the briefing was at ten o'clock in the morning. I remember it vividly because we were told we were going to drop the most powerful bomb ever produced and take off at 2:45 a.m. How they expected us to go and get some sleep is absolutely beyond me. Tibbets did not sleep. Ferebee did not sleep. I did not sleep. How do I know that, because we were all in the same poker game. I do not remember who won, but if it went true to form it was Tom Ferebee.[518]

Guards with submachine guns surrounded the area. The briefing was intense. You knew this was something very important. We left and some of the people said they went to Confession, some went to church, and some played poker. Along nine or ten o'clock at night, we were called to go to the final briefing and the final breakfast. At the conclusion Chaplain Bill Downey offered a small prayer, which he always did at the end of the briefing. I did not consciously pray.

Tibbets ended his talk at the final briefing: "Do your jobs. Follow your orders. Don't cut corners and don't take chances."[519]

Our mess officer Charlie Perry had prepared a special breakfast for us. Paul Tibbets loved pineapple fritters, so Charlie fixed fritters. I did not care much for them, but ate them anyhow. Perry packed individual lunches for each of us with apples and oranges to excess. Then we got into the trucks and went down to the airplane.

My navigation equipment was ready. I was always prepared. The day before several things happened. Lewis' regular crew was a little bit loose on things that didn't belong on board like a pair of female panties from Omaha. Tom Ferebee and I went through the airplane and cleaned it out since it was probably going to get a lot of public notice. That is when I took my instruments to the airplane and made sure that everything was there. In celestial navigation you had to have the right books along to make your calculations. Each book covered about forty degrees of latitude. I needed all the latitude changes between Tinian and Hiroshima.

"Routes in all cases were to be planned to pass by Iwo Jima on the way to the target. Landfall and land's end were to be selected on the basis of location, radar and visual check points, and flak. All aircraft were to be instructed to return to base via Iwo Jima. Altitudes to and from the target area were to be dependent upon engineering and weather factors. En route to the target the altitude was to be 10,000 feet or less. The return altitude to be specified was to be at 18,000 feet when passing Iwo Jima in order to prevent unnecessary alerting of defenses."[520]

Dutch ~ My navigation kit included things like pencils, the logbook, the drift meter, and the Weems Plotter. The compass was fixed on the airplane. I wrote on the log in pencil.

TABLE 11.1 — NAVIGATOR'S CHECKLIST

*Radio time tick	*Sextant correction
*Navigation kit	*Calibration instruments
*Astrograph	*Astro compass
*Lighting System	*Drift Meter
*Maps, charts	*Mission data
*Flight plan	*Precomputation
*Weather conditions	*Correct time
*Oxygen equipment	*Parachute, clothing
*Life Vest	*Headset/microphone
*Altimeter	*Synchronization of timepieces
*Flux-gate compass gyro	

Source: Adapted from *The B-29* Pilot Flight Operating Instructions Manual, January 25, 1944, and *The B-29* Airplane Commander Training Manual for the Superfortress, revised February 1, 1945.

PART - V

WEATHER SUMMARY

PLANNING FORECAST

Special Bombing Mission 13   6 August 1945

Base: 3-5/10 low cloud base 2000 ft, tops 6000 ft; scattered middle
       and high clouds.
Route: To 18°N: Same as bases.
       To 22°N: 6/10 low cloud base 2000 ft, tops 8-12,000 ft with
                 occasional showers; layered middle and high clouds in
                 thin and broken layers.
       To coast: 4-5/10 low cloud base 1800 ft, top 5000 ft, scattered
                 thin middle cloud.
Targets: Tokyo and Nagoya: 6-8/10 low cloud base 2000 ft, tops 6000 ft
         with large clear areas near north and east facing slopes.
         Rest: 3-5/10 low clouds base 2000 ft tops 6000 ft with large
                areas of 6-8/10 coverage on south and west facing slopes.
                     OPERATIONAL FORECAST

Base at Take-Off:
         Broken low and scattered middle and high clouds with light showers.

Route: There will be scattered low and high clouds with occasional light
         showers to 21°N. From 21°N to 24°N there will be broken low,
         middle and high clouds with moderate showers. From 24°N to 32°N
         there will be scattered low, middle and high clouds. From 32°N
         to target there will be broken low and scattered middle and high
         clouds.

Target: Hiroshima: 6/10 stratocumulus, base 2000 ft, top 5000 ft; 3/10
         altostratus, base 18,000 ft, top 20,000 ft. Winds at 28,000 ft
         will be 270°N at 30 knots.

Base on Return:
         Scattered low and middle and broken high clouds with light showers.

                     OBSERVED WEATHER

Base at Take-Off:
         Scattered low clouds with light showers.

Route: There were scattered middle and high clouds and scattered low
         clouds becoming broken to 25°N. From 25°N to 29°N there were
         overcast low becoming broken and broken high clouds. From 29°N
         to 33°N there were scattered low becoming broken and overcast
         high clouds.

Target: Hiroshima: 3/10 stratocumulus, base 2000 ft, top 3000 ft; 1-3/10
         altostratus, tops 14-16,000 ft; 1-3/10 cirrus at
         34,000 ft (1/10 clouds obscured target). Winds at
         28,000 ft were 165° at 15 knots.

Base on Return:

         Broken low clouds.

Weather Summary Planning Forecast (National Archives)

Forecast Weather (National Archives)

Dutch ~ Some of the guys in the group I understand brought good luck charms, but I never had anything like that. I did not write a letter to my wife and figured that if I was gone, I was gone.

Bob Caron had a baseball cap on. I wore a regular overseas cap with a flap opened up. It was almost impossible to wear a headset and keep it on with a regular cap. Generally, I wore the headset. If Tibbets wanted to talk to me he turned around and told me "put your damn headset on."

Ten of us rode on the back of a big old truck and sat on the railings. Tibbets and Parsons sat up in the front.

We were armed for defense in case we got shot down. I carried the same pistol on every mission in Europe and over in Japan. Someone said to Parsons "you are not armed."[521] Just before he got on the aircraft he borrowed a .45 caliber pistol from another captain.

August 6, 1945, Van Kirk's "Individual Flight Record" for the month of August certified by Capt. George W. Marquardt on August 6: Aircraft Type: B-29, 1 Landing, 12:15 hours, 3:00 hours night navigation.[522]

Dutch ~ I had other flights that month, but the flight records were kept casually.

The *Enola Gay* was one of the fifteen B-29s known as *Silverplate* aircraft specifically for the atomic bomb missions. Gun turrets (except in the tail) and armor plate had been removed, Curtiss reversible pitch propellers installed, the bomb-bay adapted to accommodate the uranium or plutonium bombs known as *Little Boy* and *Fat Man* respectively, and pneumatically operated bomb doors.[523] Markings of other B-29 groups were used to deceive the Japanese.

"Getting ready to take off"

Dutch ~ When we reached the plane the crowd looked like a Hollywood premiere and lots of picture taking was going on. People held small, small by today's standards, wire recorders. The Manhattan Project was doing this. The only media person on the island was Bill (William L.) Laurence of the *New York Times*. He knew what was going on with the Manhattan Project all the way through.

While getting their photographs taken Caron felt Van Kirk's boot against his backside.[524] Caron described Van Kirk as the good-looking captain, a perfectionist, with an easy laugh, and confident manner.[525] "Studious and perfectionist" were frequently used in era aviation manuals as essential attributes for navigators.

Dutch ~ "I had to have a pencil too."

The weather planes took off from the North Field to report on cloud cover, which was critical for visual bombing only. Capt. Claude Eatherly in *Straight Flush* headed to the primary target, Hiroshima, the command headquarters for the Japanese Army, and major armament factories. Maj. John Wilson commanded *Jabbitt III* headed for Kokura, the secondary target and a highly industrialized city. Maj. Ralph Taylor's *Full House* checked the cloud cover over Nagasaki, home to major shipbuilding and the Mitsubishi Steel Plant where the bombs and torpedoes were manufactured that rained destruction on Pearl Harbor.

Some of the *Enola Gay* flight and ground crew.

TABLE 11.2 — WEATHER AIRCRAFT CALL SIGNS FOR SPECIAL
MISSION NO. 13

Aircraft Call Sign	Target Observed
21V675	Primary – Hiroshima
7V675	Secondary – Kokura
12V675	Tertiary – Nagasaki

Source: Field Orders No. 13 by command of Lieutenant General Twining,
National Archives.

Dutch ~ We boarded the airplane and Paul hollered out the window to get
the cameras out of the way. Somebody said, "Wave at us" and that became the
famous picture of Tibbets waving out the window.

"Takeoff"

Dutch ~ We taxied down Runway A for Able and sat on the end of the runway and revved up the engines. Captain Bob Lewis, the co-pilot, called the tower at 2:45 "Dimples eight-two ready to roll." Cleared for takeoff, we started our run.

Tibbets had a special way of flying. The B-29s veered to the right down the runway as all four engines did. Typically pilots brake with the left hand brake in order to keep it straight. Paul would not do that. He would feed in the engines, the right hand engines first without braking, and gradually build up speed and get all the engines up to power while taking off. It saved another ten feet maybe of runway. So now we are going down the runway heavily loaded and know it is going to be tight.

We were loaded extremely heavy that day. Normally a B-29 loaded would be about 135,000 pounds. We were 150,000 pounds that day not because of the bomb in the front bomb bay and that was a lot of weight. We carried extra fuel to get the balance of the airplane right, which was especially critical on takeoff. The weight of the bomb in the front bay was balanced by the fuel weight in the back. We did not really need all the fuel.

Lewis wrote in his log that at the last minute before take off the cruising altitude had been changed from 9,000 to 4,000-pressure altitude.[526]

"Navigator's Log"

Point APO 247 Tinian
Time Takeoff 0245

Dutch ~ I looked out and could see the water, so we must have got off the ground. We proceeded out there a ways and made a left hand turn. You did not gain altitude very fast in a B-29. In any propeller driven plane it is a very gradual climb. We had to build up a lot of speed before pulling back and start gaining altitude and making a turn. I wanted to make sure I had a very good checkpoint for starting and picked up the north tip of Saipan. I misspelled Saipan by the way. The north tip was my checkpoint for getting a good starting point for time and space.[527]

 Position: N Tip Siapan (*sic*), Time 0255 ½, True Course 336, Drift Corr(ection) +2, Var(iation) 0, Mag(netic) Head(ing) 338, Comp(ass) Head(ing) 338, True Head(ing)

338, Temp(erature) C +22, Altitude 4700, Air Speed Ind(icated) 213, To Destination Dist(ance) 622[528]

- Time 0310, Comp. Head. 338, Temp. C +22, Altitude 4700, Air Speed Ind. 223, Air Speed Cal. 191, Air Speed True 209, To Next Check Point ETA 265, Meteorological Observation Weather 08KW

- Time 0321½, Comp. Head. 335, Temp. C +22, Altitude 4600, Air Speed Ind. 219

- Position: 17º 14N 145º 00E, Time 0332, Comp. Head. 336, Temp. C +22, Altitude 4600, Air Speed Ind. 219, Ground Speed 210, Run Time 36 1/2, Run Dist. 128, To Destination Dist. 494, To Destination Time 2:24, To Destination ETA 05:56

- Time 0345, Comp. Head. 336, Temp. C +22, Altitude 4700, Air Speed Ind. 221

- Position: 18º 43'N 144º 21E, Time 0400, True Course 337, True Head. 337, Var. 0, Mag. Head. 337, Comp. Head. Av. 337, Temp. C +22, Altitude 4600, Air Speed Ind. 222, Ground Speed 208, Run Time 28, Run Dist. 97

- Position: Δ18º 49'N 144º 07'E, Time 0402, True Course 332, Drift Corr. +4, True Head. 336, Mag. Head 336, Comp. Head. Av. 336, Temp. C +22, Altitude 4700, Air Speed Ind. 222, Air Speed True 207, Wind Dir. 80º, Wind Force 16K, Ground Speed 212, Run Time 1:06 ½, Run Dist. 235, To Destination Dist. 387, To Destination Time 1:50, To Destination ETA 0552

The calculations for this entry, Δ18º 49'N 144º 07'E, would have noted the three stars I used. I had sheets of paper, sheets and sheets of paper. Tibbets used to watch me and comment that if the navigation didn't come out right I would tear it up and start all over again. I knew approximately where I was from dead reckoning. If I took a celestial fix and it showed I was on the other side of the ocean, I knew something was wrong so I would tear it up and start over. Someone examined my log after the war and told me we bombed some place over in Egypt!

Time 0420, Comp. Head. 340, Temp. C +23, Altitude 4600, Air Speed Ind. 223

• Time 0435, Comp. Head. 340, Temp. C +23, Altitude 4600, Air Speed Ind. 223, Reset Compass Var.

During darkness until about 4:45 celestial sightings on the star Polaris gave the latitude readings and therefore good speed lines on the course we were flying.

According to Lewis' log, Tibbets "old Bull" caught a few winks while Lewis looked after the autopilot nicknamed George.[529]

Time 0450, Comp. Head. 340, Temp. C +23, Altitude 4600, Air Speed Ind. 220

• Position: Δ21º 33'N 142º 50'E Time 0459, True Course 335, Comp. Head. 340, Temp. C +23, Altitude 4600, Air Speed Ind. 217, Ground Speed 194, Run Time 57, Run Dist. 184

• Time 0515, Alter C(ourse) to 334º, Comp. Head. 340, Temp. C +23, Altitude, 5200, Air Speed Ind. 218

About this time there was a red glow in the east, a typical daybreak.

Time 0530, Comp. Head. 331, Temp. C +22, Altitude 5500, Air Speed Ind. 220

I did three celestial fixes on the mission. The triangle with a point in the middle on the log was a celestial fix. You shoot a star getting its altitude to take a celestial fix. Make the calculations and for every four seconds you are off, you are off a mile. That is the reason for an accurate clock. Every navigator carried a master clock for an accurate time, make calculations, and get a line on the map. That line presumably went all the way around the world. You get three lines on different headings and always shoot Polaris. After shooting three stars and if you do it perfectly the lines will all cross at one point and that is where you are.

I always looked for Polaris because it cuts the calculation by about seventy percent. Polaris is almost always within one degree of your latitude line. The correction of one degree that is off is relatively simple.

It was a pretty clear sky from Iwo Jima. You do not see celestial navigation on the log from there because it got to be daylight.

The method of celestial navigation during the daytime is called sun line. You shoot the sun and are getting just one line. I believe that is what Fred Noonan was trying to do with Amelia Earhart by the way. He was trying to do sun lines. By shooting sun lines you are trying to find a small island and you purposely fly off to one side or the other of the island. You shoot sun lines until you get a sun line that goes through the island. When you come up to the sun line you try to fly it to the island. If you put yourself off to the right side of the island and do the sun line perfectly you fly right to your destination. If you do it to the wrong side of the island you are in deep trouble. I did not like that method very well.

Other calculations were taken to determine the time to the destination.

 Position: 23º 53'N 141º 45'E Time 0539, Comp. Head. 331, Temp. C +22, Altitude 5500, Air Speed Ind. 209, Ground Speed 200, To Destination Dist. 60, To Destination Time 18, To Destination ETA 0557

We were just a little bit above the clouds at 5,500 feet so it was very rough. I always got airsick and thought why not get another 2,000 feet or so and it would be smoother. Parsons was told to go ahead and arm the bomb.[530] He and Jeppson went back in the bomb bay to put the black powder charge in the breach of the small cannon. The uranium projectile fired to the other part of fissionable uranium bringing them to an explosive state known as critical mass. There were three fuses on the bomb: a time fuse (we did not want it to go off too close to the airplane), a barometric fuse, and the final fuse, a radar proximity fuse, which exploded the bomb at about 1,800 feet above the ground. The radar fuse is the one that operated on a very obscure frequency.

The plutonium bomb that would be dropped on Nagasaki and all the subsequent bombs operated on an implosion principle. They had a ring of explosives around the nose and had to be fired in a very precise and timed sequence, which compressed the plutonium into a critical mass.

We did not know Morris "Dick" Jeppson, the assistant weaponeer, well.

He was the last guy to get on the plane. He assisted Captain Parsons. We did not know what to expect from Jeppson. He was not a flying officer and did not wear wings. Right away Tom and I were quick to form opinions. If Dick was going to be the assistant for Parsons, he is going to be good. We had that much respect for Parsons.

Parsons and Jeppson stood on that very narrow catwalk with nothing beneath them but thin aluminum doors, which I do not think would have held them if they had fallen while arming the bomb. While they were in the bomb bay we stayed at a low altitude up to Iwo Jima. It took them as I recall roughly an hour. When Parsons finished his fingertips and hands were bloody from the fine sharp wire threads on the end of the bomb. He informed Tibbets the bomb was armed.

Tibbets reported back to General Farrell on Tinian that "Judge," Parson's code name, had armed the bomb.

I advised Tibbets periodically about the time remaining to get to Iwo, when we would be at the Initial Point, and on the return to the base gave him an ETA. Tibbets trusted me, or he would have stuck his nose in it a little bit more. He was a pretty good navigator himself. For example, over the intercom I would say that this is the navigator and we will be at Iwo Jima in about thirty minutes. I made sure that Tibbets was on the right heading and advised him very quickly with course corrections as necessary.

Just before we reached Iwo, Tibbets crawled through the tunnel and gave Caron, Beser, and Stiborik a pep talk. Caron asked, "Colonel are we splitting atoms today?"

We gained more altitude to about nine thousand feet approaching Iwo Jima and made one big wide turn into the island. We had been in the air about three hours. As if by magic (Charles) Sweeney was on one wing and George Marquardt on the other.[531] Sweeney's *The Great Artiste* carried the monitoring instruments and Marquardt's No. 91 (later named *Necessary Evil*) the photograph equipment.

Position: IWO, Time 0555, Circleing (*sic*) Left For Rend(ezvous), Temp. C +16, Altitude 9300, Air Speed Ind. 205

• Position: IWO, Time 0607 ½, True Course 325, Drift Corr. -1, True Head. 324, Var. +3, Mag. Head. 327, Dev. Corr. - , Comp. Head. 327, Temp. C +16, Altitude 9200, Air Speed Ind. 203, To Destination

Dist. 340, Reset Compass Var(iation) + A.P.I.

The map was in nautical miles. I would make calculations then Tibbets decides to climb a little bit and throws them all off. When you climb or let down the true air speed changes every minute and the best thing you can do is by guess and by God use your head and make educated guesses.

The computer, not a computer like today, a flat instrument like a circular slide rule, corrected air speed by setting the air speed, temperature, and altitude on the instrument. Then it gave the true air speed.[532]

Top Secret commanded by Capt. Charles McKnight stood by at Iwo Jima preparing to replace No. 82 if she got into trouble.

The Army Air Corps Type E-6b computer (and later model MB-4 DR) was an important navigational tool for dead reckoning computations, wind drifts, and conversion for true airspeed and altitude and statute miles to nautical miles.[533]

Periodically I reset the compass variation. The difference between true north and magnetic north changes depending where you are at in the world.

The mission was picture perfect. Everything went exactly the way it was supposed to. From Iwo at 6:07 I gave Tibbets a new heading for Japan, and we stayed at about 9,200 feet until 7:40 that morning.

 Position: 25° 24'N 140° 58'E, Time 0618 ½, Drift Corr. -6, Comp. Head. 324, Temp. C +16, Altitude 9300, Air Speed Ind. 205, 06:24 D = -6, A(lter) C(ourse) to 320°

- Position: 26° 00'N 140° 30'E, Time 0629 ½, True Course 327, Drift Corr. -5, True Head. Av. 322, Temp. C +16, Altitude 9300, Air Speed Ind. 205, Air Speed Cal. 175, Air Speed 206, Wind Ind. 190°, Wind Force 25K, Ground Speed 223, Run Time 22, Run Dist. 82, To Destination Dist. 258, To Destination Time 1:09, To Destination ETA 0738 ½

- Time 0640, Drift Corr. -2, True Head. 320, Temp. C +17, Altitude 9400, Air Speed Ind. 205

- Time 0650, Drift Corr. -2, True Head. 320, Temp. C +18, Altitude 9300, Air Speed Ind. 206, Air Speed Cal. 176, Air Speed True 207, Wind Dir. 186, Wind Force 10, Ground Speed T. 214[534]

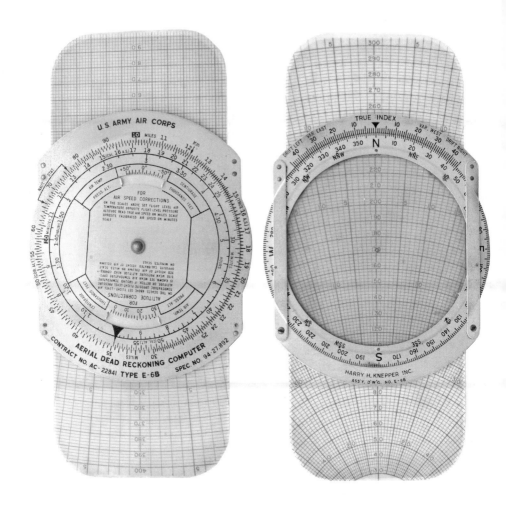

The computer can calculate the effect of wind on the aircraft and temperature on air speed, and perform mathematical computations.

ONC

- Position: Δ27° 30'N 139° 14E, Time 0700 ½, True Head. 320, Temp. C +18, Altitude 9200, Air Speed Ind. 206, Ground Speed 214, Run Time 31, Run Dist. 111, To Destination Dist. 150, To Destination Time 42, To Destination ETA 0742 ½

- Position: DR[535] 28° 53'N 138° 05'E, Time 0715, Drift Corr. 0, True Head. 322, Temp. C +18, Altitude 9200, Air Speed Ind. 206, Wind Dir.

A long line of volcanic islands sticking up between Japan and Iwo showed up on radar. Sgt. Joseph "Joe" Stiborik our radar operator was pretty damn good. He was what men call a solid citizen, a guy you liked, and wanted to be around. Joe gave me a point. If you could identify the point and pick it up on radar, you could get a fix on it.[536]

ONC meant that I saw myself as "on course." There were two fixes here of latitude and longitude. That was probably when Joe gave me the fix off the volcanic islands.

Tech. Sgt. Wyatt "Duze" Duzenbury was another very fine guy and probably the best flight engineer in the group. Duze cared for and babied the engines. There were no engine problems during the mission. Sgt. Robert Shumard assisted Duzenbury. Tom Ferebee and I being up in the group did not know the enlisted men all that well and only came in contact with them when we were flying.

The bomb operated on a very obscure frequency. If the Japanese had been on that frequency by accident, they could have exploded the bomb aboard our airplane. Jake Beser, the radar counter measures person, monitored the frequencies.

 Time 0730, True Course 322, Drift Corr. 0, True Head. 322, Temp. C +18, Altitude 9200, Air Speed Ind. 205, Ground Speed 216, Run Time 29 ½, Run Dist. 107[537]

- Position: 29° 24'N 137° 40'E, Time 0740, True Course 325, Drift Corr. 0, True Head. 325, Temp. C +18, Altitude 9200, Air Speed Ind. 205, Ground Speed 216, STC1. Reset Compass V.

We started our climb up to 10,000 feet. Morris Jeppson went back in the bomb bay again and took out the three green safety plugs and put in the red ones activating the bomb's internal batteries.[538]

The plugs isolated the testing system voltage from the bomb. Jeppson said at that point the bomb was running itself.[539]

Parsons made adjustments on the console that controlled the bomb's circuitry. I looked at Morris and asked him what happens if the green lights on the console go out and the red lights go on. He looked at me, shook his head, and said, "We are in a hell of a lot of trouble."

How did I feel? Carrying the bomb did not bother me, but the fact they were fooling around with black powder did. It is not something to fool around with. But when the talk started that "we have a live atomic bomb on board" I started thinking, an atomic bomb, holy mackerel, what are we going to do today! The only people on board who knew it was an atomic bomb prior to the mission were Tibbets, Parsons, and Ferebee.

We started to climb and we climbed slowly. It took about an hour to climb to 33,000 feet because we climbed so slowly. I was recording on the log all the way.

 Time 0750, Drift Corr. 0, True Head. 324, Temp. C +14, Altitude 13000, Air Speed Ind. 206

Page 2

- Position: DR 30° 11'N 137° 03'E, Time 0755, True Course 325, Drift Corr. 0, True Head. 325, Temp. C +8, Altitude 15000, Air Speed Ind. 204, Air Speed True Av 217, Ground Speed 227, Run Time 15, Run Dist. 52

Over water you identify the position by longitude and latitude. Here I am at 30 degrees (DR 30°) eleven minutes north (11'N) 137 degrees 3 minutes east (137° 03'E) time 0755 that is a spot over the water.

The air speed changes while climbing, the higher the altitude the faster the aircraft in terms of relative air speed.

It was a very clear day. I could see the coast of the Island of Shikoku a good hundred miles away. We had to cross the island and then the Inland Sea in order to get to Hiroshima on the main island of Honshu. When we were over Shikoku, I wish that I had recorded it in my log for historical purposes. The city of Mishima was visible from probably seventy-five miles away.

Where the hell are the fighters, I asked. There were none. No one commented.

I had all kinds of maps with me. After the war a Japanese writer came to see me and told me what their radar said we did during the mission. I told him, "I don't give a damn what your radar said." He did not know what he was talking about. We came right over Shikoku.

Time 0800, True Head. 325, Temp. C +2, Altitude 17500, Air Speed Ind. 203

The air raid alert sounded at 7:09 a.m. (Hiroshima time) as *Straight Flush* appeared over Hiroshima.[540] After two passes the plane flew away at 7:25 a.m. and the all clear sounded.[541]

Time 0807, True Head. 325, Temp. C -3, Altitude 20500, Air Speed Ind. 200

- Position: 31º 15'N 136º 12'E, Time 0815, True Head. 325, Temp. C -8, Altitude 23500, Air Speed Ind. 197 Av, Air Speed True Av 240 ½, Wind Dir. Met 240, Wind Force 20, Ground Speed 238, Run Time 20, Run Dist. 76

- Time 0823, True Head. 327, Temp. C -14, Altitude 26500, Air Speed Ind. 195

At 0830 Dick Nelson took the message in Morse code from Eatherly's *Straight Flush*, "Y-3, Q-3, B-2, C-1." The cloud cover was "2/10 lower and middle lower, 2/10 at 15,000 feet."[542]

Tibbets gave the word to the crew, "It's Hiroshima."

Position: 32º 08'N 135º 34'E, Time 0830, True Head. 329, Temp. C -20, Altitude 29000, Air Speed Ind. 194, Air Speed True Av. 258, Ground Speed 258, Run Time 15, Run Dist. 64, IFF OFF

Identification friend or foe, IFF, you better have the radio frequency on when flying near the Americans and have it off when flying near the Japanese, and record it in the log. PFC Richard Nelson, the youngest guy on the crew twenty-years old, was our radio operator.

The inter-plane command channel to be used was Channel G (143.01 mcs) of the An/ARC-3. The strike aircraft retuned Channel 7 of An/ART-13 transmitter to 7455 kcs. If any strike plane had to abort, the Field Orders were to "immediately call the Twentieth Air Force Weather Station, Iwo Jima, call sign 00V181, on 7455 kcs and transmit message saying aborting." The 313th Wing Station would be monitoring.[543]

The Field Orders defined the IFF rule. "Turn IFF to position #1 immediately before take-off. Turn IFF off when 50 miles from coast of Japanese mainland. Turn IFF on at land's end (enemy coast) when returning from target. Turn IFF off when landing."

This was just like any other mission except no one was shooting at us. I had more time to keep a nice log. When the enemy is shooting at you, it makes keeping the log more difficult. The missions in Europe were shorter and not so deep, so it was not as important as keeping the log here.

 Position: 32º 40'N 134º 53'E, Time 0840, Radar, True Head. 344, Temp. C -24, Altitude 30700, Air Speed Ind. 197

"Time 0840" "Time 0845" I probably just guessed since we were just a little further along.
• Time 0845, True. Head. 353, Temp. C -25, Altitude 30700, Air Speed Ind. 200, Air Speed True 285, Radar Wind 170º 08K

Ferebee, Tibbets, Parsons, and myself checked and agreed we had the target, the T-shaped bridge. We wanted to make sure. Then we set the bomb run for a good five minutes. Ferebee turned to me and said, "Dutch, if we had stayed on a bomb run this long while we were in Europe, they would have blasted us out of the sky."

The Japanese did not have any defense against high-flying airplanes.

 Position IP, Time 0912, True Head. 264, Temp. C -22, Altitude 30700, Altitude True 31060, <u>Large</u> 8 Ships in Harber (*sic*) at Mishima

An air sea rescue was planned for this mission. Along our route were surface ships. We knew their location and had radio frequencies if we had to contact them.

Tom Ferebee told me, "If we have trouble make sure you land close to a ship so I don't get my damn feet wet." We did have life preservers, the Mae Wests, you can guess why the name.

A submarine was in the Inland Sea of Japan between Shikoku and Honshu, so if we had to go down hopefully they would pick us up. I could see land and knew I was on course.

We went right in and hit our IP at 9:12 and stayed at an altitude of 30,700 feet until the bomb dropped. The IP is the initial point, the place where you start your bomb run. We changed course from 344 to 264. I had wanted to be at a heading of 270, but missed it a little so we ended up at 264. The IP was over a small town east of Hiroshima because we wanted to bomb on a westerly heading.[544]

The city of Mihara, east of Hiroshima on the east coast of Honshu, is at approximately 34°24'N and 132°05'30"E.

I looked down through the drift meter for a reference on the ground. By now I am doing it visually, by guess and by God.

Navigator to pilot, I called to Tibbets. He responded, "pilot."

Turn to heading 270.

I had been getting winds for Tom all the way up and now am standing behind Tom. He had dozed off on the way up. Tom could sleep anytime.

By this time our nose was on the target. "Do you see the bridge," I said.

"I see it," exclaimed Tom. Parsons, Tibbets from his seat, and Lewis looked over the nose. We got around to 264.

Tom said, "I have the target."

Parsons and I look at the winds. Tom adjusts the Norden bombsight for the winds, three degrees to the right. He has to be careful. Then I sat down and fastened my seat belt. We had warned Parsons and Jeppson about the turn.

We made a left hand turn, found our target, and bombed it and that is exactly what this log shows. After increasing our altitude to 30,700 at 8:40 we stayed up there until the bomb dropped at 9:15:15. I made a note here that we had eight large ships in the harbor of Mishima. It was important for the navigator to make observations and record them and I did.

Tom Ferebee said he wanted to bomb into the wind to get the maximum accuracy.

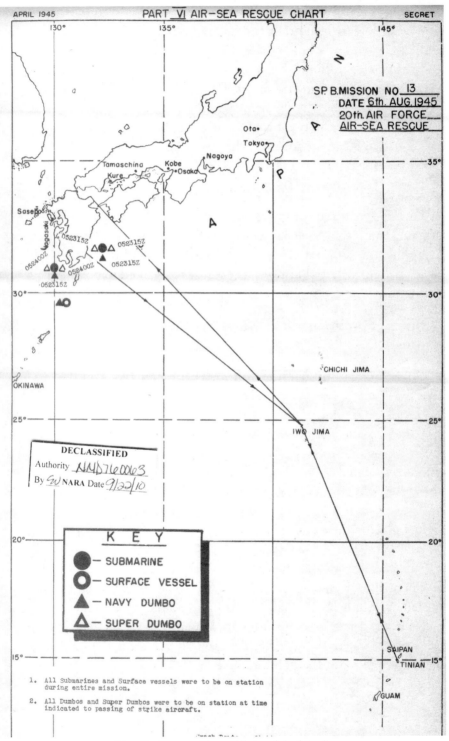

Air - Sea Rescue Chart (National Archives)

He said, "I did not care how long we sit over the target as long as I get maximum accuracy."[545]

All the while this was going on at about every 5,000 feet, I am telling Tibbets to change his course to fly a triangle, a little to the east, and turn around slightly to get the wind drift on three different headings. Then I could get a good idea of what the wind was at that altitude. I advised Tom before we ever turned onto the IP what his wind and drift would be. Almost as soon as we reached the IP the bombsight can be in extended vision, which flips all the optics a little bit forward. But do not make a mistake and drop your bomb when you are in extended vision or you will be very short. Tom and I had seen other bombardiers do this, but Tom never did. He flipped up the extended vision and saw the AP (aiming point) right away, the Aioi Bridge. Tom chose the target.[546] The bombardier is flying the airplane now. Tom has control flying through his bombsight. He is keeping the crosshairs on the target. If he does it right and put the information in his bombsight correctly, he is going to hit the target.

Either Tibbets or Lewis made the announcement, "We are on the final bomb run. Be sure you put your goggles on." Everyone put them on except Ferebee who forgot.[547] The instructions were to adjust the goggles to total darkness, extinctions as they put it. While on the bomb run the radio tone went out.[548]

We stay on the heading and go in until suddenly the bombsight releases the bomb automatically. Nobody pushes a button. There were two indices: one index was set and the other a movable index. When the indices crossed the bomb dropped and the instruments on parachutes fell out of Sweeney's airplane. The bomb detonated 1,890 feet above the ground and 800 feet from the AP.

The airplane surged from the lost weight of the bomb. Tibbets flipped off the automatic pilot, takes manual control, goes into the 155 degrees turn to the right, 60 degree bank, pushed the throttles all forward, and runs like hell. Sweeney was doing the same thing behind us a ways going to the left. The shock wave hit almost as soon as we leveled off. The tail gunner saw the shock wave coming.

It took about forty-five seconds to make the turn. Paul could not see to fly with his goggles on and the first thing I know as we go into the turn – zing, back through the airplane comes a pair of goggles.

In order to protect friendly aircraft from radioactivity in the immediate area above the explosion, airplanes were restricted from entering a fifty mile radius from any of the targets during a period of four hours prior to and six hours subsequent to the strike time.[549]

 Position Bomb Away, Time 0915[15], True Course 265, Drift Corr. -3, True Head. 262, Temp. C " (C – 22), Altitude 30700, Altitude True 31060, Air Speed Ind. 200, Ground Speed 285, Circle E of Target[550]

A sixty-degree bank at that altitude is a particularly violent maneuver. When Paul trained our pilots initially he told them, "Always make your bank tight enough that you feel the tail start to stall, then you have it tight enough." A good pilot can feel the tail starting to stall and then we ran away from it.

I am timing the bomb using my watch, timing the forty-three seconds, looking through my radarscope, and holding on. The scope was our best method of measuring the distance away from the bomb when it exploded. I was a busy guy looking at two things at the same time. We were all belted in tight. We were not going to pull a Blanchard. I pitied Morris Jeppson and Parsons sitting on the floor next to me. Jeppson had his parachute on. I wondered if he knew something that I didn't. Our parachutes were still hanging on the hooks. Sometimes you can get too familiar. We might have been a little nonchalant about the whole damn business.

One, two, . . . forty-three seconds and nothing. Everyone on that airplane was timing the forty-three seconds and I think we all concluded it was a dud because nothing happened. After another second or two there was a bright flash in the air. The bomb detonated. It worked! It was a success![551] At the same time the radarscope showed we were almost twelve miles away and felt our first shock wave. Some funny things happened when the bomb dropped. A B-29 was a pressurized airplane. Compared to the B-17 it was like getting into a Cadillac for heavens sake instead of a Ford Model A. You were supposed to depressurize before you went over the target. We did not depressurize. We were up at 30,000 feet. What the hell, if something was going to happen, we were going to get killed anyway so why depressurize.

Suddenly the airplane snapped like a piece of sheet metal cracking. Someone hollered and called out "flak." No one said anything until the first shock wave. We felt the jolt very similar to a burst of flak and close under the wing. Now it had to be either Paul or Tom or me, because we were the only three who had experienced it up until that time. I knew it was not me. Later on Tibbets admitted he was the one.

Tech. Sgt. George "Bob" Caron, the tail gunner, was a good guy and had worked with Tibbets on the test program of the B-29. I do not know why we had a tail gunner, but we did. The time between the shock waves wasn't long, maybe thirty seconds. Bob called up, "No, it wasn't flak. It was a shock wave and here comes another one."

The atomic bomb set up visible shock waves very similar to my way of thinking of dropping a pebble into still water the way the waves come up and out. Two shock waves hit us at Hiroshima. The second wave hit us at about eighteen miles away.

The first one measured at about 3½ Gs. It does not seem like much to a fighter pilot, but in a B-29 at 30,000 feet it seems like a hell of a lot.

We kept going away from the explosion for about a minute to make sure we weren't going to get any more shock waves and that the airplane was okay before we started doing any maneuvers. Boeing built good airplanes. Tibbets banked around to the left to see what happened. The first sight was that large white cloud. I had no way of measuring but guessed the cloud was already up to 45,000 feet. Obviously a tremendous amount of energy had been released.

The ground was covered with thick black smoke and dust and dirt. It looked like a pot of boiling black oil covering practically the entire city of Hiroshima. The only thing visible was the fire burning outside of the smoke on the southern perimeter. Everyone had a good look. We couldn't make any other visible observation, so we turned around to go back to the base. In the meantime Ferebee made his strike report. He was fairly nonchalant "bombing excellent" and so forth. Parsons said excellent and that it looked more powerful than the test in New Mexico.

Capt. William S. "Deak" Parsons prepared the coded report to transfer to General Farrell and Groves: Able Line 1, Line 2, Line 6, Line 9. The message gave an account that the results were good, effects greater than the Trinity test, the target was Hiroshima, and that the conditions were normal in the aircraft.[552]

Conversations started. I think the first thing out of a lot of mouths and what crossed everybody's mind was that "this war is over!" We did not see how people could stand up to such a force and keep fighting.

George Marquardt's plane was exactly where it was supposed to be that day and the camera did not work. Caron took pictures from a hand held camera from the tail of our plane. Some other guys on Marquardt's plane also had some private hand held cameras.

Position Mishima, Time 0931, True Head. 150, Temp. C -18, Altitude 29000, Air Speed Ind. 225

- Position 33º 14'N 134º 01'E, Time 0942, True Head. 142, Temp. C -18, Altitude 29200, Air Speed Ind. 215

- Position: 32º 35'N 134º 36'E, Time 0952 ½, True Head. 140, Temp. C -16, • Altitude 28000, Air Speed Ind. 211

- Position: 31º 49'N 135º 10'E, Time 1005, True Head. 140, Temp. C -11, Altitude 26000, Air Speed Ind. 213, Air Speed Cal. 183, Air Speed True 291, Ground Speed 274, Run Time 23, Run Dist. 105

I emphasize we did NOT CIRCLE THE TARGET, we flew a little bit in the southeast quadrant of Hiroshima after we made our turn around and could not make any visible observation. Everyone said let's go home. I think that's when Tibbets relaxed and started smoking his pipe again. I am not sure you are supposed to smoke incidentally. I used to smoke in a B-17 and got so I could do it under my oxygen mask. You had to be desperate to do that.

We started playing a game of how far can we see that cloud, that white cloud. By this time the cloud was at about 50,000 feet and could still see it from more than 200 miles away.[553]

Now it was up to the navigator to get them home and the mission was over.

Position: 30º 37'N 136º 13'E, Time 1025, True Head. 142, Temp. C -11, Altitude 25000, Air Speed Ind. 206, Air Speed True 278, Ground Speed 263, Run Time 20, Run Dist. 88

"CLOUD GONE"

Position: 29º 43'N 137º 03'E, Time 1041, True Head. 142, Temp. C -10, Altitude 25000, Air Speed Ind. 206, Air Speed Cal. 176, Air Speed True 270, Ground Speed 260, Run Time 16, Run Dist. 69, To Destination Dist. 220, To Destination Time 51, To Destination ETA 11:32, St Lefd, Remarks 10:52 Cloud Gone

- Time 1100, True Head. 140, Temp. C -9, Altitude 24000, Air Speed Ind. 209, Air Speed Cal. 178, Air Speed Time 270, Ground Speed 260

- Time 1115, True Head. 140, Temp. C -9, Altitude 23800, Air Speed Ind. 209

- Time 1120, True Head. 140, Temp. C -9, Altitude 23800, Air Speed Ind. 240

- Time 1140, True Head. 140, Temp. C 0, Altitude 19000, Air Speed Ind. 230

- Position: 26° 20'N 139° 25'E, Time 1146, True Head. 140, Temp. C 0, To Destination ETA 12:20

- Position: 25° 10'N 140° 40'E, Time 1208, True Head. 130, Temp. C +2, Altitude 18000, Air Speed Ind. 221

- Position 10' R IWO, Time 1219, True Head. 155, Temp. C +2, Altitude 18000, Air Speed Ind. 220

When we got to Iwo we changed course. We were on a true heading of about 140, and then changed the heading to about 150. Gradually, we changed a little more as we got closer to home, which Amelia Earhart did not do.

Nelson monitored the radio, but there was no report of surrender from Japan.

I got a good fix when we left Iwo and the next fix was dead reckoning. A compass heading gave me the direction and then I corrected it. That is the horizontal line. Starting off with a compass heading, then a deviation, which gives the true magnetic heading. It is not true north it is magnetic north. You have a variation between true north and magnetic north and make that correction, which gives a true heading. The drift meter reading gives the drift the wind is blowing the airplane. Now you have the true course and that is what you are really flying. That is how you get the course in dead reckoning. Using the computer I calculated the forecast winds from flying on three different headings. By applying the wind you have your direction and now have to get true air speed. True airspeed is airspeed corrected for air pressure and temperature. You set your indicated air speed, temperature, and altitude.

Now you have true air speed and true course. With dead reckoning you can say, that is where I am. That is one way to get a good fix.

 Position: 23° 14'N 141° 43'E, Time 1243, True Course 160, Drift Corr. -5, True Head. 155, Temp. C +4, Altitude 17400, Air Speed Ind. 221, Air Speed Cal. 188, Airspeed True 253, Wind Dir. 110, Wind Force 26K (IWO written over the wind notations), Ground Speed 237, Run Time 24, Run Dist. 95, To Destination Dist. 317, To Destination Time 1:20, To Destination ETA 14:03

- Position: 22° 45'N 141° 50'E, Time 1253, True Head. 150, Temp. C +4, Altitude 17500, Air speed Ind. 220

Page 3

August 6, 1945
Time Takeoff 0245
Time Landed 1458

- Position: 22° 15'N 142° 03'E, Time 1300, True Head. 150, Temp. C +3, Altitude 17500, Air Speed Ind. 220, Air Speed Cal. 188, Air Speed True 245

- Time 1304, True Course 156, Drift Corr. – 6, True Head. 150, Temp. C +3, Altitude 16500, Air Speed Ind. 220, Wind Dir. 105°, Wind Force 32, Ground Speed 222, Run Time 21, Run Dist. 78, To Destination Dist. 228, To Destination Time 1:01, To Destination ETA 14:05 (L.D. written above 14:05) – 15:11 Base

- Time 1310, True Heading 150, Temp. C +3, Altitude 16500, Air Speed Ind. 245, Air Speed Cal. 210, Air Speed True 278, Ground Speed 255, Run Time 06, Run Dist. 22, To Destination Dist. 206, To Destination Time 48, To Destination ETA 1358 – 15:00 Base

- Time 1350, True Head. 153, Temp. C +3, Altitude 15600, Air Speed Ind. 238

- Position: 18° 44'N 143° 52'E, Time 1400, True Head. 154, Altitude 14500, Air Speed Ind. 235

Time 1415, True Head. 154, Temp. C +10, Altitude 12800, Air Speed Ind. 235

- Time 1422 ½

- Position BASE, Time 1458

"White House Reaction"

Adm. Richard S. Edwards from the White House map room sent a top secret memo to Admiral Leahy (Eyes Only).[554] "Following information regarding MANHATTAN received: Hiroshima bombed visually with only 1-10th cover at 052315Z. There was no fighter opposition and no flak. Results clear cut successful in all respects. Visible effects greater than any test. Conditions normal in airplane following delivery."[555]

Captain Graham delivered the top secret message from the Secretary of War Stimson to President Truman. "Big bomb dropped on Hiroshima 5 August at 7:15 p.m. Washington time. First reports indicate complete success which was even more conspicuous than earlier test." Truman exclaimed, "This is the greatest day in history."[556]

President Truman ~ "Sixteen hours ago an American airplane dropped one bomb on Hiroshima, an important army base. That bomb had more power than 20,000 tons of TNT. It had more than 2,000 times the blast power of the British Grand Slam, which is the largest bomb ever yet used in the history of warfare . . . Let there be no mistake; we shall completely destroy Japan's power to make war. It was to spare the Japanese people from utter destruction that the ultimatum of July 26 was issued at Potsdam. Their leaders promptly rejected that ultimatum. If they do not now accept our terms they may expect a rain of ruin from the air, the like of which has never been seen on this earth. Behind this air attack will follow sea and land forces in such numbers and power as they have not yet seen and with the fighting skill of which they are already well aware."[557]

The Enola Gay taxiing to the hard stand upon returning from the first atomic bomb strike.
(Official photograph 509th Composite Group Photographic Laboratory
United States Army Air Forces)

"I am going to correct some Things"

Dutch ~ Lewis uttered a few profane remarks like, "My God, look at that
son of a bitch go." That was more accurate than what he wrote.[558] Almost all
his log was written after we returned to Tinian.[559]

We did not put on flak jackets. We did not have any flak jackets.

Jake Beser wrote in his book that a fighter plane came up, flew along side
of us for a little while, did a roll, and left. I have to shake my head. There were
no fighter planes, no other aircraft period.[560] If a fighter had been spotted, all
hell would have broken loose!

Beser was in addition to the crew and in charge of radar countermeasures.
Tom and I both said, "What the hell is he doing here" We didn't know. Beser
was with us at Wendover and flew with all the crews out there. He always

c. The A/C directed to attack the Utsube Oil Refinery 90.20 -
1684 MPI 066009 aborted.

SECTION E

SUBJECT: Analysis of Attack
Reference F.O. No. 13 Special Bombing Mission No. 13.

1. A/C 6292 was directed to attack the Hiroshima Urban Industrial area 90.30 AP - 063096. A/C was to carry a special (Atomic)
bomb load. Result: A/C 6292 made a visual attack on the above primary target, with excellent results. Weather over the target area was
good. Strike and Post Strike Photos were obtained. (See damage assessment reports).

SECTION F

Above: Section E - "Analysis of Attack" (National Archives)
Below: Post Strike Hiroshima Damage Assessment image (National Archives)

POST STRIKE
HIROSHIMA 90.30 URBAN
DAMAGE ASSESSMENT REPORT 192
CIU 20 AF   2965 C 35 PTU

DECLASSIFIED
Authority _NND760063_

brought a bunch of gadgets on board. Nobody really knew what he did. He was not one of my favorite characters.[561]

Some guys have said they flew top cover for us. I don't know how they could have flown higher since we were as high as you could get. Everyone was instructed to stay fifty miles away, so I don't know how anybody saw it.

We did not circle the target. We flew a little bit in the southeast quadrant, but were not able to make an observation of the city.

On the way back to the base there was a lot of sleeping. It seemed like everybody was getting a nap except the navigator. Tibbets took a nap and Bob Lewis flew. Then Lewis took a nap while Tibbets flew. We were all still pretty keyed up. I wouldn't think to comment on what Parsons felt. He must have been elated. His bomb was his baby and it worked just the way he said it would. Deak Parsons was older than the rest of us, the consummate gentlemen at all times. He was the kind of fellow you wanted to know.

I did not get airsick this time. A crowd waited for us to land.[562] The wire recorder of our comments during the mission was turned over to intelligence and disappeared after that. We got out of the airplane and someone called out "attention." Tooey Spaatz came forward greeted us and awarded Tibbets the Distinguished Service Cross.

We arrived tired having been up for more than thirty-six hours without much sleep, without shaving, without brushing our teeth, without doing anything. The plane was checked for radiation and about a two second check of our person. Then, we were offered a shot of bourbon. I did not take it because there was still the debriefing. Only the strike crew was present.

"Debriefing"

Dutch – We didn't get to the party because we had to be debriefed. I went through the important points of the log. Paul Tibbets stood right behind me. There were more generals and admirals there then I had ever seen in my life. If the Japanese had bombed the base that day they could have ended the war in the Pacific.

By this time everybody is pleased and happy. It is more like a bull session than a debriefing. Our operations officer Hazen Payette asked me what time the bomb dropped. Tibbets said "9:15 and 12 seconds."

I said, "9:15 and 15 seconds."

PART II - ENEMY FIGHTER REACTION

Section A - Missions 1 through 12

1. Enemy air opposition to these missions was nil. Only 3 fighters were sighted, on the 24 July strikes in the Kobe-Osaka area. No attacks occurred and crewmen made no claims.

2. Lack of air opposition was primarily attributable to the fact that these strikes were run during the period of least enemy activity, the month of July. In addition, the small force of B-29's and the very high altitude at which bombing took place reduced the enemy's capability to intercept.

Section B - Special Missions 13 and 16

Enemy fighter opposition was nil.

Section C - Special Missions 14, 15, 17 and 18

Japanese fighter opposition on these missions was nil.

*****

PART III - ENEMY ANTIAIRCRAFT

Section A - Missions 1 through 12

1. Due to the extreme altitude flown, flak was insignificant on these missions. The following table summarizes the flak encountered:

Mission No.	Target	No. A/C	Altitude	Flak
1	Koriyama	3	28,000	Nil (3 bursts)
2	Fukushima	1	29,000	Nil
3	Nagaoka	2	28,000	Nil
4	Toyama	3	29,000	Nil (1 burst)
5	Sumitomo	3	28,000	Nil
6	Kobe	4	28,700	Moderate and accurate
7	Yokkaichi	3	28,000	Meager and inaccurate
8	Nagaoka	4	28,500	Nil
9	Toyama	6	29,000	Nil
10	Ube	3	28,000	Nil
11	Koriyama	3	29,000	Nil
12	Wakayama	1	28,000	Moderate and inaccurate
	Maizuru	1	25,000	Nil

2. No aircraft were lost to flak on these missions, and of 37 aircraft bombing all targets, only one or 2.7 per cent, sustained flak damage. This aircraft was damaged over the Osaka area.

Section B - Missions 13 and 16

1. Due to the extreme altitude flown, flak was insignificant on these missions. The following table summarizes the flak encountered:

Mission No.	Target	No. A/C	Altitude	Flak
13	Hiroshima	1	30,200	Very meager and inaccurate
16	Nagasaki	1	28,000	Very meager and inaccurate.

2. No aircraft were lost or damaged as a result of flak.

The Enemy Fighter Reactions for the special and atomic missions. (National Archives)

Van Kirk reviewing the navigation at the debriefing.

Payette looked at me and asked, "Why were you late?" I could have shot him. A few days later I went to Hazen Payette and asked to have my log back and to keep it.

He said, "I am supposed to keep it in my intelligence file records."

The regulations said you have to keep "a" log. A copy would be just as good. So I talked Haze into a copy. We did not have copiers. I sat down and made a hand penciled copy for his files. When we went to Roswell, all those files came with us.

Deak Parsons pinned the Silver Star on me in the briefing room.[563]

For some reason or another and I did not know why, Dick (Morris) Jeppson didn't go to the debriefing with us. Dick told us this story. He had walked back to his tent and found some old Navy friends from back home waiting for him. After some conversation the group went to the mess for dinner. We had a pretty good mess at our end of the island. After dinner they returned to the Navy tents and asked each other questions. What did you do in the war? What are you doing for the war? When it came to Dick's turn and he replied nonchalantly, "Why we won the war today." His buddies responded, "You are full of shit!" The next day Dick's friends called him and said, "You bastard. You were right you did."

After the debriefing I went to bed. I was tired. Not only was it a long trip and I didn't get any rest on it, but I also did not get any sleep the day before planning the trip and had been in a poker game. I was dead. I did not even get a free hot dog or a free beer for heavens sakes.

The next morning I had breakfast. I was hungry. Whatever was my assignment I did it and am sure it was not arduous. I am not sure but probably pulled tower duty for four hours the next day. We did not have flight controllers like at Wendover. An operations or flying officer had to be on duty in the tower at all times. I hated it because there were a lot of steps and no elevator. A captain came over. "Do any of you guys know anything about that bomb you dropped yesterday?" He was in charge of fire fighting on the island and wanted to know "what do we do if one of your planes crashes on take off? Do we rush in and try to put out the fire or do we run the other way?"

We talked about it and I told him, "It does not make a bit of difference. You cannot run away fast enough to get away from it."

The top secret report wired from Tinian at 0645Z 6 August following the debriefing and received in Washington at 0845Z (4:45 EWT) speculated that the effects of the bomb "may be attributed by the Japanese to a huge meteor."[564]

"Family Reacts to News"

The newsmen called on my wife early in the morning.[565] As I recall, Tinian was nineteen hours ahead of Northumberland. Mary Jane was up feeding the baby. "What do you think of what your husband did," they asked.

My wife responded, "What did he do?"

After the reporters told Mary Jane what happened she said something intelligent like "I knew they were doing something special out there, but I did not know what." The main thing the press made a big deal of was that our son Tom was named for Tom Ferebee, his godfather.

Jean ~ Jean Van Kirk was with her Snyder grandparents on August 6, 1945. "Grandpa was a caretaker for a little farm back of Selinsgrove, a little town. I graduated one day and then went to work for a dentist, Doctor Simington, the next day. He was the only dentist in town during the war. I was on vacation with grandpa and grandma Snyder. They had a radio, but we didn't have the radio on. Aunt Martha telephoned and said 'have you heard what happened?'

Left to right, Thomas Ferebee, Paul Tibbets, Dutch Van Kirk, and Robert Lewis
(National Archives)

I did not know what in the world she was talking about. Of course we didn't know. Ted never, never said what was going on with all those missions. Then I think grandpa got a newspaper someplace and we were reading about it in the paper."

"As a teenager I was very idealistic and not too happy thinking about what happened. I was ambivalent and was not too sure what I thought about it. I changed my way of thinking afterwards. Mick's favorite expression was always 'He saved my ass.'"

"Ted was hailed as a hero in the town. We were all in awe of him, the whole town. We did not know what to think. This is Ted. This is Teedy. Somebody like him did not do things like that. He came home soon after the mission. They had Tommy by then too. He and Mary Jane went to dinner. The manager of the restaurant someplace in Sunbury gushed all over them. My father was very, very proud of Ted and to think that a kid from Northumberland was chosen for a mission like that." Mick added, "and to haul Eisenhower and Clark around!"

Mick ~ "The captain (of the *Tranquillity*) announced the crew of the *Enola Gay* on the seventh. I went wild when he read Ted's name."

August 7, 1945, the Saipan headquarters of the CINCPAC Psychological Warfare Section had prepared the text for the leaflets to be dropped daily for nine days on Japanese cities with populations greater than 100,000. The text was taken to the Twentieth Air Force headquarters in Guam. Japanese officers assigned to the psych section made the translation.

A recording of a "Nisei" reading the leaflet text was broadcast on the Office of War Information radio station to Japan beginning August 8th at 1830, every thirty minutes until the evening of August 10th.

The 73rd Bombardment Wing was assigned to drop 75 M-16 bomb cases, each containing 32,000 leaflets. The revised text AB-12 was created the morning of August 10th as a result of the Soviet declaration of war against Japan.[566]

"Leaflet Translation for AB-11"

TO THE JAPANESE PEOPLE

America asks that you take immediate heed of what we say on this leaflet.

We are in possession of the most destructive explosive ever devised by man. A single one of our newly developed atomic bombs is actually the equivalent in explosive power to what 2000 of our giant B-29's can carry on a single mission. This awful fact is one for you to ponder and we solemnly assure you it is grimly accurate.

We have just begun to use this weapon against your homeland. If you still have any doubt, make inquiry as to what happened to Hiroshima when just one atomic bomb fell on that city.

Before using this bomb to destroy every resource of the military by which they are prolonging this useless war, we ask that you now petition the Emperor to end the war. Our President has outlined for you the thirteen consequences of an honorable surrender: We urge that you accept these consequences and begin the work of building a new, better, and peace-loving Japan.

You should take steps now to cease military resistance. Otherwise, we shall resolutely employ this bomb and all our other superior weapons to promptly and forcefully end the war.

EVACUATE YOUR CITIES[567]

"AB-12 Leaflet"

この恐るべき事実は諸君が広島に唯一の箇所だけに投下された際如何なるかはそれを見れば判る此の判断を誤らず軍事のみを以て戦争を長引かせる状態を惹き起したかはそれを見れば判る

[vertical Japanese leaflet text, AB-12]

(National Archives)

ATTENTION JAPANESE PEOPLE EVACUATE YOUR CITIES

Because your military leaders have rejected the thirteen-part surrender declaration, two momentous events have occurred in the last few days.

The Soviet Union, because of this rejection on the part of the military has notified your Ambassador Sato that it has declared war on your nation. Thus, all powerful countries of the world are now at war against you.

Also because of your leaders' refusal to accept the surrender declaration that would enable Japan to honorably end this useless war, we have employed our atomic bomb.

A single one of our newly developed atomic bombs is actually the equivalent in explosive power to what 2000 of our giant B-29s could carry on a single mission. Radio Tokyo has told you that with the first use of this weapon of total destruction, Hiroshima was virtually destroyed.

Before we use this bomb again and again to destroy every resource of the military by which they are prolonging this useless war, petition the Emperor now to end the war. Our President has outlined for you the thirteen consequences of an honorable surrender: We urge that you accept these consequences and begin the work of building a new, better, and peace loving Japan.

Act at once or we shall resolutely employ this bomb and all our other superior weapons to promptly and forcefully end the war.

EVACUATE YOUR CITIES.[568]

LeMay launched more B-29s with conventional bombs against Japan. The 509th flew Special Bombing Missions Nos. 14 and 15.

Dutch ~ Bill Laurence from the *Times* went on the second atomic mission to Nagasaki. Tibbets told Tom Ferebee and me to get Bill all the equipment he needed. We hung on him every piece of equipment we could find. Bill's small stature was weighed down and he could hardly move.

"Nagasaki Mission"

Operations Order No. 39 for Special Mission No. 16 assigned Maj. Charles W. Sweeney, commander of the 393rd Squadron, to pilot aircraft No. 44-27297 victor No. 77, nicknamed *Bock's Car,* sometimes called *Bockscar* or *Bocks Car.*[569]

Dutch ~ We waited after Hiroshima to see the reaction of the Japanese. Anyone who had seen the effects of the uranium bomb was thinking we were going to hear the order of surrender almost any minute. In my opinion the reason the Japanese did not surrender was because they had an atomic program too. The Russians did. The Germans did. The Russians were the only ones we really worried about.

Later, we found out that the Japanese program was based on uranium-235, like *Little Boy*, the bomb we dropped at Hiroshima. The next bomb, *Fat Man*, was a plutonium bomb. The Japanese did not learn, nor the Germans, how to make a bomb out of plutonium. If you never made a bomb out of plutonium and only out of 235 you would logically think that you only had enough uranium for one bomb. We used all the uranium-235 made at Oak Ridge, Tennessee, in our bomb.

Before we dropped the bomb, the Twentieth Air Force dropped probably several million leaflets over about a dozen Japanese cities before we dropped the bomb telling them what was going to happen. So the Japanese were warned. I have been told that if a Japanese citizen were found with one of those leaflets at the time that he would have been killed. If I had been in Tokyo during the big fire bombings, I would have surrendered the next day for heavens sake, any logical person would have in my opinion.

Nothing happened not until after the second bomb was dropped. Sweeney was to fly the next mission. In retrospect Tibbets was asked why he did not fly that mission and responded, "We had fifteen trained crews and they all deserved an opportunity to drop the bomb."

Various things happened on the next mission.[570] Sweeney and his crew regularly flew *The Great Artiste*, which had been fitted with observation instruments for the Hiroshima flight.[571] Instead of taking the instruments out, a decision was made to switch airplanes. That is the reason Sweeney flew *Bock's Car*.[572] The decision to drop the second bomb as soon as possible was to make sure that Japan understood we had more bombs of this type. The rush to drop the second bomb was in part why I believe such a lousy job was done.

The mission took place during bad weather. In planning the navigation you work backwards from the time you want to drop the bomb to take off. Based on the meteorological data for the Nagasaki mission, I planned the navigation, the legs, and so forth, but usually the meteorological conditions changed and adjustments had to be made during the flight.

A small island off the coast of Japan was chosen for the rendezvous of the three planes, which necessitated a high altitude at 30,000 feet. I said, "You cannot do it fellows." The instruments were not precise enough. At high altitude the visibility would make it difficult to get the planes together.

Sweeney said, "Yes we can."

That was Sweeney for you.

(Charles) Don Albury and Jim Van Pelt did the best write up of the mission. One of the airplanes, *Big Stink*, was not at the rendezvous point.[573] So Sweeney waited there for forty minutes.[574] The instructions were to wait five minutes. In Sweeney's book he said that Jim Hopkins got his airplane up to 39,000 feet. He would have had to be jet propelled scared to get it up to that altitude. That was a crock of malarkey. They just did not have the visibility.

A bad front was coming through and Iwo Jima would have been socked in weather wise and could not be used as a rendezvous point to go into Nagasaki. The other reason was that going to Iwo would have made the mission longer too because of the distance to Iwo and a left turn into the target city.

After Nagasaki Paul told me to look over their logs, and tell him what happened. I am convinced that the airplanes circled the island at the same time but two were going in one direction and the third in the opposite one. They never saw each other. Ashworth and Sweeney never did like each other; let me put it that way. They were not getting along and did not communicate real well.

The weather, which had been reported good, turned sour while Sweeney waited at the rendezvous. Finally, they decided to go on to Kokura, their primary target. He went in on the bombing run on the planned heading. Beahan couldn't see the target to drop the bomb and said don't drop. They swung around again and came in on a different heading with the same result and Beahan still couldn't see the ground. Three bomb runs were made on Kokura wasting more time and in addition to running low on fuel. We had lots of fuel left on our mission. The only thing we could figure out was that Chuck must have had the plane on automatic rich all the time or something like that.[575] He made a lot of mistakes.

If Sweeney's crew couldn't drop the bomb visually, they were to drop it in the ocean and find a place to land the airplane. Okinawa was the closest land base at that particular point in time. "We had strict orders that the bomb <u>must</u> be released under visual conditions, that is that the bombardier must be able to sight the target through his bombsight...only enough fuel remained for one bomb run," wrote Beahan in 1984 in a note about the mission.

Sweeney decided to go to the secondary target, Nagasaki, and lined up on a radar run, which they were not supposed to do. (Navy Officer) Dick Ashworth said, "We will drop it by radar if necessary" and took responsibility for that to his credit. Ashworth shared his recollection sixty years later in the Anniversary Special issue of *Time* magazine. He went to Sweeney and said, "We're going to be able to make one run on this target if we're lucky" and to be prepared to use radar.

On a radar run the navigator drops the bomb through the radarscope. I never did because Ferebee never let me. Jim Van Pelt lined up on the radar run and got ready to drop after a fifteen second bomb run. The visibility was very poor. At the last minute the clouds opened up and Beahan sees the target, "I got it. I got it," about a fifteen second bomb run.

The bomb missed the target by about two miles. It was a good miss. A lot of people's lives were saved at Nagasaki because of that miss.

Bock's Car lined up on a radar run. If you want my particular analysis, they did drop it by radar. Beahan did not have enough of a bomb run to drop it visually. If he had, he would not have dropped it two miles from the target. He needed more time. They were on top of the target before he could pick it up visually, unfortunately.

Beahan comes back and said, "I dropped the bomb visually."

Bombed Nagasaki 090158Z visually. No opposition. Results technically successful. Visible effects about equal to Hiroshima. Proceeding to Okinawa. Fuel problem.

We know he didn't. He knew he didn't, but the war is over. Why make a big fuss about it. That is about the story of that mission. Sweeney tried to land on Okinawa, a fighter base, but didn't have the call sign for the airfield. One of their engines had stopped in addition to being low on fuel. Sweeney said to fire the flares for low on fuel. The crew did not know which flare. "Fire every damn flare," he said. All the flares went out: wounded on board, high ranking officer on board, low on fuel, and everything. Fred Olivi and Jim Van Pelt both said they fired the flares.

On the return to Tinian, Ashworth recalled they tuned into some local news and received word on the radio that Japan had approached the Swiss about surrendering. The mission was a "major contribution" to bringing an end to the war, but came with a "gnat's eyebrow of being a disaster," according to Ashworth.[576]

In the meantime they were trying to land on Okinawa, which was a busy fighter base with aircraft taking off and landing. To Sweeney's credit he did put the airplane in a fighter pattern and practically burned out the brakes to get stopped before the end of the runway. Fighters being smaller and more maneuverable flew a much tighter pattern than bombers. The turns were sharper.

Ashworth, Sweeney, Beahan, Van Pelt, and Albury conferred under the wing with a map trying to decide where the bomb hit and to get word back to Tinian of what happened. The communications officer initially refused to let them send the message until they found General Doolittle on the island. He knew about the bomb. Then a message was sent back to Tinian. After refueling *Bock's Car* returned to Tinian. And that is the story of that particular mission.

The casualties reported for the Hiroshima and Nagasaki missions vary widely. The Manhattan Engineer District estimated total casualties for Hiroshima as 66,000 dead and 69,000 injured, and for Nagasaki 39,000 dead and 25,000 injured.[577] Japanese estimates of Hiroshima bomb were 71,000 dead/missing and 68,000 wounded.[578] The initial reports from Japan's officials underestimated the losses at Nagasaki.[579] In Robert F. Dorr's *B-29 Superfortress*

Units he compared the Hiroshima, Nagasaki, and Tokyo fire raid total casualties as 140,000 – 150,000, 75,000 – 80,000, and 185,000 and land damage of 4.7, 1.8, and 15.8 square miles respectively.[580]

James Starnes ~ *August 9, 1945,* aboard the *Missouri* "Admiral Halsey said, 'Looks like it is coming to an end.' A day or two later we got word that the *Missouri* was going to be the place where the surrender would take place. I thought we should get out our swords and shine them."

President Truman in a letter responding to Senator Richard Russell wrote "My objective is to save as many American lives as possible but I also have a humane feeling for the women and children in Japan."[581]

The Psychological Warfare plan proceeded with the drop of 50 M-16 bombs containing 768,000 copies of leaflet AB-11 on Osaka, Fukuoka, and other cities. The following day another fifty bombs with 1,600,000 copies of the revised AB-12 leaflet were dropped on Kumamoto, Yawata, Omuta, and Yokohama.[582]

August 10, 1945, Truman ordered the continuation of bombing Japan. B-29s targeted Amagasaki and Tokyo was to be next.

"A Third Atomic Bomb Mission"

Dutch ~ We organized a little trip down to Guam and met the media. While we were in LeMay's office he asked Tibbets, "Do you have another bomb?"

Tibbets said, "Yes sir. We have a third one back at Wendover."

LeMay turned to Tibbets and said, "Get it out here and you are going to fly it."

Sweeney started to leave the room. LeMay told Sweeney that he sure fouled up. Sweeney knew he did not do a good job on that mission. Of course LeMay telling Paul he was going to fly the next one if we got the bomb out here was further proof of it.

I am personally glad there was not a third bomb because the next mission I might have screwed up on and done a worse job and then I wouldn't be able to say these things about Sweeney.

Anyway, LeMay did not have the authority to give the order, and the components would have to be assembled like the other bombs.

August 11, 1945, armored Russian columns had hammered a hundred miles into Manchuria against the Kwantung Army while the United States Marines took control of several of the Marianas Islands. Headlines on the home front announced the news of the big four Allied powers conditional acceptance of Japan's offer to end the war. The two key conditions of acceptance mandated the Emperor subject himself to the orders of a supreme Allied commander and that a government be established in Japan in accordance of "the freely expressed will of the Japanese people."[583]

August 14 -15, 1945, the Superforts renewed attacks on the railway yards, shipping off the Kure naval base, naval and army arsenals, and oil refineries on Honshu.

During the night of the fourteenth a coup d'état to stop the surrender of Japan and attempt to place Hirohito under house arrest failed. A small group of middle echelon young military officers killed Gen. Takeshi Mori, the commanding general of Hirohito's personal guard. A forged order was created in an attempt to surround the palace. Another conspirator with a squad of men tried to stop the radio broadcast of the Emperor's surrender message.[584] The dissident soldiers burned the private homes of the former Premier Kantaro Suzuki and President of the Privy Council Kiichiro Hiranuma.[585]

Secretary of State James Byrnes handed Truman the telegram from the Japanese Foreign Office to the Allied powers that "His Majesty the Emperor has issued an Imperial rescript regarding Japan's acceptance to the provisions of the Potsdam Declaration."

The president addressed reporters and announced that the Japanese had surrendered unconditionally. "This is a great day...the day we've been waiting for. This is the day for free governments in the world. This is the day when fascism and police government ceases in the world."

To the military personnel preparing for the invasion of Kyushu the news that the war was over saved their lives. They had a future.

Mick ~ "The bomb dropped at Hiroshima then Nagasaki. We did not go ashore. We got a notice that said, 'Forces will not invade.' I am not alone and I can talk to many people my age who were in the service who are going to say, 'Ted saved my life' and damn it they are right; he did. I didn't know them all up and down the coast of Japan but Ted, the crew, the *Enola Gay* then Nagasaki, then on the twelfth and they issued the surrender. That is how close we were to the truth of the invasion of Japan. My name stood on the list but we didn't go ashore. The estimate of loss was 500,000 American military

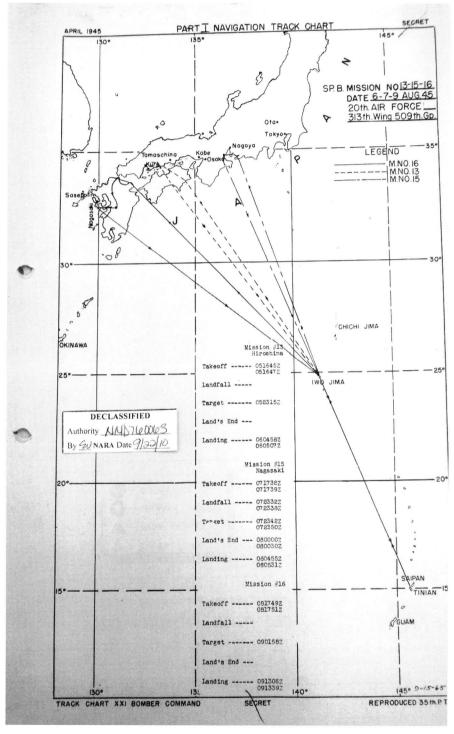

Navigational Tract Chart for Missions #13, 15, and 16. (National Archives)

personnel. Ted saved my life."

From then on the *Tranquillity* picked up survivors and military wounded to take them to Guam, which became the major hub before Hawaii.[586]

August 15, 1945
United States Naval Dispatch
From: Supreme Commander For The Allied Powers
Action: The Japanese Emperor, The Japanese Impereal (sic)
Government, The Japanese Imperial Headquarters

I have been designated as the Supreme Commander for the Allied Powers (the United States, the Republic of China, the United Kingdom and the Union of Soviet Socialist Republics) and emporered (sic) to arrange directly with the Japanese authorities for the earliest practicable date for the cessation of hostilities. It is desired that a radio station in the Tokyo area be officially designated for continuous use in handling radio communications between this headquarters and your headquarters. Your reply to this message should give the call signs, frequencies and station designation. It is desired that the radio communication with my headquarters in Manila be handled in English text. Pending designation by you of a station in the Tokyo area for the use as above indicated, Station Jum on frequency 13705 Kilocycles will be used for this purpose and WTA will reply on 15965 day and 7090 night. Upon receipt of this message, acknowledge.

Signed: MacArthur.[587]

The temporary promotion was announced of Theodore J. Van Kirk's promotion from captain to major by command of Lieutenant General Nathan Twining.[588]

Decades later, John A. Swen (president of the August 15, 1945 Foundation), wrote to Van Kirk.[589]

As a boy of 13 I was placed with 900 boys between age 10 – 16 in a cloyster in Semarang Java Indonesia. We were sick starved and near death when rolling out my mat between the 30 odd boys on our room infested with lice and bed bugs. I nightly said my child prayer for the American servicemen who died so we might live.

It gives me great pleasure to have this opportunity as president and as editor to honor your deed of bravery as a 24 year old boy.

May God give you peace for your soul eternally.

Yours respectfully

John Swen

HEADQUARTERS
UNITED STATES ARMY STRATEGIC AIR FORCES
APO 234

15 August 1945.

TO: All Personnel, Headquarters, USASTAF.
Commanding General and all Personnel, Eighth Air Force, APO 902.
Commanding General and all Personnel, Twentieth Air Force, APO 234.

In this hour of victory, my heartiest congratulations go to the officers and men who carried out our strategic bombing program against Japan.

Although I was not with you long, I had ample opportunity for first hand observation of the magnificent job you did in the Marianas and Iwo Jima, and were preparing to do on Okinawa. I visited your installations and was impressed more than I can say. I saw all my orders carried out with a precision and fidelity that gratified me more than I can possibly express.

You have made a tremendous contribution to our victory. You who helped plan and direct our missions and operate our headquarters made a record of unmarred efficiency. You who serviced our airplanes and kept them flying set a new standard of tireless and faultless maintenance. You who flew the airplanes, on the longest over-water missions ever known, showed a courage, skill and faithfulness of the highest order.

Our crews who were lost gave up their lives in the highest type of heroism ---- in a spirit of willing sacrifice toward the good of all. To these gallant men, history will pay its tribute.

Yet in a sense you have already paid the finest kind of tribute to your fallen comrades. You carried on. In your hands our strategic bombing program reached a degree of perfection, in every respect, such as few military operations in all history could boast of. I am proud of all of you for what you have accomplished.

CARL SPAATZ,
General, U.S. Army,
Commanding.

Gen. Carl Spaatz letter (National Archives)

August 28, 1945, the headquarters of the United States Army Strategic Air Forces distributed the Lovett to Spaatz letter to the Twentieth and Eighth Air Forces "All personnel will be greatly satisfied with the following extracts of a letter . . ."

> Robert A. Lovett
> War Department
> The Assistant Secretary for Air
> Washington, DC

General Carl Spaatz
Hq., USSTAT
APO 234, San Francisco
Dear Tooey:

Now that the Jap envoys are on their way to Manila I am prepared to accept as face value the almost incredible fact that the fighting stage of the war is over. The decisive factor in the sudden collapse seems to have been air power and the old myth of not being able to defeat a major country with its armies intact except by invasion seems to have been shattered once and for all . . .

We are terribly proud of the Air Force. I am sure it's the greatest team the world has ever seen . . . I send you and all in your Command my warm congratulations and my grateful thanks for your part in the magnificent victory.

Very Sincerely yours
/s/ Bob Lovett[590]

"Signing the Surrender"

James Starnes ~ A few days before "we took the ship into Sagami Bay and could see Mount Fuji. Japanese river pilots led us into Tokyo Bay to avoid mine fields. We called the pilot Mr. Moto. He spoke impeccable English. All of a sudden we went from hatred and death to friendship. We asked him questions. Could we go into Tokyo? Were some Japanese sore losers? Moto responded, 'the Emperor said . . . ' We anchored in the Bay, not moored. The destroyers brought the press on the port side."

September 2, 1945, "I was the Officer of the Deck from 0800 to 1200. Every four hours there was a different Officer of the Deck, third in command under the captain and the executive officer. My job was to make sure we did not screw up.[591] We flew the flag of the top most Commander aboard: first, Halsey, a four star admiral, then Nimitz's, a five star admiral; we hauled down Halsey's flag, and raised MacArthur's, a five star general, twin flags."[592]

The Deck Log-Remarks Sheet signed by J. L. Starnes, Jr., Lt. Comdr., U.S.N.R., reported on 08-12:

"Anchored as before. 0803, U.S.S. Buchanan (DD484) came alongside to port with various general officers of the Army and foreign representatives to witness surrender ceremonies. 0805, Fleet Admiral C. W. Nimitz came aboard and his personal flag was broken at the mainmast. 0824, U.S.S. Buchanan (DD484) cast off. 0838, U.S.S. Nicholas (DD449) came alongside to port with General of the Army Douglas MacArthur.[593] 0843, General of the Army Douglas MacArthur came aboard and his personal flag was broken at the mainmast alongside the personal flag of Fleet Admiral C. W. Nimitz. 0848, U.S.S. Nicholas (DD449) cast off."[594]

The admiral's barge brought the Japanese officials.[595] Eight side boys, four on each side stood at the top of the gangplank. "The Japanese asked permission to come aboard, and we responded 'permission granted.' Halsey and Nimitz took the Japanese one deck higher, to the surrender deck."[596]

In Tokyo Bay latitude 35° 21' 17" north, longitude 139° 45' 36" east, General Douglas MacArthur and his staff watched as Mamoru Shigemitsu "by Command and behalf of the Emperor of Japan, and the Japanese government," and Gen. Yoshijiro Umezu, Chief of the Army General Staff, "by Command and in behalf of the Japanese Imperial General Headquarters," signed the terms of surrender. General Douglas MacArthur, Allied Supreme Commander for the Allied Forces, signed and accepted at 0908 hours for "all nations," Fleet Adm. Chester W. Nimitz for the United States, Gen. Hsu Yung-Chang for the Republic of China, Adm. Sir Bruce Fraser for the United Kingdom, Lt. Gen. Kuzma Nikolayevich Derevyanko for the USSR, Gen. Sir Thomas Blamey for Australia, Col. Lawrence Moore Cosgrave for Canada, Gen. Philippe Leclerc for the Provisional Government of the French Republic, Adm. Conrad E. L. Helfrich for the Kingdom of the Netherlands, and Air Vice Marshall Leonard M. Isitt for New Zealand.[597]

"It's over. After all the devastation and cruelty, I looked up from the quarterdeck to the upper deck and could see all these Allied officers. It was a feeling of tremendous elation," remembered Starnes.

MacArthur concluded with "let us pray that peace be now restored to the world and that God will preserve it always. These proceedings are closed."

According to the log the ceremony was completed at 0925. "There was a plan to have huge groups fly over the deck. MacArthur turned to Halsey and said, 'Where are the damn planes?' As the Japs came off the deck the bombers

Japanese delegation arriving for the surrender ceremony.
(Army Pictorial Service, National Archives)

blackened the sky." Four hundred fifty carrier planes from the Third Fleet followed by the bombers flew overhead.[598] One of the pilots Richard C. Kahl flew "the power mission with several hundred other B-29s over the deck at about 300 feet to make a display for the Japanese. The noise was incredible."[599] Starnes said, "The message was don't fool with us anymore."

The surrender ceremony broadcast to the world took twenty-three minutes. The war was over!

"Return to Hiroshima September 15, 1945"

Dutch ~ Tibbets, Albury, Sweeney, Van Pelt, Lewis, Ferebee, and myself and other guys from the 509th flew to Tokyo on two C-54s. A lot of materials were being unloaded at the Atsugi Airfield. MacArthur had issued orders that if a plane couldn't get back off the ground and unloaded within a certain length of time to shove it over the hill to the dump. Tibbets said, "I guess I better

USS *Missouri* (Army Pictorial Service, National Archives)

do something about that." I do not know how he did it but Tibbets got the authority to let our C-54s sit there for a period of time while we went into the city and waited for the Japanese scientists who wanted to survey from the ground the bomb damage.

We stayed at The Dai-Ichi Hotel in Tokyo. Their bathtubs were sloped and small. If you were big and fat you could get wedged in there. I wasn't. We had a central mess and got a ration of beer everyday. The best thing about Japan was the rice beer. We found a lot of things to do around there. Bob Lewis found some girls. I don't know where he found them, but he found a bunch of them.

One night we met three flight nurses and they had to take off at a certain time. I was there, Don Albury, and Tom Ferebee.

Tom piped up, "We can take you there."

Now this was a pretty good ride. So we got or stole two jeeps from somewhere and took the nurses. At the airfield Don Albury said he was hungry. He was also drunk, looks around, and says, "They must have food in those warehouses." So he was going to break into those warehouses until he found food, but we talked him out of it.

From the airport to downtown was a distance of about ten miles. MPs with rifles stood at checkpoints along the way. I was in front in my jeep and Don and Tom were the other one. Tom was driving. Every time I slowed down to get ready to stop at a checkpoint, Tom ran into me. He bumped me and yelled, "Come on Dutch. Get going! Don't stop at the checkpoint." At one point he pushed me through the damn checkpoint.

Some American GIs, our Japanese-speaking interpreters, rounded up the Japanese scientists who were to go with us.[600] Finally we take off to go to

Hiroshima and Nagasaki, but couldn't land at Hiroshima.

We flew into a little airport Omura about twenty miles from Nagasaki. When we landed our C-54, the head officer wanted to give somebody his sword. A soldier, he just wanted to go home.

We were given two 1927 vintage buses. Both vehicles broke down before we ever got to the city. Sweeney and I sat on the cab on top of the bus laughing while Paul Tibbets tried to explain to the Japanese operator what was wrong with the bus. The driver and the Japanese officer with us couldn't speak English. For two days we walked all around the city.

While we were in Nagasaki an old Japanese soldier carrying a knapsack was walking to his home. He was devastated finding his home destroyed. It made you think, what if we came home and found our homes in that kind of condition, how we would feel about it. You had a feeling for the enemy.

At Nagasaki the railroad ties were burned out underneath the tracks and a bridge moved about six feet from the blast. The steel mill was bent at an angle. The city had been cleaned up, no bodies anywhere.

Ever since people asked me, "Didn't you get a deadly dose of radiation while you were there?" My answer always is "if I did I am going back to get more because I am eighty-nine and need another shot."

We flew back to Tinian. Another crew took the Japanese scientists back. We were in Tinian for a day or two and received word that Tibbets, Ferebee, and myself were supposed to go home, just the three of us. I remember it distinctly because I had a bad case of dysentery and had to navigate all the way home. Tom Ferebee, nothing wrong with him, slept all the way and when we landed at Honolulu Tom said, "Hey Honolulu this is great! Let's go out and do something."

I'm dead tired. All I wanted to do was to go to bed. Good old Tom could sleep through anything. When we got to Pearl Harbor I believe that is where we saw Eisenhower going the other way. Eisenhower made a comment to us that I always appreciated. "You guys started it, and you guys ended it." Recognizing what we had done during the war was rather nice.

We spent the night, got a good sleep, and then took off for California. We landed to refuel and told to go down to Roswell. A lot of things started happening not in any particular chronological sequence.

September 20, 1945
Headquarters Twentieth Air Force
APO 234, c/o Postmaster
San Francisco, California

AWARD OF THE SILVER STAR – By direction of the President... dated 6 August 1945, announcement is made of the award of the Silver Star to the following named officers and enlisted men of the 509th Composite Group:

For gallantry in action while engaged in aerial flight against the Japanese Empire on 6 August 1945. These individuals were combat crewmembers of the B-29 aircraft which flew from a base in the Marianas Islands to drop on the city of Hiroshima, Japan, the first atomic bomb to be used in warfare. Flying 1500 miles over open water to the coast of Japan, they manned their assigned positions and crossed the island of Shikoku and the Inland Sea. They constantly faced the danger of being hit by anti-aircraft fire, enemy fighters, or suffering mechanical or other failures which would intensify the risks of carrying this powerful missile. Throughout the mission the element of hazard from the unknown prevailed, for this was the first time this bomb, much more destructive than any other in existence, had been dropped from an airplane. The effect it would have on the airplane and these crew members was only to be estimated. Shortly after 0900 they brought the plane in over the city, and at 0915 the bomb release was pressed. The bomb cleared, and fell towards the planned objective. They then headed from the area and, despite a minor effect from the detonation, returned safely to their home base. By their courage and skillful performance of duty achieved in outstanding fashion despite the dangers involved in accomplishment of this historic mission, these individuals distinguished themselves by extraordinary achievement and reflect great credit on themselves and the Army Air Forces.

- Major Thomas W. Ferebee, 0443490, Air Corps, United States Army, as Bombardier.
- Captain Robert A. Lewis, 0668015, Air Corps, United States Army, as Co-Pilot.
- Captain Theodore J. Van Kirk, 0659024, Air Corps, United States Army, as Navigator.
- First Lieutenant Jacob Beser, 0855461, Air Corps, United States Army, as Radar-Counter-Measure Officer.
- Second Lieutenant Morris R. Jeppson, 0868456, Air Corps, United States Army, as Electronics Officer.
- Staff Sergeant George R. Caron, 12143134, Air Corps, United States Army, as Central Fire Control Gunner. (Tail gunner)
- Staff Sergeant Wyatt E. Duzenbury, 36181546, Air Corps, United States Army, as Flight Engineer.
- Sergeant Robert H. Shumard, 20641486, Air Corps, United States Army, as Airplane Mechanic – Gunner. (Asst. Engineer)
- Sergeant Joseph S. Stiborik, 18190899, Air Corps, United States Army, as Radar Operator

- Private First Class Richard H. Nelson, 39706799, Air Corps, United States Army, as Radio Operator[601]

By Command of Lieutenant General Twining

September 23, 1945, Colonel Tibbets and Majors Ferebee and Van Kirk, of the HQ 509th Composite Group, by order of Tibbets were TDY for approximately fifteen days to Washington, DC, on matters pertaining to operations. Travel directed by organization aircraft.[602]

September 27, 1945, by order of Colonel Tibbets, Majors Darby, Ferebee, Hubly, Lucke, and Van Kirk were awarded the Bronze Service Star to the Asiatic Pacific Theatre Ribbon for participation in the Eastern Mandates Campaign.[603]

TABLE 11.3 — VAN KIRK'S NAVIGATION RECORD FOR SEPTEMBER 1945

Day	Aircraft	No. Landings	NAV. Time	Night Nav. Time
09/15/1945	C-54	1	6:50	
09/19/1945	C-54	1	3:15	
09/20/1945	C-54	1	2:55	
09/21/1945	C-54	2	7:05	
09/23/1945	C-54	1	4:25	
09/23/1945	C-54	1	5:25	
09/24/1945	C-54	1	4:55 (O)	
09/24/1945	C-54	1	5:00	
09/25/1945	C-54	2	7:00	
09/25/1945	C-54	1	7:15	
09/26/1945	B-29	1	6:05	

Source: Major Van Kirk's Individual Flight Records. September's record certified correct by Maj. George W. Marquardt, Asst. Operations Officer.

Dutch ~ *October 27, 1945,* we flew to New York City for a big celebration and parades on Army-Navy day. We were with Bing Crosby and Grace Kelly at *Life Goes to a Party.* Bob Lewis thought he was going to take Grace Kelly home until he saw her leave with Crosby. He wasn't in the same class for Christ's sakes. At Tinker Field we had our plane waxed. We did a lot of things like that.

On *November 12, 1945,* President Truman proclaimed November 22, 1945, Thanksgiving Day, in the year of victory over German fascism and Japanese militarism. He acknowledged the sacrifice and service of all Americans. "We have won them (blessings from 'Almighty Providence') with the courage and the blood of our soldiers, sailors, and airmen. We have won them by the sweat and ingenuity of our workers, farmers, engineers, and industrialists. We have won them with the devotion of our women and children. Triumph over the enemy has not dispelled every difficulty. Many vital and far-reaching decisions await us as we strive for a just and enduring peace."

Truman urged Americans to preserve at home and in the world devotion to the essential freedoms and rights of mankind and to the high principles of citizenship.[604]

Dutch ~ The rest of the 509th arrived and reported to Roswell, our new home base. Shortly after that we were given a forty-five day leave, which fell over the period between Thanksgiving and Christmas 1945. I got to spend that entire period at home. I am trying to think how I got home on that particular one. I didn't walk. I think Tibbets probably flew me up into Harrisburg or D.C. At the end of the leave Tibbets probably came in and picked me up. He liked to go into Cincinnati and had a lot of friends there. He would fly in and out of there and pick me up on the way.

By this time Mary Jane had read all the papers and did not have a lot of questions. She did tell me one thing via a wire before I got home. Oh by the way I bought a house while you were gone.[605] It was a big old fancy concrete blockhouse. I did not exactly like the idea. I did not know what I was going to do. Buying a house pins you down a bit but she got a good deal, a very good buy. I think she paid about three thousand dollars. When I saw the house I was happy. About that time I thought about going back to college at Bucknell and living in that house for a while.

December 31, 1945, under the Selective Service System 945,862 men entered the military during the year.

Chapter Eleven — Endnotes

503 The troops named the mess hall the "Dog Patch Inn."

504 Celestial navigation studies also included general theory, time and hour angle, instruments, and astronomical triangles. The students also studied meteorology of different weather conditions such as thunderstorms and icing conditions. Norman Carlisle, ed., *The Air Forces Reader*, (New York: NY, The Bobbs-Merrill Company, 1944), 198.

505 The targets selected for Mission No. 13 were Primary Target: Hiroshima Urban Industrial Area, Secondary Target: Kokura Arsenal and City, and Tertiary Target: Nagasaki Urban area. One of the largest arsenals was located in Kokura and also manufacturing facilities of light automatic weapons, smaller type anti-aircraft and anti-tank guns, and also combat vehicles. The arsenal was reported to have equipment for mixing poison gas.

506 Charles W. Sweeney at twenty-five years old was the only pilot who flew on both the Hiroshima and Nagasaki missions.

507 The entire northeastern and eastern sides of the city were military zones. Both Kokura and Nagasaki had prisoner of war camps nearby. Nagasaki was important as a major military port, the production of naval ordnance, and a shipbuilding center.

508 During the interview for the April 5, 2009, *Culpeper Star-Exponent* McAllister said, "I dealt mostly with Marines, who were a tough breed and still are. I never saw guys like that who said, 'We'll go ashore and we'll whip their ass no problem.' And I have admired and respected the Marines all my life for all they do."

509 Doug Stanton, *In Harm's Way*, 213 to 217.

510 The LCVP (Landing Craft, Vehicle, Personnel) were built in New Orleans by Higgins Industries. Higgins boats were used in every major amphibious operation in the European and Pacific theatres. The National World War II Museum, New Orleans, LA.

511 "We backed off from the immediate scene and sent small landing craft. The men's skin almost pulled off from being in the water so long when they tried to pull themselves up. We sent small landing craft to pick them up at water level and backed off from the immediate scene," said McAllister.

512 The *Tranquillity* had been anchored off Ulithi.

513 McAllister thought he was chosen to administer the penicillin so if it killed McVay he would get the blame rather than somebody important.

514 Doug Stanton, *In Harm's Way*, 243. In 1999 Michael N. Kuryla, Jr., a survivor of the *Indianapolis* and friend of Van Kirk testified before the Senate to exonerate the military record of Captain McVay for the loss of the ship and the men lost in the tragedy.

515 "Psychological Warfare," Tactical Mission Report, Mission No. 312, 313, 314, and 316, Headquarters Twentieth Air Force, Record Group 18, National Archives Building, MD.

516 The "consolidated statistical summary of combat operations" of the Twentieth Air Force reported 513 aircraft airborne, 469 aircraft bombing primary targets, 2 aircraft lost, 6 aircraft damaged, and 1 crew member casualty for Mission No. 312, 313, 314, and 316 Field Order No. 14, National Archives.

517 Tibbets had written that General Spaatz arrived on Guam near the end of July to take

command of the Pacific Strategic Forces with an order drafted by General Groves authorizing the dropping of the "special bomb" on Hiroshima, Kokura, Nagasaki, or Niigata. Victor numbers 82, 89, 91, 90, and 88 in the above order were identifiers for the combat strike aircraft. Copy of Operational Orders No. 35 addressed to the 509th Composite Group, Office of the Operations Officer, Van Kirk personal papers.

518 Bob Lewis, the co-pilot, on the *Enola Gay* lost half a month's salary to Ferebee during a poker game. Thomas and Witts, *Enola Gay*, 48.

519 The Greenwich Workshop, Inc., "Honor The Men Who Brought The Dawn" brochure, May 1995 and Van Kirk.

520 "Navigator's Plan" under operational procedures for the Hiroshima mission and for the earlier twelve Special Bombing missions in the *Tactical Mission Report*, National Archives.

521 In *Day One* Before Hiroshima and After by Peter Wyden, General Farrell asked Parsons, "Where's Your gun?" (New York: Simon and Schuster, 1984), 243. Van Kirk remembered Farrell being present.

522 Van Kirk's flight record for August only listed the mission on the sixth.

523 Robert F. Dorr, *B-29 Superfortress Units of World War 2*, (Oxford, UK: Osprey Publishing Limited, 2002), 93.

524 S/Sgt. George R. Caron graduated from Brooklyn Polytechnic Institute and as a civilian had worked as a mechanical designer on ballistic computing instruments, range finders, and power gun mounts. Enola Gay biographies, Van Kirk personal papers.

525 Caron joked in his autobiography about feeling Van Kirk's boots and that most officers would like to kick a few enlisted men in the derriere, but he believed Van Kirk did not feel that way. George R. Caron and Charlotte E. Meares, *Fire Of A Thousand Sons* The George R. "Bob" Caron Story – Tail Gunner of the Enola Gay, (Westminster, CO: Web Publishing Company, 1995), 235.

526 Lewis kept the log at the request of William Laurence who after the mission made corrections in pencil and rephrased some entries. Lewis wrote the log in almost complete darkness and at Iwo ran out of ink. "Lewis Log," Harry S. Truman Library.

527 The Navigator's instrument panel on the B-29 had an altimeter, compass, air speed indicator, and clock. *The B-29* Pilot Flight Operating Instructions For the Army Model B-29 Airplanes, revised January 25, 1944.

528 First entry from the Navigator's Log of the *Enola Gay*, page 1. The military times were local Tinian time, one hour ahead of Hiroshima. Speed and distance figures were nautical miles (knots). The Δ had a dot in the center to identify a position determined by celestial navigation.

529 The previous thirty minutes Lewis wrote were spent dodging large cumulus clouds. Robert A. Lewis, "Notes Taken During Mission of the Enola Gay to Bomb Hiroshima, August 6, 1945," Collection HS-ABC: Atomic Bomb Collection 1939 – 1996, Harry S. Truman Library.

530 Parsons practiced arming the bomb on the ground. He believed it would be safer to arm the bomb in flight after seeing several earlier crashes prior to the mission.

531 Charles Sweeney, Robert Lewis, and Charles "Don" Albury served with Tibbets during the B-29 testing program. Thomas and Witts, *Enola Gay*, 29.

532 Van Kirk's navigational computer was fundamentally a circular slide rule for solving mathematical problems involving navigation and for determining the effect of the wind

on the aircraft. Department of the Air Force, Air Navigation Manual, 4-11.
533 Martin Bowman, *B-17 Combat Missions*, (New York, NY: Barnes & Noble, 2007), 53.
534 T. 214 was an approximation made by Van Kirk.
535 DR noted a position ascertained by Dead Reckoning.
536 Wheeler's examination book defines a "fix" as the intersection at some point on the earth of two lines or circles of position. In celestial navigation, it is the intersection of two circles from the position of two different stars.
537 Tibbets recalled Parsons made adjustments on the console at 7:30, *The Tibbets Story*, 219.
538 The bomb was armed so that the fusing system could deliver a firing signal. Jeppson explained that the bomb used a "naval gun to fire a block of U235 into a second U235 block within the bomb to produce a nuclear explosion" and should be detonated in the air. Morris R. Jeppson, "What are Hiroshima bomb "safety" plugs," December 7, 1966.
539 Jeppson described his role on the mission in "The Men Who Dropped the Bombs," *Time*, August 1, 2005.
540 The details in George R. Caron and Charlotte E. Meares *Fire Of A Thousand Sons* The George R. "Bob" Caron Story – Tail Gunner of the Enola Gay about times during the mission generally followed Van Kirk's log.
541 Teller wrote that Japanese officials assumed the *Enola Gay* and the instrument and photograph B-29s were on reconnaissance flights and did not sound a second alarm. Edward Teller with Allen Brown, *The Legacy of Hiroshima*, (Garden City, NY: Doubleday & Company, Inc., 1962), 3.
542 Gurney in the *B-29 Story* quoted part of the decoded message. Tibbets responded to the advice "C-1" to bomb the primary target as "quite unnecessary."
543 Nelson monitored at 7310 kcs to intercept in-flight reports from the weather planes over the targets.
544 The Field Orders for the primary target of Hiroshima listed (a) Aiming point: 063096. Reference: XXI BombCom Litho-Mosaic Hiroshima Area, No. 90.30 – Urban, (b) IP: 3424N – 1330530E and (c) Breakaway (if target is bombed): Right turn of at least 150 degrees 2400N – 13334E.
545 "The bombing altitude at 28,000 to 30,000 feet hopefully prevented self -destruction. The initial points to be selected were to be chosen because of radar and visual reference features. The axis of attack was to (1) entail no more than 5 degrees drift on the bomb run, (2) permit at least eight minutes for synchronization, and (3) to be upwind if at all possible...Little consideration was given to flak on the run because of the bombing altitude and the relatively undefended type of target. Bombing air speed, which was 5 miles per hour faster than S.O.P. (standard operating procedure) due to the higher cruising speed of the particular aircraft employed, its lack of turrets and its individual operation." The Bombardier's Plan from the Tactical Mission Report was for the pumpkin bomb missions as well as Hiroshima and Nagasaki. "Mission Report," National Archives Building, MD.
546 Tom Ferebee said, "It was the best aiming point I ever saw."
547 Ferebee felt a stabbing pain from his eyes to his brain fearing he would lose his sight as he watched the bomb explode. "Zero Hour," *Newsweek*, July 29, 1985.
548 Ferebee turned the radio tone switch on sixty seconds before the scheduled bomb release. The tone turned off at the same moment the pneumatic bomb bay doors

opened automatically and *Little Boy* dropped.

549 "Field Orders Number 13," authorized by the Commanding General of the Twentieth Air Force Guam, August 2, 1945.

550 Approximately 78,000 were killed, an estimated 51,000 injured, five square miles of the city destroyed, and Japan did not surrender.

551 "The first atomic bomb dropped from 30,600 feet. It exploded 43 seconds late at 8:15 a.m. Hiroshima time about 1,800 feet above the ground. The City of Hiroshima was devastated, but millions of lives both the Allies and Japanese were saved. Days later the war ended and the killing stopped." Written by Van Kirk on a photograph of the *Enola Gay*.

552 David Kahn, *The Code Breakers* The Story of Secret Writing, (New York, NY: Scribner, 1996), 548 – 549. Tibbets also sent a radio message advising the primary target bombed visually and no fighter opposition or anti-aircraft fire. *The Tibbets Story*, 228.

553 The cloud was observed from 363 nautical miles at 25,000 feet according to the memo report wired to the Chief of Staff following the briefing.

554 During the war, Admiral Edwards served as Deputy Chief of Staff and Aide to the Commander in Chief United States Fleet, then Deputy Commander in Chief United States Fleet, and Deputy Chief of Naval Operations. Admiral William D. Leahy served as Chief of Staff to President Truman from 12 April 1945 to 29 March 1948.

555 Top Secret Memo, Declassified E.O. 11652, "The Decision to Drop the Atomic Bomb," Truman Library, www.trumanlibrary.org [accessed October 6, 2010].

556 David McCullough, *Truman*, (New York: Simon & Schuster, 1992), 454; Stimson Memo, Harry S. Truman Library & Museum; and Harry S. Truman, "Greatest Thing In History," *Life*, October 24, 1955.

557 "Statement by the President of the United States," Truman Library. D. M. Giangreco's *Hell to Pay* is a comprehensive reference for the documentation of Operation Downfall, the invasion of Japan, and the Japanese defensive plans if Japan did not surrender.

558 Four out of seven pages of Lewis's log were written after he ran out of ink. His explanation of how he felt after the bomb dropped: " . . . explain this or J ("I might say" was written over the letter J x-ed out and the following phrase added: "My God what have we done.")

559 Sweeney also related in *War's End* about incidents that he believed distorted the historical record of the two atomic bomb missions. Sweeney characterized Lewis as erratic and sometimes disagreeable as time progressed following his perception of a change in his close relationship with Tibbets and a comment like "My God, what have we done" was out of character. According to what other members of the crew told Sweeney and his personal observations, the entire crew was elated by the success of the mission. While still on Tinian, Sweeney recalled that Claude Eatherly frequently remarked he planned to make money off the bombings after the war and that his claim to have seen the blast was inaccurate.

560 Beser wrote that a fighter pulled up along side the *Enola Gay*, dropped its wheels and flaps to slow down, then did a slow roll and sped away. Jacob Beser, *Hiroshima and Nagasaki Revisited* (Memphis, Tenn.: Global Press, 1988), 112.

561 Only Lt. Jacob Beser flew on both strike aircraft for the Hiroshima and Nagasaki missions.

562 In the 1992 interview with Susan Grace about the atomic bomb Van Kirk said, "You have to remember at that particular time scientists were speaking in glowing terms about all the positive things they could do with this like using it for fuel and energy" and compared the moment to inventions like the telephone.

563 General Spaatz pinned the Distinguished Service Cross on Tibbets when the *Enola Gay* landed. *Stars and Stripes* quoted Tibbets, "We selected Hiroshima as the target when we made land fall. There was no opposition, conditions were clear and we dropped the bomb visually at 9:15 a.m. "Hiroshima Dissolved In Flame and Smoke Says Superfort Crew," Pacific Edition, August 8, 1945.

564 Top secret memo to the Chief of Staff dated 6 August 1945. Photocopy of the declassified document in the unit heritage article on the 509th Composite Group in *Wings of Flame.*

565 The Associated Press called Mary Jane Van Kirk at midnight to inform her of the news. Mary Jane said that her husband had not written about any bombing missions against Japanese territory since his arrival in the Pacific. "Captain Van Kirk First Atom Bomb Raid Navigator," *Sunbury Daily Item*, August 1945.

566 The Nisei used for recording also did the calligraphy on the leaflet. Translation for AB-12 and plan for leaflet drops, "Psychological Warfare" Introduction, Tactical Report, National Archives Building, MD.

567 "Translation of leaflet dropped on the Japanese (AB-11)," Miscellaneous Historical Documents Collection, Truman Library: The Decision to Drop the Atomic Bomb Online Research File, August 6, 1945, http://www.trumanlibrary.org/ [accessed March 1, 2011].

568 Translation of AB-12 "Part I – Psychological Warfare," declassified 8-17-67, National Archives Building, College Park, MD, and also on-line at the Harry S. Truman Library, http://www.trumanlibrary.org/.

569 *Bockscar* and the nose art on the aircraft were removed for the mission. Sweeney's crew for the mission: Charles Donald Albury (co-pilot), Frederick J. Olivi (a third pilot), James F. Van Pelt, Jr. (navigator), Kermit Beahan (bombardier), John D. Kuharek (flight engineer), Raymond G. Gallagher (assistant engineer), Edward K. Buckley (radar operator), Abe M. Spitzer (radio operator), Albert T. Dehart (tail gunner) Frederick L. Ashworth (weaponeer), Philip M. Barnes (assistant weaponeer), and Jacob Beser (radar countermeasures).

570 Aviation writer and historian C. V. Glines in an article on the Nagasaki mission in the September 1995 issue of *Aviation History* concluded that Sweeney did not make stupid mistakes, but that the mission "seemed jinxed." Tibbets used the word "fiasco" although not the fault of Sweeney.

571 William Laurence, science writer for the *Times*, incorrectly identified the strike aircraft name for the Nagasaki mission, but the correct number "77." Laurence was present at the briefing and loading of the bomb according to his press release. He won a Pulitzer Prize for his reporting.

572 Sweeney's crew C-15 flew several practice missions including the night before the Nagasaki mission in *Bockscar*. Campbell, *The Silverplate Bombers*, 113-114.

573 *Big Stink* carried sophisticated photographic equipment. According to Sweeney, while Maj. James Hopkins, Jr., taxied to the runway he discovered that Dr. Robert Serber, a civilian and the *Project Alberta* photographic expert, did not have his parachute, a

violation of military regulations. Hopkins stopped and ordered Serber off the airplane.

574 Yakushima, 30°43'N 130°3E, was the rendezvous point.

575 Fuel consumption was also high at 30,000 feet. Sweeney's autobiography published in 1997 described a fuel reserve issue during the pre-flight checklist. His flight engineer Sergeant Kuharek advised that 600 gallons in the reserve tank were trapped due to a malfunction in the auxiliary transfer fuel pump in the rear bomb bay bladder. It would take several hours to replace the pump. Sweeney advised Tibbets and decided to take off with 6,400 gallons of fuel instead of 7,000 gallons. Kermit K. Beahan in his "Thoughts Concerning the Nagasaki A-bomb Mission" dated December 12, 1984, wrote that the fuel pump issue was discovered while climbing.

576 "Frederick L. Ashworth, 93," *Time*, August 1, 2005.

577 The Manhattan District report in *A Bombing Of Hiroshima and Nagasaki* points to the lack of pre-raid population data, utter confusion following the explosions, destruction of civil installations, and fires that totally consumed bodies for the difficulty in making estimates.

578 Groves did not give Japanese estimates for the Nagasaki bomb, and noted discrepancies in casualty estimates. Leslie R. Groves, *Now It Can Be Told,* 319.

579 Chun, *Japan 1945 From Operation Downfall to Hiroshima and Nagasaki*, 71.

580 The total casualties were the sum of dead and wounded in Dorr's appendix. Dorr, *B-29 Superfortress Units of World War II*, (Botley, Oxford: Osprey Publishing, 2003), 203.

581 Truman's letter in response to Russell's correspondence to the President dated two days earlier urged "If we do not have available a sufficient number of atomic bombs with which to finish the job immediately, let us carry on with TNT and fire bombs until we can produce them...We should cease our appeals to Japan to sue for peace. The next plea for peace should come from an utterly destroyed Tokyo." Truman Library: The Decision to Drop the Atomic Bomb Online Research File, "Online Documents," http://www.trumanlibrary.org/ [accessed March 20, 2011].

582 The leaflet drop program stopped during the night of August 10th when the Japanese government first expressed its willingness to discuss peace negotiations. "Psychological Warfare," Tactical Report, National Archives Building, MD.

583 Jack Bell, "Mikado Must Subject Himself To Orders Of Supreme Allied Chief; People To Decide on Government," (AP), *Niagara Falls Gazette*, August 11, 1945.

584 Some Kamikaze pilots dived to their death in Tokyo Bay after hearing the Emperor's speech. Russell Brines, "Jap Fanatics Slew Palace Guard Trying to Stop Surrender Order," *The Leader-Republican* (AP), September 7, 1945.

585 The *Asahi* (newspaper) account carried in the AP article did not report the fate of the conspirators. "Suzuki Escaped Jap Fanatics," *The New York Sun*, September 21, 1945.

586 "I was part of history because I was there. I didn't kill anybody. I took care of all the patients that I could and did what I was told to do. I don't have any hero in me," reflected Mick McAllister.

587 Copy of United States Naval Dispatch, August 15, 1945. Van Kirk personal papers.

588 Headquarters Twentieth Air Force, APO 234, c/o Postmaster, San Francisco, CA, special Orders No. 31, 15 August 1945. Van Kirk personal papers.

589 John A. Swen, Abbotsford, B.C., president of "The August 15, 1945 Foundation," letter to Mr. Van Kirk, Feb. 2, 1993.

590 Letter to General Spaatz dated August 19, 1945. Record Group 18, National Archives.

591 Starnes worried that the peg-legged Japanese Minister of Foreign Affairs Mamoru Shigemitsu might fall down the stairs. Bill Torpy, "65 years, just down the street," *The Atlanta Journal-Constitution*, August 28, 2010.

592 Lt. Commander James L. Starnes, Jr., account of the signing of the terms of surrender by the Japanese.

593 A letter dated September 28, 1965, from the Department of the Navy to Victor Gondos, Head, Army-Navy Branch, stated that "based on an examination of the logs and war diaries of *Buchanan* and *Nicholas* it is clear that *Buchanan* transported General MacArthur to *Missouri* for the Japanese surrender ceremonies," National Archives.

594 Log of the USS *Missouri* for September 2, 1945, Harry S. Truman Library, Independence, MO.

595 Foreign Minister Mamoru Shigemitsu led the Japanese emissaries.

596 At 0856, Japanese representatives came aboard. At 0902 according to the log, the ceremony commenced and the Instrument of Surrender presented to all parties including representatives of the United States, Republic of China, United Kingdom, British Pacific Fleet, Union Soviet Socialist Republic, Commonwealth of Australia, Dominion of Canada, Republic of France, Commonwealth of New Zealand, United Kingdom of Netherlands, Japanese Empire, United States Navy, and United States Army.

597 Deck Log of J. L. Starnes, Jr., Lt. Comdr., U.S.N.R., Harry S. Truman Library.

598 "Surrender of Japan, 2 September 1945, Aircraft Flyover as the Ceremonies Conclude," United States Navy Naval History & Heritage Command, http://www.history.navy. mil/index.html [accessed August 30, 2010].

599 Richard C. Kahl, interview with author, Youngstown, NY, for *Honor Thy Fathers & Mothers* publication, May 17, 2007. Kahl assigned to a B-29 bomber group on Tinian participated in the incendiary bombing raids on Japanese cities. Prior to the briefings for the B-29s missions, the bartender at the Officer's Club, a Japanese POW, correctly identified for Kahl the "secret" targets.

600 Tibbets identified the interpreters as six Nisei, born in Hawaii, and part of his security detachment. Radiology professor Masao Tsuzuki from the medical school of Tokyo University flew to the field near Nagasaki with the Tibbets group and some American scientists. Paul W. Tibbets autobiography chapter on the "End of the War."

601 The original "Orders for the Silver Star" incorrectly identified Stiborik as Radio Operator and Nelson's as the Radar Operator. Copy of General orders No. 69, Van Kirk personal papers.

602 Headquarters 509th Composite Group, Special Orders No. 97, Van Kirk personal papers.

603 Special Orders No. 6, Headquarters 509th Composite Group, APO 336, c/o Postmaster, San Francisco, CA, Van Kirk personal papers.

604 "Proclamation 2673," Proclamations Harry S. Truman 1945-1953, Harry S. Truman Library & Museum, Thanksgiving Day 1945.

605 Mr. and Mrs. Theodore J. Van Kirk resided at 244 Water Street, Northumberland, PA.

Chapter Twelve

"No regrets"

"Wing Commander for Navigation"

Dutch ~ In the military of that day there were West Pointers and non West Pointers. Paul Tibbets, Tom Ferebee, and I were non West Pointers. The West Pointers always took care of themselves. In the 509th when we came back from Tinian and out in New Mexico we were all given forty-five days leave to go home. When we came back I had been replaced. Tom had been replaced. Paul had been replaced too. Butch Blanchard, a West Pointer, was now the commanding officer of the 509th. We now had a new wing bombardier and a new wing navigator of the 509th, both West Pointers.

Tibbets was made advisor to the wing commander and Tom advisor to the wing commander of bombing. I became advisor to the wing commander for navigation. We were all given nice offices, all given a secretary, and did not have a damn thing to do. Every morning we had a leisurely breakfast and called the office to inquire, "Do you have anything for me today?"

The answer was always no. We spent our days shooting skeet, bowling, playing handball, and all kinds of athletic things. Every month we got a paycheck. I was probably in the best shape of my life because I was not working and getting a lot of exercise.

"Roswell Army Air Field"

April 26, 1946, by Special Orders No. 116 the following named, by military aircraft to PAE Hamilton Field, California, are ordered to report to the CG for necessary processing and instructions and then WP to

Roswell, New Mexico

Kwajalein by air via the route specified by the CG ATC. This movement constitutes a TEMPORARY change of station for approximate six (6) months duration. Upon completion of TDY all persons will return to proper organization at Roswell Army Air Field.

Shipment Number 4421-BZ

Col. Paul W. Tibbets, Jr.	0361713	AC	B-29 Airplane
Maj. Theodore J. Van Kirk	0659024	N	Number
Maj. Thomas W. Ferebee	0443490	B	44-86292
Capt. Kermit K. Beahan	0432331	Passenger	

The Crew A-1 was also so ordered.[606]

"Operation Crossroads"

The United States conducted nuclear weapons tests at Bikini Atoll during the summer of 1946 to study the effect on naval vessels. The *Operation Crossroads* tests were the fourth and fifth nuclear explosions, which followed the Trinity test and the bombings of Hiroshima and Nagasaki. These tests were held in the Marshall Islands and the first to be publicly announced in advance.[607]

Dutch ~ We flew into Washington on several occasions as consultants at the beginning of the planning for the Bikini atomic bomb test. We spoke through Tibbets and let him stick his neck out in the discussions with a bunch of generals. We were asked how many planes would be needed, how many men and so forth. Our recommendation was for ten airplanes and three hundred men to do it. In the end, there were over twenty thousand men and so many airplanes we couldn't park them all.

The decision of which crew would drop the bomb was to be a contest of six crews including us. Let me tell you our average error while dropping six bombs was one-half the average error from the target of the next closest crew.

On one of the bombing missions our target was a twenty-five foot by twenty-five foot shack. We were bombing from thirty thousand plus feet. Several days before Beahan and Ferebee were in the officer's club. Beahan says, "I will bet you a case of whiskey against a drink that you will never hit one of those shacks."

The very next practice mission we go out on, Ferebee is looking out through the nose. I am looking out through the bomb bay and that bomb goes right down through that shack. We made allowances for the wind going up. Nobody else was doing this. We were so far advanced above the other people it was not even funny. We even made allowances for the earth's rotation while the bomb was dropping. To Beahan's credit by the time we get back to the base at Roswell and landed, he had a case of whiskey on the ramp waiting for us.

While we were out in the Pacific, I took bets from the crew that I could split Johnston Island, one of my navigational fixes, right down the middle. We were between Pearl Harbor and Kwajalein. The crew did not know I was homing in on a Loran line. Ferebee caught on to what I was doing and wouldn't fall for it.

Another Northumberland son, 2nd Lt. Leroy V. Fenstermacher, participated in the competition at Bikini. Co-pilot Fenstermacher flew with Col. Clarence McPherson.[608]

"Artist Peter Hurd"

Dutch ~ During our time at Roswell, we reconnected with artist Peter Hurd. Pete married into the famous Brandywine family. We met Pete over in Africa and England because he had been commissioned by *Time* magazine

Grand Council, Exclusive
Order of Guinea Pigs
Sty No. 1 Kwajalein, Marshall Islands

To all loyal Brother Pigs, Greetings: Know Ye: that

MAJOR   THEODORE J VAN KIRK   0-659024

having through an exaggerated sense of patriotism subjected his body to the rigors attendant to atom bombs, hundred-foot tidal waves, mermaids, vampires, sandfleas, typhoons, mal-de-mer, cannibals, canned beer, etc., is by this writing accorded full status as a Brother Pig and all brothers are hereby commanded to give him due recognition as same under penalty of being driven from the common trough.

Given under my hand this 1ST day of MAY 1946

R M Ramey
Grand Guinea Swine.

Attested:

William T Blanchard
Little Guinea Swine
John R Pocoke Lt Col
Keeper of the Trough

Order of Guinea Pigs

to do a series on water in the southwest, I think, and then in England on the Eighth Air Force. Pete had a ranch near Roswell. We visited with him and would go out to a barn where he hid his bottle and drink with him. His wife would get annoyed, but it did not seem to bother Pete too much. He was one of the real characters of this world.

"Practical Joke on Beahan"

Dutch ~ One of the best practical jokes I ever played in my life, which I took great pride in, was on Beahan. Tom Ferebee, Kermit Beahan, and I, and maybe a couple of other guys were at Tinker Field, Oklahoma City, having a party in a hotel room. Beahan was one of the single guys and had a girl with him. I was there. Ferebee was there. Beahan said, "I think I am going to have to marry this girl."

I said, "Oh, I can do that I am a chaplain." I took the phone book and made off as a chaplain and performed the ceremony and wrote something out on an advertisement for the hotel that "I chaplain Theodore J. Van Kirk married Captain Kermit Beahan."

Later on we got to thinking about it. I talked to Tom and said, "We can play a good joke on Beahan."

"What do you have in mind," said Tom.

We knew the girls in the legal department at Tinker and asked them to type a letter on the legal department's stationery to the commanding officer at the base, Cliff Heflin. At the time he was a good friend of ours. The letter went something like this: Subject: marriage Kermit Beahan. Appeared before me, name of the girl, on such and such a day claiming she was married to Captain Beahan and had a card from chaplain Theodore J. Van Kirk stating that he performed the ceremony. The letter went on to say, "It is my duty to inform you that this constitutes a legal marriage in Oklahoma." We planned this whole thing. Heflin calls Beahan into his office.

Beahan reports, "Yes sir. What can I do for you?"

Heflin tosses the letter across his desk and said, "I know you guys were going out drinking and that some of you were going to get in trouble. Look at this Beahan. You are married." He looks at it and his face goes white. Tibbets, Ferebee, and I were in the next room looking through a crack in the door. We decided to go and get our morning coffee and so we go walking.

Heflin goes on and asks, "Bea, do you have a picture of your wife? Don't feel bad I might be able to get you a house on the base."

The nurses were in on it too and playing songs on the record player like "Put that ring on my finger." Bea really thinks he is married.

About four o'clock in the afternoon, I walked into the officer's club and there is Beahan in the telephone booth on the phone. I stop and ask him, "What are you doing?" He was trying to call the girl in question and tells me he is planning to desert and go to Mexico. He has called his attorney and was trying to get out of it.

I thought this joke had gone far enough and had to tell him. "Bea, you are not married."

He said, "What do you mean I am not married?"

I tell him he is not really married and that it was just a joke.

Bea had been an all American football player at Rice University before he got in the service. First, he had a feeling of relief, and then he started to get mad. The next thing you know he started chasing me yelling, "I will kill you, you bastard." By this time Tom walks in the officer's club and Beahan asks if Tom was in on it too.

Tom says, "Yeah Bea I was in on it too. It really was a joke."

Beahan started chasing us both around the officer's club and is going to kill us both. He finally calmed down, got all the details, and decided it was a great practical joke too. When he passed away in Houston, Texas, Tom and I attended his funeral and his daughter asks, "Are you the two guys that made my father think he was married?"

Apparently, Beahan thought it was so funny he even told his children the story.

"Ferebee Drove Off the Bridge"

Dutch ~ An automobile dealer gave Tom Ferebee a new 1946 Ford, one of the first to come out after the war. Tom brought it to Roswell. We had the habit of going up to a little town called Ruidoso, in New Mexico, a big horse racing area in the mountains. Now Tom liked to go out and have a few drinks at night. We were crossing a bridge. Anyhow, he had two wheels on the bridge and the other two off. I don't know how many bridges Tom saw when the car rolled over upside down into the creek below. No one was hurt. We managed to get out, walked through the water, and got back up on the bridge. We started walking back and Tom said, "Hell, now wait a minute."

He turned around and walked back down to the creek, and crawled into the car. Tom came back and said, "I forgot to turn off the lights." The car was a wreck.

"Bikini Contest and the Bomba Club"

Dutch ~ During the practices if you were within one hundred feet of your target dropping at thirty thousand feet it was considered practically a zero error. There has to be some luck if you hit one of them. Our average was some three hundred odd feet. The next closest was six hundred fifty feet. That crew that "won the contest" would drop the bomb for the Bikini test on a battleship painted red. The other ships were all arranged in a nice target stance and nobody was shooting at the B-29.[609]

We did not lose a single airplane or man in the 509th Group, but while practicing for the Bikini test a plane was lost doing the sharp maneuver when it snapped the tail off. Boeing had sent a letter that they did not accept responsibility for our airplanes for doing that turn at that altitude.

Another crew was picked. We won the contest hands down, but did not drop the bomb. Before the bomb was dropped Ferebee and Beahan looked over their calculations and said that the bomb was going to drop short and to the left. It missed the target and was sixteen hundred yards short and to the left and nobody was shooting at them. A mass of water from the explosion came up over the ships, now very radioactive. You couldn't predict what that was going to do.

How could they be so stupid, I thought. If you are in the contest you think you know the rules and then something entirely opposite happens. At one of the reunions I spoke with Tom White, one of the navigators in my class. Somehow he had finagled his way into the staff that was making the Bikini decision.

White said, "You did not take into account the ballistic winds." He did not know what he was talking about.

I said to White, "Tom, you know you are full of shit to put it bluntly."

Tom Ferebee and I always took the winds and the rotation of the earth into account.

I was on the island of Kwajalein during the test. A lot of landing craft and wrecked boats from the invasion had been abandoned. We salvaged and fixed up two diesel marine engines and an old crashed boat. We ran around in the lagoon with the boat and had a great time for the few days we were there. We had to leave so damn fast we did not get the chance to bring the engines we overhauled with us.

That night after the test there was a big old party with Congressmen and all that sort of thing. Beahan had formed the Bomba Club (bounce up and bite my ass). All the guys wanted to join the club not knowing what Bomba stands for. At the party Tibbets, Ferebee, and I walk in, have a drink, and try to keep to ourselves.

On the island quarters were divided into field grade officers' quarters for major and above, and company grade officers for captain and lower rank. We were all eligible to live in the field grade quarters, but Tibbets said, "Hell no. We are not going to live up there with those guys. We are going to live down with the hoi polloi."

If Tibbets said that is where we are going to live then that is where we are going to live. During the party LeMay walks in. He had been late getting there and sees the three of us. All of a sudden you could hear this roar go up and LeMay says, "Over there are three guys who will tell me where that bomb hit." Almost immediately we were pulled out of the party and told to fly the pictures of that drop back to Washington as soon as possible. They wanted to get us the hell off the island. And that was the story of the first Bikini atomic bomb over there.

"A Military or Civilian Career"

July 20, 1946, Maj. Theodore J. Van Kirk began processing out at 1245 from Building T-619, Fort George G. Meade, Maryland.[610] Simultaneously, Van Kirk received an appreciation letter from Maj. Gen. Edward F. Witsell for acceptance of an appointment as an officer in the Reserve Corps.

Dutch ~ Washington ignored us to put it bluntly. This was my first lesson in the power of the West Pointers and the learning point that they took care of themselves. I did not want to be involved in this process and only be a reserve officer. My thinking culminated in the decision to return to college and get into civilian work. I did not stop to think that when I went to work at DuPont it was going to be as bad, just different bosses.

On twenty-twenty hindsight I wish my work had been more connected to aviation like airport management or something of that type.

Hazen Payette and his brother invited Ferebee and me and our wives to their cabin in Roscommon, Michigan, way up north. We used an outhouse and even in Michigan during the fall it was cold. I hadn't used an outhouse in a long time. My grandparents had an outhouse.

We went to a local bar and were told that we couldn't buy a drink on Sunday. The bartender put out a bottle of scotch and bourbon and said, "There is nothing that says I can't give it away." Ferebee and I sat there drinking and killed the bottle of scotch between the two of us. While we were walking out the bartender said, "I have seen some pretty fancy drinkers in my day, but you two guys take the cake."

We came back to Detroit. Boats, like the old paddle wheelers, ran from Detroit to Buffalo (New York). My wife and I took the boat. It was a nice trip. We stopped in Niagara Falls and stayed at the Red Coach Inn. I didn't know that I was going to be living in Niagara Falls for heaven's sake. We did the usual touristy stuff around the Falls before heading to Northumberland, and I started back to college.

July 22, 1946, Miss Ann Elizabeth Gwin, daughter of Mr. and Mrs. Clyde Q. Gwin of Houston, Texas, and Maj. Tom W. Ferebee, of Mocksville, North Carolina, culminated their romance at the First Baptist Church in Oxford. Maj. Theodore J. Van Kirk of Northumberland, Pennsylvania, served as the best man and Col. Paul Tibbets of Orlando, Florida, ushered. Ferebee was assigned to duty at Roswell, New Mexico.[611]

"Bucknell University"

Dutch ~ I was discharged from the service rather suddenly, and applied late to Bucknell University in Lewisburg, Pennsylvania; their classes were full.[612] Arnold Seasholtz, Mary Jane's "brother," intervened. He worked with Andy Mathieson at a steel company. Mathieson (Class of 1920) served on Bucknell's Board of Trustees and wrote a letter to the university president, Dr. Herbert Spencer.[613] So, by special dispensation I started school in 1946.[614]

Dear Dr. Spencer,

This is to confirm our recent conversation with respect to the admittance of Theodore Van Kirk for the fall term. Van Kirk is a brother-in-law of Mr. Arnold P. Seasholtz, a Bucknell graduate.

Van Kirk entered the service as a private and advanced to major. He has a marvelous record, having a great deal to do with the preparation of advance training of the air corps. He was the navigation officer on the plane that dropped the first atomic bomb, and is scheduled to be the chief navigation officer on the plane that will drop the test bomb this summer.

He has been offered a very fine position with Pan-American Airlines but appreciates the value of college training.

He plans to study chemical engineering and metallurgy.

From all the information I have Van Kirk is a very unusual fellow with great possibilities, and should go far in his chosen field. I believe we will be missing a good bet if he is not admitted to the University this fall.

Sincerely yours,

A. R. Mathieson[615]

Master's Degree. Van Kirk on graduation day standing in front of his
black 1949 Pontiac "slowpoke."

Dutch ~ Then I did one of the most stupid things of my life and decided
not to repeat any of my chemistry courses. I started in Qualitative Analysis and
damn near killed myself in that class, but got through it with an A too.

I was at Bucknell when Truman came through Northumberland on his
whistle stop tour.

Japanese visitors came to the campus, and I always had to be available for
an interview. Bucknell was a religious college.[616] One of the visitors was from
Hiroshima. We had a big confab about it.

Rev. Kiyoshi Tanimoto, a Japanese Christian minister, lived a mile from
the center of the Hiroshima explosion in 1945. He spoke twice to student
groups and also at Sam House for a question and answer hour during the
evening. Tanimoto rebuilt his church and cared for homeless and orphaned
children after the war.[617]

Each time I received a diploma, Leslie Groves showed up to give a speech
during the convocation. He would invite me to dinner and tried to put the
strong arm around me to come back in the service after I completed my
degrees. At one point Groves said, "I will make you a lieutenant colonel in the
Engineering Corps."[618]

I looked at him and asked, "But General why? I am already a major in the Air Corps. Why would I want to be a lieutenant colonel in the Engineering Corps?" He got a little mad at me.

Attending Bucknell was kind of a rough time. The courses were hard, but I got good grades. I think I snowed all my teachers. We were living on seventy-five to ninety-five dollars a month. Fortunately, I had saved some money in the service or we would have starved to death. I didn't have a car of my own and borrowed my dad's car. We got by. It was not my most financially successful period, but I worked hard. The GI Bill paid for my undergraduate and Master's degree too since I had plenty of eligibility.

One summer between my sophomore and junior year I worked with the Pennsylvania State Highway Department.[619] We built a new road down along Herndon, Pennsylvania. Every other guy working in that gang of laborers was from Shamokin, the coal region, and they used a wide shovel. I couldn't pick up that shovel. It was the most miserable summer I ever spent in my life. Creosote rubbed off on your body while we unloaded the timbers from the rail cars, and it burned. Afterwards we went down to the Susquehanna with a cake of soap to wash off. It was a miserable job. After about a week or so an old civil engineer running the job found out that I was going to college and could read blueprints so I helped him. That highway is still there by the way.

I argued with Dr. Albert Cooper, the head of the engineering department.[620] The undergraduate degree requirements for chemical engineering were 144 hours and the other disciplines were only 120, which really burned me. Chemical engineering was not an easy course. I asked Dr. Cooper if the additional hours could be applied to a Master's Degree since I had a lot more hours than I needed to simply graduate. After some discussion he said only if I accepted a job to instruct while I was there. That was fair enough.

During this time I taught Engineering Metallurgy for one semester, was assistant in the unit operations laboratory for one summer, and had built or rebuilt much unit operations equipment. I was not only an instructor at Bucknell, but also the favorite chaperone for all the fraternity parties because the administration knew I would not allow anything to go on.[621]

My brother-in-law Al Young lived with us. He was studying commerce and finance, which on campus we called the frolic course. Al was very bright and became an accountant. He essentially raised my oldest son Tom. I can still picture him with Tommy on his shoulders watching the steam engines run through Northumberland. Thank God for Al. He just took over and did everything for Tommy during that period.

"Speaking About the Mission"

Dutch ~ I started speaking at Bucknell and local Kiwanis and Rotary Clubs, even church socials or anyone who called up and asked. People wanted to hear about the mission. They also wanted to see what this unusual guy looked like. If you could think of a question I probably have been asked it like, were you scared? Yes, I was scared. Usually the questions are very commonplace.

The other crew members I presume, also spoke but not as often. Tom Ferebee did not talk much because he stayed in the military. Whatever Tom would say would have been on behalf of the military; so he didn't. Most of us were pretty free to talk because we did not have any restrictions on us. The military probably figured I did not know much.

Jean ~ "Ted did not talk a lot about the mission. He was going to Bucknell and he was trying to finish. He was getting both degrees. I had my life and I was still a snot nose teenager. Ted and Mary Jane were married and had a son. As we got older we talked about it, but did not go on and on about it. You had to pry it out of him. He talked to Mick more. After we got married we never lived in the same town. We were raising two girls. Ted was raising four children. After Mick and I retired we saw him more than ever before."

January 26, 1951 *"Above and Beyond"*

Dear Dutch,

Of all the - - you are it. Tom and I have spent many an hour calling you all the names we could make up. How come you do not let us know what you are doing in order that we may fulfill a threat we once made a long time ago. We are assuming that you are now teaching classes, and we feel that, if this is the case, we should come up there and tell the students what kind of a guy their instructor used to be.

Beirne Lay is in the process of writing a story concerning my life and military career to include the Air Force version and participation in the Atomic Bombing project. This story when completed, if acceptable to the Department of Defense and Metro-Goldwyn-Mayer Studios, may be made into a movie. In the event this is done, it will be necessary to have your consent to portray you and the part that you played.

Enclosed are some release forms prepared for your signature, which I would appreciate greatly your signing and returning to me in order that I might have them available in the event the story is successful. It will be necessary for you to return two of the three attached copies with your signature; retain the other for your use.

I can personally assure you that, in the event you are portrayed in the movie, that

OFFICE OF THE USAF PLANT REPRESENTATIVE
AIR MATERIEL COMMAND
Boeing Airplane Company
Wichita, Kansas

IN REPLY ADDRESS BOTH
COMMUNICATION AND EN-
VELOPE TO USAF PLANT
REPRESENTATIVE, BOEING
AIRPLANE CO., WICHITA 1,
KANSAS. ATTENTION BY SYM-
BOL NUMBER:

26 January 1951

Theodore J. Van Kirk
252 Water Street
Northumberland, Pa.

Dear Dutch,

Of all the - - you are it. Tom and I have spent many an hour calling you all the names we could make up. How come you do not let us know what you are doing in order that we may fulfill a threat we once made a long time ago. We are assuming that you are now teaching classes, and we feel that, if this is the case, we should come up there and tell the students what kind of a guy their instructor used to be.

Beirne Lay is in the process of writing a story concerning my life and military career to include the Air Force version and participation in the Atomic Bombing project. This story when completed, if acceptable to the Department of Defense and Metro-Goldwyn-Mayer Studios, may be made into a movie. In the event this is done, it will be necessary to have your consent to portray you and the part that you played.

Enclosed are some release forms prepared for your signature, which I would appreciate greatly your signing and returning to me in order that I might have them available in the event the story is successful. It will be necessary for you to return two of the three attached copies with your signature; retain the other for your use.

I can personally assure you that, in the event you are portrayed in a movie, that your part will reflect credit upon you and your career in the military service. This also applies to Bob, Tom and Duzenbury, whom I am contacting to receive their release as requested of you.

I am out here at Wichita, Kansas, primarily to service test the B-47, and Tom is at Eglin Field, but will be out here very shortly to run bombing test with the airplane.

Please drop us a line and let us know what you are doing, and, if by chance you start getting inquiries from the Air Force concerning recall, let me know at once because I would surely like to reform the old team once again.

Give my best to Mary Jane.

Regards,

your part will reflect credit upon you and your career in the military service. This also applied to Bob, Tom and Duzenbury, whom I am contacting to receive their release as requested of you.

I am out here at Wichita, Kansas, primarily to service test the B-47 and Tom is at Elgin Field, but will be out here very shortly to run bombing test with the airplane.

Please drop us a line and let us know what you are doing, and, if by chance you start getting inquiries from the Air Force concerning recall, let me know at once because I would surely like to reform the old team once again.

Give my best to Mary Jane.

Regards,

Paul [622]

Dutch ~ When *Above and Beyond* came out, I was living in Niagara Falls. I don't think Paul Tibbets was as good-looking as Robert Taylor. There was not much about me in the movie. The actor who portrayed me must have been better looking than I am for heaven's sake.

The film opened in Buffalo, New York, at Shea's Theater on 498 Pearl Street. Van Kirk viewed the film at a special screening and shared some of his experiences with Vincent R. McFaul, general manager of the theater.[623]

"DuPont"

About a quarter mile from the south entrance to Old Fort Niagara, Major Theodore "Dutch" Van Kirk was the principal speaker at the Parent Teacher Association meeting of the Youngstown school.[624] At the time, he lived at 918-93rd Street in the Love Canal area of the City of Niagara Falls employed as a chemical engineer with DuPont in the Falls. The *Niagara Falls Gazette* reported that Van Kirk "held his audience spellbound as he related his experiences as a navigator on the plane that dropped the atomic bomb on Hiroshima."[625]

Van Kirk began his thirty-five year career at the DuPont chemical plant in the Falls with a hard hat and goggles making $400.00 a month as a process engineer.[626]

Dutch ~ Jim Young, one of my bosses at DuPont, asked me to speak in Youngstown. Jim was from Gainesville, Georgia, and the only guy in Niagara Falls with a southern accent. He lived on top of the escarpment in Lewiston and attended the Youngstown Presbyterian Church.[627]

I had an affinity for chemistry but DuPont said the hell with chemistry, you are a marketing man. After about two years in Niagara Falls and a transfer to Charlotte, North Carolina, I built a home in Columbus, Georgia. After living in the brand new house for one night I almost immediately was moved to Wilmington, Delaware, to specialize in DuPont products for government use. We produced hydrogen peroxide and worked with the military on using the product in the jet engines, which would burn in a short period of time to give added thrust.

The nomadic career continued to Cincinnati as branch manager of Electrochemicals, then to Cleveland, Ohio, and back to Wilmington again before becoming manager of the sales office in San Francisco, California, in 1978. The last move was to Stone Mountain, Georgia, about six years ago.

"Reactions After the War"

Dutch ~ At first when I came home we were all heroes. You never found a GI out in the Pacific, very few, extremely few, practically zero that were not in favor of the atomic bomb.[628] I could influence my teachers in college partly because of it, the stature that I had. They thought I knew something because of dropping the atomic bomb. From that standpoint things were rosy until

Van Kirk at
DuPont

maybe the mid sixties around the Vietnam period during the war protests.
The protestors did not differentiate between World War II and Vietnam. The
mantra about the war became the people who were engaged in dropping the
atomic bomb did not do a good thing.

Knowledge about the atomic bomb started to decrease. Today, unless you
get a very good teacher, the students have practically no knowledge about
why we dropped the bomb. I ask the students, "What do you know about
the atomic bomb?" The only thing kids know today is that the bomb caused
tremendous casualties. So you get tarred with that brush. I ask, "Do any of you
know why we dropped the atomic bomb?" They have very little knowledge
about that particular subject and very little knowledge that the bomb did bring
an end to the war, an end to the killing, and probably saved more lives than
it took. You show the students photographs of General Wainwright and my
friend next door, Captain Granston, who would have been killed if the bomb
had not ended the war. Even not considering the invasion, the bomb saved
lives and considering the invasion it saved lives.

In one hour you don't have time to re-educate them. So I don't know how
much good you do. I ask the kids, "What was World War II about?"

Some kids answer, "That is when we and the Germans were fighting the Russians."

But that is what they think. Occasionally, someone knows something on the subject; otherwise the students leave the talk and say, "Where is McDonalds?"

Today, even the teachers don't know enough about it and cover the topic in half a day. This is not enough. I would rather sometimes they would forget it instead of saying the bomb was dropped just to create a lot of casualties. The military is still passing out Purple Hearts ordered for the planned invasion of the home islands of Japan.[629] The initial request for body bags for the invasion was 250,000.[630]

At the D-Day Museum in New Orleans, I had attended a luncheon organized by Bill Devlin with their Board of some history profs to decide the direction of the museum. We had one of the best conversations ever in my life with intelligent people who knew what they were talking about, and also asked questions. There was not a naysayer in the bunch. One fellow who really impressed me was Donald Miller from Lafayette, a history professor. He wrote the book *D-Days in the Pacific*. I got to know him.

Barton Bernstein's team had a different response. I was living in California and Barton was at Stanford University. Every summer I gave a talk to teachers teaching advanced history courses on why we dropped the atomic bomb. We would have a semi-friendly discussion. Barton was one of the guys leading the charge for the initial Smithsonian exhibit. He said it wasn't necessary to drop the bomb. I told Barton, "It is not your job to rewrite history, but to report history. Your job is to report what we did and what happened." He never agreed with me on that. I could answer intelligent questions and misconceptions about the bomb. Questions like: Why did we have three pilots on the Nagasaki mission? Tibbets did not know that Fred Olivi (a third pilot) was going along on the mission. Why couldn't they bomb Kokura? Why did we have to bomb the target visually?

To us Hiroshima was just another mission. Paul Tibbets, Tom Ferebee and I flew a lot of missions. We were just going to go up in the airplane and drop another bomb. It went the way it was exactly supposed to go. The whole country became more anti-war and that reflected on the atomic bomb. People knew less and less about the bomb and the less they knew the more anti-bomb they became in general. That about sums it up.

At an air show in Ohio during the early 1980s, a group of Catholic priests picketed the air show. Another time a security guard removed someone who was deranged while we were in Canton, Ohio. I can't recall any personal thing to me.[631]

I was not present at the time while Tibbets was base commander at MacDill Field. He was ordered to give a cocktail party for some "important people," a Japanese delegation. One of the representatives came over to Tibbets who was standing off to the side minding his own business and asked, "Do you want to talk about it?"

Tibbets said, "Sir, I don't understand you."

The fellow said, "I am (Captain Mitsuo) Fuchida. I led the raid on Pearl Harbor. You sure surprised the hell out of us."

"What the hell did you think you did to us," Tibbets responded.

Other Japanese thanked us for dropping the bomb. I asked, "Why do you say that?" One man told me that he was a serf farmer in Japan prior to the war and would have remained on a lower socio-economic scale if it had not been for us. But we dropped the atomic bomb and he replied, "Today, I am the president of my own company." We got quite a bit of that.

Another time in Louisville a man introduced himself as a former kamikaze pilot and of course I usually had something flippant to say about most of these things. I looked at him and said, "Well he wasn't very good was he." But the pilot went on to say that we saved him from carrying out his kamikaze mission, saved his life, and that he was eternally grateful.

"The Best Family"

Front, left to right, Mary Jane, Joanne (Gotelli) standing, Tom holding (his son)
Tom Jr. back, left to right Dutch, Vicki (Triplett), and Larry.
(Courtesy Vicki Van Kirk Triplett)

Dutch ~ I am thoroughly convinced that mine is the best family in the world and there is no conflict between any of them: Tom, Larry, Vicki, and Joanne. In 1975 we were living in Charlotte, North Carolina. Mary Jane was up in Pennsylvania visiting family. Her sister-in-law called me. I am always cheerful and said, "What's up?"

Hazel said, "Ted it isn't good."

"What is it," I asked.

She said, "Mary Jane had a heart attack and died last night" just like that. It was very sudden and very sad, very sad. I was left alone with three teenage children. Tom was already practicing law. I learned to cook in a hurry. My best dish was hamburger helper.

A couple of years later down in Mobile to see some customers, I met Jean (Imogene Cumbie Guest). She was the receptionist. I mentioned something about going on a fishing trip with some people. Jean commented that she liked to fish too. "You can come if you want to," I told her and she did. It was a quick courtship.

"Roger Mudd"

Dutch ~ In 1982 a radio network came up with the idea to have a program to compete with 20/20. Roger Mudd was going to be the anchor and Steve Skinner, the director. One of the first programs was going to be on the atomic bomb. I lived in California at the time. The network people went through all my boxes and followed me to work taking pictures and did the same thing with Ferebee and Tibbets. It was going to be a big production.

The producers took us to Washington, DC, and one of our first trips to the Smithsonian, which I thought was significant at the time. This was prior to even a discussion about an exhibit. We got up into the *Enola Gay* cockpit and were being filmed reminiscing about the flight to Hiroshima. To all of our way of thinking, it was probably the best thing we ever made and it disappeared and never went on the air. After one program the show was cancelled because it couldn't compete with 20/20.

This is my favorite picture of any we may have had together

"Reunions with the Guys"

Dutch ~ At first when our *Red Gremlin* crew got together, they asked about the Hiroshima mission. We told them once that it was an easy mission and that was it. Dick Wiley wrote to us after the bomb was dropped. "You two guys told me you were going over to win the war and you were right." We teased each other and often repeated the story of Willie Tittsworth shooting Herman Hague.

The 393rd Bomb Squadron

Dutch,

This inscription will be inadequate in expressing my feelings Toward you, (I TOLD TOM THE SAME) because you as well as Tom have always been SPECIAL as far as I am concerned. During The war I considered us as a three legged stool —Together we stood; Sometime against big odds. Post war you took a different path but I did and I know Tom felt that you were "not that far away" Since our retirements I think we may be even "closer" and That's The way it will remain— Paul 9/26/89

Paul Tibbets' inscription to Dutch.

started having reunions, not the 509th Group. Jake Beser was part of the 393rd Squadron. Tibbets, Ferebee, and I were never invited to their squadron reunions. A lot of people held the idea that there was Tibbets, Ferebee, and Van Kirk, and the rest of the 509th. That was the way it was. However, I found myself in Salt Lake City on business at the same time of a reunion and went invited or not. Protestors appeared outside and Jake Beser insisted on going out and confronting them, which I did not agree with. About the mid 1980s Herman Zahn, one of our pilots, took over as chairman and changed the reunions to include the 509th and then we were all invited.[632] Dick Jeppson and I met at a reunion and got to know each other real well. Around 2000 we went with Dick and his wife Molly, my daughter Joanne, and Paul Tibbets and his agent Ed Humphreys to Tinian.[633]

While attending an air show with Paul Tibbets and Dick Wiley, a friend took Dick for a ride in a twin-engine B-25. The pilot sat on the left and put Dick in the pilot seat, right hand on the controls. He "let" Dick land the plane and as they were coming in saying: you are fifty-feet off, twenty-five feet off and so forth. It was a good landing really the pilot's, not Dick's because he was blind. But when they taxied in on the flight line, Dick Wiley had the biggest grin on his face. Even though he couldn't see a thing, he got to fly again. I told him, "Dick that was the best landing you ever made."

My wife and I visited Dick and Nancy Nelson in California. Dick had the most beautiful orange grove in California and shipped most of his citrus to Japan.

Ran into Bob Lewis once after leaving the service while he was promoting a diet program. I never saw Stiborik, Shumard, or Parsons after the war.[634] Even though the crew was not in touch generally, we knew we could call and count on each other and that was especially true of Tibbets, Ferebee, and myself, and the officers on the crew.

"The Smithsonian Exhibit"

The 103d United States Congress passed House Resolution 531 on September 19, 1994, and the Senate passed and agreed to Senate Resolution 257 without amendment four days later in memorializing the role of the United States in armed conflict and under Federal law to portray history in the proper context of the times. The House resolved that "any exhibit displayed by the National Air and Space Museum with respect to the *Enola Gay* should reflect appropriate sensitivity toward the men and women who faithfully and selflessly served the United States during World War II and should avoid impugning the memory of those who gave their lives for freedom."

Dutch ~ In 1995 the Air and Space Museum of the Smithsonian gave a luncheon for us in the hanger in front of the *Enola Gay*. Tibbets, Ferebee, and myself and I think Jake Beser and Dick Nelson attended. The Director announced a one hundred year restoration on the plane. One of the curators putting the exhibit together wrote his doctoral thesis on the fact that we should not have dropped the bomb. Another person planning the exhibit was enamored with the Japanese culture. Scripts were written and modified several times. One line said something to the effect that for the Japanese the bombing was primarily a campaign of vengeance and alleged American racism. Another stated that we all went crazy. I responded, "You know we all did not go crazy." We went back and forth repeatedly.

In the first exhibit it appeared that the war started with the fire bombings of Tokyo. The ratio of photographs of Japan to the Americans was about twenty to one. The writers forget about what happened in the Philippines, what happened at Guadalcanal, what happened at Tarawa, as if these battles did not exist. The Smithsonian sent the script to Japan for their approval. That is what burned us.

The Air Force Association and magazine to their credit really carried the ball and the American Legion too for their dialogue with the Smithsonian, which resulted in the first film not being used. Changes in the administration at the Smithsonian occurred during all of this. The efforts too of the Greenwich Workshop, Tibbets, the *Air and Space* magazine, others, and myself also helped.

Martin Harwit wrote *An Exhibit Denied* after he was fired as the director. He did point out that despite the scale of the destruction, Japan did not give up immediately. We had shared with him our feelings of pride serving our country on dangerous missions and contributing to the rapid end of a terrible and long war, horror at the destruction and loss of life, but hope that harnessing nuclear power will make total war unthinkable forever. Dropping the bomb saved more lives than it took. That was certainly Paul Tibbets' view.

Ray Gallagher, the assistant flight engineer on the Nagasaki mission had answered a Japanese reporter's often asked question of us, "Are you sorry you dropped the bomb?"

Ray answered, "I don't know. God must have been with me that day. You know mister at that time there was a monster loose, that monster was war. It was killing people, destroying homes, mothers, fathers, oh gosh so many heartaches and other things and here this bomb came along and stopped it. If you had it you would have used it. We had it and we used it and we stopped it. Many, many, many people got to go home." It was the best thing Ray ever said.

"Psychological Impact"

Dutch ~ I never had nightmares about the war during or after military service. People reacted differently to combat. Ninety percent of it was the fact that you didn't want to let your buddies down. This would be very obvious during a briefing when suddenly the curtain was taken off the map and you could see the red line to where you were going to bomb. I wasn't on the mission but I can imagine how guys felt when the target was Schweinfurt for example, which was a very long mission and losses were going to be extremely heavy. There was also a certain degree of machoism.

Van Kirk, Tibbets, Ferebee, and Nelson in a visit to the Marine Corps Air Station Yuma spoke publicly about their Hiroshima mission. They all agreed that given the circumstances they would do the same thing again "absolutely and without doubt." Van Kirk has had Japanese thank him because the bomb destroyed the caste system in Japan.[635]

"Going Home"

Mick ~ "He (Dutch) is a Mason, a master Mason, a fifty year veteran of the Masonic order, the blue lodge, the basic lodge; they presented him with his fifty year pin. I went up to be with him at our home lodge in Northumberland. It was pretty nifty."

Jean ~ "I am immensely proud of Ted. My ancestors, my parents, they were good, honest, hard working people. I don't think they had any idea what a chemical engineer was and that he had the grit, the courage, and yes, the drive and discipline to accomplish what he accomplished. I am amazed and admire him. I always tease Ted, 'You got all the good genes and I got the lousy ones.' He calls me and says, 'Remember I got all the good genes.'"

Jean Van Kirk McAllister, who had "about a hundred reasons" why she loved her big brother Ted, died September 13, 2011. In 1985 Jean received the Baden Powell Fellow Award from the King of Sweden. Jean, a Lutheran and member of the Eastern Star, was active in scouting with her husband of sixty-one years, Mick McAllister, and also survived by daughters Nancy (William) Kleindienst and Katie (John) Neuhauser.

Mick ~ "Ted has a warm heart."

Dutch ~ I still can go to my hometown Northumberland to the people that I know. They don't treat me like someone who was on the *Enola Gay*. They treat me like Ted Van Kirk who is home just getting something good to eat. I look at other crewmen's families and they have their little differences and their big differences. I have none of that. I have been blest so greatly in that respect and with the family I have.

I have no regrets. It has been a charmed life, a good life, a real good life.

"509th Reunions"

Dutch ~ We were at a reunion in St. Louis. I had a saying "always buy the first round. The crowd never gets smaller." A bunch of us from the 509th were having dinner at an Italian restaurant. I was sitting next to Bill Downey, our chaplain. I leaned over and asked Bill, "Are you going to say grace tonight?"

He said absolutely and stood up and not only said grace but gave a little sermon. "These are my people and we went to war together." Bill pointed out two guys in another booth who did not pay attention during the blessing and that he wanted to go and say something. I told him to forget it. He had already had several drinks. We used to accuse him of having a still in his basement.

Anyhow, we finished our meal and the other two men came over to Bill and said, "Chaplain, we just wanted to come over and say congratulations to you. We are both of the faith and we don't know if we would have had the guts to do what you just did."

Paul Tibbets and I were in a mall signing books and a Baptist minister John Butler Book videoed us, and later we visited his Christian school in Orlando. Bill Downey fell asleep on the soft easy chairs and the next thing I hear is honk honk. He is sound asleep. Tom Ferebee goes over to Bill and says, "Wake up you are disturbing the service."

John Book called while I was living in California. The conversation went like this. "John, what can I do for you?"

"Dutch, what are your plans for passing on?"

I don't know if I am going to pass on.

John persisted. "What are Paul's plans for passing on?"

John, I don't think Paul has any plans and if you don't mind I do not think we will do it. He volunteered to conduct our services when we died. I told him, "If it is all the same to you, why don't you practice on Paul and Tom first." That is my final John Butler Book story.

"Sorry if we had to invade Japan"

In 1985 Chaplain Col. William Downey of the 509th Composite Group responded to the psychologist who criticized the crew of the atomic mission. "There's no qualitative difference between killing (Japanese) in a Burma jungle with a rifle slug or killing 125,000 in an incendiary raid over Tokyo or killing a couple hundred thousand with nuclear bombs." He would not apologize or ask forgiveness from the Japanese, but offered an option that he was sorry the whole war happened and the bombing of Pearl Harbor, the killing of thousands of Americans, the invasion of the Philippines, and the barbaric Bataan Death March. Downey added that he would have been sorry if the United States had not dropped the atomic bombs, and had to invade Japan. Many more Japanese would have died.[636]

Dutch ~ Eatherly's behavior after the war contributed to the rumor that we all went crazy, which was not true. I never had post-traumatic stress disorder or difficulty sleeping.

"The passing of Thomas Wilson Ferebee"

(1918 – 2000)
Thomas W. Ferebee being awarded the Distinguished Flying Cross.
(National Archives)

Col. Thomas Wilson Ferebee retired from the Air Force in 1970. He always argued that the Hiroshima bomb was necessary. "I'm convinced that the bombing saved many lives by ending the war," Ferebee told *Newsweek* in 1970. Ferebee, the third of eleven children, was born in 1918 and grew up on a farm outside Mocksville, North Carolina. He served as deputy wing commander for maintenance of several B-47 Stratojet commands and was rated as a bombardier, a navigator, and radar operator. Ferebee served on B-52's during the Vietnam War. His wife of nineteen years, Mary Ann Conrad Ferebee, and four sons survived him.[637]

Dutch ~ Tom and I were at an air show and I told him there was something wrong and he should get to a doctor. He did and when I asked what did the doctor say Tom said, "It is not good. I have six months. Will you say something nice at my funeral?"
I said, "I will if I can think of anything."
Tom wanted a simple ceremony. His funeral was one of the best I had

ever seen. The church was packed to the hills. When driving up to Mocksville for the funeral, all the flags were at half-staff for Tom. Paul Tibbets said a few good words. So did I and added, "I will bet money there is a big poker game going on in heaven some place and I can tell you at least three people that are in on it: Tom Ferebee, Kermit Beahan, and Jim Van Pelt. All I can do is hope that they save a place for me if I go there too."

The funeral procession was a good two miles long. The State Police blocked off all the on-ramps and exits of I-40. People stood along the route. George Hicks looked at me and asked, "Dutch, did you notice anything about all those people? They are all dressed up. They all had their best clothes on, their best shirts, their best overalls" in tribute.

I want to be buried in the same plot with my mother and dad, Mary Jane, and my grandmothers and grandfathers at Riverview Cemetery in Northumberland. Reading their headstones I can trace my ancestors back to the Revolutionary War. My sister Jean married the boy right across the street, and she is going to be buried there too. When we all get together in heaven or that other place, we will have a big party. I have no desire to be buried in Arlington. I just want to go home!

"Why Did We Bomb?"

Dutch ~ When I speak to kids all they know is that the bomb caused great casualties. Yes it did, but it was the lesser of the evils. Hiroshima was picked as the target city because it was the headquarters for the Japanese Fifth Army, the people charged with the defense of Japan in case of invasion. There were other significant military targets in the city.

Anyone who understands the history of that particular time realizes that this ended the war with the least number of casualties. We dropped hundreds of thousands of leaflets over Japan before we dropped the first atomic bomb and another hundred thousands between the first and second.

Think of all the lives saved Japanese and Americans by ending the war. I have received dozens of letters that usually start out: I was a boy of sixteen at such and such a camp in the Dutch East Indies. The Japanese were no longer feeding us or giving us medical attention. They were just simply guarding us and I would not have lasted, and the prisoners of war like my next door neighbor Captain Grantson. All these people were saved.

"What If"

Dutch ~ During an HBO videotape program on the survivors of the atomic bomb called "White Light Black Rain" a panel discussion was held afterwards with a couple of survivors from Hiroshima and Nagasaki. I philosophized with the panel. "I don't know how to fight a war without killing people. You people are anti-nuclear warfare. What you should really be doing is be anti-war period." In my way of thinking we cannot possibly again have a war of the magnitude of World War II without it going nuclear.

Tom Ferebee was deputy commander for the B-47 wing during the Cuban Missile Crisis. He told me, "I had many bombers loaded with nuclear weapons all over the southeast, not only at the military bases. They were sitting at Hartsville near Nashville, and at Birmingham and Montgomery. Any place a runway was long enough for a nuclear bomber, we had one loaded and ready to go. If we had been given the word, Cuba would have been blown off the map."

President Kennedy was the right man during the Cuban crisis. He held off LeMay who was raring to go too as he usually was. I have all the respect in the world for the military, very smart guys, but you have to remember and not forget that they were trained for war. I think George Patton liked war. He would try to start one just to get into it. You need civilian control; level minds, good and smart people, and hope that the other side has the same thing.

In considering "what if" the bomb had not been dropped, "I come up with the same thing: the war would have continued, the bombs would have continued, the kamikaze attacks would have continued."[638] Without the bomb an invasion would have occurred, and it would have been bloody for both sides.

When I speak to students I try to give them an understanding of the nature of an atomic bomb and the fact that it should never be used again. The bombs today are so much worse, more powerful than what we had in 1945, and have the potential for destroying all life on earth. We hope and the students should hope that we should never see atomic bombs used in warfare again.

The focus should not be anti-nuclear warfare, but doing all we can to avoid war.

Chapter Twelve — Endnotes

606 Special Orders Number 116, Headquarters Roswell Army Air Field, Roswell, New Mexico, April 26, 1946. See appendix for Crew A-1. B-29 44-86354 and Crew A-4 were also included with this order.

607 Aubrey O. Cookman, Jr., aviation editor of *Popular Mechanics* and during the war a lieutenant colonel, described his observations of the Bikini Test in "Report From Bikini," Vol. 86 No. 2, August 1946. Cookman stated that scientific stations all over the world aided in the 10,000 measurements and analysis of the test results and the effect on humans.

608 Col. Millard Young, Chief of Staff for the Army Air Force's Bikini Task Force, considered the McPherson and Tibbets' crews among the top four of the competition. "Navigator In Lead Plane Of Atom Test," *The Morning News*, April 9, 1946.

609 Able dropped from the B-29 *Dave's Dream* formerly *Big Stink* of the 509th Composite Group. Another bomb was dropped later in July.

610 Operations Branch Separation Center Roster No. 0-200 C listed twenty men including Major Van Kirk scheduled for final physical, counseling and classification, finance, final papers, orders and ceremony. Van Kirk personal papers.

611 "Army Airmen Come From Hiroshima To Local Wedding," *Anniston Star* (Anniston, Alabama), July 23, 1946.

612 Place of separation Fort George G. Meade, MD, September 21, 1946, last wage received $611.00 a month, Van Kirk's DuPont employment application. Battles and Campaigns on the Report of Separation: Air Offensive Japan, Eastern Mandates, Algeria French Morocco, Tunisia, Sicily, and Air Offensive Europe. Decorations and Citations: Air Medal with 9 OLC GO 7 AF 12th HQ 42, American campaign Medal, European African Middle Eastern Campaign Medal, Asiatic Pacific Campaign Medal, World War II Victory Medal, and Silver Star Medal.

613 In August 1949 while Van Kirk attended Bucknell, Horace Hildreth became the University president. He had served as the Governor of Maine and in 1948 lost the Republican nomination for the United States Senate to Margaret Chase Smith. From 1953 to 1957, Hildreth served the Eisenhower administration as United States Ambassador to Pakistan.

614 "Flyer On First Atomic Raid Enrolls Here As Sophomore," *The Bucknellian*, Vol. LI., No. 1, September 19, 1946. The student newspaper for Bucknell University reported Van Kirk as "one of Pennsylvania's most decorated heroes," chosen for the atomic bomb mission "from a list of thousands of candidates," and married with a one year old son would resume his studies commuting to the campus from his home in Northumberland.

615 Copy of letter from A. R. Mathieson to Dr. Spencer dated May 3, 1946, courtesy of Thomas L. Van Kirk. Andy Mathieson sent a note to Seasholtz that Dr. Spencer indicated "a great deal of interest" and assured him "that Van Kirk would be given every consideration."

616 Freshmen, sophomores, and juniors were required to attend at least half of the chapel services held in the Beaver Memorial Methodist Church every Wednesday. Bucknell University Catalogue 1947 – 1948.

617 Born and educated in Japan Tanimoto also attended Emory University, Atlanta, GA. "Rev. Tanimoto Japanese Christian To Address Student Groups Sunday," *The Bucknellian*, No. 23, March 24, 1949.

618 Groves believed that the group's officers for the atomic bomb program should have been men who would have remained in the service after the war. Groves, *Now It Can Be Told*, 258.

619 Van Kirk received $0.94 an hour for summer construction employment for the Pennsylvania Dept. of Highways. Van Kirk personal papers.

620 Dr. Albert H. Cooper became head of the Chemical Engineering Department in 1946. Bucknell University archives.

621 Bucknell University paid Van Kirk $100.00 a month as a graduate assistant in Chemical Engineering from February 1949 to February 1950. Van Kirk personal papers.

622 Van Kirk personal papers.

623 Ed Meade, Advertising Director for New Buffalo Amusement Corporation, Buffalo Theatre Bldg., 646 Main St., Buffalo, NY, wrote and thanked Major Van Kirk for his cooperation during the screening of the motion picture with several complimentary tickets and information about the showings at the Shea's Bellevue in Niagara Falls starting January 28, 1953. The Bellevue Theatre opened in 1921 at 1711 Main Street.

624 Fort Niagara, also known as "New Fort Niagara" was an Induction Center and a major prisoner of war camp during World War II. New Fort Niagara was the brick barracks, officers' quarters, rifle range etc. constructed south of the colonial era buildings and fortifications known as "Old Fort Niagara" in the Town of Porter, Niagara County, NY. The area became Fort Niagara State Park. Youngstown High School, known as the Red Brick, is the Youngstown Civic Center today.

625 "Tells PTA About Bombing Jap City," *Niagara Falls Gazette*, January 16, 1952. Richard Tower, a World War II veteran and neighboring farmer of Dietz, introduced Van Kirk who also spoke at the Men's Brotherhood meeting of the Youngstown First Presbyterian Church on March 16, 1951, on "The Atomic Bombing of Hiroshima." The Lake Road division served supper at the meeting.

626 Van Kirk interview in 1985 with *Newsweek* magazine for a special report on the Hiroshima mission.

627 Two supporting actors in *Above and Beyond* were from Buffalo, James Whitmore and Marilyn Erskine. "Falls A-Bomber Sees Film Story of Deadly Flight," *Buffalo Evening News*, January 13, 1953.

628 Responding to the Smithsonian exhibit controversy reported in the *Washington Post* on September 26, 1994, ex-POW Garyford Payne said, "All of us who were prisoners in Japan…revere the *Enola Gay*. It saved our lives. Does anybody really think that the Japanese, faced with the same situation, wouldn't have used the atomic bomb on us"?

629 *The Washington Post* reported that 157,530 Purple Hearts were awarded during the Korean War and 211,324 in Vietnam, which had to be polished due to age. Medals as late as the Vietnam War had the six-digit serial number from 1942. D. M. Giangreco and Kathryn Moore, "Half a Million Purple Hearts," *American Heritage Magazine*, December 2000.

630 Van Kirk's numbers for the body bags are the same figures in the display at the D-day Museum in New Orleans.

631 Mick McAllister remembered his brother-in-law receiving threatening letters.

632 Capt. Herman S. Zahn commanded Crew C-12, which flew two training missions, but no combat or practice bombing missions. Their B-29 No. 44-86346 was unnamed on Tinian. Campbell, *The Silverplate Bombers*, 137.

633 The first reunion of the 393rd BS was held on August 17, 1962, in Chicago, IL.

634 Rear Admiral William Sterling Parsons born 1901, died December 5, 1953, buried in Arlington National Cemetery, Plot: Section 3, Lot 2167. "Find a grave," http://www.findagrave.com [accessed February 10, 2011].

635 While at the Marine Station, the *Enola Gay* crew members also made presentations to high school groups. Joyce Christie, "Fly Boys, *The Yuma Daily Sun*, (Yuma, AZ), March 21, 1997.

636 "Psychologist: Bombers don't feel guilt," *The Gettysburg Times*, August 6, 1985.

637 Douglas Martin, "Thomas Ferebee Died at 81: Dropped First Atomic Bomb," *New York Times,* March 18, 2000.

638 Van Kirk interview with Susan Grace, May 26, 1992.

Epilogue

World War II was a war that not only had to be fought, but a war that had to be won. On the day Roosevelt died he wrote, "More than an end to war, we want an end to the beginning of all wars." Roosevelt and Truman knew that the greatest failure of the Treaty of Versailles following World War I was that it did not win the peace. The demand for unconditional surrender from Germany and Japan attempted to address that.

The inevitable course of the science and technology of the atomic bomb began long before we define the beginning of the Second World War. The development of nuclear power, knowledge of the Asiatic Pacific Theatre, Japanese resources and plans for the invasion of Kyushu, and the repeated failure of the controlling military leaders of the Empire to surrender are fundamental for the educational studies and the public's understanding of World War II. Edward Teller wrote that the decision to use the bomb was within the framework of our great democracy even though he had first wanted a noncombat demonstration of the bomb to the Japanese. Teller and other Manhattan Project scientists were hopeful for the eventual peacetime uses of atomic energy.

Our fathers and mothers sacrificed on the home front. They fought and spilled their blood on the battlefields of land, sea, and air for those who died and suffered from the oppression of dictators and fascists, for the victims of the holocausts in Europe and in Asia, and for the millions more who would have died and their progeny who would not have been born if the war had continued. In spite of losses across the Pacific, incendiary bombings that destroyed most of their major cities on the home islands, countless deaths of civilians and military, displacement and suffering of millions, and two atomic bombs some militant leaders of Japan refused to accept the inevitable and were willing to sacrifice tens of millions of their people rather than accept defeat.

This publication has been an effort to compile primary source documents with interviews to chronicle the life and honor the military service of Theodore "Dutch" Van Kirk who like all the sixteen million men and women fought to bring an end to the war. Thousands of students and adults over the course of more than sixty years have listened to Van Kirk's Lesson 101 on Special Mission No. 13. Dutch, a sharp and witty teacher, hoped to inspire his listeners to study the war and more importantly to be part of a society that works diligently to settle conflict peacefully. This is the key for making the world the kind of place that many of our forefathers from the "greatest generation" and William and Robert Young died for. Their sacrifices need to be honored.

The evolution of humanity rests on our knowledge and insight into the past. Courage and wisdom are central to the decision to mold our swords into plowshares and at other times forge our plowshares into swords. This does not glorify the loss of life caused by one bomb, one bomber, or one man holding a rifle. But, we are part and parcel of a global community that is faced with a choice when our fellow humankind suffers or dies at the hands of oppressive governments.

World War II was an epic moment in history. The painful nature of war is that some live and some die, and for both the American and Japanese people war was a horror. To debate the past is unproductive. To study the past is vital to preserve the future for all.

Abraham Lincoln ~ "from these honored dead we take increased devotion to that cause for which they gave the last full measure of devotion that we here highly resolve that these dead shall not have died in vain."

Acknowledgments

In appreciation for the important contributions of the following individuals and groups in the creation of this historical work in alphabetical order:

Brian Anderson, David Bauman, Col. Nelson L. Beard, USAF (Ret), Gretchen H. Brosius, Bucknell University Special Collections and University Archives, Thomas G. Casey, Lt. Col. Richard E. Cole, USAF (Ret), Maureen Fennie Collura, Charles Cutler, Sr., Lt. Col. Lance E. Dickinson, USAF (Ret), Cynthia Young Diette, Barbara Berrien DuBell, Wes Fields, Louise Fossa, Amy Lynn Freiermuth, Joan L. Gearin, Seth Andrew Geller, D. M. Giangreco, Paula Giglio, Janet Gilgore, Gerry Gilstrop, Col. Carroll V. Glines, USAF (Ret), Capt. Robert W. Granston, USN (Ret), Sharon Granston, Gary Grossman, Marie Anne Simon Gwinn, Derrick Hart, Wesley Johnston, Ed Joscak, William Kelley, Wanda Langley, John Lindermuth, Michael Lombardi, Jerry Mack, Mark Mallett, Jean Van Kirk McAllister, Elwood "Mick" McAllister, National Archives at College Park, National Archives at Waltham, Naval Institute Press, Niagara Aerospace Museum, Niagara Falls Local History Library, Northumberland County Historical Society, Carol Parkinson, Rebecca Pepkowitz, Priestley-Forsyth Memorial Library, Holly Reed, Linda Reinumagi, Jane Richardson, John Richardson, Betty Santangelo, Nannette M. Simon, Schindler's Studio, Joseph Solomon, Randy Sowell, James L. Starnes, Jr., Bruce Strahan, Sam Strahan, Susan Strahan, Vicki Strahan, Schindler's Studio, Texas Woman's University Library, *The Daily Item* and *The Danville News,* Vicki Van Kirk Triplett, Harry S. Truman Library and Museum, University of Central Arkansas, Imogene "Jean" Van Kirk, Leroy "Jim" Van Kirk, Nancy Gautsch Van

Kirk, Thomas L. Van Kirk, Lt. Col. Richard H. Waring, USAF (Ret), Sarah Whittington, Lynn L. Williams, Youngstown Free Library, Youngstown Post Office, Allen Zobrist, Howard "Ted" Zobrist, and Jackie Zobrist.

A special thank you to those who read the manuscript for their corrections and suggestions: Nelson L. Beard, Jessica S. Dietz, Carol L. Force, D. M. Giangreco, and Yvonne S. Schiffer; and to all the veterans especially Richard E. Cole, Carroll V. Glines, Robert W. Granston, William Kelley, and James L. Starnes, Jr.

I am forever grateful to my high school sweetheart Raymond for taking notes, research assistance, endless editing, encouragement, cooking, and a million and one ways that helped this publication come to fruition.

It has been my privilege to sit at the kitchen table with Dutch Van Kirk. May this work honor him and all who served during World War II.

Abbreviations, Acronyms, and Log Definitions

AAF	Army Air Forces
AAFSETC	Army Air Forces Southeast Training Command
AD	Active Duty
(B)	Bombardier
AUS	Army of the United States
BG	Bombardment group
BS	Bombardment squadron
CINCPAC	Commander in Chief Pacific Command
(CP)	Co-pilot
DUKW	Amphibious tank
FEAF	Far Eastern Air Force
FTC	Flying Training Command
(G)	Gunner
(H)	Heavy
HQ	Headquarters
JASCO	Joint Assault Signal Company
(Maint)	Maintenance
(N)	Navigator
(P)	Pilot
PB	practice bombing
Pink	pumpkin
(R)	Radio Operator
TDN	travel directed is necessary in military service
TDY	temporary duty yonder also known as temporary duty assignment
Tng	training and orientation
TPA	Travel by officer or his dependents by privately owned automobile is authorized
VHB	Very Heavy Bomber
VLR	Very Long Range Bomber
WIA	Wounded in action
WP	will proceed to
True Course	intended direction of travel over the surface of the earth, written as an angle measured clockwise from true north 000° through 360.°

Drift Correction	rate of lateral displacement of the aircraft by the wind is expressed in plus or minus degrees and applied to the true course to obtain the True Heading.
True Heading	angle measured clockwise from true north through 360° to the longitudinal axis of the aircraft.
Magnetic Heading	heading of the aircraft with reference to magnetic north. The compass heading reading is taken from the compass.
True Air Speed	rate of motion of an aircraft relative to the surrounding air mass.
Ground Speed	rate of motion of the aircraft relative to the earth's surface expressed in nautical miles per hour/knot.
	1 knot = 1 nautical mile per hour = 6076 feet per hour.

Source: Department of the Air Force, *Air Navigation* Manual No. 51-40A, (Washington, DC: United States Government Printing Office, 1962).

Appendix A

Lieutenants Rated Aircraft Observers
(Aerial Navigators)

#23. The following-named Second Lieutenants, Air Corps Reserve are rated Aircraft Observers (Aerial Navigators), under the provisions of Army Regulations…

#24. The following named Second Lieutenants, Air Corps Reserve, each of whom holds an aeronautical rating, are hereby required to participate in regular and frequent aerial flights, at such times as they are called to active duty with the Air Corps, U.S. Army, under competent authority and are authorized to participate in regular and frequent aerial flights while on an inactive status…

Elias Bacha

Jess Francis Baker

John Richard Bannon

Ralph Allen Birk, Jr.

William Page Buckle, Jr.

Jones Lucias Callaway

John Holbrook Chalmers

Eldon Arthur Chappell

Charles Russel Cook

William Newton Dorsett

Abraham Jacob Dreiseszun

James Walter Dunn

Leo Odean Frazier

George Frank Freyer

Theodore Ragnvald Hokenstad

Marvin Edwards Kay

Edward Leroy Leonard

Louis Sterling McKnight

Arnold Jay Mellon

Jack Dean Nole

Harry Charles Nuessle

Levon L. Ray

Melvin John Robertson

John Clifford Roysden

Ben Hailey Rushing

Harold Spire

James Woodrow Stubbs

Theodore Jerome Van Kirk

Ralph Lloyd Vincent

William Tho White

Dave Weldon Williams

Source: Personnel Orders No. 78, By command of Lieutenant General Arnold, War Department Headquarters of the Army Air Forces, Washington, April 1, 1942, Van Kirk personal papers.

Appendix B
Other Bolero 340th Bombardment Squadron crews

B-17 E No. 41-9051

(P)	2nd Lt. John C. Summers
(CP)	2nd Lt. Andrew Kundrew
(N)	2nd Lt. William T. White
(B)	2nd Lt. Howard W. Blank
(AE)	Cpt. John B. Movota
(AAE)	Pvt. Zackie T. Gowan, Jr.
(R)	Pvt. Paul E. Price
(AR)	Cpl. Harold F. Weir
(G)	Pvt. Andy J. Lucero

B-17E No. 41-2588

(P)	1st Lt. Charles D. Lee
(CP)	2nd Lt. Glen V. Leland
(CP)	2nd Lt. Kenneth L. Ogle, Jr.
(N)	2nd Lt. Levon L. Ray
(B)	Sgt. Almus Sawyer
(AE)	Cpl. Franciso Rebello
(AAE)	Pvt. Joseph F. Cummings
(R)	Pvt. Zane A. Gemmill
(AR)	Pvt. Chester C. Love
(G)	Pvt. Richard A. William
(Maint)	T/Sgt. George Kendall

B-17E No. 41-9175

(P)	2nd Lt. Clarence W. Lipsky
(CP)	2nd Lt. David C. Howard
(B)	2nd Lt. William A. Loudermilk
(N)	2nd Lt. David McCorkle
(AE)	Cpl. Herman S. Haag
(AAE)	Pvt. William H. Warren
(R)	S/Sgt. William J. Watson
(AR)	Cpl. Charles A. Travinek
(G)	Pvt. William F. Peltier
(Maint)	S/Sgt Raymond M. Gentsch
(X)	Cpt. Randall G. Mosher

B-17E No. 41-2578

(P)	2nd Lt. Harold H. Beasley
(CP)	2nd Lt. Richard N. Wilson
(B)	2nd Lt. Wilfred L. Smith
(N)	2nd Lt. John R. Bannon
(AE)	Sgt. John L. Baird
(AAE)	Pvt. Vance H. Kirby
(R)	Cpl. Thomas T. Maston
(AR)	Pvt. George Fry
(G)	Pvt. Harold J. Snelp
(Maint)	S/Sgt. Andrew J. Flegal

B-17E No. 41-2626

(P)	2nd Lt. Jesse O. Wikle*
(CP)	2nd Lt. Roy N. Neilsen
(N)	2nd Lt. Ralph A. Birk
(B)	2nd Lt. Alfred D. Blair
(AE)	Sgt. Edward H. Smith
(AAE)	Sgt. Charles M. Nease
(R)	Cpl. Svend J. W. Hansen
(AR)	1st Sgt. John Burger
(G)	Pvt. William E. Beach
(Maint)	S/Sgt. Graham C. Hancock
(X)	Cpl. Warren H. Gresham

B-17E No. 41-2629

(P)	2nd Lt. Arthur E. Aenchbacher
(CP)	2nd Lt. Joseph F. DiSalvo
(N)	2nd Lt. Arnold J. Mellon
(B)	2nd Lt. Robert J. Art
(AE)	S/Sgt. Robert M. Moffitt
(AAE)	Pvt. Robert E. Hawkins
(R)	Pvt. Lee O. Walker
(AR)	Pvt. Theodore J. Elfrink
(G)	Pfc. Paul H. Biery
(Maint)	S/Sgt. Morris T. Quate
(X)	Pvt. Joseph E. Conchiglio

B-17E No. 41-9107

(P)	1st Lt. David C. Hoffmann
(CP)	2nd Lt. John D. Davenport
(P)	2nd Lt. Fredric G. Altman
(N)	2nd Lt. Charles C. Cutforth
(AE)	S/Sgt. Pasquale Prata
(AAE)	Pfc. Theodore Haas
(R)	S/Sgt. Robert H. Knowles
(AR)	Pfc. Charles T. Krest
(G)	Pfc. Gerald C. Freligh
(Maint)	S/Sgt. John F. Vlad
(X)	2nd Lt. John A. Cognetta

Source: Operations Orders No. 3, Headquarters 97th Bombardment Group (H), Army Air Force Office of the Operations Officer, Sarasota, Florida, May 11, 1942. Van Kirk papers.

* Capt. Jesse O. Wikle, Jr., 340th Bomb Squad, 97th Bomb Group, died February 1, 1943, buried in the American Cemetery, Carthage, Tunisia, Plot H Row 13, Grave 16. Source: American Battle Monuments Commission. http://www.abmc.gov.

Appendix C
Airplane Call Letters for 414th, 341st, and 359th Bomb Squadrons

341st BS
41-9105 1CAH   (Lieutenant Staples)
41-9101 1CAI   (Lieutenant Hanna)
41-9022 1CAJ   (Lieutenant Paine)
41-2628 1CAK   (Lieutenant Taylor)
41-9025 1CAM   (Lieutenant Cronkhite)
41-9114 1CAN   (Lieutenant Ijams)
41-9018 1CAO   (Lieutenant Kimmel)
41-9044 1CAP   (Lieutenant Duncan)
41-9013 3YDM   (Lieutenant McCorkle)

342nd BS
41-9017 WR9I   (Lieutenant Kelly)
41-9032 WR9K   (Lieutenant Stinson)
41-9026 WR9L   (Lieutenant Sammons)
41-9042 WR9M   (Lieutenant Burges)
41-9043 WR9O   (Lieutenant Dallas)
41-9115 WR9P   (Lieutenant Schwarzenbeck)
41-9108 WR9Q   (Lieutenant Holmes)
41-9090 WR9S   (Lieutenant Nichols)

359th BS
41-9098 F7XQ   (CO) (Major Thomas)
41-9074 F7XT   (Captain Hughes)
41-9125 F7XU   (Lieutenant Blair)
41-9129 F7XV   (Lieutenant Schmoldt)
41-9121 1CAQ   (Lieutenant Bennett)
41-9085 1CAR   (Lieutenant Johnson)
41-9132 1CAS   (Lieutenant Pett)
41-9073 1CAT   (Lieutenant Riley)
41-9148 WR9U   (Lieutenant Connors)

414th BS

41-9089	3YDB	(Lieutenant Starks)
41-9100	3YDC	(Lieutenant Borders)
41-9030	3YDE	(Lieutenant Sauders)
41-9045	3YDF	(Lieutenant Schley)
41-9024	3YDG	(Lieutenant Thacker)
41-9019	3YDH	(Lieutenant Baker)
41-9021	3YDI	(Lieutenant Smartt)
41-9103	3YDJ	(Lieutenant Lawrence)
41-9023	B6RY	(Lieutenant Dowswell)

419th BS

41-9119	WR9V	(CO) (Lieutenant Traylor)
41-9112	WR9W	(Lieutenant Stoddard)
41-9154	WR9X	(Lieutenant Coulter)
41-9127	3YDK	(Lieutenant Wilson)
41-9082	3YDL	(Lieutenant Teague)

Source: Signal Operations Instructions June 16, 1942, World War II Combat Operations Report, Record Group 18, National Archives, College Park, MD. Names typed as in the record.

Appendix D
Northumberland's World War II dead

James W. Beatty
Henry Brecht
John E. Bucher
Roy V. Capwell
Carl Cellitti
John S. Clark
Frank Cooper
Leonard Diehl
Carmen DiRocco
Richard Furman
Maurice O. Gautsch, Jr.*
Marlin K. Glass
Charles Goshy
Austin Gross
Albert J. Helt
Joseph Henahan

Charles Hock
Frank Holtzapple
H. Elwood Keener
Joseph Marotto, Jr.
Horace Middleton
George C. Miller
Elwood L. Moser
Clifford Reed
Kenneth Sassaman
William Skrutt
Richard Wagner
Geo. Wheeland
Robert D. Young
William C. Young
Eugene Zerbe, Jr.

Source: *General Marshall's Victory Report*, Biennial Report of the Chief of Staff of the United States Army, 1943 to 1945, to the Secretary of War, Washington, DC, September 1, 1945.

*Gautsch was the older brother of Nancy Gautsch Van Kirk.

Appendix E
Text of 509th Composite Group monument
Wendover, Utah

This monument is dedicated to the members of the 509th Composite Group, United States Army Air Force, who trained at the Wendover, Utah Army Air Force Base in 1944-45, for the vital, secret mission of delivering the first atomic bombs on Japanese targets in August 1945. The combined efforts of all members of the United States Army and the United States Navy who created the massive armed service support of this historic endeavor share this important dedication that brought World War II to a much earlier conclusion.

Recognition is given to the scientific teams who created this awesome weapon, those who sacrificed their lives in the Pacific Theatre, Allied forces in other theatres of action during World War II, and all who contributed to bring this dreadful war to an end.

The loss of lives of the people of Hiroshima and Nagasaki, Japan are especially recognized in this memorial for their sacrifice to mankind's struggle for a more peaceful world.

May this monument stand as a symbol of hope that mankind will reason and work together for the ultimate goal of world peace.

Erected by members and Friends of the 509th Composite Group (Wendover, NM)
August 25, 1990

Additional funding provided by the Division of Historic Preservation and Archaeology

Appendix F
509th Composite Group Outstanding Unit Award (With Valor)

By direction of the Secretary of the Air Force, the 509th Composite Group has been awarded the Air Force Outstanding Unit Award (with Valor) for exceptionally outstanding achievement in combat for the period 1 July 1945 to 14 August 1945.

By Order of the Secretary of the Air Force
Willie Key, MSGT, USAF, Superintendent, SAF Personnel Council

The 509th Composite Group distinguished itself by exceptionally outstanding achievement in combat from 1 July 1945 to 14 August 1945. The 509th Composite Group was the first Army Air Force group to be trained, organized, and equipped, in adverse conditions for atomic warfare. Despite the awesome rigors of war, they carried out complex and highly secret missions without any breech of security and without losing a single plane or a single life. As President George Bush stated on 20 August 1990, "When elite, highly trained crews of the 509th Composite Group carried out their decisive atomic bombing missions of Hiroshima and Nagasaki during World War II, they ushered in a new era in military warfare. These historic missions helped to bring a swift end to the hostilities in the Pacific, saving countless American and Allied lives and reaffirming our determination to secure peace through strength." The distinctive accomplishments of the members of the 509th Composite Group reflect great credit upon themselves and the United States Air Force.

Source: Special Order BG-294, Department of the Air Force, September 2, 1999. Van Kirk papers.

Bibliography

BOOKS

Appleman, Roy E. James M. Burns, Russell E. Gugeler, and John Stevens. *Okinawa: The Last Battle*. Washington: Defense Dept., Army Center of Military History, 1948.

Baggott, Jim. *The First War Of Physics* The Secret History of the Atom Bomb 1939 – 1949. New York: Pegasus Books, 2010.

Bureau of Yards and Docks. *Building the Navy's Bases in World War II: History of the Bureau of Yards and Docks and the Civil Engineers Corps 1940 – 1946*, Volume II. Washington, DC: Government Printing Office, 1947.

Beser, Jacob. *Hiroshima and Nagasaki Revisted*. Memphis, TN: Global Press, 1988.

Blumenson, Martin. *Kasserine Pass* Where America Lost Her Military Innocence. Boston, MA: Houghton Mifflin Company, 1966.

Bonner, Kermit. *Final Voyage*. Paducah, KY: Turner Publishing Co., 1996.

Bowman, Martin. *B-17 Combat Missions*. New York, NY: Barnes & Noble, 2007.

Bowman, Martin W. *Flying to Glory* The B-17 Flying Fortress in war and peace. Somerset: UK, Patrick Stephens Limited, 1992.

Berger, Carl. *B29 The Superfortress*. New York, NY: Ballantine Books, 1970.

Burrell, Dr. Robert S. *The Ghosts of Iwo Jima*. Williams-Ford Texas A & M University Military History Series, 2006.

Campbell, John M. & Donna. *Talisman* A Collection of Nose Art. West Chester, PA: Schiffer Military History, 1992.

Campbell, Richard H. Foreword by Paul W. Tibbets. *The Silverplate Bombers* A History and Registry of the *Enola Gay* and Other B-29s Configured to Carry Atomic Bombs. Jefferson, NC: McFarland & Co., Inc., 2005.

Carlisle, Norman, ed. *The Air Forces Reader*. New York: NY, The Bobbs-Merrill Company, 1944.

Caron, George R. and Charlotte E. Meares. *Fire Of A Thousand Sons* The George R. "Bob" Caron Story – Tail Gunner of the *Enola Gay*. Westminster, CO: Web Publishing Company, 1995.

Carruth, Gordon and Associates, ed. *The Encyclopedia of American Facts and Dates*. New York, NY: Thomas Y. Crowell Company, Inc., 1972.

Chang, Iris. *The Rape of Nanking* the Forgotten Holocaust of World War II. New York, NY: Basic Books, 1997.

Christman, Al. *Target Hiroshima* Deak Parsons and the Creation of the Atom Bomb. Annapolis, MD: Naval Institute Press, 1998.

Chun, Clayton K. S. *Japan 1945* From Operation Downfall to Hiroshima and Nagasaki. Oxford, UK: Osprey, 2008.

Chun, Clayton K. S. and Howard Gerrard. *The Doolittle Raid 1942: America's First Strike Back at Japan*. Oxford, UK: Osprey, 2006.

Conant, Jennet. *109 East Palace* Robert Oppenheimer And The Secret City of Los Alamos. New York, NY: Simon & Schuster, 2005.

Culley, Thomas F. et. al. *The Hour Has Come (Venit Hora) The 97th Bomb Group in World War II*. Dallas, TX: Taylor Publishing Co., 1993.

Daniel, Clifton, ed. *Chronicle of the 20th Century*, Mount Kisco, NY: Chronicle Publications, 1987.

Dietz, Suzanne Simon. *Porter* Images of America. Charleston, SC: Arcadia Publishing Company, 2005.

Dietz, Suzanne Simon. *POWs Interned At Fort Niagara* A Reference Work. Youngstown, NY: BeauDesigns, 2009.

Dornberger, Walter. *V-2 The Nazi Rocket Weapon*. New York, NY: Ballantine Books, 1954.

Dorr, Robert F. *B-29 Superfortress Units of World War 2*. Oxford, UK: Osprey Publishing Limited, 2002.

Dowell, Ernest R. *Flying Fortress* The Boeing B-17. Carrollton, TX: Squadron/Signal Publications, 1987.

Dower, John W. *Cultures Of War:* Pearl Harbor | Hiroshima | 9-11 | Iraq. New York, NY: W. W. Norton & Company, Inc., 2010.

Feifer, George. *The Battle of Okinawa* The Blood and The Bomb. Guilford, CT: The Lyons Press, 2001.

Ferrell, Robert H. Editor. *Dear Bess* The Letters from Harry to Bess Truman 1910-1959. New York: W. W. Norton & Company, 1983.

Fredriksen, John C. *The United States Air Force A Chronology*. Santa Barbara: ABC-CLIO, LLC, 2011.

Freeman, Roger A. *Airfields of the Eighth Then and Now*. London, UK: Battle of Britain Prints International Ltd., 1997.

Freeman, Roger A. *The Mighty Eighth In Color*, Stillwater, MN: Specialty Press, Inc, 1992.

Freeman, Roger A. with Alan Crouchman and Vic Maslen. *Mighty Eighth War Diary*. New York, NY: Jane's Publishing Incorporated, 1981.

Freeman, Roger A. with David Osborne. *The B-17 Flying Fortress Story*, London, UK: Arms & Armour Press, 1998.

Garrod, Charles and Bill Korst. *Alvino Rey and His Orchestra Plus The King Sisters 1938 – 1948*. Portland, OR: Joyce Record Club, 1997.

Giangreco, D. M. and Kathryn Moore. *Dear Harry...*Truman's Mailroom 1945-1953. Mechanisburg, PA: Stackpole books, 1999.

Giangreco, D. M. *Hell To Pay Operation DOWNFALL and the Invasion of Japan, 1945-1947*. Annapolis, MD: Naval Institute Press, 2009.

Glines, Carroll V. *The Doolittle Raid* America's daring first strike against Japan. New York, NY: Orion Books, 1988.

Glusman, John A. *Conduct Under Fire* Four American Doctors and Their Fight for Life as Prisoners of the Japanese, London (England): Penguin Book Ltd., 2005.

Groom, Winston. *1942: The Year That Tried Men's Soul*. New York: Grove Press, 2005.

Groves, Leslie R., Gen. U.S. Army, Retired. *Now It Can Be Told* The Story of the Manhattan Project. New York: Harper & Brothers, 1962.

Gurney, Major Gene, USAF. *B-29 Story* The Plane That Won The War, Greenwich, CN: Fawcett Publications, Inc., 1963.

Hess, William. *B-17 Flying Fortress*. New York, NY: Random House, 1974.

Hopp, George G., Series Editor. Translated by H. G. Geiss. *Luftwaffe Gunnery Techniques* The Official Gunnery Techniques Instruction for German Fighter Pilots and Air Gunners, 1943-1945. Ottawa: Valkyrie Publications, 1979.

Hoyt, Edwin Palmer. *Yamamoto The Man Who Planned Pearl Harbor*. NY: McGraw Hill, 1990.

Kahn, David. *The Code Breakers* The Story of Secret Writing. New York, NY: Scribner,

1996.

Kakehashi, Kumiko. *So Sad To Fall In Battle*: An Account of War Based On General Tadamichi Kuribayashi's Letters from Iwo Jima. New York: Presidio Press, 2007.

Krauss, Robert and Amelia, ed. *The 509th Remembered* A History of the 509th Composite Group As Told by the Veterans That Dropped the Atomic Bombs on Japan. Buchanan, MI: Krauss, 2009.

Kurzman, Dan. *Day Of The Bomb* Countdown to Hiroshima. New York: McGraw-Hill Book Company, 1986.

Langley, Andrew. *Hiroshima and Nagasaki* Fire from the Sky. Minneapolis, MN: Compass Point Books, 2006.

Langley, Wanda. *Flying Higher* The Woman Airforce Service Pilots of World War II. North Haven, CT: Linnet Books, 2002.

McCullough, David. *Truman*. New York: Simon & Schuster, 1992.

Miller, Donald L. *Masters of the Air* America's Bomber Boys Who Fought The Air War Against Nazi Germany. New York: NY, Simon & Schuster Paperbacks, 2006.

Morrison, Wilbur H. *Point Of No Return* The Story of the Twentieth Air Force. New York: Times Books, 1979.

Newcomb, Richard F. *Iwo Jima* The Dramatic Account of the Epic Battle that Turned the Tide of World War II. New York: Henry Holt & Company, LLC, 1965.

Nobleman, Marc Tyler. *The Sinking of The Indianapolis*. Minneapolis, MN: Compass Point Books, 2007.

Northumberland The Story Of An Old Town 1829 – 1929. Northumberland, PA: The Susquehanna Press, 1929.

Page, Thomas Nelson. *Robert E. Lee: Man & Soldier*. New York: Charles Scribner's Sons, 1911.

Price, Dr. Alfred. *Targeting The Reich* Allied Photographic Reconnaissance Over Europe, 1939-1945. London, UK: Lionel Leventhal Limited, 2003.

Roscoe, Theodore. *United States Destroyer Operations in World War II*. United States Naval Institute, 1953.

Senior Class Northumberland High School. *The Pine-Knotters Yearbook*. Northumberland, PA, 1938.

Smith, John N. *Airfield Focus* 48 Polebrook. England: Polebrook Gms Enterprises, 2001.

Smith, Lawrence G. *History of the 9th Bombardment Group (VH)* 1st, 5th, and 99th Squadrons as a B-29 Superfortress Unit in World War II. Princeton, NY: The 9th Bomb Group Assoc., 1995.

Stanton, Doug. *In Harm's Way* The Sinking of the USS *Indianapolis* and the Extraordinary Story of Its Survivors. New York, NY: Henry Holt & Co., LLC, 2001.

Steinbeck, John. *Bombs Away* The Story Of A Bomber Team. New York: NY, The Viking Press, 1942.

Stewart, Irvin. *Organizing Scientific Research for War* The Administrative History of the Office of Scientific Research and Development. Boston, MA: Little Brown and Co., 1948.

Stone, Justin F. ed. *Bushido: The Way of the Samurai* (based on the Hagakure by Tsunetomo, original translation by Minoru Tanaka). Garden City, NY: Square One Publishers, 2002.

Sullivan, Edward T. *The Ultimate Weapon* The Race to Develop the Atomic Bomb. New

York, NY: Holiday House, 2007.

Sweeney, Maj. Gen. Charles W., U.S.A.F. (Ret) with James A. Antonucci and Marion K. Antonucci. *War's End* An Eyewitness Account of America's Last Atomic Mission. New York, NY: Avon Books, 1997.

Tedder, Arthur W. *Air Power in War.* Tuscaloosa, AL: The University of Alabama Press, 2010.

Teller, Edward with Allen Brown. *The Legacy of Hiroshima.* Garden City, NY: Doubleday & Company, Inc., 1962.

Tibbets, Paul W. with Clair Stebbins and Harry Franken. *The Tibbets Story.* New York: Stein and Day, 1978.

Thomas, Gordon and Max Morgan Witts. *Enola Gay.* New York, NY: Stein and Day, 1977.

Ulanoff, Col. Stanley M., ed., *Bombs Away!* True Stories of Strategic Airpower from World War I to the Present, New York, NY: Doubleday & Company, Inc., 1971.

Walters, Thomas S. *Why, Must The World Be Like This.* New York, NY: Vantage Press, Inc., 2006.

Williams, Neville, ed. *Chronology of the Modern World* 1763 to the Present Time. New York, NY: David McKay Company, Inc., 1967.

MANUALS, MAGAZINES, PAMPHLETS

Aero Medical Laboratory. *Your Body In Flight.* Dayton, OH: Air Service Command Patterson Field, 1943.

Alexander, Jack. "Secretary of the Navy Frank Knox." *Life* Magazine, March 10, 1941.

"American Planes Bomb Continent U.S. Air Force enters European operations with daylight raids," *Life* Magazine, September 14, 1942.

Beahan, Kermit K. "Thoughts Concerning the Nagasaki A-Bomb Mission," 12 December '84.

Birdsall, Steve. *Pride of Seattle* The Story of the First 300 B-17s. Squadron/Signal Publications, 1998.

Campbell, Richard M. "A Brief History of the *Enola Gay.*" 509th Composite Group 60th Anniversary Reunion. Washington, DC, October 20-23, 2005.

Cookman, Aubrey O., Jr. "Report From Bikini." *Popular Mechanics*, Vol. 86 No. 2, August 1946.

Courtney, Capt. Godfrey B. "General Clark's Secret Mission" *Life*, Vol. 13 No. 26, December 28, 1942.

Davis, James Martin. *Top Secret* The Story of the Invasion of Japan. Omaha: NE, Ranger Publications, 1986.

Department of the Air Force. *Air Navigation* Manual No. 51-40A. Washington, DC: United States Government Printing Office, 1962.

"Flyer On First Atomic Raid Enrolls Here As Sophomore." *The Bucknellian*, Vol. LI. No. 1, September 19, 1946.

Giangreco, D. M. and Kathryn Moore. "Half a Million Purple Hearts." *American Heritage Magazine*, December 2000.

Glines, C. V. "The Bomb That Ended World War II." *Aviation History*, September 1995.

Gosling, F. G. *The Manhattan Project* Making the Atomic Bomb. United States Department of Energy, 1999.

Grew, Joseph C. "Report from Tokyo An Ambassador Warns of Japan's Strength." *Life*, December 7, 1942

Headquarters, AAF, Office of Flying Safety. "B-17 Pilot Training Manual for the Flying Fortress."

"How One Brother Helped to Shape History." *The Pennsylvania Freemason*, Vol. LIV No. 4, November 2007.

Jeppson, Morris R. "What are Hiroshima bomb "safety" plugs?" December 7, 1966.

National Aeronautics Council, Inc. *Aeronautics Aircraft Spotters' Guide*, Issue No. 1, Jan. 15, 1942.

Oleynikov, Pavel V. "German Scientists in the Soviet Atomic Project." *The Non Proliferation Review*, Summer 2000.

Painton, Frederick C. "Secret Mission to North Africa." *The Reader's Digest*, Vol. 42, No. 253, May 1943.

Pilot's Notes For Fortress, Air Ministry A.P. 2099 B, C, D, E & F. – P.N., Supersedes A.P. 2099 B, December 1942.

"Plutonium is Discovered, Glenn T. Seaborg," *Explorers Journal*, Vols. 51-53, December 1973.

"Rev. Tanimoto, Japanese Christian To Address Student Groups Sunday," *The Bucknellian*, No. 23, March 24, 1949.

Roberts, Dr. Jeffery J. "Peering through Different Bombsights Military Historians, Diplomatic Historians, and the Decision to Drop the Atomic Bomb," *Airpower Journal*, Spring 1998.

The B-29 Airplane Commander Training Manual for the Superfortress, revised February 1, 1945.

The B-29 Pilot Flight Operating Instructions manual, January 25, 1944.

"The Men Who Bombed Hiroshima." *Coronet*, August 1960.

"The Men Who Dropped the Bombs." *Time*, August 1, 2005.

"The Zero Zero Reunion Program," Army Air Forces Navigation School Selman Field, Monroe, Louisiana 1942-1946.

Thompson, Warren. "509th Bomb Group." *Wings of Fame* The Journal of Classic Combat Aircraft, Vol. 7, 1997.

"U.S. High-Altitude Bombers Hit Nazis." *Life* magazine, Vol. 13 No. 16, October 19, 1942.

Zachary, G. Pascal. "Vannevar Bush Backs the Bomb." *Bulletin of the Atomic Scientists*, December 1992.

"Zero Hour Forty-Three Seconds Over Hiroshima." Special Report. *Newsweek*, July 29, 1985.

REPORT DOCUMENTS

"1st Air Division: YS Reports of 97th Bomb Group Aug. 17 – Oct. 21, 1942." Record Group 18. National Archives Building, College Park, MD.

"8th Air Force: 97th Bomb Group, Call Signs of Pilots and Airplanes 1942." Record Group 18. National Archives Building, College Park, MD.

"97th Bomb Group: Mission Reports Nov. 16, 1942 – Oct. 18, 1944." Record Group 18, Records of the Army Air Forces 1902 – 1964. National Archives Building, College Park, MD.

"Bolero File April – Sept 1942." Record Group 337. National Archives Building, College Park, MD.

Carter, Kit C. and Robert Mueller. *U.S. Army Air Forces in World War II Combat Chronology 1941 – 1945*. Washington, DC: Center for Air Force History, 1991.

Complete Examination Questions and Answers Aerial Navigation for Student, Private, and Commercial Pilots. Ithaca, NY: Carlton L. Wheeler, Certified Instructor, 1941.

General Headquarters United States Army Forces In The Pacific, "DOWNFALL," Strategic Plan for Operations in the Japanese Archipelago, 1st Edition, 28 May 1945.

General Marshall's Victory Report, Biennial Report of the Chief of Staff of the United States Army, 1943 to 1945, to the Secretary of War, Washington, DC, September 1, 1945.

Lewis, Maj. Robert A. "Notes Taken During Mission of the Enola Gay to Bomb Hiroshima, August 6, 1945." Collection HS-ABC: Atomic Bomb Collection 1939 – 1996, Harry S. Truman Library.

"Minutes of Meeting held at the White House on Monday, 18 June 1945 at 1530." Miscellaneous Historical Documents Collections, Harry S. Truman Library.

Operations Reports Twelfth Air Force. Box 5866, National Archives Building, College Park, MD.

Pepkowitz, Leonard P. Personnel file. Los Alamos National Laboratory, Los Alamos, NM.

Records of United States Air Force Commands, Acts and Organization. Record Group 342, Box 186, National Archives Building, College Park, MD.

Reports and Memos – Operations Analysis Division 20th Air Force, Box 5866, National Archives Building, College Park, MD.

"Tactical Mission Report." Mission No. Special flown 20 July – 14 Aug '45, Copy No. 2, Headquarters Twentieth Air Force, National Archives Building, College Park, MD.

The Manhattan Engineer District, *A Bombing of Hiroshima And Nagasaki*. Reprint Breinigsville, PA: Kessinger, 2011.

"World War II Combat Operations Report 1941-46 Eighth Air Force," Record Group 18 Box 5668, National Archives Building, College Park, MD.

"World War II Combat Operations Reports 1941-1946 97th Bomb Group," Records of the Army Air Forces, Record Group 18 Box 688, National Archives Building, College Park, MD.

"World War II War Crimes Records: Far East," Record Group 238, National Archives Building, College Park, MD.

NEWSPAPER ARTICLES

"12 Japanese Cities Are Earmarked for Ruin From B-29's," *The Kingston Daily Freeman* (Kingston, NY), July 31, 1945.

"Admiral Yamamoto Killed, Japs Report," *The Herald Statesman*, (Yonkers, NY), May 21, 1943.

"Army Airmen Come From Hiroshima To Local Wedding." *Anniston Star* (Anniston, AL). July 23, 1946.

Ashley, Beth. "Navigator recounts bombing." *Marin Independent Journal*, August 20, 1995.

Bell, Jack. "Mikado Must Subject Himself To Orders Of Supreme Allied Chief; People To Decide on Government" (AP). *Niagara Falls Gazette*, August 11, 1945.

"Bizerte, Sfax, Tunis Battered; Axis Plane Losses Reach 277" (AP) Allied Headquarters

North Africa. *The Philadelphia Inquirer*, December 28, 1942.

Brines, Russell. "Jap Fanatics Slew Palace Guard Trying to Stop Surrender Order." *The Leader-Republican* (AP), September 7, 1945.

"Christians Should Join Jews In Special Day Of Prayer," *Brooklyn Eagle*, December 1, 1942.

Considine, Bob. "Jap Balloon Barrage Was Sidetracked." *Evening Recorder* (Amsterdam, NY), May 15, 1965.

Counts, Ron. "Boogie Woogie Bugle Boy." *Culpeper Star-Exponent*, April 6, 2009.

___. "The Times Of His Life." *Culpeper Star-Exponent*, April 5, 2009.

"Crippled Major (General) Plans Vets' Aid." *Stars and Stripes*, July 28, 1946.

Christie, Joyce, "Fly Boys," *The Yuma Daily Sun*. (Yuma, AZ), March 21, 1997.

Diblin, Joe. "The story of the man who dropped the 'bomb," *The Standard Journal* (Milton, PA), a series of four articles, 2002.

"Falls A-Bomber Sees Film Story of Deadly Flight," *Buffalo Evening News*, January 13, 1953.

Gallagher, Wes. "U.S. Fliers Blast Lille In Biggest Day Raid; 4 of 600 Planes Lost." (AP). *The Philadelphia Inquirer*, October 1942.

Grace, Susan. "Dropping the Bomb." *The Free Lance-Star*, (Fredericksburg, VA), May 26, 1992.

Greene, Bob. "I tell myself that they've gone on vacation," *Chicago Tribune*. March 19, 2000.

Gruson, Lindsey. "Robert A. Lewis, 65, Co-pilot on Mission over Hiroshima," *New York Times*, June 20, 1983.

"Heroic Crew Lands Flying Fort, Shot Up Like Sieve." (UP) News clipping, September 1942.

"Hiroshima Dissolved In Flame and Smoke Says Superfort Crew," *Stars and Stripes* Pacific Edition, August 8, 1945.

"Jap Admiral, 80, Dies," *Binghamton Press*, July 7, 1949.

"Jews to Observe Day of Mourning," *New York Evening Post*, November 30, 1942.

Lee, Clark. "General MacArthur Confers With Aides On Fall Of Bataan." *Schenectady Gazette*, April 10, 1942.

"Mareth Line Falls, Trap Closing on Axis," *Stars And Stripes*, London, England, Vol. 3 No. 126, March 30, 1943.

Martin, Douglas. "Thomas Ferebee Died at 81: Dropped First Atomic Bomb," *New York Times,* March 18, 2000.

"Morris Jeppson" obituary. *Las Vegas Review-Journal*. April 4, 2010.

"Navigator In Lead Plane Of Atom Test." *The Morning News*, (Danville, PA), April 9, 1946.

Newcomb, Richard F. "20 Years Ago Marines Landed on Iwo Jima." (AP) *Niagara Falls Gazette*, February 14, 1965.

Niagara Falls Gazette (Niagara Falls, NY).

___. "Barges in Cavite Navy Yard Burn After Jap Raid," April 1, 1942.

___. "Church Services for Palm Sunday at Youngstown; Van Kirk to Address Men," March 16, 1951.

___. "Complete Plans For Entertainment Here Of Japanese Party." October 1, 1935.

___. "Falls Marine Prays During Lull in Iwo Battle." October 1, 1935.

___. "Formally Enter Nanking" Shanghai (UP). December 17, 1937.

___. "Other Japanese Visitors," October 2, 1935.

___. "Ploesti Oil Raid Commander Dies, Ill Since 1944," March 6, 1948.

__. "Report Commander Executed, Shanghai." (UP), December 17, 1937.

__. "Russian War," January 8, 1943.

__. "Six Are Killed by Jap Balloons," May 31, 1945.

__. "Strikes Interfere with Production of Super-fortresses, Liberators." (AP), September 9, 1944.

__. "To Be Guests at Niagara Falls Tomorrow," September 30, 1935.

__. "War Grows More Grave Tojo Admits," June 5, 1943.

"Northumberland Proud Of Air Heroes Exploits," *The Evening News* (Harrisburg, PA), February 16, 1950.

"Paul Warfield Tibbets, Jr." obituary, *Columbus Dispatch* (Columbus, OH). November 3, 2007.

"Psychologist: Bombers don't feel guilt." *The Gettysburg Times*, August 6, 1985.

"Results First Game at St. Louis," *Brooklyn Eagle* Sports, (Brooklyn, NY). October 5, 1942.

"Sailors Get Series News In Quick Time." *Brooklyn Eagle* Sports, October 5, 1942.

Schenectady Gazette (Schenectady, NY).

__. "Bataan Falls Defense Exhausted," April 10, 1942.

__. "Japan Reports Resistance On Okinawa," April 3, 1945.

__. "List 8 New Jap Cities for Quick Destruction," August 1, 1945.

__. "Mt. Suribachi, on Southern Tip of Iwo Isle Is Captured By Hard Fighting Marines," February 23, 1945.

"Should U.S. keep 'first use' option." *USA Today*, March 30, 2010.

Stars and Stripes London Edition.

__. "6 Jap Divisions Destroyed on Luzon, Remainder in Peril," March 7, 1945.

__. "8th Fighters Add 200 To Bag of Nazi Planes," April 18, 1945.

__. "1,300 8th Heavies Again Blast Reich as Nazis Hide," April 12, 1945.

__. "Draft Drops to 93,000 A Month After June 30," March 24, 1945.

__. "House Unit Agrees To 18-Year-Old Ban," April 28, 1945.

__. "It's an Ill Volcano That Belches No Good," March 5, 1945.

__. "Japs Using Piloted Rockets; Yanks Wedge Okinawa Line" (ANS), April 28, 1945.

__. "New Fire Bomb Burns Hot Enough to Cut Steel," March 22, 1945.

__. "RAF Uses 10-Tonner, War's Biggest Bomb," March 15, 1945.

__. "Reds End Jap Neutrality Pact," April 4, 1945.

__. "U.S. Prepared to Fight Japanese Until 1949." July 21, 1943.

Sunbury Daily Item (Sunbury, PA).

__. "Believe Flier No. 1 Navigator of U.S. Raiders," Fall 1941.

__. "Captain Van Kirk First Atom Bomb Raid Navigator," August 1945.

__. "Ex-Orphanage Ward Killed In Saipan Battle," July 1944.

__. "Ganging Up on Flying Fortresses." News clipping, September 1942.

__. "Germans Seek Revenge After Smashing Raid." (UP) London news clipping, October 1943.

__. "Guns Fire Leaflets at Nazis in Tunisia," April 29, 2011.

__. "Hold Farewell Party For Theodore Van Kirk," September 1941.

__. "Kiwanis Given Real Thrill By Lieut. Van Kirk," 1943.

__. "Lieut. Van Kirk Leaves For Texas Assignment," December 1941.

__. "Lieut. Van Kirk 'Veteran' of Air War, Home," June 1943.

__. "Lt. Van Kirk At Mather Field for Refresher," 1943.

__. "Lt. Van Kirk, Miss Young Wed In South," September 1943.

__. "Miss Young To Marry Aviator," 1943.

__. Moore, John L. "Remembering Hiroshima," June 7, 1992.

__. "North'd. Flier In Attack On Tunisia Base" (UP), November 21 (delayed), 1943.

__. "Teddy Van Kirk Now A Captain," 1943.

"Suzuki Escaped Jap Fanatics." *The New York Sun*, September 21, 1945.

Talmadge, Eric (AP), "Bodies, mass graves found on Iwo Jima," *Buffalo News*, October 22, 2010.

"Three to Five Per Cent Of Jap Balloons Arrived," *Amsterdam Recorder*, July 25, 1946.

The Kingston Daily Freeman

__. "Suzuki Says He Won't Quit His Nation in Defeat." (AP) June 14, 1945.

The Washington Post (Washington, DC).

__. "Remembering World War II," July 26, 1995.

__. "The *Enola Gay*'s Turbulent Flight in History," September 26, 1994.

Torpy, Bill. "65 years, just down the street." *The Atlanta Journal-Constitution*, August 28, 2010.

Troan, John. "Analysis: Truman justified in use of A-bombs on Japan." *Pittsburgh Tribune Review*, August 6, 2010.

Turner, Richard L. "Most of American-Filipino Soldiers Believed Killed or Captured By Enemy." *Schenectady Gazette*, April 10, 1942.

"U.S. Airmen Get Many Decorations General Doolittle Does Pinning." *The Brownsville Herald* (Brownsville, TX), December 20, 1942.

Van de Velde, James R. "*Enola Gay* Saved Lives, Period." *The Washington Post*, February 10, 1995.

"Walter Nicholas "Buck" Dietzen," obituary. *San Diego Union-Tribune*, October 26, 2005.

Weller, George. "Cruise of Death" series. *Chicago Daily News Foreign Service*, Fall 1945.

"U.S. Precision Bombing for Germany Near." (UP) News clipping, September 1942.

"U.S. Prepared to Fight Japanese Until 1949." *Stars And Stripes*, Vol. 3 No. 222, July 21, 1943.

VIDEOS/Other

Geller, Seth Andrew. DVD film of Geller interview of Theodore J. Van Kirk, Stone Mountain, GA, October 27 - 29, 2008.

Geller, Seth Andrew. DVD film of Theodore J. Van Kirk presentation to the "Silver Wings Group" of the 352nd Fighter Group, Atlanta area, GA, October 29, 2008.

General Paul Tibbets An Oral History interview by Dawn Letson, Women Airforce Service Pilots Oral History Project, February 24, 1997.

Return to Ground Zero. NHK Nagasaki Station, August 2001.

The Greenwich Workshop, Inc. *The Men Who Brought the Dawn*. VHS, 1995.

Van Kirk, Dutch. *Red Gremlin Reunion 1991 and Larry, Vicki etc.* Home VHS video.

Van Kirk, Dutch. *The Red Gremlin and Willie Tittsworth*. Home VHS video.

Woodside, Patricia A. *Enola Gay: In Their Own Words*. National Air & Space Museum, DVD, 1995.

Index

Asaka Yasuhiko, 22
Ashworth, Frederick L., 489, 490, 508, 509
Associated Press, 279, 402
Atkinson, Joseph H., 282, 343
atomic bomb targets, 431
Atomic Energy Commission, 438
Attlee, Clement R., 426, 431
Attu, 236, 392
Battle of Attu, 406
Austin, Charles, 245
Australia, 19, 258, 331, 497

B-17s, 237, 242, 248, 259, 264, 273, 284,
    292, 307, 312, 322, 332, 362, 409,
    443, See Red Gremlin
  B-17E Rockett's crew, 227
  B-17E Tibbets' crew, 227
  E-model, 183, 202, 207, 209, 211, 232,
    241, 248, 255, 276, 285
  F-model, 276, 277, 290, 366
  G-model, 290
B-18, 259
B-19, 155
B-24 Liberator, 270, 278, 291, 292, 377,
    378, 381, 409
B-25 Mitchell, 220, 236, 322, 378, 381,
    530
B-26 Marauder, 322
B-29 Superfortress, 7, 199, 377, 386, 394,
    398, 404, 406, 408, 415, 417, 419,
    420, 424, 427, 432, 434, 435, 449,
    455, 458, 473, 486, 487, 491, 498
  aircraft No. 44-86292, 422
  Ladybird, 372
  prototype XB-29, 281, 333
B-47 Stratojet, 523, 535, 537
B-52, 535
Bangor, Maine, 234, 238, 240, 243
Bannon, John R. "Jack", 208, 210, 212, 351
Bard, Ralph A., 416
Barnes, Philip, 508
Bataan Death March, 2, 4, 6, 27, 270
  fall of Bataan, 216
Batista Army Airfield, 394

Beahan, Kermit, 259, 420, 429, 489, 490,
    508, 509, 512, 513, 515, 516, 517,
    536, 560
Beecher, Commander, 7
Belgium, 17, 19, 268
Bell Aircraft, 199, 383, 406
Bell, Larry, 199
Berlin, 409, 415, 428
Berlin Sleeper II, 366
Bernstein, Barton, 526
Beser, Jacob "Jake", 424, 440, 462, 465,
    478, 501, 507, 508, 530, 531
Bickel, Charmaine, 177
Bickel, Mrs. R. S., 176
Biega family, 15
Big Stink, 488, 508, 539
Bikini atomic bomb test, 513, 516
Bilibid prison, 4, 6
Bing, Andrew, 313
biological warfare, 221
Biskra Air Base, 326, 331, 341, 355
Bizerte, 310, 315, 326, 336, 345, 346
  Bizerte docks, 321, 322, 328, 334, 341
  Bizerte Harbor, 316, 337
  bombing of Bizerte, 307
  Sidi Ahmed aerodrome, 308, 344
Blamey, Thomas, 497
Blanchard, William, 421, 427, 435, 511
Bluie West Eight, 248
Bluie West One, 248
Boccadifalco aerodrome, 342
Bockscar, 487, 508
body bags, 1, 526
Boeing, 374, 409, 517
Boeing Airplane Company
  B-17E, 209
  B-17F production, 277
  Boeing 314, *Dixie Clipper*, 323
  Fortress No. 41-24444, 245
  test pilot Edmund Allen, 333
Bohr, Niels Henrik David, 17, 342
Bolling Field, 389
Book, John Butler, 534
Bostian, Robert B. "Bucky", 23, 35, 155,
    181, 184, 270, 294, 298
Boston Red Sox, 211

V-2 Rocket. See Walter Dornberger
Van Kirk, Charles Theodore "Dory", 329
Van Kirk, Daniel, 14
Van Pelt, James, 387, 390, 429, 488, 489, 490, 498, 536
Vandenberg, Hoyt S., 356
Veterans of Foreign Wars of the United States, 21
Vietnam, 525, 535

Wainwright, Jonathan, 4, 525
Wake Island, 237, 400
Wallace, Henry A., 29
War Between the States, 14
War Department, 335, 367, 431, 496, 548
Washington Naval Treaty, 21
Washington, University of, 3
WASP. See Women Air Force Service Pilots
Weis Pure Food Stores, 13, 24, 39, 55, 68
Welk, Lawrence, 371
Welsh, William, 307, 308
Wendover Air Base, 384
Westinghouse, 36, 174, 175, 185, 420
White House, 342, 399
  map room, 477
  meeting of Joint Chiefs, 422
White, Margaret Bourke, 263, 264, 289
Wiley, Charles "Dick", 227, 295, 324, 330, 333, 348, 357, 380, 416, 529
Wilkins, Chuck, 3
Wise, Jack V., 436
Witsell, Edward F., 518
Women Air Force Service Pilots, 361, 362, 372, 373, 392, 394
Works Progress Administration (WPA), 13
World War I, 16, 18, 21, 51, 67, 183, 343, 378
Wormley, Neil, 23, 48, 65, 66, 75, 154
Wright Junior College, 371
Wright, William, 389
Wright-Patterson, 230

Yamamoto Isoroku, 104, 341
Yankee Doodle, 259
Young, Albert, 18, 27, 350, 521

Young, Mary Jane, 18, 26, 27, 31, 33, 366, 424
  letters to Van Kirk, 25, 32, 199, 218
  wedding to Van Kirk, 365
Young, Ray, 18, 26
Young, Robert D., 195, 228, 294, 326, 345, 350, 376
Young, William C., 226, 270

Zale, John S., 6, 11
Zobrist, Howard "Ted", 415, 436
Zong, William P., 67, 152

About the Author

Photo by Frank Fletcher-Broucek

Suzanne Simon Dietz is the historian for the Town of Porter, Niagara County, and the Aero Club of Buffalo, New York. She has lectured in Western New York on local history topics and in particular German Prisoners of War held at Fort Niagara, a major POW camp during World War II.

Dietz is the author of *Porter Images of America, Lewiston Images of America, Honor Thy Fathers & Mothers* Niagara Frontier's Legacy of Patriotism and Survival, *POW's Interned at Fort Niagara* A Reference Manual, and co-author with Amy Lynn Freiermuth for *Lewiston Then & Now*.

Mrs. Dietz writes and researches for the Niagara Aerospace Museum; and presently is working on a collection of veterans' stories from World War II, Korea, and Vietnam. She has consulted for the history of the Tuscarora Indian Nation and also contributed to several books on Niagara County history and numerous local history publications.

The author's father, the late John Victor Simon, served during the Second World War as a scout in the United States Army with the 353rd Infantry Regiment, 89th Infantry Division.